FIFTH EDITION

CANADIAN CRIMINOLOGY TODAY

THEORIES AND APPLICATIONS

FRANK SCHMALLEGER
Distinguished Professor Emeritus
The University of North Carolina at Pembroke

REBECCA VOLK
Algonquin College

PEARSON

Toronto

Vice-President, Editorial Director: Gary Bennett
Editor-in-Chief: Michelle Sartor
Acquisitions Editor: Carolin Sweig
Marketing Manager: Lisa Gillis
Team Leader, Development: Madhu Ranadive
Developmental Editor: Joanne Sutherland
Project Manager: Susan Johnson
Production Editor: Nidhi Chopra, Cenveo® Publisher Services
Copy Editor: Marcia Gallego
Proofreader: Patricia Jones
Compositor: Cenveo Publisher Services
Photo Researcher: Marta Johnson, PreMedia Global
Permissions Researcher: Haydee Hidalgo, Electronic Publishing Services
Art Director: Zena Denchik
Interior Designer: Julia Hall
Cover Designer: Alex Li
Cover Image: © Biddy O'Neill/Corbis

10 9 8 7 6 5 4 3 2 1 [CKV]

Library and Archives Canada Cataloguing in Publication

Schmalleger, Frank, author
        Canadian criminology today : theories and applications/Frank Schmalleger,
Rebecca Volk. -- Fifth edition.
Includes bibliographical references and index.
ISBN 978-0-13-293575-3 (pbk.)
        1. Criminology--Textbooks. 2. Criminology--Canada--
Textbooks. I. Volk, Rebecca, author II. Title.
HV6025.S34 2013   364   C2013-902224-4

PEARSON

ISBN 978-0-13-293575-3

Brief Contents

Contents

Part II Crime Causation 113

Preface

Almost half a century ago, the noted criminologist Austin Turk began the preface to his book *Criminality and Legal Order* with these words:

> Embarrassment provided much of the initial push that led to the writing of this book. I was embarrassed at my lack of good answers when confronted by students who wondered, somewhat irreverently, why criminology is "such a confused mish-mash." . . . Some of these students were especially bothered by the "unreality" of criminological studies, by which they meant the lack of sustained attention to connections between the theories and statistics about crime and what they heard every day about relations among social conflicts, political manoeuvers, and law violation and enforcement.*

Much has changed since Turk's time, yet much remains the same. Crime is still with us in the 21st century and is becoming more complex and difficult to understand. Issues of national security and how to ensure it have left pundits questioning just how much freedom people should be willing to sacrifice to enhance security. In addition to the realities of everyday conventional crime, we are now faced with transnational and international activities. Computers and cyberspace mean that criminal actors and activities can more easily cross national and international boundaries. Worldwide recessions, corporate scandals, and stock market losses have all challenged our faith in the integrity of big business and those who control it. Added to the mix by the beginning of 2011 were new acts of criminality that emanated from all corners of the world: the explosion of human trafficking and smuggling, sexually explicit content involving minors accessible on the internet, increased numbers of mass shootings at schools and public venues, environmental transgressions such as oil and chemical spills, and thefts of hundreds of thousands of personal identities. This last issue constitutes an intimate crime that can literally cause a person to face the loss of his or her social self in a complex culture.

In the past few years, crime and criminals have changed in ways that few people had previously imagined would occur, and these changes hold considerable significance for each of us. Criminologists find themselves wondering how to embrace the challenges of this new reality as policymakers and criminal justice personnel strive to remain one step ahead of the emerging trends in crime and criminality. For the student of crime and criminal behaviour the crucial question that still remains to be answered is *why?*—why, despite all the theorizing and studies, can we not "solve" the crime puzzle? Do some people commit acts of mass shootings because they are "born violent"? Or, is their exposure to violence in childhood responsible? Why does the affluent chief executive officer of a corporate conglomerate engage in financial fraud while the young person living in a high-crime neighbourhood remains crime-free? What is it that motivates one person and not another to violate social norms? And does this motivation vary according to the type of law broken?

THEME OF SOCIAL PROBLEMS VERSUS SOCIAL RESPONSIBILITY

This fifth edition of *Canadian Criminology Today: Theories and Applications* continues to examine these questions and offer students a clear, contemporary, and comprehensive introduction to criminology that encourages critical thinking about the causes of crime and crime-prevention strategies. The thematic approach of *Canadian Criminology Today* is dualistic. On the one hand, it presents a social problems framework, which holds that crime may be a manifestation of underlying cultural issues such as poverty, discrimination,

---

*Austin Turk, *Criminality and Legal Order* (Chicago: Rand McNally, 1969), p. vii.

and the breakdown of traditional social institutions. On the other, it contrasts the social problems approach with a social responsibility perspective, which claims that individuals are fundamentally responsible for their own behaviour and maintains that they choose crime over other, more law-abiding courses of action. The thematic contrast is an important one, for it provides students with a useful framework for integrating the voluminous material contained within the field of criminology. Contrasting the two perspectives, as this book does, provides fertile ground for discussion and debate, allowing students to better understand the central issues defining contemporary criminology and to reach their own conclusions about the value of criminology theory.

AN APPLIED FOCUS

Canadian Criminology Today meets the needs of students preparing for careers in the Canadian criminal justice system. Its applied focus on the explanations of crime and deviance and their application to real-life examples of criminal behaviour reflects the learning outcomes of introductory criminology courses. The text addresses the latest social issues and discusses innovative criminological perspectives in an interesting and accessible manner; it makes use of attention-getting stories, news briefs, images, charts, and graphs. Study tools such as learning objectives, margin definitions, and end-of-chapter review and multiple-choice questions serve to reinforce student learning.

The goal is that today's students will find *Canadian Criminology Today* relevant, interesting, informative, and useful. It is designed to assist them in understanding the reasons and motivations behind criminal and deviant behaviour, to allow them to draw their own conclusions about the most effective ways to address such behaviour, and ultimately, to prepare them for their future careers within the criminal justice system. After all, it is only by understanding the reality of crime and criminal behaviour that we can ever hope to come close to solving and preventing it.

FEATURES IN THE FIFTH EDITION

Learning features in the fifth edition of *Canadian Criminology Today* build on those found in the fourth edition. They include the following:

- ■ Numbered *Learning Objectives* align with each of the major sections within the chapter.
- ■ Current crime stories opening each chapter pique interest and alert students to key topics.
- ■ Updated *Crime in the News* boxes provide students with reality-based studies.
- ■ *Who's Responsible—the Individual or Society?* boxes are found in every chapter and provide case studies and critical thinking questions to help students focus on the book's overall theme of social problems versus social responsibility.
- ■ NEW! Theories Applied graphic features appear at the end of Chapters 5 to 10, putting complex theories into context for students. These features present questions about the chapter-opening case study, encouraging students to apply each of the theories presented in the chapter.
- ■ An increased use of visuals in the form of additional graphics, boxed information, and photos enhance reader focus and support comprehension.
- ■ Margin definitions provide students with immediate comprehension and application of key terms.
- ■ Marginal icons highlighting relevant videos and activities in *MySearchLab* appear throughout chapters to provide students with further learning resources.
- ■ The end-of-chapter *Summary of Learning Objectives* is numbered, and each point relates directly to start-of-chapter learning objectives in order to help students focus on the important material covered in each section.

■ New! End-of-chapter *Multiple-Choice Questions* allow students another opportunity to test their understanding of chapter material and reinforce their learning.

NEW AND UPDATED CONTENT IN THE FIFTH EDITION

■ expanded discussion of technology and crime, including an examination of technology in the fight against crime and biometric technologies

■ expanded look at cybercrime to include cyberbullying

■ updated analysis of various legislation, including the *Safe Streets and Communities Act* and the National Crime Prevention Strategy

■ updated chapters examining crime statistics and patterns of crime with expanded use of Canadian and international examples and case studies

■ updated case studies and *Crime in the News* stories

STUDENT SUPPLEMENT

MySearchLab® with eText provides access to an online interactive version of the text and features writing, grammar, and research tools to help you with your writing and research assignments. Just like the printed text, you can highlight and add notes to the eText online. You can also access the eText on your iPad or Android tablet by downloading the free Pearson eText app.

Special features of this MySearchLab® include chapter learning outcomes, chapter quizzes, engaging media resources (videos and activities), glossary flashcards, and interactive animations. This site also includes access to the Cybrary, an extensive criminal justice directory, a variety of academic journals, and the Associated Press news feeds.

For more information and to redeem or purchase an access code please visit www.mysearchlab.com.

INSTRUCTOR SUPPLEMENTS

The following supplements can be downloaded by instructors from a password-protected location on Pearson Canada's online catalogue (**www.pearsoncanada.ca/highered**). Navigate to your book's catalogue page to view a list of those supplements that are available. See your local sales representative for details and access.

■ The Instructor's Manual (ISBN 978-0-13-339937-0) includes learning objectives for each chapter, a brief chapter outline, and detailed lecture outlines with teaching tips.

■ The PowerPoint Presentations (ISBN 978-0-13339940-0) summarize the key points for each chapter.

■ The Test Item File (ISBN 978-0-13-339941-7) is a comprehensive test bank featuring multiple-choice, true–false, and essay questions with references to text page numbers, level of difficulty, and skill level.

■ MyTest (ISBN 978-0-13-339939-4) from Pearson Canada is a powerful assessment generation program that helps instructors easily create and print quizzes, tests, and exams, as well as homework or practice handouts. Questions and tests can all be authored online, allowing instructors ultimate flexibility and the ability to efficiently manage assessments at any time, from anywhere.

peerSCHOLAR

Firmly grounded in published research, peerScholar is a powerful online pedagogical tool that helps develop students' critical and creative thinking skills through creation, evaluation, and reflection. Working in stages, students begin by submitting written assignments. peerScholar then circulates their work for others to review, a process that can be anonymous or not, depending on instructors' preferences. Students immediately receive peer feedback and evaluations, reinforcing their learning and driving development of higher-order thinking skills. Students can then re-submit revised work, again depending on instructors' preferences.

Contact your Pearson representative to learn more about peerScholar and the research behind it.

ACKNOWLEDGMENTS

The fifth edition of *Canadian Criminology Today: Theories and Applications* would not have been possible without the support from the team at Pearson Canada. It has been a pleasure to work with Carolin Sweig and Joanne Sutherland once again. My sincere gratitude to both—Joanne for her patient guidance and sage advice, and to Carolin for her vision and leadership. Thanks also to Susan Johnson, Nidhi Chopra, and Marcia Gallego, whose editorial talents and feedback have ensured that this edition is accessible and easy to read.

Reviews and insights from colleagues have helped to make this book relevant and up-to-date. Special recognition and thanks are due to long-time colleague Oliver Stoetzer of Fanshawe College for his ongoing support and for sharing his understanding of the field with me. Thanks also to Jane Barker of Nipissing University, Jarkko Jalava of Okanagan College, Hannele Jantti of Douglas College, Jamie Levitt of Niagara College, Melanie Marchand of Georgian College, Karen Moreau of Niagara College, Alexander Shvarts of Humber College, Laurel Whitney of Capilano University, and Michael Young of Camosun College for all their feedback.

Finally, my strength and resolve come from Martin, Monica, and Aaron; thank you, as always.

The future of criminology lies in the minds and hearts of those students in whom the passion for the discipline has been ignited. I salute them and encourage them to take up the challenges presented by the realities of crime and criminality in our ever-changing world, always with the goal of bettering the lives of all those affected.

Rebecca Volk

About the Authors

Frank Schmalleger, Ph.D., is professor emeritus at the University of North Carolina at Pembroke, where he was recognized as Distinguished Professor. Dr. Schmalleger holds degrees from the University of Notre Dame and Ohio State University, having earned both a master's (1970) and a doctorate in sociology (1974) from Ohio State University with a special emphasis in criminology. From 1976 to 1994, he taught criminal justice courses at the University of North Carolina at Pembroke. For the last 16 of those years, he chaired the university's Department of Sociology, Social Work, and Criminal Justice. Frank Schmalleger is the author of numerous articles and many books, including *Criminal Justice Today: An Introductory Text for the 21st Century*; *Juvenile Delinquency*; *Criminal Justice: A Brief Introduction*; *Criminal Law Today*; *Computers in Criminal Justice*; *Criminal Justice Ethics*; *Finding Criminal Justice in the Library*; *A History of Corrections*; and *The Social Basis of Criminal Justice*. Schmalleger is also founding editor of the journal *Criminal Justice Studies* (formerly *The Justice Professional*). Schmalleger's philosophy of both teaching and writing can be summed up in these words: "In order to communicate knowledge we must first catch, then hold, a person's interest—be it student, colleague, or policymaker. Our writing, our speaking, and our teaching must be relevant to the problems facing people today, and they must—in some way—help solve those problems."

Rebecca Volk currently oversees the Centre for Organizational Learning at Algonquin College in Ottawa, Ontario, after many years as a coordinator and professor in the Police Foundations Program at the college. She holds a bachelor's degree in political science from Queen's University in Kingston, Ontario, and an applied master's degree in criminology from the University of Ottawa. She is also co-author of *Police Ethics: A Matter of Character*.

Volk's professional experience has included involvement with a variety of offender aftercare and advocacy agencies, federal and provincial correctional institutions and residential centres, legal aid services, and various police agencies. She serves on the boards of several organizations devoted to promoting social justice for the most vulnerable among us.

Chapter 1

What Is Criminology?

Matt Barnes/Disney ABC Television Group/Getty Images

Rather than attributing crime and all that is evil to a relatively small group of people, I am saying that crime and socially harmful behaviour is widely (although not evenly) dispersed in society.

—*Thomas Gabor*[1]

LEARNING OBJECTIVES

After reading this chapter, you should be able to

1.1 Understand what crime is and how it is defined in this book.

1.2 Recognize the difference between criminal and deviant acts, and the complexity of this distinction.

1.3 Discuss who decides what should be criminal and how such decisions are made.

1.4 Explain what criminologists do.

1.5 Define what criminology is and the role of theoretical criminology.

1.6 Appreciate the role of research and experimentation in theory building in criminology.

1.7 Explain how social policy in the area of crime control is determined.

1.8 Discuss the theme of this book and explain the distinction between the social problems and social responsibility perspectives of crime causation.

1.9 Understand what it means to say that "criminal activity is diversely created and variously interpreted."

1.10 Discuss the discipline that has contributed the most to the theoretical understandings of crime causation over the past century.

INTRODUCTION

The TV megahit series *NCIS* (Naval Criminal Investigative Service) is recognized as one of the most popular scripted TV shows in the world.[2] With over 20 million dedicated viewers, the show has achieved heights that most other programs can't even dream of. Another immensely popular television series is the *CSI* franchise, which follows teams of crime-scene investigators in New York City and other locales. In 2012, *CSI* was declared the most watched show in the world.[3]

The popularity of prime-time television crime shows is not limited to *NCIS* or *CSI*. Other widely followed series include the Canadian police shows *Rookie Blue* and *Continuum* and the popular American hits *Criminal Minds*, *White Collar*, *The Wire*, *Cold Case*, and *Law and Order*—along with the *Law and Order* spin-offs, *Law and Order: Criminal Intent* and *Law and Order: Special Victims Unit*. Social commentators note that the plethora of crime shows bombarding the airwaves today reveals a penchant among North American TV viewers for crime-related entertainment and a fascination with criminal motivation and detective work.

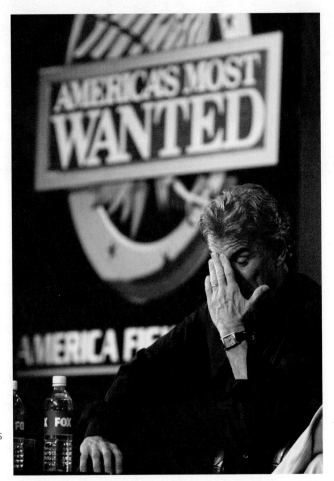

The public's interest in real-life stories of criminal victimization, revenge, and reform has given birth to reality-TV crime shows such as *America's Most Wanted*.

Reed Saxon/AP Photo

The public's interest in real-life stories of criminal victimization, revenge, and reform has given birth to reality-TV crime shows, including *America's Most Wanted*, *Cops*, *World's Wildest Police Videos*, and Canada's *The Beat*, which follows a group of Vancouver police officers as they patrol the city's lower east side. Similarly, video magazine shows like *The Fifth Estate*, *W5*, *60 Minutes*, *20/20*, and *Nightline* frequently focus on justice issues, and any number of movies—including *Sherlock Holmes*, *The Departed*, *Training Day*, *The Green Mile*, *Runaway Jury*, *The Shawshank Redemption*, *The Collector*, *Whiteout*, and *Minority Report*—play off the public's fascination with crime and the personal drama it fosters.

WHAT IS CRIME?

BEFORE WE BEGIN THE DISCUSSION OF CRIMINOLOGY IN EARNEST, WE NEED TO consider just what the term *crime* means. Crime can be defined in a variety of ways, and some scholars have suggested that at least four definitional perspectives can be found in contemporary criminology. These diverse perspectives see crime from (1) legalistic, (2) political, (3) sociological, and (4) psychological viewpoints. How we see any phenomenon is crucial because it determines the assumptions that we make about how that phenomenon should be studied. The perspective that we choose to employ when viewing crime determines the kinds of questions we ask, the nature of the research we conduct, and the type of answers that we expect to receive. Those answers, in turn, influence our conclusions about the kinds of crime-prevention and crime-control policies that might be effective.

Legalistic Perspective

Seen from a legalistic perspective, **crime** is *human conduct in violation of the criminal laws of a state, the federal government, or a provincial or local jurisdiction that has the power to make such laws.* Without a law that circumscribes a particular form of behaviour there can be no crime, no matter how deviant or socially repugnant the behaviour in question may be.

> **Crime** Human conduct in violation of the criminal laws of a state, the federal government, or a provincial or local jurisdiction that has the power to make such laws and for which there is some form of authorized sanction.

The notion of crime as behaviour[4] that violates the law derives from earlier work by criminologists who defined crime as "an intentional act in violation of the criminal law . . . committed without defense or excuse, and penalized by the state as a felony or misdemeanor."[5] Edwin Sutherland, one of the best-known criminologists of the last century, said of crime that its "essential characteristic . . . is that it is behavior which is prohibited by the State as an injury to the State and against which the State may react . . . by punishment."[6]

A serious shortcoming of the legalistic approach to crime is that it yields the moral high ground to powerful individuals who are able to influence the making of laws and the imposition of criminal definitions on lawbreakers. By making their own laws, powerful but immoral individuals can escape the label "criminal." In Chapter 10, we will explore this issue further and focus on the process of criminalization, which is the method used to **criminalize** some forms of behaviour—or make them illegal—while other forms remain legitimate. While we have chosen to adopt the legalistic approach to crime in this book, it is important to realize that laws are social products, so crime is socially relative in the sense that it is created by legislative activity.

> **Criminalize** To make illegal.

Another problem with the legalistic perspective is its insistence that the nature of crime cannot be separated from the nature of law, as the one explicitly defines the other. Not always recognized by legalistic definitions of crime, however, is the social, ethical, and individual significance of fundamentally immoral forms of behaviour. Simply put, some activities not yet contravened by **statute** still call out for a societal response, sometimes leading commentators to proclaim, "That ought to be a crime!" or "There should to be a law against that!"

> **Statute** A formal written enactment of a legislative body.

The legalistic definition of crime also suffers from its seeming lack of recognition that formalized laws have not always existed. Undoubtedly, much immoral behaviour occurred in past historical epochs, and contemporary laws probably now regulate most such behaviour. English common law, for example, upon which much of Canadian **statutory law** is based, judged behaviour in terms of traditional practice and customs and did not make use of written statutes. Although Canada has enacted a comprehensive legal code, it still adheres to a common-law tradition. (The exception to this is Quebec provincial law, which operates under the civil-law system used in many continental European countries. Dating back to the law of the Romans, the modern civil-law system is based on the Napoleonic Code of the early 19th century.) In such "common-law states," individuals may be prosecuted for violating traditional notions of right and wrong, even though no violation of written law took place. Common law is discussed in more detail in Chapter 5. (See Box 1.1 for the distinction between three primary forms of law.)

Changes in the laws will undoubtedly continue to occur, perhaps even legitimizing former so-called crimes where fundamentally moral or socially beneficial forms of behaviour have been criminalized. Over the last few years, for example, the federal government, along with members of the general public, has debated the pros and cons of euthanasia and certain forms of biomedical research, especially those involving human cloning and the use of human stem cells.

In what is seen as a landmark case in the euthanasia debate, in 1993, Sue Rodriguez, a 42-year-old British Columbia woman, challenged before the Supreme Court of Canada the statute that criminalizes the act of assisted suicide. Suffering a slow and painful death from amyotrophic lateral sclerosis (ALS), also known as "Lou Gehrig's disease," Ms. Rodriguez felt that the law forbidding a third party to assist in her death violated her rights under the *Canadian Charter of Rights and Freedoms*. "If I cannot give consent to my own death, whose body is this? Who owns my life?" asked the Victoria woman.[7] The Supreme Court ruled against Rodriguez, and she committed suicide two years later.

The debate has continued since. In 1995 and 2000, Special Senate Committees considered and made recommendations regarding the issue of euthanasia, concluding that "the principles, expertise, and medical infrastructure for the care of people facing death were

Box 1.1   PRIMARY FORMS OF LAW

Criminal law

Regulates actions that have the potential to harm interests of the state. Categories of criminal law include

- *indictable offences:* serious crimes including murder, robbery, sexual assault, hostage taking, perjury, and passing counterfeit money, among others. Carry a sentence of incarceration of 14 years or longer.

- *summary conviction offences:* less serious crimes including making indecent telephone calls, being found in a common bawdy house, causing a disturbance in or near a public place, and loitering on private property at night. Carry a maximum sentence of six months of incarceration.

- *hybrid offences (dual procedure):* may be tried either as indictable or summary conviction offences. The decision on how to treat a hybrid offence is made by the Crown attorney and is based on the circumstances surrounding the offence and the accused. They include pointing a firearm, driving while disqualified, and uttering death threats.

Civil law

Exists primarily for the purpose of enforcing private rights and deals with arrangements between individuals, such as contracts and claims to property.

Administrative law

Regulates many daily business activities. Violation of such regulations generally results in warnings or fines, depending on their adjudged severity. For example, decisions of the British Columbia Crime Victim Assistance Program or the Ontario Workplace Safety and Insurance Board constitute part of administrative case law.

The debate over assisted suicide highlights the changing nature of criminal activity. Sue Rodriguez used her personal situation to attempt to get the Supreme Court to strike down section 241(b) of the *Criminal Code of Canada*, which makes it illegal to assist someone in committing suicide. She was unsuccessful, and the law stands.

Chuck Stoody/Canadian Press Images

evolving far too slowly."[8] In June 2008, MP Francine Lalonde introduced in the House of Commons Bill C562, an act to amend the *Criminal Code* calling for the right to die with dignity. In 2012, the British Columbia Supreme Court ruled in the case of Gloria Taylor that the federal ban on assisted suicide contravenes section 15 of the *Canadian Charter of Rights and Freedoms*. This case will be heard by the Supreme Court in 2013.[9]

Political Perspective

A second perspective on crime is the political one, where crime is the result of criteria that have been built into the law by powerful groups and are then used to label selected undesirable forms of behaviour as illegal. Those who adhere to this point of view say that crime is a definition of human conduct created by authorized agents in a politically organized society. Seen this way, laws serve the interests of the politically powerful, and crimes are merely forms of behaviour that are perceived by those in power as direct or indirect threats to their interests. Thus, the political perspective defines crime in terms of the power structures that exist in society and asserts that criminal laws do not necessarily bear any inherent relationship to popular notions of right and wrong.

Some criminologists insist that the field of criminology must include behaviours that go beyond those defined as crimes through the political process; not doing so, they say, restricts rather than encourages inquiry into relevant forms of human behaviour.[10]

Sociological Perspective

Watch

Sociologists' Approach to Crime and Deviance

Adherents of our third perspective, the sociological viewpoint, would likely agree with this statement by Canadian criminologist Ezzat Fattah who saw crime as "an antisocial act of such a nature that its repression is necessary or is supposed to be necessary to the preservation of the existing system of society."[11] Some criminologists have gone so far as to claim that any definition of crime must include all forms of antisocial behaviour.[12]

Ron Claassen, a modern-day champion of restorative justice, suggested, for example, that "crime is primarily an offense against human relationships, and secondarily a violation of a law—since laws are written to protect safety and fairness in human relationships."[13] A more comprehensive sociological definition of crime was offered by Herman Schwendinger and Julia Schwendinger in 1975: crime encompasses "any harmful acts," including violations of "the fundamental prerequisites for well-being, [such as] food, shelter, clothing, medical services, challenging work and recreational experiences, as well as security from predatory individuals or repressive and imperialistic elites."[14] The Schwendingers have challenged criminologists to be less constrained in what they see as the subject matter of their field, saying that violations of human rights may be more relevant to criminological inquiry than many acts that have been politically or legally defined as crime. Jeffrey H. Reiman, another contemporary criminologist, asked similar questions. "The fact is that the label 'crime' is not used in America to name all or the worst of the actions that cause misery and suffering to Americans," said Reiman. "It is primarily reserved for the dangerous actions of the poor." Writing about unhealthy and unsafe workplaces, Reiman asked, "Doesn't a crime by any other name still cause misery and suffering? What's in a name?"[15] While a sociological approach to understanding crime is attractive to many, others claim that it suffers from wanting to criminalize activities that cause only indirect harm, that is, it is easier for most people to appreciate the criminality involved in a robbery or a sexual assault than in the cost-cutting efforts made by a businessperson.

Psychological Perspective

Finally, a psychological perspective states that "crime is a form of social maladjustment which can be designated as a more or less pronounced difficulty that the individual has in reacting to the stimuli of his environment in such a way as to remain in harmony with that environment."[16] Seen this way, crime is problem behaviour, especially human activity that contravenes the criminal law and results in difficulties in living within a framework of generally acceptable social arrangements. According to Matthew B. Robinson, "The maladaptive view of crime does not require any of the [traditional] elements . . . in order for an act to be a crime: no actual harm to others; no prohibition by law before the act is committed; no arrest; and no conviction in a court of law. Any behavior which is maladaptive ... would be considered crime. If criminologists adopted this view of crime," said Robinson, "the scope of criminology would be greatly expanded beyond its current state. All actually or even potentially harmful behaviors could be examined, analyzed, and documented for the purpose of gaining knowledge about potentially harmful behaviors and developing strategies to protect people from all harmful acts, not just those that are called 'crime' today."[17]*

As this discussion shows, a unified or simple definition of crime is difficult to achieve. The four points of view that we have discussed here form a kind of continuum, bound on one end by strict legalistic interpretations of crime and on the other by much more fluid behavioural and moralistic definitions.

1.2 LEARNING OBJECTIVE

◉⌐Watch

Piercings Perceived as Deviance

✱⌐Explore

Deviance

CRIME AND DEVIANCE

SOCIOLOGICALLY SPEAKING, MOST CRIMES CAN BE REGARDED AS DEVIANT FORMS OF behaviour—that is, as behaviours that are in some way abnormal. Piers Beirne and James Messerschmidt, two contemporary criminologists, defined deviance as "any social behavior or social characteristic that departs from the conventional norms and standards of a community or society and for which the deviant is sanctioned."[18] Their definition, however, does not count as deviant any sanctionable behaviour that is not punished or

*Matthew B. Robinson, "Defining 'Crime,'" http://www.appstate.edu/~robinsnmb/smokeharms.htm [Accessed November 4, 2006]. Reprinted with permission from Matthew B. Robinson.

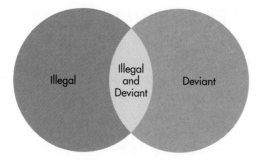

Figure 1.1 The Overlap between Deviance and Crime

punishable. Hence, the definition of **deviant behaviour** that we will use in this book is as follows: *deviant behaviour is human activity that violates social norms.*

Abnormality, deviance, and crime are concepts that do not always easily mesh. Some forms of deviance are not criminal, and the reverse is equally true (see Figure 1.1). Deviant styles of dress, for example, although perhaps outlandish to the majority, are not circumscribed by criminal law, unless (perhaps) decency statutes are violated by a lack of clothing. Even in such cases, laws are subject to interpretation and may be modified as social norms change over time. A little over a decade ago, the Court of Appeal in Ontario overturned the conviction of Gwen Jacob, who had been charged with committing an indecent act after she walked topless down a city street on a hot summer's day. The three judges on the panel ruled that there had to be a sexual connotation for the act to be considered indecent, and they found that Jacob had no such motivation. The Topfree Equal Rights movement that has emerged across Canada and the United States highlights the role that societal interpretation plays in defining a criminal offence.

Some types of behaviour, although quite common, are still against the law even if those who engage in them do not think of them as deviant. Speeding on provincial highways, for example, although probably something that most motorists engage in occasionally, is illegal. Complicating matters further is the fact that some forms of behaviour are either illegal or defined differently in various jurisdictions. For example, every province in Canada has some form of distracted-driving law banning the use of cell phones to call or text-message while driving, but this legislation varies widely.[19]

Deviant behaviour Human activity that violates social norms.

Deviance is relevant to the social context within which it occurs, as these licensed sex workers in Amsterdam show. Why is sex for hire against the law in most Canadian jurisdictions?

Peter Dejong/AP Photo

WHAT SHOULD BE CRIMINAL?

As you have probably realized by now, the question "What is crime?" is quite different from the question "What should be criminal?" Although most people agree that certain forms of behaviour, such as murder, sexual assault, burglary, and theft, should be against the law, there is far less agreement about the appropriate legal status of things like drug use, gambling, and "deviant" forms of consensual adult sexual behaviour.

While the question "What should be criminal?" can be answered in many different ways, the social and intellectual processes by which an answer is reached can be found in three contrasting points of view: (1) the consensus perspective, (2) the pluralist perspective, and (3) the conflict perspective. Each sees the relationship between the law and the social order somewhat differently; indeed, a criminologist's choice of perspective can influence his or her approach in explaining the causes of crime and criminal behaviour and, in turn, his or her suggestions for their prevention or control.

The Consensus Perspective

Consensus perspective
An analytical perspective on social organization that holds that most members of society agree about what is right and wrong and that various elements of society work together toward a common vision of the greater good.

The **consensus perspective** is built around the notion that most members of society agree on what is right and wrong, and that the various elements of society—including institutions such as churches, schools, government agencies, and businesses—work together toward a common vision of the greater good. The consensus viewpoint holds that laws should be enacted to criminalize given forms of behaviour when members of society generally agree that such laws are necessary. According to Raymond J. Michalowski, whose excellent analytical work is used to describe each of the three major approaches discussed in this section, the consensus perspective is characterized by four principles:[20]

1. Most members of a society believe in the existence of core values. The consensus perspective holds that shared notions of right and wrong characterize the majority of society's members.

2. Laws reflect the collective will of the people. Law is seen as the result of a consensus achieved through legislative action and represents a kind of social conscience.

3. Law serves all people equally. From the consensus point of view, the law not only embodies a shared view of justice but also is perceived to be just in its application.

4. Law violators represent a unique subgroup with distinguishing features. The consensus approach holds that law violators must somehow be improperly socialized, be psychologically defective, or suffer from some other lapse that leaves them unable to participate in what is otherwise widespread agreement on values and behaviour.

The consensus perspective is most applicable to homogeneous societies or those characterized by shared values, norms, and belief systems. In a multicultural and diverse society like Canada, however, a shared consensus may be difficult to achieve. In such a society, even relatively minor matters may lead to complex debates over the issues involved.

Contrary to the assumptions made by consensus thinkers, it has become quite plain to most observers of the contemporary social scene that not everyone agrees on what the law should say. Society today is rife with examples of conflicting values and ideals. Consensus is hard to find. Modern debates centre on issues such as abortion, euthanasia, the death penalty, the purpose of criminal justice agencies in a diverse society, social justice, the rights and responsibilities of minorities and other underrepresented groups, women's issues, the proper role of education, economic policy, social welfare, the function of the military in a changing world, environmental concerns, and appropriate

Should Polygamy Be a Protected Religious Practice?

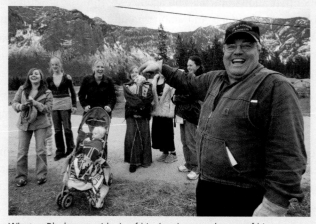

Winston Blackmore with six of his daughters and some of his grandchildren.

Jonathan Hayward/Canadian Press Images

The rural town of Bountiful in the southeastern interior of British Columbia is a community of about 1000 residents, all of whom are members of the Fundamentalist Church of Jesus Christ of Latter Day Saints (FLDS). The community is openly polygamous, in accordance with the most well-known tenet of the religion.

In January 2009, the Royal Canadian Mounted Police (RCMP) arrested Winston Blackmore, 52, and James Oler, 44, of Bountiful, charging them each with one count of practising polygamy under section 293 of the *Criminal Code of Canada*. The charges against Blackmore were linked to his marriages to 19 women, dating back to May 2005. The charges against Oler were linked to his marriages to three women, dating back to November 2004. It was alleged that Mr. Blackmore had as many as 26 wives, including one who was under the age of 16, and more than 100 children.

The RCMP investigated the case starting in 2005, interviewing over 90 people in British Columbia and the United States. After the investigation, British Columbia's Crown prosecutors remained reluctant to lay polygamy charges for fear they would be declared unconstitutional on the basis of religious freedom, recommending that the government get

a court ruling on the constitutionality of Canada's anti-polygamy laws. The then attorney general of British Columbia, Wally Oppal, finally appointed a third special prosecutor and charges were laid.

In September 2009, the Supreme Court of British Columbia dismissed the charges against Blackmore and Oler, ruling that the attorney general did not have the authority to appoint a new special prosecutor to consider the cases given that prosecutors had recommended against charges. The province appealed the ruling to the British Columbia Supreme Court and, in November 2011, that court upheld Canada's polygamy laws, ruling that while the law does infringe on religious freedom, it is justified given the harm that polygamy causes to children, women, society, and the institution of monogamous marriage.

The issue is clearly one of *Charter* rights of the individual versus the criminal law of the state. Canadians see American authorities cracking down on FLDS sects, such as one in Texas where over 400 children, including at least one Canadian, were taken into custody and another in Utah where a sect leader was charged with polygamy and the rape of a child. There has not been similar action in Canada, however.

Think about it:

1. What rights should members of minority faiths have when they advocate or engage in behaviour that goes beyond social norms or violates the law? Give some examples.

2. Would the rights you identified above extend to the practice of polygamy? Why or why not?

3. What is the legal history of the practice of polygamy in Canada? When did it become illegal? Why?

Based on CBC News, "Canada's polygamy laws upheld by BC Supreme Court," November 23, 2011, www.cbc.ca/news/canada/british-columbia/story/2011/11/23/bc-polygamy-ruling-supreme-court.html; CBC News, "Polygamy charges in Bountiful B.C. thrown out," September 23, 2009, www.cbc.ca/news/canada/british-columbia/story/2009/09/23/bc-polygamy-charges-blackmore-oler-bountiful.html; CTV News, "Polygamy charges laid against Bountiful, B.C. leaders," January 9, 2010, www.ctvnews.ca/polygamy-charges-laid-against-bountiful-b-c-leaders-1.358027; *The Fifth Estate*, "Bust-up in Bountiful," April 12, 2008, www.cbc.ca/fifth/bustupinbountiful/.

uses of high technology. As many contemporary public forums would indicate, there exists within Canada today a great diversity of social groups, each with its own point of view regarding what is right and what is wrong, and each with its own agenda. (See the discussion in the Who's Responsible? box.)

The Pluralist Perspective

Pluralist perspective
An analytical approach to social organization that holds that a multiplicity of values and beliefs exists in any complex society but that most social actors agree on the usefulness of law as a formal means of dispute resolution.

The second perspective, the **pluralist perspective**, mirrors the thought that a multiplicity of values and beliefs exists in any complex society and that different social groups will have their own respective sets of beliefs, interests, and values. A crucial element of this perspective is the assumption that although different viewpoints exist, most individuals agree on the usefulness of law as a formal means of dispute resolution. From pluralist perspective, the law exists as a peacekeeping tool that allows officials and agencies within the government to settle disputes effectively between individuals and among groups; whatever settlement is reached will be acceptable to all parties because of their agreement on the fundamental role of law in dispute settlement. The basic principles of the pluralistic perspective include the following:[21]

- Society consists of many diverse social groups. Differences in age, gender, sexual preference, ethnicity, and the like often provide the basis for much naturally occurring diversity.

- Each group has its own characteristic set of values, beliefs, and interests. Variety in gender, sexual orientation, economic status, ethnicity, and other forms of diversity produces interests that may unite like-minded individuals but that may also place them in natural opposition to other social groups.

- A general agreement exists on the usefulness of formalized laws as a mechanism for dispute resolution. People and groups accept the role of law in the settlement of disputes and accord decisions reached within the legal framework at least a modicum of respect.

- The legal system is value-neutral, that is, free of petty disputes or above the level of general contentiousness that may characterize relationships between groups.

- The legal system is concerned with the best interests of society. Legislators, judges, prosecutors, attorneys, police officers, and correctional officials are assumed to perform idealized functions that are beyond the reach of self-serving groups, so official functionaries can be trusted to act in accordance with the greater good, to remain unbiased, and to maintain a value-free system for the enforcement of laws.

The Conflict Perspective

◉ **Watch**

Justice and Privilege

Conflict perspective An analytical approach to social organization that holds that conflict is a fundamental aspect of social life and can never be fully resolved.

The third perspective, the **conflict perspective**, maintains that conflict is a fundamental aspect of social life itself that can never be fully resolved. Formal agencies of social control merely coerce the unempowered or the disenfranchised to comply with the rules established by those in power. Laws are a tool of the powerful, useful in keeping others from wresting control over important social institutions. Rather than being the result of any consensus or process of dispute resolution, social order rests upon the exercise of power through law. Those in power must work ceaselessly to remain there, although the structures they impose on society—including patterns of wealth building that they define as acceptable and circumstances under which they authorize the exercise of legal power and military might—give them all the advantages they are likely to need. The conflict perspective can be described in terms of the following key elements:[22]

- Society is made up of diverse social groups, and diversity is based on distinctions that people hold to be significant, such as gender, sexual orientation, and social class.

- Each group holds to differing definitions of right and wrong, so moralistic conceptions and behavioural standards vary from group to group.

- Conflict between groups is both socially significant and unavoidable because groups defined by such characteristics as ethnicity, gender, and social class compete for power, wealth, and other forms of power.

- The fundamental nature of group conflict centres on the exercise of political power, which is the key to the accumulation of wealth and to other forms of power.

- Law is a tool of power and furthers the interests of those powerful enough to make it. Laws allow those in control to gain what they define as legitimate access to scarce resources and to deny such access to the politically disenfranchised.

- Those in power are inevitably interested in maintaining their power against those who would usurp it.

WHAT DO CRIMINOLOGISTS DO?

1.4 **LEARNING OBJECTIVE**

A TYPICAL DICTIONARY DEFINITION OF A **CRIMINOLOGIST** IS "ONE WHO STUDIES crime, criminals, and criminal behaviour."[23] Occasionally, the term *criminologist* is used broadly to describe almost anyone who works in the criminal justice field, regardless of formal training. There is a growing tendency, however, to reserve application of the term *criminologist* to academics, researchers, and policy analysts with advanced degrees who are involved in the study of crime and crime trends and in the analysis of societal reactions to crime. Hence, it is more appropriate today to describe specially skilled investigators, crime-laboratory technicians, fingerprint experts, crime-scene photographers, ballistics experts, and others who work to solve particular crimes as *criminalists*. A **criminalist** is "a specialist in the collection and examination of the physical evidence of crime."[24] Police officers, corrections professionals, probation and parole officers, judges, Crown attorneys, defence counsel, and others who do the day-to-day work of the criminal justice system are often referred to as criminal justice professionals.

Criminologist One who is trained in the field of criminology; also, one who studies crime, criminals, and criminal behaviour.

✳⌐Explore

Roles of Criminologists

Criminalist A specialist in the collection and examination of the physical evidence of crime.

Academic criminologists and research criminologists generally hold doctoral or master's degrees in the field of criminology or criminal justice from an accredited university. Some criminologists hold degrees in related fields such as sociology and political science and have specialized in the study and control of crime and deviance. Many academic criminologists teach either criminology or criminology-related subjects in institutions of higher learning, including universities and community colleges. Nearly all criminology professors are involved in research or writing projects, by which they strive to advance criminological knowledge. Other criminologists are strictly researchers and work for federal agencies such as the Department of Justice Canada, Public Safety Canada, or the Canadian Centre for Justice Statistics.

The results of criminological research in Canada and the United States are generally published in journals such as the *Canadian Journal of Criminology and Criminal Justice* (the official publication of the Canadian Criminal Justice Association), the *Canadian Journal of Law and Society*, the *Canadian Journal of Women and the Law*, *Criminology* (the official publication of the American Society of Criminology), *Theoretical Criminology*, *Crime and Delinquency*, and *Social Problems*.[25] International English-language journals are numerous and include the *International Review of Victimology*, the *Australian and New Zealand Journal of Criminology*, and the *British Journal of Criminology*.

People who have earned undergraduate degrees in the field of criminology often find access to police investigative or support work, probation and parole agencies, court-support activities, and correctional (prison) work. Criminologists also work for government agencies interested in developing effective social policies to prevent or fight crime.

Private security provides another career track for individuals interested in criminology and criminal justice. The number of personnel employed by private security agencies today is one-third greater than that by public law enforcement agencies, and the gap is widening.[26] Many upper- and mid-level managers working for private security firms hold criminology or criminal justice degrees. A similar trend is emerging in the field of public policing. While most Canadian police services require applicants to have a high school

Table 1.1 What Do Criminologists Do?

The term *criminologist* is usually applied to credentialed individuals, such as those holding advanced degrees in the field, who engage in the study of crime, criminal behaviour, and crime trends. The word *criminalist* is used to describe people who specialize in collecting and examining the physical evidence associated with specific crimes. Others working in the criminal justice system are called *criminal justice professionals*. This table lists some of the activities and jobs open to individuals working in the three areas.

Activities of Criminologists

Data gathering	Public service
Data analysis	Analysis of crime patterns and trends
Theory construction	Scholarly presentations and publications
Hypothesis testing	Education and training
Social policy creation	Threat assessment and risk analysis
Public advocacy	

Jobs in the Field of Criminalistics

Forensics examiner	Crime-scene photographer
Crime-laboratory technician	Polygraph operator
Ballistics expert	Fingerprint examiner
Crime-scene investigator	

Jobs in the Field of Criminal Justice

Law enforcement officer	Judge
Probation or parole officer	Defence attorney
Corrections officer	Crown attorney
Prison administrator	Cybercrime investigator
Private security officer	Young offender worker
Victims' advocate	Court support worker

diploma as a minimum, a majority of recent new recruits to the profession have attained higher levels of education.

Anyone trained in criminology has various alternatives (see Table 1.1). Some people with undergraduate degrees in criminology or criminal justice go on to law school. Some teach high school, while others become private investigators. Many criminologists provide civic organizations (such as victims' assistance and justice advocacy groups) with much-needed expertise, a few work for politicians and legislative bodies, and some appear on talk shows to debate the pros and cons of various kinds of social policies designed to fight crime. Some criminologists even write books such as this one!

WHAT IS CRIMINOLOGY?

THE ATTEMPT TO UNDERSTAND CRIME PREDATES WRITTEN HISTORY. PREHISTORIC evidence, including skeletal remains showing signs of primitive cranial surgery, seems to indicate that preliterate people explained deviant behaviour in terms of spirit possession. Primitive surgery was an attempt to release unwanted spiritual influences. In the thousands of years since, many other theoretical perspectives on crime have been advanced. This book describes various criminological theories and covers some of the more popular ones in detail.

Definition of Terms

Before beginning any earnest discussion, however, it is necessary to define the term *criminology*. As our earlier discussion of the nature of crime and deviance indicates, not only must criminologists deal with a complex subject matter—consisting of a broad range of illegal behaviours committed by frequently unknown or uncooperative individuals—they must also manage their work under changing conditions mandated by ongoing revisions of the law and fluctuating **social policy**. In addition, as we have already seen, a wide variety of perspectives on the nature of crime abound. All this leads to considerable difficulties in defining the subject matter under study.

Social policy A government initiative, program, or plan intended to address problems in society.

There is some evidence that the term *criminology* was coined by a Frenchman, Paul Topinard, in 1889;[27] he used it to differentiate the study of criminal body types within the field of anthropology from other biometric pursuits.[28] However, while Topinard may have coined the term, he did little to help define it. As with the concept of crime, various definitions of criminology can be found in the literature today.

One straightforward definition can be had from a linguistic analysis of the word *criminology*. As most people know, *-ology* means "the study of something," and the word *crimen* comes from Latin, meaning "accusation," "charge," or "guilt." Hence, linguistically speaking, the term *criminology* literally means "the study of crime." In addition to this fundamental kind of linguistic definition, three other important types of definitions can be found in the literature: (1) disciplinary, (2) causative, and (3) scientific. Each type of definition is distinguished by its focus.

Disciplinary definitions are those that, as the name implies, focus on criminology as a discipline. Seen from this viewpoint, criminology is a field of study or a body of knowledge. Some of the earliest criminologists of the past century offered definitions of their field that emphasized its importance as a discipline of study. Edwin Sutherland, considered by many the "dean of criminology," wrote in the first edition of his textbook *Criminology* in 1924, "Criminology is the body of knowledge regarding the social problem of crime."[29] Sutherland's text was to set the stage for much of North American criminology throughout the rest of the 20th century. It was reprinted in 1934 with the title *Principles of Criminology*,[30] and even after Sutherland's death in 1950, his revered text was revised for many years by Donald R. Cressey and later by David F. Luckenbill. By 1974, Sutherland's classic definition of criminology had been modified by Cressey: "Criminology is the body of knowledge regarding delinquency and crime as a social phenomenon. It includes within its scope the processes of making laws, of breaking laws, and of reacting toward the breaking of laws."[31]

Causative definitions emphasize criminology's role in uncovering the underlying causes of crime. In keeping with such an emphasis, contemporary criminologists Gennaro F. Vito and Ronald M. Holmes stated, "Criminology is the study of the causes of crime."[32]

Finally, there are those who point to the scientific nature of contemporary criminology as its distinguishing characteristic. According to Clemens Bartollas and Simon Dinitz, for example, "Criminology is the scientific study of crime."[33] Writing in 1989, Bartollas and Dinitz seemed to be echoing an earlier definition of criminology offered by Marvin E. Wolfgang and Franco Ferracuti, who wrote in 1967, "Criminology is the scientific study of crime, criminals, and criminal behavior."[34]

One of the most comprehensive definitions of the term *criminology* that is available today comes from the European Society of Criminology (ESC), which in its constitution defined *criminology* as "all scholarly, scientific and professional knowledge concerning the explanation, prevention, control and treatment of crime and delinquency, offenders and victims, including the measurement and detection of crime, legislation, and the practice of criminal law, and law enforcement, judicial, and correctional systems."[35] ESC's emphasis is on "knowledge"; even though it mentions the "practice" of what many would call criminal justice (that is, policing, courts, and corrections), it is the study and knowledge of such practice that form the crux of the ESC perspective.

For our purposes, we will use a definition somewhat simpler than that of the ESC, one that brings together the works of previous writers but also recognizes the increasingly professional status of the criminological enterprise. Throughout this book, then, we will say that **criminology** is *an interdisciplinary profession built around the scientific study of crime and criminal behaviour, including their manifestations, causes, legal aspects, prevention, and control.* As this definition indicates, criminology includes consideration of possible solutions to the problem of crime. Hence, this text (in later chapters) describes prevention and treatment strategies and social policy initiatives that have grown out of the existing array of theoretical explanations for crime.

Our definition is in keeping with the work of J.P. Gibbs, a notable 20th-century criminologist who wrote that the purpose of criminology is to offer well-researched and objective answers to four basic questions: (1) "Why do crime rates vary?" (2) "Why do individuals differ as to criminality?" (3) "Why is there variation in reactions to crime?" and (4) "What are the possible means of controlling criminality?"[36] It is important to note that our definition and Gibbs's guiding queries encompass a number of different terms that are sometimes easily confused. Criminology, **criminality**, crime, deviance, and **criminal behaviour** are five concepts used in this chapter and throughout this book, and learning the definition of each provides a good start for anyone studying in this field.

As a field of study, criminology in its present form is primarily a social scientific discipline. Contemporary criminologists generally recognize, however, that their field is *interdisciplinary*; that is, it draws upon other disciplines to provide an integrated approach to understanding the problem of crime in contemporary society and to advancing solutions to the problems crime creates. Hence, anthropology (especially cultural anthropology or ethnology), biology, sociology, political science, psychology, economics, ethology (the study of character), medicine, psychiatry, law, philosophy, ethics, and numerous other fields all have something to offer the student of criminology, as do the tools provided by statistics, computer science, and other forms of scientific and data analysis.

It is important, however, to note that although criminology may be interdisciplinary as well as cross-professional, few existing explanations for criminal behaviour have been successfully or fully integrated. Just as physicists today are seeking a unified field theory to explain the wide variety of observable forms of matter and energy, criminologists have yet to develop a generally accepted, integrated approach to crime and criminal behaviour that can explain the many diverse forms of criminality while also leading to effective social policies in the area of crime prevention and control. The attempt to construct criminological theories that are relevant to the problems of today is made all the more difficult because, as discussed earlier, the phenomenon under study—crime—is very wide-ranging and is subject to arbitrary and sometimes unpredictable legalistic and definitional changes.

A successfully integrated criminology must bring together the contributions of various theoretical perspectives and disciplines, but it must also—if it is to have any relevance—blend the practical requirements of our nation's judicial system with emotional and rational calls for morality and justice. Should capital punishment, for example, be reinstated? If so, on what basis? Is it because it is a type of vengeance and therefore deserved? Or can we continue to say that it is unjustified because many sociological studies have shown that it does little to reduce the rate of serious crime such as murder? Just what do we mean by *justice*, and what can criminological studies tell us—if anything—about what is just and what is unjust?

The editors of the journal *Theoretical Criminology*, which began publication over a decade ago, wrote in the inaugural issue that "criminology has always been somewhat of a haphazardly assembled, umbrella-like structure which nevertheless usefully shelters a variety of theoretical interests that are espoused and employed by different disciplinary, methodological, and political traditions."[37] In other words, while the field of criminology can benefit from the wide variety of ideas available via a multiplicity of perspectives, all of which seek to understand the phenomenon we call "crime," cross-discipline collaboration can be quite difficult.

Criminology An interdisciplinary profession built around the scientific study of crime and criminal behaviour, including their forms, causes, legal aspects, prevention, and control.

Criminality A behavioural predisposition that disproportionately favours criminal activity.

Criminal behaviour A way of acquiring valued resources from others by exploring and deceiving them.

Criminology examines the causes of crime and seeks ways to prevent or control it. Criminal justice examines the criminal justice system, including police, courts, and corrections. How do the two disciplines complement one another?

Richard Lautens/Toronto Star/ZUMApress.com/Alamy

As our earlier definition of *criminology* indicates, however, it is more than a field of study or a collection of theories; it is also a discipline and a profession.[38] Notably, criminology also contributes to the discipline of **criminal justice**, which emphasizes application of the criminal law and study of the components of the justice system, especially the police, courts, and corrections. As one author stated, "Criminology gives prominence to questions about the *causes of criminality*, while the *control of lawbreaking* is at the heart of criminal justice."[39]

Criminal justice The scientific study of crime, the criminal law, and components of the criminal justice system, including the police, courts, and corrections.

Theoretical Criminology

Theoretical criminology, a subfield of general criminology, is the type of criminology most often found in community colleges and universities. Theoretical criminology, rather than simply describing crime and its occurrence, posits explanations for criminal behaviour. As Sutherland stated, "The problem in criminology is to explain the criminality of behavior . . . However, an explanation of criminal behavior should be a specific part of [a] general theory of behavior and its task should be to differentiate criminal from non-criminal behavior."[40]

To explain and understand crime, criminologists have developed many theories. As we will see later in this chapter, a **theory**, at least in its ideal form, is made up of clearly stated propositions that posit relationships, often of a causal sort, between events and things under study. An old Roman theory, for example, proposed that insanity is caused by the influence of the moon and may even follow its cycles—hence the term *lunacy*.

Theories attempt to provide us with explanatory power and help us to understand a phenomenon under study. The more applicable a theory is found to be, the more generalizable it is from one specific instance to others— in other words, the more it can be applied to other situations. A **general theory** of crime is one that attempts to explain all (or at least most) forms of criminal conduct through a single, overarching approach. Unfortunately, as Don Gottfredson observed, "Theories in criminology tend to be unclear and lacking in justifiable generality."[41] When we consider the wide range of behaviours regarded as criminal—from murder, through drug use, to white-collar and computer crime—it seems difficult to imagine one theory that can explain them all or which might even explain the same type of behaviour under varying circumstances. Still, many past theoretical approaches to crime causation were **unicausal** while attempting to be all-inclusive. In other words, the approaches posited a single, identifiable source for all serious deviant and criminal behaviour.

An **integrated theory**, in contrast to a general theory, does not necessarily attempt to explain all criminality but is distinguishable by the fact that it merges (or attempts to merge)

Theory A series of interrelated propositions that attempt to describe, explain, predict, and ultimately control some class of events. A theory gains explanatory power from inherent logical consistency and is "tested" by how well it describes and predicts reality.

General theory A theory that attempts to explain all (or at least most) forms of criminal conduct through a single, overarching approach.

Unicausal Having one cause. Unicausal theories posit only one source for all that they attempt to explain.

Integrated theory An explanatory perspective that merges (or attempts to merge) concepts drawn from different sources.

concepts drawn from different sources. Put another way, "An integrative criminology . . . seeks to bring together the diverse bodies of knowledge that represent the full array of disciplines that study crime."[42] Hence, integrated theories provide potentially wider explanatory power than narrower formulations. Recognizing that no one theory can explain all criminal behaviour, Don G. Gibbons noted, "The basic idea of theoretical integration is straightforward; it concerns the combinations of single theories or elements of those theories into a more comprehensive argument. At the same time, it would be well to note that in practice, integration is a matter of degree: some theorists have combined or integrated more concepts or theoretical elements than have others."[43]

Both the general applicability and the theoretical integration of criminological theories to a wide variety of law-violating behaviours are intuitively appealing concepts. Even far more limited attempts at criminological theorizing, however, often face daunting challenges. To date, "criminologists have not managed to articulate a large collection of relatively formalized arguments in a general or integrated form."[44] Hence, although we will use the word *theory* in describing the many explanations for crime covered by this book, it should be recognized that the word is only loosely applicable to some of the perspectives we will discuss.

As we shall learn later in this chapter, many social scientists insist that to be considered theories, explanations must consist of sets of clearly stated, logically interrelated, and measurable propositions. The fact that only a few of the theories described in this book rise above the level of organized conjecture—and those offer only limited generalizability and have rarely been integrated—is one of the greatest challenges facing criminology today.

1.6 | **LEARNING OBJECTIVE**

THE EVOLVING SCIENCE OF CRIMINOLOGY

THE THEORETICAL PERSPECTIVES ADOPTED BY CRIMINOLOGISTS PROVIDE THE underpinning for the direction of their research and the development of their theories. Indeed, over the past century, criminologists have undertaken the task of building a scientific or evidence-based criminology, as distinguished from what had been the "armchair criminology" of earlier times. Armchair criminologists offered their ideas to one another as conjecture—fascinating "theories" that could be debated (and sometimes were) ad nauseam. The ruminations of armchair criminologists may have achieved a considerable degree of popular acclaim through the involvement of distinguished lecturers, the association of such ideas with celebrated bastions of higher learning, and their publication in prestigious forums, but they were rarely founded on anything other than mere speculation.

Although it is easy to dispense with armchair criminology as the relaxed musings of carefree intellectuals undertaken almost as sport, it is far more difficult to agree on the criteria necessary to move any undertaking into the realm of serious scientific endeavour. Present-day criminology is decidedly more scientific, however, than its intellectual predecessor—which means that it is amenable to objective scrutiny and systematic testing. A variety of criteria has been advanced for declaring any endeavour "scientific." Among them are these:[45]

- the systematic collection of related facts (as in the building of a database)
- an emphasis on the availability and application of the scientific method
- "the existence of general laws, a field for experiment or observation . . . and control of academic discourse by practical application"
- "the fact that it has been accepted into the scientific tradition"
- an "emphasis on a worthwhile subject in need of independent study even if adequate techniques of study are not yet available" (as in the investigation of paranormal phenomena)

Probably all the foregoing could be said of criminology. For one thing, criminologists do gather facts. The mere gathering of facts, however, although it may lead to a descriptive criminology, falls short of offering satisfactory explanations for crime. Hence, most contemporary criminologists are concerned with identifying relationships among the facts they observe and attempting to understand the many and diverse causes of crime. This emphasis on unveiling causality moves criminology beyond the merely descriptive into the realm of conjecture and theory building. A further emphasis on measurement and objectivity gives contemporary criminology its scientific flavour.

Theory Building

A few years ago, Inspector Andy Parr, of the Sussex Police Department in England, reviewed crime statistics for the town of Brighton and found that violent crime was higher on nights when the moon was full.[46] "I compared a graph of full moons and a graph of last year's violent crimes and there is a trend," Parr told the United Kingdom's *Telegraph* newspaper. "People tend to be more aggressive" when the moon is full, Parr concluded. His findings were supported, he said, by his patrol experience. "When you try to reason with people on a full moon they become more aggressive and less rational," he told reporters. "When you try to reason with them on a full moon they become more argumentative."

Ultimately, the goal of research within criminology is the construction of theories or models that allow for a better understanding of criminal behaviour and that permit the development of strategies intended to address the problem of crime. Simply put, a theory consists of a set of interrelated propositions that provide a relatively complete form of understanding (see Figure 1.2). Hence, even if we find that crime is higher when the moon is full, we must still ask why. Is it because the light from full moons makes it possible for those interested in committing crime to see better at night? If so, then we would expect crime to be higher in areas where there is no cloud cover than in areas with clouds. Likewise, lighted cities should show less of a rise in crime during full moons than rural areas and small towns. In any event, a complete lunar theory of crime causation would contain specific propositions about the causal nature of the phenomena involved.

There are many ways to define the word *theory*. One cogent definition comes from Don M. Gottfredson, a well-known criminologist of modern times: "Theories consist of postulates [assumptions], theoretical constructs, logically derived hypotheses, and definitions. Theories can be improved steadily through hypothesis testing, examination of evidence from observations, revisions of the theory, and repetitions of the cycle, repeatedly modifying the theory in light of the evidence."[47] (A hypothesis is an explanation that accounts for a set of facts and that can be tested by further investigation.) Another well-known methodologist describes theories this way: "A theory is a set of related propositions that suggest why events occur in the manner that they do. The propositions that make up theories are of the same form as hypotheses: they consist of concepts and the linkages or relationships between them."[48] Theories serve a number of purposes. For one thing, they give meaning to observations, explaining what we see in a particular setting by relating those observations to other things already understood. Hence, a theory of physics can explain the behaviour of light by saying that light has the properties of both waves and particles. Such a theory is immediately useful because we can easily grasp ideas like waves and particles even if we have trouble conceptualizing light's essence.

Theories within criminology serve the same purpose as those within the physical sciences, but they are often more difficult to test. For example, few people can intuitively understand the motivation of "lust murderers" (a term developed by the Federal Bureau of Investigation in the United States and popularized by the media to refer to men who sexually abuse and kill women, often sadistically). Some psychiatric theories (discussed in

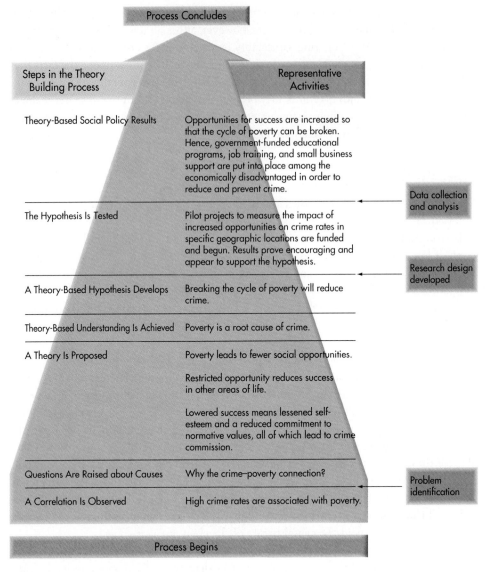

Figure 1.2 The Theory-Building Process

Chapter 7) suggest that lust murderers kill because of a deep-seated hatred of women. Hate is something that most minds can grasp, and a vision of lust murder as an extreme example of the age-old battle between the sexes provides an intellectual "handle" that at least some can comprehend. Hence, theory building dispenses with the old adage that "it takes one to know one," instead bringing at least the possibility of understanding within the reach of all. Note, however, that although such limited explanations as the one discussed here may provide a degree of understanding, they must still be tested to determine whether they are true.

The Role of Research and Experimentation

More important than the claims made by theories and by the theorists who create them are findings of fact that either support those claims or leave them without foundation. Hence, theories, once proposed, need to be tested against the real world through a variety of research strategies, including experimentation and case studies. This is equally true whether the proposed theory is relatively simple or dauntingly complex.

Reliable determinations of program effectiveness are made through research. **Research** can be defined as the use of standardized, systematic procedures in the search for

Research The use of standardized, systematic procedures in the search for knowledge.

The full moon over Toronto. It is the job of researchers to determine the validity of such claimed relationships—and of theorists to explain why such relationships hold. Are phases of the moon correlated with changes in the rate of occurrence of certain crimes?

Angelo Cavalli/Tips Images/Tips Italia Srl a socio unico/Alamy

knowledge.[49] Some researchers distinguish between applied research and non-applied or pure research. **Applied research** "consists of scientific inquiry that is designed and carried out with practical application in mind."[50] In applied research, the researcher is working toward some more or less practical goal. It may be the reduction of crime, the efficient compensation of victims of crime, or an evaluation of the effectiveness of policies implemented to solve some specific aspect of the crime problem. **Pure research**, on the other hand, is undertaken simply for the sake of advancing scientific knowledge and is not expected to be immediately relevant.

Another type of research, secondary research or secondary analysis, can be distinguished from primary research.[51] **Primary research** is "characterized by original and direct investigation,"[52] whereas **secondary research** consists of new evaluations of existing information collected by other researchers.

Scientific research generally proceeds in stages, which can be divided conceptually among (1) problem identification, (2) the development of a research design, (3) a choice of data-gathering techniques, and (4) a review of findings (which often includes statistical analysis).

Problem Identification Problem identification, the first step in any research, consists of the naming of a problem or choice of an issue to be studied. Topics may be selected for a variety of reasons. Perhaps the researcher has a personal interest in a particular issue

Applied research Research based on scientific inquiry that is designed and carried out with practical application in mind.

Pure research Research undertaken simply for the sake of advancing scientific knowledge.

Primary research Research characterized by original and direct investigation.

Secondary research New evaluations of existing information collected by other researchers.

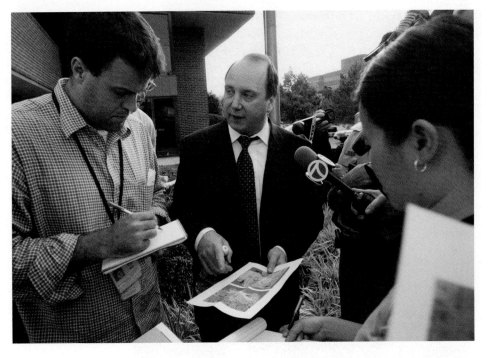

Former Vancouver Police Service detective Kim Rossmo (centre) used the hypothesis that humans—offenders included—are creatures of habit as the basis for his geographic profiling tool. How do hypotheses presented by researchers gain credibility?

Nick Wass/AP/Canadian Press Images

and wants to learn more, or maybe a professor or teacher has assigned a research project as part of the requirements for a class. Whatever the reason for beginning research, however, the way in which a research problem is stated and conceptualized will help narrow the research focus and will serve as a guide to the formulation of data-gathering strategies.

Although some criminological research undertaken today is purely descriptive, the bulk of such research is intended to explore issues of causality, especially the claims made by theories purporting to explain criminal behaviour. As such, much contemporary research in criminology is involved with the testing of hypotheses.

Hypothesis 1. An explanation that accounts for a set of facts and that can be tested by further investigation. 2. Something that is taken to be true for the purpose of argument or investigation.

Within the modern scientific tradition, a **hypothesis** serves two purposes: it is an explanation that accounts for a set of facts and that can be tested by further investigation, and it is something that is taken to be true for the purpose of argument or investigation. Some criminologists, as mentioned earlier, have observed what appears to be a correlation, or relationship, between phases of the moon and the rate of crime commission. Such observers may propose the following hypothesis: the moon causes crime. Although this is a useful starting hypothesis, it needs to be further refined before it can be tested. Specifically, the concepts contained within the hypothesis must be translated into measurable variables. A **variable** is simply a concept that can undergo measurable changes.

Variable A concept that can undergo measurable changes.

Scientific precedent holds that only measurable items can be satisfactorily tested. We might, for example, move a step further toward both measurability and specificity in our hypothesis about the relationship between the moon and crime by restating it as follows: rates of murder, rape, robbery, and assault rise when the moon's fullness increases and are highest when the moon is fullest. Once the concepts within our hypothesis are measurable, we can test the hypothesis itself; that is to say, we can observe what happens to crime rates as the moon approaches fullness, as well as what happens when the moon is full, and see whether our observations support our hypothesis.

The Development of a Research Design Research designs structure the research process. They provide a kind of road map to the logic inherent in one's approach to a research problem, and they also serve as guides to the systematic collection of data.

Research design The logic and structure inherent in an approach to data gathering.

Research designs consist of the logic and structure inherent in any particular approach to data gathering. A simple study, for example, might be designed to test the assertion that the consumption of refined white sugar promotes aggressive or violent tendencies. One could imagine researchers approaching prison officials with the proposal that inmate diets should be altered to exclude all refined sugar. Likewise, the prison canteen would be prohibited from selling items containing sugar for the duration of the experiment.

To determine whether the forced reduction in sugar consumption actually affected inmates' behaviour, researchers might look at the recorded frequency of aggressive incidents occurring within the confines of the prison before the experiment was initiated and compare such data with similar information on such incidents following the introduction of dietary changes. Researchers employing a strategy of this type would likely examine differences between the two sets of observations, one made before introduction of the experimental intervention and the other after. The difference, they may assume, would show changes in behaviour resulting from changes in diet—in this case, the exclusion of refined white sugar. Although this basic research design illustrates well the logic behind naïve experiments, it does not lend good structure to a research undertaking, because it does not eliminate other possible explanations of behavioural change. For example, during the time between the first and second observations, inmates may have been exposed to some other influence that reduced their level of aggression. Television cable service to the prison may have been disrupted, lowering the exposure inmates received to violent programming; a new warden may have taken control of the facility, relaxing prison rules and reducing tensions; or a transfer or release of especially troublesome inmates may have occurred. The possibilities for rival explanations (that is, those that rival the explanatory power of the hypothesis under study) are nearly limitless. Rival explanations such as these, called "competing hypotheses" by some researchers and **confounding effects** by others, make the results of any single series of observations uncertain.

To have the confidence that the changes intentionally introduced into a situation are the real cause of observed variations, it is necessary to achieve some degree of control over factors that threaten the certainty that experimental interventions did indeed cause the changes observed in the study group. **Controlled experiments** are those that attempt to hold conditions (other than the intentionally introduced experimental intervention) constant. In fact, some researchers have defined the word *experiment* simply as "controlled observation."

Hence, although criminologists sometimes employ true experimental designs in the conduct of their research, they are more likely to find it necessary to use **quasi-experimental designs**. These designs are especially valuable when aspects of the social setting are beyond the control of the researcher. The crucial defining feature of quasi-experimental designs is that they give researchers control over the "when and to whom" of measurement, even though others decide the "when and to whom" of exposure to the experimental intervention.

Sometimes, for example, legislators enact new laws intended to address some aspect of the crime problem, specifying the kinds of crime preventative measures to be employed and what segment of the population is to receive them. Midnight basketball, intended to keep young people off the streets at night, is an example of such legislatively sponsored intervention. The question, of course, is whether money spent in support of such an activity would actually reduce the incidence of street crime committed by youth. Unfortunately, good research data that could answer the question ahead of time are often unavailable. However, once the programs are in place, researchers can study them. Hence, although criminologists are not politically situated so as to be able to enact midnight basketball legislation, they are able to study the effects of such legislation after it has been enacted.[53]

Choice of Data-Collection Techniques

Once a research problem has been identified, concepts have been made measurable, and a design for the conduct of the research has been selected, investigators must decide on the type of data to be gathered and the techniques of data gathering they wish to employ. Ultimately, all research depends on the

Confounding effect A rival explanation, or competing hypothesis, that is a threat to the internal or external validity of a research design.

Controlled experiment An experiment that attempts to hold conditions (other than the intentionally introduced experimental intervention) constant.

Quasi-experimental design An approach to research that, although less powerful than an experimental design, is deemed worthy of use when better designs are not feasible.

use of techniques to gather information, or data, for eventual analysis. Many first-time researchers select data-gathering techniques on the basis of ease or simplicity, and some choose according to the cost or the amount of time the techniques require. The most important question to consider when beginning to gather information, however, is whether the data-gathering strategy selected will produce information in a usable form. The kind of information needed depends on the questions to be answered. Surveys of public opinion as to the desirability of the death penalty, for example, cannot address issues of the punishment's effectiveness as a crime-control strategy.

These five major data-gathering strategies typify research in the field of criminology.

Surveys: **Survey research** typically involves the use of questionnaires or surveys. Respondents may be interviewed in person or over the telephone, or queried via email or fax. Mail surveys are common, although they tend to have a lower response rate than other types of social surveys. The information produced through the use of questionnaires is referred to as *survey data*. Statistics Canada data, for example, are gathered by survey-takers who are trained periodically for that purpose. Survey data also inform the Canadian Urban Victimization Survey and other Statistics Canada–related reports produced by the Canadian Centre for Justice Statistics. Surveys have been used also in criminology to assess fear of crime and attitudes toward the police and to discover the extent of unreported crime.

Case studies: **Case studies** are built around in-depth investigations into individual cases. The study of one (perhaps notorious) offender, scrutiny of a particular criminal organization, and analysis of a prison boot camp all may qualify as case studies. Case studies are useful for what they can tell us to expect about other similar cases. If a study of a street gang, for example, reveals the central role of a few leaders, we would expect to find a similar organizational style among other gangs of the same kind. Although they may suffer from high levels of subjectivity in which feelings cannot be easily separated from fact, case studies provide the opportunity to investigate individual cases—an element lacking in both surveys and participant observations.

Participant observation: **Participant observation** "involves a variety of strategies in data gathering in which the researcher observes a group by participating, to varying degrees, in the activities of the group."[54] Some participant researchers operate undercover, whereas others make their identity and purpose known from the outset. It is possible to distinguish between at least two additional kinds of participant observation: (1) the participant as observer and (2) the observer as complete participant. When researchers make their presence known to those whom they are observing without attempting to influence the outcome of their observations or the activities of the group, they fit the category of participants who are observers. But researchers who make their presence known may inadvertently influence outcomes because people tend to act differently when they know they are being watched. When researchers become complete participants in the group they are observing, however, they run the risk of influencing the group's direction.

Self-reporting: Another subjective data-gathering technique is the **self-report**, which investigates aspects of a problem not otherwise amenable to study. When official records are lacking, research subjects may be asked to record and report rates of otherwise secretive behaviour. Self-reports may prove especially valuable in providing checks on official reports consisting of statistical tabulations gathered through channels such as police departments, hospitals, and social services agencies.

Many self-reporting techniques require the maintenance of a diary or personal journal and request vigilant and ongoing observations of the study subject's own behaviour. Hence, sex researchers may ask subjects to maintain an ongoing record of their frequency of intercourse, the variety of sexual techniques employed, and their preference in partners—items

Survey research Research using a social science data-gathering technique that involves the use of questionnaires.

Case study An investigation into an individual case.

Participant observation A strategy in data gathering in which the researcher observes a group by participating, to varying degrees, in the activities of the group.

Self-report A research investigation of subjects in order to record and report their behaviours.

of information that are not easy to come by through other means or that cannot be accurately reconstructed from memory.

Secondary analysis: Not all data-gathering techniques generate new data. **Secondary analysis** purposely culls pre-existing information from data that have already been gathered (possibly for another purpose) and examines it in new ways. The secondary analysis of existing data and the use of previously acquired information for new avenues of inquiry are strategies that can save researchers a considerable amount of time and expense.

One important source of data for secondary analysis is the Canadian Centre for Justice Statistics (CCJS), created through the National Justice Statistics Initiative (NJSI) of the federal government. The mandate of the NJSI is "to provide information to the justice community and the public on the nature and extent of crime and the administration of criminal justice in Canada."[55] Through the CCJS, the NJSI is meant to ensure the production of useful information to support legislative, policy, management, and research agendas, and to inform the public. Access to CCJS data is open to the public, and data sets are available for sale to individual researchers. (A more detailed look at the CCJS is found in Chapter 2.)

Review of Findings   Some data, once collected, are simply archived or stored, but most data are subject to some form of analysis. Data analysis generally involves the use of mathematical techniques intended to uncover correlations between variables and to assess the likelihood that research findings can be generalized to other settings. These are statistical techniques, and their use in analyzing data is called *statistical analysis*. Statistical techniques provide tools for summarizing data and also provide quantitative means for identifying patterns within the data and for determining the degree of **correlation** that exists between variables.

Quantitative versus Qualitative Methods   There are some who feel that there has been a tendency in criminology research over the past half century to overemphasize **quantitative methods** or techniques, that is, those that produce measurable results that can be analyzed statistically. To be sure, as such critics would be quick to admit, a considerable degree of intellectual comfort must be achieved in feeling that one is able to reduce complex forms of behaviour and interaction to something countable (as, say, the frequency of an offence). Intellectual comfort of this sort derives from the notion that anything expressible in numbers must somehow be more meaningful than that which is not.

It is crucial to realize, however, that numerical expression is mostly a result of how researchers structure their approach to the subject matter and is rarely inherent in the subject matter itself. Such is especially true in the social sciences, where attitudes, feelings, behaviours, and perceptions of all sorts are subject to quantification by researchers, who impose upon such subjective phenomena artificial techniques for their quantification.

Qualitative methods, in contrast to those that are quantitative, produce subjective results or results that are difficult to quantify. Even though their findings are not expressed numerically, qualitative methods provide yet another set of potentially useful criminological research tools. Qualitative methods are important for the insight they provide into the subjective workings of the criminal mind and the processes by which meaning is accorded to human experience. Introspection, life histories, case studies, and participant observation all contain the potential to yield highly qualitative data.[56]

Consider, for example, how the following personal account of the motivation needed to rob banks provides subjective insights into the life of a young offender that would otherwise be difficult to express:[57]*

> I rob banks for the money. I like the excitement and thrills, but I do it for the money. The danger is exciting, but I don't do it for that. I spend my money on drugs—a lot on coke. It really does fly. I don't know where half of it goes. I had an apartment when I was sixteen

---

*Patrick J. Desroches, Behind the Bars—Experiences in Crime (Toronto: Canadian Scholars' Press Inc./Women's Press, 1996), pp. 27–28. Reprinted by permission of Canadian Scholars' Press Inc. and/or Women's Press.

Secondary analysis   The reanalysis of existing data.

Correlation   A causal, complementary, or reciprocal relationship between two measureable variables.

Quantitative method   A research technique that produces measurable results.

(((•—Listen

Professor Turns 'Gang Leader for a Day'

Qualitative method   A research technique that produces subjective results or results that are difficult to quantify.

A member of the Aboriginal street gang known as Indian Posse. Some researchers doubt that quantitative methods can adequately assess the subjective experiences of certain kinds of offenders. What is the nature of such "subjective experiences"?

Rodrigo Abd/AP Photo

and I was really proud of it. I bought a bed, a T.V., a four-metre-long couch worth $1600. I was proud of myself. I was doing well. I was living with a chick who was 18, but she was just a friend. I'd also spend a lot of money on my family. I'd give some to my sisters. I'd spend a lot on taxis. I'd take them everywhere. On movies and amusement parks. Money is important to me. I never have enough, I always want more. If I was to get a big score, I would want another big score. After a while you start getting bigger ideas. I've thought about doing an armoured vehicle and I've watched them make deliveries.

It's only a fluke or a set-up that gets you caught. You either get caught cold-cock or you don't get caught at all. If they don't catch us in the first couple of hours, then forget it. They don't have a very good chance. This was the first time I got caught, but I think I learned a lot. Next time it will not be so easy. Once you get caught, everyone goes through a process where they don't want to do it anymore. Then after a couple of months, you're willing to do it again. I'm supposed to have a job when I hit the street, but if I have no job and no money I would do a bank for sure. It's your only means of survival. If I have no job and nowhere to stay, of course I'm going to do a bank. It's what I know. I've been trained to do that.

This passage is taken from an interview with Jules, aged 17. From a French-Canadian family of eight brothers and eight sisters, Jules started robbing banks at 15. His five older brothers have all been convicted of robbing banks and armoured vehicles.

Although the preceding is a purely personal account and may hold questions of generalizability for researchers, imagine the difficulties inherent in acquiring this kind of data through the use of survey instruments or other traditional research techniques. Autobiographical accounts, introspection, and many forms of participant observation amount to a kind of phenomenological reporting, in which description leads to understanding and intuition is a better guide to theory building than are volumes of quantifiable data. A growing number of criminologists believe that qualitative data-gathering strategies represent the future of criminological research.

VALUES AND ETHICS IN THE CONDUCT OF RESEARCH

RESEARCH, ESPECIALLY THAT CONDUCTED WITHIN THE SOCIAL SCIENCES, DOES NOT occur in a vacuum. Values enter into all stages of the research process, from the selection of the problem to be studied to the choice of strategies to address it. In short, research is never entirely free from preconceptions and biases, although much can be done to limit their impact.

The most effective way of controlling the effects of biases is to be aware of them at the outset of the research. If, for example, researchers know that the project they are working on elicits strong personal feelings but necessitates the use of interviewers, it would be beneficial to strive to hire interviewers who are relatively free of biases or can control the expression of their feelings. Data gatherers who are prejudiced against subgroups of potential respondents can represent a threat to the validity of the research results. And they may turn off some respondents, perhaps through racial innuendo, personal style, mannerisms, and so forth.

Of similar importance are ethical issues. Although they may not affect the validity of research results, these issues can have a significant impact on the lives of both researchers and research subjects. The protection of human subjects, privacy, and **data confidentiality**—which embraces the principle of protecting the confidentiality of individual research participants while preserving justified research access to needed information provided by them—are all critical ethical issues.

Informed consent, a strategy used by researchers to overcome many of the ethical issues inherent in criminological research, means that research subjects are informed as to the nature of the research about to be conducted, their anticipated role in it, and the uses that will be made of the data they provide. Ethics may also require that data derived from personal interviews or the testing of research subjects be anonymous (not associated with the names of individual subjects) and that raw (unanalyzed) data be destroyed after a specified time interval (often at the completion of the research project).

Federal regulations require a plan for the protection of sensitive information as part of grant proposals submitted to federal agencies. In Canada, the *Tri-Council Policy Statement: Ethical Conduct for Research Involving Humans* has been adopted as a common research ethics policy for those conducting, participating in, or reviewing human research. Some universities, research organizations, and government agencies have established institutional review boards tasked with examining research proposals to determine whether expectations of ethical conduct have been met before these proposals are submitted to funding organizations. Institutional review boards often consist of other researchers with special knowledge of the kinds of ethical issues involved in criminological research.

Participant observation sometimes entails an especially thorny ethical issue: should researchers themselves violate the law if their research participation appears to require it? Those researching gang activity, for example, have sometimes been asked to transmit potentially incriminating information to other gang members, to act as drug couriers, and even to commit crimes of violence to help establish territorial claims important to members of the gang. Researchers who refuse may endanger not only their research but also themselves. Compliance with the expectations of criminal groups, of course, evokes other kinds of dangers, including the danger of apprehension and prosecution for violations of the criminal law.

Although the dilemma of a participant observer, especially one secretly engaged in research, is a difficult one, some of the best advice on the subject was offered by Frank E. Hagan: "In self-mediating the potential conflicting roles of the criminal justice researcher, it is incumbent on the investigator to enter the setting with eyes wide open. A decision must be made beforehand on the level of commitment to the research endeavor and the analyst's ability to negotiate the likely role conflicts. Although there are no hard and fast rules *the researcher's primary role is that of a scientist*."[58]

Hagan also suggested that a code of ethics should guide all professional criminologists in their research undertakings. This code, said Hagan, would require the researcher to assume the following personal responsibilities:[59]

- Avoid procedures that may harm respondents.
- Honour commitments to respondents and respect reciprocity.
- Exercise objectivity and professional integrity in performing and reporting research.
- Protect confidentiality and privacy of respondents.

Data confidentiality The ethical requirement of social scientific research to protect the confidentiality of individual research participants while preserving justified research access to the information participants provide.

Informed consent The ethical requirement of social scientific research that research subjects be informed as to the nature of the research about to be conducted, their anticipated role in it, and the uses to which the data they provide will be put.

CRIMINOLOGY AND SOCIAL POLICY

IDEALLY, RESEARCH RESULTS IN THE FIELD OF CRIMINOLOGY SHOULD HAVE BOTH practical implications that can guide daily practice in relevant areas and a significant impact on those who formulate public crime-control policy. It is understood that "the normative educative model assumes that a rational use of data by policy makers, practitioners, and scientists will be of value to the field."[60] For example, studies have shown that arrests (rather than mere warnings) of domestic violence perpetrators prove effective in reducing the likelihood of reoffending, resulting in some police departments advising their officers to make such arrests and some legislators advocating passage of mandatory arrest laws.[61]

Unfortunately, publicly elected officials often either are ignorant of current criminological research or do not heed the advice of professional criminologists, seeking instead to create politically expedient policies, which has led some to proclaim the "irrelevance" of criminology.

Kevin Haggerty, from the University of Alberta, argued that

> the long-standing relationship between criminal justice policy and the advice of criminologists has been ruptured in the past two decades. Three interrelated factors help to account for this displacement of criminological thought: (1) the rise of neo-liberal forms of governance which have made traditional forms of criminological knowledge and preferred sites of intervention increasingly superfluous to the practice of governance; (2) the ascendancy of a highly symbolic public discourse about crime; and (3) the transformation of the criminal justice system by new technologies of detection, capture and monitoring.[62]

So, while the work of criminologists continues to influence the developement of specific criminal justice policies, these three realities pose additional hurdles.

A look at the three-strikes laws of our American neighbours provides one case in point. Three-strikes laws, which became popular near the end of the 20th century, require that convicted offenders receive lengthy prison sentences (often life without possibility of parole) following their third conviction. Such laws are built on the seemingly common-sense notion that "getting tough" on repeat offenders by putting them in prison for long periods should reduce the crime rate; logic seems to say that lengthy prison sentences for recidivists will reduce crime by removing the most dangerous offenders from society.

Many studies of the three-strikes laws have concluded that such legislation typically results in clogged court systems and crowded correctional facilities and encourages three-time offenders to take dramatic risks to avoid capture.[63] A particular study, dubbed "the most comprehensive study ever of crime prevention,"[64] found that "much of the research on prisons was inadequate or flawed, making it impossible to measure how much crime was actually prevented or deterred by locking up more criminals."[65] Despite this evidence suggesting otherwise, the U.S. laws that support the lock-up of more offenders remain popular with the voting public, and lawmakers have been quick to seize upon "get-tough" crime-prevention policies in the interest of getting votes.

In an even more puzzling development, current Canadian policymakers appear to be following suit. The recent introduction of Bill C-10, the *Safe Streets and Communities Act*, sees increased use of incarceration as a response to crime—including increased use of mandatory minimum prison sentences, more frequent pretrial detention, and harsher penalties of incarceration for young offenders. Detractors to this approach point to the U.S. experience, stressing that if treating offenders more harshly resulted in less crime, the United States would lead the world in crime reduction. Yet, despite a prison population that has more than doubled in the past 20 years, the U.S. crime rate has not significantly decreased. Japan, on the other hand, is an industrialized nation that has seen its crime rates decrease in recent years. It also has one of the lowest per capita incarceration rates in the world, relying on a system of "retributive shaming" or "confession, repentance and absolution."[66] (See Chapter 11 for a more in-depth look at the *Safe Streets and Communities Act*.)

Another case in point is the area of Aboriginal justice initiatives in Canada. In an article entitled "The Impact of Aboriginal Justice Research on Policy: A Marginal Past and an Even More Uncertain Future," Carol La Prairie wrote:

> The benefits of research for Aboriginal criminal justice in Canada have scarcely been tapped. There have been some issue-specific activities over the past 25 years but research has not systematically been designed and integrated into policy, practice, and project development. Because research is often negatively perceived by Aboriginal people and is of sporadic interest to government, its history of shaping justice projects and influencing policy decision-making has been marginal at best.[67]

La Prairie concluded that this apparent lack of research impact and integration results from the fact that government legislators equate Aboriginal justice issues with the self-government movement, which has largely served to portray Aboriginal justice problems (such as the over-representation of Aboriginals as offenders in the criminal justice system) as conflicts over race and culture, rooted in a colonial history of conflict and discrimination. She claimed that the emphasis of research on the race/cultural issue has failed to consider other possible explanations for problems faced by Aboriginal people, such as "community marginalization, inequity of distribution of community resources, and family breakdown and dysfunction."[68]

Professional criminologists are acutely aware of the need to link sound social policy to the objective findings of well-conducted criminological research, and they continue to work to forge this link. "So little is known about the causes of crime and about the effects of criminal justice policy on crime that new insights about the criminal justice system can often be extremely revealing and can eventually change the way people think about the crime problem or about the criminal justice system."[69]

Social Policy and Public Crime Concerns

"If it bleeds, it leads" is a phrase often used by the media to determine how much attention and coverage is given to a news story. Indeed, the news media, the internet, and social media seem to be preoccupied with delivering stories about war, disease, and incidents of violent crime. Many argue that the media are simply giving the public what it wants; others argue that the public's perception about threats to its safety and protection is skewed. A report by Julian Roberts identified a number of ways that the mass media influence public attitudes and beliefs about crime: (1) the media tend not to report or to emphasize declining crime rates; (2) national crime figures (which for the past decade have been reporting declining crime rates) are published only once a year, allowing the media the remainder of each year to concentrate on extreme, violent cases; and (3) crime stories reported by the media are rarely put in a statistical context, and the electronic and print news outlets neglect to comment on trends in crime rates over time.[70]

Although Canadian crime rates have been declining for more than a decade, concern over personal and national security, crime rates, and increasingly terrorism remains pervasive. A 2009 Canadian public opinion poll indicated that the majority of Canadians endorse the federal government's anti-crime proposals. For example, 91 percent support a mandatory two-year jail term for anyone selling drugs at or near a school, 82 percent would include all sex offenders in a national registry, and 61 percent think mandatory minimum sentences are a good idea.[71]

Fear of crime is not necessarily related to the actual incidence of crime. A Department of Justice report concluded that "despite an increasing concern for crime, the public's fears remain unrelated to actual crime rates and potential for victimization, as perceptions of criminal activity and violence are not in tune with reality."[72] Even though crime rates have declined, concern over crime remains an important determinant of public policy. Hence, political agendas that promise to lower crime rates or to keep them low, as well as those that

According to pollsters, fear of crime is a persistent concern among Canadians. Given recent statistics showing falling crime rates, is such fear realistic? What role does the media play in the perception of crime among Canadians?

Peter Alvey People/Alamy

call for changes in the conditions that produce crime, can be quite successful for candidates or incumbents who promote them in an environment where concern over crime remains high.[73] In his book entitled *Risk: The Science and Politics of Fear*, Dan Gardner contended that we are all becoming more susceptible to irrational fear, and this irrationality is caused in part by those politicians, activists, and media that promote fear for their own gain. Why is it that we find ourselves worrying about what statistics tell us are unlikely threats—terrorism, child abduction, cancer caused by chemical pollution—while we largely ignore serious risks like obesity and smoking?[74]

1.8 | **LEARNING OBJECTIVE**

Watch

Inequities in Education

Social problems perspective
The belief that crime is a manifestation of underlying social problems such as poverty, discrimination, pervasive family violence, inadequate socialization practices, and the breakdown of traditional social institutions.

THE THEME OF THIS BOOK

THIS BOOK BUILDS ON A SOCIAL POLICY THEME BY ASKING QUESTIONS ABOUT THE sources of crime and criminality and by asking what we can do to prevent and control crime. Our theme contrasts two popular perspectives (see Figure 1.3).

Social Problems Perspective

One point of view, termed the **social problems perspective**, holds that crime is a manifestation of underlying social problems such as poverty, discrimination, the breakdown of traditional social institutions, the low level of formal education among some disadvantaged groups, pervasive family violence experienced during the formative years, and inadequate

Figure 1.3 The Theme of This Book: Social Problems versus Social Responsibility

socialization practices that leave too many young people without the fundamental values necessary to contribute meaningfully to the society in which they live. Advocates of the social problems perspective, while generally agreeing that crime and violence are serious social problems, advance solutions based on what is, in effect, a public health model. Adherents of that model say that crime must be addressed in much the same way as public health concerns like AIDS or cancer.

Proponents of the social problems perspective typically foresee solutions to the crime problem as coming in the form of government expenditures in support of social programs designed to address the issues that lie at the root of crime. Government-funded initiatives, designed to enhance social, educational, occupational, and other opportunities, are perceived as offering programmatic solutions to ameliorate most causes of crime. The social problems approach to crime is characteristic of what social scientists term a *macro approach* because it portrays instances of individual behaviour (crimes) as arising out of widespread and contributory social conditions that enmesh unwitting individuals in a causal nexus of uncontrollable social forces.

Within the Canadian setting, the social problems perspective has generally influenced crime-prevention policy. In 1993, the Solicitor General and the Parliamentary Standing Committee on Justice produced a report entitled *Crime Prevention in Canada: Toward a National Strategy*. The report recommended the implementation of a "National Strategy on Community Safety and Crime Prevention" (now known as the National Crime Prevention Strategy) focused on developing new plans to look at the causes of crime and to develop partnerships with communities across the country to carry out crime-prevention activities. Phase I of the National Strategy (1994–1998) saw the creation of the National Crime Prevention Council (NCPC), whose mandate was the promotion of crime prevention through social development, with particular emphasis on early-prevention programs targeting children and youth. The NCPC identified a number of factors that place children and youth at risk of engaging in criminal behaviour. These included child poverty, inadequate living conditions, inconsistent and uncaring parenting, childhood traumas such as physical and sexual abuse, family breakdown, racism and other forms of discrimination, difficulties in school, delinquent friends, and living situations where there is alcohol, drug, and other kinds of substance abuse. Since 1998, Phase II has been building on the work done by the NCPC and focusing on helping communities develop programs and partnerships to reduce crime and victimization. The NCPC is moving toward a results- and evidence-based approach to crime prevention. Its funding programs and activities are focused on addressing known risk factors associated with crime and violence in high-risk populations and places. With this evolution, the approaches to crime prevention have become more evidence-based. In addition to focusing on children and youth, this phase places priority on Aboriginal people and women's personal safety.[75] (A detailed examination of the National Crime Prevention Strategy can be found in Chapter 11.)

Social Responsibility Perspective

A contrasting perspective lays the cause of crime squarely at the feet of individual perpetrators. This point of view holds that individuals are fundamentally responsible for their own behaviour and maintains that they choose crime over other, more law-abiding courses of action. Perpetrators may choose crime, advocates of this perspective say, because it is exciting, it offers illicit pleasures and the companionship of like-minded thrill-seekers, or it is simply less demanding than conformity. This viewpoint, which we shall call the **social responsibility perspective**, has a close affiliation with rational choice theory (discussed in Chapter 5) and is associated with a belief in the importance of free will. Advocates of the social responsibility perspective, with their emphasis on individual choice, tend to believe that social programs do little to solve the problem of crime because, they say, a

Social responsibility perspective The belief that individuals are fundamentally responsible for their own behaviour and that they choose crime over other, more law-abiding courses of action.

certain number of crime-prone individuals, for a variety of personalized reasons, will always make irresponsible choices. Hence, advocates of the social responsibility approach suggest highly personalized crime-prevention and reduction strategies based on firm punishments, imprisonment, individualized rehabilitation, and increased security, as well as a wider use of police powers. The social responsibility perspective characteristically emphasizes a *micro approach* that tends to focus on individual offenders and their unique biology, psychology, background, and immediate life experiences.

The social responsibility perspective is most evident in the approach to crime prevention and control adopted by our neighbours to the south. The *Violent Crime Control and Law Enforcement Act* of 1994, for example, expanded the number of capital crimes under federal law from a handful of offences to 52.[76] The law also made billions of dollars available to municipalities to put tens of thousands new police officers on the streets and allocated billions for states to build and operate prisons and incarceration alternatives like "boot camps." Prison funding was intended to ensure that additional prison cells would be available to put—and keep—violent offenders behind bars. A subchapter of the 1994 *Violent Crime Control and Law Enforcement Act* created a federal "Three Strikes and You're Out" law, mandating life imprisonment for criminals convicted of three violent federal felonies or drug offences. Similarly, the law increased or created new penalties for over 70 federal criminal offences, primarily covering violent crimes, drug trafficking, and gun crimes. Since the 1994 federal legislation was passed, many states have moved to toughen their own laws against violent criminals; violent juveniles and repeat offenders have been especially targeted. The *USA PATRIOT Act*—enacted in 2001 and renewed with modifications in 2006—targets terrorism and crimes committed in support of terrorist activity. The *PATRIOT Act* has been criticized by many for going too far in limiting individual freedoms and restricting personal choice, although its supporters argue that its provisions are needed to effectively fight the "war on terrorism."

A note about wording is in order. Although the social responsibility perspective might also be termed the *individual responsibility perspective*, because it stresses individual responsibility above all else, we've chosen to use the term *social responsibility perspective* instead, as it holds that individuals must be ultimately responsible to the social group of which they are a part and that they should be held accountable by group standards if they are not. In short, this perspective is one characterized by societal demands for the exercise of individual responsibility.

1.9 LEARNING OBJECTIVE ## THE SOCIAL CONTEXT OF CRIME

CRIME DOES NOT OCCUR IN A VACUUM. EVERY CRIME HAS A UNIQUE SET OF CAUSES, consequences, and participants. Crime affects some people more than others, having a special impact on those who are direct participants in the act itself—offenders, victims, police officers, witnesses, and so on. Crime, in general, provokes reactions from its victims, from concerned groups of citizens, from the criminal justice system, and sometimes from society as a whole, which manifests its concerns through the creation of new social policy. Reactions to crime, from the everyday to the precedent-setting, may colour the course of future criminal events.[77]

In this book, we shall attempt to identify and examine some of the many social, psychological, economic, biological, and other causes of crime while expounding on the many differing perspectives that have been advanced to explain both crime and criminality. Popular conceptions of criminal motivation are typically shaped by media portrayals of offender motivation, which often fail to take into consideration the felt experiences of the law violators. By identifying and studying this diversity of perspectives on criminality, we will discover the characteristic disjuncture among victims, offenders, the justice system, and society as to the significance that each assigns to the behaviour in question—and often to its motivation.

Making Sense of Crime: The Causes and Consequences of the Criminal Event

This book recognizes that criminal activity is diversely created and variously interpreted. In other words, this book depicts crime not as an isolated individual activity, but as a *social event*.[78] Like other social events, crime is fundamentally a social construction.[79] To say that crime is a social construction is not to lessen the impact of the victimization experiences that all too many people undergo in our society every day, nor does such a statement trivialize the significance of crime-prevention efforts or the activities of members of the criminal justice system. Likewise, it does not underplay the costs of crime to individual victims and to society as a whole. It does, however, recognize that although a given instance of criminal behaviour may have many causes, it also carries with it many different kinds of meanings—at least one for offenders, another (generally quite different one, of course) for victims, and still another for agents of the criminal justice system. Similarly, a wide range of social interest groups, from victims' advocates to prisoner rights and gun control organizations, all interpret the significance of law-breaking behaviour from unique points of view, and each arrives at different conclusions as to what should be done about the so-called crime problem.

For these reasons, we have chosen to apply the concept of social relativity to the study of criminality.[80] **Social relativity** refers to the fact that social events are differently interpreted according to the cultural experiences and personal interests of the initiator, the observer, or the recipient of that behaviour. Hence, as a social phenomenon, crime means different things to the offender, to the criminologist who studies it, to the police officer who investigates it, and to the victim who experiences it first-hand.

Figure 1.4 illustrates the causes and consequences of crime in rudimentary diagrammatic form. In keeping with the theme of this book, it depicts crime as a social event. The figure consists of a foreground, describing those features that immediately determine the nature of the criminal event (including responses to the event as it is transpiring), and a background, in which generic contributions to crime can be seen with interpretations of the event after it has taken place. We call the background causes of crime *contributions* and use the word *inputs* to signify the more immediate propensities and predispositions of the actors involved in the situation. Inputs also include the physical features of the setting in which a specific crime takes place. Both background contributions and immediate inputs contribute to and shape the criminal event. The more or less immediate results or consequences of crime are termed *outputs*, while the term *interpretations* appears in the diagram to indicate that any crime has a lasting impact both on surviving participants and on society. As Figure 1.4 shows, the

> **Social relativity** The notion that social events are differently interpreted according to the cultural experiences and personal interests of the initiator, the observer, or the recipient of that behaviour.

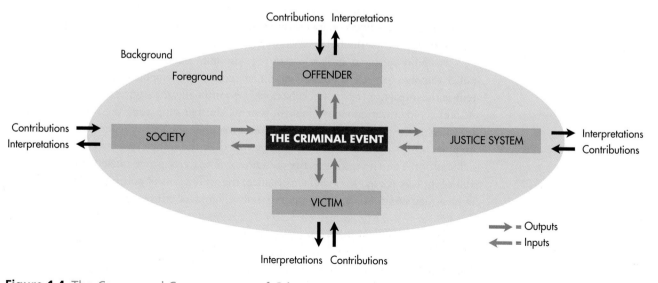

Figure 1.4 The Causes and Consequences of Crime

criminal event is ultimately a result of the coming together of inputs provided by the offender, the victim, society, and the justice system.

Crime and the Offender

Offenders bring with them certain background features, such as personal life experiences, a peculiar biology (insofar as they are unique organisms), a distinct personality, personal values and beliefs, and various kinds of skills and knowledge (some of which may be useful in the commission of crime). Background contributions to crime can be vitally important. Recent research, for example, tends to cement the existence of a link between child-rearing practices and criminality in later life. Joan McCord, reporting on a 30-year study of family relationships and crime, found that self-confident, non-punitive, and affectionate mothers tend to insulate their male children from delinquency and, consequently, later criminal activity.[81] Difficulties associated with the birthing process have also been linked to crime in adulthood.[82] Negative familial relationships and birth trauma are but two of the literally thousands of different kinds of experiences individuals may have. Whether individuals who undergo trauma at birth and are deprived of positive maternal experiences will turn to crime depends on many other things, including their own mixture of other experiences and characteristics, the appearance of a suitable victim, failure of the justice system to prevent crime, and the evolution of a social environment in which criminal behaviour is somehow encouraged or valued.

Each of the parties identified in Figure 1.4 contributes immediate inputs to the criminal event. Foreground contributions by the offender may consist of a particular motivation, a specific intent (in many cases), or a drug-induced state of mind.

Crime and the Criminal Justice System

Criminal justice system The various agencies of justice, especially police, courts, and corrections, whose goal it is to apprehend, convict, sanction, and rehabilitate law violators.

Like the offender, the **criminal justice system** (meaning the various agencies of justice such as the police, the courts, and corrections) also contributes to the criminal event, albeit unwillingly, through its failure to (1) prevent criminal activity, (2) adequately identify specific offenders prior to their involvement in crime, and (3) prevent the early release of convicted criminals who later become repeat offenders. Such background contributions can be seen in prisons (a central component of the justice system) that serve as "schools for crime," fostering anger against society and building a propensity for continued criminality in inmates who have been "turned out." Similarly, the failure of system-sponsored crime-prevention programs—ranging from the patrol activities of local police departments to educational and diversionary programs intended to redirect budding offenders—helps to set the stage for the criminal event.

On the other hand, proper system response may reduce crime. One study found that police response (especially arrest) can, under certain demographic conditions, dramatically reduce the incidence of criminal behaviour.[83] Additionally, the study found that arrest "constitutes communication to criminals in general," further supporting the notion that inputs provided by the justice system have the power to either enhance or reduce the likelihood of criminal occurrences. Immediate inputs provided by the justice system typically consist of features of the situation such as the presence or absence of police officers, the ready availability (or lack thereof) of official assistance, the willingness of police officers to intervene in pre-crime situations, and the response time required for officers to arrive at a crime scene.

Crime and the Victim

Few crimes can occur without a victim. Sometimes the victim is a passive participant in the crime, such as an innocent person killed by an impaired driver. In such cases, the victim is simply in the proverbial wrong place at the wrong time. Even then, however, merely by being present the victim contributes his or her person to the event, thereby increasing the severity of the incident (that is, the impaired driver who injures no one may still be breaking the law but is committing a far less serious crime than a similar incident in which somebody is killed).

Sometimes, however, victims more actively contribute to their own victimization through the appearance of defencelessness (having characteristics such as old age, drunkenness, or disability), by failing to take appropriate defensive measures (leaving doors unlocked or forgetting to remove keys from a car's ignition), by unwisely displaying wealth (flashing large-denomination bills in a public place), or simply by making other unwise choices (walking down a dark alley in a dangerous section of the city at 3 a.m.) In a study of Canadian victimization, Leslie W. Kennedy and David R. Forde found that violent personal victimization "is contingent on the exposure that comes from following certain lifestyles," which as especially true "for certain demographic groups, particularly young males."[84] (See Chapter 4 for a further discussion on victims of crime.)

Although lifestyles may provide the background that fosters victimization, a more active form of victimization characterizes "victims" who initiate criminal activity, such

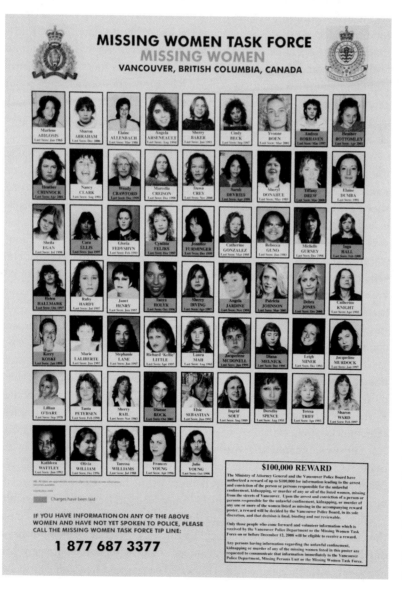

In 2007, Robert Pickton was convicted of the murders of six women and charged in the deaths of an additional twenty women (stayed in 2010), many of them prostitutes and drug users. The Missing Women Commission of Inquiry, established in 2010 by the B.C. Lieutenant-Governor, released a report that identified blatant police failure triggered by systemic bias against poor, vulnerable women of Vancouver's Downtown Eastside as the reason that Pickton was able to evade arrest for so many years.

Darryl Dyck/Canadian Press Images

as the barroom brawler who picks a fight but ends up on the receiving end of the ensuing physical violence. Victim-precipitated offences are those that involve active victim participation in the initial stages of a criminal event and that take place when the soon-to-be victim instigates the chain of events that ultimately results in the victimization.

Crime and Society

Finally, the general public (termed *society* in Figure 1.4) contributes to the criminal event both formally and informally. Society's formal contributions sometimes take the form of legislation, whereby crime itself is defined. Hence, as we shall discuss in considerable detail in Chapter 11, society structures the criminal event in a most fundamental way by delineating (through legislation and statute) what forms of activity are to be thought of as criminal.

Society's less formal contributions to crime arise out of generic social practices and conditions such as poverty, poor and informal education, various forms of discrimination by which pathways to success are blocked, and the **socialization** process (the process whereby people acquire the cultural patterns of their society). Socialization has an especially important impact on crime causation because it provides the interpretative foundation used to define and understand the significance of particular situations in which we find ourselves, and it is upon those interpretations that we may (or may not) decide to act. Date rape, for example, can occur when a man concludes that his date "owes" him something for the money he has spent on her. That feeling, however inappropriate from the point of view of the victim and the justice system, probably has its roots in early-learned experiences—including values communicated from television, the movies, and popular music—about gender-related roles under such circumstances. In other words, society, through the divergent values and expectations it places upon people, property, and behaviour under particular conditions, may provide the motivational basis for many offences.

The contributions society makes to the backgrounds of both offender and victim and to the structure of the justice system, and the influences each in turn have upon the general social order, provide for a kind of "feedback loop" in our vision of crime (the loop is not shown in Figure 1.4 for fear of unnecessarily complicating it). Through socialization, for example, individuals learn about the dangers of criminal victimization, but when victimization occurs and is publicized, it reinforces the socialization process, leading to an increased wariness of others, and so on. An example can be seen in the fact that children throughout Canada are routinely taught to avoid strangers and to be suspicious of people they do not know. A few decades ago, avoiding strangers was not ordinarily communicated to children; it entered cultural awareness following a number of horrendous and well-publicized crimes involving child victims and is now a shared part of the socialization process experienced by countless children every day throughout Canada.

The contributions made by society to crime are complex and far-reaching. Some say that the content of the mass media (movies, television, video games, the internet, popular music, etc.) can lead to crime by exposing young people to inappropriate role models and to the kinds of activity—violence and unbridled sexuality, for example—that encourage criminality.

Society's foreground contributions to crime largely emanate from the distribution of resources and the accessibility of services, which are often the direct result of economic conditions. In a study of the availability of medical resources (especially quality hospital emergency services), William G. Doerner found that serious assaults may "become" homicides when such resources are lacking but that homicides can be prevented through the effective use of capable medical technology.[85] Hence, societal decisions leading to the distribution and placement of advanced medical support equipment and personnel can effectively lower homicide rates in selected geographic areas. Of course, homicide rates will

Socialization The lifelong process of social experience whereby individuals acquire the cultural patterns of their society.

be higher in areas where such equipment is not readily available. In Doerner's words, "the causes of homicide transcend the mere social world of the combatants."[86]

The moments immediately preceding any crime are ripe with possibilities. When all the inputs brought to the situation by all those present coalesce into activity that violates the criminal law, a crime occurs. Together, the elements, experiences, and propensities brought to the situation by the offender and the victim, and those contributed to the pending event by society and the justice system, precipitate and decide the nature, course, and eventual outcome of the criminal event. While certain circumstances contribute to the criminal event as it unfolds, it is also important to note that some of the inputs brought to the situation may be inhibiting, that is, they may tend to reduce the likelihood or severity of criminal behaviour.

As mentioned earlier, the causes of crime, however well documented, tell only half the criminological story. Each and every crime has consequences. Although the immediate consequences of crime may be relatively obvious for those parties directly involved (for example, the offender and the victim), crime also has an indirect impact on society and the justice system. Figure 1.4 terms the immediate effects of crime *outputs*. As with the causes of crime, however, the real impact of such outputs is mediated by perceptual filters, resulting in what the figure terms *interpretations*. After a crime has taken place, each party to the event must make sense of what has transpired. Such interpretations consist of cognitive, emotional, and (ultimately) behavioural reactions to the criminal event.

Interpretations are ongoing. They happen before, during, and after the criminal event and are undertaken by all those associated with it. An interesting and detailed study of the interpretive activity of personnel in the criminal justice system documents what happens when callers reach the 911 dispatcher on police emergency lines.[87] Because many prank calls and calls for information are made to 911 operators, the operators must judge the seriousness of every call that comes through. What the caller says was found to be only a small part of the informational cues that the dispatcher seeks to interpret prior to assigning the call to a particular response (or non-response) category. Honest calls for help may go unanswered if the operator misinterprets the call. Hence, quite early on in the criminal event, the potential exists for a crucial representative of the justice system to misinterpret important cues and conclude that no crime is taking place.

Other interpretative activities may occur long after the crime has transpired, but they are at least as significant. The justice system, taken as a whole, must decide guilt or innocence and attempt to deal effectively with convicted offenders. Victims must attempt to make sense of their victimizations in such a way as to allow them to testify in court (if need be) and to pick up the pieces of their crime-shattered lives. Offenders must come to terms with themselves and decide whether to avoid prosecution (if escape, for example, is possible), accept blame, or deny responsibility. Whatever the outcome of these more narrowly focused interpretative activities, society—because of the cumulative impact of individual instances of criminal behaviour—will also face tough decisions through its courts and law-making agencies. Society-level decision making may revolve around the implementation of policies designed to stem future instances of criminal behaviour, the revision of criminal codes, or the elimination of unpopular laws.

Our perspective takes a three-dimensional integrative view of the social event called *crime*. We will (1) attempt to identify and understand the multiple causes giving rise to criminal behaviour, (2) highlight the processes involved in the criminal event as it unfolds, and (3) analyze the interpretation of the crime phenomenon, including societal responses to it. From this perspective, crime can be viewed along a temporal continuum as an *emergent activity* that (1) arises out of past complex causes; (2) assumes a course that builds upon immediate relationships between victim, offender, and the social order that exist at the time of the offence; and (3) elicits a formal response from the justice system, shapes public perceptions, and (possibly) gives rise to changes in social policy after it has occurred.

The advantages of an integrative perspective can be found in the completeness of the picture that it provides. The integrative point of view results in a comprehensive and inclusive view of crime because it emphasizes the personal and social underpinnings as well as the consequences of the crime. The chapters that follow employ the integrative perspective advocated here to analyze criminal events and to show how various theoretical approaches can be woven into a consistent perspective on crime.

1.10 | LEARNING OBJECTIVE

THE PRIMACY OF SOCIOLOGY

THIS BOOK RECOGNIZES THE CONTRIBUTIONS MADE BY NUMEROUS DISCIPLINES, including biology, economics, psychology, psychiatry, physiology, and political science, to the study of crime and crime causation. It is important to recognize, however, that the primary perspective from which most contemporary criminologists operate is a sociological one. Hence, a large number of today's dominant theoretical understandings of criminal behaviour are routinely couched in the language of social science and fall within the framework of sociological theory. The social problems versus social responsibility theme, around which this book is built, is in keeping with such a tradition.

Some, however, would disagree with those who claim that the sociological perspective should be accorded heightened importance in today's criminological enterprise. Those who argue for the primacy of the sociological perspective emphasize the fact that crime, as a subject of study, is a social phenomenon. Central to any study of crime must be the social context of the criminal event, which brings victims and criminals together.[88] Moreover, much of contemporary criminology rests upon a sound tradition of social scientific investigation into the nature of crime and criminal behaviour that is rooted in European and North American sociological traditions that are now well over 200 years old.[89]

One of the criticisms of the sociological perspective has been its seeming reluctance to accept the significance of findings from other fields, as well as its frequent inability to integrate such findings into existing sociological understandings of crime. Another has been its seeming difficulty in conclusively demonstrating effective means of controlling violent (as well as other forms of) crime. In the words of one prominent criminologist, "Sociological factors play a role. But they have not been able to explain why one person becomes violent and another doesn't."[90]

While sociological theories continue to develop, new and emerging perspectives ask to be recognized. The role of biology in explaining criminal tendencies, for example, appears to be gaining strength as investigations into the mapping of human DNA continue. Nonetheless, whatever new insights may develop over the coming years, it is likely that the sociological perspective will continue to dominate the field of criminology for some time to come. Such dominance is rooted in the fact that crime—regardless of all the causative nuances that may be identified in its development—occurs within the context of the social world. As such, the primary significance of crime and of criminal behaviour is fundamentally social in nature, and any control over crime must stem from effective social policy.

MySearchLab® with eText offers you access to an online interactive version of the text, extensive help with your writing and research projects, and provides round-the-clock access to credible and reliable source material.

SUMMARY OF LEARNING OBJECTIVES

1.1 In this chapter, the term *crime* was defined as a violation of the criminal law. Near the end of this chapter, we recognized the complexity of crime, calling it an *emergent activity*. In the process, crime was redefined as a law-breaking event whose significance arises out of an intricate social nexus involving a wide variety of participants.

1.2 Deviance, or deviant behaviour, refers to a violation of social norms. Some forms of behaviour (such as murder, sexual assault, and most serious crimes) are both criminal and deviant. Others may be deviant but not criminal (for example, nudity under certain circumstances), or may be criminal but not regarded as deviant by many members of society (for example, the use of marijuana).

1.3 Decisions as to what should be criminal are generally made by legislatures, at both the provincial and federal levels. Such decisions are arrived at through a political process that involves input from social interest groups, including those in favour of criminalizing certain behaviours and those opposed to criminalizing them.

1.4 The term *criminologist* is applied to credentialed individuals who engage in the study of crime, criminal behaviour, and crime trends. *Criminalist* is used to describe people who specialize in the collection and examination of the physical evidence associated with specific crimes. *Criminal justice professionals* include law enforcement officers, judges, criminal defence attorneys, prosecutors, cybercrime investigators, victims' advocates, jailers, corrections officers, and so on.

1.5 *Criminology* is an interdisciplinary profession built around the scientific study of crime and criminal behaviour, including their forms, causes, legal aspects, and control. It is a social science that endeavours to develop theories based on applied techniques of data collection and hypothesis testing. Theoretical criminology, in turn, contributes to a more complete understanding of the nature of crime and crime causation.

1.6 *Research* refers to the use of standardized, systematic procedures in the search for knowledge. Determinations of program effectiveness are made through research. Experimentation uses data collection and hypothesis testing to validate theory.

1.7 Ideally, research results in the field of criminology should have a significant impact on public crime-prevention policy. Unfortunately, publicly elected officials often either are ignorant of current criminological research or do not heed the advice of professional criminologists, seeking instead to create politically expedient policies.

1.8 This book builds on a social policy theme by asking what the sources of crime and criminality are and what we can do to prevent and control crime. The theme contrasts two perspectives: the *social responsibility perspective* holds that crime is a matter of individual responsibility; the *social problems perspective* holds that crime is a manifestation of underlying social problems beyond the control of individuals.

1.9 This book sees crime as a social event, not an isolated individual activity. A given instance of criminal behaviour may have many causes and many different kinds of meanings. *Social relativity* holds that social events are interpreted differently according to the cultural experiences and personal interests of the initiator, the observer, and the recipient of that behaviour.

The discipline of sociology has had the most impact on theoretical understandings of crime and crime causation, so a large number of today's theoretical explanations of criminal behaviour are routinely couched in the language of social science and fall within the framework of sociological theory. Nonetheless, it is important to recognize the contributions made by numerous other disciplines (biology, economics, psychology, psychiatry, physiology, political science), making the study of crime and crime causation interdisciplinary.

Questions for Review

1. What is crime? How might the notion of crime change over time?

2. What is deviance? How are crime and deviance similar? How do they differ?

3. Who decides what should be criminal? How do the three perspectives of theoretical criminology differ in how they might determine what should be criminal?

4. What are some of the employment opportunities available in the field of criminology? Do you think you might want to become a criminologist? Why or why not?

5. What is criminology? In what ways is contemporary criminology interdisciplinary?

6. What is a theory? What purposes do theories serve? What role do research and experimentation play in theory building in criminology?

7. How is social policy in the area of crime control determined?

8. What is the theme of this textbook? Upon which two contrasting viewpoints does it build?

9. How would you describe the various participants in a criminal event? How does each contribute to an understanding of the event?

10. In what ways has the discipline of sociology contributed the most to theoretical understandings of crime causation over the past century?

Multiple-Choice Questions

1. Some criminologists contend that _____ data-gathering strategies represent the future of criminological research.
    a. quantitative
    b. self-report
    c. survey
    d. case study
    e. qualitative

2. Which of the following statements about deviance and crime is/are true?
    a. All deviant behaviour is criminal.
    b. All criminal behaviour is deviant.
    c. Deviance and criminal behaviour are identical.
    d. Deviance and criminal behaviour overlap.
    e. Deviance and criminal behaviour do not overlap at all.

3. Contemporary criminologists generally recognize that their field is _____.
    a. narrowly defined
    b. interdisciplinary
    c. isolated
    d. limited
    e. all-inclusive

4. A _____ is a series of interrelated propositions that attempt to describe, explain, predict, and ultimately control some class of events.

   a. concept

   b. variable

   c. theory

   d. hypothesis

   e. research design

5. Which of the following statements about the social problems perspective is false?

   a. It suggests that crime is a symptom of underlying social problems such as poverty and discrimination.

   b. It emphasizes the development of social and educational opportunities as a way of dealing with crime.

   c. It emphasizes crime-prevention efforts such as harsher sentences.

   d. It sees crime as a public health issue as well as a criminal justice issue.

   e. It suggests that solutions to crime need to come in the form of government expenditures in support of social programs.

Chapter 2
Crime Statistics

Bart Ah You/Modesto Bee/MCT via Getty Images

Who does what? When? How often? These are the perennial questions about crime. There is no scarcity of answers. Indeed, there is a surplus. The problem is that the answers seldom satisfy. Dissatisfaction follows from the fact that our measures of crime are of doubtful accuracy.

—*John Hagen*[1]

LEARNING OBJECTIVES

After reading this chapter, you should be able to

2.1 Describe how the collection and study of crime statistics has developed through history.

2.2 Understand the usefulness and limitations of crime statistics.

2.3 Recognize various methods used to collect and disseminate crime data.

2.4 Assess the correlations that exist between the predominant social dimensions of crime and criminal behaviour.

INTRODUCTION

Seventy-seven-year-old Melissa Shepard knows little about statistics but she is familiar with crime. Shepard, also known as Melissa Stewart, Melissa Weeks, and Melissa Friedrich, lives in Nova Scotia and has been arrested and convicted on numerous occasions for crimes including grand theft forgery, fraud, misrepresentation, theft, manslaughter, and most recently in October 2012, attempted murder for trying to poison her husband. She is alleged to have administered the tranquilizer benzodiazepine to him two days after their marriage.

Shepard's most recent run-in with the law has earned her the nickname the "Internet Black Widow" for her ability to persuade grieving widowers to marry her; she then steals their money and kills them. In 1991, she killed her husband Gordon Stewart, of Prince Edward Island, on a deserted road near Halifax. He had been heavily drugged when she ran him over twice with a car. She was sentenced to six years in jail for manslaughter and was released after serving two.

Shortly after being released from jail, Melissa Stewart, as she was known at the time, travelled to Florida, where she met Robert Friedrich at a Christian retreat. They married in Nova Scotia in 2000, but a year later the Friedrich family noticed that his health was faltering; he was suffering from mysterious fainting spells, slurred his speech, and was in and out of hospital. They also said his money had started to disappear. In 2002, Friedrich died of cardiac arrest, and no one was charged in his death.

In 2005, Shepard was sentenced to five years in prison on seven counts of theft from Alexander Strategos, a Florida man she had met online. On the day they moved in together, he was taken to hospital after hitting his head. Strategos wound up being hospitalized eight times over a two-month period, and eventually a drug was found in his system. Investigators reported that Shepard syphoned about $20 000 U.S. out of his bank account. Strategos, now 81 and living in Pinellas Park, Florida, said he wasn't surprised to hear about the latest allegations. "She's a nice woman, she treated me all right until she started giving me drugs." For that incident, Shepard was sentenced to five years in a Florida prison. Upon her release in 2009, she was deported to Canada and moved to New Glasgow, Nova Scotia.

The "Internet Black Widow" will appear in court in June 2013 to stand trial for the latest charges.[2]

A HISTORY OF CRIME STATISTICS

2.1 LEARNING OBJECTIVE

MELISSA SHEPHARD IS A STATISTICAL ANOMALY. FEW PEOPLE ARE INVOLVED IN crime past middle age. Fewer still are involved in crime at Shephard's age. And even fewer are female. Data from the Canadian Centre for Justice Statistics showed that the likelihood of someone committing a crime declines with age. People 65 years of age and older, for example, commit fewer than 1 percent of all crimes, and the proportion of crimes committed by women, especially crimes of violence, is so small that it cannot be meaningfully expressed as a percentage of total crime.

Although the gathering of crime statistics is a relatively new phenomenon, population statistics have been collected periodically since pre-Roman times. Old Testament accounts of enumerations of the Hebrews, for example, provided evidence of Middle Eastern census taking thousands of years ago. In like manner, the New Testament described how the family of Jesus had to return home to be counted during an official census—providing evidence of routine census taking during the time of Christ. The *lustrum*, which was a ceremonial purification of the entire ancient Roman population after census taking, has led historians to conclude that Roman population counts were made every five years. Centuries later, the *Domesday Book*, created by the order of William the Conqueror in 1085–1086, provided a written survey of English landowners and their property. Other evidence shows that primitive societies around the world also took periodic counts of their members. The Incas, for example, a pre-Columbian indigenous empire in western South America, required successive census reports to be recorded on knotted strings called *quipas*.

Although census taking has occurred throughout history, inferences based on statistical **demographics** appear to be a product of the last 200 years. In 1798, the English economist Thomas Robert Malthus (1766–1834) published his *Essay on the Principle of Population as It Affects the Future Improvement of Society*, in which he described a worldwide future of warfare, crime, and starvation. The human population, Malthus predicted, would grow exponentially over the following decades or centuries, leading to a shortage of needed resources, especially food. Conflict on both interpersonal and international levels would be the result, Malthus claimed, as individuals and groups competed for survival.

Demographics The characteristics of population groups, usually expressed in statistical form.

André-Michel Guerry and Adolphe Quételet

As a direct result of Malthusian thought, investigators throughout Europe began to gather "moral statistics," or social enumerations, which they thought might prove useful in measuring the degree to which crime and conflict existed in societies of the period. Such statistics were scrutinized in hopes of gauging "the moral health of nations"—a phrase commonly used throughout the period. One of the first such investigators was André-Michel Guerry (1802–1866), who calculated per capita crime rates throughout various French provinces in the early 19th century.

In 1835, the Belgian astronomer and mathematician Adolphe Quételet (1796–1864) published a statistical analysis of crime in a number of European countries, including Belgium, France, and Holland. Quételet set for himself the goal of assessing the degree to which crime rates varied according to climate and people's sex and age. He noticed what is still obvious to criminal statisticians today—that crime changes with the seasons, with many violent crimes showing an increase during the hot summer months and property crimes increasing in frequency during colder parts of the year. As a consequence of these observations, Quételet proposed what he called the "thermic law." According to thermic law, Quételet claimed, morality undergoes seasonal variation—a proposal that stimulated widespread debate in its day.[3]

The first officially published crime statistics appeared in London's *Gazette* beginning in 1828 and France's 1825 *Compte generale*. Soon, comparisons (or what contemporary statisticians call *correlations*) began to be calculated between economic conditions and the rates of various types of crime. From a study of English statistical data covering the years 1810 to 1847, Joseph Fletcher concluded that prison commitments increased as the price of wheat rose. Similarly, the German writer Georg von Mayr, whose data covered the years 1836 to 1861, discovered that the rate of theft increased with the price of rye in Bavaria.

The work of statisticians such as Guerry and Quételet formed the historical basis for what has been called the **statistical school** of criminology. The statistical school anticipated the development of both sociological criminology and the ecological school, perspectives that are discussed in considerable detail later in this book.

Statistical school A criminological perspective with roots in the early 19th century that seeks to uncover correlations between crime rates and other types of demographic data.

2.2 LEARNING OBJECTIVE

👁 **Watch**

Introduction to Measurement of Crime

USEFULNESS OF CRIME STATISTICS

How many assaults were committed last year in Canada? Who committed them? Who were the most likely to be victims? What part of the country had the highest rate of assault? Why?

These are the types of questions frequently asked, not only by those with a particular interest in the study of crime and offenders, but also by members of the general public. Crime statistics help provide answers to these and other questions and paint a picture of the reality of crime in this country. Often the first step toward solving a problem is understanding it, and this certainly applies to the problem of crime. Criminologists, students of criminology, and interested members of the public must understand the crime problem before any serious attempts at controlling or preventing it can be made. Crime statistics and data can be useful toward this end in a number of ways.

Crime data assist in describing the nature and extent of crime, which is necessary to develop effective crime-prevention policies. These policies, in turn, are usually responses to public pressure. Since it is the public that is the major player in reporting crime, the types of crime it reports reflect those issues most concerning it. By providing descriptive information about criminal activity, crime data serve as a gauge of the community's well-being.

Chapter 1 provides a brief discussion of the usefulness of theory development in the study of crime and criminals. Crime data provide the empirical support for the hypotheses developed by criminologists, who attempt to explain the phenomenon of crime and criminals. Crime data ultimately provide the test for theoretical assertions.

Just as crime statistics are used as a basis for developing social policy, they are also crucial in evaluating that policy. Whether or not a get-tough approach with young offenders will reduce the amount of youth crime or the introduction of increased penalties and mandatory sentences of incarceration will reduce the amount of violent crime will ultimately be assessed through an analysis of the data (see Chapter 11 for an in-depth look at specific crime-prevention initiatives). Program evaluation is often difficult to do well, and many such evaluations fall prey to the cost factor. Some programs are introduced largely because they are more cost-effective than conventional approaches, yet they may not achieve the desired result of reducing crime. Likewise, some programs that successfully reduce crime are shelved because they are seen as too expensive.

Most criminologists agree that the prevention of crime is generally considered preferable to its punishment and prevention is largely based on prediction. What types of people are most likely to commit what types of crime and why? Where will they commit them? Criminologists and others use crime data to help provide answers to these questions. The Canadian Crime Prevention Through Environmental Design model (CPTED) is based on the theory that the proper design and effective use of a physical space can help reduce the incidence of crime in that area. This theory, in turn, is based on crime data showing that

Canadians are especially fearful of violent crime. Here police investigate the scene of a fatal shooting of a bank teller during an armed robbery. Is the public's perception of the amounts and types of crime borne out by official statistics?

Ron Bull/Toronto Star/Canadian Press Images

crime occurs more often in areas where the opportunities for criminal activity are greatest (see Chapters 8 and 11 for a further description of the CPTED model).

It is important to note that predicting criminal activity and behaviour is an inexact science open to numerous pitfalls. In the early part of the 20th century, for example, Cesare Lombroso believed he could predict future criminal behaviour based on an individual's physical characteristics, such as the size of his ears or the shape of her nose. In the search for a quick fix to the crime problem, some people subscribed to such predictors. For others, prediction models for crime and criminal behaviour seem about as accurate as flipping a coin.[4]

Finally, crime data are useful in providing a picture of risk. Public perceptions of the amount and types of crime are often inconsistent with reality. Crime statistics are useful in assessing the risk to various segments of the population. For example, does one's sex, age, or social class have any bearing on his or her risk of becoming a victim of crime or of becoming involved in criminal behaviour? The study of risk assessment, with crime data used as its basis, is a growing area of interest within criminology.

SOURCES OF CRIME STATISTICS

COMPILATION OF CRIME STATISTICS HAS CONTINUED APACE EVER SINCE CRIME-related data began to be gathered over a century ago. Crime statistics in Canada are reported in two major surveys: the **Uniform Crime Reporting Survey (UCR)** and the **Victimization Survey**, conducted through the General Social Surveys. Both fall under the auspices of Canada's national statistics department, Statistics Canada. In 1981, the Canadian Centre for Justice Statistics (CCJS) was created as a satellite of Statistics Canada, through the cooperation of the federal and provincial governments. See Box 2.1 for an overview of the CCJS.

It is important to realize at the outset that these two types of data differ. Because of the differences in methodology and crime coverage, the two approaches examine the

---

Box 2.1 THE CANADIAN CENTRE FOR JUSTICE STATISTICS (CCJS)

As the collection of crime data became more formalized through the introduction of the uniform crime reports in the 1960s and victimization and self-report surveys in the 1970s, it became apparent that Canada needed a national centre for the collection, collation, and dissemination of these data. The creation of the Canadian Centre for Justice Statistics (CCJS) in 1981 was a result of a decade of numerous task forces and ongoing federal–provincial negotiations around this issue. By 1985, the CCJS had evolved as the administrative arm of Canada's National Justice Statistics Initiative (NJSI), whose mandate is to "provide information to the justice community and the public on the nature and extent of crime and the administration of justice in Canada."[5] It is through the CCJS that the NJSI produces statistical information to be used to support the legislative, policy, management, and research agenda of the Canadian government and also to inform the public.

The CCJS is subdivided into program areas, including law enforcement, courts, legal aid, corrections, and youth justice. Each of these program areas collects and collates data to examine the incidence of crime and criminal activity in Canada in areas such as homicide, street prostitution, criminal harassment, weapons and violent crime, motor vehicle crimes and impaired driving, and violent youth crime. The work of the CCJS also includes compiling information on other aspects of the criminal justice system, including justice-system expenditures, prisons and corrections data, probation and parole populations, inmate profiles, public perceptions and fear of crime, criminal justice system personnel figures, information on the activities of adult and youth courts, and topics and issues concerning victimization. This information is made available to the public through a service bulletin known as *Juristat*, which is published periodically throughout the year. *Juristat* and other CCJS reports are made available online or in person through the CCJS in Ottawa or through a number of Statistics Canada Regional Reference Centres throughout the country. Most public, community college, and university libraries also carry this information in reference departments. Publications of the CCJS can also be obtained by telephone at 1-800-263-1136, by email at infostats@statcan.gc.ca, or through the Statistics Canada website at www.statcan.gc.ca. Statistical information is also available through this website.

nation's crime reality from unique perspectives, and results are not strictly comparable. Nevertheless, the two surveys can complement each other, and each is certainly useful in providing an overall picture of criminal activity. The two surveys are compared in detail later in the chapter.

The Uniform Crime Reporting Survey

The Uniform Crime Reporting Survey (UCR) was initiated in 1961 through the efforts of Statistics Canada and the Canadian Association of Chiefs of Police. It provides a standardized procedure by which police departments across the country can collect information about crimes that come to their attention and then report this information to Statistics Canada, specifically to the CCJS. The CCJS then collates the raw data and makes them available to the public.

Between 1962 and 1988, the official crime statistics generated from the UCR were based on summarized monthly police reports from police departments across the country. Known as the Aggregate Uniform Crime Reporting Survey, these police reports included the number of incidents and offences reported to police, the number of actual offences, the number of offences cleared, the number of adults charged, the number of youths charged, and the sex of those charged.

Changes in the UCR after 1988 shifted the emphasis of data collection away from summary or aggregate collection to include incident-based collection. The new system, known as the Revised UCR2 Survey or Incident-Based UCR, included data collection in the following areas:

- *information on victims:* age, sex, victim/accused relationship, level of injury, type of weapon causing injury, drug and/or alcohol use;

- *information on the accused:* age, sex, type of charges laid or recommended, drug and/or alcohol use; and

- *information on the circumstances of the incident:* type of violation (or crime), target of violation, types of property stolen, dollar value of property affected, dollar value of drugs confiscated, type of weapon present, time and type of location of the incident.[6]

A revised version of the UCR2 known as the UCR2.1 was introduced in 1998. This survey was designed to provide certain efficiencies in reporting for police services. In 2004, another version named UCR2.2 was introduced to take into account new violations and variables such as organized crime, cyber crime, hate crime, and geocode information. In 2008, a police-reported Crime Severity Index (PRCSI) was introduced to measure changes in the severity of crime from year to year. This index assigns a weight to each offence that is derived from actual sentences handed down by courts in all provinces and territories. Weights are calculated using the five most recent years of available sentencing data. More serious crimes are assigned higher weights, less serious offences lower weights. As a result, when all crimes are included, more serious offences have a higher impact on changes in the index.

Police services are required to respond to the survey. In the most recent year for which this information is available, more than 1200 separate police detachments comprising 204 different police forces from across the country supplied data for the complete year to the UCR2 Survey.[7] The UCR records offences cleared by charge or otherwise

Arson causes millions of dollars' worth of property damage yearly. Are UCR statistics on arson accurate?

Condor 36/Shutterstock

and rates of crime. The phrase *offence cleared by charge* refers to an offence that is closed when police have formally charged a person or when there is sufficient evidence to lay a charge against an identified person, even if that person has not been apprehended by police. *Offence cleared otherwise* refers to a case in which police cannot or do not charge a person even if they have identified a suspect and have enough evidence to support the laying of a charge. Examples include cases of diplomatic immunity, instances in which the complainant declines to proceed with charges against the accused, cases in which police have opted not to lay a charge (e.g., the uses of extrajudicial measures for youth), or cases where the alleged offender dies before being formally charged.[8] The *clearance rate* indicates the proportion of incidents that are cleared by charge or otherwise for different types of offences, compared to the total number of actual incidents.

The **crime rate** used in the UCR is based on a population of 100 000. By taking into account population, the crime picture is standardized across the country in any given year. For example, in 2011 the total number of recorded violent crimes was 424 410. The rate of crimes of violence was 1231 based on a Canadian total population of 34 476 848. This crime rate was calculated as follows:

$$\frac{\text{\# of reported violent crimes}}{\text{total population}} \times 100\ 000$$

$$\frac{424\ 410\ \text{violent crimes reported}}{34\ 476\ 848\ \text{total population}} \times 100\ 000 = 1231$$

Thus, we see that there were 1231 violent crime incidents per 100 000 population in Canada in 2011. If we consider a specific type of violent crime, such as homicide, and apply the same procedure, the equation will look like this:

$$\frac{598\ \text{homicides reported}}{34\ 476\ 848\ \text{total population}} \times 100\ 000 = 2$$

This tells us that there were approximately 2 homicides for every 100 000 Canadians in 2011.[9] A summary of the UCR findings for 2011 is reproduced in Box 2.2.

Programmatic Problems with Available Data The most significant methodological feature of the Uniform Crime Reporting Survey is indicated by its name. It is a "reporting" system. In other words, only crimes that are reported to the police (or discovered by them, or by someone else who then reports them) are included in the statistics compiled by the system. Unless someone complains to the police about a criminal incident, it will go unreported and will not appear in the UCR. Most complaints are made by victims.

Because UCR data are based on *reported* crime, the system has been criticized for underestimating the true incidence of criminal activity within Canada—a measurement that would also include unreported crimes. Unreported and under-reported criminal activity has been called the **dark figure of crime**. Some experts say that sexual assault is the most under-reported crime in the UCR. Reasons for not reporting a crime such as sexual assault are numerous and include (1) the victim's fear of the perpetrator; (2) the victim's shame, which may carry over from traditional attitudes about sexual behaviour and a woman's role in sexual encounters; (3) the victim's fear of not being believed; and (4) the victim's fear of further participation in the justice system (such as the possibility of the victim being required to go to court and testify against the offender, thereby exposing herself to potentially embarrassing cross-examination and public scrutiny). Other general reasons cited by victims for failure to report a crime include "fear of revenge," "nothing can be done," "the crime was too minor," or the incident was a "private matter."

Many other crimes are under-reported as well. Although sexual assault is indeed seriously under-reported (a conclusion drawn from comparison of UCR and Victimization Survey sexual assault statistics), the most seriously under-reported crime may in fact be

Box 2.2 HIGHLIGHTS OF THE 2011 UCR

- Police-reported crime decreased in 2011, continuing the downward trend seen over the past 20 years. Police reported about 2 million *Criminal Code* offences in 2011, about 110 000 fewer than in 2010.

- Both the crime rate, which measures the volume of crime reported to police, and the Crime Severity Index (CSI), which measures the severity of crime, dropped 6% in 2011. The drop in crime was seen in most parts of the country and for virtually all offences.

- As in past years, both the volume and severity of crime were found to be highest in the territories. Saskatchewan reported the highest CSI in 2011 among the provinces, followed by Manitoba, British Columbia, and Alberta.

- Ontario had the lowest CSI in the country, followed by New Brunswick and Prince Edward Island. Nova Scotia was the only eastern province whose CSI in 2011 was above the national index.

- All of Canada's census metropolitan areas (CMAs) reported a decrease in their CSI values. Regina continued to report the highest CSI value among all CMAs, followed by Saskatoon, Thunder Bay, and Winnipeg. The lowest CSI values were seen in Guelph, Quebec City, Toronto, and Ottawa.

- The violent crime rate and the violent CSI also declined in 2011, both down 4%. The decrease in the violent CSI marks the fifth consecutive decline.

- Declines were seen in most violent offences, including attempted murders, major assaults, sexual assaults, and robberies, as well as most non-violent offences including break-ins and motor vehicle thefts. The only offences to show an increase in 2011 were homicide, sexual offences against children, child pornography, criminal harassment, impaired driving, and most drug offences.

- The homicide rate increased in 2011, up 7%. The largest increases were reported in Alberta (+39%) and Quebec (+24%). Conversely, Ontario's rate dropped 16% to its lowest point since the mid-1960s.

- Winnipeg reported the highest homicide rate among all CMAs, followed by Halifax and Edmonton.

- Police-reported youth crime also dropped in 2011. Both the youth crime rate and the youth CSI decreased 10%. The rate of youth accused of some of the most serious violent offences also dropped: homicide (−16%), major assault (−4%), and robbery (−4%).

Source: Statistics Canada, *Juristat* 85-002-X, Released July 24, 2012. Reproduced and distributed on an "as is" basis with the permission of Statistics Canada.
It is interesting to note that changes in public attitudes about certain types of crime such as child abuse have resulted in the public's inclination to report these crimes more readily. Does an increase in the number of reported child abuse cases mean that there are more incidents of child abuse occurring or simply that more cases are being reported?

theft $5000 and under, because the theft of small items may never make it into official police reports and may even be forgotten by victims during interviews with victimization surveyors.

Another concern raised about the accuracy of UCR numbers lies with the way in which police services record and report the criminal activity that is detected. The UCR receives crime data from municipal police departments across Canada as well as from the RCMP, the Ontario Provincial Police, and the Sûreté du Québec (Quebec's provincial police force). To expect that all these police services are recording their crime statistics in a uniform manner is unrealistic, although the CCJS does work with police agencies on an ongoing basis to detect and resolve any difficulties in the reporting or transmission of data. Nevertheless, there are variations in how the police count crime, as a result of a number of factors. Changes in the number of police services and police officers will most certainly affect the number of detected crimes. Enforcement practices or mandates often vary from one police department to another. For example, if commercial break and enters are a problem in one community, local police will be more vigilant toward this type of criminal activity, which will be reflected in the crime report.

Related to police recording and reporting are methodological concerns with the way the UCR "counts" crime, especially in an incident involving multiple offences. The UCR counts only the most serious offence (MSO) in the incident. For example, if someone breaks into a store, severely assaults the security personnel, and steals a laptop, only the assault is recorded. The MSO is determined by the maximum sentence length; in the scenario just mentioned, although the break and enter and assault both carry a maximum life sentence, the crime against the person is considered more serious and takes precedence over the crime against property. As a result, less serious offences tend to be under-represented by the UCR Survey. The recent introduction of the police-reported Crime Severity Index (PRCSI) is an attempt to address this shortcoming. For the purposes of counting, even though crimes against the person take precedence over crimes against property, this is not the case when the crime rate is calculated. Recall that the crime rate is the total number of reported crimes in a given year per 100 000 population. This total encompasses all categories of crime including federal and provincial statute violations. For example, the number of reported motor vehicle thefts might skyrocket in a given year, while the number of assaults might fall. The resulting overall crime rate for that year would be higher than for the year before because both classifications of crime are assigned the same weight.

Finally, for violent crime, the UCR records the number of incidents in terms of number of victims. If one person assaults two people, two incidents are recorded. But if two people assault one person, only one incident is recorded. The exception to this scoring rule for violent crime is robbery: one occurrence of robbery is counted as one incident regardless of the number of victims. Since robbery can involve many people who could be considered victims (for example, in the case of a bank robbery), to count each one would seriously overstate the occurrence of robbery. Thus, the total number of incidents recorded in the UCR is actually equal to the number of victims of violent crimes (other than robbery) plus the number of individual occurrences of non-violent crimes and robbery.

A final concern about the accuracy of the UCR centres on the legal definition of crime. A case in point: the renaming and redefinition of rape to sexual assault in 1983 means that the types of behaviour constituting sexual assault have been more clearly defined to include those behaviours from unwanted sexual touching to aggravated sexual assault that endangers the life of the victim. Similarly, amendments to the definition of arson in 1990 now include mischief fires as arson. Both of these redefinitions have broadened the scope of these criminal activities and have resulted in a corresponding increase in the statistical incidence of these crimes.

The consistency of definition is also a concern. Part of the difficulty in measuring child abuse, for example, arises from the fact that there is no apparent consensus as to what constitutes child abuse across Canada at the provincial and territorial level, where child-welfare services are organized and delivered. For example, the maximum age of the child to be protected (under 16 in Newfoundland and Labrador to under 19 in British Columbia) and the policies underlying child protection vary across the country. It is estimated that cases of child abuse would double if threats and acts of indecent exposure were added to the definition. As well, the distinction between corporal punishment and physical abuse is not clear, which further thwarts the accurate accounting of child abuse. For the purposes of recording, the CCJS defines child abuse as incidents of physical and sexual assault and homicide where the victim is under 18 years of age.[10]

⊙⃝ Watch

Different Types of Partner Violence

Data Gathering Using Victimization Surveys

Victimization Surveys differ from the UCR in one especially significant way: rather than depending on reports of crimes to the police, the data contained in Victimization Surveys consist of information elicited through interviews with members of randomly selected households throughout the country. Hence, these surveys uncover a large number of crimes that may not have been reported and are therefore regarded by many researchers as a more accurate measure of the actual incidence of crime in Canada than is the UCR.

A number of significant Victimization Surveys have been undertaken in Canada. The first, and perhaps the most comprehensive, was the *Canadian Urban Victimization Survey* (CUVS) conducted in 1981 under the auspices of the Solicitor General of Canada.

It randomly sampled roughly 60 000 Canadians over the age of 16 in seven major cities. In telephone interviews, respondents were asked to describe any victimization experiences they had suffered in the preceding calendar year. Eight categories of crime were included in the survey: sexual assault, robbery, assault, break and enter, motor vehicle theft, theft of household property, theft of personal property, and vandalism. The survey uncovered over 700 000 personal victimizations and almost 900 000 household victimizations for the calendar year of 1981. It also revealed that fewer than 42 percent of these victimizations had been reported to the police or had otherwise come to police attention.[11]

Beginning in 1988, Statistics Canada has conducted a Victimization Survey every five years, as part of the General Social Survey (GSS). The 2009 GSS (the latest one from which victimization data are available) sampled a national target population of roughly 20 000 Canadians aged 15 and over in the provinces and territories, excluding full-time residents of institutions. Interviews were conducted by telephone from February to December 2009, using random-digit dialing techniques. In an interview lasting 30 minutes on average, respondents were asked about their experiences with the criminal justice system in the previous 12 months and specifically about eight types of criminal victimization: sexual assault, robbery (and attempted robbery), physical assault, theft of personal property, break and enter (and attempted break and enter), motor vehicle/parts theft (and attempts), attempts at and theft of household property, and vandalism. Respondents who had been victims of a crime were asked for detailed information about each incident including when and where it occurred, whether the incident had been reported to the police, and how they had been affected by the experience. Respondents were also questioned about their perceptions and fear of crime and their knowledge and perceptions of the criminal justice system. Demographic information about the respondents was also gathered, including age, sex, and marital status, as well as educational, occupational, and income levels. Highlights of the findings of the survey are presented in Figures 2.1 and 2.2. Generally, the summary indicated a slight increase in household victimization rates in the five-year period between 1999 and 2004. A significant proportion of Canadians (roughly 28 percent) were affected by one or more of the crimes covered in the 2004 GSS as compared to 26 percent in the 1999 survey. It is interesting to compare these rates of victimization with the concerns about fear of crime among Canadians, discussed in Chapter 1.

While the CUVS and subsequent GSS have helped to provide a picture of the amounts and types of crime generally in Canada, other surveys have been conducted to look at specific types of crime victims. Most notable among these is the first-ever national Violence

Figure 2.1 Self-reported Victimization Incidents Reported to the Police, 2009

Note: Excludes all incidents of spousal sexual and physical assault. Excludes data from Northwest Territories, Yukon, and Nunavut. Data for sexual assault are not shown as they are too small to produce reliable estimates. Source: Statistics Canada, General Social Survey, 2009. Reproduced and distributed on an "as is" basis with the permission of Statistics Canada.

Reasons

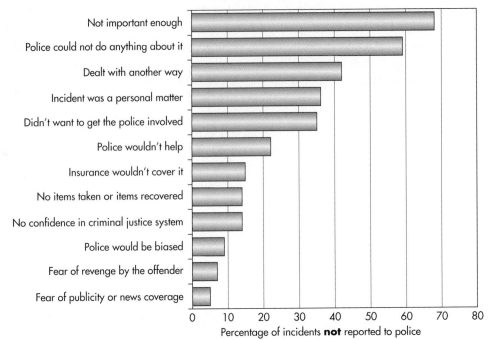

Figure 2.2 label: Percentage of incidents **not** reported to police

- Not important enough
- Police could not do anything about it
- Dealt with another way
- Incident was a personal matter
- Didn't want to get the police involved
- Police wouldn't help
- Insurance wouldn't cover it
- No items taken or items recovered
- No confidence in criminal justice system
- Police would be biased
- Fear of revenge by the offender
- Fear of publicity or news coverage

Figure 2.2 Reasons for Not Reporting Victimization Incidents to Police, 2009

Note: Excludes all incidents of spousal sexual and physical assault. Excludes data from Northwest Territories, Yukon, and Nunavut.

Source: Statistics Canada, General Social Survey, 2009. Reproduced and distributed on an "as is" basis with the permission of Statistics Canada.

Against Women Survey (VAWS), undertaken by Statistics Canada in 1993. Over 12 000 women 18 years of age and older were interviewed by telephone about their experiences of physical and sexual violence since the age of 16 and their perceptions of their personal safety. The findings of the survey indicated significantly more incidents of violence against women than had ever been previously indicated in official UCR numbers. One-half of all Canadian women reported having experienced at least one incident of violence since age 16, and almost one-half reported that this violence had been perpetrated by men known to them. A summary of the findings from the VAWS is outlined in Box 2.3.

A number of initiatives have been undertaken at the international level to compare victimization rates from country to country. The International Crime Victimization Survey (ICVS) is one such initiative, first implemented in 1989. The most recent

---

Box 2.3 HIGHLIGHTS OF THE VIOLENCE AGAINST WOMEN SURVEY (VAWS)

- About 50% of all Canadian women have experienced at least one incident of violence since the age of 16.

- Almost 50% of women reported violence by men known to them, and 25% reported violence by a stranger.

- Approximately 25% of all women have experienced violence at the hands of a current or past marital partner (includes common-law unions).

- Roughly 15% of currently married women reported violence by their spouses; 50% of women with previous marriages reported violence by a previous spouse.

- More than 10% of women who reported violence in a current marriage have at some point felt their lives were in danger.

- About 60% of Canadian women who walk alone in their own area after dark feel "very" or "somewhat" worried doing so.

- Women with violent fathers-in-law are at three times the risk of assault by their partners than are women with non-violent fathers-in-law.

Source: Statistics Canada, *The Daily* 11-001-XPE November 18, 1993. Reproduced and distributed on an "as is" basis with the permission of Statistics Canada.

- According to the results of the International Crime Victimization Survey (ICVS), in 2004 17% of Canadians aged 16 and over had been victims of at least one of the ten crimes measured by the survey. The overall international victimization rate was 16%.

- Canada's highest victimization rate was for theft from a vehicle. For almost all countries participating in the ICVS, the offences with the highest victimization rates were theft of personal property, theft from a car, and theft of a bicycle.

- Canada, along with Finland and Luxembourg, ranked relatively low with respect to the proportion of incidents (theft from a car, theft of a bicycle, burglary, attempted burglary, and theft of personal property) reported to the police. At 48%, the proportion of Canadian victims of these crimes who reported the incident to the police in 2004 was below the international average (53%).

- In 2004, 86% of Canadians aged 16 and over believed that the police were doing a good or excellent job at controlling crime in their area. Canada, along with Finland and the United States, was among the countries whose populations were the most satisfied with the job done by the police.

Source: Statistics Canada, *Juristat*, 85-002-XIE2008010 vol. 28 no. 10. Released December 15, 2008. Reproduced and distributed on an "as is" basis with the permission of Statistics Canada.

survey (2004/2005) was coordinated with the European Survey on Crime and Safety (EU ICS). Canada was one of 30 countries participating in this survey that set out to provide comparable information on the incidence of victimization around the world. People aged 16 years and older were asked through random telephone sampling for information on ten offences (robbery/attempted robbery, sexual offences, physical assaults/threats, theft of personal property, burglary of residence, attempted burglary of residence, theft of car/ van/truck, theft from car, theft of motorcycle, theft of bicycle). Respondents were asked when, where, and how often offences had occurred during the previous year and the previous five years; whether offences were reported to police; and whether victimization experiences were considered serious. Respondents were also asked for their opinion on public safety, policing, and sentencing. An average of 1000 to 5000 persons were interviewed per country. Despite some recognized methodological shortcomings, such as the likelihood of fairly large sampling errors, the findings of the survey are interesting. Seventeen percent of Canadians reported having been victimized within the previous year, which was slightly above the average of 16 percent when compared to the 29 other countries participating in the survey. A summary of the highlights of this survey can be found in Box 2.4.

Critique of Victimization Surveys   Just as the UCR has been criticized for underrepresenting the actual incidence of criminal activity in Canada, Victimization Surveys in general, and the GSS in particular, can be criticized for possible over-reporting of some crimes. It is beyond the purview of a Victimization Survey to verify the actual occurrence of any of the crimes reported to the interviewers; therefore, no measure exists to determine the number of crimes that might be over-reported. Victimization Surveys are dependent upon the ability of the respondent to not only recall incidents and their details but also to accurately place them in time. Some respondents provide more detailed and accurate accounts of their victimization experiences, which may skew the data. As well, by their nature, Victimization Surveys exclude data on homicide, kidnapping, so-called victimless crimes (public intoxication, prostitution, and gambling), impaired driving, drug offences, crimes such as vandalism and theft committed against commercial or public property, and crimes committed against children under the age of 15.

Comparing Uniform Crime Reporting Surveys and Victimization Surveys   Even though the data generated by the UCR and Victimization Surveys are based on the same categories of crime, they reveal very different pictures. Findings from the

UCR are the reports of crimes recorded by the police, who are generally alerted to the crime as a result of a call from a victim. The type and frequency of calls to police change over time and vary according to location. For example, as the community tolerance for sexual assault and family violence declines, victims or witnesses of these crimes may be more willing to report them to authorities, and authorities will be more likely to treat them as crimes.

Victimization Surveys, on the other hand, were developed to provide a way of looking at crime from the perspective of individual victims. They describe what has happened to individual Canadians and the way in which these individuals respond to their victimization experiences. Without a doubt, these surveys reveal that many Canadians do not report personal victimizations and suggest the reasons for this.

Despite their divergent focuses, UCR and Victimization Surveys can complement one another. Victimization data can help place UCR findings in context. For instance, how much change in official crime data for family violence can be attributed to changes in reporting patterns or police practices? (Police in Ontario and some other provinces are mandated to lay charges against the perpetrator in a domestic assault situation if sufficient evidence exists, regardless of the victim's willingness to concur.) How are crime trends a reflection of people's attitudes toward crime and the criminal justice system? While neither UCR nor victimization data can provide comprehensive information about crime, when considered together they are useful in providing a picture of crime and criminal activity in Canada. See Table 2.1 for a comparison of the UCR and GSS.

Data Gathering Using Self-Report Studies

Self-report study A data collection method requiring subjects to reveal their own participation in criminal behaviour.

Another approach to the production of data on the amount and types of crime is the **self-report study**. Within the field of criminology, there is a widely held belief that to understand crime, it is important to ask people about their involvement with it. There have been countless self-report studies conducted with various groups of individuals, most notably with youth. The results of the groundbreaking work by Short and Nye[12] led many to believe that traditional police data have the potential to be biased toward certain segments of society, in particular the lower socio-economic classes. Other gaps between official sources of data and self-report data have been found in the age, sex, and race of the offender. One of the most notable Canadian self-report studies was conducted by LeBlanc and Fréchette.[13]

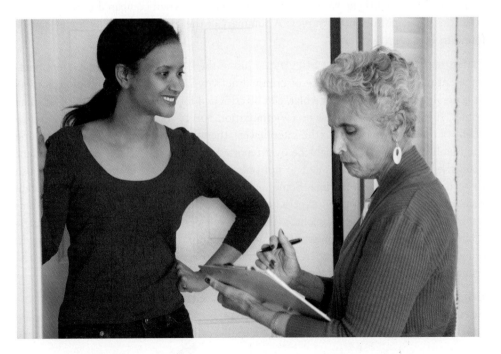

The self-report study allows criminologists to understand crime from the perspective of the perpetrator. What is a drawback to this approach of data collection?

Edbockstock/Fotolia

Table 2.1 Differences between the UCR and GSS

UCR	GSS
Data Collection Methods:	
Administrative police records	Personal reports from individual citizens
Census	Sample survey
100% coverage of all police agencies	Sample of approximately 10 000 persons using random digit dialing sampling technique
Data submitted on paper or in machine-readable format	Computer Assisted Telephone Interviewing (CATI); excludes households without telephones
National in scope	Excludes Yukon, Northwest Territories, and Nunavut
Continuous historical file: 1962 onwards	Periodic survey: 1988, 1993, 2000, 2004
All recorded criminal incidents regardless of victims' age	Target population: persons aged 15 and over, excluding full-time residents of institutions
Counts only those incidents reported to and recorded by police	Collects crimes reported and not reported to police
Scope and Definitions:	
Primary unit of count is the criminal incident	Primary unit of count is criminal victimization (at personal and household levels)
Nearly 100 crime categories	Eight crime categories
"Most serious offence" rule results in an undercount of less serious crimes	Statistics are usually reported on a "most serious offence" basis, but counts for every crime type are possible, depending on statistical reliability
Includes attempts	Includes attempts
Sources of Error:	
Reporting by the public	Sampling error
Processing error, edit failure, non-responding police department	Non-sampling error related to the following: coverage, respondent error (e.g., recall error), non-response, coding, edit and imputation, estimation
Police discretion, changes in policy and procedures	
Legislative change	

Source: Adapted from the Statistics Canada publication "An Overview of the Differences Between Police-Reported and Victim-Reported Crime 1997," 85-542-XIE 1997001, no. 1, May 14, 1997.

Using a list of 39 questions, these researchers surveyed a large group of high-risk Montreal youth on a variety of behaviours (the list of questions is reproduced in Table 2.2). LeBlanc and Fréchette hoped to use the results of their surveys to describe delinquent patterns for all high-risk Canadian male youth. Despite methodological shortcomings, including the failure to consider cultural differences between French- and English-speaking Canadians and the failure to consider delinquency rates among females, the study was important in its contribution to a general understanding of the crime picture among youth in Canada.

In general, self-report studies are recognized within the field of criminology as one means of counting crime and criminals. When considered in conjunction with other methods of information gathering, self-report studies help provide a clearer and more complete picture of crime and who commits it. They are considered to be particularly useful in

Table 2.2 Self-Report Questions from the Montreal Youth Study by LeBlanc and Fréchette

During the past 12 months, did you

1.   . . . purposely damage or destroy musical instruments, sports supplies, or other school equipment?
2.   . . . purposely damage or destroy public or private property that did not belong to you?
3.   . . . take some school property worth $5.00 or more?
4.   . . . purposely damage school building (windows, walls, . . .)?
5.   . . . take a motorcycle and go for a ride without the owner's permission?
6.   . . . take a car and go for a ride without the owner's permission?
7.   . . . purposely destroy a radio antenna, tires, or other parts of a car?
8.   . . . "beat up" someone who hadn't done anything to you?
9.   . . . take something from a store without paying?
10.   . . . threaten to beat up someone to make him do something he didn't want to do?
11.   . . . get into a place (a movie, a game, or a performance) without paying the admission price?
12.   . . . use a weapon (stick, knife, gun, rock, . . .) while fighting another person?
13.   . . . use stimulants (speed, pep pills, etc. . . .) or hallucinogens (LSD, STP, THC, etc. . . .)?
14.   . . . have a fist fight with another person?
15.   . . . take something of large value (worth $50.00 or more) that did not belong to you?
16.   . . . gamble for money with persons other than your family members?
17.   . . . sell any kind of drugs?
18.   . . . break into and enter somewhere to take something?
19.   . . . carry a weapon (chain, knife, gun, etc. . . .)?
20.   . . . take something of some value (between $2.00 and $50.00) that did not belong to you?
21.   . . . purposely set a fire in a building or in any other place?
22.   . . . take and keep a bicycle that did not belong to you?
23.   . . . take something of little value (worth less than $2.00) that did not belong to you?
24.   . . . trespass anywhere you were not supposed to go (vacant house, railroad tracks, lumber yard, etc. . . .)?
25.   . . . use marijuana or hashish?
26.   . . . make anonymous phone calls (not say who you were)?
27.   . . . use opiates (heroin, morphine, opium)?
28.   . . . send in a false alarm?
29.   . . . buy, use, or sell something that you knew to be stolen?
30.   . . . drive a car without a driver's licence?
31.   . . . have sexual relations (other than kissing) with a person of the same sex?
32.   . . . skip school without a legitimate excuse?
33.   . . . have sexual relations (other than kissing) with a person of the opposite sex?
34.   . . . take part in a gang fight between adolescents?
35.   . . . run away from home for more than 24 hours?
36.   . . . tell your parents (or those who replace them) that you would not do what they ordered you to do?
37.   . . . take money from home without permission and with no intention of returning it?
38.   . . . get drunk on beer, wine, or other alcoholic beverages?
39.   . . . "fool around" at night when you were supposed to be at home?

Source: M. LeBlanc and M. Fréchette, *Male Criminal Activity from Childhood through Youth: Multilevel and Developmental Perspectives* (New York: Springer-Verlag, 1989), pp. 195–196, cited in M.A. Jackson and C.T. With kind permission of Springer Science+Business Media.

highlighting the relationship between social class and crime and in uncovering much crime that goes undetected.[14]

Limitations of Self-Report Studies

Since their acceptance as a legitimate means of examining the reality of crime and criminals, self-report studies have consistently become more sound. Nevertheless, a number of methodological shortcomings continue to exist. For example, the accuracy of this research approach is largely predicated on the honesty and forthrightness of the respondent. Inaccurate answers may result from a number of factors, including the respondent's failure to disclose behaviour, the tendency to exaggerate behaviour, or the respondent's failure to remember. Often respondents are concerned about confidentiality and anonymity, which is understandable given the information they are being asked to reveal. This may affect the way they answer or indeed whether they even participate in the survey. Analyses of self-report studies indicate that the more offences a respondent has committed, the fewer he or she is likely to admit to. Conversely, a respondent who has committed a lesser number of offences is more likely to admit to them in a self-report survey.

Other methodological limitations include a lack of standardized data collection methods, such as comparable questions, time frames, or geographic areas. Nevertheless, there seems to be agreement that self-report studies are useful in providing a more rounded picture of the criminal, especially when compared with the picture that is often captured in official statistics based on police reports. While the official statistics provide information on tangibles such as the age and sex of an offender, self-report studies serve to reveal characteristics such as education levels, home life, peer group, and general socio-economic realities of the offender. It has been suggested that this approach could be used to include an examination of those biological and psychological factors that contribute to criminal behaviour, thereby complementing the environmental realities they already help to illuminate. Whether the findings of these self-report studies that target a specific group in a specific time and place can be used to deduce general assumptions about criminals and the crimes they commit is still open to debate.

THE SOCIAL DIMENSIONS OF CRIME

CRIME DOES NOT OCCUR IN A VACUUM. IT INVOLVES REAL PEOPLE—HUMAN perpetrators and victims. Because society defines certain personal characteristics as especially important, it is possible to speak of the "social dimensions of crime," that is, aspects of crime and victimization as they relate to socially significant attributes by which groups are defined and according to which individuals are assigned group membership. Socially significant attributes include sex and gender, ethnicity or race, age, income or wealth, profession, and social class or standing within society. Such personal characteristics provide criteria by which individuals can be assigned to groups such as "the rich," "the poor," "male," "female," "young," "old," "black," "white," "white-collar worker," "manual labourer," and so on.[15]

We have already alluded briefly to the fact that the UCR, GSS or Victimization Surveys, and self-report studies structure the data they gather in ways that reflect socially significant characteristics. The UCR, for example, provides information on reported crimes, which reveals the sex and age of perpetrators. Victimization statistics document the age and sex of crime victims and the educational, occupational, and income levels of households reporting victimizations. Self-report studies provide some insight into the age, sex, ethnic background, education levels, social habits, and socio-economic status of those engaged in delinquent or criminal behaviour.

The social dimensions of crime are said by statisticians to reveal relationships or correlations. A **correlation** is simply a connection or association observed to exist between two measurable variables. Correlations are of two types: positive and negative. If one measurement increases when its correlate does the same, then a positive correlation or positive relationship is said to exist between the two. When one measurement decreases in value

Correlation A causal, complementary, or reciprocal relationship between two measurable variables.

as another rises, a negative or inverse correlation has been discovered. Victimization data, for example, show a negative relationship between age and victimization. As people age, victimization rates decline. So, although some elderly people do become crime victims, older people as a group tend to be less victimized than younger people. Uniform Crime Report data, on the other hand, show a positive relationship between youth and likelihood of arrest—specifically, between young adulthood and arrest. Young adults, it appears, commit most crimes. Hence, as people age, they tend to be both less likely to be victimized and less likely to become involved in criminal activity.

A word of caution is in order. Correlation does not necessarily imply causation. Because two variables appear to be correlated does not mean that they have any influence on one another, or that one causes another either to increase or to decrease. Correlations that involve no causal relationship are said to be *spurious*. A study of crime rates, for example, shows that many crimes seem to occur with greater frequency in the summer. Similarly, industry groups tell us that food retailers sell more ice cream in the summer than at any other time. Are we to conclude, then, from the observed correlation between crime rates and ice cream sales that one in some way causes the other? To do so on the basis of an observed correlation alone would obviously be foolish.

Some observed correlations do appear to shed at least some light on either the root causes of crime or the nature of criminal activity, often referred to as **correlates of crime**. Our discussion now turns to these.

Correlates of crime Those variables observed to be related to criminal activity such as age, sex and gender, ethnicity, and social class.

Age and Crime

If records of persons accused are any guide, criminal activity is associated more with youth than any other stage of life. Year after year, Uniform Crime Reports consistently show that younger people, from their mid- to late teens to their early and mid-20s, account for the bulk of the crime reported in this country. Indeed, age is one of the strongest correlates of criminal behaviour.

A Statistics Canada report indicated that persons aged 15 to 24 represented 14 percent of the total population but accounted for 45 percent of those charged with property crimes and 32 percent of those charged with violent crimes.[16] See Figure 2.3 for a graphical depiction.

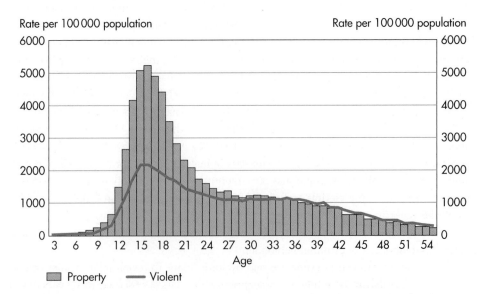

Figure 2.3 Persons Accused of Property Crimes and Violent Crimes by Age, Canada

Source: Adapted from Statistics Canada, "Exploring Crime Patterns in Canada," 85-561-MIE 2005005, no. 5, June 29, 2005.

Cautions raised by some U.S. criminologists that an impending demographic shift will result in a substantial increase in crime, and especially violent crime, have proven to be misguided.[17-20] A look at the demographic reality in Canada paints a somewhat different picture. Canadian statistics tell us that crime rates in Canada have followed population shifts, with somewhat of a time lag. According to Statistics Canada, most of the baby boomers were 15 years of age between 1960 and 1980, a time that witnessed steady increases in violent and property crime rates. Property crime rates levelled out in the 1980s as the percentage of 15- to 24-year-olds began to drop, and increased slightly in the early 1990s before declining sharply (as the percentage of 25- to 34-year-olds began to decline). It is interesting to note that violent crimes do not parallel as closely the demographic shift; the violent crime rate continued to increase steadily until 1993. The decline in the violent crime rate began several years after the start of the decline in the 15–24 age group.[21] Other studies suggest that our crime rates have steadily declined due to positive changes in economic and employment opportunities for youth today as compared with the realities of the recession years of the 1980s, which negatively affected the cohort of those born in the 1960s.[22] Further explanations for the correlation between youth and crime are raised in Box 2.5.

When considering the correlation between age and victimization, the most recent statistics show that Canadians between the ages of 15 and 24 years experienced personal victimization at rates 15 times greater than the rate for other groups. The risk of violent victimization steadily declined as age increased. For example, those 25 to 34 years of age had a rate of 165 per 1000 compared to a rate of 114 per 1000 for the group aged 35 to 44. Rates of violent victimization were lowest among those aged 65 and older. These Canadians had a rate of 19 violent incidents per 1000 population.[23] Statistics show that children are over-represented as victims of certain types of crimes. While Victimization Surveys only poll Canadians over 15 years of age, UCR statistics indicate that for offences such as sexual assault and other sexual offences (sexual interference, invitation to sexual touching, sexual exploitation, and incest), children under 13 years of age represent 15 percent and 29 percent respectively.[24]

Sex and Crime

⊙–[**Watch**

Women and Criminal Behaviour

Sex appears so closely linked to most forms of criminal activity that it has been called "the best single predictor of criminality."[25] The most recent data available indicate that males account for 77 percent of those adults accused of a criminal offence. This is particularly true when considering violent crimes; adult males make up 90 percent of all charges for homicide and 98 percent of all charges for sexual assault, child pornography, and sexual violations against children. With property crimes, adult males constitute 73 percent of overall charges related to property offences. The offences with the highest representation of females include abduction (49 percent), prostitution (45 percent), and theft under $5000 (37 percent). The most common offences for which females are accused are theft under $5000, assault level 1, and administration of justice violations (e.g., failure to appear in court, breach of probation, etc.).[26]

The continued lower rate of female criminality has been explained by some as primarily due to cultural factors, including early socialization, role expectations, and a reluctance among criminal justice officials to arrest and prosecute women. Women who are struggling with poverty, homelessness, and addiction may turn to illegal activities to support themselves and their families. Others have assumed a biological propensity toward crime and aggression among men that may be lacking in women. These and other issues are addressed in Chapters 6 to 10.

Of note is the reality that the proportion of women charged with criminal activity has increased over the past three decades. In 2009, women made up just over 21 percent of all adults charged with a *Criminal Code* offence, up from 15 percent in 1979. A similar increase can be found across offence categories. Some criminologists cite *role convergence*, or the adaptation of the role of women to more closely resemble that of men, as an explanation for this. Others see the significant increases in female involvement in offences such as shoplifting, credit card fraud, and passing bad cheques as a manifestation of the *feminization of poverty*, rather than the convergence of male and female roles.[27] As the number of poor, female single parents grows, their marginalization may be reflected in increases in certain types of female property crimes.

When women commit crime, they are more often followers than leaders. One study of women in correctional settings, for example, found that women are far more likely to assume "secondary follower rules during criminal events" than "dominant leadership roles." Only 14 percent of women surveyed played primary roles, but those who did "felt that men had little influence in initiating or leading them into crime."[28]

However, trends that focus on the relative proportion of female offenders should be interpreted with caution. Whether the rise in adult female rates of police-reported crime reflects an actual increase in female offending or a change in enforcement practices cannot be determined simply by an examination of statistical data. Changes to how police approach certain offences may affect the number of women charged.[29]

Although much female criminality has long been overlooked, criminologists are now increasingly aware of gender issues. How does the criminality of men and women appear to differ?

Stroheim Gerda/WoodyStock/Alamy

Table 2.3 Adult Victims of Violent Crime by Sex: Selected Incidents

	Males	Females
Total violent	52%	48%
Physical Assault (levels 1, 2, 3)	57%	43%
Sexual assault (levels 1, 2, 3)	30%	70%
Robbery	60%	40%

Source: Adapted from Samuel Perreault and Shannon Brennan, "Criminal Victimization in Canada, 2009," *Juristat,* 85-002-X, vol. 30, no. 2, 2010, p. 23.

While the rate of adult males charged with a criminal offence has been declining over the past 20 years, the rate of adult females charged has generally been increasing over the past decade. This difference in trends is even more pronounced for violent crime. Since 1991, the rate of males charged with violent crime has declined 32 percent, while the rate for females has increased 34 percent. However, males still accounted for more than 4 in 5 people accused of violent crime in 2011.[30]

Concerning victimization, there is very little difference in the overall risk of personal victimization for women and men. The General Social Survey (GSS) indicates that the rate of personal violent victimization in 2009 was 112 incidents per 1000 population for women as compared to 125 per 1000 for men. While men reported higher rates for physical assault (94 per 1000 population for men, 67 for women) and for robbery (16 for men, 10 for women), women were still much more likely to be victims of sexual assault at a rate of 34 per 1000 population as compared to 15 per 1000 for men.[31] (Table 2.3 looks at adult victims of violent crime based on sex for selected categories of crime.) The Violence Against Women Survey (VAWS) indicates that up to one-half of all Canadian women have experienced at least one incident of violence since the age of 16. Specifically, the VAWS findings indicate that 34 percent of women surveyed reported having experienced a physical assault, 39 percent reported having been sexually assaulted, and 15 percent had experienced unwanted sexual touching. Almost one-half of the women surveyed experienced violence by men known to them (boyfriends, dates, marital partners, friends, family, neighbours).[32] A more detailed examination of some of the current Canadian legislation aimed at assisting victims of crime, and female victims in particular, can be found in Chapter 4.

Ethnicity and Crime

Unlike data from the United States, Canadian crime statistics do not routinely report on the racial and ethnic makeup of offenders. The only official Canadian statistics that report on the correlation between ethnicity and crime derive from studies that consider incarcerated offender or inmate profiles. The number of inmates, while accurate, is not representative of the actual number of offenders and offences detected by police. Nevertheless, correctional statistics can be useful in shedding light on the reality of ethnicity and crime in Canada, especially with respect to the representation of Aboriginal Canadians. Figure 2.4 shows the representation of the adult offender population in federal custody (serving a custody sentence of two years or more) by race.

The reality of Aboriginal over-representation in the Canadian criminal justice system has been studied for some time. Public Safety Canada statistics indicate that in 2011, Aboriginals represented approximately 18.5 percent of the federal adult inmate population (32 percent of the female inmate population, 21 percent of the male inmate population) while representing 3 percent of the total Canadian adult population.[33]

A number of reasons have been cited for the disproportionate number of Aboriginals in the Canadian criminal justice system. Some maintain that this reality is a result of the

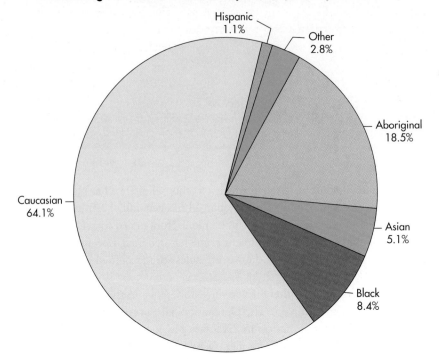

Percentage of Federal Offender Population (as of April 10, 2011)

Hispanic 1.1%

Other 2.8%

Aboriginal 18.5%

Asian 5.1%

Black 8.4%

Caucasian 64.1%

Figure 2.4 Percentage of Federal Offender Population (by Race, Canada)

Source: Corrections and Conditional Release Statistical Overview: Annual Report, page 42, Public Safety Canada, 2011. Reproduced with the permission of the Minister of Public Works and Government Services Canada, 2013.

discriminatory treatment of Aboriginals by the criminal justice system. A number of studies have concluded that "biased discretion" or selective enforcement by criminal justice officials translates into the over-represented numbers of Aboriginals in the system.[34] While there may be instances when discrimination has played a role in a police officer's decision to arrest an Aboriginal person or in the decision of a justice of the peace to deny bail to an Aboriginal offender, there is limited research evidence to support the claim of active, systemic discrimination against Aboriginals by the Canadian criminal justice system. A recent report by the federal correctional investigator criticized the federal correctional system for its "routine" discrimination of Aboriginal offenders. See the following Who's Responsible? box for one overview of the correctional investigator's report.

Other explanations look to the socio-economic realities of many Aboriginal Canadians. The role of social and economic inequality and the realities of past and current living conditions for many Aboriginals are more often cited as causes contributing to criminality among Native peoples.[35]

Research by Carol La Prairie explored the contribution that certain large Canadian cities may make to the over-representation of Aboriginal peoples in the system. She concluded that a disproportionate number of Aboriginals living in urban centres (most notably Thunder Bay, Winnipeg, Regina, and Saskatoon) experience the social realities of low income, unemployment, lack of education, unstable housing, and single-parent families. For La Prairie, what explains an Aboriginal person's likelihood of involvement in the criminal justice system is "the concentration of poor, single-parent, and poorly educated Aboriginal people in the inner core of their large cities."[36] In addition to the social realities identified by La Prairie, the role of alcohol and substance abuse in the offences committed by Aboriginals cannot be overlooked. A review of a number of Canadian studies concluded that alcohol is a major contributor to the crimes committed by Native peoples.[37] Furthermore, a significant number of Aboriginals serving provincial terms of incarceration are doing so for default of an original fine sentence. Some studies indicated that almost two-thirds of the Aboriginals in some provincial institutions are serving sentences for such defaults.[38] It is most likely that socio-economic conditions have more to do with the inability to meet fine payments than a wilful refusal to pay.

As victims of crime, 37 percent of Aboriginal Canadians report having been victimized as compared to 26 percent of non-Aboriginal Canadians. In particular, Aboriginals experience violent victimization at a rate of 223 incidents per 1000 population as compared to 84 incidents, a rate about three times as great. This difference is largely a result of the rate of physical assault, which is the most frequently occurring violent offence. The rate of violence for Aboriginal females is 2.5 times higher than that for non-Aboriginal females (279 versus 106 incidents per 1000 females), while for Aboriginal males, the pattern is different, with a rate of violent victimization that is similar (165 for Aboriginal males versus 105 incidents for non-Aboriginal males per 1000 males).[39]

WHO'S RESPONSIBLE—THE INDIVIDUAL OR SOCIETY?

Disappointing Results Continue

A 2009 report commissioned by the federal Office of the Correctional Investigator entitled *Good Intentions, Disappointing Results: A Progress Report on Federal Aboriginal Corrections* documented the fact that correctional outcomes for Aboriginal offenders continue to lag significantly behind those of non-Aboriginal offenders. The Correctional Investigator noted that Aboriginal offenders tend to be

- released later in their sentences (lower parole grant rates)
- over-represented in segregation populations
- more likely to have served previous youth and/or adult sentences
- classified as higher risk and higher need
- more likely to reoffend and have their conditional releases revoked more often

The Correctional Investigator recognized that many of the circumstances that contribute to high rates of Aboriginal incarceration such as poverty, substance abuse, discrimination, and social exclusion and isolation go well beyond the capacity of Correctional Service Canada (CSC) to address. The report did make it clear, however, that CSC has the exclusive jurisdiction and the legal mandate to ensure that Aboriginal people serving a federal sentence are given opportunity to access culturally sensitive programming and safely return to their communities.

In the 2011–2012 report of the Office of the Correctional Investigator, similar realities regarding Aboriginal inmates were noted. The Correctional Investigator stated that Aboriginal offenders

- are much more likely than others to have their parole revoked, are less likely to be granted day or full parole,

and are most often released on statutory release or held until a warrant expiry date

- are referred to proportionately more programs than their non-Aboriginal counterparts of equivalent risk and need
- return to CSC custody at a higher rate post–warrant expiry
- are twice as likely to be affiliated with a gang (male inmates)
- are disproportionately more involved in self-harm incidents

The Correctional Investigator concluded that "the gap between Aboriginal and non-Aboriginal correctional outcomes is widening over time. Based on current trends and outcomes that show no apparent sign of changing, there is every indication that the proportion of Aboriginal inmates will reach one-in-four in the near future."

Think about it:

1. Are Aboriginal offenders victimized by the Canadian correctional system? What is the correctional system's responsibility to these offenders?

2. Does the over-representation of Aboriginals in the criminal justice system indicate systemic discrimination toward Aboriginals? Defend your opinion.

3. Why do supports and programs for Aboriginal offenders "continue to lag significantly behind those of non-Aboriginal offenders"? What are some of the correctional programs that do exist for Aboriginal offenders?

Sources: Michelle Mann, *Good Intentions, Disappointing Results: A Progress Report on Federal Aboriginal Corrections* (Ottawa: Office of the Correctional Investigator, 2009); Office of the Correctional Investigator, *Annual Report, 2011–2012* (Ottawa: The Correctional Investigator Canada, 2012).

Social Class and Crime

Prior to 1960, criminologists generally assumed that a correlation existed between social class and crime. They believed that members of lower social classes were more prone to commit crime and they thought that this propensity applied to all types of criminal activity. In the early 1960s, studies of the relationship between social class and crime, which made use of offender self-reports, seemed to show that the relationship between social class and criminality was an artefact of discretionary practices within the criminal justice system.[40] Such studies of teenagers found that rates of self-reported delinquency and criminality were fairly consistent across various social classes within North American society. Similar studies of white-collar criminality seemed to show that, although the nature of criminal activity may vary between classes, members of all social classes had nearly equal tendencies toward criminality. The apparent penchant for crime among members of the lower social classes was explained partially by the fact that the types of crime traditionally committed by these groups were those most likely to come to the attention of law enforcement officials and be fully prosecuted by the criminal justice system. While there is no doubt that people from all social classes commit crimes, a number of studies have pointed to a significant correlation between lower socio-economic status and criminal activity, as we shall see below.

In 1978, a comprehensive re-evaluation of 35 earlier studies of the relationship between social class and crime concluded that previously claimed links were non-existent.[41] Publication of the report fuelled further study of the relationship between social class and crime, and in 1981 a seminal article by Australian criminologist John Braithwaite, which summarized the results of 224 previous studies on the subject, concluded convincingly that members of lower social classes were indeed more prone to commit crime.[42] In contrast to earlier studies, Braithwaite found that "socio-economic status is one of the very few correlates of criminality which can be taken, on balance, as persuasively supported by a large body of empirical evidence."

Many of the difficulties surrounding research into the relationship between social class and crime appear to stem from a lack of definitional clarity. In the many different studies evaluated by Braithwaite, for example, neither *crime* nor *class* was uniformly defined. Some researchers have similarly suggested that earlier studies may have been seriously flawed by their near-exclusive focus on young people and by their conceptualization of crime in terms of relatively minor offences (truancy, vandalism, etc.).[43] Hence, a lack of concise definitions of the subject matter, combined with inadequate measurement techniques, may have led to misleading results.

Canadian studies of street youth in Toronto and Edmonton found that many came from lower-class families and were on the street because of poor relationships at home and at school. The struggle for survival often resulted in involvement in delinquency and crime.[44] A Canadian study surveyed over 3200 grades 7 to 9 students in 177 classes in Toronto. The survey collected information on topics including family background and family bonds, attachment to school and neighbourhood, commitment to school, use of alcohol and drugs, and time devoted to paid and voluntary work. The results of the self-report survey concluded that delinquent behaviour was significantly more prevalent among students who reported consuming alcohol and drugs, those who indicated having little parental supervision, and those living in a step-family or blended family at the time of the survey.[45]

Unemployment and measures of poverty and income inequality are often cited as risk factors for criminal activity. Inasmuch as these factors can be used as indicators of social class, statistical trends indicate that unemployment rates in Canada were relatively high in the 1980s and 1990s. Similarly, overall trends in property crime were also high in the same time periods. Interestingly, rates of violent crime do not seem to follow these patterns.[46] A comparison of unemployment and crime rates is found in Figures 2.5a and 2.5b.

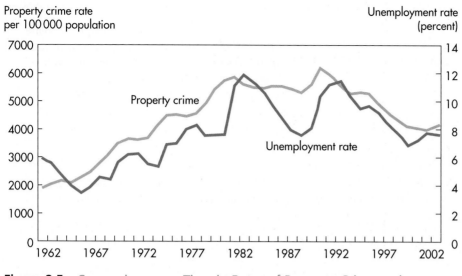

Figure 2.5a Comparison over Time in Rates of Property Crime and Unemployment, 1962 to 2003

Source: Statistics Canada, "Exploring Crime Patterns in Canada," 85-561-MIE2005005 no. 5. Released June 29, 2005. Reproduced and distributed on an "as is" basis with the permission of Statistics Canada.

Are those from the lowest socio-economic classes also most likely to be victims of crime? Victimization Survey data from the GSS indicate that those households with incomes below $20 000 had the highest violent victimization rate at 147 per 1000 population, significantly higher than the rate of those in other income categories. People with household incomes of more than $60 000 had the highest rate of theft of personal property at 143 incidents per 1000 population.[47]

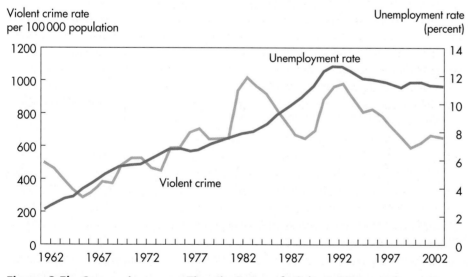

Figure 2.5b Comparison over Time in Rates of Violent Crime and Unemployment, 1962 to 2003

Source: Statistics Canada, "Exploring Crime Patterns in Canada," 85-561-MIE2005005, no. 5. Released June 29, 2005.

MySearchLab® with eText offers you access to an online interactive version of the text, extensive help with your writing and research projects, and provides round-the-clock access to credible and reliable source material.

SUMMARY OF LEARNING OBJECTIVES

 Crime statistics have been gathered in one form or another for at least 150 years. They help to paint a fairly objective picture of the reality of crime in this country.

 Often the first step toward solving a problem is understanding it, and this certainly applies to the problem of crime. Criminologists, students of criminology, and interested members of the public must understand the crime problem before any serious attempts at controlling or preventing it can be made. Crime statistics and data assist in describing the nature and extent of crime, which is necessary to develop effective crime-prevention policies and provide a picture of risk. Each approach used to collect data about crime has shortcomings that serve to skew the data.

2.3 In Canada, the Uniform Crime Reporting Survey (UCR) is administered by Statistics Canada and annually collects information on crimes reported to the police and on charges laid throughout the country. Victimization Surveys conducted by Statistics Canada as part of the General Social Survey every five years provide reports on the criminal victimization of households and individuals. Self-report studies collect data by requiring subjects to reveal their own participation in criminal activity.

2.4 Social dimensions of crime are aspects of crime and victimization as they relate to socially significant attributes by which groups are defined and according to which individuals are assigned group membership. The strongest social dimensions of crime are age, sex, ethnicity, and social class. Canadian crime statistics tell us that young men are especially over-represented in the criminal justice system, and among these men, Aboriginals account for a proportion that is vastly over-representative of their numbers in our population. Social class is a less significant indicator of criminal behaviour yet some studies do show a correlation between crime and social class as measured by employment, levels of education, etc. Whether the strong correlations between crime and age, sex, ethnicity, and social class can be explained using biological or sociological approaches is discussed in Chapters 6 to 10.

Questions for Review

1. How has the history of statistics collection had a direct impact on how we collect crime statistics today?

2. What is the usefulness of crime data? What are some of the challenges with the way crime statistics are collected?

3. What are the major differences between the UCR and Victimization Surveys? Can useful comparisons be made between these two crime indices? If so, what might such comparisons involve?

4. This chapter implies that if you are young, male, Aboriginal, and unemployed, you have a greater likelihood of being represented in Canadian criminal justice statistics. What are some of the reasons for this "reality"?

Multiple-Choice Questions

1. The revised UCR includes all the following except _____.

   a. information on the number and types of offences reported to police

   b. information on the number and sex of adults and youth charged

   c. information on victims and the accused

   d. information on circumstances of the incidents

   e. information on the genetic history of the accused

2. The term *social dimensions of crime* is used to describe aspects of crime and victimization as they relate to _____ by which groups are defined and according to which individuals are assigned group membership.

   a. common characteristics

   b. socially significant attributes

   c. socio-economic traits

   d. commonalities

   e. cultural traits

3. Based on 82 411 incidents of reported motor vehicle thefts and a total population of 34 476 848, what would the rate of crime be for motor vehicle thefts?

   a. 23.90

   b. 239.03

   c. 34.61

   d. 346.17

   e. 246.17

4. In Canada, those at the highest risk of personal victimization are between the ages of _____.

   a. 12 and 18

   b. 12 and 21

   c. 14 and 20

   d. 15 and 24

   e. 21 and 25

5. If you were to ask people to reveal their own participation in criminal behaviour using a survey, you would be participating in a _____.

   a. social dimension analysis

   b. self-report study

   c. correlation of crime analysis

   d. geographic information study

   e. self-dimension analysis

Chapter 3
Patterns of Crime

Steve Niedorf Photography/The Image Bank/Getty Images

The one thing we know with any kind of certainty is that a falling crime rate doesn't have much to do with policies related to punishment. Sending more people to prison may reduce the likelihood that they're committing offences while they're in prison but, if anything, it increases the likelihood that they'll commit offences after they've been released.

—Anthony Doob[1]

LEARNING OBJECTIVES

After reading this chapter, you should be able to

3.1 Understand how crimes are classified and identify the major categories of crime classified by the Uniform Crime Report Surveys (UCR) and the major crime rate trends in Canada.

3.2 Describe the offences classified as violent crime and apply various theories that explain why people commit acts of violence.

3.3 Describe the offences classified as property crime and apply various theories that suggest motivating factors in cases of property crime.

3.4 Describe the offences classified as crimes against the public order and apply various theories that propose explanations for public order crimes.

INTRODUCTION

It was a crime spree that was as cunning as it was insidious. After six years and ill-gotten gains of over $1 million in stolen money and property, Ken Crawford was eventually apprehended by police in Ottawa, Ontario. Known as the "Locker Room Bandit," Crawford had the look of a respectable, middle-aged businessman. During his criminal career, however, his "business" involved the theft of wallets, jewellery, and other personal possessions from health-club locker rooms across the country.

His crime spree began when Crawford, an out-of-work tool and die maker, tried to go back to school for retraining but was denied a student loan and was unable to get a part-time job to help pay for his tuition. Instead, he devised a plan that would get him the money he needed.

His scheme was simple, and it worked hundreds of times over the many years that he was actively involved in crime. He would approach a health club and ask to try out the facilities, saying that he was interested in a membership. Once inside the locker room, he would select a wealthy-looking patron and wait until he went to work out. Out of his gym bag Crawford would produce a set of bolt cutters and a combination lock. After snapping the lock off the victim's locker and emptying it of the wallet and other valuable personal items, Crawford would re-lock the locker using the combination lock he had brought. When the unsuspecting victim returned, Crawford was long gone, buying himself valuable time as the victim struggled with his lock in vain. Using the personal identification in the wallet, Crawford emptied the victims' bank accounts and took cash advances using the credit cards. Police estimated he averaged about $5000 cash for each job. When Crawford was apprehended, police found bolt cutters, 103 wallets, watches, jewellery, and thousands of dollars in cash in his home.

In return for pleading guilty to defrauding the public, possession of property obtained by crime, and possession of stolen credit cards, Crawford received a three-and-a-half-year sentence. As he handed down his sentence, Judge Paul Bélanger told Crawford, "If you have talent, it is as a talented crook. But not that talented, bearing in mind where you currently sit."[2]

CLASSIFICATIONS OF CRIME

3.1 LEARNING OBJECTIVE

A SIGNIFICANT PORTION OF THIS BOOK IS DEVOTED TO EXAMINING A VARIETY OF explanations for why people commit crime. Chapter 2 provides an overview of the ways in which crime statistics are collected so that a picture of the incidence of crime and the number and types of criminals in a given period will emerge.

But what *types* of crime are committed in Canada? How many of each type occur annually? Typically, crimes are organized into categories, or **typologies of crime**. The Uniform Crime Report Surveys (UCR) classify crimes into the following categories: violent crime, property crime, other crime, traffic offences (as defined in the *Criminal Code of Canada*), federal drug legislation offences, and other federal statute violations. Categorization helps to identify patterns that may exist within these groupings and to focus discussion concerning motivation of the offender. For example, does the person who commits murder do it for reasons distinct from those of the person who breaks into someone's home and robs it?

This chapter examines three categories of crime: violent crime, property crime, and crimes against the public order, such as counterfeiting and drug abuse. In addition to providing a snapshot of the incidence of crime committed in Canada for each of these categories, this chapter makes the link to theoretical explanations discussed in later chapters that might explain why these crimes are committed. Unless otherwise noted, all the 2011 statistics cited in this chapter are taken from 2011 UCR crime statistics, which indicate that approximately two million *Criminal Code* offences were reported in 2011, almost

Typologies of crime Classifications of crime useful in identifying patterns of criminal activity and motivations for criminal behaviour.

110 000 fewer than in 2010. Since peaking in 1991, the crime rate has generally been decreasing and in 2001 was at its lowest point since 1972.[3] Table 3.1 provides a statistical snapshot of the crime picture in Canada in 2011.

Table 3.1 Police-Reported Crime for Selected Offences, Canada, 2010 and 2011

Type of offence	2010[r]		2011		Percent change in rate 2010 to 2011	Percent change in rate 2010 to 2011
	Number	Rate	Number	Rate	Percent	
Total crime (excluding traffic)—"crime rate"	2 094 875	6 139	1 984 916	5 756	–6	–24
Violent crime						
Homicide	554	2	598	2	7	–3
Other violations causing death[1]	100	0	78	0	–23	–49
Attempted murder	668	2	655	2	–3	–19
Sexual assault level 3—aggravated	179	1	140	0	–23	–22
Sexual assault level 2—weapon or bodily harm	402	1	398	1	–2	12
Sexual assault level 1	21 795	64	21 283	62	–3	–19
Sexual violations against children[2,3]	3 684	11	3 822	11	3	...
Assault level 3—aggravated	3 481	10	3 486	10	–1	15
Assault level 2—weapon or bodily harm	51 955	152	50 184	146	–4	5
Assault level 1	175 289	514	172 770	501	–2	–19
Assault police officer[4]	15 913	47	11 943	35	–26	31
Other assaults	3 281	10	3,097	9	–7	–34
Firearms—use of, discharge, pointing	2 017	6	1 936	6	–5	–20
Robbery	30 478	89	29 746	86	–3	–13
Forcible confinement or kidnapping	4 301	13	3 774	11	–13	35
Abduction	449	1	402	1	–11	–46
Extortion	1 578	5	1 525	4	–4	–17
Criminal harassment	21 315	62	21 690	63	1	1
Uttering threats	76 347	224	71 945	209	–7	–28
Threatening or harassing phone calls	21 604	63	20 341	59	–7	–42
Other violent *Criminal Code* violations	3 830	11	4 597	13	19	9
Total	**439 220**	**1 287**	**424 410**	**1,231**	**–4**	**–16**
Property crime						
Breaking and entering	197 058	577	181 217	526	–9	–42
Possess stolen property[5,6]	30 275	89	21 496	62	–30	–28
Theft of motor vehicle	92 505	271	82 411	239	–12	–56
Theft over $5000 (non-motor vehicle)	15 649	46	15 153	44	–4	–35

Theft under $5000 (non-motor vehicle)	527 509	1 546	497 452	1 443	–7	–32
Fraud[7]	89 830	263	89 801	260	–1	–7
Mischief[8]	340 090	997	315 977	916	–8	–15
Arson	12 234	36	10 378	30	–16	–35
Total	**1 305 150**	**3 824**	**1 213 885**	**3 520**	**–8**	**–31**
Other *Criminal Code* offences						
Counterfeiting	815	2	620	2	–25	–68
Weapons violations	15 038	44	14 471	42	–5	0
Child pornography[9]	2 218	6	3 132	9	40	209
Prostitution	3 020	9	2 459	7	–19	–57
Disturb the peace	119 913	351	117 476	341	–3	17
Administration of justice violations	178 135	522	177 159	514	–2	2
Other violations	31 366	92	31 304	91	–1	–29
Total	**350 505**	**1 027**	**346 621**	**1 005**	**–2**	**2**
***Criminal Code* traffic violations**						
Impaired driving[10]	87 231	256	90 277	262	2	–2
Other *Criminal Code* traffic violations	55 615	163	55 938	162	0	29
Total	**142 846**	**419**	**146 215**	**424**	**1**	**8**
Drug offences						
Possession—cannabis	56 853	167	61 406	178	7	16
Possession—cocaine	7 325	21	7 392	21	0	23
Possession—other drugs[11]	9 761	29	10 352	30	5	97
Trafficking, production, or distribution—cannabis	18 363	54	16 548	48	–11	–26
Trafficking, production, or distribution—cocaine	9 873	29	10 251	30	3	37
Trafficking, production, or distribution—other drugs	7 047	21	7 215	21	1	41
Total	**109 222**	**320**	**113 164**	**328**	**3**	**14**
Other federal statute violations						
Youth Criminal Justice Act	11 957	35	11 619	34	–4	–44
Other federal statutes	20 767	61	21 344	62	2	0
Total	**32 724**	**96**	**32 963**	**96**	**0**	**–22**
Total—all violations	**2 379 667**	**6 973**	**2 277 258**	**6 604**	**–5**	**–21**

[r] revised

1. Includes, for example, criminal negligence causing death.

2. Sexual offences against children is a relatively new crime category with only partial data available prior to 2010; therefore, the percent change from 2001 to 2011 is not shown.

3. Includes sexual interference, invitation to sexual touching, sexual exploitation, and luring a child via a computer. Excludes incidents of child pornography due to limited information on victim characteristics.

(Continued)

4. In 2010, a system anomaly resulted in some non–peace officer assaults being coded as peace officer assaults in 2010. Comparisons between 2010 and other years should be made with caution.

5. Includes trafficking and the intent to traffic stolen goods.

6. In 2011, the UCR survey was modified to create separate categories for possession of stolen property less than or equal to $5000 and for possession of stolen property over $5000. As a result, incidents of possession under $5000 may now be reported as secondary offences when occurring in conjunction with more serious offences, leading to a decrease in the number of possession of stolen property incidents reported in 2011.

7. Includes identity theft and identity fraud.

8. Includes altering, removing, or destroying a vehicle identification number (VIN).

9. In 2002, legislative changes were made to include the use of the internet for the purpose of committing child pornography offences. As such, the percent change in this offence is calculated from 2003 to 2011 in the last column.

10. Includes alcohol and/or drug impaired operation of a vehicle, alcohol and/or drug impaired operation of a vehicle causing death or bodily harm, failure or refusal to comply with testing for the presence of alcohol or drugs, and failure or refusal to provide a breath or blood sample.

11. Includes precursors and equipment.

Note: Counts are based upon the most serious violation in the incident. One incident may involve multiple violations. Data for specific types of crime are available (in most cases) beginning in 1977. Rates are calculated on the basis of 100 000 population. Percent change based on unrounded rates. Populations based upon July 1st estimates from Statistics Canada, Demography Division.

Source: Shannon Brennan, "Police-reported crime statistics in Canada, 2011", *Juristat*, Statistics Canada, July 24, 2012. Reproduced and distributed on an "as is" basis with the permission of Statistics Canada.

VIOLENT CRIME

Violent crime incidents include homicide, attempted murder, assault, sexual assault, robbery, use of firearms, kidnapping and abduction, criminal harassment, and uttering threats. At a rate of 1231 incidents per 100 000 population in 2011, the violent crime rate fell 4 percent between 2010 and 2011, marking the fifth consecutive drop in the severity of violent crime. Similar to previous years, violent crimes accounted for about one-fifth of offences reported to police, and within the categories of offences classified as violent crime, common assault accounted for 77 percent of the total number. Across the regions of the country, violent crime rates decreased or remained stable in all provinces and territories from the previous year, with the most notable declines in Nova Scotia, Saskatchewan, and British Columbia (–7 percent) and Manitoba (–5 percent). Nunavut, Northwest Territories, and Yukon posted the highest violent crime rates in the country (9987, 8499, and 4226 per 100 000 respectively), while the province reporting the highest violent crime rate was Saskatchewan, at 2366 per 100 000. Ontario recorded the lowest rate of violent crime at 950, with Quebec having the second lowest rate at 1045 per 100 000.

Homicide

In 2003, Rene Michaud was found guilty of first-degree murder in the deaths of two Ottawa school teachers, Bob and Bonnie Dagenais. In a case that made national news, Michaud, with a 16-year-old accomplice, broke into the Dagenais' cottage in the middle of the night and then shot the couple with a shotgun when they confronted him. The Dagenais had recently retired after successful careers as teachers in the Ottawa School Board. Bob Dagenais was well known and so popular that when he was transferred from one high school to another, the students walked out to protest the move. Rene Michaud was convicted of first-degree murder and received a life sentence with no chance of parole for 25 years.[4]

The terms *homicide* and *murder* are often used interchangeably, but they are not synonymous. **Homicide** occurs when a person, directly or indirectly, by any means, causes the death of a human being. Homicide, therefore, can be either culpable or non-culpable. *Culpable homicide* is considered an offence under the *Criminal Code of Canada* and includes murder, manslaughter, and infanticide. *Non-culpable homicide* consists of justifiable and/or excusable homicide. Justifiable homicide includes legally authorized acts such as a police officer killing someone in the course of duty, while excusable homicide includes acts of self-defence, defence of others, or defence of property.

Murder (s. 229 of the *Criminal Code of Canada*) occurs when a person intentionally causes the death of another human being or intends to cause bodily harm likely to result in death. Murder is further classified into first-degree murder and second-degree murder. **First-degree murder** (defined in s. 231) describes culpable homicide that is planned and deliberate; or involves the killing of a peace officer such as a police officer or correctional worker; or occurs during the commission of another serious offence such as sexual assault, kidnapping, or hijacking. **Second-degree murder** (defined in s. 231) includes all murder that is not first degree. In other words, it is intentional and unlawful but not planned. **Manslaughter** (s. 234) is considered to be a non-intentional homicide committed in response to sudden provocation, as a result of impaired judgment due to alcohol or drug consumption, or as a result of recklessness or carelessness. **Infanticide** (s. 233) occurs when a female causes the death of her newborn child (under age 1) if her mind is considered disturbed from the effects of giving birth.

Serial murder and mass murder are two varieties of what is usually termed first-degree murder. Although most murderers kill only once in their lives, serial and mass murderers kill more than one person. **Serial murder** has been defined as culpable homicide that "involves the killing of several victims in three or more separate events."[5] These separate events are sometimes spread out over years. Infamous Canadian serial killers include Clifford Olson, who killed at least 11 young people aged 9 to 18 over a nine-month period in 1980–1981 in British Columbia. Between 1987 and 1990, Paul Bernardo committed at least 18 violent sexual assaults in Toronto and later went on to abduct, sexually assault, and strangle two teenaged girls in 1991 and 1992 in St. Catharines, Ontario. He was assisted in these murders by his wife, Karla Homolka, who subsequently testified against her husband. Allan Legère killed a grocery store owner in 1987 and went on to kill four other people in Miramichi, New Brunswick, terrorizing the rural community between 1987 and 1989 and earning for himself the nickname "The Monster of the Miramichi." Robert Pickton was found guilty on six counts of second-degree murder for the deaths of sex-trade workers who went missing between 1995 and 2002. Other notorious American serial killers include Jeffrey Dahmer, who killed and dismembered 15 young men in the 1980s; David Berkowitz, better known as "Son of Sam," who killed young men and women in New York City in the 1970s; Charles Manson, who ordered his followers to kill seven people in California; Ted Bundy, who killed many college-aged women; and the female serial killer Aileen Carol Wuornos, who killed six men who had picked her up as she hitchhiked through Florida.[6] Internationally infamous killers include Dr. Harold Shipman of Britain, who was convicted of killing 15 female patients and suspected in the deaths of 23 more, and Javed Iqbal, convicted of sexually assaulting and killing 100 street children in Pakistan and sentenced to die in the same way his victims died—by strangulation.

Similar to the serial killer is the spree killer, who kills a number of victims over a relatively short period. Andrew Cunanan, who killed fashion designer Gianni Versace and others in 1997, is an example. Cunanan's killing spree lasted three months and claimed five victims.

Homicide   When a person, directly or indirectly, by any means, causes the death of a human being. Homicide can be culpable or non-culpable.

Murder   When a person intentionally causes the death of another human being or intends to cause bodily harm likely to result in death.

First-degree murder   Culpable homicide that is planned and deliberate.

Second-degree murder   All murder that is not first-degree murder.

Manslaughter   All non-intentional homicide.

Infanticide   When a female considered disturbed from the effects of giving birth causes the death of her newborn child (under age 1).

Serial murder   Culpable homicide that involves the killing of several victims in three or more separate events.

Mass murder is different from serial murder in that it entails "the killing of four or more victims at one location, within one event."[7] On December 6, 1989, in what has become known as the "Montreal Massacre," Marc Lepine shot and killed 14 female students at Montreal's École Polytechnique. Other mass murderers in Canada include Victor Hoffman, who, at age 19, killed nine members of a family as they slept in their Saskatchewan farmhouse in 1967; Mark Chahal, a Vancouver accountant who shot dead his ex-wife and eight other members of her family at a home in Vernon, British Columbia, in 1996; Kevin Vermette, who shot three young men at a deserted campground in Kitimat, British Columbia, in 1997; and James Roszko, who ambushed and then killed four RCMP officers on his Alberta farm in 2005. Other infamous mass murders include the 31 people killed in 1991 when a man smashed his pickup truck through a cafeteria window in Texas and shot lunch-goers to death; 16 school-aged children and their teacher killed in Dunblane, Scotland, in 1996; 12 high school students and a teacher killed by two fellow students who marched through the halls of Columbine High School in Colorado targeting specific individuals in 1999; and 77 people, many of them youth, gunned down at a summer camp in Norway in 2011.

In 2011, homicides (598) and attempted murders (655) accounted for less than half of 1 percent of all violent crimes committed in Canada. While the rate of homicide increased by 7 percent from the previous year, the homicide rate has generally been decreasing since peaking in the mid-1970s. Rates of attempted murder also decreased in 2011, down 3 percent from the previous year.

Geographically, during the same time period, homicide rates increased from east to west in Canada.[8] The lowest rates were reported in Yukon, where no homicides were recorded, followed by Prince Edward Island (0.7 homicides per 100 000), Newfoundland and Labrador (0.8), New Brunswick (1.1), Ontario (1.2), and Quebec (1.3). The highest homicide rates per 100 000 were found in Nunavut (21) and Northwest Territories (6.9), followed by Manitoba (4.2). In absolute numbers, Ontario and Alberta led the country in 2011, with 161 and 109 homicides respectively, although Ontario's rate, at 1.2 per 100 000, is at the national average of 1.7. With 86 homicides in 2011 (1.5 per 100 000), Toronto reported the most homicides of any metropolitan area, a decrease by 6 percent from the previous year. However, when population differences were taken into account, rates were higher in Winnipeg (5.2), Halifax (4.4), Edmonton (4.2), Thunder Bay (3.3), Regina (3.2),

Paul Bernardo (left) and Karla Homolka (right) together abducted, sexually assaulted, and murdered two Ontario teenagers.

Left: Paul Irish/GetStock.com; Right: Peter Power/GetStock.com and Saint John (2.9). Police reports indicate 46 youth (aged 12 to 17) were charged with homicide in 2011, a decrease of 13 percent from the previous year. Despite this decrease, the youth homicide rate was the second highest since 1961. In 2010, 94 homicides were considered by police to be gang related, accounting for 17 percent of all homicides reported to police and representing a 25 percent decline from the previous year.

Among solved homicides in 2010, most victims (83 percent) knew their killer. Acquaintances made up the majority of accused persons (40 percent), followed by family members (34 percent), strangers (17 percent), and criminal relationships (9 percent). In recent years, the number of intimate partner homicides has been relatively stable. (*Intimate partners* are defined as married, common-law, or dating partners.) In 2010, there were 89 victims of homicide by an intimate partner, one above the number recorded in 2009. Women continue to be about four times more likely to be victims of intimate partner homicide than men.

Since the 1980s, the most common method used to commit homicide has fluctuated between shootings and stabbings. In 2010, 32 percent of homicides involved firearms; handguns accounted for the majority of these (64 percent), followed by rifles or shotguns (23 percent), and other firearms such as sawed-off shotguns, automatic firearms, or other firearm-like weapons (13 percent). By comparison, U.S. statistics indicate that almost 68 percent of all homicides involved the use of a firearm.[9] Thirty-one percent of the homicides were committed by stabbing, with beatings accounting for 22 percent. The remaining incidents were committed by strangulation or suffocation (8 percent) or other methods (8 percent) such as by motor vehicle, fire, poisoning, and shaken baby syndrome. Although there have been some annual fluctuations, shootings decreased from 2009 to 2010 (–7 percent), consistent with a general decline in firearm-related homicides seen over the past three decades.

Statistics Canada also collects information related to the occupation of homicide victims. Omitting illegal occupations (such as drug dealing and prostitution), there were 130 homicides from 2000 to 2010 that police believed were directly related to the victim's job. Twenty-seven of these homicides involved transportation-related occupations, such as taxi drivers, truck drivers, and bus drivers. Another one in five work-related homicides (26) involved security occupations (including police and correctional officers as well as other security personnel). Retail employees (including service station and convenience store clerks) accounted for 22 of all work-related homicides, followed by restaurant, bar, and hotel workers (19) and janitors or superintendents (6). Since 2000, police recorded that 78 prostitutes were killed as a direct result of their occupation, including 5 in 2010.

Sexual Assault

The *Criminal Code of Canada* distinguishes between three levels of sexual assault, according to the seriousness of the incident. These levels reflect amendments made to the *Criminal Code* in 1983. Prior to that year, section 143 of the *Criminal Code* defined rape to have occurred when "a male person has sexual intercourse with a female person who is not his wife (a) without her consent, or (b) with her consent if the consent (i) is extorted by threats or fear of bodily harm, (ii) is obtained by impersonating her husband, or (iii) is obtained by false or fraudulent representations as to the nature and quality of the act." Under this definition, the act was largely defined as one of sexual penetration, and the offender was presumed to be a male and the victim female. As well, under the legislation husbands could not be charged with raping their wives.

Currently, sexual assault legislation focuses on the violent nature of the act, rather than its sexual nature. **Sexual assault** is considered to be an assault committed in circumstances of a sexual nature such that the sexual integrity of the victim is violated. The

Sexual assault An assault committed in circumstances of a sexual nature such that the sexual integrity of the victim is violated. The degree of violence used determines whether the sexual assault is level 1, level 2, or level 3.

current laws allow for the accused (including legally married spouses) to be charged with sexual assault regardless of whether or not penetration occurred. As well, the offence has been "degenderized" such that perpetrators can be either male or female, as can victims. Critics charge, however, that it is overwhelmingly men who sexually assault women and that it has now been left to the discretion of the courts to determine what constitutes sexual assault, as opposed to common assault.[10] *Level 1 sexual assault* (s. 271) is the classification of least physical injury to the victim and can include unwanted sexual touching; *level 2 sexual assault* (s. 272) involves the use of a weapon or threats to use a weapon, or results in bodily harm; *level 3 sexual assault* (s. 273) is aggravated sexual assault, resulting in wounding, maiming, or disfiguring the victim, or endangering his or her life.[11]

Statistics on sexual assault collected by the UCR are delineated according to the three levels of sexual assault. In 2011, 21 821 sexual assaults were reported nationwide—97.5 percent of those were classified as level 1. In 2011, the rates for all three levels of sexual assault declined, down 3 percent from the previous year. The overall rate of sexual assault at 62 per 100 000 population was over 25 percent lower than a decade earlier but still close to one and a half times the rate in 1983 when the new definition of the offence was introduced (41 per 100 000). (Refer to Chapter 2 for a discussion of the impact of crime definitions on crime rates.) It is interesting to note that the sexual assault rate for females is effectively twice that indicated by the official figures, since any realistic tally of such crimes should compare the number of female victims assaulted with the number of females in the overall population (rather than to a count of the entire population, which includes males).

Data from the most recent UCR indicate that over 70 percent of victims of sexual assault were female, compared to 48 percent of victims of all other violent crimes.[12] Most had been victimized by a friend or acquaintance, and the remainder by a family member or stranger. Forty-five percent of all sexual assault victims reported to the police were between the ages of 15 and 24.

It is important to note that the number of sexual assaults reported to police is an undercount of the actual number of sexual assaults that occur. Self-report data from the General Social Survey have consistently shown that most sexual assaults are not brought to the attention of the police.[13] The reasons for victims' hesitancy vary: some feel they are responsible for some aspect of their social relationship that led to the sexual assault, some are ashamed or embarrassed, some believe that the incident wasn't important enough, and some feel that it's a private matter. Social media such as Facebook and Twitter are increasingly being used by sexual assault victims to "go public" about their abuse, in the hopes of raising awareness and encouraging other victims to come forward (see Box 3.1).

The ability to capture the extent of sexual violence against women remains hampered by socio-cultural factors that contribute to under-reporting. **Rape myths** are false assumptions about sexual assault that continue to characterize much of the discourse surrounding sexual violence: that women bring false sexual assault charges to get even with men, that women bring rape upon themselves by wearing provocative clothing, that women are "asking for it" by going to bars alone, and that women say no when they really mean yes. In 1980, Martha R. Burt first began researching rape myth ideology;[14] since then, numerous other studies have supported widespread acceptance of these myths.[15] Rape myths serve to undermine the traumatic nature of this offence and to discount the experiences of women by placing stereotypical parameters around who can and who cannot be sexually assaulted. Rape myths inhibit the reporting of sexual assault and normalize sexual assault as a crime of violence.[16] Largely as a result of such myths, women continue to report that the criminal justice system does not respond with sensitivity and compassion toward their victimization.

The sexual assault laws are applicable to all victims regardless of the age of the victim. The UCR also collects information on sexual violations specific to children, a category

Rape myth A false assumption about sexual assault, such as "When a woman says no, she really means yes."

Box 3.1 WHY SEX ASSAULT VICTIMS ARE GOING PUBLIC

Toronto actress Alice Moran wore a knee-length, polka dot dress the night she was sexually assaulted, one victim in a string of attacks in the city's Annex neighbourhood this summer.

"The last time I wore that dress," wrote Ms. Moran of her outfit the night she was assaulted, "it was to Easter dinner at my Gran's."

For years, victims of sexual assault have unburdened themselves on Facebook: groups such as "Sexual Assault Survivors" have helped women bond. But now, women like

Some victims of sexual assault go public in order to gain control over their stories and in some cases to "out" and shame their perpetrators.

Rick Madonik/ZUMA Press/Newscom

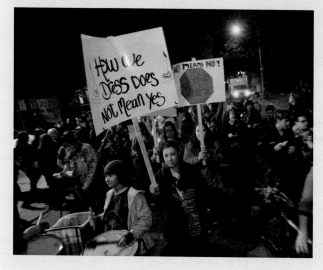

Ms. Moran are going even more broadly public, online, to gain control over their own narratives. In some cases, they're using social media to out and shame the perpetrators.

Catharsis is common for sexual assault victims who've "come out" online. But there are risks, legal and emotional, say those who work with survivors. "The absolute lack of security is foolhardy, and it presupposes a shift in culture around these issues that we haven't seen yet," says Amanda Dale, executive director of the Barbra Schlifer Commemorative Clinic, which serves women experiencing violence in Toronto.

"We don't want to reinforce the message of shame and keep these things so private that we never shift the conversation," said Ms. Dale. "That's why young women like [Alice Moran] are taking the step to go bold and go public, because they feel like they're warriors on the edge of a social taboo. But there are consequences for that."

"It is a spotlight that burns you very, very badly," said Jane Doe, the Toronto woman who successfully sued police for negligence after her 1986 rape by a known offender— the "Balcony Rapist," Paul Callow.

Jane Doe—who chose to maintain her anonymity under legislation that protects the privacy of those who experience sexual assault—questions why so much of the responsibility continues falling to women, including identifying themselves online to help catch rapists and prevent future crimes.

Source: Zosia Bielski, "Why Sex Victims Are Going Public," *Globe and Mail*, September 6, 2012. http://www.theglobeandmail.com/life/why-sex-assault-victims-are-going-public/article4524879/ [Accessed December 1, 2012].

that includes sexual interference, invitation to sexual touching, sexual interference and exploitation, and luring a child via a computer.

Police reported over 3800 incidents of sexual violations against children in 2011. The rate of sexual violations against children rose 3 percent between 2010 and 2011, making it one of the few categories of violent offences to increase in 2011. The UCR also captures data on incidents of child pornography, which encompasses publishing, distributing, and accessing material. Police reported more than 3100 incidents of child pornography in 2011, 900 more than in 2010. The rate of child pornography incidents increased 40 percent, the largest increase of any *Criminal Code* offence in 2011. (Fluctuations in the rate of child pornography are most likely reflective of police-based programs and initiatives targeting this particular offence.)[17]

Related to the offence of sexual assault is the offence of criminal harassment, often referred to as *stalking*. Legislation regarding this offence was first enacted in Canada in 1993 as a response to violence against women. The goal of the legislation is to identify and respond to criminal harassment before it escalates into serious physical harm to victims and to prohibit deliberate conduct that is psychologically harmful to others in causing them to fear for their safety. **Criminal harassment** (s. 264) is generally defined as "repeated following, watching or communicating with a person or someone known to them in a way that causes them to fear for their safety or for the safety of someone known to them" and applies equally to all victims.[18]

Criminal harassment Also known as stalking, the repeated following, watching, or communicating with a person or someone known to the person in a way that causes that person to fear for his/her safety or for the safety of someone known to him/her.

The increased use of the internet by Canadians has also led to an increase in the incidence of *cyberstalking*, or online harassment. Closely related to real-life stalking, individuals use chat rooms, message boards, and emails to threaten or post obscene messages about the victim. It is possible for cyberstalking to extend to real life as the stalker may use the internet or obtain information about the target and then use it in a conventional stalking incident. While online stalkers can be charged under the criminal harassment provision of the *Criminal Code*, the nature of the activity makes it difficult to identify stalkers. There are rarely any witnesses, and jurisdictional problems arise if the stalker is located in a city or country different from that of the victim. The limited evidence that does exist about cyberstalking indicates that the majority of the victims are women.[19] See Chapter 12 for a more in-depth look at cyber-crimes.

Statistics from the UCR on criminal harassment show 21 690 reported incidents, representing almost 17 percent of all violent crimes reported to the police or a rate of 63 per 100 000 population. Females accounted for 76 percent of all victims of criminal harassment, compared to about half (51 percent) of victims of overall violent crime.[20]

In most cases, the offender is known to the victim; 45 percent of all female victims are stalked by a former partner, 22 percent by a casual acquaintance, and 6 percent by a current partner. Other offenders include strangers (12 percent), business relations (5 percent), and other family members (5 percent). Male victims of criminal harassment are most commonly stalked by casual acquaintances (37 percent), ex-partners (22 percent), business acquaintances (12 percent), strangers (11 percent), other family members (5 percent), and current partners (2 percent).[21]

Robbery

Robbery The unlawful taking or attempted taking of property that is in the immediate possession of another by threatened or actual use of force or violence.

The crime of **robbery** (s. 343) is regarded as a violent personal crime because it is committed in the presence of a victim and involves threatened or actual use of force or violence in the commission of a theft or attempted theft from another person. Although some individuals mistakenly use the terms *robbery* and *break and enter* interchangeably (as in the phrase "my house was robbed"), it should be remembered that robbery is a personal crime and that individuals, not houses, are robbed.

The 2011 UCR reported that 29 746 robberies came to the attention of the authorities across the nation that year, meaning that the robbery rate was 86 for every 100 000 people in Canada. This was a decrease of 3 percent from the previous year and almost 20 percent lower than a decade ago.

The involvement of weapons, such as firearms or knives, to commit robbery has gradually declined while the use of physical force or threats (but no weapon) was higher than a decade earlier. Statistics for robbery in 2008 indicate that robberies without a weapon accounted for more than half (57 percent) of all incidents.

Most robberies occurred in an outdoor public location such as the street or a parking lot (50 percent). Forty percent occurred in a commercial location such as a convenience store, bank and financial institution, gas station, or school, while residential settings accounted for 10 percent.[22]

Assault

Assault (defined in s. 265) involves the intentional or threatened application of force on another person without consent. The *Criminal Code of Canada* includes several categories of assault: *level 1 assault* (s. 266), or common assault, which is the least serious type of assault and includes behaviours such as punching, pushing, slapping, shoving, or threats by act or gesture; *level 2 assault* (s. 267), which involves the use of a weapon or results in bodily harm; *level 3 assault* (s. 268), which includes assaults that wound, maim, disfigure, or endanger the life of the victim; and *other assaults*, which involve use of force against a peace officer, unlawfully causing bodily harm, and discharge of a firearm with intent.

Of the 241 480 incidents of recorded assaults in 2011, common assault (level 1) accounted for 72 percent of all assaults and 40 percent of all reported violent incidents. Overall, the rate of common assault for 2011 (501 per 100 000 population) decreased by 2 percent from the previous year. The majority of assaults continue to be perpetrated by adult males, yet, among youth aged 12 to 17, about a third of assaults are committed by females. Unlike sexual assaults, victims of assault are as likely to be male as female.

Assault The intentional or threatened application of force on another person without consent. The categories of assault include level 1—assault or common assault; level 2—assault that involves the use of a weapon or that causes bodily harm; and level 3—assault that results in wounding or endangering the life of the victim.

👁 **Watch**

The KKK

Hate crime A criminal act directed toward a person or group because of race, national or ethnic origin, religion, language, colour, sex, age, sexual orientation, or mental or physical disability. Also referred to as *hate-motivated crime*, or *bias crime*.

Hate Crime

The definition of **hate crime** has evolved out of the sections of the *Criminal Code* that address hate propaganda and the *Purpose and Principles of Sentencing*. Sections 318 and 319 of the *Criminal Code* refer to "advocating genocide, public incitement of hatred, or the wilful promotion of hatred against an identifiable group, including those distinguished by colour, race, religion, ethnic origin, or sexual orientation." Section 718.2 of the *Criminal Code*, which addresses sentencing principles, allows the courts to take into consideration whether an offence was "motivated by bias, prejudice, or hate based on race, national or ethnic origin, language, colour, religion, sex, age, mental or physical disability, sexual orientation, or any other similar factor."[23] In other words, courts now consider hate motivation as an aggravating circumstance.

There are two sources of data that can be used to measure incidents of hate crime in Canada. One is the Uniform Crime Reporting Survey and the other is the Victimization Survey (as part of the General Social Survey). Results from the most recent implementation of both these surveys showed the proportion of all crime purported to be motivated by hate to be relatively low, although the number of hate crimes reported by GSS respondents was significantly higher than that reported by police services. Findings from the last GSS conducted in 2004 indicated that only about 40 percent of hate crimes had been reported to police. Seventy-seven percent of hate crimes recorded in the GSS involved offences against the person (49 percent were assaults) compared to 58 percent of non–hate-related incidents, supporting research that shows that hate-motivated crimes are more likely to involve offences against the person and are more likely to involve excessive violence. While the most recent

Victimization Survey showed little difference in the overall rates of hate victimization by sex, results did show that younger individuals, aged 15 to 25, were twice as likely to report having experienced a hate crime, compared to those aged 25 to 34 (22 per 1000 versus 11 per 1000 population). Among visible minorities, the reported rate of hate crime was almost three times greater (19 per 1000) than for non–visible minorities (7 per 1000 population).[24]

In 2007, police services reported 765 incidents that had been motivated by hate, representing a rate of 3.1 per 100 000 population, 13 percent lower than the previous year. The most common type of hate crime was mischief, including acts of graffiti or vandalism of public property. Minor assaults (14 percent) and uttering threats (8 percent) were the most common types of violent hate crime offences. There was one homicide motivated by hate in 2007, and since 1991 there have been a total of 23 hate-motivated homicides.

There are three primary motivations for hate crimes: race or ethnicity, religion, and sexual orientation. In 2007, among incidents where the motivation was known to police, the most common was race or ethnicity, accounting for 60 percent of the incidents in that year. Religious motivations accounted for another 24 percent of hate crimes, and sexual orientation for 10 percent. The remaining 2 percent were motivated by factors such as the victim's mental or physical disability, sex, language, occupation, and political beliefs. See Box 3.2 for a summary of the police-reported hate crime in 2008.

Box 3.2 POLICE-REPORTED HATE CRIME IN CANADA, 2008: HIGHLIGHTS

Canadian police services reported 1036 hate-motivated crimes, up from 765 in 2007. This represented an increase of 35%. Changes in the number of police-reported hate crimes can vary considerably from year to year due to increased awareness by the public as well as improved policing practices. Over the past three years, the vast majority of hate crimes have stemmed from one of three motivations: race/ethnicity, religion, or sexual orientation, each of which increased in 2008 (see Figure 3.1). Non-violent offences, usually mischief, were the most common type of offences in 2008. About 6 in 10 persons accused of hate crime were between 12 and 22 years of age, the majority of whom were male.

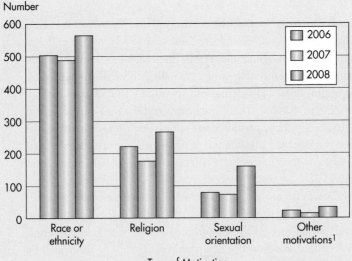

Figure 3.1 Hate Crimes Reported by Police, by Type of Motivation, 2006, 2007, and 2008

Incidents against blacks represented the largest category of racially motivated hate crimes (37%). The majority (64%) of religion-motivated hate crimes in 2008 involved crimes against the Jewish faith.

Source: Adapted from Mia Dauvergne, "Police-Reported Hate Crime in Canada, 2008," *Juristat*, vol. 30, no. 2 (Ottawa: Ministry of Industry, March 2010). http://www.statcan.gc.ca/pub/85-002-x/2010002/article/11233-eng.htm [Accessed December 1, 2012].

Theoretical Explanations of Violent Crime

Why do people commit acts of violence? What compels a man to sexually assault a woman or a youth to pick up a knife and force a convenience store clerk to hand over the money in the till? While there are no easy answers to these questions, there are certainly a number of theoretical explanations commonly accepted within the field of criminology that might provide answers.

Cases of mass or serial murder, such as the 14 women killed by Marc Lepine in Montreal on December 6, 1989, or the 6 women Robert Picton was convicted of confining, assaulting, and murdering between 2005 and 2007, often tempt us to examine the individual offender for clues. Surely people who kill others must have "something wrong with them" that compels them to commit these heinous acts. Chapters 6 and 7 examine a number of biological and psychological explanations of crime that can be applied to violent offenders. The biological theories found in Chapter 6 question whether certain individuals are predisposed to violence. Is the male sex drive, which has been developed through evolution to perpetuate the species, an explanation for man's sexual aggression toward women? Can naturally occurring levels of the male hormone testosterone be seen as a reason why males commit close to 90 percent of all violent crime in Canada? Chapter 7 outlines a number of psychological or neurological dysfunctions such as abnormal electroencephalograms, low intelligence, attention deficit disorder (ADD), or attention deficit hyperactivity disorder (ADHD), as well as psychotic symptoms such as hallucinations, paranoia, and distorted views of reality that may account for criminal behaviour. Various personality disorders, including anti-social personality disorder—psychopathy in particular—are considered as possible causes for deviant sexual behaviour. Psychological theories emphasizing personality types look to Freudian analysis and contend that it is the *id*, or that aspect of personality from which drives, wishes, urges, and desires emanate, that causes the behaviour of rapists, for example. The hostile and sadistic feelings toward women many rapists tend to display are often considered to be rooted in psychotic or personality disorders.

An inability to deal with frustration is considered by some to contribute to aggressive behaviour. Chapter 7 refers to the case of Pierre Lebrun, who killed four fellow employees after years of taunting because of a speech impediment; this apparently

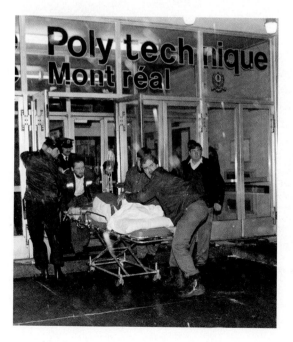

Mass murderer Marc Lepine killed 14 female students at L'École Polytechnique in Montreal. Which theories do you think work best to explain such violent criminal behaviour: those from the social responsibility perspective or those from the social problems perspective?

Shaney Komulainen/Canadian Press Images

caused him to "snap." Donald Lauzon, 19, who killed his 2-year-old daughter Samantha by repeatedly banging her head against the arm of a sofa, was at a loss to explain the anger that welled inside him and surfaced whenever he became frustrated. "The kid would do something and I would hit her," he is quoted as saying. "I wouldn't mean to actually use full force, but that's what would happen. I hit her. Kid would go flying. When it happened I'd freak out, I'd go 'Oh God. What did I do? I'm never going to do this again.'"[25]

Social learning theories assume that people learn how to behave by modelling themselves after others whom they have the opportunity to observe. Does a young boy's exposure to violence in the home account for his future violent behaviour? Violence on television and in the movies has been cited as the cause of violence in some instances, most notably in the tragic case of James Bulger, aged 2, of Liverpool, England, who was abducted from a shopping mall, beaten to death, and dumped on a railway track by two 10-year-old boys, who claimed they got the idea after watching the same violent video several times the previous day. The individual responsibility perspective contends that it is the psychological makeup of each person that determines the way in which observed behaviour is absorbed, processed, and acted upon. Some individuals may be exposed to violence in the home and never become violent themselves, while others are compelled to model their behaviour on the actions, and even deviant actions, of others.

The same issues can be examined in the debate over whether or not those children who are physically or sexually abused in the home later go on to inflict harm on others. The link between family violence and future criminality is not a direct one, and there appear to be numerous other factors that need to be taken into consideration. Some criminologists argue that, while being abused as a child may increase the risk of future violence or criminality, many people who are victims of childhood violence do not become violent adult offenders.[26]

In contrast to the individual responsibility perspective are those theories that fall under the social problems perspective. Discussed in Chapters 8, 9, and 10, these theories

Professional hockey player Steve Moore is wheeled to an ambulance after being hit from behind during a 2004 game by Vancouver Canucks hockey star Todd Bertuzzi. Moore suffered broken neck vertebrae, a concussion, and nerve damage in the incident, ending his hockey career. Bertuzzi was suspended by the National Hockey League and prevented from finishing the season. In a controversial decision, he was also charged with assault causing bodily harm and subsequently pled guilty to assault. Do you think Bertuzzi should have been criminally charged for his actions?

Chuck Stoody/Canadian Press Images

look to socialization and cultural factors as explanations for acts of violence. Are males raised to behave more aggressively? Are our cultural values responsible for sending a message to young males that the way to deal with stress and frustration is through the use of aggression? Well-known accounts of drivers who assault others as a result of what is known as *road rage* suggest that perhaps societal tolerance for the use of violence to solve disputes has increased.

The subculture of violence theory in Chapter 8 is frequently cited as an explanation for acts of violence perpetrated by individuals from a certain subculture that promotes particular values or codes of conduct. For example, the expectation that young males defend their honour and reputation at all costs naturally leads to the use of violence if that is what is necessary to achieve this end. Therefore, it is conformity to this set of values that leads to violence; violence is not seen in these subcultural settings as the result of deviant behaviour. This argument is used further to explain why victims of violence in these groups are usually members of the group and not outsiders. The account of the murder of Sylvain Leduc in Chapter 8 helps to illustrate this point.

The feminist criminology perspective discussed in Chapter 10 would explain violence against women as resulting from societal inequalities due primarily to gender. The physical and sexual assault of women is a means by which males are able to maintain their dominance over women. Thus, the sexual victimization of girls is a behaviour learned by young males in a patriarchal society.

PROPERTY CRIME

3.3 | LEARNING OBJECTIVE

PROPERTY CRIMES COMPRISE UNLAWFUL ACTS PERPETRATED WITH THE INTENT OF gaining property but without the use or threat of violence. Included in this category are breaking and entering, theft, fraud, crime involving motor vehicles, arson, mischief, and possession of stolen property.

The 2011 UCR reported 1 213 885 incidents of property crime, or a rate of 3520 per 100 000 population in that year, which represents a 4 percent drop from the previous year and the lowest recorded number since 1969. The rates of property crime declined in almost every province with the most significant drops recorded in Manitoba (–14 percent) and Alberta (–11 percent) followed by New Brunswick, Quebec, and British Columbia (–8 percent each). Ontario recorded the lowest rate in the country at 2739 per 100 000 population. Overall, the western provinces and the territories recorded the highest property crime rates, with the highest in Saskatchewan (12 272 per 100 000) and Northwest Territories (48 032 per 100 000).

Breaking and Entering

Breaking and entering (s. 348) is one of the most common and serious of property offences. This crime constitutes an invasion of personal territory or a workspace and often results in the theft or destruction of property. While most break and enters are property crimes, the potential for personal violence is inherent. Breaking and entering a dwelling house carries a maximum penalty of life imprisonment (as compared with ten years for breaking and entering of a place other than a dwelling house), reflecting the possibility of violent confrontation between the offender and the homeowner. In the UCR, police-reported breaking and entering is categorized into three different types: (1) residential—the breaking and entering of a private residence, including single homes as well as attached garages, garden homes, apartments, cottages, mobile homes, rooming houses, etc.; (2) business— the breaking and entering of a facility used for commercial or public affairs, including, for example, financial institutions, stores, and non-commercial enterprises such as government buildings, schools, churches, and non-profit agencies; and (3) other—the breaking

Breaking and entering The unlawful entry of a place to commit an indictable offence.

Rate per 100,000 population

Figure 3.2 Break and Enter and Motor Vehicle Theft Rate, Canada, 1981 to 2011

Source: Statistics Canada, *Juristat* 85-002-X, July 2012. Reproduced and distributed on an "as is" basis with the permission of Statistics Canada.

and entering of private property structures such as sheds, detached garages, or storage and transportation facilities. The UCR statistics include attempted as well as completed break and enters.

In 2011, 181 217 incidents of breaking and entering were recorded, representing a rate of 526 per 100 000 population. (See Figure 3.2 for a representation of this trend.) This is a decrease of 9 percent from the previous year, in keeping with the consistent decreases in the last four decades. In 2011, 63 percent of all break and enters were residential, while business break and enters accounted for 28 percent. The remaining 9 percent included other locations such as schools, sheds, or detached garages.

The type of property stolen from residences is quite different from that stolen from businesses. Audio/video equipment, jewellery, money, cheques or bonds, personal accessories, machinery and tools, photographic equipment, office equipment, and bicycles typify the property stolen from residences. Thefts from break and enters into businesses include money, cheques or bonds, office equipment, consumable goods (alcohol, cigarettes), audio/video equipment, machinery and tools, and personal accessories. Firearms were more frequently stolen from homes during break and enters than from businesses. The majority of these were rifles and shotguns, while the minority consisted of restricted weapons. Data from the UCR suggest that break and enters involving violence occur in fewer than 5 percent of cases. Of these, the majority involve an assault, while others involve robbery, sexual assault, abduction, and criminal harassment. Almost all violent break and enters occur at a place of residence.[27]

As has been the case for the past ten years, the highest rate of breaking and entering was recorded by Saskatchewan (858 per 100 000) despite a 9 percent decrease from 2010. Ontario and New Brunswick recorded the lowest rates, at 379 and 447 respectively.

Theft

Theft The act of dishonestly taking property belonging to another person with the intention of depriving its owner of it either permanently or temporarily.

Theft (s. 322) is defined as the act of dishonestly taking property belonging to another person with the intention of depriving its owner of it either permanently or temporarily.[28] Specific categories of theft included in the *Criminal Code of Canada* are *theft of gas, electricity, or telecommunications* (cable television) (s. 326) and *theft of credit card* (s. 342). The severity of the theft is determined largely by the monetary value placed on the property taken.

In 1995, the *Criminal Code* was amended to include *theft over $5000* and *theft $5000 and under* (prior to 1995, this amount was $1000; prior to 1986, it was $200). Not included in the category are motor vehicle theft, fraud, or possession of stolen property. Section 342 of the *Criminal Code* deals with offences against the rights of property; section 342.1 deals with the unauthorized use of a computer; and section 342.2 deals with possession of a device to obtain computer service. See Chapter 12 for a more in-depth discussion of computer-related crime trends.

In 2011, 595 016 incidents of theft accounted for about 30 percent of all *Criminal Code* incidents and 50 percent of all property crimes. Of these, over 40 percent were classified as theft $5000 and under. This figure most likely under-represents the amount of theft that occurs: theft under $5000 remains one of the crimes most under-reported by victims. Official statistics indicate that it constitutes a rate of 1443 incidents per 100 000 population, while the rate for theft over $5000 stood at 44 per 100 000 for 2011. The overall theft rate was about 7 percent lower than for the previous year and has been declining since 1991.

Compared with other types of offences, the number of females charged with theft $5000 and under is quite high—females constitute about a third of both adults and youth aged 12 to 17 charged. The majority of these females were charged with shoplifting (see Chapter 2 for a discussion of the correlation between females and criminal behaviour and the *feminization of poverty*).

Motor Vehicle Theft

Motor vehicle theft is defined as the taking of a vehicle without the owner's authorization. A motor vehicle is defined as a car, truck, van, bus, recreational vehicle, semi-trailer truck, motorcycle, construction machinery, agricultural machinery, or other land-based motor vehicle (such as a go-kart, snowmobile, all-terrain vehicle, or dune buggy).[29] Excluded from the category of motor vehicle theft is theft of airplanes, boats, trains, and spacecraft, which are counted as thefts over $5000.

In 2011, 82 411 incidents of motor vehicle theft (an average of about 226 per day) accounted for slightly more than 6 percent of all property crimes. At a rate of 239 per 100 000 population, this constitutes a 12 percent decrease from the previous year. Cars continue to be the most commonly stolen vehicles followed by trucks, minivans, and sport-utility vehicles. Motor vehicle theft is one of the least likely crimes to be solved by police; the clearance rate continues to be lower than other property-related offences. It is also a crime often associated with youth. Statistics show that over 30 percent of people charged with motor vehicle theft were youth aged 15 to 17. Of these, the vast majority were male.[30]

The rate of motor vehicle theft decreased between 2010 and 2011 in every province and territory with the exception of Newfoundland and Labrador (+6 percent), Prince Edward Island (+3 percent), and Nova Scotia (+2 percent). Nevertheless, Prince Edward Island and Newfoundland and Labrador reported the lowest rates, at 82 and 116 per 100 000 respectively, while Northwest Territories (488) and Saskatchewan (470) reported the highest rates.

Explanations for such varied provincial rates could include extra high rates of motor vehicle theft in Regina (489 per 100 000) and Saskatoon (579 per 100 000). Joyriding continues to be the primary motivation for motor vehicle theft; organized crime rings account for most of the remainder. According to the RCMP, "Anytime you see a movie that's released that has auto theft-related issues our thefts across the country peak."[31]

The Criminal Intelligence Service Canada (CISC) reports that the theft of heavy equipment in Canada has been increasing for the past several years while recovery rates are declining. Common types of heavy equipment stolen, usually by organized crime rings, include farm machinery (tractors), construction equipment (excavators, forklifts, etc.), and other heavy equipment (tractor trailers, generators, compressors, etc.). The product

Motor vehicle theft The taking of a vehicle without the owner's authorization. A motor vehicle is defined as a car, truck, van, bus, recreational vehicle, semi-trailer truck, motorcycle, construction machinery, agricultural machinery, or other land-based motor vehicle (such as a go-kart, snowmobile, all-terrain vehicle, or dune buggy).

identification number is modified and the equipment is generally smuggled out of Ontario and Quebec. The stolen equipment is shipped to a different part of Canada or is exported to destinations such as east Africa, South America, Mexico, the United Arab Emirates, and the United States.[32]

Theoretical Explanations for Property Crime

The realities surrounding property crime are complex and belie the ability to pinpoint a simple explanation. Does the person who breaks into someone's home and steals the television and laptop do this for the same reason that someone else breaks into a car and rides around in it at high speeds?

The most obvious motivating factor in many cases of property crime appears to be greed, and many criminological theories have used this notion as a starting point. These theories fall under the social problems perspective heading, because they largely assume that property crime is the manifestation of a variety of underlying social problems, not the least of which is poverty. Theories such as the strain theory (discussed in Chapter 8) and the routine activities theory (Chapter 5) suggest that there is a desire to achieve a universal goal, which is defined in terms of money and the goods, services, privileges, and prestige it can buy. The opportunity to achieve this goal through legitimate means such as schooling and employment is restricted for some people, who then turn to illegitimate or criminal opportunities to do so. If the illegitimate opportunities outnumber the legitimate ones, the temptation for some to seek this "easy route" may become too great to resist. The increase in the amount of fraud being committed using credit cards over cheques may be explained using this theory, for example.

Still other theories contend that the commission of property crimes, including motor vehicle theft, breaking and entering, and shoplifting, all satisfy a need for excitement. The subcultural theories discussed in Chapter 8 maintain that material needs are often insufficient to explain the fascination with theft some people have. These theories suggest that crime is fun and is done to achieve a sense of status and belonging within a peer group.

The social process theories outlined in Chapter 9 look to the interaction between individuals as an explanation for criminal behaviour. What influence, for example, do peer

When youth engage in property crimes such as vandalism to public property, are they behaving in response to peer pressure and simply looking to have some excitement?

Nic Cleave Photography/Alamy

pressure and group behaviour have on the behaviour of some individuals? Can association with delinquent peers promote the learning of crimes such as theft and joyriding in stolen cars? The differential association theory suggests this is so. The social control theory outlined in Chapter 9 looks to the individual's attachment to positive role models, commitment to realistic goals, involvement in recreational and school activities, and belief in conventional values as a means of decreasing the likelihood of criminal behaviour. This theory suggests that those people, especially youth, who are bored and have no positive direction in life run a much greater risk of being attracted to crimes such as theft, shoplifting, arson, and vandalism.

CRIMES AGAINST THE PUBLIC ORDER

INCLUDED IN THE *CRIMINAL CODE OF CANADA* ARE A NUMBER OF ACTIVITIES OFTEN referred to in criminological terms as *public order crimes* or *victimless crimes*. While it is debatable whether these activities do or do not victimize, it is generally agreed that though they violate prevailing morality, social policy, and public opinion, it is open to debate whether they should be classified as criminal. Such crimes against the public order traditionally refer to activities and behaviours involving sex, such as commercial sex, pornography, and erotic materials; activities involving the use, abuse, and sale of drugs and alcohol; and behaviours involving individual lifestyle choices, such as gambling and assisted suicide.

The UCR includes a category referred to as "Other *Criminal Code* Incidents" in which some of these crimes are reported. These offences represent a general catch-all category of crimes that are classified by the UCR as neither violent nor property-related. Offences in this grouping include counterfeiting, weapons violations, child pornography, disturb the peace, prostitution, administration of justice violations (bail violations), and other.

Counterfeiting

Counterfeiting (s. 448) is considered to include any unauthorized reproduction of a thing with the intention that it be accepted as genuine. Counterfeiting can thus refer to anything that is capable of reproduction, including things that are subjects of rights of private property, such as art, or things that are subject to protection as intellectual property. It most commonly refers to the reproduction of currency (s. 449); forging of credit cards or debit cards (s. 342); documents for identification, such as passports (s. 57); or any paper that represents value (e.g., stamps, travellers' cheques, or negotiable instruments, ss. 370, 376). The penalties for these activities range from a maximum penalty of 14 years' imprisonment for counterfeiting currency and forging a passport to 10 years for fraudulent credit cards.

Counterfeiting Any unauthorized reproduction of a thing with the intention that it be accepted as genuine. It can thus refer to anything that is capable of reproduction, including things that are subjects of rights of private property. It also includes the reproduction of documents for identification, such as passports, or any paper that represents value (e.g., stamps, travellers' cheques, or negotiable instruments).

Counterfeiting is somewhat unique in that, for a relatively high-volume offence, police-reported statistics show large year-to-year fluctuations. For example, between 2002 and 2004, the rate increased by 147 percent, but it has declined by 68 percent since then.

The National Anti-Counterfeiting Bureau of the RCMP is another source of information on trends in counterfeiting. The RCMP identifies *counterfeit currency* as banknotes (bills) that have been successfully passed without detection and seized notes that have been intercepted by law enforcement officials. Access to sophisticated computer devices and software and to high-quality colour photocopiers has been among the reasons for the prevalence of counterfeiting currency. The RCMP also indicates that organized crime groups have become increasingly involved in the production and distribution of counterfeit banknotes and documents. Chapter 12 takes another look at the extent of the involvement of organized crime groups in a number of criminal activities.

A number of organizations are involved in prevention, detection, and awareness-raising around the growing activity of counterfeiting, including the Bank of Canada and

Box 3.3 BANK OF CANADA POLYMER SERIES

The introduction of the *Polymer* series by the Bank of Canada features new security features as well as an educational approach (Feel.Look.Flip.) to assist the public in remembering how to check bills.

Feel the raised ink on the large number, the shoulders of the large portrait, and the words *Bank of Canada* and *Banque du Canada*. (1)

Look

- for transparency through the large window containing a metallic portrait and building (2)
- at the details in the metallic portrait in the large window. It matches the large portrait (3)
- at the details in the metallic building in the large window. Tilt the note to see sharp colour changes in the building (4)
- at the numbers in and around the large window that match the value of the note. Some of the numbers appear in reverse (5)

- at the word *Canada*. It is transparent and feels slightly raised (6)
- at the maple leaves that border the large window. Some of the leaves cross into the window (7)
- at the frosted maple leaf window to see that it has a transparent outline (8)
- at the hidden numbers by using a small light like an incandescent bulb or a pot light (added security feature) (9)

Flip the note to see the features repeated in the same colours and detail on the other side.

Source: Courtesy of The Bank of Canada.
http://www.bankofcanada.ca/banknotes/bank-note-series/polymer/ [Accessed December 2, 2012].

Feel.Look.Flip

Used with the permission of the Bank of Canada

coalitions such as the Anti-Counterfeiting Network. The Bank of Canada, for example, continues to issue banknotes with added security features (see Box 3.3). The introduction of the polymer $20, $50, and $100 banknotes in 2011 is likely to result in the reduction of illegal activity involving these denominations. Thirty-two countries around the world have successfully used this polypropylene material since it was pioneered by the Reserve Bank of Australia beginning in 1988.[33] Increased education and awareness by merchants and retailers in detecting counterfeit bills and enhanced law enforcement efforts have also contributed to the recorded drops.

Prostitution

Prostitution Most commonly used to refer to the illegal activities of publicly communicating with another person for the purposes of buying or selling sexual services, running a bawdy house, or living on the avails of the prostitution of another person.

Prostitution, or the exchange of money for sex, is not illegal in Canada. What *is* illegal is the associated activities such as publicly communicating with another person for the purposes of buying or selling sexual services (s. 213), running a bawdy house (s. 210), or living on the avails of a prostitution of another person (s. 212).

Sex trade workers and their supporters gather on the front steps of the Supreme Court of Canada building in Ottawa as they challenge Canada's criminal laws regarding adult prostitution, arguing that argues current laws put sex-trade workers at risk by making safe and secure brothels illegal, forcing sex-trade workers to ply their trade in the streets, where they're vulnerable to abuse and predators. Do you think the laws regarding prostitution should be amended?

John Major/QMI AGENCY

Prostitution is a controversial issue, and there seems to be little consensus as to the best means of dealing with it. While it is generally considered to be a voluntary activity and is therefore often classified as a victimless crime, there are serious health, social, legal, and community issues associated with it. Other forms of activity such as drug trafficking and use are often linked to it. Those neighbourhoods in which prostitutes ply their trade constantly struggle with the health and safety risks associated with discarded needles and condoms. Health concerns, such as the spread of sexually transmitted diseases, affect the prostitutes, their customers, and the families of customers.

Statistics on prostitution are very closely tied to the law enforcement practices of any given police service and therefore vary across provinces and municipalities. In 2011, the rate of prostitution incidents reported to the police decreased by 19 percent from the previous year. This decrease is most probably a reflection of changes in police enforcement practices.

Over half of the 2459 individuals charged with prostitution-related crimes were females. Of the males charged, it can be assumed that most were clients, although some were prostitutes themselves or were living on the avails of prostitution. Of those charged in 2011, official statistics indicate that less than 1 percent were youth aged 12 to 17. It is generally believed that this number vastly under-represents the actual number of youths involved in prostitution, since many in this age group are diverted by police to social services rather than charged.

Public concerns have been raised about the ever-decreasing age of prostitutes. Incidents of children being recruited and sold into a life of prostitution in Asian countries such as Thailand, Japan, India, and the Philippines are well documented.[34] The alarmingly increasing activity in the trafficking of persons for sexual exploitation is discussed in detail in Chapter 12. Of equal concern to law enforcement officials is the increased practice of what is known as "sex tourism," which involves the promotion to Canadians of travel packages designed for the purpose of illegal sexual encounters, often with minors. Box 3.4 outlines the recently amended sections of the *Criminal Code of Canada* that target this illegal activity.

Box 3.4 CANADA'S "SEX TOURISM" LAW

Donald Bakker was the first case involving charges under Canada's sex tourism law. In 2005, Bakker was charged with 22 counts of assault involving adult prostitutes and 16 counts related to children in a foreign country. His case did not proceed to trial when he subsequently pled guilty to 10 counts of sexual assault, three of which involved attacks on women in British Columbia and the rest involving children in Asian countries. A 1997 amendment to the *Criminal Code* introduced section 7.4(1)* or what has come to be known as the sex tourism law. Section 7.4(1) reads:

> Notwithstanding anything in this Act or any other Act, every one who, outside Canada, commits an act or omission that if committed in Canada would be an offence against section 151, 152, 153, 155, or 159, subsection 160(2) or (3), section 163.1, 170, 171 or 173 or subsection 212(4) shall be deemed to commit that act or omission in Canada if the person who commits the act or omission is a Canadian citizen or permanent resident within the meaning of subsection 2(1) of the *Immigration and Refugee Protection Act* who is ordinarily resident in Canada.

*The offences listed in section 7.4(1) are

- **s.151** sexual interference
- **s.152** invitation to sexual touching
- **s.153** sexual exploitation
- **s.155** incest
- **s.159** anal intercourse
- **s.160(2)** compelling the commission of bestiality
- **s.160(3)** bestiality in the presence of a child under 14/ inciting child under 14 to commit
- **s.163(1)** making, distributing, selling, or possessing child pornography
- **s.170** parent or guardian procuring sexual activity
- **s.171** householder permitting sexual activity
- **s.173** indecent acts/exposure
- **s.212(4)** prostitution of a person under 18

Do you agree that Canadian citizens should be subject to prosecution if they sexually abuse children, including engaging in child prostitution, while outside Canada?

Illicit Drugs

There is a correlation between illicit drug use and criminal activity, albeit a complex one. This examination of illicit drugs considers those related criminal activities contained in the *Controlled Drugs and Substances Act* (CDSA). Essentially, the drug law is made up of two categories of offences: *supply offences*, which include the growing and distribution (trafficking and importing) of illegal and prohibited drugs, and *possession offences*, which include the purchase and use of illegal and prohibited drugs. The official number of recorded offences is obviously sensitive to enforcement and detection practices. An increase in the number of arrests and seizures does not necessarily indicate an increase in the population's use of illicit drugs, but rather may indicate an increased circulation of drugs or stepped-up enforcement at national or international levels. Canadian government estimates indicate that the illegal drug market in Canada generates billions of dollars annually.[35]

The overall rate of police-reported drug offences in Canada has generally been increasing since the early 1990s. In 2011, police reported more than 113 100 drug crimes, of which more than half (54 percent) were for the possession of cannabis. Increases were recorded in the possession of cannabis (+7 percent) and other drugs (+5 percent), while the rate of trafficking cannabis declined by 11 percent. The second largest category of drug crimes involves cocaine offences. In 2011, cocaine offences made up nearly one-quarter of all drug offences known to police, about half of which involved possession and the other half trafficking. In contrast to the trend in cannabis offences, the rate of cocaine offences has been increasing in recent years, primarily as a result of increases in possession. Compared to other types of drug offences, those involving heroin are relatively low. According to the RCMP, heroin is one of the least-used illicit drugs in Canada.[36] Slight increases have been noted for drug offences, such as those related to PCP, LSD, ecstasy, amphetamines ("crystal meth"), barbiturates, and anabolic steroids (+2 percent). Of all categories of drugs, the "other" drug offence rate has risen the most in the past ten years, up 168 percent. Increases have occurred in virtually all provinces and across each of the major offence types. In its 2010 report on organized crime, Criminal Intelligence Service Canada (CISC) stated that Canada has become one of the primary source countries in the world for ecstasy, supplying significant quantities to the United States and to a lesser extent Japan, Australia, and New Zealand. "Super labs," used for the mass production of certain synthetic drugs, such as methamphetamine, have been located by police in British Columbia, Ontario, and Quebec.[37]

British Columbia has consistently had the highest rate of police-reported drug offences. In 2011, the cannabis crime rate in this province (424 incidents per 100 000) was significantly higher than that of Saskatchewan, the next highest province.

Theoretical Explanations of Crimes against the Public Order

The radical criminology perspectives outlined in Chapter 10 contend that behaviours are deemed to be deviant or criminal by definition. Crimes against the public order are seen by many as examples of *conflict crimes*, or those behaviours around which there is much controversy within society as to their acceptance. Social conflict criminology would contend that laws against behaviours such as prostitution and substance abuse are made by the powerful segment of society to ensure the subordination of those who engage in these activities. Feminist criminology, for example, would propose that, in the case of prostitution, women are conditioned to be subservient to men and are transformed into commodities to be bought and sold.

Many of the other social problem theories are useful to explain public order crimes. Refer to the differential association theory in Chapter 9; how can the crimes of prostitution and drug use be explained in terms of learned behaviour brought on through peer pressure? Similarly, social control theory, with its emphasis on strong bonds between the individual and the social order, might be applicable when explaining the criminal behaviour of bored and unfocused youth. Weak attachments to the family early on in life because of dysfunction within the home can compel many youth to flee and find refuge in the street, where prostitution and drug abuse are available options.

Individual responsibility theories can be seen to apply to public order crimes as well. For example, is it possible that dependency on alcohol and drugs has a genetic basis? Are addictive personality types passed on from generation to generation? Chapter 6 looks at some genetic roots of crime, while Chapter 7 examines theories of personality and asks whether there are certain personality types that are predisposed to certain types of criminal behaviour. For example, does low self-esteem, poor self-image, and anxiety result in a personality that is prone to addiction?

MySearchLab® with eText offers you access to an online interactive version of the text, extensive help with your writing and research projects, and provides round-the-clock access to credible and reliable source material.

SUMMARY OF LEARNING OBJECTIVES

3.1 The Uniform Crime Report Surveys (UCR) classify crimes into the following categories: violent crime, property crime, other crime, traffic offences, federal drug legislation offences, and other federal statute violations. Canada's overall police-reported crime rate dropped 6 percent in 2011, continuing the downward trend seen over the past 20 years. This drop in crime was seen in most parts of the country and for virtually all offences. Of the 1.9 million *Criminal Code* incidents reported, violent crime constituted 21 percent, property crimes 61 percent, and other offences such as counterfeiting, prostitution, bail violations, and mischief 18 percent.

3.2 Violent crime incidents include homicide, attempted murder, assault, sexual assault, robbery, use of firearms, kidnapping and abduction, criminal harassment, and uttering threats. Social problems theories look to socialization and cultural factors as explanations for acts of violence, while social learning theories assume that people learn how to behave by modelling themselves after others they have observed. However, the individual responsibility perspective contends that it is the psychological makeup of each person that determines the way in which observed behaviour is absorbed, processed, and acted upon. Biological theories question whether certain individuals are predisposed to violence.

3.3 Property crimes comprise those unlawful acts perpetrated with the intent of gaining property but do not involve the use or threat of violence. Included in this category are breaking and entering, theft, fraud, crime involving motor vehicles, arson, mischief, and possession of stolen property. The social problems perspective largely assumes that the motivating factor in many cases of property crime is greed, while social process theories emphasize the role of peer pressure and group behaviour.

3.4 Crimes against the public order traditionally refer to activities and behaviours involving sex; activities involving the use, abuse, and sale of drugs and alcohol; and behaviours involving individual lifestyle choices, such as gambling and assisted suicide. Crimes against the public order are seen by many as examples of conflict crimes, or those behaviours around which there is much controversy within society as to their acceptance.

Questions for Review

1. How are typologies of crime useful in understanding patterns of crime? What are the categories used by the Canadian Uniform Crime Reporting Survey (UCR)?

2. Which of the categories of crime discussed in this chapter do you think has the most accurate crime count? Why?

3. How does the definition of a crime affect the counting of it? How do police enforcement activities affect the count?

4. This book emphasizes a social problems versus social responsibility theme. Which perspective best explains the reality of crime in this country? Is one perspective more appropriate when considering violent crime? Property crime? Crime against the public order?

Multiple-Choice Questions

1. Most victims of sexual assault are victimized by _____.

    a. a stranger

    b. a friend or acquaintance

    c. a family member

    d. a spouse

    e. a sibling

2. Which of the following offences is *not* classified as a violent offence?

    a. robbery

    b. abduction

    c. sexual assault

    d. use of a firearm

    e. possession of stolen property

3. Which of the following acts is not illegal in Canada?

    a. publicly communicating with another person for the purpose of buying sexual services

    b. publicly communicating with another person for the purpose of selling sexual services

    c. exchanging money for sex

    d. running a bawdy house

    e. living on the avails of prostitution

4. Currently, sexual assault legislation focuses on _____.

    a. the sexual nature of the act

    b. the gender of the victim

    c. the relationship between the victim and the accused

    d. the violent nature of the act

    e. the gender of the accused

5. Typically, crimes are organized into categories, or _____.

    a. classifications of crime

    b. typologies of crime

    c. subtexts of crime

    d. textures of crime

    e. layers of crime

Multiple Choice Answers: 1b, 2e, 3a, 4d, 5b

Chapter 4

Victimology: The Study of the Victim

Eric Gay/AP Photo

Victims' rights have become far too important to relegate them to mere abstract statements of principle and the time has come to translate symbolic recognition into a practical and meaningful law reform agenda.

—*Alan Young*[1]

LEARNING OBJECTIVES

After reading this chapter, you should be able to

4.1 Discuss the development of the field of victimology and the realities of being a victim of crime.

4.2 Describe the emergence of victims' rights.

4.3 Identify current directions in victimology and the services available to victims of crime.

4.4 Understand the concept of victim restitution and describe how the process works in Canada.

4.5 Assess future directions in the field of victimology.

INTRODUCTION

In March 2003, the grief-stricken family of Andy Moffitt left an Ottawa courtroom unable to believe or understand the five-year prison sentence just handed down to the man who had killed their son.

Several years earlier, Moffitt, a computer engineering student at the University of Ottawa, was celebrating the end of his exams with some friends at a neighbourhood bar and grill. Just after midnight, Moffitt and his friends witnessed a scuffle between a man and the bar manager. One of Moffitt's companions ran to the aid of the manager but was immediately attacked. Moffitt rushed to help his friend and was stabbed once in the chest by the assailant. Moffitt was pronounced dead later at the hospital. "This guy was a great kid and he was trying to be a Good Samaritan by smoothing out the fight," Detective Dale Hayes said. "For trying to help, he got shanked."[2]

Several hours later, a man telephoned 911, asking police to come and pick him up. Henry Danninger, a 26-year-old student also attending the University of Ottawa, was apprehended and charged with second-degree murder. Danninger had gone to the restaurant that evening looking for a roommate whom he believed had taken some drugs belonging to him. The bar manager was trying to remove Danninger from the establishment when Moffitt stepped in to help. Danninger and Moffitt had never met before. Moffitt was simply in the wrong place at the wrong time.

The five-year sentence of incarceration was a shock to Moffitt's family. They had hoped for a much stiffer penalty, but a plea-bargain arrangement reduced the charge from second-degree murder to manslaughter. That, in conjunction with the time Danninger had spent in pretrial custody and the fact that he had no prior criminal record, compelled Justice Roydon Kealey to impose the sentence. "I'm speechless," said the victim's mother, Paulette Moffitt of Brockville, who'd been hoping for a sentence twice as long. "I hope for the remainder of his life that he thinks about what he did to Andy," she railed before walking away from the courthouse one final time.[3] "I will never forget having to phone Andy's older brother to tell him his brother was dead," said Ms. Moffitt. "I was the one (who) broke his heart, telling him the most dreadful news imaginable. To witness the pain that Andy's two brothers and my husband have endured because of Henry Danninger is like his knife is slowly piercing my heart."[4]

The governor general of Canada honoured Andy Moffitt in 2003 with a Medal of Bravery for the heroic deed that cost him his life. In 2005, a private member's bill, Bill C-393, was introduced into the House of Commons, proposing the introduction of mandatory minimum sentences for carrying a concealed weapon and for manslaughter of an unarmed person inflicted with a knife that was previously concealed. The bill was passed in 2008 and continues to await final assent. The Andrew Moffitt Memorial Scholarship has awarded thousands of dollars to engineering students at the University of Ottawa since it was established. In 2010, an Ottawa park was renamed Andy Moffitt Trail to honour him.

THE DYNAMICS OF VICTIMIZATION

4.1 | LEARNING OBJECTIVE

JUST AS CRIMINALS HAVE BEEN STUDIED TO DETERMINE WHAT KINDS OF SOCIAL AND personal experiences they have, so too have criminologists advocated close scrutiny of victims. The development of the field of **victimology**, or the study of victims, has closely paralleled the development of criminology. As was characteristic of the wider body of criminological theory, early victimologists stressed constitutional factors that propelled the victim toward victimization. The adjudged degree of an individual's potential for victimization was termed **victim-proneness**.

One of the earliest writers in the field, Hans von Hentig, depicted crime as a duet played by two.[5] "In a sense," wrote von Hentig, "the victim shapes and moulds the criminal."[6]

Victimology The study of victims and their contributory role, if any, in the criminal event.

Victim-proneness The degree of an individual's likelihood of victimization.

Von Hentig created a typology, or classificatory scheme, of victims based on what he saw as biological or situational weaknesses that could be physically, socially, psychologically, or environmentally based. He also wrote of "victim areas," or parts of the country to which tourists and others with money are drawn. Similarly attracted are the criminals who prey upon them. Recent incidents involving Canadian and other foreign tourists in destinations such as Mexico and Florida were presaged by this kind of thinking. Likewise, inner-city areas rich in crime were seen as creating a special relationship between victim and criminal.

Von Hentig used colloquial information, pre-existing statistical data, and documented individual experiences and personal observations to support his concepts. Although he did not undertake any empirical research of his own, von Hentig's ideas helped propel the importance of the victim into the forefront of criminological thinking during the 1950s and 1960s.

Some criminologists trace the development of the field of victimology to even earlier writings, including those of Benjamin Mendelsohn. In 1937, Mendelsohn, a European defence attorney, published a paper advocating the study of victims.[7] Like von Hentig, Mendelsohn created his own classification of victim types. Mendelsohn's typology was based on the degree of guilt that the victim brought to the criminal event.

Mendelsohn is generally credited with coining the term *victimology* and developing the concept of the **penal couple**, which describes the relationship between victim and criminal. He also coined the term *victimal* to describe the victim counterpart of the criminal and the word *victimity*, which signified the opposite of criminality. In his writings, Mendelsohn called for the development of victimology as a field of study independent from criminology. He foresaw the creation of an international institute for victimological research as part of the United Nations and called for the creation of an international society of victimology with its own journal. The *International Review of Victimology* continues to publish victimological research.

Henry Ellenberger introduced the concept of **victimogenesis** in 1954 to explain how people can undergo life experiences that eventually place them in circumstances that contribute to their future victimization.[8] Just as a criminal experiences events in life that lead to criminality, Ellenberger argued that many victims undergo a process of socialization that results in less caution, a proclivity to associate with possible offenders, an increased likelihood of frequenting places associated with criminal activity, and a generally higher risk of criminal victimization.

A decade later, writing in collaboration with Thorsten Sellin, Marvin E. Wolfgang introduced a typology of victims based on victim–offender relationships which described

- primary victimization—in which an individual falls victim to crime
- secondary victimization—in which an impersonal agency such as a business is victimized
- tertiary victimization—in which the government or public order is offended, perhaps through regulatory violations
- mutual victimization—in which the participants willingly involve themselves in a crime (e.g., drug sales, gambling, prostitution)
- no victimization—a category reserved for offences committed by youth that could not be committed by an adult (e.g., purchase of cigarettes by an underage person)[9]

The advent of routine, state-sponsored, nationwide victimization surveys such as the Canadian Urban Victimization Survey, first conducted in 1982, led to the further development of theoretical models of victimizations. Experts attempted to explain why certain groups of individuals and locations were especially prone to victimization, but also developed new theories to offer explanations for the variations in the rates of victimization and for the phenomenon of repeat victimization.

Penal couple A term that describes the relationship between victim and criminal.

Victimogenesis The contribution to victimization made by the background of a victim.

One of the most important theories of victimology was tabled by Michael Hindelang, Michael R. Gottfredson, and James Garofalo in 1978.[10] Known as the **lifestyle model,** the theory holds that the likelihood that an individual will suffer a personal victimization depends heavily on the concept of lifestyle, which is influenced by social roles played by people, the position one occupies in the social structure, and how one chooses to process options based on life experiences.

A year later, Lawrence E. Cohen and Marcus Felson proposed the notion of the **routine activity approach,** arguing that occurrences of personal victimization are dependent upon the "routine" or "daily activities" of people and are the outcome of three elements: the motivated offender, a suitable target, and the absence of a capable guardian. Central to this approach are opportunity, proximity/exposure, and facilitating factors. The risk of criminal victimization will vary in keeping with the circumstances and locations in which people place themselves and their property.[11]

The **opportunity model** posited by Lawrence E. Cohen, J.R. Kluegel, and Kenneth Land in 1981 incorporates elements from the lifestyle and routine activity theories, contending that the risk of criminal victimization depends largely on people's lifestyle and daily activities that bring them and their property into direct contact with potential offenders in the absence of capable guardians.[12]

Ezzat Fattah, a Canadian criminologist recognized as one of the leading thinkers in the field of victimology, attempted to integrate the various lifestyle/opportunity theories into a comprehensive scheme. He contended that this scheme comprised ten components,[13] which he identified as

1. *Opportunities*, which are closely linked to the characteristics of potential targets and to the activities and behaviour of these targets

2. *Risk factors*, particularly those related to socio-demographic realities such as age, sex, area of residence, etc.

3. *Motivated offenders* who do not choose their victims/targets at random but select them according to specific criteria

4. *Exposure* of the victim to potential offenders and to high-risk situations that increase the risk of criminal victimization

5. *Associations* between offenders and victims so that those who are in close personal, professional, or social contact with offenders run a greater risk of being victimized

Lifestyle model The theory that the likelihood that an individual will suffer a personal victimization depends heavily on the concept of lifestyle.

Routine activity approach The theory that occurrences of personal victimization are dependent upon the "routine" or "daily activities" of people and are the outcome of three elements: the motivated offender, a suitable target, and the absence of a capable guardian.

Opportunity model The contention that the risk of criminal victimization depends largely on people's lifestyle and daily activities that bring them and their property into direct contact with potential offenders in the absence of capable guardians.

A purse-snatcher in action. How could a victim's lifestyle be a factor in a crime such as this one?

Elizabeth Robertson/AP Photo

6. *Dangerous times and dangerous places*, which include evenings, weekends, and places of public entertainment

7. *Dangerous behaviours* such as provocation, which increases the risk especially of violent victimization, and other behaviours such as negligence and carelessness, which enhance chances of property victimization

8. *High-risk activities*, which increase the potential for victimization and can include deviant and illegal activities

9. *Defensive/avoidance behaviours*, which tend to contribute to the reduction in the risk of victimization; those who take precautions are less likely to be victimized than those who are risk-takers

10. *Structural/cultural proneness* of people, which means that those who are powerless and culturally stigmatized and marginalized are more likely to be criminally victimized

It is interesting to note that the findings of the most recent General Social Survey in Canada indicate that the risk of victimization is greatest for those who are 15 to 24 years of age, who are single, whose main activity is classified as "student," who occupy the lowest household income categories, who live in an urban setting, and who participate in evening activities outside the home more than 30 times per month, reflecting the fact that youths partake in more than one activity per evening.[14]

Realities of Being a Victim

Some authors have identified a number of procedural models that can be applied to a study of the victimization process, the experience the victim undergoes during and following victimization.[15] The "victims of crime model" developed by Morton Bard and Dawn Sangrey postulated that three stages are involved in any victimization: (1) the stage of impact and disorganization, during and immediately following the criminal event; (2) recoil, during which the victim formulates psychological defences and deals with conflicting emotions of guilt, anger, acceptance, and desire for revenge (the state of recoil is said to last from three to eight months); and (3) the reorganizational stage, during which the victim puts his life back together and gets on with daily living in a more or less normal fashion.[16] Some victims do not successfully adapt to the victimization experience, and a maladaptive reorganizational stage may last for many years.

The model developed by Elizabeth Kübler-Ross to describe the stages that dying persons go through has some applicability to the victimization process. Kübler-Ross described a five-part transitional process of denial, anger, bargaining, depression, and acceptance.[17] Victims often either deny the likelihood of their own victimization or believe that "this can't be happening to me." After the victimizing event, many victims feel anger, and some express rage toward their victimizers. Bargaining occurs when victims negotiate with themselves as well as with family members, representatives of the criminal justice community, and social service providers over how the victimization experience should be personally interpreted and officially handled. Acceptance occurs when the victim finally acknowledges that victimization has occurred, and the victim makes the adjustments necessary to go on with life. Of course, as in the case of other models, the Kübler-Ross model allows for maladjustment in the final phase as some victims never successfully integrate the victimization experience into their psyches in a way that avoids reduction in the quality of their lives.

Countless studies examining the psychological well-being of victims[18] have concluded that criminal victimization

■ can leave psychological scars that last as long as or longer than any physical or financial loss

- can result in anxiety disorders, depression, drug and alcohol abuse, fear, flashbacks, lowered self-esteem, sexual dysfunction, thoughts of suicide, suspiciousness, and a feeling of social isolation

- can result in the development of post-traumatic stress disorder (PTSD)

- can result in feelings of guilt, with victims of violence experiencing the greatest level of guilt

- can result in a decreased sense of satisfaction with life and a perception that the world is less caring

In addition to the literature examining the psychological realities of criminal victimization, there has been much discussion about the **post-crime victimization** or **secondary victimization** created by the criminal justice system in its treatment of victims during the criminal process. In an often-cited article, Dean Kilpatrick and Randy Otto contended that "promising victims' rights that are not delivered may involve a certain danger: providing rights without remedies would result in the worst of consequences, such as feelings of helplessness, lack of control and further victimization. Ultimately, with the victims' best interests in mind, it is better to confer no rights than 'rights' without remedies."[19]

Two Canadian studies concluded that victims of rape and child sexual abuse suffer from psychological distress years after victimization, but the studies were less conclusive about the psychological ill effects of non-sexual offences. These studies concluded by highlighting a lack of coordination among social psychologists, clinical psychologists, social support providers, and criminologists in the study of the impact of criminal victimization on victims.[20] A growing body of literature has emerged examining the role of social workers and other health-care professionals in dealing with victims of crime. Much of this literature has been critical of the role of these individuals, noting that they are often ill-equipped and improperly trained.

Post-crime victimization or secondary victimization Problems in living that tend to follow from initial victimization, some of which may be related to the victim's interaction with the criminal justice system.

EMERGENCE OF VICTIMS' RIGHTS

4.2 | LEARNING OBJECTIVE

FUELLED LARGELY BY THE EXPANSION OF THEORETICAL STUDY WITHIN THE FIELD OF criminology of the victim as a participant in the criminal event, a focus on the victim's role in the formal criminal justice process took hold in Canada in the late 1980s and early 1990s. The emergence of victims' advocacy and support organizations served to further highlight the need to critically examine the role and rights of victims within the criminal justice system.

A Historical Overview of Victim Responses to Crime

In early times, victims took the law into their own hands. If they were able to apprehend their victimizers, they enacted their own form of revenge and imposed some form of personal retaliation. One of the earliest known legal codes, the **Code of Hammurabi** (circa 1750 BC) required that many offenders make restitution; if the offender could not be found, the victim's family was duty bound to care for the needs of the victim. This early period in history has been called the Golden Age of the Victim, because victims not only were well cared for but also had considerable say in imposing punishments upon apprehended offenders.

Eventually crimes came to be understood as offences against society, and the victim was forgotten. By the late Middle Ages, the concept of "King's Peace" had emerged, wherein all offences were seen as violations of imperial law. The notion of private injury became one of public wrong, and the law of wrongdoing became the law of crime. It became the duty of local governments to apprehend, try, and punish offenders, effectively removing the victim from any direct involvement in judicial decision making. Victims were expected only to provide evidence of a crime and to testify against those who had offended them. Society's

Code of Hammurabi An early set of laws established by the Babylonian King Hammurabi, who ruled the ancient city from 1792 to 1750 BC.

moral responsibility toward making victims "whole again" was forgotten, and victims as a class were moved to the periphery of the justice process. Justice for the victim was forgotten, translated instead into the notion of justice for the state.

It is widely believed that this movement was largely a power play by the state to enhance its own coffers.[21] The previous practice of a compensatory award made to the victim by the offender for a harm done now became a fine for the benefit of the state. In the 13th century, fines levied by the courts constituted one-eighth of all revenue to the king.[22] By the 14th century, the victim was no longer the focus of the criminal process and the notion of an active role for the victim did not re-emerge until the 19th century. Nils Christie saw this as the theft of criminal conflicts from the real parties to the conflict, stating,

> So, in a modern criminal trial, two important things have happened. First, the parties are being represented. Second, the one party that is represented by the state, namely the victim, is so thoroughly represented that she or he for most of the proceedings is pushed completely out of the arena, reduced to the trigger-off of the whole thing. She or he is a sort of double loser; first vis-à-vis the offender, but secondly and often in a more crippling manner by being denied rights of full participation in what might have been one of the most important ritual encounters in life. The victim has lost the case to the state.[23]*

The situation remained largely unchanged until the 20th century, when renewed interest in the plight of victims led to a resurgence of positive sentiments around the world. Discussion of the role of the victim in the formal criminal justice process ensued, with supporters and detractors of the victim's right to participate in the process lining up on opposite sides of the argument. Much of the current academic debate continues to centre on the discussion of whether or not increased protection for victims can be achieved only at the expense of the rights of the accused. Much of this debate is focused on the participatory rights of the victim in the formal court process. For example, some victims' rights advocates recommend that victims be allowed to express an opinion or recommendation as to a convicted offender's sentence at the sentencing portion of the formal court process.

Commemorative vigils like this one have been held every year on December 6 since the Montreal Massacre in 1989 when 14 women died at the hands of gunman Marc Lepine. Do you think that this type of public memorial helps to raise the awareness of victims' rights?

Ryan Remiorz/Canadian Press Images

*Nils Christie, "Conflicts as Property," British Journal of Criminology, vol. 17(1): 1-15 (1977), pp. 3–4. Used by permission of Oxford University Press.

Those who caution against the increased participation of victims in the court process argue that this will only serve to whittle away at the accused's right to due process and turn the sentencing into an opportunity for victims to seek revenge.[24]

Within the emerging discipline of victimology, academic discussion focused on the development of a pedagogical basis for the growing victims' rights movement. This discussion centred largely around the two models of criminal justice put forth by Herbert Packer in 1968. In *The Limits of the Criminal Sanction*, Packer presented the *crime control model* and the *due process model*.[25] The former model describes an assembly-line approach to justice, focusing on the efficient repression of crime and the safety of the community. The latter model discusses an approach to criminal justice that emphasizes civil liberties and the importance of the verdict rather than the efficiency of the process. For many involved in the victims' rights movement, Packer's time-tested theory failed to provide the underpinning required to support the role of victims in the criminal process. In the late 1990s, Kent Roach, then dean of law at the University of Saskatchewan, proposed a third model as a theoretical base for victims' rights, referring to it as the *victims' rights model* and calling for more laws and prosecutions, a greater role for the victim in the trial, and more services and support for victims.[26]

Roach developed his model by distinguishing between what he identified as the *punitive* victims' rights model and the *non-punitive* victims' rights model. He described the punitive approach as one resembling the crime control model because it focuses on the enactment of criminal law, prosecution, and punishment as ways to control crime. Under this approach, he said that

> victim advocacy is often focused on creating new criminal laws in the hope that they will prevent future victimization. Feminist reforms of sexual assault laws and new laws targeting the sexual abuse of children are designed not only to protect the privacy and integrity of the victims, but to make convictions easier to obtain. Victim impact statements and victim involvement at sentencing and parole hearings are often directed toward greater punishment. Much more directly than due process, victims' rights can enable and legitimate crime control.[27]

His non-punitive model of victims' rights, on the other hand, looked away from the reliance on criminal sanction and punishment and toward the prevention of crime and restorative justice. He stated that

> both the processes of prevention and restoration can be represented by a circle. One manifestation of the circle may be the gated community with its own private police force. Another example would be successful neighbourhood watch or the self-policing of families and communities. Once a crime has occurred, the circle represents the processes of healing, compensation, and restorative justice. Normatively, the circle model stresses the needs of victims more than their rights and seeks to minimize the pain of both victimization and punishment.[28]

Roach went on to advocate that the non-punitive approach would seek to shift the focus of importance away from traditional crime-control strategies and agents such as the police, prosecutors, defence lawyers, and judges and toward the victim, the offender, families, and supporters. Victims, in turn, would play the most significant role in determining how the offender should be dealt with.

CURRENT DIRECTIONS IN VICTIMOLOGY AND VICTIMS' RIGHTS

4.3 LEARNING OBJECTIVE

AGAINST THIS BACKDROP OF INCREASING RECOGNITION FOR VICTIMS, A FLURRY OF laws and legislation have been developed, the earliest of which were intended to provide compensation primarily to victims of violent crimes.

Compensation for criminal injury is not unknown throughout history. The Code of Hammurabi specified that

> if a man has committed robbery ... that man shall be put to death. If the robber is not caught, the man who has been robbed shall formally declare what he has lost ... and the city ... shall replace whatever he has lost for him. If it is the life of the owner that is lost, the city or the mayor shall pay one maneth of silver to his kinfolk.

The first modern victim compensation statute was adopted by New Zealand in 1963. Known as the *Criminal Injuries Compensation Act*, it provided an avenue for claims to be filed by victims of certain specified violent crimes. A three-member board was empowered to make awards to victims. One year later, partially in response to a movement led by the social reformer Margaret Fry, Great Britain established a similar board. In 1965, California passed the first piece of U.S. legislation intended to assist victims of crime, and today all 50 states have passed similar legislation.

The first Canadian criminal injuries compensation plan was created in Saskatchewan in 1967. By 1988, a compensation program was available in every province and territory, providing financial compensation for injuries or death resulting from a crime of violence committed by another person. Each provincial compensation program is unique, but all include time limits on the filing of an application and set maximum award amounts per applicant, varying from $5000 to $30 000. In addition, most plans allow surviving relatives of murder victims and those injured while preventing a crime to qualify for compensation. Payments are not generally awarded for victims with injuries caused by motor vehicle accidents. In all plans, payments for lost wages, medical expenses, and prescription drugs are commonly made. Some provincial plans compensate victims for general damages, including pain and suffering caused by the offence. Victims who are responsible in some significant way for their own victimization may receive a lower reward or be disqualified completely. Factors such as intoxication, prior knowledge of the offender's criminalistic tendencies, and provocation of the offender can all result in reduced awards.

Although many tout the benefits of victim compensation programs, some studies of the effectiveness of government-sponsored compensation programs have found that most crime victims are reluctant to seek compensation and that those who do are generally from households with higher incomes. Frustrations with delays, poor information about the programs, and unmet expectations regarding assistance with psychological and support needs as well as financial needs were also cited as limitations.[29]

A 2007 report by the ombudsman of Ontario, entitled *Adding Insult to Injury*, strongly criticized that province's Criminal Injuries Compensation Board, calling it a "colossal failure that needlessly revictimizes people." In his report, the ombudsman claimed that the board has become mired in bureaucratic red tape that serves only to delay or deny compensation to victims. Compared to Quebec and British Columbia, where the average time to process a victim's claim is about four months, it takes an average of three years to do so in Ontario. He detailed the cases of several victims, including one who was forced to choose between buying food and burying his murdered daughter and another who had his claim returned because he had failed to dot an *i* on his form.[30] Shortly after the report's publication, the government of Ontario announced a $20 billion infusion into the Criminal Injuries Compensation Board to bolster payments to claimants and hire staff to address backlogs in processing claims.[31]

At the 1979 Federal–Provincial Conference of Ministers Responsible for Criminal Justice, the issue of victims' rights was raised by provincial ministers and subsequently formally brought to the attention of the federal government. A loose coalition of Canadian feminist organizations, Canadian victim assistance programs, and the strengthening U.S. victims' rights movement came together to move the issue into the forefront. A number of grassroots lobby groups were influential in promoting awareness of victims' issues. Most notable of these were Victims of Violence (now known as Victims of Violence, Canadian Centre for Missing Children), founded by Gary and Sharon Rosenfeldt, the parents of one of Clifford Olson's victims, and Canadians Against Violence Everywhere Advocating its Termination (CAVEAT), founded by Priscilla de Villiers, whose daughter was murdered. (CAVEAT was closed in 2001.)

This raising of awareness resulted in the creation of the 1983 Federal–Provincial Task Force on Justice for the Victims of Crime. The task force made 79 recommendations addressing the needs of victims and the requirements for effective victim services, many of which are in place today. Among these are provisions for improvements in emotional and practical assistance for victims, as well as provisions within the *Criminal Code of Canada* that ensure criminal injuries compensation, the increased use of restitution, and the introduction of the idea of a victim impact statement in the pre-sentence report.

International attention to the issue saw a number of nations sign on to the 1985 United Nations Declaration of Basic Principles of Justice for Victims of Crime and Abuses of Power, which is essentially a declaration of general principles. In adopting the declaration, the General Assembly of the United Nations stated that it was "cognizant that millions of people throughout the world suffer harm as a result of crime and abuse of power, and that the rights of these victims have not been adequately recognized."[32] Despite the lack of concrete details regarding implementation of these rights for victims, the document served as a catalyst for similar documents around the world, not the least of which was the **Canadian Statement of Basic Principles of Justice for Victims of Crime**, endorsed by the provincial and territorial ministers of justice in 1988 and amended in 2003 (see Box 4.1).

Canadian Statement of Basic Principles of Justice for Victims of Crime A document promoting access to justice, fair treatment, and provision of assistance for victims of crime.

Box 4.1 CANADIAN STATEMENT OF BASIC PRINCIPLES OF JUSTICE FOR VICTIMS OF CRIME, 2003

In honour of the United Nations' Declaration of Basic Principles of Justice for Victims of Crime, and with concern for the harmful impact of criminal victimization on individuals and on society, and in recognition that all persons have the full protection of rights guaranteed by the *Canadian Charter of Rights and Freedoms* and other provincial Charters governing rights and freedoms; that the rights of victims and offenders need to be balanced; and of the shared jurisdiction of federal, provincial, and territorial governments, the federal, provincial, and territorial Ministers Responsible for Criminal Justice agree that the following principles should guide the treatment of victims, particularly during the criminal justice process.

The following principles are intended to promote fair treatment of victims and should be reflected in federal/provincial/territorial laws, policies and procedures:

1. Victims of crime should be treated with courtesy, compassion, and respect.

2. The privacy of victims should be considered and respected to the greatest extent possible.

3. All reasonable measures should be taken to minimize inconvenience to victims.

4. The safety and security of victims should be considered at all stages of the criminal justice process and appropriate measures should be taken when necessary to protect victims from intimidation and retaliation.

5. Information should be provided to victims about the criminal justice system and the victim's role and opportunities to participate in criminal justice processes.

6. Victims sho uld be given information, in accordance with prevailing law, policies, and procedures, about the status of the investigation; the scheduling, progress and final outcome of the proceedings; and the status of the offender in the correctional system.

7. Information should be provided to victims about available victim assistance services, other programs and assistance available to them, and means of obtaining financial reparation.

8. The views, concerns and representations of victims are an important consideration in criminal justice processes and should be considered in accordance with prevailing law, policies and procedures.

9. The needs, concerns and diversity of victims should be considered in the development and delivery of programs and services, and in related education and training.

10. Information should be provided to victims about available options to raise their concerns when they believe that these principles have not been followed.

Source: Canadian Statement of Basic Principles of Justice for Victims of Crime, 2003, http://www.justice.gc.ca/eng/rp-pr/cj-jp/victim/03/princ.html Department of Justice Canada, 2003. Reproduce with the permission of the Minister of Public Works and Government Services Canada, 2013.

These principles have served to guide the development of policy and legislation for the victims of crime at both the federal and the provincial levels. A 1998 report from the House of Commons Standing Committee on Justice and Human Rights entitled *Victims' Rights—A Voice, Not a Veto* made a number of recommendations regarding further amendments to the *Criminal Code* to strengthen the voice of victims of crime. Most provinces and territories in Canada have enacted legislation to promote and protect the interests of victims.

In 2005, a National Office for Victims was established under the auspices of Public Safety Canada. As a central resource for victims of offenders under federal responsibility, the office provides general information for victims and the public and makes referrals on behalf of victims to Correctional Service Canada and the National Parole Board, when required.[33] Two years later, the independent Office of the Federal Ombudsman for Victims of Crime was created. By facilitating access of victims to existing programs, addressing complaints of victims about legislative compliance, enhancing awareness of criminal justice personnel and policymakers about the needs of victims, and identifying emerging trends that may adversely affect victims, the Office of the Ombudsman works to ensure that the federal government meets its responsibilities to victims of crime.[34] The Policy Centre for Victim Issues within the Department of Justice engages in legislative reform, consultation, policy development, research, and project funding.[35]

The provincial governments are primarily responsible for the provision of individual welfare rights and as such have almost all enacted legislation to recognize the rights of victims. In 1986, Manitoba was the first province to incorporate principles from the UN declaration into its own law.[36] Many of these provincial bills emphasize the notion of empowerment for the victim and provide rights of participation and notification. Ontario's legislation, known as *An Act Respecting Victims of Crime—Victims' Bill of Rights*, is emblematic of the rights enshrined in most provincial and territorial legislation. Box 4.2 reproduces the principles for the treatment of victims found in the act.

Box 4.2 AN ACT RESPECTING VICTIMS OF CRIME—VICTIMS' BILL OF RIGHTS (ONTARIO)

Section 2(1)

The following principles apply to the treatment of victims of crime:

1. Victims should be treated with courtesy, compassion, and respect for their personal dignity and privacy by justice system officials.

2. Victims should have access to information about,

    i. the services and remedies available to victims of crime,

    ii. the provisions of this Act and of the *Compensation for Victims of Crime Act* that might assist them,

    iii. the protection available to victims to prevent unlawful intimidation,

    iv. the progress of investigations that relate to the crime,

    v. the charges laid with respect to the crime and, if no charges are laid, the reasons why no charges are laid,

    vi. the victim's role in the prosecution,

    vii. court procedures that relate to the prosecution,

    viii. the dates and places of all significant proceedings that relate to the prosecution,

    ix. the outcome of all significant proceedings, including any proceedings on appeal,

    x. any pretrial arrangements that are made that relate to a plea that may be entered by the accused at trial,

    xi. the interim release and, in the event of conviction, the sentencing of an accused,

    xii. any disposition made under section 672.54 or 672.58 of the *Criminal Code* (Canada) in respect of an accused who is found unfit to stand trial or who is found not criminally responsible on account of mental disorder, and

    xiii. their right under the *Criminal Code* (Canada) to make representations to the court by way of a victim impact statement.

3. A victim of a prescribed crime should, if he or she so requests, be notified of,

    i. any application for release or any impending release of the convicted person, including release

>

in accordance with a program of temporary absence, on parole or on an unescorted temporary absence pass, and

   ii. any escape of the convicted person from custody.

4. If the person accused of a prescribed crime is found unfit to stand trial or is found not criminally responsible on account of mental disorder, the victim should, if he or she so requests, be notified of,

   i. any hearing held with respect to the accused by the Review Board established or designated for Ontario pursuant to subsection 672.38(1) of the *Criminal Code* (Canada),

   ii. any order of the Review Board directing the absolute or conditional discharge of the accused, and

   iii. any escape of the accused from custody.

5. Victims of sexual assault should, if the victim so requests, be interviewed during the investigation of the crime only by police officers and officials of the same gender as the victim.

6. A victim's property that is in the custody of justice system officials should be returned promptly to the victim, where the property is no longer needed for the purposes of the justice system.

Section 2(2)

The principles set out in subsection (1) are subject to the availability of resources and information, what is reasonable in the circumstances of the case, what is consistent with the law and the public interest, and what is necessary to ensure that the resolution of criminal proceedings is not delayed.

Source: Ontario Statues and Regulations, Service Ontario e-Laws, http://www.e-laws.gov.on.ca/html/statutes/english/elaws_statutes_95v06_e.htm [Accessed October 5, 2012].

Current Services for Victims

In addition to the development of statements of principles, the movement to recognize the needs and rights of victims has led to the development of a variety of services and programs across the country. Services offered to victims cover a wide range, from general information and compensation to health services and counselling. According to a recent victim services review, there are 884 victim services across the country, provided at a cost of $179 million (excluding compensation programs).[37] These services are largely found within various components of the criminal justice system and assist and support an individual's involvement with the system as a victim. Most of these were not available as recently as 30 years ago. A number of these services are highlighted in Box 4.3.

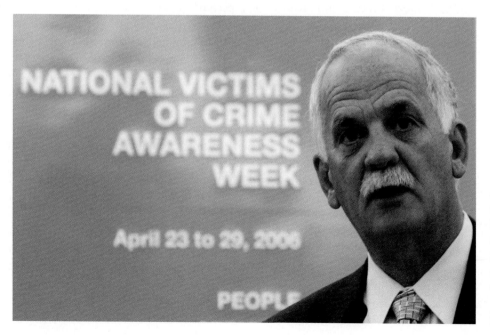

An annual National Victims of Crime Awareness Week has been sponsored by the Canadian government since 2004. How do such events engage all Canadians to assist victims of crime?

Jonathan Hayward/Canadian Press Images

Box 4.3 PROVINCIAL/TERRITORIAL VICTIM SERVICES

Alberta

Edmonton Police Service—Victim Services Unit

http://www.edmontonpolice.ca/CommunityPolicing/
FamilyProtection/VictimServices.aspx

Staffed by trained police officers, civilians, and volunteers, this unit provides crisis response, personal support, follow-up assistance, court preparation, and trauma debriefings for victims of crime.

British Columbia

Ministry of Public Safety and the Solicitor General— Court Prep

http://www.courtprep.ca

This interactive information site provides an overview of criminal court procedures for youth, including the roles of victims and witnesses of crime.

Newfoundland and Labrador

Department of Justice—Services for Victims

http://www.justice.gov.nl.ca/just/victim_services/
index.html

Eleven regional offices throughout the province provide support to victims through information about the justice system, their court cases, pre-court preparation, assistance with victim impact statements, referrals to specialized community resources, and short-term emotional support and counselling.

Ontario

Ministry of the Attorney General—SupportLink

http://www.attorneygeneral.jus.gov.on.ca/english/
ovss/programs.asp#supportLink

Located in 20 communities across the province, this service provides safety planning, follow-up contact, and, where appropriate, wireless phones pre-programmed to 911 to people at high risk of sexual assault, domestic violence, and stalking.

Quebec

Justice Québec—Crime Victims Assistance Centres (CAVACs)

http://www.cavac.qc.ca/english/index.html

Located in most urban centres throughout Quebec, CAVACs provide free and confidential services including post-traumatic shock counselling and support to victims through the court process.

Yukon

Department of Justice—Domestic Violence Treatment Option Court (DVTO Court)

http://www.yukoncourts.ca/courts/territorial/dvtoc.
html

Specially assigned judiciary, Crown attorneys, and defence council deal with domestic assault cases only in this court, which sits one afternoon a week. Probation officers, counsellors, and victim-services personnel provide assistance to the process as well as the victim. Disposition in this court often involves the offender's participation in the Spousal Assault Program (SAP).

Police-Based Victim Services Forty percent of all victim services are police-based.[38] Usually located in police departments, these types of programs are designed to help victims as soon as possible after their contact with the criminal justice system begins. These types of services typically include death notification, information about the investigation, assistance with various applications for compensation, and referrals. In order to provide this support to victims, many police services across Canada now have in-house victim services units.[39] Usually staffed by civilians and volunteers, these services are available 24 hours a day for immediate victim support. For example, in the case of a fatal car accident, responding police officers can call upon their department's victim services unit to provide crisis intervention at the scene of the accident. Such services not only allow police officers to resume their duties but also ensure that the victim is supported by a trained professional. Many victim services units also use volunteers who represent various cultural, ethnic, and linguistic groups to help meet the specific needs of victims.

Some provinces have also established and funded independent crisis intervention services that provide victim support through referrals from police. In Ontario, the Victim Crisis Assistance and Referral Service (VCARS) is found in 48 centres across the province. A full-time coordinator and a group of trained volunteers, who are available as support to police at the scene of a crime, staff most VCARS programs. Available 24 hours a day and 7 days a week, VCARS personnel help victims cope with the impact of the crime or tragic circumstance. This may mean helping an elderly woman clean up after her home has been burglarized or spending time with survivors of a fatal car accident. Follow-up is often provided in the form of referrals for ongoing counselling if required.

Crown/Court-Based Services   Most court-based victims programs are located within the courthouses and work closely with the Crown's office. Most assist those victims whose cases have resulted in prosecution. They emphasize court preparation and are designed to assist the victim through the trial process. One such program is the **Victim/Witness Assistance Program** located throughout Ontario. It provides services such as notification of court dates and adjournments, guided tours through the courtroom, explanations of court proceedings, and emotional support throughout the trial, especially on the day(s) of victim testimony.[40] Many provinces also provide specialized court-based support programs for child victims and witnesses.

The recognition of the victim's involvement and the need for support throughout the court process has resulted in a number of provisions outlined in the *Criminal Code of Canada* with special attention to victims of violence. For example, section 722 allows victims to record a statement describing the emotional suffering, trauma, and/or financial hardship experienced as a result of their victimization. Known as a **victim impact statement**, these accounts are introduced into court after conviction and prior to sentencing (see Box 4.4). They are most common in cases of interpersonal victimization, and judges are expected to consider these statements in arriving at an appropriate sanction for the offender. The extent to which victim impact statements affect a judge's sentencing determination is debatable, and most victims do not submit one. Proponents of victim impact statements

Victim/Witness Assistance Program   A program in Ontario that counsels victims, orients them to the justice process, and provides a variety of other services such as transportation to court, child care during court appearances, and referrals to social service agencies.

Victim impact statement   A written document that describes the losses, suffering, and trauma experienced by the crime victim or by the victim's survivors. Judges are expected to consider these effects in arriving at an appropriate sentence for the offender.

Box 4.4 VICTIM IMPACT STATEMENT

In November 1999, Elaine Rose Cece, 41, and Barbara Taylor, 31, were found guilty of first- degree murder in the August 4, 1998, slaying of Toronto police constable William Hancox. The following is an excerpt from the transcript of the victim impact statement submitted by Kim Hancox, wife of the murdered officer.

I have attempted to write this victim impact statement several times and each time had to give up in fear of returning to a place in my life that I may not be able to escape from again. In order to relate to anyone the experience I have been through and continue to go through on a daily basis requires me to journey into the very depths of my existence, a dark, lonely and truly horrifying place. It has taken me over a year to be able to control, to some degree, the haunting capabilities of that place which eats away at my soul day and night. The images of my husband, my best friend, my soulmate, the father of my children, being savagely attacked with a butcher knife. The very look of horror that I imagine being on his face, a look of sheer terror and helplessness. . . .

What were his thoughts, were they only thoughts of survival or were they thoughts of never seeing his daughter again, never seeing his new baby, never seeing me? Did he struggle in vain to stay alive, knowing that to be left without him would break me into pieces? I walk through these images daily whether I

want to or not and even put myself in the passenger's seat of his van so he doesn't have to die alone. . . .

The completely selfish act of two people has not only left my husband dead, it has left me on the brink of insanity, struggling only to survive to the next day. I was in a wonderful spot in my life, married to a man I simply adored, with a beautiful daughter who was a mirror image of her father, and expecting another child. All that was reduced to an existence where I just get up and remember to breathe. . . .

My daughter will never have that golf lesson with her dad. My son will never play that hockey game with his father. I will never be able to fill his shoes. I am learning to live without him, but it requires just settling with what life has dealt me rather than living every moment to the fullest. Nothing is the same. . . . I am not the same. Bill would be destroyed to know the suffering everyone has had to endure, and that is hard to live with.

I believe Bill was put on this earth just for me and me for him. We truly had a wonderful relationship. I try to appreciate that I was lucky enough to have true love in my life, even if it was for a short time. Some people never get it at all.

Source: Kim Hancox and *The Canadian Police Association Express.* Used with permission.

---

contend that they allow victims to have their say and feel involved in the criminal justice process, providing, for many, a cathartic emotional outlet.[41]

A number of other *Criminal Code* provisions are aimed at reducing the secondary victimization often experienced by people who appear as witnesses at trials. In order to protect the identity of victims, a trial judge may override the fundamental principle of justice that trials be public and issue an order to "exclude all or any members of the public from the courtroom for all or part of the proceedings" (s. 486(1)). Rarely done, this action is meant to allow for the "proper administration of justice" by allowing a victim or witness to testify free from stress or fear. These public-exclusion orders are most often used in cases involving child witnesses.

Additionally, section 486(3) states that judges can order "the identity of the complainant or of a witness and any information that could disclose the identity of the complainant or of a witness shall not be published in any document or broadcast in any way." These publication bans can be imposed in specific types of cases only, such as those involving sexual assault, incest, extortion, or a sexual offence involving children. Contravention of a publication ban is a summary conviction offence. Subsections 276.2 and 276.3 restrict the publication of proceedings to determine the admissibility of evidence regarding a sexual assault complainant's sexual history.

Other provisions intended to facilitate the participation of witnesses include subsection 486(1.2), which permits a support person to be present in court with a witness under the age of 14 in sexual-offence proceedings, and subsection 486(2.1), which permits a sexual offence complainant who is under the age of 18 to provide his or her testimony from behind a screen or by closed-circuit television. This provision has recently been expanded to include victims and witnesses in prostitution and assault cases. Subsection 715.1 permits, as evidence, a videotaped version of a witness's testimony in proceedings relating to sexual offences where the victim or witness was under the age of 18 at the time of the offence.

Victims and Corrections   Victim involvement with the criminal justice system often continues after the offender is convicted and sentenced. The federal *Corrections and Conditional Release Act* (CCRA), for example, outlines the role of the victim in the parole process. In addition to those victims' rights highlighted in Box 4.5, the victim and/or any other interested party may attend a parole hearing, provided a written

---

Box 4.5 VICTIMS' RIGHTS AND THE CORRECTIONAL PROCESS

How do victims receive information about the offenders who harmed them?

To receive information about an offender, a victim must request it in writing from Correctional Services Canada (CSC) or the National Parole Board (NPB). This is commonly known as "registering." A victim can contact CSC by telephone; however, in order to confirm registration, a victim must submit a written request or complete and sign an *Information Request for Victims Form* to CSC or NPB. A person can register as a victim or authorize someone else in writing to act as his or her representative.

Is the offender notified when a victim registers?

No. Offenders do not have the right to be notified when a victim registers with the CSC or the NPB for victim notification.

Do victims have to receive information directly?

No. If victims do not want to receive information directly, they can appoint in writing a representative or agent to receive the information on their behalf.

Does a victim's registration ever expire?

Registration for victim notification does not expire. The file may be inactivated if any of the following situations occur:

■ The offender's sentence expires. However, if the offender receives a subsequent federal sentence, the victim will be notified and asked if he or she wants to receive ongoing notification again.

■ The victim advises the NPB or CSC that he or she no longer wants to receive victim notification.

>

- The offender dies while incarcerated or under CSC supervision in the community.

Can victims request no contact from an offender?

Yes. Victims can request that an offender have no contact with them at various times during the criminal justice process.

Can victims share the impact of the crime with CSC or NPB?

Yes. CSC and NPB encourage victims to provide a Victim Statement describing the impact of the crime on their lives and/or other information related to the correctional and conditional release process.

CSC uses victim information in

- Deciding the offender's institutional security level;
- Recommendations to the NPB about whether the offender should be granted conditional release and what special conditions, if any, should be placed on the offender;
- Decisions about whether the offender should be released on a temporary absence or a work release; and
- Evaluations of the offender's programming needs and overall risk of reoffending.

NPB uses victim information in

- Decisions with respect to community releases (UTA, day parole, full parole, statutory release) that may or may not have special conditions imposed.
- Personal information about a victim, such as address and telephone number, will *not* be made available to the offender. However, the law requires that CSC and NPB

disclose to offenders any information that will be considered when they make decisions on such things as an offender's parole application, conditions of release, etc.

- Victims can submit a victim statement anytime during the correctional process. However, to present a victim statement at a National Parole Hearing, victims must complete and sign a *Request to Present a Victim Statement at a Hearing Form* and submit it to the NPB.

Can a victim find out about the institution where the offender is placed?

Yes. Victims can find out more about CSC institutions on the Regions and Facilities page of CSC's website.

How is an offender released into the community?

CSC releases eligible federal offenders into the community under various types of conditional release: temporary absence, day parole, full parole, statutory release, or accelerated parole. In each case offenders are subject to strict monitoring and control. Conditions may include regular meetings with a parole officer, curfews, or drug testing.

Public safety is the number one consideration in all decisions related to an offender's release. If an offender's risk becomes unmanageable in the community, his or her release will be suspended, and in many cases, revoked by the NPB or conditions will be applied.

By law, CSC must release offenders who have reached the warrant expiry date of their sentence.

Source: Adapted from "Victim Services at CSC, Frequently Asked Questions," *Correctional Services Canada*, http://www.csc-scc.gc.ca/victims-victimes/faq-faq-eng.shtml [Accessed October 5, 2012].

---

request has been made in advance of the hearing. Victims must travel to the location of the hearing and absorb any associated costs. Written transcripts of the hearing are made available upon request to those victims who cannot attend a hearing. In addition, some provinces have adopted legislation and procedures allowing the victim to remain informed of changes in the status of incarcerated offenders. Amendments made to the CCRA in 2007 ensure that victims can receive advance notice and reasons for offender transfers to minimum security facilities or temporary absences from institutions, as well as information about offender program participation and any convictions for any serious disciplinary offences.

In British Columbia, the Victim Safety Unit of the Ministry of Justice operates an automated Victim Notification System. Victims can register to be notified of changes in the custody status of an offender. The notification system provides victims with a personal identification number to access such information about their cases.

System-Based Services This approach to the provision of assistance to victims emphasizes a system-based approach instead of one that is police- or Crown/court-based. It allows victims to receive all their services from one location so that they don't have to deal with various components of the system independently. Both Nova Scotia and Prince Edward Island have implemented the system-based model.

VICTIM RESTITUTION

Restitution A criminal sanction, in particular the payment of compensation by the offender to the victim.

THE VICTIMS' MOVEMENT HAS ALSO SPAWNED A REBIRTH OF THE CONCEPT OF restitution. **Restitution** is punishment through imposed responsibility—in particular, the payment of compensation to the victim. Restitution encompasses the notion that criminal offenders should shoulder at least a portion of the financial obligations required to make the victim whole again and places responsibility for the process back upon the offender who caused the loss of wholeness initially. Restitution, which works through court-imposed fines and garnishments, has many advocates who claim that it benefits society by leading to an increased sense of social and individual responsibility on the part of convicted offenders.

At one time in Canada, the responsibility for requesting restitution lay with the victim. Many who were not aware of this option failed to petition the court, and restitution was not ordered. Currently, a judge can unilaterally order restitution or do so at the request of the Crown; it can be so ordered as a stand-alone sentence or as part of another, such as a probation order or a conditional sentence. These types of sentences help ensure that beneficiaries of the restitution order receive payment. Failure to pay in either instance can lead to a breach of the sentence and incarceration. Beneficiaries can also use civil courts to enforce a restitution order.

A relatively recent addition to the *Criminal Code of Canada* has extended the use of restitution to criminal cases involving criminal injury. Subsection 738(1) allows a judge to impose a sentence of restitution to cover expenses to the victim relating to things such as loss of income or support, costly dental work, or physiotherapy expenses. In addition, in the case of an offence causing bodily harm to the offender's spouse or child in instances of family violence, this subsection allows restitution to be ordered for readily ascertainable

WHO'S RESPONSIBLE—THE INDIVIDUAL OR SOCIETY?

13-Year-Old Boy an Offender or a Victim?

In Ottawa in the mid-summer of 2009, a 13-year-old boy was arrested with four friends as they fled the third bank they had robbed that day. Not only was he charged with robbery but was also the only one in the group who faced weapons and obstructing police charges as well. How had he found himself in this place?

Not long after the boy was born, his mother moved in with a man who was violent. The boy was frequently beaten, tied to a pole in the basement and left in the dark for hours. The boy's mother was often whipped with a skipping rope and his 15-year-old sister was frequently woken at night by her stepfather's belt lashing her thighs. The boy's mother feared for her life and told no one of the abuse.

Forbidden to even speak at home, the boy took to stealing. He shoplifted toys from a department store before he was ten years old, he stole an MP3 player from his doctor's office, and then escalated to stealing a car from a construction site. The boy's sister describes him as "addicted to stealing." "He thinks stealing is going to make it better," she says.

When he began to disappear for days at a time, his mother placed her son in a group home from which he constantly ran away. In fact, he was missing from a group home in the days before the bank robberies.

His sister blames their stepfather for her brother's problems. While she is finishing high school and intending to go to university for nursing, her stepfather's treatment has left her timid and shy. "My brother listens to me," she says. "If he's out with me he doesn't get into trouble . . . He's got a lot of things in there different from everybody else. He needs someone to figure him out and get inside his head."

Think about it:

1. Is this young boy an offender or a victim? Why?

2. How should our criminal justice system treat youth like this young boy?

Source: Tony Spears, "Only 13, but in Trouble Once Again," *The Ottawa Citizen*, June 17, 2009, p. A1. Material reprinted with the express permission of Ottawa Citizen Group Inc., a CanWest Partnership.

expenses incurred by the victim as a result of moving out of the offender's household, for temporary housing, child care, food, and transportation.

Section 737 of the *Criminal Code of Canada* requires a **victim surcharge** to be automatically imposed in addition to any other sanction handed down to an offender convicted of an offence in the *Criminal Code* or the *Controlled Drugs and Substances Act*. The revenue raised by this surcharge remains in the province or territory where it is imposed and is to be used specifically to fund programs and initiatives providing assistance to victims of crime. This provision further stipulates that the maximum victim fine surcharge is 15 percent of any fine imposed or, where no fine is imposed, is not to exceed $50 for an offence punishable by summary conviction and $100 in the case of an offence punishable by indictment. The sentencing judge may waive the victim fine surcharge where the imposition of the surcharge would cause undue hardship. Most provinces and territories have also enacted legislation imposing a surcharge on provincial offences such as highway traffic violations. This revenue is also used to fund victim programs and services.

Victim surcharge A mandatory, judicial imposition of a monetary fine administered in addition to a criminal sentence and used to finance victim services.

FUTURE DIRECTIONS IN VICTIMOLOGY

INITIATIVES TAKEN BY THE FEDERAL AND PROVINCIAL GOVERNMENTS IN CANADA IN recent decades have done much to emphasize and highlight the rights and role of victims within our criminal justice system. However, despite this recognition, there is still concern that the needs of victims are not being fully met. A recent Department of Justice survey designed to gauge Canadians' level of public confidence in the criminal justice system concluded that "confidence in the criminal justice system is generally low compared to other public systems, such as health and education. The central concern appears to be around sentencing practices and the need for reparation, accountability and ultimately rehabilitation to prevent future criminal behaviour."[42] (See the Who's Responsible? box for a discussion of a case where victimization may have led to criminal behaviour.)

Indeed, some assert that the victims' movement has been adopted by governments to boost ratings and opinion polls and justify a platform of increased penalties for offenders as the primary way of recognizing victims' rights. Ezzat Fattah asserted, "Crime victims are not the first group whose cause is exploited by unpopular governments seeking a higher rating in public opinion polls, by opportunistic politicians seeking electoral votes, or by incompetent public officials trying to detract attention from their failure to control crime or reduce its incidence."[43] Others, such as Kent Roach, believe that there needs to be a fundamental structural change away from an adversarial approach to our criminal justice system and toward a restorative, victims-centred approach before victims' rights can be truly respected. Until that time, any recognition of victims' rights and roles in the criminal process cannot be considered as anything more than "window dressing," and the modern crime victim can be seen only as a participant who is "all dressed up with nowhere to go."[44]

Various victims' bills of rights state that victims should have access to information and notification of services, investigation, court progress, and the like, but no means of ensuring compliance with these requirements exists. Police and prosecutors are not legally obligated to ensure that victims are notified and may violate a bill of rights with impunity.

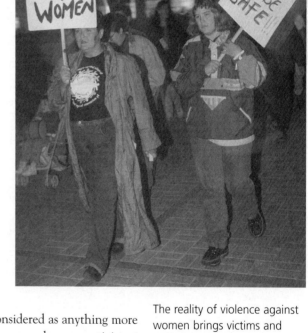

The reality of violence against women brings victims and their supporters together in Take Back the Night marches like this one. Do you think that there are currently sufficient services for victims of crime?

QMI Agency

Additionally, even if notification is given, the legislation does not allow a victim's role in the process to override that of the prosecution. In other words, delays or stays of prosecutions and plea-bargaining decisions all remain at the discretion of the Crown and can be made without victim notification or involvement. Much of the victims' rights legislation does not include language that mandates the right of victims to participate in the proceedings. For example, many require that victims' views be heard only insofar as it is "appropriate and consistent with criminal law and procedure."[45] Finally, while victims of crime are now provided with a wide range of legal rights, most legislation still does not provide for legal representation to ensure that these rights are exercised.

Irvin Waller, a leading Canadian academic, advocate in the field of victimology, and president of the International Organization for Victims' Assistance, suggested that much of what is needed to support victims of crime has already been agreed upon through the international recognition of the Declaration on Basic Principles of Justice for Victims of Crime and Abuse of Power, adopted by the General Assembly of the United Nations in 1985. Waller stated that "there is much rhetoric on doing justice and support for victims. Indeed there are often laws and a patchwork of services to implement those laws. But much needs to be done to make support services universal, to get restitution paid, and to provide equitable compensation." He went on to contend that

> it is time in legal systems such as that in New Zealand or Canada to move beyond token victim impact statements or restorative justice processes which do not guarantee victims' participation. By combining the criminal and civil jurisdictions in one court process, we would enable victims to have standing to defend their personal interests in their safety, reparation and truth.[46]

The struggle to recognize crime victims' needs and rights continues. There is no doubt that victims have been left out of the criminal process for too long. Governments at all levels have formally acknowledged this. Waller contended that the time is now for all nations to adopt domestic legislation for victims that clearly

- defines a victim of crime,
- makes a commitment to the reduction of victimization,
- provides for access to justice and fair treatment for victims of crime, protection of victims, witnesses and experts, information, assistance, restorative justice, restitution and compensation, and
- sets out how to ensure implementation and monitoring.[47]

SUMMARY OF LEARNING OBJECTIVES

4.1 Just as criminals have been studied to determine what kinds of social and personal experiences they have, so too have criminologists advocated close scrutiny of victims. The emergence of a formal study of the dynamics of victimization in the 1950s and 1960s is known as victimology. The role that victims play in the criminal event has been defined as victim-proneness and victimogenesis, while lifestyle and routine activities of victims have been seen to contribute to whether or not victimization occurs. Victimization brings with it significant psychological and in some cases physical challenges.

4.2 The Code of Hammurabi (circa 1750 BC) required that many offenders make restitution. By the late Middle Ages, the concept of "King's Peace" had emerged, wherein all offences were seen as violations of imperial law. The situation remained largely unchanged until the 20th century. The emerging discipline of victimology was focused on the strengthening of the victims' rights movement. A focus on the role of the victim in the formal criminal justice process took hold in Canada in the late 1980s and early 1990s.

4.3 Provincial and federal governments in Canada have enacted legislation to recognize and support victims' rights, services, and programs. A Canadian Statement of Basic Principles of Justice for Victims and individual provincial victims' bills of rights are meant to enshrine these rights. Current services for victims of crime are made available in conjunction with police, the Crown/courts, and correctional services across the country.

4.4 Restitution is a criminal sanction, in particular the payment of compensation by the offender to the victim. Restitution works through court-imposed fines and garnishments. A judge can unilaterally order restitution or do so at the request of the Crown; restitution can be so ordered as a stand-alone sentence or as part of another, such as a probation order or a conditional sentence.

4.5 Questions continue to be asked about the needs of victims, the impact of the criminal justice process on the well-being of victims, the role of the victim in the justice process, and whether our current criminal justice structure ensures the true participation of victims.

Questions for Review

1. What are some of the realities of victimization? What is meant by *secondary victimization*?
2. What is the difference between the *punitive* victims' rights model and the *non-punitive* victims' rights model as described by Kent Roach?
3. What are some of the existing services for victims of crime? Do you think they adequately address the concerns of victims?
4. What is the purpose of victim restitution? Does restitution benefit society? Why or why not?
5. Should the role of victims in the criminal process be changed from its current status? Can our current adversarial approach to justice ever allow this to happen? Explain your position.

Multiple-Choice Questions

1. _____ is generally credited with creating the terms *victimology* and *penal couple*.
   a. Henry Ellenberger
   b. Ezzat Fattah
   c. Margaret Fry
   d. Hans von Hentig
   e. Benjamin Mendelsohn

2. _____ counsel(s) victims, orient(s) them to the justice process, and provide(s) a variety of other services such as transportation to court, child care during court appearances, and referrals to social service agencies.
   a. Victimogenesis
   b. Victim impact statements
   c. Victim/witness assistance programs
   d. Victim crisis and referral services
   e. Victims' Bill of Rights

3. The offender is directly involved in victim _____ programs.
   a. compensation
   b. impact
   c. assistance
   d. witness
   e. restitution

4. _____ describe(s) the consequences of a crime from the perspective of the victim or the victim's survivors.
   a. Victim impact statements
   b. Victim/witness assistance programs
   c. Social process theories
   d. Cohort analysis
   e. Victim Crisis and Referral Service

5. According to the most recent General Social Survey in Canada, _____ are at the greatest risk of victimization.
   a. married individuals
   b. mentally ill individuals
   c. those with the highest household income
   d. those who are single
   e. those who are employed

Multiple Choice Answers: 1e, 2c, 3e, 4a, 5d

Chapter 5

Classical and Neoclassical Thought

David Levenson/Alamy

*The more promptly and the more closely punishment follows upon the
commission of a crime, the more just and useful will it be.*

—*Cesare Beccaria*[1]

LEARNING OBJECTIVES

After reading this chapter, you should be able to

5.1 Discuss the major principles of the classical school of criminology.

5.2 Name some of the forerunners of classical thought in criminology and explain
the relevance of the history of criminology and its early thinkers to current
views of crime and criminality.

5.3 List some important thinkers of the classical school of criminology and understand what heritage their way of thinking provides.

5.4 Define neoclassical criminology and describe how it differs from the classical
perspective.

5.5 Explain the role of punishment in neoclassical criminology.

5.6 Discuss the policy implications of the classical school.

5.7 Assess the shortcomings of the classical approach.

INTRODUCTION

The Canadian criminal justice system plays a balancing act between upholding and protecting the rights of each individual Canadian as enshrined in the *Charter of Rights and Freedoms* and upholding and protecting the collective rights of Canadian society as a whole as embodied in the *Criminal Code* and other statutes. A landmark incident in Canadian jurisprudence illustrates this challenge. On April 10, 1995, Canada Customs officials seized and confiscated computer disks from John Robin Sharpe that contained a text authored by Sharpe and entitled, "Sam Paloc's Flogging, Fun, and Fortitude—A Collection of Kiddiekink Classics." Sharpe was charged with simple possession of child pornography contrary to section 163.1(4) of the *Criminal Code of Canada* and possession of child pornography for the purpose of distribution and sale, contrary to section 163.1(3). Thirteen months later police again charged Sharpe under sections 163.1(4) and 163.1(3) after confiscating a collection of books, manuscripts, stories, and photographs depicting child pornography from his home near Surrey, British Columbia.

At trial, Sharpe argued that section 163.1(4) infringed upon his individual freedoms, especially his freedom of expression guaranteed and protected under section 2(b) of the *Canadian Charter of Rights and Freedoms* since many of the articles seized were written or drawn by him. The trial judge, Justice Duncan Shaw, accepted this submission, finding section 163.1(4) to be unconstitutional. Sharpe was acquitted on the counts of possession. The Crown appealed the court's ruling to the British Columbia Court of Appeal, where it was dismissed. An appeal to the Supreme Court of Canada was heard in early 2001. In a unanimous decision, the Supreme Court upheld the sections of the *Criminal Code* restricting the possession of child pornography; however, the Court remained split as to whether there should be exceptions based on freedom of expression. In a 6–3 ruling, the Supreme Court ruled that people can't be prosecuted for creating photographic or written material intended solely for their own use as long as real pictures or videos do not show illegal acts.

In 2002, Sharpe returned to court to face the original charges of possession and distribution of child pornography. Sharpe admitted guilt to the possession of pornographic pictures of children but was found not guilty of possessing or distributing written child pornography. He was sentenced to a four-month conditional sentence of house arrest.

The Sharpe case ignited public controversy across the nation. Those who opposed the courts' decisions protested that the protection of an individual's right to freedom of expression should not come at the expense of public safety, especially that of children. Child advocacy groups such as Alliance for the Rights of Children and Beyond Borders were concerned that the Supreme Court ruling created a loophole for pedophiles. They argued that literature of the type possessed by Sharpe ignores the rights of children and serves to sexually excite pedophiles and romanticize violent acts against children. Others, like the Canadian Civil Liberties Association (CCLA), believed that the Sharpe case highlighted concerns about Canadians' freedom to write, draw, or imagine anything they want. The CCLA cited the case of Toronto artist Eli Langer, who was charged with having created "child pornography" because of a number of drawings he had on display in an art gallery that depicted youngsters in sexual situations. The charges were ultimately withdrawn and Langer's work was deemed by the court to have "artistic merit." In this case, as in Sharpe's, the constitutionality of the child pornography law was upheld; the CCLA contended that legitimate artists who deal with such subject matter will continue to risk criminal charges. Indeed, the CCLA pointed out, those parents who take and keep photographs of their nude babies run a similar risk.

The controversy sparked by the Sharpe case is an excellent example of the debate between individual rights versus the collective rights of Canadians. Some argue that an overemphasis on individual rights comes at the expense of the rights of the group. Others fear that the erosion of individual rights may make the state too powerful. This debate has roots in the Enlightenment and the emergence of the classical school of criminology, both of which are discussed in this chapter.

MAJOR PRINCIPLES OF THE CLASSICAL SCHOOL

5.1 LEARNING OBJECTIVE

THIS BRIEF SECTION SUMMARIZES THE CENTRAL FEATURES OF THE CLASSICAL school of criminological thought. Each of the points listed in this discussion can be found elsewhere in this chapter; this overview is intended to provide a summation and to be a guide to the rest of this chapter (see Table 5.1).

✳–⎡**Explore**

The Classical School of Thought in Criminology

◉–⎡**Watch**

Basic Principles of the Classical Perspective

Most classical theories of crime causation make the following basic assumptions:

- Human beings are fundamentally rational, and most human behaviour is the result of free will coupled with rational choice.

- Pain and pleasure are the two central determinants of human behaviour.

- Punishment, a necessary evil, is sometimes required to deter law violators and to serve as an example to others who would also violate the law.

- Root principles of right and wrong are inherent in the nature of things and cannot be denied.

- Society exists to provide benefits to individuals that they would not receive in isolation.

- When men and women band together for the protection offered by society, they forfeit some of the benefits that accrue from living in isolation.

- Certain key rights of individuals are inherent in the nature of things, and governments that contravene those rights should be disbanded.

- Crime disparages the quality of the bond that exists between individuals and society and is therefore an immoral form of behaviour.

FORERUNNERS OF CLASSICAL THOUGHT

5.2 LEARNING OBJECTIVE

THE NOTION OF CRIME AS A VIOLATION OF ESTABLISHED LAW DID NOT EXIST IN MOST primitive societies. Lack of lawmaking bodies, absence of formal written laws, and loose social bonds precluded the concept of crime as law violation, but all human societies from the simplest to the most advanced did evidence their own widely held notions of right and wrong.

Table 5.1	The Classical School and Neoclassical Thinkers	
Theory	**Classical Criminology**	**Neoclassical Criminology**
Period	1700s–1880s	1970s–present
Theorists	Cesare Becarria, Jeremy Bentham, and others	Lawrence Cohen, Marcus Felson, Ronald V. Clarke, Derek B. Cornish, and others
Concepts	Free will, deterrence through punishment, social contract, natural law, due process, Panopticon	Rational choice, routine activities, capable guardians, situational crime prevention, just deserts, determinate sentencing, specific deterrence, general deterrence

Sociologists term such fundamental concepts of morality and propriety as *mores* and *folkways*. *Mores*, *folkways*, and *law* were terms used by William Graham Sumner to describe the three basic forms of behavioural strictures imposed by social groups upon their members.[2] Mores and folkways govern behaviour in relatively small primitive societies, whereas in large complex societies, they are reinforced and formalized through written laws.

Mores consist of proscriptions covering potentially serious violations of a group's values (for example, murder, sexual assault, and robbery). **Folkways** are time-honoured customs; although they carry the force of tradition, their violation is less likely to threaten the survival of the social group. The fact that North American men have traditionally worn little jewellery illustrates a folkway that has given way in recent years to various types of male adornment, including earrings, gold chains, and even makeup. Mores and folkways, although they may be powerful determinants of behaviour, are nonetheless informal, because only laws have been codified into formal strictures wielded by institutions and created specifically for enforcement purposes.

Another method of categorizing socially proscriptive rules is provided by some criminologists who divide crimes into the dual categories of *mala in se* and *mala prohibita*. Acts that are **mala in se** are said to be fundamentally wrong, regardless of the time or place in which they occur (for example, forcing someone to have sex against his or her will and the intentional killing of children). Those who argue for the existence of *mala in se* offences usually point to some fundamental rule, such as religious teachings (the Bible's Ten Commandments, the Koran, etc.), to support their belief that some acts are inherently wrong.

Offences termed **mala prohibita** offences are said to be wrong in areas where they are prohibited (for example, prostitution, gambling, drug use, and premarital sexual behaviour). The status of such behaviours as *mala prohibita* is supported by the fact that they are not necessarily crimes in every jurisdiction; gambling, for example, is legal in parts of Canada, mainly because of the huge revenue potential it holds.

The Demonic Era

Since time began, humankind has been preoccupied with what appears to be an ongoing war between good and evil. Oftentimes evil has appeared in impersonal guise, as when the great bubonic plague (the "Black Death"), ravaged Europe and Asia in the 14th century, leaving as much as three-quarters of the population dead in a mere span of 20 years. At other times, evil has seemed to wear a human face, as when the Nazi Holocaust claimed millions of Jewish lives during World War II.

Whatever its manifestation, the very presence of evil in the world has begged for interpretation, and sage minds throughout human history have advanced many explanations for the evil conditions that individuals and social groups have at times been forced to endure. Some forms of evil, such as the plague and the Holocaust, appear cosmically based, whereas others—including personal victimization, criminality, and singular instances of deviance—are the undeniable result of individual behaviour. Cosmic-level evil has been explained by ideas as diverse as divine punishment, karma, fate, and the vengeful activities of offended gods. Early explanations of personal deviance ranged from demonic possession to spiritual influences to temptation by fallen angels.

Early Sources of the Criminal Law

The Code of Hammurabi
Modern criminal law is the result of a long evolution of legal principles. The Code of Hammurabi is one of the first known bodies of law to survive for study today. King Hammurabi ruled the ancient city of Babylon from 1792 to 1750 BC and created a legal code consisting of strictures that were originally intended to establish

Mores Behavioural proscriptions covering potentially serious violations of a group's values. Examples might include strictures against murder, sexual assault, and robbery.

Folkways Time-honoured customs. Although folkways carry the force of tradition, their violation is unlikely to threaten the survival of the group.

Mala in se An act thought to be wrong in and of itself.

Mala prohibita An act that is wrong only because it is prohibited.

property and other rights and that were crucial to the continued growth of Babylon as a significant commercial centre. Hammurabi's law spoke to issues of theft, property ownership, sexual relationships, and interpersonal violence. Well-known criminologist Marvin Wolfgang observed, "In its day, 1700 BC, the Hammurabi Code, with its emphasis on **retribution**, amounted to a brilliant advance in penal philosophy mainly because it represented an attempt to keep cruelty within bounds."[3] Prior to the code, captured offenders often faced the most barbarous retribution, frequently at the hands of revenge-seeking victims, no matter how minor their transgressions had been.

Early Roman Law

Of considerable significance for our own legal tradition is early Roman law. Roman legions under Emperor Claudius I (10 BC–AD 54) conquered England in the middle of the first century, and Roman customs, law, and language were forced upon the English population during the succeeding three centuries under the Pax Romana—a peace imposed by the military might of Rome.[4]

Early Roman law derived from the **Twelve Tables**, a collection of basic rules regulating family, religious, and economic life written around 450 BC. They appear to have been based on common and fair practices generally accepted among early tribes that existed prior to the establishment of the Roman Republic; only fragments of the tables survive today.

The best-known legal period in Roman history occurred during the reign of Emperor Justinian I (AD 527–565). By the end of the 6th century, the Roman Empire had declined substantially in size and influence and was near the end of its life. Possibly to preserve Roman values and traditions, Justinian undertook the laborious process of distilling Roman laws into a set of writings. The Justinian Code, as these writings came to be known, actually consisted of three lengthy legal documents—the Institutes, the Digest, and the Code itself—and distinguished between two major legal categories: public and private laws. Public laws dealt with the organization of the Roman state, its Senate, and governmental offices. Private law concerned itself with contracts, personal possessions, the legal status of various types of persons (citizens, free people, slaves, freedmen, guardians, husbands and wives), and injuries to citizens. It contained elements of our modern civil and criminal law and influenced Western legal thought through the Middle Ages.

Common Law

Common law refers to a traditional body of unwritten legal precedents created through everyday practice in English society. It was based on shared traditions and standards and was supported by court decisions during the Middle Ages. As novel situations arose and were handled by British justices, their declarations became the start for any similar future deliberation.

Common law was given considerable legitimacy in the 11th century with the official declaration by the English king Edward the Confessor (AD 1042–1066) that it was the law of the land. The authority of common law was further reinforced by the decision of William the Conqueror to use popular customs as the basis for judicial action following his subjugation of Britain in 1066.

Eventually, court decisions were recorded and made available to barristers (English trial lawyers) and judges. As criminologist Howard Abadinsky wrote, "Common law involved the transformation of community rules into a national legal system. The controlling element [was] precedent."[5] Today, common law forms the basis for much of our statutory and case law and has been called the major source of modern criminal law in English-speaking countries around the world.

The Magna Carta

The Magna Carta (literally, "great charter"), another important source of modern laws and legal procedure, was signed on June 15, 1215, by King John of England at Runnymede, under pressure from British barons who took advantage of his military defeats to demand a pledge to respect their traditional rights and to be bound by law. At the time of its signing, the Magna Carta (63 chapters in length) was little more than a feudal document listing specific royal concessions.[6] Its original purposes were to ensure

The Magna Carta, an important source of modern Western laws and legal procedure. What are some other important sources of modern criminal law?

Bettmann/Corbis

feudal rights, to guarantee that the king would not encroach on the landowning barons' privileges, and to ensure respect for the customs of towns.

Its wording, however, was later interpreted during a judicial revolt in 1613 to support individual rights and jury trials. Sir Edward Coke, chief justice under James I, held that the Magna Carta guaranteed basic liberties for all British citizens and ruled that any acts of Parliament that contravened common law would be void.[7] Section 7 of the *Canadian Charter of Rights and Freedoms* assures this fundamental right for Canadians today. Similarly, a specific provision of the Magna Carta, designed originally to prohibit the king from prosecuting the barons without just cause, was expanded into the concept of due process of law, a cornerstone of modern legal procedure. Because of these later interpretations, the Magna Carta has been called "the foundation stone of our present liberties."[8]

The Enlightenment

The Enlightenment A social movement that arose during the late 17th and 18th centuries and built upon ideas such as empiricism, rationality, free will, humanism, and natural law.

The Enlightenment (or the Age of Reason), a highly significant social movement that occurred during the late 17th and 18th centuries, was built upon ideas developed by many important thinkers. Because of their indirect contributions to classical criminological thought, it is worthwhile to briefly discuss the writings of a few of these historical figures.

Thomas Hobbes The English philosopher Thomas Hobbes (1588–1679) developed what many writers regard as an extremely negative view of human nature and social life, which he described in his momentous work, *Leviathan* (1651). Fear of violent death, he said, forces human beings into a **social contract** with one another to create a state that demands the surrender of certain natural rights and submission to the absolute authority of a sovereign while offering protection and succour to its citizens. The social contract concept significantly influenced many of Hobbes's contemporaries, but much of his writing was condemned for assuming an overly pessimistic view of both human nature and existing governments.

Social contract The Enlightenment-era concept that human beings abandon their natural state of individual freedom to join together and form society. Although in the process of forming a social contract individuals surrender some freedoms to society as a whole, government, once formed, is obligated to assume responsibilities toward its citizens and to provide for their protection and welfare.

John Locke In 1690, the English philosopher John Locke (1632–1704) published his *Essay Concerning Human Understanding*, in which he put forth the idea that the natural human condition at birth is akin to that of a blank slate upon which interpersonal encounters and other experiences indelibly inscribe the traits of personality. In contrast to earlier thinkers, who assumed that people are born with certain innate propensities and even rudimentary intellectual concepts and ideas, Locke ascribed the bulk of adult human qualities to life experiences.

In the area of social and political thought, Locke further developed the Hobbesian notion of the social contract and contended that human beings, through a social contract, abandon their natural state of individual freedom and lack of interpersonal responsibility to join together and form society. Although individuals surrender some freedoms to society, government, once formed, is obligated to assume responsibilities toward its citizens, to provide for their protection and welfare, and to guarantee them certain inalienable rights such as the right to life, health, liberty, and possessions. A product of his times, during which the dictatorial nature of monarchies and the Roman church were being much disparaged, Locke stressed the duties that governments have toward their citizens while paying very little attention to the responsibilities of individuals to the societies of which they are a part, and he argued that political revolutions, under some circumstances, might become an obligation incumbent upon citizens.

Locke also developed the notion of checks and balances between divisions of government, a doctrine elaborated on by French jurist and political philosopher Charles Louis de Secondat Montesquieu (1689–1755). In *The Spirit of Laws* (1748), Montesquieu wove Locke's notions into the concept of a separation of powers between divisions of government. The Canadian parliamentary system is based on these very principles.

Jean-Jacques Rousseau   Swiss-French philosopher and political theorist Jean-Jacques Rousseau (1712–1778) further advanced the notion of the social contract in his treatise of that name (*Social Contract*, 1762), stating that human beings are basically good and fair in their natural state, but historically were corrupted by the introduction of shared concepts and joint activities such as property, agriculture, science, and commerce. As a result, the social contract emerged when civilized people agreed to establish governments and systems of education to correct the problems and inequalities brought on by the rise of civilization.

Rousseau also contributed to the notion of **natural law**, a concept originally formulated by St. Thomas Aquinas (1225–1274), Baruch Spinoza (1632–1677), and others to provide an intuitive basis for the defence of ethical principles and morality. Natural law was used by early Christian church leaders as a powerful argument in support of their interests. Submissive to the authority of the church, secular rulers were pressed to reinforce church doctrine in any laws they decreed. Thomas Aquinas wrote in his *Summa Theologica* that any human-made law that contradicts natural law is corrupt in the eyes of God. Hence, natural law was incorporated into English common law throughout the Middle Ages.

Rousseau agreed with earlier writers that certain immutable laws are fundamental to human nature and can be readily ascertained through reason. Human-made law (or "positive law"), in contrast, derives from human experience and history, both of which are subject to continual change, and thus changes from time to time and from epoch to epoch. Rousseau expanded the concept of natural law to support emerging democratic principles.

Natural law   The philosophical perspective that certain immutable laws are fundamental to human nature and can be readily ascertained through reason. Human-made laws, in contrast, are said to derive from human experience and history—both of which are subject to continual change.

Thomas Paine   Thomas Paine (1737–1809), an English-American political theorist and author of *The Rights of Man* (1791 and 1792), defended the French Revolution, arguing that only democratic institutions could guarantee individuals' **natural rights**. For example, commentators have cited the "crimes against humanity" committed by Nazis during World War II as indicative of natural law principles. The chilling testimony of Rudolf Hess,[9] Hitler's deputy, during the 1945 war crimes trial in Nuremberg, Germany, as he recalled the "Fuehrer's" order to exterminate millions of Jews indicates the extent of the planned "final solution":

Natural rights   Rights that, according to natural law theorists, individuals retain in the face of government action and interests.

> In the summer of 1941 I was summoned to Berlin to Reichsfuehrer SS Himmler to receive personal orders. He told me something to the effect—I do not remember the exact words—that the Fuehrer had given the order for a final solution of the Jewish question. We, the SS, must carry out that order. If it is not carried out now then the Jews will later on destroy the German people. He had chosen Auschwitz on account of its easy access by rail and also because the extensive site offered space for measures ensuring isolation.[10]

Who could argue against the premise, natural law supporters ask, that Hitler's final solution to the Jewish "problem" was inherently wrong?

Although the concept of natural law has waned somewhat in influence over the past half century, many people today still maintain that the basis for various existing criminal laws can be found in immutable moral principles or some other identifiable aspect of the natural order. Modern-day advocates of natural law claim that it comes from outside the social group and that it is knowable through some form of revelation, intuition, or prophecy.

The present debate over abortion is an example of modern-day use of natural law arguments to support both sides in the dispute. Those who oppose abortion (frequently called "pro-lifers" or "right-to-lifers") claim that an unborn fetus is a person, that he or she is entitled to all the protection we would give to any other living human being, and that such protection is basic and humane and lies in the natural relationship of one human being to another and within the relationship of a society to its children. Advocates of the present law (which allows abortion upon request under certain conditions) maintain that abortion is a "right" of any pregnant woman because she is the only one who should be in control of her body and claim that the legal system must address the abortion question by offering protection for this natural right.

5.3 | LEARNING OBJECTIVE

THE CLASSICAL SCHOOL

THE ENLIGHTENMENT FUELLED THE FIRES OF SOCIAL CHANGE, LEADING EVENTUALLY to the French and American revolutions. It also inspired other social movements and freed innovative thinkers from the chains of convention. As a direct consequence of Enlightenment thinking, superstitious beliefs were discarded and men and women began to be perceived, for the first time, as self-determining entities possessing a fundamental freedom of choice; free will and rational thought came to be recognized as the linchpins of all significant human activity. In effect, the Enlightenment inspired the re-examination of existing doctrines of human behaviour from the point of view of rationalism.

Classical school A criminological perspective of the late 18th and early 19th centuries that had its roots in the Enlightenment. It held that men and women are rational beings, that crime is the result of the exercise of free will, and that punishment can be effective in reducing the incidence of crime to the degree that it negates the pleasure to be derived from crime commission.

Within criminology, the Enlightenment led to the development of the **classical school** of criminological thought. Crime and deviance, which had been previously explained by reference to mythological influences and spiritual shortcomings, took their place in Enlightenment thought alongside other forms of human activity as products of the exercise of free will. Once people were seen as having control over their lives, crime came to be explained as a particularly individualized form of evil—that is, as a moral wrongdoing fed by personal choice.

👁—Watch

Cesare Beccaria

Cesare Beccaria

Cesare Beccaria (1738–1794) was born in Milan, Italy, the eldest of four children; he was trained at Catholic schools and earned a doctor of laws degree by the time he was 20. In 1764, Beccaria published his *Essay on Crimes and Punishments*, which consisted of 42 short chapters covering a few major themes to communicate his observations on the laws and justice system of his time. In the *Essay*, Beccaria distilled the notion of the social contract into the idea that "laws are the conditions under which independent and isolated men united to form a society."[11] More than anything else, his writings consisted of a philosophy of punishment. Beccaria claimed that the purpose of punishment should be deterrence rather than retribution, and punishment should be imposed to prevent offenders from committing additional crimes. Beccaria saw punishment as a means to an end and not an end in itself, and crime prevention was more important to him than revenge.

To help prevent crimes, Beccaria argued, adjudication and punishment should both be swift and, once punishment is decreed, certain: "The more promptly and the more closely punishment follows upon the commission of a crime, the more just and useful it will be." Punishment that is imposed immediately following crime commission, according to Beccaria, is connected with the wrongfulness of the offence, both in the mind of the offender and in the minds of others who might see the punishment imposed and thereby learn of the consequences of involvement in criminal activity.

Beccaria concluded that punishment should be only severe enough to outweigh the personal benefits to be derived from crime commission and that any additional punishment would be superfluous. "In order," he said, "for punishment not to be, in every instance, an act of violence of one or of many against a private citizen, it must be essentially public, prompt, necessary, the least possible in the given circumstances, proportionate to the crimes, [and] dictated by the laws."

Beccaria distinguished among three types of crimes: those that threatened the security of the state, those that injured citizens or their property, and those that ran contrary to the social order. According to Beccaria, punishment should fit the crime—theft should be punished through fines, personal injury through corporal punishment, and serious crimes against the state (such as inciting revolution) through the death penalty. (Beccaria was opposed to the death penalty in most other circumstances, seeing it as a kind of warfare waged by society against its citizens.)

Beccaria condemned the torture of suspects, a practice still used in the 18th century, saying that it was a device that ensured that weak suspects would incriminate themselves, while strong ones would be found innocent. Torture was also unjust because it punished individuals before they had been found guilty in a court of law. In Beccaria's words,

> No man can be called guilty before a judge has sentenced him, nor can society deprive him of public protection before it has been decided that he has in fact violated the conditions under which such protection was accorded him. What right is it then, if not simply that of might, which empowers a judge to inflict punishment on a citizen while doubt still remains as to his guilt or innocence?

Beccaria's *Essay* touched upon a variety of other topics. He distinguished, for example, between two types of proof: "perfect proof," where there was no possibility of innocence, and "imperfect proof," where some possibility of innocence remained. Beccaria also believed in the efficacy of a jury of one's peers, recommending that half of any jury panel consist of the victim's peers and half consist of the accused's peers.

Beccaria's ideas were widely recognized as progressive by his contemporaries. His principles were incorporated into the French penal code of 1791 and significantly influenced the justice-related activities of European leaders such as Catherine the Great of Russia, Frederick the Great of Prussia, Emperor Joseph II of Austria, and the framers of the American Constitution. Perhaps more than anyone else, Beccaria is responsible for the contemporary belief that criminals have control over their behaviour, that they choose to commit crimes, and that they can be deterred by the threat of punishment.

Jeremy Bentham

⊙ Watch

Jeremy Bentham

Jeremy Bentham (1748–1832), another founder of the classical school, wrote in his *Introduction to the Principles of Morals and Legislation* (1789) that "nature has placed mankind under the governance of two sovereign masters, pain and pleasure."[12] To reduce crime, or, as Bentham put it, "to prevent the happening of mischief," the pain of crime commission must outweigh the pleasure to be derived from criminal activity. Bentham's claim rested upon his belief, spawned by Enlightenment thought, that human beings are fundamentally rational and that criminals will weigh in their minds the pain of punishment against any pleasures thought likely to be derived from crime commission.

Bentham advocated neither extreme nor cruel punishment—only punishment sufficiently distasteful to the offender that the discomfort experienced would outweigh the pleasure to be derived from criminal activity. The more serious the offence is, the more reward it holds for its perpetrator and therefore the more weighty the official response must be. "Pain and pleasure," said Bentham, "are the instruments the legislator has to work with" in controlling anti-social and criminal behaviour.

Bentham's approach has been termed **hedonistic calculus** or **utilitarianism** because of its emphasis on the worth any action holds for an individual undertaking it. Bentham stated, "By the principle of utility is meant that principle which approves or disapproves of every action whatsoever, according to the tendency which it appears to have to augment or diminish the happiness of the party whose interest is in question; or, what is the same thing . . . to promote or to oppose that happiness." In other words, Bentham believed that individuals could be expected to weigh the consequences of their behaviour before acting to maximize their pleasure and minimize their pain, based on intensity, duration, certainty, and immediacy (or remoteness) in time.

Like Beccaria, Bentham focused on the potential held by punishment to prevent crime and to act as a deterrent for those considering criminal activity. Regarding criminal legislation, he wrote that "the evils of punishment must be made to exceed the advantage of the offence."

Utilitarianism is a practical philosophy, and Bentham was quite practical in his suggestions about crime prevention. He recommended the creation of a centralized police force focused on crime prevention and control—a recommendation that found life in the English *Metropolitan Police Act* of 1829, which established London's New Police under the direction of Sir Robert Peel. This model of policing was adopted in the creation of Canada's first national police force, the Dominion Police Force, in 1867.

Bentham's other major contribution to criminology was his suggestion that prisons be designed along the lines of what he called a "Panopticon House." The **Panopticon** was to be a circular building with cells along the circumference, each clearly visible from a central location staffed by guards. Panopticons were to be constructed near or within cities so that they might serve as an example to citizens of what would happen to them should they commit crimes. Bentham also wrote that prisons should be managed by contractors who could profit from the labour of prisoners and that the contractor should "be bound to insure the lives and safe custody of those entrusted to him." Although a Panopticon was never built

Hedonistic calculus or utilitarianism   The belief, first proposed by Jeremy Bentham, that behaviour holds value to any individual undertaking it according to the amount of pleasure or pain that it can be expected to produce for that person.

Panopticon   A prison designed by Jeremy Bentham that was to be a circular building with cells along the circumference, each clearly visible from a central location staffed by guards.

Jeremy Bentham (1748–1832), whose work is closely associated with the Classical School of criminology. What are the key features of the Classical School?

Bettmann/CORBIS

in Bentham's England, French officials funded a modified version of such a prison which was eventually built at Lyon, and three prisons modelled after the Panopticon concept were constructed in the United States.

Bentham's critics have been quick to point out that punishment often does not seem to work and that even punishment as severe as death appears not to have any effect on the incidence of crimes such as murder (discussed in greater detail later in this chapter). Such critics forget Bentham's second tenet: for punishment to be effective, "it must be swift and certain."

Heritage of the Classical School

The classical school was to influence criminological thinking for a long time and has been instrumental in moulding the way in which thinkers on the subject of crime have viewed the topic for more than 200 years. The heritage left by the classical school is still operative today in the following five principles:

1. *Rationality*: Human beings have free will and the actions they undertake are the result of choice.

2. *Hedonism*: Pleasure and pain, or reward and punishment, are the major determinants of choice.

3. *Punishment*: Criminal punishment is a deterrent to unlawful behaviour, and deterrence is the best justification for punishment.

4. *Human rights*: Society is made possible by individuals cooperating together. Hence, society owes to its citizens respect for their rights in the face of government action and for their autonomy insofar as such autonomy can be secured without endangering others or menacing the greater good.

5. *Due process*: An accused should be presumed innocent until proven otherwise, and an accused should not be subject to punishment before guilt is lawfully established.

Some of these concepts are easily recognizable in the *Canadian Charter of Rights and Freedoms*, the *Criminal Code of Canada*, and the *Youth Criminal Justice Act*.

NEOCLASSICAL CRIMINOLOGY

BY THE END OF THE 19TH CENTURY, CLASSICAL CRIMINOLOGY, WITH ITS EMPHASIS on free will and individual choice as the root causes of crime, had given way to another approach known as *positivism*. Positivism (discussed in greater detail in Chapter 6) made use of the scientific method in studying criminality and was based on an acceptance of **hard determinism**: the belief that crime results from forces beyond the control of the individual. The original positivists completely rejected the notion of free will and turned their attention to the impact of socialization, genetics, economic conditions, peer group influences, and other factors that might determine criminality. Acceptance of the notion of hard determinism implied that offenders were not entirely (if at all) responsible for their crimes and suggested that crime could be prevented by changing the conditions that produced criminality.

While positivism remains an important component of contemporary criminology, many of its assumptions were undermined in the 1970s by studies that seemed to show that offenders could not be rehabilitated no matter what was tried, a growing and widespread public fear of crime that led to "get tough on crime" policies, and a cultural reaffirmation of the belief that human beings had a rational nature. The resulting resurgence of classical ideals, called **neoclassical criminology**, focused on the importance of character (a kind of middle ground between total free will and hard determinism) and the dynamics of character

5.4 | **LEARNING OBJECTIVE**

◉ | **Watch**

Neoclassical Thought

Hard determinism   The belief that crime results from forces beyond the control of the individual.

Neoclassical criminology   A contemporary version of classical criminology that emphasizes deterrence and retribution, with reduced emphasis on rehabilitation.

development, as well as the rational choices that people make when faced with opportunities for crime.

The neoclassical movement appears to have had its start with a number of publications produced in the 1970s, such as Robert Martinson's national survey of rehabilitation programs. In an often-quoted article entitled *What Works?* Martinson found that, when it came to the rehabilitation of offenders, nothing seemed to work, as most resumed their criminal careers after release from prison.[13] "Nothing works!" became a rallying cry of conservative policymakers, and the nothing-works doctrine received much public attention. Many conservative politicians and some criminologists began calling existing notions of crime prevention and rehabilitation into question and claimed that enhanced job skills, increased opportunities for employment, and lessened punishment did nothing to stem what was a rising tide of crime.

In 1975, political scientist James Q. Wilson wrote *Thinking about Crime*, in which he suggested that crime is not a result of poverty or social conditions and cannot be affected by social programs.[14] He argued for the lengthy incarceration of offenders and for the elimination of criminal opportunity.

Rational Choice Theory

Rational choice theory, a product of the late 1970s and early 1980s, mirrors many of the principles found in classical criminology. The theory rests upon the belief that individuals make a conscious, rational, and at least partially informed choice to commit crime. It employs cost-benefit analysis (as in the field of economics), viewing human behaviour as the result of personal choices made after weighing both the costs and the benefits of available alternatives. "[Rational choice] predicts that individuals choose to commit crime when the benefits outweigh the costs of disobeying the law. Crime will decrease when opportunities are limited, benefits are reduced, and costs are increased."[15]

Two varieties of rational choice theory can be identified. One builds on an emerging emphasis on victimization and is called *routine activities theory*; the second, largely an extension of the rational choice perspective, is called *situational choice theory*.

Routine activities theory (also termed *lifestyle theory*) was proposed by Lawrence E. Cohen and Marcus Felson in 1979.[16] Cohen and Felson stated that lifestyles contribute significantly to both the volume and the type of crime found in any society and suggested that changes in American society during the 1960s and 1970s (specifically increased personal affluence and greater involvement in social activities outside the home) brought about increased rates of household theft and personal victimization by strangers. Central to the routine activities approach is the claim that crime is likely to occur when a motivated offender and a suitable victim come together in the absence of a "capable guardian," meaning one who effectively discourages crime, and that a person who has taken crime-prevention steps is less likely to be victimized. According to Cohen and Felson, "The risk of criminal victimization varies dramatically among the circumstances and locations in which people place themselves and their property."[17] For example, a person who routinely uses an automated teller machine late at night in an isolated location is far more likely to be preyed upon by robbers than is someone who stays home after dark. Lifestyles that contribute to criminal opportunities are likely to result in crime because they increase the risk of potential victimization.[18]

Although non-criminal lifestyles at a given point in one's lifetime are partly the result of unavoidable social roles and assigned social positions, those who participate in a given lifestyle generally make rational decisions about specific behaviours (such as going to a particular automated teller machine at a certain time). The same is true of criminal lifestyles. Hence, the meshing of choices made by both victims and criminals contributes significantly to both the frequency and the type of criminal activity observed in society.

Mapping Out Sex Crimes Arrest

An alleged sexual predator on the loose for a year was snared by geo-profiling.

Sex Crimes Unit investigators called upon D/Const Manny San Pedro, a geographic profiling analyst at Corporate Planning, to put his knowledge to work on a long series of occurrences involving a man exposing himself to children.

Over the course of a year, there had been 20 similar occurrences in North York and Scarborough, in which a man drove up to early-teen and preteen girls and exposed himself while in his vehicle.

"It had become an issue," said lead investigator Sex Crimes Unit Det. Kim Hancock, noting the man had been targeting young girls quite often. Area schools sent out notices to parents while police issued news releases.

"Escalation of his behaviour was a community concern." There was a partial licence plate, a description of the vehicle and a composite picture of the suspect but all efforts to identify and find him had yielded nothing.

After putting together his profile of coloured maps and graphs using the Rigel Analyst software, San Pedro was left with a 292 square-kilometre area, crisscrossed by highways 404 and 401, to find a place where the man would strike again. Two distinct areas where occurrences had occurred stood out. He identified a peak area of seven square kilometres.

Adding the schools in the area and a five-minute walking buffer around them for children walking home, he was left with a good target area for investigators.

"You identify the routine activity space for potential victims," he said, of looking for a future occurrence.

"By the offender's behaviour so far, he's likely to return to that area," said San Pedro, who also looked for times the offender struck when children were en route to and from school.

Because the case qualified as a sex crime and was more complex, San Pedro consulted with Ontario Provincial Police geoprofiler D/Sgt Brad Moore who offered his advice on the case.

San Pedro prescribed a one-month project, targeting the areas on specific days of the week at certain times of day, briefing officers from 33 and 41 Divisions where the crimes had taken place and handing them a geo-profile package.

"You could see the pattern, certain days and school hours," Hancock said. "Manny inputted all the information, got rid of the peripheral stuff and gave us an area to focus on."

Teams of officers were then dispatched to the roads San Pedro had highlighted as potential offender trolling areas.

Within 33 minutes of setting up on a driveway at a street, Consts. Jessica McInnis and Colleen Sweetnam, 41 Division's school liaison officers, saw a van matching the description pass them. They followed the van and eventually pulled

The mapping system shows hot spots where the suspect allegedly exposed himself to children.

THE BADGE, Newspaper at the Toronto Police Service

it over after the man is alleged to have driven for several blocks.

Hancock said the profile helped focus the search.

"It was wonderful," Hancock said, of the profile. "It helped focus us. We had officers driving around a bigger catchment area the week before."

The man is charged with invitation to sexual touching, criminal harassment and dangerous operation of a motor vehicle, four counts of exposure to person under 14 years, and 10 counts of indecent act.

"It's great to see we can net some good results," San Pedro said. "The analysts don't solve crimes, we provide investigative leads—it's all about the strategic deployment of resources so you're not wasting our efforts."

He said gathering more eyewitness accounts and other evidence makes the geo-mapping process more powerful because it thrives off information. He said the open lines of communication between himself and Sex Crimes investigators helped a great deal.

"It's not an exact science— it's based on probabilities," said San Pedro. "What I do is not evidence; it's up to investigators to collect that. I provide leads to assist detectives with investigative strategies."

Discussion Questions

1. How is the practice of geographic profiling supported by the routine activities theory?

2. Are there any other theories that would support this police practice?

Source: "Mapping Out Sex Crimes Arrest", *The Badge, The Newspaper of the Toronto Police Service*, January 2007, http://www.ecricanada.com/wp-content/themes/arjuna-x/images/TPS200701pg01.pdf. Reprinted with permission from Toronto Police Service.

See the Crime in the News box for an examination of a Canadian geographic profiling system used to track down criminals that is based on this notion of routine activities.

In a later work, Felson suggested that a number of "situational insights" might combine to elicit a criminal response from individual actors enmeshed in a highly varied social world, pointing out that "individuals vary greatly in their behaviour from one situation to another" and that criminality might flow from temptation, bad company, idleness, or provocation.[19] Convenience stores, for example, create temptations toward theft when they display their merchandise within easy reach of customers. Other authors have defined the term *situation* to mean "the perceptive field of the individual at a given point in time" and have suggested that it "can be described in terms of who is there, what is going on, and where it is taking place."[20]

Situational choice theory provides an example of **soft determinism**, which views criminal behaviour "as a function of choices and decisions made within a context of situational constraints and opportunities."[21] The theory suggests that the probability of criminal activity can be reduced by changing the features of a given social situation or of the surrounding environment. Ronald V. Clarke and Derek B. Cornish, collaborators in the development of the situational choice perspective, analyzed the choice-structuring properties of a potentially criminal situation, defining them as "the constellation of opportunities, costs, and benefits attaching to particular kinds of crime."[22] Clarke and Cornish suggested the use of situational strategies to lower the likelihood of criminal victimization in given instances. They also recognized that the rationality of criminal offenders is inevitably bounded or limited, as it is for all of us, by the amount and accuracy of information available to them at the time they are weighing the costs and consequences of future actions.[23]

In brief, rational choice theorists concentrate on "the decision-making process of offenders confronted with specific contexts . . . [shifting] the focus of the effort to prevent crime from broad social programs to target hardening, environmental design or any impediment that would [dissuade] a motivated offender from offending."[24]

Earlier approaches focused largely on the balance between pleasure and pain as the primary determinant or preventative of criminal behaviour, whereas rational choice theory tends to place less emphasis on pleasure and emotionality and more on rationality and cognition. Some rational choice theorists distinguish among the types of choices offenders make as they move toward criminal involvement. One type of choice, known as *involvement decisions*, has been described as "multi-stage" and is said to "include the initial decision to engage in criminal activity as well as subsequent decisions to continue one's involvement or to desist."[25] Another type of choice, *event decisions*, relates to particular instances of criminal opportunity (such as the decision to rob a particular person or to let him or her pass); in contrast to involvement decisions, which may take months or even years to reach, these are usually made quickly.

Situational Crime-Control Policy

Building on the work of rational and situational choice theorists, Israeli criminologist David Weisburd described the advantages of a situational approach to crime prevention:

> Crime prevention research and policy have traditionally been concerned with offenders or potential offenders. Researchers have looked to define strategies that would deter individuals from involvement in crime or rehabilitate them so they would no longer want to commit criminal acts. In recent years crime prevention efforts have often focused on the incapacitation of high-rate or dangerous offenders so they are not free to victimize law-abiding citizens. In the public debate over crime prevention policies, these strategies are usually defined as competing approaches.[26]

However, Weisburd pointed out that "they have in common a central assumption about crime prevention research and policy: that efforts to understand and control crime must begin with the offender. In all of these approaches, the focus of crime prevention is on people and their involvement in criminality."

Situational choice theory
A brand of rational choice theory that views criminal behaviour "as a function of choices and decisions made within a context of situational constraints and opportunities."

Soft determinism The belief that human behaviour is the result of choices and decisions made within a context of situational constraints and opportunities.

A new approach developed in large part as a response to the failures of traditional theories and programs. "Although this assumption [the focus on people] continues to dominate crime prevention research and policy," said Weisburd, "it has begun to be challenged by a very different approach that seeks to shift the focus of crime prevention efforts." For many scholars and policymakers, this meant having to rethink assumptions about criminality and how offenders might be prevented from participating in crime, with some suggesting that a more radical reorientation of crime-prevention efforts was warranted. They argued that the shift must come not in terms of the specific strategies or theories that are used, but in terms of the unit of analysis that forms the basis of crime-prevention efforts. Rather than focusing on people who commit crime, they called for an emphasis on the context in which crime occurs.

This approach, which is called **situational crime prevention**, looks to develop greater understanding of crime and more effective crime-prevention strategies through concern with the physical, organizational, and social environments that make crime possible.[27] The situational approach does not ignore offenders; it merely places them as one part of a broader crime-prevention equation that is centred on the context of crime. It demands a shift in the approach to crime prevention from one concerned primarily with why people commit crime to one that looks primarily at why crime occurs in specific settings. It moves the context of crime into central focus and sees the offender as only one of a number of factors that affect it. Situational crime prevention is closely associated with the idea of a "criminology of place," discussed in Chapter 8.

Weisburd suggested that a "reorientation of crime prevention research and policy from the causes of criminality to the context of crime provides much promise. . . . At the core of situational prevention is the concept of opportunity."[28] In contrast to offender-based approaches to crime prevention, which usually focus on the dispositions of criminals, situational crime prevention begins with the opportunity structure of the crime situation, meaning the immediate situational and environmental components of the context of crime. This approach to crime prevention tries to reduce the opportunities for crime in specific situations through efforts as simple and straightforward as **target hardening** or access control.

The value of a situational approach lies in the fact that criminologists have found it difficult to identify who is likely to become a serious offender or to predict the timing and types of future offences that repeat offenders are likely to commit. Weisburd explained that "legal and ethical dilemmas make it difficult to base criminal justice policies on models that still include a substantial degree of statistical error." He added that "if traditional approaches worked well, of course, there would be little pressure to find new forms of crime prevention. If traditional approaches worked well, few people would possess criminal motivation and fewer still would actually commit crimes."

Situational prevention advocates argue that the context of crime provides a promising alternative to traditional offender-based crime-prevention policies.[29] They assume that situations provide a more stable and predictable focus for crime-prevention efforts than do persons. In part, this assumption develops from common-sense notions of the relationship between opportunities and crime. Shoplifting, for example, is by definition clustered in stores and not residences, and family disputes are unlikely to be a problem outside of the home. High-crime places, in contrast to high-crime people, cannot flee to avoid criminal justice intervention, and crime that develops from the specific characteristics of certain places cannot be easily transferred to other contexts.

In short, situational crime control works by removing or reducing criminal opportunity. If we accept that opportunity is a cause of crime equal in importance to the personal and social characteristics that other researchers point to as causes, then, according to Felson and Clarke, we have a "criminology that is not only more complete in its theorizing, but also more relevant to policy and practice."[30] If Felson and Clarke are correct in what they say, then much of the crime-prevention work that is already being done by police

Situational crime prevention A social policy approach that looks to develop greater understanding of crime and more effective crime-prevention strategies through concern with the physical, organizational, and social environments that make crime possible.

Target hardening The reduction in criminal opportunity for a particular location, generally through the use of physical barriers, architectural design, and enhanced security measures.

agencies, private security, and businesses aimed at reducing criminal opportunity directly affects the basic causes of crime. The Crime Prevention Through Environmental Design (CPTED) approach is one used by police services across Canada; it is discussed in more detail in Chapter 11.

Critique of Rational Choice Theory Rational choice theory (as well as situational choice and routine activities theories) can be criticized for an overemphasis on individual choice and a relative disregard for the role of social factors in crime causation, such as poverty, poor home environment, and inadequate socialization. In one study, for example, Laura J. Moriarty and James E. Williams found that the routine activities approach explained 28 percent of property crimes committed in socially disorganized (high-crime) areas of a small Virginia city and explained only 11 percent of offences committed in low-crime areas.[31] In the words of the authors, "This research demonstrates more support for routine activities theory in socially disorganized areas than in socially organized areas."[32] Hence, although one could argue that the kinds of routine activities supportive of criminal activity are more likely to occur in socially disorganized areas, it is also true that the presence (or absence) of certain ecological characteristics (that is, the level of social disorganization) may enhance (or reduce) the likelihood of criminal victimization. As the authors stated,

> Those areas characterized by low socio-economic status will have higher unemployment rates, thus creating a larger pool of motivated offenders. Family disruption characterized by more divorced or separated families will result in more unguarded living structures, thus making suitable targets more available. Increased residential mobility will result in more non-occupied housing, which creates a lack of guardianship over the property and increases the number of suitable targets.[33]

Rational choice theory seems to assume that everyone is equally capable of making rational decisions when such is probably not the case. Some individuals are more logical by virtue of temperament, personality, or socialization, whereas others are emotional, hotheaded, and unthinking. Empirical studies of rational choice theory have added scant support for the perspective's underlying assumptions, tending to show instead that criminal offenders are often unrealistic in their appraisals of the relative risks and rewards facing them.[34] Similarly, rational and situational choice theories seem to disregard individual psychology and morality with their emphasis on external situations; moral individuals, when faced with easy criminal opportunities, may rein in their desires and turn their backs on temptation, say critics.

Finally, the emphasis of rational and situational choice theories upon changing aspects of the immediate situation to reduce crime has been criticized for resulting in the **displacement** of crime from one area to another.[35] Target hardening,[36] a key crime-prevention strategy advocated by such theorists, has sometimes caused criminals to find new targets of opportunity in other areas.[37]

Displacement A shift of criminal activity from one spatial location to another.

PUNISHMENT AND NEOCLASSICAL THOUGHT

PUNISHMENT IS A CENTRAL FEATURE OF BOTH CLASSICAL AND NEOCLASSICAL thought. Whereas punishment served the ends of deterrence in classical thought, its role in neoclassical thinking has been expanded to support the ancient concept of retribution. Those advocating retribution see the primary utility of punishment as revenge.

If a person is attracted to crime and chooses to violate the law, modern neoclassical thinkers argue, then he or she *deserves* to be punished because the consequences of the crime were known to the offender before the crime was committed. Moreover, the criminal *must* be punished so that future criminal behaviour can be curtailed.

Notions of revenge and retribution are morally based on a sense of indignation at criminal behaviour and on the sense of righteousness inherent in notions of morality and propriety. Both philosophies of punishment turn a blind eye to the mundane and practical consequences of any particular form of punishment. Hence, advocates of retributive philosophies of punishment easily dismiss critics of the death penalty, who frequently challenge the efficacy of court-ordered capital punishment on the basis that such sentences do little to deter others. Wider issues, including general deterrence, become irrelevant when a person focuses narrowly on the emotions that crime and victimization engender in a given instance. From the neoclassical perspective, some crimes cry out for vengeance while others demand little more than a slap on the wrist or an apology from the offender.

Just Deserts

The old adage "he got what was coming to him" well summarizes the thinking behind the **just deserts model** of criminal sentencing. *Just deserts* refers to the concept that criminal offenders deserve the punishment they receive at the hands of the law and that any punishment that is imposed should be appropriate to the type and severity of crime committed. The idea of just deserts has long been a part of Western thought, dating back at least to Old Testament times. The Old Testament dictum of "an eye for an eye, and a tooth for a tooth" has been cited by many as divine justification for strict punishments, although some scholars believe that in reality the notion of "an eye for an eye" was intended to *reduce* the barbarism of existing penalties, whereby an aggrieved party might exact the severest of punishments for only minor offences (even petty offences were often punished by whipping, torture, and sometimes death).

According to the neoclassical perspective, doing justice ultimately comes down to an official meting out of what is deserved. Justice for an individual is nothing more or less than what that individual deserves when all the circumstances surrounding that person's situation and behaviour are taken into account.

Just deserts model The notion that criminal offenders deserve the punishment they receive at the hands of the law and that punishments should be appropriate to the type and severity of the crime committed.

Deterrence

True to its historical roots, **deterrence** is a hallmark of modern neoclassical thought. In contrast to early thinkers, however, today's neoclassical writers distinguish between deterrence that is specific and that which is general. **Specific deterrence** is a goal of criminal sentencing that seeks to prevent a particular offender from engaging in repeat criminality. **General deterrence** works by way of example, seeking to prevent others from committing crimes similar to the one for which a particular offender is being sentenced.

Following their classical counterparts, modern-day advocates of general deterrence frequently stress that for punishment to be an effective impediment to crime, it must be swift, certain, and severe enough to outweigh the rewards flowing from criminal activity. Those who advocate punishment as a deterrent are often frustrated by the complexity of today's criminal justice system and the slow and circuitous manner in which cases are handled and punishments are meted out. Punishments today, even when imposed by a court, are rarely swift in their imposition; the wheels of modern criminal justice are relatively slow to grind to a conclusion, given the many delays inherent in judicial proceedings and the numerous opportunities for postponement and appeal. Certainty of punishment is also anything but a reality. Certain punishments are those that cannot be easily avoided, but even when punishments are ordered, they are frequently not carried out—at least not fully.

If the neoclassicists are correct, ideally, criminal punishments should prevent a repetition of crime or **recidivism**—the repetition of criminal behaviour by those already involved in crime. (The definition becomes more complicated when the question of what constitutes this repeat criminal behaviour is considered. Does *recidivism* refer to the perpetration of a new offence? To a return to the criminal justice system? Or to a return to

Deterrence The prevention of crime.

Specific deterrence A goal of criminal sentencing that seeks to prevent a particular offender from engaging in repeat criminality.

General deterrence A goal of criminal sentencing that seeks to prevent others from committing crimes similar to the one for which a particular offender is being sentenced.

Recidivism The repetition of criminal behaviour.

the correctional system? Does it include any breach of release conditions or only a breach of the most serious conditions?)[38] Despite the definitional challenges, recidivism can also be used to measure the success of a given approach to the problem of crime. When so employed, it is referred to as a **recidivism rate**, expressed as the percentage of convicted offenders who have been released from a correctional facility and who are later rearrested for a new crime or a violation of the conditions of their release (known as a *technical violation*). While the public perception is that recidivism rates in Canada are high, the reality is somewhat different. In the last comprehensive study issued by the Canadian federal government, offenders were tracked for up to two years after their release into the community. The study found that reconviction rates for offenders released from federal institutions were 43 percent. Non-violent offences accounted for the majority of reconvictions. The violent reconviction rate was 13 percent, while the sexual reconviction rate was very low, at 0.7–1.7 percent. The study also indicated that more than half of the reconvictions occurred after the sentence was completed when the offender was no longer under supervision.[39]

The Death Penalty   Notions of deterrence, retribution, and just deserts all come together in **capital punishment**, the legal imposition of a death sentence. The many different understandings of crime and crime control, along with arguments over free will and social determinism, combine with varying philosophies of punishment to produce considerable disagreement over the efficacy of death as a form of criminal sanction.

Opponents of capital punishment make ten claims:

1. Capital punishment does not deter crime.
2. The death penalty has been imposed on innocent people, and no workable system is currently in place to prevent the accidental execution of innocents (see the Crime in the News box for cases of wrongful imprisonment).
3. Human life, even the life of a murderer, is sacred.
4. State-imposed death lowers society to the same moral (or amoral) level as the murderer.
5. The death penalty has been (and may still be) imposed in haphazard and seemingly random fashion.
6. The death penalty is imposed disproportionately upon ethnic minorities.
7. Capital punishment goes against the most fundamental precepts of almost every organized religion.
8. The death penalty is more expensive than imprisonment.
9. Capital punishment is widely viewed as inhumane and barbaric internationally.
10. There is a better alternative (usually said to be life in prison without possibility of parole).

Advocates of capital punishment generally discount each of these claims, countering with the notion that death is *deserved* by those who commit especially heinous acts, and that anything short of capital punishment under certain circumstances is an injustice in itself; some people deserve to die for what they have done. Evolving from a natural law perspective, such arguments are sometimes supported on religious grounds and are based on the notion of just deserts (discussed earlier).

Strong feelings on both sides of the issue have generated a plethora of studies of the efficacy and fairness of capital punishment as a criminal sanction. Although one might expect study results to have produced some agreement, just the opposite seems to have happened—and a relative impasse exists as to how those studies should be interpreted. The extent to which the death penalty acts as a general deterrent has been widely examined. Some researchers have compared murder rates between U.S. states that have eliminated the death penalty and those that have retained it, finding little variation in the rate at

Recidivism rate   The percentage of convicted offenders who have been released from prison and who are later rearrested for a new crime.

Capital punishment   The legal imposition of a sentence of death upon a convicted offender.

which murders are committed.[40] Others have looked at variations in murder rates over time in jurisdictions that have eliminated capital punishment, with similar results.[41] A now classic 1988 Texas study provided a comprehensive review of capital punishment by correlating homicide rates with the rate of executions within the state between 1930 and 1986.[42] The study, which was especially important because Texas has been quite active in the capital punishment arena, failed to find any support for the use of death as a deterrent.

While capital punishment has not been legal in Canada since 1976, there are some Canadians who would like to see its reinstatement. It is practised in many states in the United States and in other countries including Japan, Russia, and China.

Canada's Wrongful Convictions: Cases Where The Courts Got It Wrong

Joyce Milgaard makes a phone call after the release of a Saskatchewan report into the wrongful conviction of her son, David Milgaard, in September 2008. The report praised her "epic struggle" in seeking David's release during his more than 22 years behind bars.

Geoff Howe/The Canadian Press Images

They languished behind bars for years, wrongfully jailed for crimes they did not commit.

But the high-profile ordeals of Donald Marshall Jr., David Milgaard and others have put a spotlight on what has been called the fallibility of Canadian justice.

These cases are not unique and certainly not isolated to Canada, although estimates of the actual number of wrongful convictions vary widely.

Each miscarriage of justice, however, deals a blow to a society's confidence in the legal system, experts say.

"Wrongful convictions undermine the two prongs of the criminal justice system's legitimacy," states a 1992 report prepared by the Library of Parliament. "If someone is wrongfully convicted, that person is punished for an offence he or she did not commit and the actual perpetrator of the crime goes free."

To make it worse, advocates say many who were ultimately exonerated watched their applications stall for years in the federal review board process.

In 2000, federal Justice Minister Anne McLellan announced plans to try to prevent such cases from happening again. The changes, since enacted in the Criminal Code of Canada, enable the justice minister to use his or her discretion to respond to persons who believe they have been wrongfully convicted.

Groups such as the Association in Defence of the Wrongfully Convicted have also advocated on behalf of those they say have been jailed unfairly.

Here are some of the major cases in recent Canadian history:

Donald Marshall Jr.

In 1971, Marshall was wrongfully convicted of murdering his friend, Sandy Seale, in a Sydney, N.S., park. Marshall was just 17 years old when he received a life sentence.

He was released in 1982 after RCMP reviewed his case. He was cleared by the Nova Scotia Court of Appeal the following year. Though the Appeal Court declared him not guilty, Marshall was told he had contributed to his own conviction and that any miscarriage of justice was more apparent than real.

Marshall, a Mi'kmaq, was exonerated by a royal commission in 1990 that determined systemic racism had contributed to his wrongful imprisonment. The seven-volume report pointed the finger at police, judges, Marshall's original defence lawyers, Crown lawyers and bureaucrats.

Roy Ebsary, an eccentric who bragged about being skilled with knives, was eventually convicted of manslaughter in Seale's death and spent a year in jail.

Marshall died in a Sydney hospital in August 2009 after a lengthy illness. He was 55.

David Milgaard

Milgaard was charged with the 1969 murder of Saskatoon nursing aide Gail Miller and in January 1970 was sentenced to life in prison. Appeals to the Saskatchewan Court of

(Continued)

Canada's Wrongful Convictions: Cases Where The Courts Got It Wrong

Appeal and Supreme Court of Canada in the two years after his conviction were unsuccessful.

Milgaard's mother, Joyce, believed from the day he was arrested that her son was innocent. She kept his case alive, talking to whoever would listen—and many who didn't—while he spent more than two decades in prison.

In 1991, Justice Minister Kim Campbell directed the Supreme Court of Canada to review the conviction. The Supreme Court of Canada set it aside in 1992, and Milgaard was subsequently cleared by DNA evidence five years later.

The Saskatchewan government awarded Milgaard $10 million for his wrongful conviction in 1999. That same year, Larry Fisher was found guilty of the rape and stabbing death of Gail Miller.

A provincial judicial inquiry, which released a comprehensive 815-page report in September 2008, concluded that "the criminal justice system failed David Milgaard." The inquiry also found that Milgaard might have been released from jail years sooner if police had followed up on a lead they received in 1980.

Guy Paul Morin

Christine Jessop, a nine-year-old girl, disappeared from her Queensville, Ont., home in October 1984. Her body was found in a farmer's field two months later. Guy Paul Morin, the Jessops' next-door neighbour in the community about 60 km north of Toronto, was later charged with her murder.

Morin was acquitted in 1986, but a new trial was ordered by the Ontario Court of Appeal. At this second trial, Morin was convicted and sentenced to life in prison. He appealed and in 1995 was exonerated by DNA testing.

A public inquiry into the case was called, and its report was tabled in 1998. It concluded that mistakes by the police,

prosecutors and forensic scientists combined to send an innocent man to jail.

Steven Truscott

In 1959, Truscott was sentenced to be hanged at age 14 for a schoolmate's murder, becoming Canada's youngest death-row inmate. After the original conviction, he spent four months in the shadow of the gallows until his death sentence was commuted to life imprisonment. Paroled in 1969, Truscott disappeared into an anonymous existence in a southern Ontario city.

On August 28, 2007—48 years later—the Ontario Court of Appeal unanimously overturned Truscott's conviction and acquitted him, declaring the case "a miscarriage of justice" that "must be quashed." The judges went on to say, however, that "the court is not satisfied that the appellant has been able to demonstrate his factual innocence." In July 2008, the Ontario government announced it would pay Truscott $6.5 million in compensation for his ordeal.

Discussion Questions

1. Canada abolished capital punishment in 1976. If this criminal sanction had still been an option, what might have happened to these men?

2. How do cases of exoneration, like the ones described in this box, influence public opinion about capital punishment?

3. What are your feelings about capital punishment? Explain.

Source: "Canada's Wrongful Convictions: Cases Where The Courts Got It Wrong," CBC News, October 14, 2010, http://www. cbc.ca/news/canada/story/2009/08/06/f-wrongfully-convicted.html [Accessed October 21, 2012].

5.6 | LEARNING OBJECTIVE

POLICY IMPLICATIONS OF THE CLASSICAL SCHOOL

A FEW YEARS AGO, LAWRENCE W. SHERMAN DESCRIBED FOUR PARADIGMS OF JUSTICE, shown in Figure 5.1.[43] As the figure illustrates, each form of justice can be described in terms of whether it presumes a rational or an emotional basis for crime, as well as a rational or an emotional societal response to criminality. According to Sherman, two types of justice—one rational (focused on deterrence) and the other emotional (focused on retribution)—"have competed for primacy" since the dawn of the modern era. Combining those two perspectives on justice with notions of either a rational or an emotional offender yields the four paradigms in the figure.

The first paradigm, which Sherman termed *expressive economics*, assumes that crime is a rational act but that the justice philosophy that undergirds it uses "punishment as a symbolic *expression* of the emotions of anger and outrage by the state and society at the act of a criminal." Expressive economics finds an emotional society using the criminal law

	Offender Rational	Offender Emotional
Law Emotional	Expressive Economics	Expression
Law Rational	Rational Economics	Emotional Intelligence

Figure 5.1 Lawrence W. Sherman's Paradigms of Justice

Source: Lawrence W. Sherman, "Reason for Emotion: Reinventing Justice with Theories, Innovations, and Research: The American Society of Criminology 2002 Presidential Address," *Criminology*, vol. 41, no. 1 (2003), pp. 1–37. Reprinted with permission.

and the justice system as a combined means of expressing its feelings and inflicting retribution on offenders who have made the decision to violate the law. This, said Sherman, is the "paradigm that dominates current practice." It is also, he explained, the reason that so many people come away from the justice process feeling unfulfilled: "Few of us expect much justice from an expressive state that dramatizes its outrage at a rational offender who coolly calculates costs and benefits."[44] According to Sherman, it was Beccaria's attacks on expressive punishment as immoral that led to abolition of the death penalty in Canada and many European countries.

Another important justice paradigm is a kind of *rational economics*, under which an assumed-to-be-purposeful offender encounters a justice system based on rational—rather than emotional—principles. Such a system employs punishment to make the economics of crime more favourable to law-abiding than to law-breaking behaviour. This kind of rational economics favours deterrence and most closely mirrors the principles of classical and neoclassical thought.

During the past several decades, a mixed justice philosophy of expressive and rational economics has led to the advent of such seemingly rational punishment practices as determinate sentencing and to such emotional consequences as lengthened prison terms. **Determinate sentencing** is a strategy that attempts to address the issue of sentencing certainty. This approach mandates a specific and fixed amount of time to be served for every offence category. Under determinate sentencing schemes, for example, judges might be required to impose seven-year sentences on offenders convicted of armed robbery, but only one-year sentences on those convicted robbers who used no weapon. Determinate sentencing schemes build upon the two notions of classical thought: (1) the pleasure of a given crime can be somewhat accurately assessed, and (2) a fixed amount of punishment necessary for deterrence can be calculated and specified. Proponents contend that determinate sentences may also reduce sentencing bias since disparity based on race or social status would be eliminated. Canadian judges have voiced the concern that determinate sentencing models limit the amount of discretion or personal judgment they can exercise when meting out a sentence. It is unlikely that determinate sentencing models will be fully adopted in Canada, although increasing numbers of *Criminal Code* offences carry a mandatory minimum sentence from which Canadian judges cannot vary. Official statistics indicate that that there were about 38 000 adults incarcerated in 2010–2011 (140 per 100 000), an increase of 1 percent since 2009–2010.[45] By comparison, the state and federal prison population in the United States stood at 1 613 656 inmates, or approximately 740 per 100 000 in 2010.[46] See Chapter 11 for a further discussion of this "getting tough on crime" approach.

Imprisonment is one component of a strategy of **incapacitation**—the use of imprisonment or other means to reduce the likelihood that an offender will be capable of committing future offences. Proponents of modern-day incapacitation often distinguish between the terms *selective incapacitation*, in which crime is controlled via the imprisonment of specific individuals, and *collective incapacitation*, whereby changes in legislation and/or sentencing patterns lead to the removal from society of entire groups of individuals judged

Determinate sentencing A criminal punishment strategy that mandates a specified and fixed amount of time to be served for every offence category.

Incapacitation The use of imprisonment or other means to reduce the likelihood that an offender will be capable of committing future offences.

to be dangerous. Advocates of selective incapacitation as a crime-prevention strategy point to studies that show the majority of crimes are perpetrated by a small number of hard-core repeat offenders. The most famous of those studies, conducted by University of Pennsylvania professor Marvin Wolfgang, focused on 9000 men born in Philadelphia in 1945.[47] By the time this cohort of men had reached age 18, Wolfgang was able to determine that 627 "chronic recidivists" were responsible for the large majority of all serious violent crimes committed by the group. Other more recent studies have similarly shown that a small core of criminal perpetrators is probably responsible for most criminal activity.

Such thinking has led to the development of incapacitation as a modern-day treatment philosophy and to the creation of innovative forms of incapacitation that do not require imprisonment—such as house arrest, use of halfway houses, or provision of career-training centres for convicted offenders. Similarly, such thinkers argue, the decriminalization of many offences and the enhancement of social programs designed to combat what they see as the root causes of crime—including poverty, low educational levels, general lack of skills, and inherent or active discrimination—will lead to a much reduced incidence of crime in the future, making high rates of imprisonment unnecessary.

Before leaving our discussion of Sherman, however, it should be pointed out that the figure implies the existence of two other justice paradigms. One of these, which he termed quite simply *expression*, results from the combination of an emotional offender and an emotional society. In this particular interface—of emotion upon emotion—Sherman explained that "the state is morally obliged to take an explicitly *emotional* stance towards a presumably emotional offender, without regard for harm to the state's self-interest in the effects of its action on the offender's future behavior."[48] See the Who's Responsible? box for an inside look at crime and emotion.

It is the fourth paradigm—*emotional intelligence*—in which Sherman placed the most hope for the future. Under such a paradigm, individuals within the criminal justice system

Criminal Behaviour: Rational Choice or Adrenalin Rush?

Following his arrest for the theft of a police car, Moonbeam Kittaro met with one of his friends in the visiting area of the local jail. Here's what he said:

I stole a cop car and s***, was it exciting!

I mean, the thing was just sitting there running in the parking lot with the keys in it. Who wouldn't take it?

I've never been so high on pure adrenaline. It was an adrenaline rush being behind the wheel of that f***ing car.

It turned my girlfriend on too.

I drove over to her place with the lights and siren on, and as soon as she saw the car she wanted to go for a ride.

We must have hit 140 on the Interstate!

Then we pulled into a rest stop and made love in the back seat.

It was the whole illegal thing that got her so excited.

But that's when we got arrested.

The cops surrounded the car, guns drawn and all that s***.

We didn't even hear them coming.

Think about it:

1. Why did Kittaro steal the car? Do you think that he knew, before he stole it, that the theft would lead to so much excitement?

2. Can the desire for excitement explain crimes like Kittaro's? Can the same desire explain other kinds of crimes? If so, what might they be?

3. If excitement explains crime commission, then why doesn't everyone commit crime for the excitement that it brings?

4. What kinds of crime-prevention programs might be based on the principles illustrated here?

Note: This example is a fictionalized one intended to encourage critical thinking.

would control their emotions and would work with offenders and victims to bring about a reasonable resolution of the situation that would repair the harm caused by the crime. Sherman cited the 32 percent drop in executions that occurred nationwide in the United States following the growing availability of DNA evidence that helped to exonerate those wrongfully convicted of capital crimes as evidence of how intelligence and reason can ameliorate emotions in even the most egregious crimes.

CRITIQUE OF CLASSICAL THEORIES

5.7 LEARNING OBJECTIVE

CLASSICAL AND NEOCLASSICAL THOUGHT REPRESENTS MORE A PHILOSOPHY OF JUSTICE than it does a theory of crime causation. As some writers have observed, however, "the true test of Beccaria's essay can be judged by the influence it has had over time on our justice system."[49] The influence of Beccaria, the Enlightenment, and classical thinkers remains today in the *Canadian Charter of Rights and Freedoms*, in "get-tough" approaches to crime, and in a continuing emphasis on individual rights. The classical school "has left behind a legacy that we see in almost every aspect of our present-day justice system."[50]

Critics charge, however, that the classical school lacks explanatory power over criminal motivation, other than to advance the simple claim that crime is the result of free will and individual choice. Such critics point out that classical theory is largely bereft of meaningful explanations for the deeper fonts of personal motivation, including those represented by human biology, psychology, and the social environment. Moreover, the classical school, as originally detailed in the writings of Beccaria and Bentham, lacked any scientific basis for the claims it made. Although neoclassical writers have advanced the scientific foundation of classical claims (via studies such as those showing the effectiveness of particular forms of deterrence), many still defend their way of thinking by reference to philosophical ideals, such as just deserts.

CLASSICAL AND NEOCLASSICAL THEORIES APPLIED

Crime is a result of rational choices made by individuals seeking various kinds of illicit rewards. Neoclassical criminology is a contemporary perspective built on classical principles.

NEOCLASSICAL CRIMINOLOGY

holds that it is character and character development, as well as the choices people make when faced with opportunities for crime, that determine criminal behaviour.

Is the case of John Robin Sharpe one that can be explained using the notions of rational choice and opportunity?

CLASSICAL CRIMINOLOGY

holds that human beings are fundamentally rational, pain and pleasure are the two central determinants of human behaviour, and punishment is necessary to deter law violators and to serve as an example to others.

How do the classical tenets of individual rights versus the rights of society apply to the case of John Robin Sharpe?

SUMMARY OF LEARNING OBJECTIVES

5.1 The classical school in criminology posits that at least some illegal activity is the result of rational choices made by individuals seeking various kinds of illicit rewards. The classical perspective sees human beings as fundamentally rational, portrays pain and pleasure as the two central determinants of human behaviour, and sees punishment as necessary to deter law violators and to serve as an example.

5.2 The classical school grew out of the Enlightenment. Notions of free will, individual choice, deterrence as a goal of the justice system, and punishment as a natural consequence of crime owe much of their contemporary influence to the classical school. Influential thinkers of the Enlightenment era include Thomas Hobbes, John Locke, Thomas Paine, Montesquieu, and Rousseau.

5.3 Two important thinkers of the classical school of criminology, Cesare Beccaria and Jeremy Bentham, saw crime as providing pleasure to those who commit it and believed in punishment as the way to prevent it.

5.4 Neoclassical criminology is a contemporary perspective built on classical principles emphasizing the importance of character and character development, as well as the choices people make when faced with opportunities for crime. Rational choice theory recognizes the opportunities for crime and the important role that capable guardians play in preventing it.

5.5 In neoclassical criminology, punishment is seen as providing both a deterrent and just deserts. Just deserts implies that criminal offenders deserve the punishment they receive and that any criminal punishment meted out should be appropriate to the type and severity of the crime committed.

5.6 Policy implications of the classical school revolve around the idea of a rational offender punished by a system working purposefully toward the goals of crime reduction and prevention of recidivism. Determinate sentencing, truth in sentencing, and capital punishment are all strategies developed from classical school principles.

5.7 Classical perspectives can be criticized for their lack of comprehensive explanatory power over criminal motivation and for their lack of both meaningful explanations as to how a choice for or against criminal activity is made and any appreciation for the deeper fonts of personal motivation.

Questions for Review

1. What are the central concepts that define the classical school of criminological thought? Which of those concepts are still alive? Where do you see evidence for the survival of those concepts?

2. Name the various pre-classical thinkers identified in this chapter. What ideas did each contribute to Enlightenment philosophy? What form did those ideas take in classical criminological thought?

3. Who were the important thinkers of the classical school of criminology, and what heritage did their way of thinking provide?

4. This book emphasizes a theme of social problems versus social responsibility. Which perspective is more clearly supported by classical and neoclassical thought? Why?

5. How would you define *recidivism*? What is a recidivism rate? Why are recidivism rates so high today? What can be done to lower them?

6. What are the policy implications of the classical school? What kinds of crime-prevention and crime-control programs might be based on classical principles?

7. What are the shortcomings of the classical school and neoclassical thinking about crime and punishment?

Multiple-Choice Questions

1. The _____ was a social movement that arose during the 18th century and built upon ideas such as empiricism, rationality, free will, humanism, and natural law.

   a. Code of Hammurabi

   b. classical school

   c. Enlightenment

   d. social contract

   e. Magna Carta

2. Which of the following is an example of a *mala in se* offence?

   a. assault

   b. prostitution

   c. drug use

   d. vagrancy

   e. assisted suicide

3. _____ is based upon the belief that behaviour holds value to any individual undertaking it according to the amount of pleasure or pain that it can be expected to produce for that person.

   a. Retribution

   b. The social contract

   c. Natural law

   d. Hedonistic calculus

   e. Recidivism

4. The heritage left by the classical school is still operative today in which of the following statements?

   a. Society is made possible by individuals cooperating together.

   b. An accused person should be presumed guilty until proven otherwise.

   c. Retribution is the best justification for punishment.

   d. Human behaviour is determined by social forces.

   e. Punishment is ineffective in deterring criminal behaviour.

5. _____ seeks to prevent a particular offender from engaging in repeat criminality.

   a. General deterrence

   b. Retribution

   c. Specific deterrence

   d. Recidivism

   e. Rehabilitation

Multiple Choice Answers: 1c, 2a, 3a, 4c, 5b

Chapter 6
Biological Roots of Criminal Behaviour

Steve Baccon/Photodisc/Thinkstock

Social programs aim to eradicate educational, social, and economic inequities. These efforts can only be undermined by statements stressing the importance of genetic factors in determining criminality.

—*Julian V. Roberts and Thomas Gabor*[1]

LEARNING OBJECTIVES

After reading this chapter, you should be able to

6.1 Identify the basic principles that characterize biological theories of crime causation.

6.2 Understand how biological perspectives might explain human aggression.

6.3 Be aware of the research linking genetics and crime.

6.4 Consider the contribution of sociobiology to the study of criminality.

6.5 Explain how criminality can be explained from a biosocial perspective.

6.6 Identify modern-day social policy that reflects the biological and biosocial approaches to crime causation.

6.7 Assess the shortcomings of biological theories of criminal behaviour.

INTRODUCTION

At a recent annual meeting of the American Neurological Association, two neuroscience researchers reported on the case of a man with no history of pedophilia who began molesting children after developing an egg-sized brain tumour.[2] According to the neuroscientists, Russell Swerdlow and Jeffrey Burns, friends of the man told investigators that the 40-year-old married teacher had never previously exhibited abnormal impulses but suddenly started visiting prostitutes, making sexual advances toward children, and spending time on websites selling child pornography. Soon, they reported, his wife left him and he was arrested and convicted on child molestation charges. Although he entered a treatment program for pedophiles, he propositioned women at the facility and was expelled from treatment. About the same time, he began having headaches and went to a hospital emergency room, where he reported experiencing strong sexual urges and said that he feared he would rape his landlady. Attending neurologists noticed other symptoms indicative of neurological problems, such as poor balance and the inability to copy simple drawings. An MRI scan conducted at the hospital showed that the man had a large tumour in the right frontal cortex of his brain. The tumour was removed, and the man's abnormal urges disappeared. Later, however, they reoccurred, and another scan showed that the tumour had returned. Once again it was removed, and the man's behaviour returned to normal. Swerdlow and Burns reported that the tumour was located in the part of the brain associated with social judgments and self-control, and they speculated that it was the cause of the man's pedophiliac urges. "We're dealing with the neurology of morality here," said Swerdlow.

Can a brain tumour cause crime? We may never be sure; however, many biological theories have been advanced to explain criminality. Abnormalities of the brain, genetic predispositions, vitamin deficiencies, an excess of hormones such as testosterone, hypoglycemia (low blood sugar), fetal alcohol syndrome (FAS), a relative lack of neurotransmitters such as serotonin in the brain, and blood abnormalities are among the many current biological explanations of crime available today.

The field of criminology has been cautious about giving credence to biological theories of human behaviour. One reason for this, as noted in Chapter 1, is that contemporary criminology's academic roots are firmly grounded in the social sciences. As the well-known biocriminologist C. Ray Jeffery, commenting on the historical development of the field, observed,

> The term *criminology* was given to a social science approach to crime as developed in sociology. Sutherland's (1924) text *Criminology* was pure sociology without any biology or psychology; beginning with publication of that text, criminology was offered in sociology departments as a part of sociology separate from biology, psychology, psychiatry, and law. . . . Many of the academicians who call themselves criminologists are sociologists.[3]

Another challenge with biological theories is that the link between biology and crime is rarely as clear as the example that opened this chapter. The influence of biology on behaviour of any kind is more often the result of an *interaction* among genetic, hormonal, and other biological features of an individual and his or her social and physical environments. Noted biosocial researcher and writer Anthony Walsh observed that "biological theories are theories of criminality, not crime."[4] Walsh explained that crime is a "legal label" that is placed on specific behaviours violating criminal law. Criminality, on the other hand, said Walsh, "is a property of individuals, a continuous trait that is itself an amalgam of other continuous traits, and thus belongs to a more inclusive kind of criminology."[5] According to Walsh, criminality can be seen as the willingness to violate individual rights and social norms, whether or not such behaviour is against the law. Criminality, Walsh pointed out, consists of "a relative lack of empathy, conscience, self-control, and fear, as well as self-centeredness, and a penchant for risky behavior."[6] Seen this way, biological explanations of criminality are more likely to be couched in terms of a propensity for violence, aggression, deceit, recklessness, fearlessness, and so on.

Society tends to shy away from biological explanations for criminality and disordered behaviour because of concern with concepts such as genetic determinism, which have come to be seen as synonymous with inevitability since the physical makeup of a person is hard to change. Open inquiry, however, requires objective consideration of all points of view and an unbiased examination of each for its ability to shed light upon the subject under study. Hence, for an adequate consideration of biological theories as they may relate to crime and crime causation, we need to turn to literature outside of the sociological and psychological mainstream.

MAJOR PRINCIPLES OF BIOLOGICAL THEORIES

6.1 | **LEARNING OBJECTIVE**

THIS BRIEF SECTION SERVES TO SUMMARIZE THE CENTRAL FEATURES OF **BIOLOGICAL theories** of crime causation. Each of these points can be found elsewhere in this chapter, so this section is meant to be a guide (see Table 6.1).

Biological theories of crime causation make certain fundamental assumptions:

Biological theory A theory that maintains that the basic determinants of human behaviour, including criminality, are constitutionally or physiologically based and often inherited.

- The brain is the organ of the mind and the locus of personality. In the words of C. Ray Jeffery, "The brain is the organ of behavior; no theory of behavior can ignore neurology and neurochemistry."[7]

- Basic determinants of human behaviour, including criminal tendencies, are constitutionally or genetically based to a considerable degree.

- Observed gender and racial differences in rates and types of criminality may be at least partially the result of biological differences between the sexes and between racially distinct groups.

- Basic determinants of human behaviour, including criminality, may be passed on from generation to generation; that is, a penchant for crime may be inherited.

- Much of human conduct is fundamentally rooted in instinctive behavioural responses such as territoriality and acquisitiveness that are characteristic of biological organisms everywhere.

Watch

Major Principles of the Biological Perspective

Table 6.1 Biological Theories

Theory	Early Positivism	Constitutional Theories	Body Chemistry Theories	Sociobiology	Biosocial Criminology
Period	1890s–1930	1930s–1940s; 1960s–present	1940s–present	1975–present	1987–present
Theorists	Franz Joseph Gall and others	Ernst Kretschmer and others	Ellen G. Cohen and others	Edwin O. Wilson	James Q. Wilson, Richard J. Herrnstein
Concepts	Phrenology, atavism, born criminals, criminaloids	Somatotyping, mesomorph, ectomorph, endomorph, XYY supermale, twin studies	Conduct norms, focal concerns, subculture, socialization, subculture of violence	Altruism, tribalism, survival of the gene pool	Constitutional factors, genetic inheritance

- Biological roots of human conduct have become increasingly disguised, as modern symbolic forms of indirect expressive behaviour have replaced more primitive and direct ones.

- At least some human behaviour is the result of biological propensities inherited from more primitive developmental stages in the evolutionary process, meaning that some human beings may be further along the evolutionary ladder than others, and their behaviour may reflect that fact.

- The interplay between heredity, biology, and the social environment provides the nexus for any realistic consideration of crime causation.

6.2 LEARNING OBJECTIVE

BIOLOGICAL ROOTS OF HUMAN AGGRESSION

IN 1966, KONRAD LORENZ PUBLISHED HIS NOW FAMOUS WORK ON AGGRESSION.[8] In it, Lorenz described how aggression permeates the animal kingdom and asked, "What is the value of all this fighting?" "In nature," he said, "fighting is such an ever-present process, its behavior mechanisms and weapons are so highly developed and have so obviously arisen under the pressure of a species-preserving function, that it is our duty to ask this question."[9]

Lorenz accepted the evolutionary thesis of the 19th-century biologist Charles Darwin that intraspecies aggression favoured the strongest and best animals in the reproductive process, but he concluded that aggression served a variety of other purposes as well. Aggression, said Lorenz, ensures an "even distribution of animals of a particular species over an inhabitable area" and provides for a defence of the species from predators.[10] Human aggression, he claimed, meets many of the same purposes but can take on covert forms. The drive to acquire wealth and power that was so characteristic of Western men at the time of his writing is part of the human mating ritual, whereby a man might "win" a prized woman through displays of more civilized forms of what could otherwise be understood as intraspecies aggression.

Charles Darwin (1809–1882), founder of modern evolutionary theory. How might evolutionary theory relate to criminality?

Bettmann/CORBIS

Lorenz's greatest contribution to the study of human behaviour may have been his claim that all human behaviour is, at least to some degree, "adapted instinctive behavior": in other words, much of human conduct is fundamentally rooted in instinctive behavioural responses characteristic of biological organisms everywhere and present within each of us in the form of a biological inheritance from more primitive times. Even rational human thought derives its motivation and direction from instinctual aspects of human biology, and the highest human virtues, such as the value placed on human life, "could not have been achieved," said Lorenz, "without an instinctive appreciation of life and death."[11]

Building upon the root functions of aggression, Lorenz concluded that much of what we today call "crime" is the result of overcrowded living conditions combined with a lack of legitimate opportunity for the effective expression of aggression. Crowding increases the likelihood of aggression, while contemporary socialization works to inhibit it. In the words of Lorenz, "In one sense we are all psychopaths, for each of us suffers from the necessity of self-imposed control for the good of the community."[12] When people break down, said Lorenz, they become neurotic or delinquent, and crime may be the result of stresses that have been found to typically produce aggression throughout the animal kingdom.

The brain is indeed "the organ of the mind" as early criminologists claimed. Here, a computer-enhanced image shows areas of activity within the brain. Do you think biology may play a role in crime?

Scott Camazine/Science Source

Lorenz's explanations, like many of the biologically based theories we will encounter in this chapter, appear more applicable to violent crime than to other forms of criminal offence. But it is important to recognize that modern frustrations and concomitant manifestations of aggression may be symbolically, rather than directly, expressed. Hence, a stockbroker who embezzles a client's money, spurred on by the need to provide material goods for an overly acquisitive family, may be just as criminal as the robber who beats his victim and steals her purse to have money to buy liquor.

Early Biological Theories

◉—[Watch

Phrenology

Numerous perspectives on criminal biology predate Lorenz's work. Some of the perspectives fall into the category of **criminal anthropology**, the scientific study of the relationship between human physical characteristics and criminality. One of the earliest criminological anthropologists was Franz Joseph Gall (1758–1828). Gall hypothesized in his theory of **phrenology** (also called *craniology*) that the shape of the human skull was indicative of the personality and could be used to predict criminality. Gall's approach contained four themes:

1. The brain is the organ of the mind.

2. Particular aspects of personality are associated with specific locations in the brain.

3. Portions of the brain that are well developed will cause personality characteristics associated with them to be more prominent in the individual under study, whereas poorly developed brain areas lead to a lack of associated personality characteristics.

4. The shape of a person's skull corresponds to the shape of the underlying brain and is therefore indicative of the personality.

Gall was one of the first Western writers to firmly locate the roots of personality in the brain. Prior to his time, it was thought that aspects of personality resided in various organs throughout the body—a fact reflected in linguistic anachronisms surviving into the present day (for example, when someone is described as being "hard-hearted" or as having

Criminal anthropology The scientific study of the relationship between human physical characteristics and criminality.

Phrenology The study of the shape of the head to determine anatomical correlates of human behaviour.

"a lot of gall"). Greek philosopher Aristotle was said to believe that the brain served no function other than to radiate excess heat from the body, so Gall's perspective, although relatively primitive by today's standards, did much to advance physiological understandings of the mind–body connection in Western thought.

Although Gall never tested his theory, it was widely accepted by many of his contemporaries because it represented something of a shift away from theological perspectives prevalent at the time and a move toward scientific understanding—a trend that was well underway by the time of his writings. Phrenology also provided for systematic evaluation of suspected offenders and was intriguing for its ease of use. One of Gall's students, Johann Gaspar Spurzheim (1776–1853), brought phrenological theory to North America and helped to spread its influence through a series of lectures and publications on the subject. Phrenology's prestige in North America extended into the 20th century, finding a place in classification schemes used to evaluate newly admitted prisoners. Even Arthur Conan Doyle's fictional character Sherlock Holmes was described as using phrenology to solve a number of crimes.

The Positivist School One of the best-known early scientific biological theorists—19th-century Italian army prison physician Cesare Lombroso (1836–1909)—coined the term **atavism** to suggest that criminality was the result of primitive urges that, in modern-day human throwbacks, survived the evolutionary process. He described "the nature of the criminal" as "an atavistic being who reproduces in his person the ferocious instincts of primitive humanity and the inferior animals."[13]

At the same time, Charles Darwin was making a substantial impact on the scientific world with his theory of biological evolution. Darwin proposed that human beings and other contemporary living organisms were the end products of a long evolutionary process governed by rules such as natural selection and survival of the fittest. Lombroso adapted elements of Darwin's theory to suggest that primitive traits survived in present-day human populations and led to heightened criminal tendencies among individuals who harboured them. Darwin himself had proposed this idea when he wrote, "With mankind some of the worst dispositions, which occasionally without any assignable cause make their appearance in families, may perhaps be reversions to a savage state, from which we are not removed by very many generations."[14]

Lombroso has been called the father of modern criminology because he was the first criminologist of note to employ the scientific method—particularly measurement, observation, and attempts at generalization—in his work. Other writers, more specific in their pronouncements, have referred to him as the "father of the Italian School" of criminology, in recognition of the fact that 19th-century positivism began in Italy.

Positivism, as mentioned in Chapter 5, was built on two principles: (1) an unflagging acceptance of social determinism, or the belief that human behaviour is determined not by the exercise of free choice but by causative factors beyond the control of the individual, and (2) application of scientific techniques to the study of crime and criminology. The term *positivism* had its roots in the writings of Auguste Comte (1798–1857), who proposed use of the scientific method in the study of society in his 1851 work *A System of Positive Polity*.[15] Positivism holds that social phenomena are observable, explainable, and measurable in quantitative terms. For a strict positivist, reality consists of a world of objectively defined facts, which can be scientifically measured and—ultimately—controlled.[16]

Lombroso's scientific work consisted of postmortem studies of the bodies of executed and deceased offenders, which he measured in many different ways. The body of one such well-known criminal, named Vilella, provided Lombroso with many of his findings and reinforced his belief that most offenders were genetically predisposed toward criminality. When he examined Vilella's brain, Lombroso found an unusual depression, which he named "the median occipital fossa" and identified features of Vilella's brain as being

Atavism A term used by Cesare Lombroso to suggest that criminals are physiological throwbacks to earlier stages of human evolution.

👁 **Watch**

Positivism

👁 **Watch**

Cesare Lombroso

Positivism The application of scientific techniques to the study of crime and criminals.

similar to those found in lower primates. Study of another offender, an Italian soldier whom Lombroso called Misdea in his writings and who "attacked and killed eight of his superior officers and comrades," supported his conclusions.[17]

In addition to his examinations of Vilella and Misdea, Lombroso conducted autopsies on another 65 executed offenders and examined 832 living prison inmates, comparing physical measurements of their body parts with measurements taken from 390 soldiers. As a result of his work, Lombroso claimed to have found a wide variety of bodily features predictive of criminal behaviour. Among them were exceptionally long arms, an index finger as long as the middle finger, fleshy pouches in the cheeks "like those in rodents," eyes that were either abnormally close together or too far apart, large teeth, ears that lacked lobes, prominent cheekbones, a crooked nose, a large amount of body hair, a protruding chin, large lips, a non-standard number of ribs, and eyes of differing colours or hues. Lombroso went so far as to enumerate characteristics of particular types of offenders. Murderers, whom he called "habitual homicides," had "cold, glassy eyes, immobile and sometimes sanguine and inflamed; the nose, always large, is frequently aquiline or, rather, hooked; the jaws are strong, the cheekbones large, the hair curly, dark, and abundant; the beard is frequently thin, the canine teeth well developed and the lips delicate."[18]

Atavism implies the notion that criminals are born that way. Lombroso was continuously reassessing his estimates of the proportion, from among all offenders, of **born criminals**. At one point, he asserted that fully 90 percent of offenders committed crimes because of atavistic influences; he later revised the figure downward to 70 percent, admitting that normal individuals might be pulled into lives of crime. In addition to the category of the born criminal, Lombroso described other categories of offenders, including the insane, "criminaloids," and criminals incited by passion. The insane were said to include mental and moral degenerates, alcoholics, drug addicts, and so forth. **Criminaloids**, also termed "occasional criminals," were described as persons who were pulled into breaking the law by virtue of environmental influences. Nevertheless, most criminaloids were seen by Lombroso as exhibiting some degree of atavism and hence were said to "differ from born criminals in degree, not in kind." Those who became criminals by virtue of passion were said to have surrendered to intense emotions, including love, jealousy, hatred, or an injured sense of honour.

Although he focused on physical features, Lombroso was not insensitive to behavioural indicators of criminality. In his later writings, he claimed that criminals exhibited acute sight, hearing abilities that were below the norm, an insensitivity to pain, a lack of moral sensibility, cruelty, vindictiveness, impulsiveness, a love of gambling, and a tendency to be tattooed.

In 1893, Lombroso published *The Female Offender*.[19] In that book, he expressed his belief that women exhibit far less anatomical variation than do men but insisted that criminal behaviour among women, as among men, derived from atavistic foundations. Lombroso saw the quintessential female offender as the prostitute, who was "the genuine typical representative of criminality" among women.[20] Prostitutes, he claimed, act out atavistic yearnings and, in doing so, return to a form of behaviour characteristic of humankind's primitive past.

Born criminal An individual who is born with a genetic predilection toward criminality.

Criminaloids A term used by Cesare Lombroso to describe occasional criminals who were pulled into criminality primarily by environmental influences.

Evaluations of Atavism   Following in Lombroso's positivistic footsteps around the turn of the 20th century, the English physician Charles Buckman Goring (1870–1919) conducted a well-controlled statistical study of Lombroso's thesis of atavism. Using newly developed but advanced mathematical techniques to measure the degree of correlation between physiological features and criminal history, Goring examined nearly 3000 inmates at Turin prison beginning in 1901. Enlisting the aid of London's Biometric Laboratory, he concluded that "the whole fabric of Lombrosian doctrine, judged by the standards of science, is fundamentally unsound."[21] Goring compared the prisoners with students at Oxford and Cambridge universities, British soldiers, and non-criminal hospital patients, and published his findings in 1913 in his lengthy treatise *The English Convict: A Statistical Study.*[22]

A similar study was conducted between 1927 and 1939 by Earnest A. Hooton, a professor of anthropology at Harvard University. In 1939, Hooton published *Crime and the Man*, in which he reported having evaluated 13 873 inmates from ten states, comparing them along 107 physiological dimensions with 3203 non-incarcerated individuals who formed a control group.[23] His sample consisted of 10 953 prison inmates, 2004 county jail prisoners, 743 criminally insane, 173 "defective delinquents," 1227 "insane civilians," and 1976 "sane civilians."

Hooton distinguished between regions of the country, arguing that "states have favorite crimes, just as they have favorite sons." He reported finding physiological features characteristic of specific criminal types in individual states. He was drawn to the conclusion that "crime is not an exclusively sociological phenomenon, but is also biological."[24]

Hooton stated that "it is impossible to improve and correct environment to a point at which these flawed and degenerate human beings will be able to succeed in honest social competition," making it clear that he did not believe that rehabilitation programs could have much effect upon most offenders, and suggesting banishing them to a remote location.[25] Hooton concluded that criminals showed an overall physiological inferiority to the general population and that crime was the result of "the impact of environment upon low grade human organisms."[26]

Hooton, an example of whose work is provided in Figure 6.1, was quickly criticized along a number of dimensions. In the words of Stephen Schafer, a contemporary criminologist,

> The major criticisms were that his criminal population was not a representative sample of all criminals, that his control group was a fantastic conglomeration of non-criminal civilians, . . . that he emphasized selected characteristics and disregarded others, that he gave no convincing evidence that the criminal's "inferiority" was inherited, and that he failed to explore other important data that were available.[27]

Figure 6.1 Ernest A. Hooton's "Massachusetts Criminal"

Source: Reprinted by permission of the publisher from "Old American Criminals—Massachusetts: Mosaic of Cranial, Facial, and Morphological Features" in *Crime and the Man* by Earnest Albert Hooton, p. 57, Cambridge, MA: Harvard University Press. Copyright © 1939 by the President and Fellows of Harvard College. Copyright © renewed 1967 by Mary C. Hooton.

Perhaps even more significant, Hooton failed to recognize that members of his non-criminal control group might, in fact, have been involved in crime but managed to elude capture and processing by the criminal justice system; in other words, the most successful criminals may not have appeared in Hooton's study group of inmates because they had eluded the law, thereby making their way into his supposedly non-criminal control group. His study might have simply demonstrated that "inferior" criminal specimens are the ones who get caught and end up in prison.

Nonetheless, claims that physical abnormalities may be linked to crime persist into the present day. In a study of teenage boys reported in 2000, for example, Canadian researchers L. Arseneault and Richard E. Tremblay conducted hormonal, anthropometric, psychophysiological, neuropsychological, and psychiatric evaluations of 1037 boys who had attended kindergarten in 1984 in a socially and economically disadvantaged area of Montreal.[28] Using evaluations provided years later by parents, teachers, classmates, and the children themselves, Arseneault and Tremblay concluded that subtle physical abnormalities, including minor abnormalities in the shape of the ears, tongue, and teeth, were associated with an increased risk of behavioural and psychiatric problems in later years. The researchers suggested that such minor physical abnormalities might have resulted from genetic problems or prenatal insults associated with exposure to toxins, concluding that "both the total count of minor physical anomalies and the total count of minor physical anomalies of the mouth were significantly associated with an increased risk of violent delinquency in adolescence, beyond the effects of childhood physical aggression and family adversity." Arseneault and Tremblay recognized, however, that abnormalities of the type they identified might be associated with neurological deficits and that abnormalities of the mouth could lead to feeding problems in the first months after birth, which might somehow cause problems in development or socialization.

Body Types

Constitutional theories are those that explain criminality by reference to offenders' body types, genetics, or external observable physical characteristics. A constitutional, or physiological, orientation that found its way into the criminological mainstream during the early and mid-20th century was that of **somatotyping** (classifying according to body types), primarily associated with the work of Ernst Kretschmer and William H. Sheldon. Kretschmer, a professor of psychiatry at the German University of Tubingen, proposed a relationship between body build and personality type and created a rather detailed "biopsychological constitutional typology" that revolved around three basic mental categories: cycloids (also called "cyclothymes"), schizoids (or "schizothymes"), and displastics. **Cycloids**, who were associated with a heavyset, soft type of body, vacillated between normality and abnormality, lacked spontaneity and sophistication, and committed mostly non-violent property offences. **Schizoids**, who tended to possess muscular, athletic bodies but could also be thin and lean, were seen as more likely to be schizophrenic and to commit violent types of offences. **Displastics** were a mixed group described as highly emotional and often unable to control themselves, and thought to commit mostly sexual offences and other crimes of passion.

Influenced by Kretschmer, Sheldon utilized measurement techniques to connect body type with personality.[29] Sheldon felt that Kretschmer had erred in including too large an age range in his work, so he limited his study to 200 boys between the ages of 15 and 21 at the Hayden Goodwill Institute in Boston. Sheldon concluded that four basic body types characterized the entire group (see Figure 6.2):

1. The **endomorph** is soft and round, with "digestive viscera [that] are massive and highly developed" (the person is overweight and has a large stomach).

Watch
William Sheldon

Explore
Evidence—Somatotypes

Constitutional theory A theory that explains criminality by reference to offenders' body types, inheritance, genetics, or external observable physical characteristics.

Somatotyping The classification of human beings into types according to body build and other physical characteristics.

Cycloid A term developed by Ernst Kretschmer to describe a particular relationship between body build and personality type. The cycloid personality, which was associated with a heavyset, soft type of body, was said to vacillate between normality and abnormality.

Schizoid A person characterized by a schizoid personality disorder. Such disordered personalities appear to be aloof, withdrawn, unresponsive, humourless, dull, and solitary to an abnormal degree.

Displastic A mixed group of offenders described by theorist Ernst Kretschmer as highly emotional and often unable to control themselves.

Endomorph A body type described as soft and round or overweight.

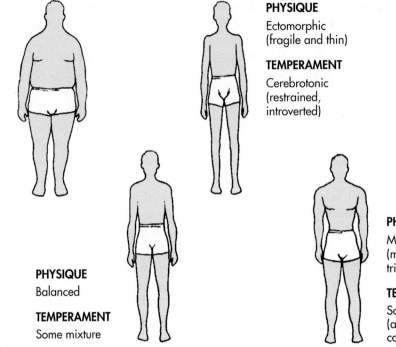

PHYSIQUE
Endomorphic
(soft and round)

TEMPERAMENT
Viscerotonic
(sociable, loves
to eat)

PHYSIQUE
Ectomorphic
(fragile and thin)

TEMPERAMENT
Cerebrotonic
(restrained,
introverted)

PHYSIQUE
Balanced

TEMPERAMENT
Some mixture

PHYSIQUE
Mesomorphic
(muscular and
triangular)

TEMPERAMENT
Somatotonic
(adventurous,
competitive)

Figure 6.2 Sheldon's Somatotypes

Source: BARTOL, CRIMINAL BEHAVIOR: A PSYCHOSOCIAL APPROACH., 1st Ed., ©1980, p. 23. Reprinted and Electronically reproduced by permission of Pearson Education, Inc., Upper Saddle River, New Jersey.

Mesomorph A body type described as athletic and muscular.

Ectomorph A body type described as thin and fragile, with long, slender, poorly muscled extremities and delicate bones.

2. The **mesomorph** is athletic and muscular, with "somatic structures[that] are in the ascendancy" (the person has larger bones and considerable muscle mass).

3. The **ectomorph** is thin and fragile and has "long, slender, poorly muscled extremities, with delicate, pipestem bones."

4. The balanced type is a person of average build, not overweight, thin, or exceedingly muscular.[30]

Individuals (excluding the balanced type) were ranked along each of the three major dimensions using a seven-point scale. A score of 1–1–7, for example, would indicate that a person exhibited few characteristics of endomorphology or mesomorphology but was predominantly ectomorphic. Sheldon claimed that varying types of temperament and personalities were closely associated with each of the body types he identified: Ectomorphs were said to be "cerebrotonic," or restrained, shy, and inhibited; endomorphs were "viscerotonic," or relaxed and sociable. Mesomorphs, or muscular body types, were most likely to be associated with delinquency or "somatotonia," which he described as "a predominance of muscular activity and vigorous bodily assertiveness." Sheldon's work was supported by constitutional studies of juvenile delinquents conducted by Sheldon and Eleanor Glueck and reported in 1950.[31] The Gluecks compared 500 known delinquents with 500 nondelinquents, matching both groups on age, general intelligence, ethnic–racial background, and place of residence. Like Sheldon, the Gluecks concluded that mesomorphy was associated with delinquency.

Early biological theorists like Gall, Lombroso, and Sheldon provide an interesting footnote to the history of criminological thought. Today, however, their work is mostly relegated to the dustbins of academic theorizing. Modern biological theories of crime are far more sophisticated than their early predecessors, and it is to these we now turn.

Chemical and Environmental Precursors of Crime

Recent research in the area of nutrition has produced some limited evidence that the old maxim "you are what you eat" may contain more than a grain of truth. Biocriminology has made some strides in linking violent or disruptive behaviour to eating habits, vitamin deficiencies, genetics, inheritance, and other conditions that affect the body. Studies of nutrition, endocrinology, and environmental contaminants have all contributed to advances in understanding such behaviour.

One of the first studies to focus on chemical imbalances in the body as a cause of crime was reported in the British medical journal *Lancet* in 1943.[32] The authors of the study linked murder to **hypoglycemia**, or low blood sugar. Low blood sugar, produced by too much insulin in the blood or by near-starvation diets, was said to reduce the mind's capacity to effectively reason or to judge the long-term consequences of behaviour. More recent studies have linked excess consumption of refined white sugar to hyperactivity, excitability, and impairment of the ability to make reasoned decisions. Popular books such as *Sugar Blues* provide guides for individuals seeking to free themselves from the negative effects of excess sugar consumption.[33]

Hypoglycemia A medical condition characterized by low blood sugar.

To some degree, even courts have accepted the notion that excess sugar consumption may be linked to crime. In the early 1980s, for example, Dan White, a former San Francisco police officer, was given a reduced sentence after his lawyers used what came to be known as the "Twinkie Defence." They argued that White's night-long binge on large numbers of Coca-Colas and Twinkies before he murdered San Francisco Mayor George Moscone and City Councillor Harvey Milk was evidence of White's unbalanced mental state. The consumption of junk food was presented as evidence of depression since White was normally very health conscious. More than ten years later, however, a well-conducted 1994 study reported in the *New England Journal of Medicine* seemed to contradict the notion that sugar may lead to hyperactivity;[34] similarly, neither sugar nor artificial sweeteners were shown to have any link to an increase in learning disabilities. In the study, researchers at Vanderbilt University and the University of Iowa varied the diets of supposedly sugar-sensitive youngsters from ones that were high in sugar to a diet that was low in sugar but contained the artificial sweetener aspartame; a third experimental diet contained very little sugar but had added saccharin. After surveying parents, teachers, and babysitters and testing the study group for changes in memory, concentration, and math skills, the researchers concluded, "We couldn't find any difference in terms of their behavior or their learning on any of the three diets."[35] Hence, to date, the evidence concerning sugar's impact on behaviour is less than clear.

Allergic reactions to common foods have been reported as the cause of violence and homicide by a number of investigators.[36] Some foods—including milk, citrus fruit, chocolate, corn, wheat, and eggs—are said to produce allergic reactions in sensitive individuals, leading to a swelling of the brain and the brain stem; such swelling is thought to impede the higher faculties, reducing people's sense of morality and creating conditions that support impulsive behaviour. Involvement of the central nervous system in such allergies may reduce the amount of learning that occurs during childhood and may contribute to delinquency as well as to adult criminal behaviour.

Some studies have implicated food additives, such as the flavour enhancer monosodium glutamate, dyes, and artificial flavourings in producing criminal violence.[37] Other research has found that coffee and sugar may trigger anti-social behaviour;[38] researchers were led to these conclusions through finding that inmates consumed considerably greater amounts of coffee, sugar, and processed foods than others.[39] It is unclear, however, whether inmates drink more coffee because of boredom, or whether "excitable" personalities feel a need for the kind of stimulation available through coffee consumption. On the other hand, habitual coffee drinkers in non-prison populations have not been linked to crime, and other studies show no link between the amount of sugar consumed by inmates and hyper-activity.[40] Nonetheless, some prison programs have been designed to limit intake of dietary stimulants through nutritional management and the substitution of artificial sweeteners for refined sugar.

Vitamins have also been examined for their impact on delinquency. At least one researcher found that disruptive children consumed far less than optimal levels of vitamins B_3 and B_6 than did non-problem youths.[41] Some researchers have suggested that the addition of these vitamins to the diets of children who were deficient in them could control unruly behaviour and improve school performance.

Other nutrients have been studied to assess their possible behavioural impact. In 2003, for example, Ingrid B. Helland reported that maternal diet during pregnancy can strongly affect IQ and early infant behaviour and concluded that it might also determine the risk of delinquency and criminality in later life.[42] Helland and her colleagues supplemented the diets of pregnant and lactating women with either omega-3 (DHA) or omega-6 fatty acids and followed the development of their offspring for years after the supplementation program had ended; they found that children receiving dietary omega-3 supplementation had significantly higher IQ levels by age 4 and performed better on problem-solving tests than those receiving omega-6 fatty acids.

A year later, a study of the relationship between omega-3 intake levels and chronic hostility among 3600 urban young adults concluded that higher consumption of omega-3 fatty acids was related to significantly lower levels of hostility. Researchers concluded that "high dietary intake of DHA and consumption of fish rich in omega-3 fatty acids may be related to lower likelihood of high hostility in young adulthood."[43] Similarly, a 2007 study conducted in the United Kingdom found that anti-social behaviour could be reduced in children through dietary supplementation with poly-unsaturated fatty acids.[44]

In a study designed to test the hypothesis that dietary supplementation could reduce violence among prison populations, C. Bernard Gesch and colleagues supplemented the diets of 115 English young adult prisoners and compared their behaviour with 116 inmates receiving placebos.[45] The experiment lasted 142 days, and supplements included vitamins, minerals, and essential fatty acids. Researchers found a 35.1 percent reduction in offence rates in the supplement group, with the greatest reduction for the most serious incidents, including violence. The Gesch study supported the findings of Stephen Schoenthaler and his colleagues, who found that nutritional supplementation could reduce anti-social acts by incarcerated offenders in California, citing a 30 percent decrease in the rate of serious rule violation for persons receiving dietary supplements similar to those used in the Gesch study.[46]

In 1997, British researchers Roger D. Masters, Brian Hone, and Anil Doshi published a study purporting to show that industrial and other forms of environmental pollution cause people to commit violent crimes.[47] The study used statistics from the FBI's Uniform Crime Reporting Program and data from the U.S. Environmental Protection Agency's Toxic Release Inventory. A comparison between the two data sets showed a significant correlation between juvenile crime and high environmental levels of both lead and manganese. Masters and his colleagues suggested an explanation based on a neurotoxicity hypothesis. Another author stated,

> According to this approach, toxic pollutants—specifically the toxic metals lead and manganese—cause learning disabilities, an increase in aggressive behavior, and—most importantly—loss of control over impulsive behavior. These traits combine with poverty, social stress, alcohol and drug abuse, individual character, and other social and psychological factors to produce individuals who commit violent crimes.[48]

According to Masters, the presence of excess manganese lowers levels of serotonin and dopamine in the brain, both of which are associated with impulse control and planning.

Low brain levels of serotonin are known to cause mood disturbances, poor impulse control, and increases in aggressive behaviour.[49] Masters also claimed that children who are raised from birth on infant formula and who are not breastfed will absorb five times as much manganese as do breastfed infants; calcium deficiency is known to increase the absorption of manganese and "a combination of manganese toxicity and calcium deficiency adds up to 'reverse' Prozac."[50]

In defence of his thesis, Masters cited other studies, the largest of which was an examination of 1000 African-American children in Philadelphia that showed that levels of exposure to lead was a reliable predictor of the number of juvenile offences among the exposed male population, the seriousness of juvenile offences, and the number of adult offences. More recent studies seem to support his thesis.[51]

Masters reasoned that toxic metals affect individuals in complex ways. Because lead diminishes a person's normal ability to detoxify poisons, it may heighten the effects of alcohol and drugs; industrial pollution, automobile traffic, lead-based paints, and aging water delivery systems are all possible sources of contamination. In a recent interview, Masters noted, "The presence of pollution is as big a factor [in crime causation] as poverty. It's the breakdown of the inhibition mechanism that's the key to violent behavior."[52] When brain chemistry is altered by exposure to heavy metal and other toxins, he said, people lose the natural restraint that holds their violent tendencies in check.

In addition to chemical substances likely to be ingested that may affect behaviour, other environmental features have also been linked to the likelihood of aggressive behaviour. During the early 1980s, for example, Alexander Schauss and his followers found that the use of a specific shade of pink could have a calming effect on people experiencing feelings of anger and agitation.[53] Findings indicated that exposure to pink produced an endocrine change that had a tranquilizing effect on the muscles which was not subject to conscious control. As a result of such studies, jail cells in a number of locales were painted pink in hopes that aggressive tendencies among inmates might be reduced. Researchers supported such measures, saying that "the use of pink color in reducing aggression and causing muscular relaxation of inmates is humane and requires no medication or physical force."[54]

More recent studies have focused on prenatal exposure to substances like marijuana, tobacco smoke, and alcohol. In 2000, results of a ten-year study that monitored the development of the children of more than 600 low-income women found that prenatal marijuana use was significantly related to increased hyperactivity, impulsivity, inattention symptoms, increased delinquency, and externalizing problems.[55] The findings remained significant even when researchers controlled for other lifestyle features.

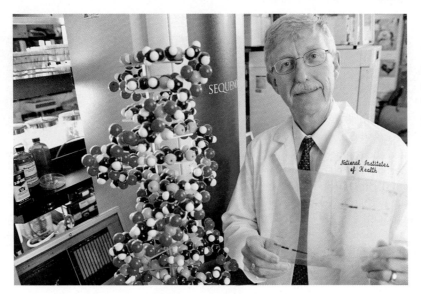

Dr. Francis Collins, former director of the Human Genome Project and current director of the National Institutes of Health. The international Human Genome Project is a research program undertaken to determine the complete nucleotide sequence of human DNA. What are some of the ethical, legal, and social implications of such a project?

Michael Ventura/Alamy

Similarly, a study of 1022 New Zealand children who had been followed for 18 years found that "children whose mothers smoked one pack of cigarettes or more per day during their pregnancy had mean rates of conduct disorder symptoms that were twice as high as those found among children born to mothers who did not smoke during their pregnancy."[56] The observed relationship was twice as strong among male teens as among females. Similar relationships between prenatal smoking and aggression and hyperactivity in later life have been reported by Dutch researchers.[57] A 2006 meta-analysis by researchers at Washington State University also found that smoking by pregnant mothers contributed slightly to their children's subsequent anti-social behaviour.[58]

Prenatal alcohol exposure also seems to be linked to delinquency and psychiatric problems later in life. A 1999 study of 32 children found that alcohol-exposed children exhibited greater delinquency and less intelligence than a control group of children who had not suffered from alcohol exposure while in the womb. The researchers concluded that their findings, which are consistent with the work of other researchers,[59] showed that "alcohol-exposed children, although less impaired intellectually, are more likely than children with mental retardation to exhibit antisocial behaviours, lack of consideration for the rights and feelings of others, and resistance to limits and requests of authority figures."[60]

Hormones and Criminality

Testosterone The primary male sex hormone. It is produced in the testes, and its function is to control secondary sex characteristics and sexual drive.

Hormones have also come under scrutiny as potential behavioural determinants. The male sex hormone **testosterone** has been linked to aggression (see the following Who's Responsible? box). Most studies on the subject have consistently shown an apparent relationship between high blood testosterone levels and increased aggressiveness in men. More focused studies have unveiled a direct relationship between the amount of the chemical present and the degree of violence used by sex offenders;[61] other researchers have linked steroid abuse among bodybuilders to destructive urges and psychosis.[62] Some contemporary investigations have demonstrated a link between testosterone levels and aggression in teenagers,[63] and others have shown that adolescent problem behaviour and teenage violence rise in proportion to the amount of testosterone levels in the blood of young men.[64] In 1987, for example, a Swedish researcher, Dan Olweus, reported that boys aged 15 to 17 showed levels of both verbal and physical aggression that correlated with the level of testosterone present in their blood, stating that boys with higher levels of testosterone "tended to be habitually more impatient and irritable than boys with lower testosterone levels."[65] He concluded that high levels of the hormone led to increased frustration and habitual impatience and irritability.

WHO'S RESPONSIBLE—THE INDIVIDUAL OR SOCIETY?

Hormones and Criminal Behaviour

Lamont Ridgeway, 22, was arrested and charged with sexual assault after 21-year-old Nicole Bachman called police to her home at 2:00 A.M. Ridgeway and Bachman had met in an evening class at the local community college, and Bachman invited Ridgeway to her apartment for a beer after the class was over. Officers couldn't help but notice that Bachman was an unusually attractive young woman whose clothes were in disarray and that she was visibly intoxicated and slurred her words as she spoke; Ridgeway was passed out on her couch, apparently after having had far too much to drink.

"He raped me!" Bachman told the two officers who responded to her call for help. "I told him to stop, and he wouldn't," she said.

(Continued)

Hormones and Criminal Behaviour

Ridgeway was roused from sleep, arrested, searched, handcuffed, and taken to jail, where he was booked and charged with sexual assault. After being advised of his rights not to speak and to have a lawyer represent him, he decided to tell the officers who were questioning him that it wasn't really sexual assault. "She came on to me," he said. "She took her blouse off, then her pants. And she gave me a lot to drink. Yeah, she said 'No,' but by then we were already there. I couldn't stop. Why would she want to, anyway?"

When Ridgeway's lawyer arrived, he advised Ridgeway not to say anything more. The lawyer, hired by Ridgeway's wealthy parents, read the statement that he had given to the police and then hired a psychiatrist to help in building a defence that might stand up in court.

When the case went to trial two months later, the psychiatrist testified as an expert witness for the defence. He told the jury that blood tests showed that Ridgeway had abnormally large amounts of testosterone naturally occurring in his blood, that testosterone was the chemical messenger responsible for the male sex drive (which, he said, differed substantially from that of women), and that Ridgeway had consequently been unable to control his behaviour on the night of the alleged assault. "The young man was simply doing what his hormones made him do," the psychiatrist testified. "It's my professional opinion," he concluded, "that with that amount of testosterone affecting his judgment, he really didn't have much choice in his behavioural responses once he was offered alcohol and was then visually stimulated by the young woman's removal of her clothes. If this was my patient," the psychiatrist added, "I'd treat him with the testosterone antagonist Depo-Provera, and we would see the strength of his sex drive substantially diminished. You could be sure that this kind of thing wouldn't happen again."

In response, the prosecution called its own expert, a noted biochemist who, citing various studies, said that there was no clearly established link between blood levels of testosterone and aggressive sexual behaviour in human beings. "Even if there were," he said, "people are not mindless animals. We have free choice. We are not so driven by our blood chemistry that we cannot decide what we are going to do in any given situation."

Think about it:

1. With which expert witness do you agree more—the psychiatrist or the biochemist? Why?

2. Do you believe that blood chemistry can ever be an explanation for behaviour? For crime?

3. How do our understandings of criminal motivation and crime causality influence our policies on the treatment, punishment, and reformation of those who violate the law?

Note: This example is a fictionalized one, intended to encourage critical thinking.

In what may be the definitive work to date on the subject, Alan Booth and D. Wayne Osgood concluded that there is a "moderately strong relationship between testosterone and adult deviance," but suggested that the relationship "is largely mediated by the influence of testosterone on social integration and on prior involvement in juvenile delinquency."[66] In other words, measurably high levels of testosterone in the blood of young men may have some effect on behaviour, but those effects are likely to be moderated by the social environment.

A 1997 study by Paul C. Bernhardt found that testosterone might not act alone in promoting aggression.[67] Bernhardt discovered that aggressive behaviour in men may be influenced by high testosterone levels combined with low brain levels of the neurotransmitter serotonin and postulated that testosterone's true role is to produce dominance-seeking behaviour, but not necessarily overt aggression. According to Bernhardt, when individuals are frustrated by their inability to achieve dominance, serotonin acts to reduce the negative psychological impact of frustration, producing calmer responses. Men whose brains are lacking in serotonin, however, feel the effects of frustration more acutely and therefore tend to respond to frustrating circumstances more aggressively, especially when testosterone levels are high.

A few limited studies have attempted to measure the effects of testosterone on women. Although women's bodies manufacture roughly 10 percent of the amount of the hormone secreted by men, subtle changes in testosterone levels in women have been linked to changes in personality and sexual behaviour.[68] One such study showed that relatively high

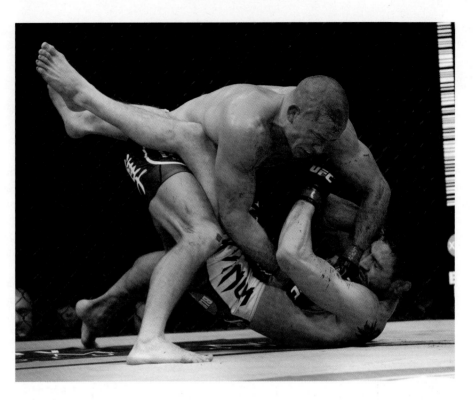

Canadian UFC welterweight champion Georges St-Pierre pins Nick Diaz.
Sex hormones such as testosterone have been linked to aggressive behaviour. Testosterone also enhances secondary sexual characteristics such as body hair and muscle mass in males. What kinds of crimes might be hormonally influenced?

Ryan Remiorz/Canadian Press Images

blood levels of testosterone in female inmates were associated with "aggressive dominant behaviour" in prison.[69]

Some researchers believe that a drop in serotonin levels in the female brain just prior to menstruation might explain the agitation and irritability sometimes associated with premenstrual syndrome.[70] Serotonin has been called a "behaviour-regulating chemical," and animal studies have demonstrated a link between low levels of the neurotransmitter present in the brain and aggressive behaviour. For example, monkeys with low serotonin levels have been found more likely to bite, slap, and chase others of their kind. Studies at the National Institute on Alcohol Abuse and Alcoholism in Bethesda, Maryland, have linked low serotonin levels in humans to impulsive crimes. Men convicted of premeditated murder, for example, have been found to have normal serotonin levels, whereas those convicted of crimes of passion have lower levels.[71]

One 1998 study of 781 men and women age 21 found a clear relationship between elevated *blood* levels of serotonin (which correspond to lower *brain* levels of the chemical) and violence in men.[72] The study controlled for a host of possible intervening factors, including gender, diet, psychiatric medications, illicit drug use, season of the year (during which the blood test was done), plasma levels of tryptophan (the dietary precursor of serotonin), alcohol and tobacco use, psychiatric diagnoses, platelet count, body mass, socioeconomic status, IQ, and history of suicide attempts. The relationship held true when both court records and self-reports of violence were assessed. No relationship between serotonin levels and aggression was seen in female subjects.

Similar research by Swedish neuropsychiatrists in 2003 found that a "dysregulation of serotonin" in the brain and central nervous system could lead to increased impulsivity, irresponsibility, aggression, and need for stimulation.[73] The researchers examined the cerebrospinal fluid (CSF) of 28 violent and sexual offenders and noted that an imbalance between levels of serotonin and dopamine was highly associated with psychopathic traits.

Other hormones, such as cortisol and the thyroid hormone T_3, have also been implicated in delinquency and poor impulse control. A few years ago, two separate Swedish studies found evidence suggesting that elevated levels of the thyroid hormone T_3 were related to alcoholism, psychopathy, and criminality.[74] Blood serum levels of the thyroid hormone T_4 (thyroxine), on the other hand, were negatively related to anti-social behaviour. The researchers concluded that the results of their studies indicate an intimate relationship between T_3 and T_4 and abuse and anti-social behaviour. They emphasized the importance of further studies on T_3 as a biological marker for abuse, social deviance, and repeated violent behavior.[75]

Finally, a few years ago a different kind of link between hormones and crime was identified when Swiss researchers published a study in the well-known journal *Nature* identifying what they called a "trust hormone."[76] Greater quantities of the hormone, a small protein called oxytocin, appear to make people more trusting, and the researchers showed that trust levels could be manipulated by having men inhale oxytocin. (Oxytocin has also been called the "love hormone" because its levels in the brain spike when people make love as well as when women breast-feed.) Those commenting on the research suggested that fraud scams might one day be perpetrated by con men (or women) spraying oxytocin in the air.[77]

GENETICS AND CRIME

Criminal Families

6.3 | LEARNING OBJECTIVE

Watch

Genetics and Crime

Some scholars have suggested that a penchant for crime may be inherited and that criminal tendencies are genetically based. Early studies of this type often focused on criminal families or families that appeared to exhibit criminal tendencies through several generations.

In 1877, Richard L. Dugdale (1841–1883) published a study of one such family—the **Juke family**.[78] Dugdale traced the Juke lineage back to a notorious character named Max, a Dutch immigrant who arrived in New York in the early 18th century. Two of Max's sons married into the notorious "Juke family of girls," six sisters, all of whom were said to be illegitimate. Max's male descendants were reputed to be vicious, and one woman named Ada had an especially bad reputation and came to be known as "the mother of criminals." By the time of the study, Dugdale was able to identify approximately 1200 of Ada's descendants; included among their numbers were 7 murderers, 60 habitual thieves, 90 or so other criminals, 50 prostitutes, and 280 paupers. Dugdale compared the crime-prone Jukes with another family, the pure-blooded progeny of Jonathan Edwards, a Puritan preacher and one-time president of Princeton University. Descendants of Edwards included American presidents and vice-presidents and many successful bankers and businesspeople, and no one was identified from among the Edwards lineage who had a run-in with the law. In 1916, Arthur H. Estabrook published a follow-up to Dugdale's work, in which he identified an additional 715 Juke descendants, including 378 more prostitutes, 170 additional paupers, and 118 other criminals.[79]

Juke family A well-known "criminal family" studied by Richard L. Dugdale.

Following in the tradition of family-tree researchers, Henry H. Goddard (1866–1957) published a study of the **Kallikak family** in 1912.[80] Goddard attempted to place the study of deviant families within an acceptable scientific framework by providing a kind of control group, so for comparison purposes he used two branches of the same family. One branch began as the result of a sexual liaison between Martin Kallikak, a Revolutionary War soldier, and a barmaid whose name is unknown. As a result of this illegitimate union, a son (Martin Jr.) was born. After the war, Kallikak returned home and married a righteous Quaker girl, and a second line of descent began. The legitimate branch produced only a few minor deviants, but the illegitimate line resulted in 262 feeble-minded births and various other epileptic, alcoholic, and criminal descendants. (The term *feeble-minded*, which was much in vogue at the time of Goddard's study, was later recast as *mentally retarded*, and today people exhibiting similar characteristics might be referred to as *mentally handicapped* or *mentally challenged*.) Because feeble-mindedness appeared to occur with some predictability in Goddard's study but criminal activity seemed to be only randomly represented among the descendants of both Kallikak lines, Goddard concluded that a tendency toward feeble-mindedness was inherited but that criminality was not.

Kallikak family A well-known "criminal family" studied by Henry H. Goddard.

Eugenics The study of hereditary improvement by genetic control.

Today, the work of Dugdale and Goddard has been discredited.[81] Nevertheless, studies like these, which focused on inherited mental degeneration, led to the **eugenics** movement of the 1920s and early 1930s and to the development of a branch of criminology that held that the root causes of criminality were largely passed from generation to generation in the form of "bad genes."[82] Social policies developed during the eugenics movement called for the sterilization of mentally handicapped women to prevent their bearing additional offspring. In Canada, sexual sterilization laws in Alberta and British Columbia resulted in the sterilization of almost 3000 citizens between 1928 and 1972. During this period, the legislation targeted not only those with mental illness but also the poor, Aboriginal people, unwed mothers, and non-English-speaking immigrants.[83]

The eugenics movement, as it existed in North America before World War II, was largely discredited by intense condemnation of Nazi genetic research, mass sterilization, and eugenics programs, including those that led to the Holocaust. As a consequence, research attempting to ferret out the biological underpinnings of behavioural traits remains suspect in the minds of many today.

The XYY "Supermale"

Developments in the field of human genetics have led to the study of the role of chromosomes, and sex-linked chromosomes in particular, in crime causation. The first well-known study of this type was undertaken by British researcher Patricia A. Jacobs[84] and her colleagues, who in 1965 examined 197 Scottish prisoners for chromosomal abnormalities through a relatively simple blood test known as karyotyping.[85] Twelve members of the group displayed chromosomes that were unusual, and seven were found to have an XYY chromosome. Normal male individuals possess an XY chromosome structure; normal female individuals are XX. Some other unusual combinations might be XXX, wherein a woman's genetic makeup contains an extra X chromosome, or XXY, also called Klinefelter's syndrome, in which a man might carry an extra X, or female, chromosome. Klinefelter's men often are possessed of male genitalia but are frequently sterile and evidence breast enlargement and intellectual retardation. The XYY man, however, whose incidence in the prison population was placed at around 3.5 percent by Jacobs, was quickly identified as potentially violent and termed a **supermale**.

Supermale A male individual displaying the XYY chromosomal structure.

Following the introduction of the supermale notion into popular consciousness, a number of offenders attempted to offer a chromosome-based defence. In 1969, for example, Lawrence E. Hannell, who was adjudged a supermale, was acquitted of murder in Australia on the grounds of insanity.[86] Such a defence, however, did not work for Richard Speck, another claimed XYY man, convicted of killing eight Chicago nursing students in 1966. It was later learned that Speck did not carry the extra Y chromosome.

To date, there have been nearly 200 studies of XYY males. Although not all researchers agree, taken as a group these studies tend to show that supermales have the following characteristics:[87]

- taller than average height (often 6 feet 1 inch or taller)
- acne and other skin disorders
- below-average intelligence
- over-representation in prisons and mental hospitals
- family tree with above-average history of crime or mental illness

The supermale phenomenon (also called the XYY syndrome) was more sensationalism than fact. Little evidence suggests that XYY men actually commit crimes of greater violence than do other men, although they may commit somewhat more crimes overall. A 1976 Danish study of 4000 men born in Copenhagen between 1944 and 1947 may have helped put the issue to rest with its finding that the incidence of XYY men was less than 1 percent in the general male population.[88] More recent research has concluded that "studies done thus far are largely in agreement and demonstrate rather conclusively that males of the XYY type are not predictably aggressive."[89]

Chromosomes and Modern-Day Criminal Families

In 1993, Dutch criminologists caught worldwide attention with their claim that they had uncovered a specific gene with links to criminal behaviour. Researcher H. Hilger Ropers, geneticist Han G. Brunner, and collaborators studied what media sources called "the Netherlands' most dysfunctional family."[90] Although members of the unnamed family displayed IQs in the near-normal range, they seemed unable to control their impulses and often ended up being arrested for violations of the criminal law; the arrests, however, were always of men. Tracing the family back five generations, Brunner found 14 men whom he classified as genetically given to criminality. None of the women in the family displayed criminal tendencies, although they were often victimized by their crime-prone male siblings.

According to Ropers and Brunner, because men have only one X chromosome, they are especially vulnerable to any defective gene, whereas women, with two X chromosomes, have a kind of backup system in which one defective gene may be compensated for by another wholesome and correctly functioning gene carried in the second X chromosome. After a decade of study, Ropers and Brunner announced that they had isolated the specific mutation that caused the family's criminality. The gene, they said, is one that is responsible for production of an enzyme called monoamine oxidase A (MAOA), which is crucially involved in the process by which signals are transmitted within the brain by breaking down the chemicals serotonin and noradrenaline. Both are substances that, when found in excess in the brain, have been linked to aggressive behaviour in human beings. Because men with the mutated gene do not produce the enzyme necessary to break down chemical transmitters, the researchers surmised, their brains are overwhelmed with stimuli, resulting in uncontrollable urges and, ultimately, criminal behaviour.

Twin Studies

Studies of the criminal tendencies of fraternal and identical twins have provided a methodologically sophisticated technique for ferreting out the role of inheritance in crime causation. Fraternal twins, or **dizygotic (DZ) twins**, develop from different fertilized eggs and share only that genetic material common among siblings. Identical twins, or **monozygotic (MZ) twins**, develop from the same egg and carry virtually the same genetic material. Hence, if human behaviour had a substantial heritable component, twins would display similar behavioural characteristics despite variations in their social environment, with any observed relationship being stronger among MZ twins than among DZ twins.

One of the first studies to link MZ twins to criminality was published in the 1920s by German physician Johannes Lange.[91] Examining 13 pairs of MZ twins and 17 pairs of DZ twins, he found that in 10 of the 13 MZ pairs both twins were criminal, whereas only 2 of the 17 DZ twins exhibited such similarity. Lange's findings drew considerable attention, even though his sample was small and he was unable to adequately separate environmental influences from genetic ones. A much larger twin study was begun in 1968 by the European researchers Karl O. Christiansen and Sarnoff Mednick, who analyzed all twins (3586 pairs) born on a selected group of Danish islands between 1881 and 1910.[92] Christiansen and Mednick found significant statistical support for the notion that criminal tendencies are inherited: 52 percent of identical twins and 22 percent of fraternal siblings displayed the same degree of criminality within the twin pair. Such similarities remained apparent even among twins separated at birth and raised in substantially different environments.

Dizygotic twins Twins who develop from a separate ovum and carry the genetic material shared by siblings.

Monozygotic twins Twin who develop from the same egg and carry virtually the same genetic material.

In 1996, British researchers studying 43 MZ and 38 DZ same-sex twins through the use of self-report questionnaires stated that "common bad behaviors of the sort admitted to by the majority of adolescents have a substantially heritable component. Additive genetic effects account for most of the variation, with no evidence of a contribution from shared environment."[93] The researchers also determined that genetic effects on behaviour appear to increase with age. The British research was supported by the findings of a joint U.S.–Australian examination of 2682 adult twin pairs; in that study, researchers found "a substantial genetic influence on risk for conduct disorder" (defined to include chronic stealing, lying, bullying, arson, property destruction, weapons use, cruelty to animals or people, fighting, aggression, truancy, and running away from home).[94]

Twin studies appear to point to criminal genes that, once inherited, inevitably produce anti-social behaviour. Such a conclusion, however, is not necessarily warranted; genes may simply influence the way people respond to their surroundings, that is, so-called criminal genes may essentially be genetic predispositions to respond in certain ways to a criminogenic environment.

Male–Female Differences in Criminality

A number of contemporary writers have proposed that criminologists need to recognize that "the male is much more criminalistic than the female."[95] With the exception of crimes such as prostitution and shoplifting, the number of crimes committed by men routinely far exceeds the number of crimes committed by women in almost all categories. The data on the extent of male–female criminality show a degree of regularity over time: the proportion of homicides committed by men versus women has remained more or less constant for decades (see Table 6.2).

Despite the mounting evidence that criminality is genetically determined, many criminologists continue to recognize socialization and culture as having the major roles in determining criminality. Hence, as changes in socialization practice and cultural roles increase the opportunity for women to commit what had previously been regarded as traditional male offences, evidence of crime committed by women should reflect an increase in their criminal involvement. In Canada, with the exception of crimes against the person, the gap between male and female crime rates has been narrowing in the past 30 years. Overall, the percentage of *Criminal Code* offences committed by females has increased from 9 percent to 17 percent. Increases were seen particularly in offences classified as serious thefts (from 9 to 23 percent), fraud (from 11 to 30 percent), and minor theft (from 22 to 38 percent).[96]

Interestingly, the situation in the United States is somewhat different. Women are arrested for only 19 percent of all violent crimes and 37 percent of property crimes—a proportion that has remained surprisingly constant over the years since the Federal Bureau of Investigation began gathering crime data more than half a century ago. Such

Table 6.2	Male and Female Murder Perpetrators as a Percentage of All Homicide Suspects, 1966–2010								
1966		**1979**		**1986**		**1998**		**2010**	
Male	Female	Male	Female	Male	Female	Male	Female	Male	Female
85.6%	14.4%	87.3%	12.7%	85.4%	14.6%	91.5%	8.5%	88.5%	11.5%

Sources: Adapted from M.A. Jackson and C.T. Griffiths, *Canadian Criminology: Perspectives on Crime and Criminality* (Toronto: Harcourt Brace, 1995), p.149; Statistics Canada, *Homicide Statistics* 1979 (Cat. 85-209) (Ottawa: Minister of Supply and Services, 1980); Statistics Canada, *Homicide in Canada* 1986: *A Statistical Perspective* (Ottawa: Minister of Supply and Services, 1997); S. Tremblay, "Canadian Crime Statistics, 1988," *Juristat*, vol. 19, no. 9 (Ottawa: Minister of Industry, 1999); and Tina Hotten Mahoney, "Homicide in Canada, 2010", *Juristat* article, (Ottawa: Minister of Industry, 2011).

apparent differences not only have existed over time but can also be seen in cross-cultural studies.[97]

In evaluating the criminality of women based on statistics alone, however, there is a danger of misidentifying causal factors operative in the behaviour itself. Although men consistently commit more murders than women, we should not jump to the conclusion that this bit of evidence shows a genetic predisposition toward interpersonal violence in men that is absent in women. To do so would fail to recognize the role of other causal factors. For example, observable racial variation in crime rates has provided some writers with a basis for claiming that some racial groups are disproportionately violent, attributing such violence to genetics. While Canadian crime statistics do not routinely report on the racial and ethnic makeup of offenders, two studies of Canadian inmate populations have concluded that offenders from non-Aboriginal, visible ethnic minorities were under-represented.[98]

The reality for Aboriginal people in Canada is quite different. Numerous studies over the years have consistently demonstrated that Aboriginals are over-represented in the criminal justice system. Robert Silverman and Leslie Kennedy found that the proportion of Aboriginals involved in homicide is at least five times greater than is their representation in the population.[99] Work by Mary Hyde and Carol La Prairie indicated that Aboriginal peoples are implicated in more offences involving alcohol, in fewer property offences, and in more violent offences.[100] In all provinces and territories, the representation of Aboriginal adults in correctional services exceeds their representation in the general population.[101] By comparison, a look at the statistics in the United States shows that African-Americans are more than six times more likely than Caucasians to commit murder, three times as likely to commit rape, seven times as likely to rob, and twice as likely to commit any kind of crime.[102]

Such statistics, however, can be inherently misleading because—unlike the undeniable and easily observable biological differences that exist between men and women—racial groupings are defined more by convention than by genetics. Some writers have suggested that "pure" racial groups no longer exist, and that even historical racial distinctions were based more on political convention than on significant genetic differences.

The criminality of women (or its lack) may be culturally determined to a considerable degree, but data routinely show that women continue to be less likely than men to be involved in most property crimes and less likely still to commit violent crimes. We have already evaluated the role that testosterone may play in increasing the propensity toward violence and aggression among men. A few authors have suggested that testosterone is the agent primarily responsible for male criminality and that its relative lack in women leads them to commit fewer crimes. Some evidence supports just such a hypothesis. Studies have shown, for example, that female fetuses exposed to elevated testosterone levels during gestation develop masculine characteristics, including a muscular body build and a demonstrably greater tendency toward aggression later in life.[103] However, genetically based behavioural differences between men and women are so overshadowed by aspects of the social environment, including socialization, the learning of culturally prescribed roles, and the expectations of others, that definitive conclusions are difficult to reach.

One proposed social-psychological explanation for homicidal behaviour among women, for example, suggested that men who kill tend to do so out of a need to control a situation, whereas women who kill tend to do so because they have lost control over themselves.[104] The theorists stated that "women as a group are more 'controlled' than men, particularly with respect to their experience and expression of anger" and that such control emanates from the fact that "men are always the subjects and women the objects in [a] male-centric universe."[105] As a consequence of our culture's overemphasis on women's looks rather than on their performance, women internalize a self-image based on their appearance rather than on their character, resulting in low self-esteem and low self-confidence; low self-esteem necessitates greater self-control and results in lower criminality among women. Such a perspective suggests that women tend to commit homicides only when driven past the brink of self-control, thus offering an explanation for why homicides committed by women are generally spontaneous rather than planned, why they usually involve the killing of intimates, and why they generally occur in the home. "Women generally view themselves as part of a collective of relationships around them," these theorists stated, "and evaluate their self-worth based on the value and success of these relationships."[106] Hence, when relationships break down, a woman's self-worth may be negated, resulting in a lessening of control—and homicide may ensue.

6.4 LEARNING OBJECTIVE

SOCIOBIOLOGY

Sociobiology The systematic study of the biological basis of all social behaviour.

IN THE INTRODUCTION TO HIS ARTICLE SUMMARIZING SOCIOBIOLOGY, ARTHUR Fisher wrote, "Every so often, in the long course of scientific progress, a new set of ideas appears, illuminating and redefining what has gone before like a flare bursting over a darkened landscape."[107] To some, **sociobiology**—a theoretical synthesis of biology, behaviour, and evolutionary ecology brought to the scientific community by Edward O. Wilson in his seminal 1975 work *Sociobiology: The New Synthesis*—holds the promise of just such a new paradigm, or model.[108] In his book, Wilson defined sociobiology as "the systematic study of the biological basis of all social behavior [that is] a branch of evolutionary biology and particularly of modern population biology." Through his entomological study of social insects (especially ants), Wilson demonstrated that particular forms of behaviour could contribute to the long-term survival of the social group. Wilson focused on altruism (selfless, helping behaviour); contrary to the beliefs of some evolutionary biologists, he found that helping behaviour facilitated the continuity of the gene pool found among altruistic individuals, and the primary determinant of behaviour, including human behaviour, was the need to ensure the survival and continuity of genetic material from one generation to the next.

Territoriality, according to Wilson's writings, explains many of the conflicts, including homicide, warfare, and other forms of aggression between and among human beings. In Wilson's words, "Part of man's problem is that his intergroup responses are still crude and primitive, and inadequate for the extended extraterritorial relationships that civilization has thrust upon him." The "unhappy result," as Wilson termed it, may be "tribalism," expressed through the contemporary increase of street gangs, racial tension, and hardened encampments of survivalist and separatist groups.

Sociobiological theory not only tells us that the violence and aggressiveness associated with territoriality are often reserved for strangers but also explains intragroup aggression (violence occurring within groups). Wilson's theory suggests that within the group "a particularly severe form of aggressiveness should be reserved for actual or suspected adultery. In many human societies where sexual bonding is close and personal knowledge of the behavior of others detailed, adulterers are harshly treated. The sin is regarded to be even worse when offspring are produced."[109] Hence, territoriality and acquisitiveness extend to location, possessions, and even other people. Human laws, in Wilson's view, are designed to protect genetically based relationships people have with one another as well as their material possessions and their claimed locations in space, so violations of these intuitive relationships result in crime and in official reactions by the legal system.

Wilson's writing propelled researchers into a flurry of studies intended to test the validity of his assertions. A Canadian study by Martin Daly and Margo Wilson of violence in the homes of adoptive children found that stepchildren run a risk 70 times greater of being killed by their adoptive parents than do children living with their natural parents.[110] Some writers have concluded that "murderous behavior, warfare, and even genocide were unavoidable correlates of genetic evolution, controlled by the same genes for territorial behavior that had been selected in primate evolution."[111] Others have suggested that biological predispositions developed during earlier stages of human evolution colour contemporary criminal activity; male criminals, for example, tend toward robbery and burglary—crimes in which they can continue to enact their "hunter" instincts developed long ago—whereas the criminality of women often involves shoplifting and simple theft, more typical of "gatherer" instincts.

Human behavioural predilections can be studied in a variety of ways. In the 1989 book *Evolutionary Jurisprudence*, John H. Beckstrom reported on his examination of over 400 legal documents as well as legal claims and court decisions spanning over 300 years of judicial activity that showed support for Wilson's contentions that humans tend to act to preserve territorial claims, their likelihood of successful reproduction, and the continuation of their own particular genetic material.[112] Other theorists have gone so far as to imply that, among humans, there may be a gene-based tendency to experience guilt and to develop a conscience and that notions of right and wrong, whether embodied in laws or in social convention, may flow from such a naturalistic origin.

As sociobiology began to receive expanded recognition from investigators (most of whom are American), some social scientists began to treat it as "criminology's anti-discipline."[113] Criticisms included charges that

- sociobiology fails to convey the overwhelming significance of culture, social learning, and individual experiences in shaping the behaviour of individuals and groups
- sociobiology is fundamentally wrong in its depiction of the basic nature of human beings—there is no credible evidence of genetically based or determined tendencies to act in certain ways
- sociobiology is just another empirically unsupported rationale for the authoritative labelling and stigmatization of despised, threatening, and powerless minorities
- human beings are so thoroughly different from other animal species, even other primates, that there is no rational basis for the application to humans of findings from animal studies

In the words of one observer, "Most criminologists, like most academicians, were wedded to a **paradigm**, . . . the idea that one great problem solution can permit the explanation of nearly all the unexplained variation in the field."[114] Today, many scholars are beginning to sense the growing need for a new synthesis, a way to consider the impact of biological theories such as sociobiology along with other long-accepted perspectives such as sociology and psychology. Gail Anderson, internationally renowned Canadian professor of forensic entomology (the use of insect evidence at crime scenes), provided an integrative approach to considering criminal behaviour by examining the role of biology in criminal behaviour and how biology interacts with sociological forces to lead to crime.[115] Indeed, the field of criminology appears ripe for a new multicausal approach.

Paradigm An example, model, or a theory.

BIOSOCIAL CRIMINOLOGY

IN THE MID-1980S, ARNOLD L. LIEBER DELIVERED AN ADDRESS AT THE ANNUAL meeting of the American Psychological Association. He used the forum to describe his research on biology and crime, which linked phases of the moon to fluctuations in the incidence of violence among human beings (nights around full moons show a significant rise in crime).[116]

Shortly after Lieber's presentation, criminologist James Q. Wilson and psychologist Richard J. Herrnstein teamed up to write *Crime and Human Nature*, a book-length treatise that reiterates many of the arguments proposed by biological criminologists over the previous century.[117] Part of their purpose was to reopen discussion of biological causes of crime. "We want to show," Herrnstein said, "that the pendulum is beginning to swing away from a totally sociological explanation of crime."[118] Their avowed goal was "not to state a case just for genetic factors, but to state a comprehensive theory of crime that draws together all the different factors that cause criminal behavior."[119]

Wilson and Herrnstein cited several constitutional factors contributing to crime:[120]

- *Gender:* "Crime "has been predominantly male behavior."
- *Age:* "In general, the tendency to break the law declines throughout life."
- *Body type:* "A disproportionate number of criminals have a mesomorphic build."
- *Intelligence:* Criminality is said to be clearly and consistently associated with low intelligence.
- *Personality:* Criminals are typically aggressive, impulsive, and cruel.

Although personality, behavioural problems, and intelligence may be related to environment, the authors said that "each involves some genetic inheritance." Wilson and Herrnstein recognized social factors in the development of personality but suggested that constitutional factors predispose a person to specific types of behaviour, and that societal *reactions* to such predispositions may determine, to a large degree, the form of continued behaviour. Research continues into the interaction between biology and the environment and the impact on human behaviour, including criminality. **Biosocial criminology** theory contends that biological factors do not operate in an environmental vacuum, nor do environmental factors operate in a biological vacuum.

Biosocial criminology A theoretical perspective that sees the interaction between biology and the environment as key to understanding human behaviour, including criminality.

POLICY IMPLICATIONS OF BIOLOGICAL THEORIES

BIOLOGICAL THEORIES OF CRIME CAUSATION PRESENT UNIQUE CHALLENGES TO policymakers. C. Ray Jeffery proposed the following as part of a comprehensive biologically based program of crime prevention and crime control:[121]

- "pre- and post-natal care for pregnant women and their infants" to monitor and address potentially detrimental developmental conditions that could lead to heightened aggression and crime later in life
- monitoring of children throughout the early stages of their development to identify "early symptoms of behavioral disorder"
- monitoring of children in their early years to reduce the risk of exposure to violence-inducing experiences such as child abuse and violence committed by other children
- neurological examinations, including CAT, PET, and MRI scans, to be used "when the need is evident"
- biological research conducted in prisons and treatment facilities to better identify the root causes of aggression and violence, and changes to laws that prevent the experimental use of prison subjects, the analysis of the bodies of executed prisoners, and other similar types of biological investigations

Jeffery added that the fundamental orientation of the legal system must change so as to acknowledge contributions of biological criminologists, replacing or supplementing our current "right to punishment" doctrine with a "right to treatment" philosophy. Jeffery concluded his analysis by saying, "If legal and political barriers prevent us from regarding antisocial behavior as a medical problem, and if we do not permit medical research on criminal behavior, how can we ever solve the crime problem?"[122]

The dangers of too great a dependence on biological approaches to crime, however, raise the spectre of an Orwellian bogeyman in charge of every aspect of human social life—from conception to the grave—and include the possible abortion of defective fetuses, capital punishment in lieu of rehabilitation, and enforced sterilization. Precedent for such fears can be found in cases such as that of Leilani Muir, who, during the 1950s, was placed in Alberta's Provincial Training School for Mental Defectives at the age of 10. Based on a single IQ test, she was labelled a "moron" and, at the age of 14, was sterilized without her consent. The operation was sanctioned under Alberta's *Sexual Sterilization Act.*

Potential links between race and crime, suggested by some researchers, are especially repugnant to many who criticize biological criminology. Canadian criminologists Julian Roberts and Thomas Gabor observed, "People who accept the view that variations in crime rates reflect genetic factors may also embrace an underlying message about crime prevention. Social programs aim to eradicate educational, social, and economic inequities. These efforts can only be undermined by statements stressing the importance of genetic factors in determining criminality."[123] Ronald Walters, a political scientist at Howard University, similarly observed that "seeking the biological and genetic aspects of violence is dangerous to African-American youth. When you consider the perception that black people have always been the violent people in this society, it is a short step from this stereotype to using this kind of research for social control."[124]

Although biological theories of crime have problems, some criminologists believe that to ignore the potential contributions of biological theorists does a disservice to the science of criminology and denies the opportunity for compassionate and objective researchers to realistically assist in the process of crime prevention and reduction. In 1997, in an attempt to bring biological theorizing into the criminological mainstream, Lee Ellis and Anthony Walsh expanded on the theme of genetic predispositions, noting that

> in the case of behavior, nearly all of the effects of genes are quite indirect because they are mediated through complex chains of events occurring in the brain. This means that there are almost certainly no genes for something as complex as criminal behavior. Nevertheless, many genes may affect brain functioning in ways that either increase or reduce the chances of individuals learning various complex behavior patterns, including behavior patterns that happen to be so offensive to others that criminal sanctions have been instituted to minimize their recurrence.[125]

CRITIQUE OF BIOLOGICAL THEORIES

6.7 LEARNING OBJECTIVE

IN A CRITIQUE OF BIOLOGICAL THEORIES OF CRIME, NOTED CRIMINOLOGIST NICOLE Hahn Rafter argued against the possible development of a contemporary eugenics movement based upon the findings of modern-day genetics. In *Creating Born Criminals,* Rafter attempted to demonstrate the need for contemporary researchers and policymakers to know how eugenic reasoning worked in the past so that they would be able to recognize the dangers posed by any theory that interprets social problems in biological terms and that sees what might be innate differences as evidence of biological inferiority.[126] While genetic solutions to human problems may seem to offer a near-future panacea, Rafter warned that policymakers must always be on their guard against the danger of oversimplifying social issues as complex as crime.

A focused critique of biological perspectives on crime causation was provided by Glenn D. Walters and Thomas W. White, who contended that "genetic research on crime has been poorly designed, ambiguously reported, and exceedingly inadequate in addressing the relevant issues."[127] Walters and White highlighted these specific shortcomings of studies in the area of genetics:

- Few biological studies adequately conceptualize criminality. Several studies "have defined criminality on the basis of a single arrest."[128]

- Twin studies, in particular, have sometimes failed to properly establish whether a pair of twins is MZ or DZ because some MZ twins are not identical in appearance, and only a few twin studies have depended on biological testing rather than on a simple evaluation of appearances.

- Problems in estimating the degree of criminality among sample populations are rife in biological (and many other) studies of criminality. Interview data are open to interpretation, and existing statistical data on the past criminality of offenders are not always properly appreciated.

- Methodological problems abound in many studies attempting to evaluate the role of genetics in crime: lack of control or comparison groups, small sample sizes, dropping out of subjects from study groups, biased sampling techniques, and the use of inappropriate forms of statistical analysis.

- Results obtained in other countries may not be applicable to the country in question. Twin studies conducted in Sweden and Denmark provide an example of this potential lack of generalizability.

Walters and White nevertheless concluded that "genetic factors are undoubtedly correlated with various measures of criminality," adding that "the large number of methodological flaws and limitations in the research should make one cautious in drawing any causal inferences at this point in time."[129]

BIOLOGICAL THEORIES APPLIED

CONSTITUTIONAL THEORIES

holds that criminals can be explained by body type, inheritance, genetics, or external observable physical characteristics.

Could the sexually deviant behaviour of the 40-year-old man described in the introduction be in any way attributed to the factors for criminal behaviour held by constitutional theories?

Crime is a result of many behavioural predispositions, including aggression and criminality, which are constitutionally or physiologically based and inherited. Early proponents of biological theories argued that at least some human behaviour is the result of biological propensities inherited from more primitive developmental stages in the evolutionary process.

SOCIOBIOLOGY AND BIOSOCIAL CRIMINOLOGY

holds that criminal behaviour is linked to an individual's biological makeup and the interaction between biology and the environment.

How could the crime prevention and control approach advocated by sociobiology have helped the deviant man described in the introduction?

BODY CHEMISTRY

holds that criminal behaviour is a result of chemical influences, including hormones, food additives, allergies, vitamins, and other chemical substances.

Was there any evidence that chemical or hormonal imbalance played a role in the deviant sexual behaviour presented by the man described in the introduction?

MySearchLab® with eText offers you access to an online interactive version of the text, extensive help with your writing and research projects, and provides round-the-clock access to credible and reliable source material.

SUMMARY OF LEARNING OBJECTIVES

6.1 Biological theories of crime causation adhere to the principle that many behavioural predispositions, including aggression and criminality, are constitutionally or physiologically influenced and inherited. Early proponents of biological theories argued that at least some human behaviour is the result of biological propensities inherited from more primitive developmental stages in the evolutionary process.

62 According to some, human behaviour is, to some degree, adapted instinctual behaviour, and aggression is a form of biological inheritance from more primitive times. Aggression today may manifest as criminal behaviour when environmental conditions conspire to elicit such instinctive responses.

6.3 Some scholars have suggested that a penchant for crime may be inherited and that criminal tendencies are genetically based. Beginning in the late 1800s, researchers in the field of criminal anthropology focused on criminal families. More recently, developments in the field of genetics have led to the study of the role of chromosomes in crime causation. One of the first ideas to make use of chromosomes as an explanation for violent crime was the XYY, or supermale, notion of criminality.

6.4 Sociobiology is a theoretical perspective developed by Edward O. Wilson that can be described as "the systematic study of the biological basis of all social behaviour." Wilson believed that the primary determinant of human behaviour was the need to ensure the survival and continuity of genetic material from one generation to the next. Sociobiologists often focus on explaining the violence and aggression associated with territoriality. Sociobiology has been employed to explain intergroup and intragroup aggression.

6.5 The biosocial perspective sees the interaction between biology and environment as key to understanding human behaviour, including criminality. Genetic predispositions and their interaction with the surrounding social and physical environments may combine to produce criminality.

6.6 Proponents of the biological roots of criminal behaviour argue that it is only when the impact of biology on human behaviour is fully recognized that effective social policies—including those aimed at controlling crime—can be developed. Such crime-prevention approaches would monitor and address detrimental developmental conditions during prenatal and early development years of children and include biological research on prison inmates.

6.7 Few biological studies adequately conceptualize criminality, methodological problems have been found in many studies attempting to evaluate the role of genetics in crime, and results obtained outside North America may not be applicable within this country. Many criminologists have concluded that while biology provides a context for human behaviour, biological predispositions are overshadowed by the role of volition, mechanisms of human thought, and undeniable influences of socialization and acculturation.

Questions for Review

1. What are the central assumptions of biological theories of crime? How do such theories differ from other perspectives that attempt to explain the same phenomena?

2. How might biological perspectives explain human aggression?

3. What have research studies in the field of genetics had to say about possible causes of crime?

4. What is sociobiology? How do sociobiologists explain criminality?

5. How is criminality explained from a biosocial perspective?

6. What are the policy implications of biological theories of crime? What Canadian example discussed in this chapter might presage a type of policy based on such theories?

7. Why have biological approaches to crime causation encountered stiff criticism? Do you agree or disagree with those who are critical of such perspectives? Why?

Multiple-Choice Questions

1. According to C. Ray Jeffrey, a comprehensive biologically based program of crime prevention and crime control would include _____.
   a. trephination
   b. eugenics
   c. phrenology
   d. atavisms
   e. prenatal and postnatal care for pregnant women and their infants

2. Constitutional factors that James Q. Wilson and Richard J. Herrnstein cite as contributing to crime include age, body type, intelligence, personality, and _____.
   a. upbringing
   b. gender
   c. educational attainment
   d. crowding
   e. socio-economic status

3. The somatotypology developed by _____ consisted of the endomorph, mesomorph, ectomorph, and balanced type.
   a. Willaim H. Sheldon
   b. Frank Joseph Gall
   c. Johann Gasper Spurzheim
   d. Richard J. Herrnstein
   e. Sheldon and Eleanor Glueck

4. _____ is the concept used by Cesare Lombroso to suggest that criminality is the result of primitive urges that survived the evolutionary process.
   a. Ectomorph
   b. Criminaloid
   c. Schizoid
   d. Cycloid
   e. Atavism

5. The study of crime and criminals through the use of scientific techniques is referred to as _____.
   a. positivism
   b. somatotypology
   c. displastics
   d. sociobiology
   e. phrenology

Multiple Choice Answers: 1e, 2b, 3a, 4e, 5a

Chapter 7

Psychological and Psychiatric Foundations of Criminal Behaviour

Nathan Denette/The Canadian Press/AP Photo

Psychopaths are social predators who charm, manipulate, and ruthlessly plow their way through life, leaving a broad trail of broken hearts, shattered expectations, and empty wallets.

—*Robert Hare*[1]

LEARNING OBJECTIVES

After reading this chapter, you should be able to

7.1 Recognize the major principles of psychological perspectives on criminal behaviour.

7.2 Identify some early psychological and psychiatric theories offered to explain criminality.

7.3 Discuss how criminality can be seen as a form of maladaptive behaviour.

7.4 Discuss how criminality can be seen as a form of adaptive behaviour.

7.5 Describe how the modelling theory of aggression explains how aggressive patterns of behaviour, once acquired, can be activated.

7.6 Understand how behaviour theory explains the role of rewards and punishments in shaping behaviour.

7.7 Consider the unique characteristics of those found "not criminally responsible by reason of mental disorder."

7.8 Identify current social policy reflecting the psychological approach to criminal behaviour.

7.9 List some assumptions underlying the practice of criminal psychological profiling.

INTRODUCTION

Some crimes defy explanation. In December 2002, Germans were horrified by a story sweeping the nation about a respectable engineer and software specialist who was alleged to have mutilated and eaten a 43-year-old microchip engineer. As police investigators descended upon the home and property of Armin Meiwes on the outskirts of Kassel, Germany, the gruesome details of ritualistic torture and cannibalism unfolded. Frozen human flesh that had been bagged and labelled by body part was found in a freezer, and human bones were discovered discarded in the gardens around the house.

Using advertisements on the internet such as "Wanted: young, well-built 18–30-year-old for slaughter," Meiwes lured scores of men from around the world to his chat room, where he confessed his cannibalistic tendencies. Some of the chat room participants agreed to meet with Meiwes; one 27-year-old conference organizer from London, England, allowed Meiwes to chain him to a bed and stick pins in his body, marking out his liver, a kidney, and other organs to be consumed. Yet another, a 34-year-old cook from southern Germany, allowed Meiwes to string him up on meat hooks in a slaughter parlour in his house. Both men decided that the fantasy had gone far enough and did not proceed to the ultimate conclusion.

One man, Bernd Brandes, did not leave, however. A leading microchip designer who lived in a luxury penthouse suite, Brandes sold his car and other valuables and met with Meiwes at his home in March 2001. Details of their meeting were recorded on a videotape made by Meiwes; together the two men planned a grisly ritual and then executed it as they amputated, fried, and ate part of Brandes's body. Meiwes then stabbed Brandes to death. He sliced his flesh into small chunks, which he wrapped and stored in the freezer. He confessed to eating about 20 kilograms of the flesh in the months between the killing and his arrest.

Armin Meiwes was charged with first-degree murder only, since cannibalism is not legally prohibited in Germany. Thousands of printed emails and internet exchanges were presented as evidence in court. Details of Meiwes's life revealed that he had lived alone with his mother until her death. His father left the family when Meiwes was 8 years old and his mother subsequently married and divorced three times. Psychologist Heinrich Wilmer testified at the trial that Meiwes was neither mentally ill nor motivated by sexual gratification. Rather, he lacked male role models, was incredibly lonely, and made up imaginary friends whom he imagined eating so that they would never go away.[2] The defence argued that Meiwes's victim had volunteered for sacrifice; Meiwes was merely assisting Brandes to fulfill his death wish. Prosecutors, on the other hand, argued that Meiwes premeditated the murder of his victim and did it for his own sexual satisfaction. In one email read at his trial, Meiwes, who became known around the world as the "Cannibal of Rotenburg," wrote that cannibalism should be promoted as a form of development aid. "We could solve the problem of overpopulation and famine at a stroke," he stated. He also told the court that his cannibalism stemmed from an acute sense of loneliness and that his desperate need for a brother led him to consume a male so he would be "bound to me forever."[3] Meiwes was found guilty of manslaughter in January 2004 and received an eight-and-a-half-year sentence. In 2005, an appeal by the prosecution argued that Brandes was not legally capable of agreeing to his killing due to apparent mental challenges and alcohol over-consumption. At the trial, a psychologist testified that Meiwes still had fantasies about consuming human flesh and was a threat to reoffend. The court agreed, and Meiwes was sentenced to life in prison in May 2006.[4]

In 1989, in a very violent incident that has since heightened the public's awareness of violence against women, 14 female students at L'École Polytechnique in Montreal were shot to death by Marc Lepine, an embittered misogynist. Lepine entered a classroom and shouted, "I want the women," and then, "You're all a bunch of feminists, and I hate feminists."[5] After ordering all the men to leave the room, Lepine shot six women dead. Over the next 20 minutes, the 25-year-old Lepine methodically stalked the cafeteria, the classrooms, and the corridors of the school, leaving 8 other women dead and 13 injured. He finally turned the gun on himself. In the three-page suicide note found in his pocket, Lepine blamed feminists for ruining his life. Lepine's actions were explained by Dr. Renée Fugère, forensic psychiatrist at Montreal's Allan Memorial Institute, as those of a delusional man who repeatedly failed to achieve his ambitions in work—and with women. "Lepine probably did not have the capacity to mourn his failed relationships," she said, "so he kept it inside. Those feelings piled up and finally exploded."[6]

What motivates people to kill or maim—or even to commit other, less serious, offences? How can many killers "seem so normal" before their crimes, giving no hints of the atrocities they are about to commit? For answers to questions such as these, many people turn to psychological theories. Psychologists are the pundits of the modern age of behaviourism, offering explanations rooted in determinants lying within individual actors. Psychological determinants of deviant or criminal behaviour may be couched in terms of exploitive personality characteristics, poor impulse control, emotional arousal, an immature personality, and so on. Canadian criminal psychologists Don Andrews and James Bonta observed that "the major sources of theoretical development in criminology have been—and continue to be—psychological. A theory of criminal conduct is weak indeed if uninformed by a general psychology of human behavior."[7] Other writers have gone so far as to claim that any criminal behaviour is only a symptom of a more fundamental psychiatric disorder.[8]

Before beginning a discussion of psychological theories, however, it is necessary to provide a brief overview of the terminology used to describe the psychological study of crime and criminality. **Forensic psychology**, one of the fastest-growing subfields of psychology, is the application of the science and profession of psychology to questions and issues relating to law and the legal system.[9] Forensic psychology

Forensic psychology The application of the science and profession of psychology to questions and issues relating to law and the legal system. Also known as *criminal psychology*.

Armin Meiwes used the internet to lure victims into his cannibalistic ritual. What explains the public's fascination with bizarre killers?

Uwe Zucchi/Ddp/Getty Images

is sometimes referred to as *criminal psychology*, and forensic psychologists are also called *criminal psychologists*, *correctional psychologists*, and *police psychologists*. Unlike forensic psychologists (who generally hold doctoral degrees), forensic psychiatrists are medical doctors, and forensic psychiatry is a branch of psychiatry having to do with the study of crime and criminality. Its practitioners apply psychiatry to the needs of crime prevention and solution, criminal rehabilitation, and issues of the criminal law.[10]

What is the fundamental distinguishing feature of psychological approaches as opposed to other attempts to explain behaviour? Two contemporary criminologists offered the following insight: "Theories are psychological insofar as they focus on the individual as the unit of analysis."[11] Another writer, Curt Bartol, defined psychology as "the science of behavior and mental processes"; he went on to say, "Psychological criminology is the science of the behavior and mental processes of the criminal."[12]

MAJOR PRINCIPLES OF PSYCHOLOGICAL THEORIES

7.1 | **LEARNING OBJECTIVE**

THIS BRIEF SECTION SUMMARIZES THE CENTRAL FEATURES OF PSYCHOLOGICAL THEORIES of crime causation.[13] This cursory overview is intended to provide more than a summary; it is meant to be a guide to the rest of this chapter (see Table 7.1).

👁 **Watch**

Basic Principles of the Psychological Perspective

Most psychological theories of crime causation make the following fundamental assumptions:

- The individual is the primary unit of analysis.

- Personality is the major motivational element within individuals because it is the seat of drives and the source of motives.

- Crimes result from abnormal, dysfunctional, or inappropriate mental processes within the personality.

- Criminal behaviour may be purposeful for the individual insofar as it addresses certain felt needs. Behaviour can be judged "inappropriate" only when measured against external criteria purporting to establish normality.

- Normality is generally defined by social consensus (what the majority of people in any social group agree is "real," appropriate, or typical).

- Defective, or abnormal, mental processes may have a variety of causes, including a diseased mind, inappropriate learning or improper conditioning, the emulation of inappropriate role models, and adjustment to inner conflicts.

Psychological theory A theory derived from the behavioural sciences that focuses on the individual as the unit of analysis. Psychological theories place the locus of crime causation within the personality of the individual offender.

Table 7.1 Types of Psychological and Psychiatric Theories

Theory	Psychoanalytic Criminology	Frustration–Aggression	Psychiatric Criminology	Modelling
Period	1920s–present	1940s–present	1930s–present	1950s–present
Theorists	Sigmund Freud and others	J. Dollard, Albert Bandura, Richard H. Walters, S.M. Halleck	Hervey Cleckley, Robert Hare, and others	Albert Bandura and others
Concepts	Id, ego, super-ego, sublimation, psychotherapy, Thanatos, neurosis, psychosis	Frustration, aggression, displacement, catharsis, alloplastic and autoplastic adaptation	Psychopath, sociopath, anti-social, asocial personality	

PERSPECTIVES OF EARLY THEORIES

Psychological Perspective

Conditioning A psychological principle holding that the frequency of any behaviour can be increased or decreased through reward, punishment, or association with other stimuli.

Twin threads ran through early psychological theories and constituted the early field of psychological criminality. One strand emphasized behavioural **conditioning**; the other focused mostly on personality disturbances and diseases of the mind. The concept of conditioned behaviour was popularized through the work of the Russian physiologist Ivan Pavlov (1849–1936), whose work with dogs won the Nobel Prize in Physiology or Medicine in 1904. The dogs, who salivated when food was presented to them, were always fed in the presence of a ringing bell. Soon the dogs salivated when the bell alone was rung—even when no food was present. Hence Pavlov demonstrated that animal behaviour could be predictably altered through association with external changes arising from the environment surrounding the organism.

Psychopathology The study of pathological mental conditions.

The other thread wending its way through early psychological theories was that of mental disease, or **psychopathology**. In the psychology literature, the word *psychopathology* "refers to any sort of psychological disorder that causes distress either for the individual or for those in the individual's life."[14] Depression, schizophrenia, attention deficit/hyperactivity disorder, alcoholism, and bulimia can all be considered forms of psychopathology.

The concept of psychopathology has been called "one of the most durable, resilient and influential of all criminological ideas."[15] In its original formulation, psychopathology embodied the notion of a diseased mind. It described a particular form of insanity referred to as "moral idiocy," which was thought to have a constitutional, or physiological, basis. The concept is summarized in the words of Nolan Lewis, who wrote during his tenure as director of the New York State Psychiatric Institute and Hospital at Columbia University during World War II that "the criminal, like other people, has lived a life of instinctive drives, of desires, of wishes, of feelings, but one in which his intellect has apparently functioned less effectually as a brake upon certain trends. His constitutional makeup deviates toward the abnormal, leading him into conflicts with the laws of society and its cultural patterns."[16]

Psychiatric Perspective

Psychiatric criminology Theories derived from the medical sciences, including neurology, which, like other psychological theories, focus on the individual as the unit of analysis. Psychiatric theories form the basis of psychiatric criminology.

Forensic psychiatry A branch of psychiatry having to do with the study of crime and criminality.

Psychological criminology, with its historical dual emphasis on early forces shaping personality and conditioned behaviour, can be distinguished from **psychiatric criminology** (also known as **forensic psychiatry)**, which envisions a complex set of drives and motives operating from hidden recesses deep within the personality to determine behaviour. Psychiatrist David Abrahamsen explained crime this way: "Antisocial behavior is a direct expression of an aggression or may be a direct or indirect manifestation of a distorted erotic drive. . . . Crime may . . . be considered a product of a person's tendencies and the situation of the moment interacting with his mental resistance."[17] The key questions to be answered by psychiatric criminology, according to Abrahamsen, are "What creates the criminal impulse?" and "What stimulates and gives it direction?" A later forensic psychiatrist answered these questions this way: "Every criminal is such by reason of unconscious forces within him."[18] Forensic psychiatry explains crime as being caused by biological and psychological urges that are mediated through consciousness; little significance is placed on the environment after the first few formative years of life. Psychiatric theories are derived from the medical sciences, including neurology, and, like other psychological theories, focus on the individual as the unit of analysis.

CRIMINAL BEHAVIOUR AS MALADAPTATION

The Psychoanalytic Perspective

◉ Watch

Sigmund Freud

Perhaps the best-known psychiatrist of all time is Sigmund Freud (1856–1939), who coined the term **psychoanalysis** in 1896 and based an entire theory of human behaviour on it. From the point of view of psychoanalysis, criminal behaviour is maladaptive, or the product of inadequacies inherent in the offender's personality. Significant inadequacies may result in full-blown mental illness, which in itself can be a direct cause of crime. The psychoanalytic perspective encompasses diverse notions such as personality, neurosis, psychosis, and more specific concepts such as transference, sublimation, repression, and the Oedipus complex (the desire to have sexual intercourse with the parent of the opposite sex and to kill the parent of the same sex). **Psychotherapy** is the attempt to relieve patients of their mental disorders through the application of psychoanalytical principles and techniques.

According to Freud, the personality is made up of three components: the id, the ego, and the superego (see Figure 7.1). The **id** is that fundamental aspect of the personality from which drives, wishes, urges, and desires emanate and operates according to the pleasure principle, seeking full and immediate gratification of its needs. From the Freudian perspective, we carry within our id the prerequisite motivation for criminal behaviour—we are all potential murderers, sexual aggressors, and thieves, and our drives and urges are kept in check only by other controlling aspects of our personalities.

A second component of the personality, the **ego**, is primarily charged with reality testing. (Freud's use of the word *ego* should not be confused with popular usage, whereby a person might talk about an "inflated ego" or an "egotistical person.") For Freud, the ego was primarily concerned with how objectives might be best accomplished. The ego effects strategies that maximize pleasure and minimize pain, laying out various paths of action for wish fulfillment, but inherently recognizes that it may be necessary to delay gratification to achieve a more fulfilling long-term goal.

The **superego**, the third component of the personality, is like a moral guide to right and wrong. If properly developed, it assays the ego's plans, dismissing some as morally

Psychoanalysis The theory of human psychology founded by Freud and based on the concepts of the unconscious, resistance, repression, sexuality, and the Oedipus complex.

Psychotherapy A form of psychiatric treatment based on psychoanalytical principles and techniques.

Id The aspect of the personality from which drives, wishes, urges, and desires emanate. More formally, it is the division of the psyche associated with instinctual impulses and demands for immediate satisfaction of primitive needs.

Ego The reality-testing part of the personality; also called the *reality principle*. More formally, it is the personality component that is conscious, most immediately controls behaviour, and is most in touch with external reality.

Superego The moral aspect of the personality; much like the conscience. More formally, it is the division of the psyche that develops by the incorporation of the perceived moral standards of the community, is mainly unconscious, and includes the conscience.

Figure 7.1 The Psychoanalytic Structure of Personality

inappropriate while accepting others as ethically viable. When the dictates of the super-ego are not followed, feelings of guilt may result. The superego also contains what Freud called the *ego-ideal*, a symbolic representation of what society values, and differs from the conscience in that it is less forceful in controlling behaviour in the absence of the likelihood of discovery.

Although Freud wrote little about crime per se, he did spend much of his time attempting to account for a variety of abnormal behaviours, many of which might lead to violations of the criminal law. One way in which a person might be led into crime is as the result of a poorly developed superego: his or her mind is left to fall back on the ego's reality-testing ability, and the ego, operating without a moral guide, may select a path of action that, although expedient at the time, violates the law. Individuals suffering from poor superego development are likely to seek immediate gratification without giving much thought to the long-term consequences.

Freud held that many outstanding accomplishments of the human species are due to **sublimation**—the psychological process whereby one item of consciousness comes to be symbolically substituted for another—when powerful sexual and aggressive drives are channelled into socially constructive activity, but that inadequate sublimation can be another cause of crime. For example, a man may hate his mother, his hatred being perhaps the faulty by-product of the striving for adult independence. If he is unable to give voice to that hatred directly, he may act out this hatred by attacking other women whom he symbolically substitutes in his mind for the mother. Sublimation, like many other psychoanalytical concepts, is a slippery idea. Mother hatred, for example, is difficult to demonstrate, and the link between such hidden feelings and adult action is impossible to prove.

Freud also postulated the existence of a death instinct, which he called **Thanatos**. According to Freud, all living things have a fundamental desire to descend into an inanimate state, or death. Living takes energy and cunning; death, at least at some level, is an easier choice because it releases the organism from the need for continued expenditure of energy. Thanatos was seen as contributing to many of the advances of the human species because if there was no wish to die at some instinctual level, according to Freud, few people would have the courage to take risks—and without risks, little progress would be possible in any sphere of life. An innate death wish has been used to explain why some offenders seem to behave in ways that ensure their eventual capture—serial killers who send taunting messages to the police, terrorists telling the media of their planned activities or taking credit for public attacks, rapists "accidentally" leaving their wallets at the scene, or burglars breaking into occupied dwellings.

From the Freudian perspective, **neurosis** is a minor form of mental illness. Neurotic individuals are in touch with reality but may find themselves anxious, fearful of certain situations, or unable to help themselves; fear of heights, compulsive hand washing, and eating disorders are examples. Most neuroses do not lead to crime but some can. A few years ago, for example, a man from Iowa was sentenced to nearly six years in prison and fined $200 000 for the theft of more than 21 000 rare books from hundreds of libraries.[19] The offender, whose compulsive interest in rare books began at yard sales and with searches in trash receptacles, may have seen himself as involved in a messianic mission to preserve recorded history. Well-heeled individuals may be manifesting a compulsive neurosis when the powerful need to steal drives them to risk arrest and jail.

Recently, the field of psychiatry has seen a rekindling of interest in Freudian psychology. The reason, according to some contemporary thinkers, is that psychopharmacology, or the use of drugs to treat psychiatric symptoms and disorders, has been unable to provide an alternative grand theory of personality, emotion, and motivation.[20] Moreover, today's neuroscientists are busily creating a chemical map of the mind that seems to validate the

Sublimation The psychological process whereby one aspect of consciousness comes to be symbolically substituted for another.

Thanatos A death wish.

Neurosis A functional disorder of the mind or of the emotions involving anxiety, phobia, or other abnormal behaviour.

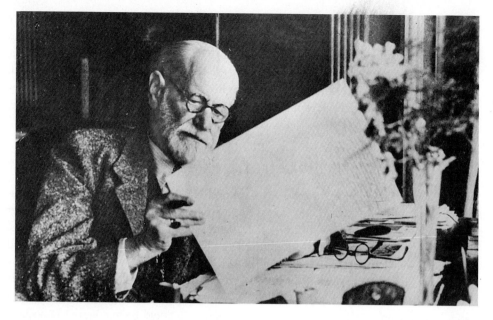

Sigmund Freud (1856–1939), examining a manuscript in the office of his Vienna home, circa 1930. How have Freud's theories influenced contemporary criminology?

Bettmann/Corbis

general sketch that Freud provided decades ago, and soon a new and unified perspective that reconciles the work of neurologists and psychiatrists may emerge. The recognition of just such a possibility prompted Eric R. Kandel, the 2000 Nobel laureate in physiology or medicine, to say that psychoanalysis is "still the most coherent and intellectually satisfying view of the mind."[21]

Personality Types and Crime

In 1964, Hans Eysenck, a British psychiatrist, published *Crime and Personality*, a book-length treatise in which he explained crime as the result of fundamental personality characteristics linked to individual central nervous system characteristics.[22] Eysenck described three personality dimensions with links to criminality: psychoticism, extroversion, and neuroticism.

Psychoticism, which Eysenck said "is believed to be correlated with criminality at all stages,"[23] is defined by characteristics such as a lack of empathy, creativeness, tough-mindedness, and anti-sociability. Psychoticism, according to Eysenck, is also frequently characterized by hallucinations and delusions, leading to the personality type described as psychotic. Extroverts, the second personality type, are described as carefree, dominant, and venturesome, operating with high levels of energy. "The typical extrovert," Eysenck wrote, "is sociable, likes parties, has many friends, needs to have people to talk to, and does not like reading or studying by himself."[24] Neuroticism, the third of the personality characteristics Eysenck described, is said to be typical of people who are irrational, shy, moody, and emotional.

According to Eysenck, psychotics are the most likely to be criminal because they combine high degrees of emotionalism with similarly high levels of extroversion. Individuals with such characteristics are especially difficult to socialize and to train and do not respond well to the external environment. Eysenck cited many studies in which children and others who harboured characteristics of psychoticism, extroversion, and neuroticism performed poorly on conditioning tests designed to measure how quickly they would respond appropriately to external stimuli. Conscience, according to Eysenck, is fundamentally a conditioned reflex, so an individual who does not take well to conditioning will not fully develop a conscience and will continue to exhibit the asocial behavioural traits of a very young child.

Central to Eysenck's approach was his belief that personality traits are fundamentally dependent upon physiology, specifically upon the individual's autonomic nervous system (ANS). Some individuals possess nervous systems that cannot handle a great deal of stimulation, and these introverts shun excitement, are easily trained, and rarely become criminal. However, those who possess nervous systems in need of constant stimulation seek excitement and are far more likely to turn to crime. Up to two-thirds of all behavioural variance, claimed Eysenck, could be attributed to genetics.

The Link between Frustration and Aggression

In his early writings, Freud suggested that aggressive behaviour is a response to frustration and limitations imposed upon a person. The frustration–aggression thesis was later developed more fully in the writings of J. Dollard, Albert Bandura, Richard H. Walters, and others. Dollard's frustration–aggression theory held that although frustration can lead to various forms of behaviour—including regression, sublimation, and aggressive fantasy—direct aggression toward others is its most likely consequence.[25] Because everyone suffers frustration at times in life, beginning with weaning and toilet training, aggression is a natural consequence of living. However, that aggression could be manifested in socially acceptable ways (such as through contact sports, military or law enforcement careers, or simple verbal attacks) and/or engaged in vicariously by observing others who are acting violently (as in movies, on television, and in fiction). Dollard applied the psychoanalytical term *displacement* to the type of violence that is vented on something or someone who is not the source of the original frustration and suggested that satisfying one's aggressive urges via observation was a form of "catharsis."

The story of Pierre Lebrun, a former employee of a public transit company, provides an example of the frustration–aggression theory applied to real-life crime. In April 1999, the 40-year-old Lebrun entered the maintenance garage at a public bus company in Ottawa and opened fire with a high-powered .30-06-calibre hunting rifle, killing four people and wounding two others before taking his own life. In his suicide note left at his parents' home, Lebrun expressed his anger toward certain former co-workers whom, he claimed, had teased him for a speech impediment. Ironically, none of the men on his "hit list" were victimized. He had been fired by his company several years earlier but his union fought the dismissal and won. Lebrun had resigned from the company four months before the killing. It appears he was acting out of the frustrations born of his experiences with his co-workers.[26]

Some psychologists have tried to identify what it is that causes some individuals to displace aggression or to experience it vicariously (through catharsis), while others respond violently and directly toward the immediate source of their frustrations. Andrew F. Henry and James F. Short, Jr., for example, suggested that child-rearing practices are a major determining factor in such a causal nexus.[27] Restrictive parents who both punish and love their children, said Henry and Short, will engender in their children the ability to suppress outward expressions of aggression. But when one parent punishes and the other loves, or when both punish but neither shows love, children can be expected to show anger directly and perhaps even immediately because they will not be threatened with the loss of love. Physical punishment rarely threatens the loss of love, and children so punished cannot be expected to refrain from direct displays of anger.

In 1960, Stewart Palmer studied murderers and their siblings to determine the degree of frustration they had been exposed to as children.[28] He found that male murderers had experienced much more frustration than their brothers and that more than twice as many frustrating experiences—ranging from difficult births to serious illnesses, childhood beatings, severe toilet training, and negative school experiences—were reported by the murderers than by their law-abiding siblings.

The Psychotic Offender

For many law-abiding citizens, extreme forms of criminal behaviour are often difficult to understand, as the gruesome story of Vince Li illustrates[29] (see the Who's Responsible? box on p. 186 of this chapter).

Some seemingly inexplicable forms of criminality may be the result of **psychosis**. Neurotic individuals often face only relatively minor problems in living. Psychotic people are out of touch with reality in some fundamental way, possibly suffering from hallucinations, delusions, or other breaks with reality. Psychoses may be either organic (resulting from physical damage to, or abnormalities in, the brain) or functional (having no known physical cause). Canadian criminologist Gwynn Nettler said, "Thought disorder is the hallmark of psychosis. People are called crazy when, at some extremity, they cannot 'think straight.'"[30] She identified three characteristics of psychotic individuals: "(1) a grossly distorted conception of reality, (2) moods, and swings of mood, that seem inappropriate to circumstance, and (3) marked inefficiency in getting along with others and caring for oneself."[31] Psychotics have also been classified as schizophrenic or paranoid schizophrenic. **Schizophrenics** are said to be characterized by disordered or disjointed thinking, in which the types of logical associations they make are atypical of other people. **Paranoid schizophrenics** suffer from delusions and hallucinations.

Unfortunately, psychiatrists have not been able to agree on definitive schizophrenic criteria that would allow for convenient application of the term. One prominent psychiatrist wrote about "how varying schizophrenia may appear, ranging from no striking symptoms at all to conspicuous psychotic features. Thus on the surface the schizophrenic may appear normal and, to some extent, lead a conventional life."[32] The same author later explained, "Schizophrenia is not a clearly defined disease. It is characterized rather by a kind of alteration of thinking or feeling."[33] Schizophrenia is disorganization of the personality and in its most extreme form, it may manifest itself in seemingly irrational behaviour as well as hallucinations and delusions.

Psychoses may lead to crime in a number of ways. In a highly publicized case in Ottawa, Ontario, Jeffrey Arenburg waited outside a local television station and shot and killed well-known sportscaster Brian Smith as he left work. Arenburg, who had a history of paranoid schizophrenia, believed that radio and television stations were broadcasting his thoughts through the fillings in his teeth. His assault on Smith was his attempt to stop these broadcasts.

Refer to the section of this chapter entitled "Mental Illness and the Law" for an understanding of how our criminal justice system deals with those who are afflicted with a recognized psychosis such as paranoid schizophrenia.

The Psychopath

The term *psychopathy* comes from the Greek words *psyche* (meaning "soul" or "mind") and *pathos* ("suffering" or "illness"). The word appears to have been coined by the 19th-century German psychiatrist Richard von Krafft-Ebing (1840–1902),[34] making its way into English psychiatric literature through the writings of Polish-born American psychiatrist Bernard Glueck[35] (1884–1972) and William Healy (1869–1963).[36] The **psychopath**, also called a **sociopath**, has been historically viewed as perversely cruel, often without thought or feeling for his victims.[37]

The concept of a psychopathic personality, which by its very definition is asocial, was fully developed by Georgian neuropsychiatrist Hervey Cleckley in his important 1964 book *The Mask of Sanity*.[38] He described the psychopath as a "moral idiot," as one who does not feel empathy with others even though that person may be fully cognizant of what is objectively happening around him or her. The central defining characteristic of a psychopath

Psychosis A form of mental illness in which sufferers are said to be out of touch with reality.

Schizophrenic A mentally ill individual who is out of touch with reality and suffers from disjointed thinking.

Paranoid schizophrenic A schizophrenic individual who suffers from delusions and hallucinations.

Psychopath or **sociopath** A person with a personality disorder, especially one manifested in aggressively anti-social behaviour, and who is lacking in empathy.

came to be "poverty of affect" or the inability to accurately imagine how others think and feel, so it becomes possible for a psychopath to inflict pain and engage in acts of cruelty without appreciation for the victim's suffering. Cleckley described numerous characteristics of the psychopathic personality:

- superficial charm and "good intelligence"
- absence of delusions, hallucinations, or other signs of psychosis
- absence of nervousness or psychoneurotic manifestations
- inability to feel guilt or shame
- unreliability
- chronic lying
- ongoing anti-social behavior
- poor judgment and inability to learn from experience
- self-centredness and incapacity to love
- unresponsiveness in general interpersonal relations
- impersonal, trivial, and poorly integrated sex life
- failure to follow any life plan

Cleckley stated that "psychopathy was defined by a constellation of dysfunctional psychological processes as opposed to specific behavioral manifestations."[39] Even though psychopaths have a seriously flawed personality, they can easily fool others into trusting them—hence the title of Cleckley's book.

According to Cleckley, indicators of psychopathy appear early in life, often in the teenage years, and include lying, fighting, stealing, and vandalism. Even earlier signs may be found, according to some authors, in bedwetting, cruelty to animals, sleepwalking, and fire-setting.[40] In a recent report prepared for the Correctional Service of Canada, psychopaths were described as "individuals who display impulsiveness, callousness, insincerity, pathological lying and deception, egocentricity, poor judgment, an impersonal sex life, and an unstable life plan."[41] The most definitive modern measure of psychopathy can be found in the Psychopathy Checklist (PLC), developed by Robert Hare, of the University of British Columbia.[42] This series of ratings by qualified experts using information from subject interviews and official records assessed degree of psychopathy using two kinds of indicators: affective and interpersonal traits (glibness, emotional detachment, egocentricity, superficial charm, and shallow affect) and traits associated with a chronic unstable and anti-social lifestyle (irresponsibility, impulsivity, criminality, and proneness to boredom).[43] Hence, psychopathy has both emotional and behaviour components.

A 2004 study of eight Canadian maximum-security male prisoners classified as psychopaths according to the PCL found that the men were not only impaired emotionally but also unable to efficiently process abstract words, perform abstract categorization tasks, understand metaphors, and process emotionally weighted words and speech.[44] During a test on abstract concepts, the men's brains were scanned using functional magnetic resonance imaging (fMRI); scans showed that a section of their brains did not activate as it should have. The researchers concluded that their findings "support the hypothesis that there is an abnormality in the function of the right anterior superior temporal gyrus in psychopathy."[45]

Some have questioned whether psychopaths merely lack empathy or really don't know the difference between right and wrong. Recent research by Marc Hauser, professor and director of the Cognitive Evolution Laboratory at Harvard, seems to show that the ability to tell right from wrong is something that human beings are born with, that the human brain is hard-wired to make moral distinctions, and that the same distinctions tend to be made across cultures. "The question," explained Hauser, "is whether emotions are causally necessary for moral judgment. Take psychopaths: we know they have some kind of

Clifford Olson never showed any guilt or remorse for the 11 young people he murdered in British Columbia in the early 1980s. During his years of incarceration, he tormented the families of the victims by sending them letters with comments about the murders. Do you think he is the prototypical psychopath?

Regina Leader-Post-Bryan Schlosser/ Canadian Press

emotional deficit because they don't seem to feel remorse or empathy for their victims. Does this deficit corrupt their moral judgment because emotions are necessary to make the right decision? Or is their moral judgment actually intact, but their behavior is screwed up because their emotions don't stop them from doing the wrong thing? My guess is the latter—that emotions flow from moral judgments and control behavior."[46]

It is important to note that the terms *psychopath* and *criminal* are not synonymous. Cleckley and others have noted that one can be a psychopath and not a criminal. Individuals manifesting many of the characteristics of a psychopathic personality, however, are likely to run afoul of the law.

Anti-Social Personality Disorder

In the attempt to identify sociopathic individuals, some psychologists started to place greater emphasis on the type of behaviour exhibited rather than on the identifiable personality traits. By 1968, the American Psychiatric Association (APA) had discontinued using the words *sociopath* and *psychopath* in its *Diagnostic and Statistical Manual of Mental Disorders* (DSM-II), replacing them with the terms *anti-social* and *asocial personality*.[47] In that year, the APA manual changed to a description of **anti-social (asocial) personality** types as

> individuals who are basically unsocialized and whose behavior pattern brings them repeatedly into conflicts with society. They are incapable of significant loyalty to individuals, groups, or social values. They are grossly selfish, callous, irresponsible, impulsive, and unable to feel guilt or to learn from experience and punishment. Frustration tolerance is low. They tend to blame others or offer plausible rationalization for their behavior.[48*]

Anti-social personality or **asocial personality** An individual who is unsocialized and whose behaviour pattern brings him or her into repeated conflict with society.

*Reprinted with permission from the Diagnostic and Statistical Manual of Mental Disorders, Second Edition, (Copyright ©1968). American Psychiatric Association. All Rights Reserved.

In most cases, individuals exhibiting an anti-social personality are said to be suffering from **anti-social personality disorder** (sometimes referred to in clinical circles as APD or ASPD).

Individuals manifesting characteristics of ASPD are likely to run afoul of the law. As one writer stated, "The impulsivity and aggression, the selfishness in achieving one's own immediate needs, and the disregard for society's rules and laws brings these people to the attention of the criminal justice system."[49] Moreover, studies of individuals who score high on psychological inventories designed to measure the degree of psychopathy have found to exhibit high rates of both criminality and recidivism.[50]

The causes of ASPD are unclear. Somatogenic causes (those based on physiological features) are said to include a malfunctioning of the central nervous system, which is characterized by a low state of arousal driving the sufferer to seek excitement, and brain abnormalities which may have been present since birth. Work by Robert Hare shows that an **electroencephalogram (EEG)** taken of an individual diagnosed as having ASPD is frequently abnormal, reflecting "a malfunction of some inhibitory mechanisms," making it unlikely that persons characterized by ASPD will "learn to inhibit behavior that is likely to lead to punishment."[51] It is difficult, however, to diagnose ASPD through physiological measurements because similar EEG patterns also show up in patients with other types of disorders. Psychogenic causes (those rooted in early interpersonal experiences) include inability to form attachments to parents or other caregivers early in life, sudden separation from the mother during the first six months of life, and other early forms of insecurity during the first few years of life. In short, a lack of love, or the sensed inability to unconditionally depend on one central loving figure (typically the mother in most psychological literature), immediately following birth is often posited as a major psychogenic factor contributing to the development of ASPD.

Most studies of ASPD have involved male subjects. Only rarely have researchers focused on women with anti-social personalities, and it is believed that only a small proportion of those afflicted with ASPD are women.[52] What little research there is suggests that females with ASPD possess many of the same definitive characteristics as their male counterparts and that they assume their anti-social roles at similarly early ages.[53] The lifestyles of anti-social females, however, appear to include sexual misconduct and abnormally high levels of sexual activity, but such research can be misleading because the cultural expectations of female sexual behaviour inherent in early studies may not always have been in keeping with reality. In other words, early researchers may have so little accurate information about female sexual activity that the behaviour of women judged to possess anti-social personalities may have actually been far closer to the norm than originally believed.

One Canadian study of penitentiary inmates in Quebec, which attempted to classify criminal offenders by type of mental disorder, determined that ASPD characterizes 46.6 percent of all inmates; schizophrenics, 6.3 percent; manic-depressives, 1.6 percent; drug-disordered persons, 18.6 percent; depressed individuals, 8.1 percent; and alcohol abuse–related sufferers another 33.1 percent.[54] A review of 20 such studies found great variation in the degree and type of disorder said to be prevalent among incarcerated offenders.[55] The studies categorized from 0.5 to 26 percent of all inmates as psychotic, 2.4 to 28 percent as mentally subnormal, 5.6 to 70 percent as ASPD, 2 to 7.9 percent as neurotic, and 11 to 80 percent as suffering from mental disorders induced by alcoholism or excessive drinking. Such studies usually concluded that few convicted felons are free from mental impairment of one sort or another. It is important to note, however, that the results from studies like these and others are dependent upon the characteristics used in the diagnostic tool. If the diagnostic criteria change, so too will the perceived prevalence of ASPD. It is important to note that the distinction in definitions between the anti-social personality and the psychopath means that, while most psychopaths meet the criteria for ASPD, most individuals with ASPD are *not* psychopaths. This failure to distinguish between psychopathy and anti-social personality disorder means that offenders are often mistakenly diagnosed as psychopaths rather than individuals with ASPD. Psychopathy is usually considered an aggravating rather than a mitigating circumstance, with the prognosis for treatment being low and the prediction of reoffending being high. Diagnostic confusion about the two disorders has the potential of harming both psychiatric offenders and society. There is hope that this situation of diagnostic confusion will be addressed with the publication of the *Diagnostic and Statistical Manual of Mental Disorders V* scheduled for release in 2013.[56]

CRIME AS ADAPTIVE BEHAVIOUR

SOME PSYCHIATRIC PERSPECTIVES HAVE HELD THAT "CRIME IS A COMPROMISE, representing for the individual the most satisfactory method of adjustment to inner conflicts which he cannot express otherwise. Thus, his acting out the crime fulfills a certain aim or purpose."[57] One pressing need of many criminals, according to psychiatric theory, is the need to be punished, which arises from a sense of guilt. Psychiatrists who suggest that the need to be punished is a motivating factor in some criminal behaviour are quick to point out that this need may be a closely guarded secret, unknown even to the offender, because many drives, motives, and wishes are unconscious or repressed by people who harbour them. Repression occurs when the mind chooses to keep certain aspects of itself out of consciousness, possibly because of shame, self-loathing, or a simple lack of adequate introspection. However the desire for punishment sometimes comes to the fore. In the mid-1990s, for example, Westley Dodd was hanged by authorities in Washington State for the kidnapping, rape, and murder of three little boys four years earlier. Dodd, who said he had molested dozens of children over the course of a decade, sought the death penalty after he was convicted, saying he deserved to die and vowing to sue the American Civil Liberties Union or anyone else who sought to save him.[58]

Crime can be adaptive in other ways, such as the adaptation to life's stresses. According to Seymour L. Halleck, turning to crime can provide otherwise disenfranchised individuals with a sense of power and purpose.[59] In Halleck's words, "During the planning and execution of a criminal act the offender is a free man. The value of this brief taste of freedom cannot be overestimated. Many of the criminal's apparently unreasonable actions are efforts to find a moment of autonomy."[60]

When the choice of crime reduces stresses that the individual faces by producing changes in the environment (empowerment), it is referred to as an **alloplastic adaptation**. When crime leads to stress reduction as a result of internal changes in beliefs, value systems, and so forth, it is called **autoplastic adaptation**. The offender who is able to deny responsibility for other failures by turning to crime is said to be seeking autoplastic adaptation. Because other forms of behaviour may also meet many of the same needs as does crime, Halleck pointed out, individuals may choose crime only when no reasonable alternatives are available or when criminal behaviour has inherent advantages, as under instances of economic or social oppression. For example, individuals who are actively discriminated against may find personal and political significance in violating the laws of the oppressing society.

From Halleck's point of view, crime "has many advantages even when considered independently of the criminal's conscious or unconscious needs for gratification."[61] Even though crime can be immediately rewarding or intensely pleasureful, such a reward is more like a "fringe benefit"; its central significance is that it "is an action which helps one survive with dignity."[62] Halleck explained that "we cannot understand the criminal unless we appreciate that his actions are much more than an effort to find a specific gratification."[63] Another approach to stress as a causative agent in crime commission suggests that stress may lead to aggression toward others and toward oneself (through self-destructive behaviour such as suicide, smoking, and abuse of alcohol).[64] This approach measured stress at the societal level, arguing that although the relationship between stress and aggression

Alloplastic adaptation A form of adjustment resulting from changes in the environment surrounding an individual.

Autoplastic adaptation A form of adjustment resulting from changes within an individual.

Modelling theory contends that we learn how to behave by observing others. Do you think this theory can help to explain a link between violent computer games and violent crime?

Paul Sakuma/Canadian Press Images

has been studied at the individual level, "the neglect of social stress as an explanation for society-to-society differences in aggression may be partially due to a lack of an objective means of comparing the stressfulness of life in different societies."[65] Concluding that societal stress levels heighten levels of aggression, adherents of this approach suggested that social policies should be created to reduce the impact of stressful events such as having to stop work, foreclosing on a mortgage, and dropping out of school.

People's perceptions vary, so although criminal behaviour may appear to be a valid choice for some individuals who are seeking viable responses to perceived stresses and oppression, their perceptions may not be wholly accurate. Misperceived stress and oppression may still lead to crime, even when far simpler solutions may be found in a more realistic appraisal of the offender's situation.

7.5 LEARNING OBJECTIVE

◉—Watch

Emergence of Learning Theory

◉—Watch

Gabriel Tarde

MODELLING THEORY

GRAND THEFT AUTO III, SOLDIER OF FORTUNE, POSTAL,[2] MANHUNT, MORTAL Kombat, Carmageddon, Thrill Kill—do violent computer games lead to violent crime? While the jury is still out on that question, some courts have acted to ensure the continued availability of such software. In 2011, for example, the U.S. Supreme Court struck down a California law that banned the sale of violent video games to minors. While the court looked at the constitutionality of a single state statute, it largely ignored the broader significance of imitation and modelling in shaping behaviour that has long been studied. One of the earliest attempts to explain crime and deviance as learned behaviour can be found in the work of Gabriel Tarde (1843–1904), a French social theorist who discounted the biological theories of Lombroso and others so prevalent in his day and suggested that it was possible to infer certain laws that appeared to govern the social world. The basis of any society, Tarde believed, was imitation, and he developed a theory of human behaviour built on three laws of imitation and suggestion.[66] Tarde's first law held that individuals in close intimate contact with one another tend to imitate each other's behaviour (children tend to imitate their parents). His second law stated that imitation moves from the top down (poor people tend to imitate wealthy people, youngsters tend to emulate older people). The third law was that of insertion, meaning that new acts and behaviours tend to either reinforce or replace old ones (the music of each generation replaces the music of the preceding one, the politics of young people eventually become the politics of the nation).

Albert Bandura developed a comprehensive **modelling theory** of aggression. Bandura stated that "a complete theory of aggression must explain how aggressive patterns are developed, what provokes people to behave aggressively, and what sustains such actions after they have been initiated."[67] Although everyone is capable of aggression, "people are not born with repertories of aggressive behavior. They must learn them." Bandura went on to say, "The specific forms that aggressive behavior takes, the frequency with which it is expressed, the situation in which it is displayed, and the specific targets selected for attack are largely determined by social learning factors."[68]

Modelling theory, a form of social learning theory, asserts that people learn how to act by observing others. Early on, Bandura experimented with children who observed adult role models striking inflatable cartoon characters. When these children were observed following their encounter, they exhibited similarly aggressive behaviour. Bandura also studied violence on television and concluded that "television is an effective tutor. Both laboratory and controlled field studies in which young children and adolescents are repeatedly shown either violent or non-violent fare disclose that exposure to film violence shapes the form of aggression and typically increases interpersonal aggressiveness in everyday life."[69] A later study by other researchers showed that even after ten years, the level of violence engaged in by young adults was directly related to the degree of violent television they had been exposed to as children.[70] One 2010 meta-analysis (a study of other studies) found that playing violent video games increases the frequency of aggressive thoughts and behaviours and leads to a decrease in empathy.[71] The study analyzed data from studies of more than 130 000 gamers in the United States, Europe, and Japan from elementary school through college.

Once aggressive patterns of behaviour have been acquired, it becomes necessary to show how they can be activated. Aggression can be provoked, Bandura suggested, by people experiencing physical assaults as well as verbal threats and insults, and by having their hopes thwarted or their behaviour obstructed (see the Crime in the News box). Deprivation and other adversities in life are also potential triggers of aggression.

Another form of reward flowing from aggression is what Bandura called "reduction of aversive treatment." For example, standing up to a bully is the most effective way of dealing with the harassment; "the squeaky wheel gets the grease" means simply that aggressive people often get what they go after.

Bandura recognized that everyone has self-regulatory mechanisms that can ameliorate the tendency toward aggression and that people reward or punish themselves according to internal standards they have for judging their own behaviour. Hence, aggression may be inhibited in people who value religious, ethical, or moral standards of conduct like compassion, thoughtfulness, and courtesy. People who devalue aggression may still engage in it via a process he called "disengagement," whereby rationalizations are constructed to overcome

Modelling theory A form of social learning theory that asserts that people learn how to behave by observing others.

How a Bright Kid with Excellent Self-Esteem Slaughtered His Whole Family

An example of aggression that resulted from thwarted goal seeking, and which may have been seen as holding future benefits for the boy involved, occurred in the early 1990s when Gavin Mandin shot and killed his parents and two sisters. Mandin, who was 15 at the time, waited in the family farmhouse not far from Edmonton, Alberta, for the rest of his family to return from a shopping trip. When the car pulled into the driveway, Mandin sighted through the scope of his pump-action, .22-calibre rifle and fired through a window and screen in the house. A bullet penetrated his stepfather Maurice's temple as he stepped out of the car, killing him instantly. His mother, Susan, still in the car, looked up as another shot crashed through the car's windshield and entered her brain. Mandin then shot his two sisters, Islay, 12, and Janelle, 10, at point-blank range as they sat in the back seat of the car, first in the head and then with the rifle pressed against their chests. Mandin then drove the car with the bodies in it to an area of thick bush nearby. Using ropes and an all-terrain vehicle, Mandin dragged his stepfather's body further into the bush.

By all accounts, Mandin's home life had been normal enough. Mandin was, reportedly, the "apple of his mother's eye" and she would defend him in all circumstances. However, there were signs that Mandin was not as enamoured of his family. Notes found behind Mandin's bed read, "I hate Janelle, I hate Susan, I hate Islay," and "Susan can't make me do anything. I wish she were dead." One particularly disturbing treatise said, "There will come the day when I rule. I will be the leader of the universe. All I love and desire will be mine. I will be the most powerful man on earth. I will have all the world it will be my backyard, all my enemies will die by my hand." During his interrogation by RCMP investigators, Mandin cited many reasons for his actions. He stated that he was made to clean his room, carry groceries into the house, and wash dishes. He disliked going to church services with the family, so he put a lock on his door to keep them from disturbing him. Mandin told RCMP investigator Corporal Ted Lachuk,

Sometimes, like, I will have something important to say to my mother and she will be sitting down and eating and I will come up to her and say "mom" and she won't do anything and I'll just keep calling her again and again. One time I called her eight or nine times and she didn't even answer. A couple of times I even tapped her on the shoulder and she ignores me and it really makes me angry.

Shortly after being taken into custody, Mandin declared, "I guess I get the house now, eh?" Later he stated that he intended to use a $1000 bond his mother had saved for him as an investment, to become a "zillionaire."

Mandin was denied parole in 2001, largely owing to his lack of remorse for his crime. He underwent many psychological reports while incarcerated, some of which labelled him a psychopath; however, he has never met the criteria of the Hare Psychopathy Checklist. In 2012, Gavin Mandin applied for and was granted full parole; he is living in the community and goes by the name Gavin Ian Maclean. Since he was originally given a life sentence, he will be monitored in the community for the rest of his life.

Discussion Questions

1. Some individuals become aggressive because they are rewarded for doing so. Do you think Gavin Mandin's criminal behaviour be explained this way?

2. Albert Bandura posited that some who engage in aggressive behaviour justify it by placing blame on their victims. Was this part of Gavin Mandin's rationalization for his actions?

3. Gavin Mandin was tested for psychopathic tendencies. Do you think he fits the profile of a psychopath?

Sources: Adapted from Jim Demers, "'I Am Gavin.' How a Bright Kid with Excellent Self-Esteem Slaughtered His Whole Family," Alberta Report, December 6, 1993, pp. 18–22. Ryan Tumilty, "At 20-year mark, one question lingers in Mandin murder case", St Albert Gazette, August 10, 2011, http://www.stalbertgazette.com/article/20110810/SAG0801/308109968/at-20-year-mark-one-question-lingers-in-mandin-case.

internal inhibitions, including (1) placement of blame on their victim; (2) dehumanization through bureaucratization, automation, urbanization, and high social mobility; (3) vindication of aggressive practices by legitimate authorities; and (4) desensitization resulting from repeated exposure to aggression.

Modelling theory has been criticized for lacking comprehensive explanatory power. How can striking differences in sibling behaviour be explained when early childhood experiences were similar? Why do apparent differences exist between the sexes in degree and type of criminality, irrespective of social background and early learning experiences? More recent versions of modelling theory, sometimes called "cognitive social learning theory,"[72] attempt to account for such differences by hypothesizing that reflection and cognition play a significant role in how a person interprets what is observed and then forms responses. Few people behave precisely as others do because they have their own ideas about both the meanings of observed behaviour and the consequences of emulation.

BEHAVIOUR THEORY

7.6 **LEARNING OBJECTIVE**

BEHAVIOUR THEORY HAS SOMETIMES BEEN CALLED THE STIMULUS–RESPONSE approach to human behaviour. "At the heart of behavior theory is the notion that behavior is determined by environmental consequences which it produces for the individual concerned."[73] When an individual's behaviour results in rewards or feedback seen as pleasurable or rewarding, the behaviour is reinforced and will likely become more frequent, but when punishment follows the behaviour, the frequency of that behaviour will probably decrease.

The individual's responses are termed **operant behaviour**, because his or her choices effectively operate on the surrounding environment to produce consequences for him or her. Similarly, stimuli provided by the environment become behavioural cues that serve to elicit conditioned responses from individual. Behaviour theory is often employed by parents seeking to control children through a series of **punishments** and **rewards**. Young children may be punished with spanking, the temporary loss of a favoured toy, or a turned-off television. Older children are often told what rules to obey and what rewards to anticipate if they adhere to those rules and what punishments to expect if they do not.

In behaviour theory, rewards and punishments have been divided into four conceptual categories: (1) positive rewards that increase the frequency of approved behaviour by adding something desirable to the situation (a "good" child is given a toy); (2) negative rewards that increase the frequency of approved behaviour by removing something distressful (a "good" child is permitted to skip the morning's chores); (3) positive punishments that decrease the frequency of unwanted behaviour by adding something undesirable (a "bad" child is spanked); and (4) negative punishments that decrease the frequency of unwanted behaviour by removing something desirable (a "bad" child has candy taken away). It is through the application of rewards and punishments that behaviour is shaped.

Behaviour theory differs from other psychological theories in that the major determinants of behaviour are envisioned as existing in the environment surrounding the individual rather than in the individual. B.F. Skinner (1904–1990), the best-known proponent of behaviour theory, rejected unobservable psychological constructs, focusing instead on patterns of responses to external rewards and stimuli. Skinner did extensive animal research involving behavioural concepts and created programmed instruction, which allows students to work at their own pace and provides immediate rewards for learning accomplishments.

Although behaviour theory has much to say about the reformation of criminal offenders through the imposition of punishment, the approach is equally significant for its contributions to understanding the genesis of such behaviour. As one writer explained, "It is the balance of reinforcement and punishment in an individual's learning history which will dictate the presence or absence of criminal behavior."[74] According to the behavioural model, crime results when individuals "receive tangible rewards (positive reinforcement) for engaging in delinquent and criminal behavior, particularly when no other attractive alternative is available."[75]

Behaviour theory has been criticized for ignoring the role that cognition plays in human behaviour. A martyr, for example, persists in what society may define as undesirable behaviour even in the face of severe punishment, including the loss of his or her own life; no punishment deters a martyr from answering this higher calling. Criminals who are

Watch
Behaviour Theory

Watch
Punishment vs. Reward

Behaviour theory A psychological perspective positing that individual behaviour that is rewarded will increase in frequency, and behaviour that is punished will decrease.

Operant behaviour Behaviour that affects the environment so as to produce responses or further behavioural cues.

Punishments Undesirable behavioural consequences likely to decrease the frequency of occurrence of that behaviour.

Rewards Desirable behavioural consequences likely to increase the frequency of occurrence of that behaviour.

punished for official law violations may find that their social group interprets criminal punishment as status enhancing. According to behaviour theory, criminal punishments are in danger of losing sway over many forms of human behaviour today because society's fragmented value system leads to various interpretations of criminal punishments, thereby changing the significance of experiences such as arrest, conviction, and imprisonment. In the past, criminal offenders were often shunned and became social outcasts, but today those who have been adjudicated criminal may find that their new status holds many rewards.

7.7 LEARNING OBJECTIVE

MENTAL ILLNESS AND THE LAW

UNFORTUNATELY FOR CRIMINOLOGISTS, PSYCHOLOGICAL CONCEPTIONS OF MENTAL illness, ASPD, and even psychopathy are not readily applicable to the criminal justice system, which relies instead on the legal concept of insanity. Seen this way, *insanity* is a term that refers to a type of defence allowable in criminal courts. While the legal concept of insanity is based upon claims of mental illness, it has no precise counterpart in the jargon of contemporary psychologists or psychiatrists, who speak in terms of mental status or psychosis or personality disorder, so legal and psychiatric understandings of mental impairment rarely coincide.

The *Criminal Code of Canada* defines **mental disorder** as a "disease of the mind." Whether a specific condition is a disease of the mind, however, is a question of law. While medical evidence is used to assist a judge in deciding whether the accused suffers a disease of the mind, the Supreme Court of Canada has stated that the protection of public safety must also be considered. The Court has ruled that if the accused suffers from a recurring condition that may continue to present a danger to the public, the accused's condition should be treated as a mental disorder.[76] A number of mental disorders are recognized by the courts as diseases of the mind, including schizophrenia, paranoia, senile dementia, melancholia, various types of epilepsy, and delirium tremens caused by alcohol abuse. Self-induced states caused by alcohol or drugs, and temporary conditions such as hysteria and concussion, are excluded.[77] The burden of proving a claim of "not criminally responsible on account of mental disorder," however, falls upon the defendant. Just as a person is assumed to be innocent at the start of any criminal trial, so too is the person assumed to be sane.

Mental disorder (psychological) Disease of the mind including schizophrenia, paranoia, senile dementia, melancholia, various types of epilepsy, and delirium tremens caused by alcohol abuse; **Mental disorder (legal)** A legally established inability to understand right from wrong, or to conform one's behaviour to the requirements of the law. Also, a defence allowable in criminal courts.

WHO'S RESPONSIBLE—THE INDIVIDUAL OR SOCIETY?

Tragedy on a Greyhound Bus

On July 30, 2008, at 5:55 p.m., 22-year-old Tim McLean boarded a Greyhound bus in Erickson, Manitoba, bound for Winnipeg. He was returning home from a summer employment on the carnival circuit. He took a seat at the back of the bus, several rows behind Vince Li, who had already been travelling on the bus for a day and was headed to Thunder Bay.

The bus stopped between Brandon and Portage la Prairie, where both men got off for a break. Upon re-boarding, Vince Li moved to the back of the bus and sat beside Tim McLean. The two men did not exchange any words.

At approximately 8:30 p.m., in an unprovoked attack and for no apparent reason, Vince Li began to repeatedly stab Tim McLean. Despite his efforts to defend himself and get out of his seat, McLean was trapped at the back of the bus, the seats in front of him barring him from escape. He fell to the floor while Li continued to stab him, apparently oblivious to the screams of the other passengers and the bus driver exhorting him to stop. Only after the passengers vacated the bus did Li attempt to escape through the front door, but he was trapped when the bus driver managed to close the door on his arm. Li pulled his arm free and

>

returned to the body of McLean, continuing to defile it with cuts and stabs.

As panicked passengers waited for emergency personnel, Li attempted again to exit the bus, now holding Tim McLean's severed head in one hand, his bloodied buck knife in the other. The quick-thinking bus driver had managed to cut the power to the door and a truck driver who had stopped to help barricaded the door with a snipe bar. Trapped, Li went back to McLean's torso and continued to mutilate it.

Upon their arrival, RCMP officers ordered Vince Li to throw the knife out of the bus window. He refused and continued to cut McLean's body with the knife and a pair of scissors. Witnesses reported seeing Li licking blood from his fingers, and placing some of McLean's internal organs and body parts in plastic bags.

After several hours, Li decided to surrender, jumping out a window of the bus. After a scuffle, he was subdued by the RCMP and formally arrested. Charged with second-degree murder, Li appeared in court several months later. At his trial, psychiatrists testified Li was schizophrenic and suffering a major psychotic episode at the time of the killing. Li heard voices from God telling him that McLean, sitting next to him on the bus, was an evil threat that needed to be eliminated, psychiatrists said. Even after the killing, Li believed McLean might come back to life and threaten him. Li was found "not criminally responsible on account of mental disorder" (NCRMD), the judge ruling that he was suffering hallucinations from untreated schizophrenia at the time of the attack. Li was sent to a secure psychiatric facility where he continues to be treated and held until he is deemed well enough to be released.

A shocked public reacted to the tragic event, and McLean's mother, Carol deDelley, led a very public crusade to change Canada's laws. Launching a petition, she called on the federal government to enact "Tim's Law," an amendment to the *Criminal Code* that would ensure that those who are found not criminally responsible for crimes on account of a mental disorder are jailed for a minimum period of time.

In May 2013, the Criminal Court Review Board ruled that Vince Li be granted escorted full-day passes as far away as Winnipeg.

Think about it:

1. Most people with diagnosed mental illness never commit acts of violence. In rare cases such as the one described here, how should perpetrators be dealt with?

2. Do you agree with the legal definition of NCRMD? Should Vince Li have been deemed to be "not responsible" for his violent acts?

3. Do our current laws regarding the criminally insane sufficiently recognize the rights of victims?

Sources: Adapted from "Accused in Manitoba Bus Killing Fit to Stand Trial: Court," *CBC News*, October 6, 2008, http://www.cbc.ca/canada/manitoba/story/2008/10/06/beheading-court.html [Accessed October 23, 2012]; Tom Broadbeck, "The Story of Vince Li," March 4, 2009, http://blogs.canoe.ca/raisinghell/2009/03/page/2/ [Accessed October 23, 2012]; "Bus Slaying's Grim Anniversary Marked," *CBC News*, July 30, 2009, http://www.cbc.ca/canada/manitoba/story/2009/07/29/greyhound-beheading-anniversary073009.html [Accessed October 23, 2012]; and Vince Li gets Winnipeg visitation privileges", CBC News, May 17, 2013, http://www.cbc.ca/news/canada/manitoba/story/2013/05/17/mb-vince-li-granted-winnipeg-visits-cp.html [Accessed May 25, 2013].

The McNaughten Rule

One of the first instances within Western legal tradition where insanity was accepted as a defence to criminal liability can be found in the British case of Daniel McNaughten (also spelled M'Naughton and M'Naghton). McNaughten was accused of the 1844 killing of Edward Drummond, the secretary of British prime minister Sir Robert Peel. McNaughten had intended to kill Peel, but because he was suffering from mental disorganization, he shot Drummond instead, mistaking him for Peel. At his trial, the defence presented information to show that McNaughten was suffering from delusions, including the belief that Peel's political party was, in some vague way, persecuting him. The court accepted his lawyer's claims and the defence of insanity was established in Western law. Other jurisdictions were quick to adopt the **McNaughten rule**, as the judge's decision in the case came to be called, which holds that individuals cannot be held criminally responsible for their actions if at the time of the offence either (1) they did not know what they were doing, or (2) they did not know that what they were doing was wrong.

Today, the McNaughten rule is still followed in Canada when mental disorder is at issue in criminal cases. Critics of the McNaughten rule say that, although the notion of intent inherent within it appeals well to lawyers, "it is so alien to current concepts of human behavior that it has been vigorously attacked by psychiatrists. An obvious difficulty

McNaughten rule A standard for judging legal insanity that requires that offenders did not know what they were doing, or if they did, that they did not know it was wrong.

with the McNaughten rule is that practically everyone, regardless of the degree of his criminal disturbance, knows the nature and quality and rightness or wrongness of what he is doing."[78]

Fitness to Stand Trial and Not Criminally Responsible on Account of Mental Disorder

When the question of mental fitness arises, two standards are assessed. First, is the accused fit to stand trial; that is, does he or she understand the nature of charges against him or her? If a court-ordered psychiatric assessment determines that the accused is unfit to stand trial (UST), then that individual is usually placed in a psychiatric facility or released under community supervision for ongoing treatment. The individual's case is reviewed annually, and the Crown is responsible for bringing it before the courts every two years. If the individual becomes fit to stand trial, he or she may do so at that time.

The second standard of fitness is the accused's mental state at the time of the offence. A finding of "**not criminally responsible on account of mental disorder**" (NCRMD) acknowledges that the accused committed the offence but finds that the accused suffered from a mental disorder that made him or her incapable of appreciating the nature and quality of his or her actions or that the actions were wrong. When such a verdict of NCRMD is made, a disposition hearing is ordered to assess whether or not the accused poses any threat to the public or to him- or herself. If not, that accused may be released under supervision to the community. Otherwise, the accused may be detained in a secure hospital, under certain conditions.

Not criminally responsible on account of mental disorder (NCRMD) A finding that offenders are responsible for committing the offence that they have committed and, because of their prevailing mental condition, should be sent to a psychiatric hospital for treatment rather than to prison. The maximum length of stay is predetermined.

The length of time in hospital detention has been a subject of controversy in recent years. The Supreme Court decision *R. v. Swain* resulted in an overhaul of the existing legal insanity criteria and practices, most notably the automatic and indefinite detention for those found legally insane. In that decision, the Court held not only that "the duty of the trial judge to detain is unqualified by any standard whatsoever" but also that "insanity acquitees should be detained no longer than necessary to determine whether they are currently dangerous due to their insanity."[79] Amendments to the *Criminal Code* passed in 1992 (see Box 7.1) reflect the basic principle of Canadian criminal law that to convict someone of a crime, the state must prove not only a wrongful act, but also a guilty mind. In the words of then Minister of Justice Kim Campbell, "The mental disorder provisions of the *Criminal Code* needed to be updated to reflect the evolution of society and the law. These changes will ensure that individuals are not deprived of their *Charter* rights. At the same time, the amendments offer protection of the public from dangerous mentally disordered persons who come into conflict with the law."[80]

Interestingly, other countries use a variety of definitions of legal insanity. In the United States, where the issue falls within the jurisdiction of the individual state, a number of alternatives exist. In addition to the McNaughten rule, the irresistible-impulse test is employed in 18 states and holds that a defendant is not guilty of a criminal offence if the person, by virtue of his or her mental state or psychological condition, was not able to resist committing the action in question. Several U.S. states have adopted the "guilty but mentally ill" (GBMI) standard. A GBMI verdict means that a person can be held responsible for a specific criminal act, even though a degree of mental incompetence may be present in his or her personality. Individuals adjudicated GBMI are found guilty of the criminal offence with which they are charged but, because of their mental condition, are generally sent to psychiatric hospitals for treatment rather than to prison.[81] Other standards include the Durham rule and the Brawner rule.

Provisions for Individuals Found NCRMD Part XX.1 of the *Criminal Code of Canada* makes provisions for the treatment of individuals found NCRMD. Procedures for

Box 7.1 MENTAL DISORDER AS A DEFENCE

The *Criminal Code of Canada* permits the defence of insanity, as follows:

Defence of Mental Disorder	**16.** (1)	No person is criminally responsible for an act committed or an omission made while suffering from a mental disorder that rendered the person incapable of appreciating the nature and quality of the act or omission or of knowing that it was wrong.
Presumption	(2)	Every person is presumed not to suffer from a mental disorder so as to be exempt from criminal responsibility by virtue of subsection (1), until the contrary is proved on the balance of probabilities.
Burden of Proof	(3)	The burden of proof that an accused was suffering from a mental disorder so as to be exempt from criminal responsibility is on the party that raises the issue.

Source: *Criminal Code of Canada*, R.S.C. 1985, c. C-46, s.16 [as amended S.C. 1991, c. 43, s. 2].

dealing with those found NCRMD stipulate that such a person must attend a disposition hearing, which can either be held by the trial court or be referred to a provincial review board made up of lawyers, psychiatrists, and other appointees, which is the usual course of action. This disposition hearing must be held within 45 days of the NCRMD finding. If the court holds the hearing and makes an order other than an absolute discharge, the review board must review the case within 90 days. The NCRMD person may be present at the disposition, may be represented by counsel, and may cross-examine witnesses. The disposition hearings are public and "may be conducted in as informal a manner as is appropriate in the circumstances."[82] The recommendation of the review board for the treatment of the NCRMD individual is expected to reflect the least intrusive or restrictive option consistent with the protection of society. For example, the court or review board might allow someone who committed a theft, who is not dangerous, and who is willing to submit to psychiatric treatment on an outpatient basis to stay at home rather than be sent to a hospital setting. Such a condition would be subject to the supervision of medical staff giving the treatment and to periodic reviews; changes may be effected as required. The review board in such a case would have the authority to revoke this status and order hospitalization, should the person's condition deteriorate.

The former practice of indefinite hospitalization under the Warrants of the Lieutenant-Governor has been replaced with a system of "caps," or maximum periods of deprivation of liberty. The "capping" provides a rough equivalence between the way in which the criminal law treats sane and mentally disordered offenders. For example, in cases of murder, the outer limit is life. In cases of offences against the person, the outer limit is ten years or the maximum penalty stipulated by the *Criminal Code*, whichever is shorter. For all other offences, the "cap" is the lesser of two years or the maximum penalty stipulated by the *Criminal Code*. If at the expiration of the "cap" the NCRMD person is still considered a danger, he or she can be involuntarily committed to a secure hospital under the authority of provincial mental health legislation. The initial length of hospitalization is determined by the review boards. Each province is required to have a review board and each NCRMD case must be reviewed annually. All decisions rendered by the review boards are binding.

Despite public perception, the defence of mental disorder has not been used successfully in a large number of cases in Canada. Yet some argue that this defence is being used

André Dallaire, a diagnosed paranoid schizophrenic, was declared not criminally responsible for attempting to kill Prime Minister Chrétien after breaking into his home. How does the Canadian criminal justice system deal with people such as Dallaire?

Fred Chartrand/Canadian Press Images

more often since the introduction of the 25-year minimum life sentence for first-degree murder in 1976.[83] A study of mentally accused and the criminal justice system by the Canadian Centre for Justice Statistics indicated that the total number of active cases before review boards in the early 2000s (including UST and NCRMD cases) was fewer than 3000.[84] Some high-profile Canadian cases in which the defence of mental disorder was used successfully include those of André Dallaire, the paranoid schizophrenic who tried unsuccessfully to assassinate then Prime Minister Chrétien; Dorothy Joudrie, who attempted to murder her husband with five blasts from a shotgun in Calgary; and Elizabeth Elliott, who stepped in front of a transport truck on a highway near Perth, Ontario, while carrying her five-year-old daughter. Elliott's schizophrenia and bipolar disorder had caused her to have religious delusions that were responsible for her behaviour.[85]

7.8 | LEARNING OBJECTIVE

SOCIAL POLICY AND FORENSIC PSYCHOLOGY

PSYCHOLOGICAL THEORIES CONTINUE TO EVOLVE. RESEARCH IN THE FIELD HAS shown a stability of aggressiveness over time. That is, children who display early disruptive or aggressive behaviour are likely to continue their involvement in such behaviour as adults.[86] Some researchers have found that aggressiveness appears to stabilize over time.[87] Children who demonstrate aggressive traits often evidence increasingly frequent episodes of such behaviour until it becomes a major component of their adolescent or adult personality. Therefore, it is possible to conclude that problem children are likely to become problem adults.

This research holds considerable significance for those who are attempting to assess dangerousness and identify personal characteristics that would allow for the prediction of dangerousness in individual cases, which is of great concern to today's policymakers. In the late 1990s, Jean Gerald Dionne, a convicted sex offender, was charged with the kidnapping, forcible confinement, and sexual assault of a teenaged girl. Dionne at the time had a record of assaulting a 58-year-old woman in 1980, of criminal negligence causing death in the drowning of a 2-year-old boy in 1982, and of sexually assaulting an 8-year-old, wheelchair-bound girl in 1991.[88]

Can past behaviour predict future behaviour? Do former instances of criminality presage additional ones? Are there other identifiable characteristics violent offenders might manifest that could serve as warning signs to criminal justice decision makers faced with the dilemma of whether to release convicted felons? One study found a strong relationship between childhood behavioural difficulties and later problem behaviour: "Early antisocial behavior is the best predictor of later antisocial behavior. It appears that this rule holds even when the antisocial behavior is measured as early as the preschool period."[89] Using children as young as 3 years old, researchers were able to predict later delinquency, leading them to conclude that "some antisocial behavioral characteristics may be components of temperament." A second study, tracking a sample of male offenders for over 20 years, found that stable but "unmeasured individual differences" account for the positive association that exists between past criminal behaviour and the likelihood of future recurrence.[90] An 1996 analysis of recidivism studies by Canadians Paul Gendreau, Tracy Little, and Claire Goggin found that criminal history, pre-adult anti-social behaviour, and "criminogenic needs" (measurable anti-social thoughts, values, and behaviour) were all predictors of recidivism.[91]

Prediction requires more than generalities; it necessitates the ability to predict which specific individuals will engage in future violations of criminal law. **Selective incapacitation** is a policy based on the notion of career criminality.[92] Career criminals (also called *habitual offenders*) are people who repeatedly violate the criminal law. Research has shown that only a small percentage of all offenders account for most crimes reported to the police—some studies found as few as 8 percent of all offenders committing as many as 60 serious crimes

Selective incapacitation A social policy that seeks to protect society by incarcerating those individuals deemed to be the most dangerous.

per year.[93] The strategy of selective incapacitation has been criticized by some authors for yielding a rate of "false positives" of over 60 percent.[94] Potentially violent offenders are not easy to identify, even on the basis of past criminal records, and sentencing individuals to long prison terms simply because they are thought likely to commit crimes in the future would no doubt violate their *Charter* rights.

Part XXIV of the *Criminal Code of Canada* deals with dangerous and long-term offenders. The Crown Attorney can make application upon conviction (but before sentencing) to have an offender designated as "dangerous." The dangerous offender designation brings with it an indefinite or indeterminate sentence of incarceration and a lengthened period of parole ineligibility. One intention of the indeterminate sentence is that these offenders will receive mental health treatment. Whether or not this happens effectively is debatable. The past decade has seen an increase in the use of the dangerous offender designation to deal with repeat and violent offenders. The 2011 annual report of Public Safety Canada reported 473 offenders designated as dangerous; the majority of these were convicted of offences involving sexual aggression.[95] The *Tackling Violent Crime Act* of 2008 introduced changes to the dangerous offender provisions by putting the onus on an individual who has been convicted of specific violent or sexual crimes three or more times to convince the court why he or she should not be designated a dangerous offender.

Definitions of *dangerousness* are fraught with difficulty because "dangerousness is not an objective quality like obesity or brown eyes, rather it is an ascribed quality like trustworthiness."[96] Dangerousness is not necessarily a personality trait that is stable or easily identifiable, but even if it were, some studies of criminal careers seem to show that involvement in crime decreases with age.[97] One author stated that if "criminality declines more or less uniformly with age, then many offenders will be 'over the hill' by the time they are old enough to be plausible candidates for preventive incarceration."[98]

No discussion of social policy relating to the insights of criminal psychology would be complete without mention of **correctional psychology**, which is concerned with the diagnosis and classification of offenders, the treatment of correctional populations, and the rehabilitation of inmates and other law violators. One of the most commonly used classification instruments in correctional facilities today is the Minnesota Multiphasic Personality Inventory, better known as the MMPI. Based on results of MMPI inventories, an offender may be assigned to a security level, a correctional program, or a treatment program. Psychological treatment typically takes the form of individual or group counselling such as psychotherapy, guided group interaction, cognitive therapy, behavioural modification, and various forms of interpersonal therapy. Canadian Paul Gendreau is internationally recognized for his research on techniques for improving the practice of correctional psychology and reducing the risk of criminal reoffending. In 2007, Gendreau was appointed an officer of the Order of Canada in recognition of his service to Canada.

Correctional psychology
The branch of forensic psychology concerned with the diagnosis and classification of offenders, the treatment of correctional populations, and the rehabilitation of inmates and other law violators.

Social Policy and the Psychology of Criminal Conduct

A practical synthesis of psychological approaches to criminal behaviour is offered by Canadians Donald A. Andrews and James Bonta in their book *The Psychology of Criminal Conduct*.[99] Andrews and Bonta used the term "psychology of criminal conduct" (PCC) to distinguish their point of view from what they called "the weak psychology represented in mainstream sociological criminology and clinical/forensic psychology."[100] They stated that any useful synthesis of contemporary criminal psychology should be fundamentally objective and empirical, as opposed to many currently well-accepted perspectives that "placed higher value on social theory and political ideology than [on] rationality and/or respect for evidence."[101] Andrews and Bonta explained,

The majority of perspectives on criminal conduct that are most favored in mainstream criminology reduce people to hypothetical fictions whose only interesting characteristics are their location in the social system. Almost without exception, the causal significance of social location is presumed to reflect inequality in the distribution of social wealth and power [which] is a major preoccupation of mainstream textbook criminology, even though such a focus has failed to significantly advance understanding of criminal conduct.[102]

In *The Psychology of Criminal Conduct*, Andrews and Bonta did not attempt to develop a new behavioural theory but asked for the objective application of what is understood about the psychology of crime, behaviour, and criminal offenders possible through the application of readily available high-quality psychological findings. Based on nearly 500 published reports on "controlled evaluations of community and correctional interventions," they concluded that treatment reduces recidivism "to at least a mild degree."[103] Targeting higher-risk cases and using treatments outside of formal correctional settings (such as the offender's family and peers) are elements of the most effective treatment strategies. Along with objective measures of the success of rehabilitation programs and strategies, effective intervention and treatment services based on the use of psychological assessment instruments that have already demonstrated their validity, empirically established risk factors that can be accurately assessed, and accurately measured community crime rates are all ready and waiting to make a practical psychology of criminal conduct available to today's policymakers. In the words of Andrews and Bonta, "There exists now an empirically defensible general psychology of criminal conduct (PCC) that is of practical value. It should speak to policy advisors, policy makers and legislators who must come to see that human science is not just [a] relic of a positivistic past."[104] They concluded that the major remaining issue "on which work is only beginning, is how to make use of what works."[105]

7.9 | LEARNING OBJECTIVE

CRIMINAL PSYCHOLOGICAL PROFILING

DURING WORLD WAR II, THE U.S. WAR DEPARTMENT RECRUITED PSYCHOLOGISTS and psychoanalysts in an attempt to predict future moves enemy forces might make, and the psychological and psychoanalytical techniques were applied to the study of German leader Adolf Hitler, Italian leader Benito Mussolini, Japanese general and prime minister Hideki Tojo, and other Axis leaders. Such psychological profiling of enemy leaders may have given the Allies the edge in battlefield strategy.

Psychological profiling The attempt to categorize, understand, and predict the behaviour of certain types of offenders based on behavioural clues they provide; also called *criminal profiling* and *behavioural profiling*.

Today, **psychological profiling** (also called *criminal profiling* and *behavioural profiling*) is used to assist criminal investigators seeking to better understand individuals wanted for serious offences. Profilers develop a list of typical offender characteristics and other useful principles by analyzing crime scene and autopsy data, in conjunction with interviews and other studies of past offenders, in the belief that almost any form of conscious behaviour (including behaviour engaged in by the offender during a criminal episode) is symptomatic of an individual's personality. The way a kidnapper approaches victims, the manner of attack used by a killer, and the specific sexual activities of a rapist might all help paint a picture of the offender's motivations, personal characteristics, and likely future behaviour. Sometimes psychological profiles can provide clues as to what an offender might do following an attack. Some offenders have been arrested, for example, after returning to the crime scene, a behaviour typically predicted by specific behavioural clues left behind, and a remorseful type can be expected to visit the victim's grave, permitting fruitful stakeouts of cemeteries.

While criminal profiling is not necessarily useful in every case, it can help narrow the search for an offender in repetitive crimes involving one offender, such as a serial rape or murder. Knowledge gleaned from profiling can also help in the interrogation of suspects and can be used to identify and protect possible victims before the offender has a chance to strike again.

Profiles have also contributed significantly to the scientific literature in criminology. In a well-known study of lust murderers (men who kill and often mutilate victims during or following a forced sexual episode), Robert R. Hazelwood and John E. Douglas distinguished between the organized non-social and the disorganized asocial types.[106] The organized non-social lust murderer exhibits complete indifference to the interests of society and is completely self-centred, methodical, cunning, and "fully cognizant of the criminality of his act and its impact on society."[107] The disorganized asocial lust murderer was described this way:

> [He] exhibits primary characteristics of societal aversion. This individual prefers his own company to that of others and would be typified as a loner. He experiences difficulty in negotiating interpersonal relationships and consequently feels rejected and lonely. He lacks the cunning of the non-social type and commits the crime in a more frenzied and less methodical manner. The crime is likely to be committed in close proximity to his residence or place of employment, where he feels secure and more at ease.[108]

During the 1980s, the Federal Bureau of Investigation (FBI) in the United States led the movement to develop psychological profiling techniques through its concentration on violent sex offenders and arsonists. Much of that work continues at the FBI's Training Academy in Quantico, Virginia, in the Behavioral Science Unit (BSU), whose official mission continues to focus on serial killers, lust murderers, domestic terrorists, and the like and aims to develop and provide programs of training, research, and consultation in the behavioural and social sciences for the FBI and the law enforcement community. The unit's activities have been popularized by movies and television shows such as *Silence of the Lambs* (1991) and *Criminal Minds*; however, media representations may lead the public to put too much stock in behavioural techniques such as psychological profiling. "It's not the magic bullet of investigations," said retired agent Robert Ressler, "it's simply another tool."[109]

Based on training acquired at the FBI Training Academy, Canadian police officials have developed an automated case linkage system that uses some of the behavioural principles of psychological profiling to identify and track violent serial criminals. Through the pioneering work of Inspector Ron MacKay of the RCMP and Sergeant Greg Johnston of the Ontario Provincial Police (OPP), the **Violent Crime Linkage Analysis System (ViCLAS)** was introduced in 1995. ViCLAS is a centralized computer bank containing details of violent crimes, allowing police to recognize patterns among violent offences. In cases of solved or unsolved homicides and sexual assaults, missing persons, and nonparental abductions, police investigators must respond to over 200 questions covering details of all aspects of an incident, including victimology, modus operandi, forensics, and behavioural information. The information is then forwarded to one of the ViCLAS centres throughout the country, where trained ViCLAS specialists input it and interpret the results. There is a ViCLAS centre in every province except for Prince Edward Island. Seven sites are maintained by the RCMP, and one each maintained by the OPP and the Sûreté du Québec. These sites perform data entry, conduct quality reviews, and await further processing and/or analysis. As of 2007, there were approximately 300 000 cases on the system and over 3200 linkages made.[110]

Most initial operational difficulties have been worked out, and the system has been adopted internationally in countries such as Belgium, Australia, and the United Kingdom. Advocates of ViCLAS believe it is serving to facilitate communication between investigators with the common goal of solving serious serial criminal acts and protecting the public from dangerous repeat offenders. In the words of RCMP Inspector Ron MacKay, "The linking of a series of crimes committed by the same offender not only increases investigative efficiency, it also enhances the grounds for multiple charges and dangerous offender status, with resultant indefinite/longer sentences for serial offenders."[111]

Violent Crime Linkage Analysis System (ViCLAS) A centralized computer bank containing details of violent crimes that assists police in recognizing patterns among violent offences and offenders.

PSYCHOLOGICAL AND PSYCHIATRIC THEORIES APPLIED

PSYCHOANALYTIC CRIMINOLOGY
holds that criminal behaviour can be explained by considering the role of personality to determine human behaviour.
Armin Meiwes demonstrated an overactive id, which could not be controlled by his superego.

Psychological and psychiatric theories of criminal behaviour emphasize individual propensities and characteristics in the genesis of criminality. Whether the emphasis is on conditioned behaviour, development of parental attachment, or psychoanalytic structure of the human personality, these approaches see the wellsprings of human motivation, desire, and behavioural choice as being firmly rooted in the personality.

Can the bizarre perversions of Armin Meiwes and the murderous actions of Marc Lepine be explained from a psychological and/or psychiatric perspective?

MODELLING THEORY
holds that criminal behaviour is learned by modelling others whom an individual has the opportunity to observe.
Marc Lepine was unable to self-regulate his aggression and engaged in the process of disengagement to justify his violent outburst.

FRUSTRATION–AGGRESSION THEORY
holds that criminal behaviour is a form of adaptation to reduce stress caused by frustration.
Marc Lepine was frustrated and angry at the female students who had succeeded in studying engineering at Montreal's L'École Polytechnique when he had not; he blamed them for his failure.

PSYCHIATRIC CRIMINOLOGY
holds that criminal behaviour is linked to a complex set of drives and motives operating from the recesses deep within the personality.
Armin Meiwes was described as a lonely man who made up imaginary friends whom he fantasized about eating so they would be with him always.

SUMMARY OF LEARNING OBJECTIVES

7.1 Psychological and psychiatric theories of criminal behaviour emphasize individual propensities and characteristics in explaining criminality. Whether the emphasis is on conditioned behaviour, development of parental attachment, or psychoanalytic structure of the human personality, these approaches see the wellsprings of human motivation, desire, and behavioural choice as being firmly rooted in the personality.

7.2 Early psychological theories used the concept of behavioural conditioning to explain most human activity. Criminality was seen as a form of mental disease, or psychopathy. Psychiatric criminology, or forensic psychiatry, saw crime as caused by biological and subconscious psychological urges mediated through consciousness.

7.3 From the point of view of psychoanalysis, criminal behaviour is maladaptive, the product of inadequacies in the offender's personality. The psychoanalytic perspective, advanced by Sigmund Freud in the early 1900s, encompasses diverse notions like personality, neurosis, and psychosis as well as transference, sublimation, and repression.

7.4 Some psychiatric perspectives see criminality as a form of adaptive behaviour to stresses, holding that law violation represents an individual's most satisfactory method of adjustment to inner conflicts that he or she cannot otherwise express.

7.5 Modelling theory asserts that people learn how to act by observing others. Once aggressive patterns of behaviour have been thus acquired, aggression can be activated by people experiencing physical assaults or verbal threats and insults, having their hopes thwarted, or having their goal-seeking behaviour obstructed.

7.6 Behaviour theory (or the stimulus–response approach to human behaviour) holds that behaviour is directly determined by the environmental consequences it produces for the individual exhibiting the behaviour. When an individual's behaviour results in rewards or positive feedback, that behaviour will increase in frequency; when punishment follows behaviour, that behaviour will decrease.

7.7 Psychological and psychiatric conceptions of mental illness, anti-social personality, and even psychopathy are not readily applicable to the criminal justice system, which relies instead on the legal concept of insanity. While the legal concept of insanity is based upon claims of mental illness, it has no precise counterpart in the jargon of contemporary psychologists or psychiatrists.

7.8 Some theorists now consider that psychological criminology can be used for the development of consistent and dependable social policy in the prediction of dangerousness and the rehabilitation of offenders and that selective incapacitation may be a workable policy to prevent future criminality.

7.9 Psychological profiling of criminal offenders, based on the belief that almost any form of conscious behaviour is symptomatic of the individual's personality, is a serious crime-fighting undertaking that may change the nature of localized crime-prevention strategies.

Questions for Review

1. What are the major principles of psychological perspectives on criminal behaviour?

2. What were some early psychological and psychiatric theories offered to explain criminality?

3. From a psychological perspective, how can criminal behaviour be seen as a form of maladaptive behaviour?

4. How can crime be a form of adaptation to one's environment? Why would an individual choose such a form of adaptation over others that might be available?

5. How does the modelling theory of aggression explain how aggressive patterns of behaviour, once acquired, can be activated?

6. How does behaviour theory explain the role of rewards and punishments in shaping behaviour?

7. What is the difference between the person diagnosed as a psychopath and the person deemed to be "not criminally responsible on account of mental disorder"?

8. What types of crime-control policies might be based on psychological understandings of criminality?

9. What are some assumptions underlying the practice of criminal psychological profiling?

Multiple-Choice Questions

1. _____ are said to be characterized by disordered or disjointed thinking, in which the types of logical associations they make are atypical of other people. They suffer from delusions and hallucinations.

    a. Psychopaths

    b. Persons with asocial personalities

    c. Schizophrenics

    d. Persons with anti-social personalities

    e. Sociopaths

2. Those defendants found "not criminally responsible on account of mental disorder" (NCRMD) are hospitalized _____.

    a. for life.

    b. for an indefinite period of time.

    c. until they are mentally well.

    d. to a maximum period of time as stipulated in the *Criminal Code*.

    e. to a maximum period of time as stipulated by the *Mental Health Act*.

3. According to _____, crime is the result of fundamental personality characteristics linked to individual central nervous system characteristics.

    a. Sigmund Freud

    b. B.F. Skinner

    c. Albert Bandura

    d. Hans Eysenck

    e. Robert Hare

4. _____ is defined as the likelihood that a given individual will later harm society or others.

    a. Irresistible impulse

    b. Dangerousness

    c. Guilty but mentally ill

    d. Psychological profiling

    e. Psychopathy

5. _____ refers to a form of adjustment resulting in changes in the surrounding environment.

   a. Alloplastic adaptation

   b. Autoplastic adaptation

   c. Operant behaviour

   d. Neurosis

   e. Psychosis

Chapter 8

The Meaning of Crime:
Social Structure Perspective

Monkey Business Images/Shutterstock

If we would change the amount of crime in the community, we must change the community.

—*Frank Tannenbaum*[1]

LEARNING OBJECTIVES

After reading this chapter, you should be able to

8.1 Understand the nature of sociological theorizing, and discuss some of the assumptions of the sociological perspective of crime causation.

8.2 Describe the major principles of social structure theories of criminal behaviour.

8.3 Distinguish between the three types of social structure theories discussed in this chapter.

8.4 Identify social policy that reflects the social structure approach.

8.5 Assess the shortcomings of the social structure approach.

INTRODUCTION

In March 1994, police responded to a 911 call reporting a collapsed man on a busy street in Ottawa, Ontario. It soon became apparent that the man had been shot through the chest; he died on the sidewalk before he could be taken to hospital. The incident shocked the nation's capital when details of the case revealed that Nicholas Battersby, a 27-year-old British-born engineer, had been the victim of a so-called drive-by shooting. An employee at a local high-tech firm, Battersby had simply been out for a stroll at 7:30 in the evening when a bullet from a sawed-off .22-calibre rifle shot from within a Jeep hit him in the chest.

After several days of an intensive police manhunt, three local teens, Rubens Henderson, Brian Raymond, and Cory Cyr, were charged with Battersby's murder. All three youths had long records of trouble with the law. Henderson, who had been adopted from a Brazilian orphanage, never really adapted to life in Ottawa. Despite sincere attempts by his mother to provide support, Henderson soon became known as a troublemaker in school. In grade six, he assaulted a student, a teacher, and a vice-principal and was expelled from the school with grades ranging from C to F. He soon acquired a Young Offenders' record, which included break and enter, assault, joyriding in stolen cars, being unlawfully at large, and the use of illicit drugs. His activities brought him into contact with Brian Raymond and Cory Cyr. Raymond was raised by a single mother in a neighbourhood where there was a motorcycle gang clubhouse. Psychologists used words like "dull" and "borderline" when labelling Raymond's language, math, and reasoning skills. Yet he knew how to hot-wire cars and get his hands on all sorts of drugs. Cory Cyr had spent many of his 16 years in group homes. Two days before the Battersby shooting, he had been released from jail after serving a 30-day sentence for assaulting a youth into unconsciousness after losing a Nintendo game to him. In 1996, Rubens Henderson received a life sentence for second-degree murder, while Cory Cyr and Brian Raymond received five- and four-year sentences, respectively, for manslaughter.[2]

The motivation behind the killing of Nicholas Battersby is not entirely clear. There is no doubt that the three youths were intoxicated on drugs and alcohol as they rode around in the stolen Jeep taking random shots at storefronts and people. What is also certain is that all three had socially deprived backgrounds. They lacked educational achievement and the basic skills needed for success in the modern world. Academic failure, and subcultural values that focused on excitement and greed, dictated the direction their lives were to take—and all but ensured their fateful encounter with Nicholas Battersby.

SOCIOLOGICAL THEORIES

IN CONTRAST TO MORE INDIVIDUALIZED BIOLOGICAL AND PSYCHOLOGICAL THEORIES (discussed in Chapters 6 and 7), which have what is called a *micro focus*, sociological approaches utilize a *macro focus*, stressing the type of behaviour likely to be exhibited by group members rather than attempting to predict the behaviour of specific individuals.

As noted in Chapter 1, sociological thought has influenced criminological theory construction more significantly than any other perspective during the past half century, due (at least in part) to a widespread concern with social issues, including civil rights, the women's movement, issues of poverty, and the changing influence of many traditional social institutions such as the family, government, organized religion, and educational systems.

Sociological theories examine both institutional arrangements within a **social structure** (i.e., interrelationships among society's institutions) and **social processes** (i.e.,

◉ Watch

Introduction to Social Culture

8.1 LEARNING OBJECTIVE

Sociological theory A perspective that focuses on the nature of the power relationships that exist between social groups and on the influences that various social phenomena bring to bear on the types of behaviours that tend to characterize groups of people.

Social structure The pattern of social organization and the interrelationships among institutions characteristic of a society.

Social process The interaction between and among social institutions, groups and individuals.

interactions between and among different social institutions, groups, and individuals) as they affect socialization and have an impact on **social life** (i.e., social interaction).

Social life   The ongoing structured interaction—including socialization and social behaviour in general—that occurs between persons in a society.

Although all sociological perspectives on crime share a common starting point, particular theories give greater or lesser weight to selected components of social life. We can identify three key sociological explanations for crime:

1. Crime is the result of an individual's location within the structure of society. This approach focuses on the social and economic conditions of life, including poverty, alienation, social disorganization, weak social control, personal frustration, relative deprivation, differential opportunities, alternative means to success, and deviant subcultures and subcultural values that conflict with conventional values. (These are the primary features of *social structure theories*, which are discussed in this chapter.)

2. Crime is the end product of various social processes. This approach stresses inappropriate socialization and social learning as well as interpersonal relationships, strength of the social bond, and personal and group consequences of societal reactions to deviance as they contribute to crime. (These are the primary characteristics of the *social process theories*, which are discussed in Chapter 9.)

3. Crime is the product of class struggle. This perspective emphasizes existing power relationships between social groups, ownership of the means of production, and economic and social structures of society as they relate to social class and social control. (These are the primary features of the *social conflict theories*, which are discussed in Chapter 10.)

8.2   LEARNING OBJECTIVE

MAJOR PRINCIPLES OF THE SOCIAL STRUCTURE PERSPECTIVE

Social structure theory   A theory that explains crime by reference to the economic and social arrangements in society. This type of theory emphasizes relationships among social institutions and describes the types of behaviour that tend to characterize groups of people rather than individuals.

THE THEORIES IN THIS CHAPTER ARE TERMED SOCIAL STRUCTURE THEORIES. THESE THEORIES look at the formal and informal social and economic arrangements (or structure) of society as the root causes of crime and deviance. These theories also see the negative aspects of societal structure, such as disorganization within the family, poverty or income inequality, and disadvantages due to lack of success in the educational process, as producers of criminal behaviour.

Although different kinds of social structure theories have been advanced to explain crime, they all have one thing in common: they highlight those arrangements within society that contribute to the low socio-economic status of identifiable groups as significant causes of crime. Social structure theorists view members of socially and economically disadvantaged groups as being more likely to commit crime, and they see economic and social disenfranchisement as fundamental causes of crime. Poverty, lack of education, absence of saleable skills, and subcultural values conducive to crime are all thought to be predicated on the social conditions surrounding early life experiences, and they provide the causal underpinnings of social structure theories.

Environmental influences, socialization, and traditional and accepted patterns of behaviour are all used by social structuralists to portray the offender as a product of his or her social environment, and the immediate social environment is viewed as a consequence of the structure of the society to which the offender belongs. Although criminality is recognized as a form of acquired behaviour, it is depicted as the end result of social injustice, racism, and feelings of disenfranchisement to which existing societal arrangements give rise. When these arrangements are unfair and relatively unchangeable, they perpetuate the fundamental conditions that cause crime. Crime is seen largely as a lower-class phenomenon, and the criminality of the middle and upper classes is generally discounted as less serious, less frequent, and less dangerous.

As this chapter will show, the social structure theories of crime causation are quite diverse; however, most such perspectives build upon the following fundamental assumptions:

- Social groups, social institutions, arrangements of society, and social roles all provide the focus for criminological study.

- Group dynamics, group organization, and subgroup relationships form the causal nexus out of which crime develops.

- The structure of society and its relative degree of organization or disorganization are important factors contributing to the prevalence of criminal behaviour.

TYPES OF SOCIAL STRUCTURE THEORIES

8.3 | LEARNING OBJECTIVE

THIS CHAPTER DESCRIBES THREE MAJOR TYPES OF SOCIAL STRUCTURE THEORIES: (1) social disorganization theory (also called the *ecological approach*), (2) strain theory, and (3) culture conflict theory (see Table 8.1). All have a number of elements in common, and the classification of a theory into a subcategory is often more a matter of which aspects a writer chooses to emphasize than the result of any clear-cut definitional elements inherent in that theory.

Social Disorganization Theory

Social disorganization theory (which depicts social change, social conflict, and lack of social consensus as the root causes of crime and deviance) is closely associated with the ecological school of criminology. *Ecology* is a term borrowed from biology that describes the interrelationships between living organisms and their environment; social scientists use the term *human ecology* to describe the interrelationship between human beings and the physical and cultural environments in which they live.[3] Pioneers in the human ecology movement saw cities as superorganisms that incorporated areas adapted to specific groups, including ethnic groups ("Little Italy," "Chinatown"), which were functional enclaves within a larger organized whole that possessed its own dynamics.

The idea of the community as a functional whole that directly determines the quality of life for its members was developed and explored around the beginning of the 20th century by sociologists like Emile Durkheim.[4] Durkheim believed that crime was a normal part of all societies and that law was a symbol of social solidarity, so an act was "criminal when it offend[ed] strong and defined states of the collective conscience."[5]

Some of the earliest sociologists to study communities were W.I. Thomas and Florian Znaniecki. In *The Polish Peasant in Europe and America*, Thomas and Znaniecki described the problems Polish immigrants faced in the early 1900s when they left their homeland and moved to American cities.[6] The authors noted that crime rates rose among displaced people and hypothesized that the cause was the social disorganization that resulted from immigrants' inability to successfully transplant guiding norms and values from their home cultures into the new one.

Watch

Introduction to Social Disorganization and the Chicago School

Listen

Crime Study Challenges Past Assumptions (on Deviance)

Social disorganization theory
A perspective on crime and deviance that sees society as a kind of organism and crime and deviance as a kind of disease or social pathology.

Table 8.1 Social Structure Theories

Theory	Social Disorganization	Strain	Culture Conflict
Period	1920s–1930s	1930s–present	1920s–present
Theorists	Robert Park and others	Robert Merton and others	Thorsten Sellin and others
Concepts	Social ecology, Chicago school, concentric zones, criminology of place	Anomie, goals, means, opportunity structures, reaction formation, general strain theory	Conduct norms, focal concerns, subculture, socialization, subculture of violence

Emile Durkheim

👁️⎯Watch

Introduction to Chicago School

👁️⎯Watch

Concentric Zone Theory Social
Structure

👁️⎯Watch

Concentric Zone Theory

Social ecology An approach to
criminological theorizing that attempts
to link the structure and organization
of a human community to interactions
with its localized environment.

Chicago School Some of the earliest sociological theories to receive widespread recognition can be found in the writings of Robert Park and Ernest Burgess. In the 1920s and 1930s at the University of Chicago, they developed what became known as **social ecology**, or the ecological school of criminology.[7] With the rapid influx of immigrant populations at the beginning of the 20th century, American cities in particular were caught up in swift social change, and Park and Burgess saw them as an ideal focus for study of social change and disorganization. They viewed cities as having five concentric zones, much like the circles on a target, each with unique characteristics and populations (see Figure 8.1). Park and Burgess referred to the central business zone as Zone I or the "loop," where retail businesses and light manufacturing were located; Zone II, surrounding the city centre, was home to recent immigrant groups and was characterized by deteriorated housing, factories, and abandoned buildings; Zone III contained mostly working-class tenements; Zone IV was occupied by middle-class citizens with single-family homes; and Zone V, the suburbs, was called the "commuter zone." Park and Burgess noticed that residents of inner-city zones tended to migrate to outer zones as their economic positions improved.

Clifford Shaw and Henry McKay, other early advocates of the ecological approach, applied the concentric zone model to the study of juvenile delinquency, conducting empirical studies of arrest rates for juveniles in Chicago during the years 1900–1906, 1917–1923, and 1927–1933. These years were associated with high rates of neighbourhood transition, during which one immigrant group after another moved in rapid succession from the inner city toward the suburbs—a process that was repeated with the arrival of each new wave of immigrants. Shaw and McKay found that rates of offending remained relatively constant over time within zones of transition, and they concluded, therefore, that delinquency was caused by the nature of the environment in which immigrants lived rather than by characteristics of the immigrant groups themselves.[8] Shaw and McKay saw social disorganization as the inability of local communities to solve common problems, and they believed

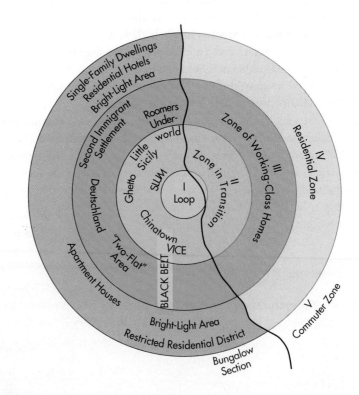

Figure 8.1 Chicago's Concentric Zones

Source: Robert E. Park, Ernest W. Burgess, and R. D. McKenzie, *The City* (Chicago: University of Chicago Press, 1925), p. 55. Copyright © 1969; University of Chicago Press. Reprinted with permission.

that the degree of disorganization in a community was largely predicated upon the extent of residential mobility and racial heterogeneity present in that community. In effect, as a new immigrant group, like the Polish, replaced an old immigrant group, like the Irish, and became dominant in a particular location, the process of succession was complete.

Early **ecological theories** focused on selected geographic areas; thus, their methodology came to be known as *area studies*. Because 1920s Chicago served as the model for most of these studies, they became collectively referred to as the **Chicago school of criminology**. Although the applicability of these early studies to other time periods may be questionable, the Chicago school demonstrated the tendency of criminal activity to be associated with urban transitional zones, which were typified by social disorganization, turmoil, lower property values, poverty, and lack of privacy.

The greatest contribution the ecological school made to criminological literature can be found in its claim that society wields a major influence on human behaviour.[9] Ecological theorists of the Chicago school used two sources of information: (1) population statistics and official crime and (2) ethnographic data. Population statistics (demographics), when combined with crime information, provided empirical material that gave scientific weight to ecological investigations; ethnographic information, gathered in the form of life stories (ethnographies), described the lives of city inhabitants. By comparing one set of data with the other—demographics with ethnographies—ecological investigators were able to show that life experiences varied from one location to another and that personal involvement in crime was strongly associated with place of residence.

The work of Canadian Carol La Prairie, which looks at the reality of high crime rates on some First Nations reserves in Canada, is representative of the ecological approach. In a recent study, La Prairie concluded that those Aboriginal communities that remained "institutionally complete" had significantly lower rates of crime compared with those reserves that experienced rapid change due to economic and cultural pressures.[10] Later studies by La Prairie used the concepts of social ecology to help explain the variation in rates of incarceration of Aboriginal peoples between the eastern and western provinces. In her comparison of two eastern and two western urban centres, La Prairie noted significant differences in the degree of integration of the Aboriginal populations. While the eastern centres showed more social integration of inner-city Aboriginal residents, the western cities had displaced most of the Aboriginal population to communities outside the city centres. Not surprisingly, the incarceration rate of Aboriginal peoples was significantly higher in the western centres. La Prairie's findings recognized the importance of social organization from a social-ecological point of view. The author also stressed the additional need for efforts to stabilize Aboriginal populations within urban centres through the provision of, for example, decent, affordable housing.[11]

Criminology of Place

Ecological approaches to crime causation have found a modern birth in the **criminology of place** (also called **environmental criminology**), which builds on the contributions of routine activities theory and situational crime prevention (both of which were discussed in Chapter 5). It emphasizes the importance of geographic location and architectural features in terms of prevalence of victimization. Hot spots of crime can include neighbourhoods, specific streets, and even individual houses and businesses. Lawrence W. Sherman and colleagues cited a study that revealed that 3 percent of places (addresses and intersections) in Minneapolis produced 50 percent of all calls to the police and noted that crime in Minneapolis, although relatively rare, was geographically concentrated.[12]

Reflecting on the questions first addressed by Shaw and McKay, another contemporary researcher, Rodney Stark, asked, "How is it that neighborhoods can remain the site of high crime and deviance rates despite a complete turnover in their populations? . . . There must be something about places as such that sustains crime."[13] Stark developed a theory of deviant neighbourhoods consisting of 30 propositions, including the following:[14]

Ecological theory A type of sociological approach that emphasizes demographics (the characteristics of population groups) and geographics (the mapped location of such groups relative to one another) and sees the social disorganization that characterizes delinquency areas as a major cause of criminality and victimization.

Chicago school of criminology An ecological approach to explaining crime that examines how social disorganization contributes to social pathology.

Criminology of place or **environmental criminology** An emerging perspective that emphasizes the importance of geographic location and architectural features as they are associated with the prevalence of criminal victimization.

- To the extent that neighbourhoods are dense and poor, homes will be crowded.

- Where homes are more crowded, there will be a greater tendency to congregate outside the home in places and circumstances that raise levels of temptation and opportunity to deviate.

- Where homes are more crowded, there will be lower levels of supervision of children.

- Reduced levels of child supervision will result in poor school achievement, with a consequent reduction in stakes in conformity and an increase in deviant behaviour.

- Poor, dense neighbourhoods tend to be mixed-use neighbourhoods.

- Mixed use increases familiarity with and easy access to places offering the opportunity for deviance.

Broken window thesis A perceptive on crime that holds that physical deterioration in an area leads to increased concerns for personal safety among area residents and to higher crime rates in that area.

Central to the criminology of place is the **broken windows thesis**, first advanced in a 1982 article by James Q. Wilson and George Kelling entitled "Broken Windows: The Police and Neighborhood Safety."[15] The thesis holds that physical deterioration and an increase in unrepaired buildings leads to increased concerns for personal safety among area residents.[16] These concerns lead to further decreases in maintenance and repair; to increased delinquency, vandalism, and crime; and to even further deterioration in safety and the physical environment—all resulting in offenders from other neighbourhoods being increasingly attracted by the area's perceived vulnerability. Physical disorder, left unchecked, leads to crime by driving residents indoors and sending a message to would-be offenders that a neighbourhood is out of control.[17]

Even within high-crime neighbourhoods and neighbourhoods characterized by urban decay, crimes tend to be concentrated at specific locations such as street blocks or multiple-family dwellings, and some units within specific apartment buildings are more likely to be the site of criminal occurrences. Therefore, the criminology of place employs the concept of **defensible space**, which evolved from a 1994 conference at Washington University in St. Louis, Missouri. Defensible space encompasses "the range of mechanisms—real and symbolic barriers, strongly defined areas of influence, and improved opportunities for surveillance—that combine to bring an environment under the control of its residents."[18] The St. Louis conference brought criminologists, police officers, and architects face-to-face and focused on crime problems characteristic of public-housing areas. Conference findings demonstrated that specific architectural changes that enhanced barriers, defined boundaries, and removed criminal opportunity could do much to reduce the risk of crime—even in the middle of high-crime neighbourhoods.

Defensible space The range of mechanisms that combine to bring an environment under the control of its residents.

The criminology of place holds that location can be as predictive of criminal activity as lifestyles of victimized individuals or social features of victimized households. (*Place* has been defined by researchers as "a fixed physical environment that can be seen completely and simultaneously, at least on its surface, by one's naked eyes."[19]) Places can be criminogenic because they have certain routine activities associated with them or because they provide the characteristics that facilitate crime commission.

Crime Prevention Through Environmental Design (CPTED) A crime-prevention strategy based on the premise that the design and effective use of the built environment can lead to a reduction in the incidence and fear of crime.

Recognizing the criminology of place, the Peel Regional Police Service (Peel region is located just west of Toronto) introduced to the Canadian market in the early 1980s a program of **Crime Prevention Through Environmental Design (CPTED)**. It is based on the theory that the proper design and effective use of a physical environment can help reduce the incidence and fear of crime. The CPTED program revolves around three strategies: (1) natural surveillance (keeping potential intruders under observation); (2) natural access control (decreasing the opportunity for crime); and (3) territorial reinforcement (extending a sphere of influence through physical design to develop a sense of ownership by users). In an example cited by Peel Regional Police, a CPTED review of a restaurant recommended the following changes: (1) improvement of sightlines to the outside by removing unnecessary clutter such as bushy plants and promotional material from the take-out window;

London's Metropolitan Police officers view displays from TV cameras around London in the Special Operations Room of their Central Communications Command. Defensible space can be defined in terms of barriers to crime commission and preventive surveillance opportunities. How might such features be enhanced in high-crime areas?

Oli Scarff/Getty Images

(2) improvement of sightlines within the restaurant by removing planters that divided the dining room and waiting area; and (3) improvement of lighting by repairing defective ceiling lamps and increasing the number of light fixtures. These changes resulted in a more intimidating and less private target to would-be offenders while also giving staff the ability to better observe potential offenders before a robbery.[20] (See Chapter 11 for an in-depth look at the CPTED model.)

More recent studies of the broken windows thesis have cast doubt on the assertion made by Wilson and Kelling that police intervention into the process that links disorder and crime can be effective in reducing crime.[21] It may be that disorder and crime have common roots and that one is more associated with the other than produced by it.[22] Hence, efforts to target quality-of-life offences in urban areas that are experiencing high levels of social disorganization may not have the desired effect of reducing crime.

Strain Theory

The second type of social structure theory discussed in this chapter is strain theory. *Strain* can be defined as the pressure that individuals feel to reach socially determined goals.[23] The classic statement of **strain theory**—which depicts delinquency as a form of adaptive problem-solving behaviour committed in response to problems involving frustrating and undesirable social environments—was offered in 1938 by Robert K. Merton, who also developed the concept of **anomie** (a French word meaning "normlessness").

Anomie was popularized by Émile Durkheim in his 1897 book, *Suicide*, in which he used the term to explain how a breakdown of predictable social conditions can lead to feelings of personal loss, dissolution, and a lack of a sense of belonging.[24] Merton's use of the term *anomie* was somewhat different and meant a disjunction between socially approved means to success and legitimate goals.[25] Merton maintained that legitimate goals, such as wealth, status, and personal happiness, are generally defined as desirable for everyone. But the widely acceptable means to these goals, such as education, hard work, and financial savings, are not equally available. As a consequence, crime and deviance tend to arise as an alternative means to success when individuals feel the strain of being pressured to succeed in socially approved ways but find that the tools for such success are unavailable to them. In Merton's words, "It's not how you play the game, it's whether you win."[26] Merton's emphasis on the felt strain resulting from the lack of fit between goals and means led to his approach being called strain theory.

Complicating the picture further, Merton maintained that not everyone accepts the legitimacy of socially approved goals. Merton described the disjuncture between possible combinations of goals and means. In speaking of what he called *conformity*, Merton

Watch
Introduction to Strain Theory

Watch
Robert Merton

Strain theory A sociological approach that posits a disjuncture between socially and subculturally sanctioned means and goals as the cause of criminal behaviour.

Anomie A social condition in which norms are uncertain or lacking.

labelled those who accept the goals that society holds as legitimate for everyone, and who have ready availability of the means for achieving those goals. The mode of adaptation associated with this combination of goals and means typifies most middle- and upper-class individuals.

Innovation arises when the emphasis on approved goal achievement combines with a lack of opportunity to participate fully in socially acceptable means to success. This form of adaptation is experienced by many lower-class individuals who have been socialized to desire traditional success symbols (expensive cars, large homes, big bank accounts) but who do not have ready access to approved means of acquiring them (educational opportunity).

Innovative behavioural responses, including crime, can be expected to develop when individuals find themselves so deprived. Merton said that "poverty as such, and consequent limitation of opportunity, are not sufficient to induce a conspicuously high rate of criminal behavior. Even the often mentioned 'poverty in the midst of plenty' will not necessarily lead to this result."[27] It is when those who find themselves in poverty are pressured to achieve material success and acquire other associated symbols of status that innovation results.

Merton went on to describe what he referred to as *ritualism*, or the type of behaviour arising when members of society participate in socially desirable means but show little interest in goal achievement. A ritualist may get a good education, work every day in an acceptable occupation, and appear to be leading a solid middle-class lifestyle yet care little for the symbols of success, choosing to live an otherwise independent lifestyle.

Retreatism describes the behaviour of those who reject both the socially approved goals and the means. They may become dropouts, drug abusers, or homeless persons, or participate in alternative lifestyles, such as communal living. Such individuals are often socially and psychologically separate from the larger society around them.

Merton's last category, *rebellion*, describes the actions of a person who wishes to replace socially approved goals and means with some other system. Political radicals, revolutionaries, and anti-establishment agitators may fit into this category. Merton believed that conformity was the most common mode of adaptation prevalent in society, whereas retreatism was least common.

A contemporary application of Merton's strain theory was offered by Margaret Beare in her examination of the increased involvement of Canadian Mohawks in the smuggling of cigarettes. High taxes on Canadian cigarettes tempted many smokers to turn to cheaper contraband U.S. cigarettes. In Ontario and Quebec, residents of some Aboriginal communities along the Canada–U.S. border were the main sources of contraband cigarettes. The last time statistics were available, it was believed that almost one-quarter of the cigarettes smoked in Canada were illegal.[28]

General Strain Theory   In 1992, strain theory was reformulated by Robert Agnew and others who moulded it into a comprehensive perspective called *general strain theory* (GST).[29] GST sees law-breaking behaviour as a coping mechanism enabling those who engage in it to deal with the socio-emotional problems generated by negative social relations.

According to GST, strain occurs when others do the following: (1) prevent or threaten to prevent an individual from achieving positively valued goals; (2) remove or threaten to remove positively valued stimuli that a person possesses, such as the death of a loved one; or (3) present or threaten to present someone with noxious or negatively valued stimuli, like physical abuse. Agnew explained that strains most likely to cause crime include child abuse and neglect; negative secondary-school experiences; abusive peer relations; chronic unemployment; marital problems; parental rejection; erratic, excessive, and or/harsh supervision or discipline; criminal victimization; homelessness; racial, ethnic, or gender discrimination; and a failure to achieve selected goals. Factors that increase the likelihood of criminal coping include poor conventional coping skills and resources; availability of criminal skills and resources; low levels of conventional social support; routine association with criminal others; personal beliefs and values favourable to crime; frequent exposure to situations where the costs of crime are low; low levels of social control, including weak bonds to conventional others; and lack of investment in conventional institutions. Agnew's strategies for reducing exposure to strains include eliminating strains conducive to crime, altering strains to make them less conducive to crime, removing individuals from exposure to strain, and equipping individuals with the traits and skills needed to avoid strains conducive to crime.

General strain theory expands on traditional strain theory in several ways. First, it significantly expands the focus of strain theory to include all types of negative relations between an individual and others. Second, GST maintains that strain is likely to have a cumulative effect on delinquency after reaching a certain threshold. Third, GST provides a more comprehensive account of the cognitive, behavioural, and emotional adaptations to strain than do traditional strain approaches. Finally, GST more fully describes the wide variety of factors affecting the choice of delinquent adaptations to strain.

Agnew saw the crime-producing effects of strain as cumulative and concluded that whatever form it takes, "strain creates a predisposition for delinquency in those cases in which it is chronic or repetitive."[30] Predispositions may be manifested in the form of negative affective states, meaning emotions such as anger, fear, depression, and disappointment. An analysis by Agnew of other strain theories found that all such theories share at least two central explanatory features.[31] Strain theories, Agnew said, focus "explicitly on negative relationships with others; relationships in which the individual is not treated as he or she wants to be treated" and argue that "adolescents are pressured into delinquency by the negative affective states—most notably anger and related emotions—that often result from negative relationships."[32]

A 1994 study tested some of the assumptions underlying GST through an analysis of American data.[33] It found partial support for GST and discovered that negative relations with adults, feelings of dissatisfaction with friends and school life, and the experience of stressful events (e.g., family dissolution) were positively related to delinquency, as was living in an unpleasant neighbourhood (one beset by social problems and physical deterioration). When conceived of more broadly as exposure to negative stimuli, the study found general strain to be significantly related to delinquency.

Contrary to Agnew's hypothesis, however, the study found no evidence that the effects of strain were increased when they were experienced for longer periods of time or that they were diminished when adolescents classified that part of their life in which they experienced strain as "unimportant." Consistent with earlier findings, the study also found that feelings of general strain were positively related to later delinquency, regardless of the number of delinquent peers, moral beliefs, self-efficacy, and level of conventional social support.[34] Some support was found for the belief that general strain leads to delinquency by weakening the conventional social bond and strengthening the unconventional bond with delinquent peers.

Culture Conflict Theory

The third type of social structure theory discussed in this chapter is **culture conflict theory**, which suggests that the root cause of criminality can be found in a clash of values

Culture conflict theory A sociological perspective on crime that suggests that the root cause of criminality can be found in a clash of values between variously socialized groups over what is acceptable or proper behaviour.

between differently socialized groups over what is acceptable or proper behaviour. The culture conflict concept is inherent in ecological criminology (discussed earlier in this chapter) and its belief that zones of transition tend to be in flux and harbour groups of people whose values are often at odds with those in the larger society.

The culture conflict perspective found its clearest expression in the writings of Thorsten Sellin in his 1938 book *Culture Conflict and Crime*.[35] Sellin maintained that the root cause of crime could be found in different values about what is acceptable or proper behaviour. According to Sellin, **conduct norms**, which provide the valuative basis for human behaviour, are acquired early in life through childhood socialization, and it is the clash of norms between variously socialized groups that results in crime. Because crime is a violation of laws established by legislative decree, the criminal event itself, from this point of view, is nothing other than a disagreement over what should be acceptable behaviour. For some social groups, what we tend to call *crime* is simply part of the landscape—something that can be expected to happen to you unless you take steps to protect yourself. From this point of view, those to whom crime happens are not so much victims as they are simply ill-prepared.

Sellin described two types of culture conflict. *Primary conflict* arises when a fundamental clash of cultures occurs, as when an immigrant father kills his daughter's lover following an old-world tradition that demands that a family's honour be kept intact.[36] The other type of conflict, called *secondary conflict*, occurs when smaller cultures within the primary one clash, as when middle-class values (upon which most criminal laws are based) find fault with inner-city or lower-class norms, resulting in the social phenomenon we call *crime*.

Subcultural Theory Fundamental to the notion of culture conflict is the idea of **subculture**, a collection of values and preferences that is communicated to subcultural participants through a process of socialization. Subcultures differ from the larger culture in that they claim the allegiance of smaller groups of people. For example, the wider North American culture may proclaim that hard work and individuality are valuable, but a particular subculture may espouse the virtues of deer hunting, male bonding, and recreational alcohol consumption. Countercultures, which tend to reject and invert the values of the surrounding culture, and criminal subcultures, which may actively espouse deviant activity, represent extremes. **Subcultural theory** is a sociological perspective that emphasizes the contribution made by variously socialized cultural groups to the phenomenon of crime.

Early writings on subcultures include *The Gang* by Frederick M. Thrasher.[37] Thrasher studied 1313 gangs in Chicago in 1927, and his descriptive work led to a typology in which he described different types of gangs. In 1943, William Foote Whyte, drawing on Thrasher's work, published *Street Corner Society*.[38] Whyte, in describing his three-year study of the Italian slum he called "Cornerville," further developed the subcultural thesis, showing that lower-class residents of a typical slum could achieve success through the opportunities afforded by slum culture, including racketeering and bookmaking.

Focal Concerns In 1958, Walter B. Miller attempted to detail the values that drive members of lower-class subcultures into delinquent pursuits, describing *lower-class culture* as "a long-established, distinctively patterned tradition with an integrity of its own."[39] According to his article, entitled "Lower Class Culture as a Generating Milieu of Gang Delinquency," a large body of systematically interrelated attitudes, practices, behaviours, and values characteristic of lower-class culture are designed to support and maintain the basic features of the lower-class way of life. In areas where these differ from features of middle-class culture, action oriented to the achievement and maintenance of the lower-class system may violate norms of the middle class and be perceived as deliberately nonconforming.

Conduct norms Shared expectations of a social group relative to personal conduct.

Subculture A collection of values and preferences that is communicated to subcultural participants through a process of socialization.

Subcultural theory A sociological perspective that emphasizes the contribution made by variously socialized cultural groups to the phenomenon of crime.

Watch

Walter B. Miller

Miller stated, "This does not mean, however, that violation of the middle-class norm is the dominant component of motivation; it is a by-product of action primarily oriented to the lower-class system."

Miller also outlined what he termed the **focal concerns** or key values of delinquent subcultures: trouble, toughness, smartness, excitement, fate, and autonomy. Miller found that *trouble* is a dominant feature of lower-class culture. Getting into trouble, staying out of trouble, and dealing with trouble when it arises become focal points in the lives of many members of lower-class culture. Miller recognized that getting into trouble is not necessarily valued in and of itself, but is seen as an oftentimes necessary means to valued ends.

Focal concerns The key values of any culture, and especially the key values of a delinquent subculture.

Like many theorists of the time, Miller was primarily concerned with the criminality of men. The lower-class masculine concern with *toughness* may have been due to many men in the groups he examined being raised in female-headed families and may have reflected an almost obsessive concern with masculinity as a reaction to the perceived threat of over-identification with female role models.

Miller described *smartness* as the "capacity to outsmart, outfox, outwit, dupe, take, [or] con another or others and the concomitant capacity to avoid being outwitted, taken or duped oneself. . . . In its essence smartness involves the capacity to achieve a valued entity—material goods, personal status—through a maximum use of mental agility and a minimum of physical effort." *Excitement* was seen as a search for thrills—often necessary to overcome the boredom inherent in lower-class lifestyles. Fights, gambling, picking up women, and making the rounds were all described as derivative aspects of the lower-class concern with excitement. *Fate* is related to the quest for excitement and to the concept of luck or of being lucky. As Miller stated, "Many lower-class persons feel that their lives are subject to a set of forces over which they have relatively little control. These are not supernatural forces or organized religion . . . but relate more to a concept of 'destiny' or man as a pawn. This often implicit world view is associated with a conception of the ultimate futility of directed effort toward a goal."

Autonomy, manifested in statements like "I can take care of myself" or "No one's going to push me around," produces behavioural problems from the perspective of middle-class expectations when it surfaces in work environments, public schools, or other social institutions built on expectations of conformity.

Miller's work on subcultures and their focal concerns was derived almost entirely from his study of African-American inner-city delinquents in the Boston area in the 1950s. Therefore, it may be less relevant to members of lower-class subcultures in other times or in other places.

Code of the Street Work by Elijah Anderson, who studied African-American neighbourhoods along Philadelphia's Germantown Avenue and published the results in his book titled *The Code of the Street*, offered a subcultural ethnography of the social mores operating in some American inner cities today.[40] In *Code*, Anderson detailed aspects of street code that stress a hyperinflated notion of manhood resting squarely on the idea of respect: "At the heart of the code is the issue of respect, loosely defined as being treated 'right' or being granted one's 'props' (or proper due) or the deference one deserves." In street culture, a man's sense of worth is determined by the respect he commands when in public.

A crucial distinction between both families and individuals in inner-city neighbourhoods like Germantown are expressed by what residents call the "decent family" and the "street family," marking people as either trying to uphold positive values or being oriented toward the street. Street life, Anderson explained, involves displays of physical strength and intellectual prowess meant to demonstrate that "I can take care of myself" and "I can take care of my own." Those who wholeheartedly embrace the street code are proud to live the "thug life," identify with role models like Tupac Shakur and Young Jeezy, and see people and situations as obstacles to be subdued or overcome, learning to outsmart or hustle others while avoiding being hustled themselves. (See the Crime in the News story later in this chapter about gang member John Richardson and Ace Crew.)

⊙ Watch

MS13 Gang-Life

Violent Subcultures   Some subcultures are decidedly violent and are built around violent themes and around values supporting violent activities. In 1967, Franco Ferracuti and Marvin Wolfgang published their seminal work, *The Subculture of Violence: Toward an Integrated Theory of Criminology*, which drew together many of the sociological perspectives previously advanced to explain delinquency and crime.[41] Ferracuti and Wolfgang's main thesis was that violence is a learned form of adaptation to certain problematic life circumstances and that learning to be violent takes place within the context of a subcultural milieu that emphasizes the advantages of violence over other forms of adaptation. Such subcultures are characterized by songs and stories that glorify violence, by gun ownership, and by rituals tending to stress macho models. They are likely to teach that a quick and decisive response to insults is necessary to preserve one's prestige within the group. Subcultural group members have a proclivity for fighting as a means of settling disputes. Subcultures of violence both expect violence from their members and legitimize it when it occurs. In Ferracuti and Wolfgang's words, "The use of violence . . . is not necessarily viewed as illicit conduct, and the users do not have to deal with feelings of guilt about their aggression."[42] In other words, for participants in violent subcultures, violence can be a way of life.

Ferracuti and Wolfgang based their conclusions on an analysis of data that showed substantial differences in the rate of homicides between racial groups in the Philadelphia area—non-Caucasian men had a homicide rate of 41.7 per 100 000, versus only 3.4 for Caucasian men, and non-Caucasian women showed a homicide rate of 9.3, versus 0.4 for Caucasian women. Explaining these findings, Ferracuti and Wolfgang stated,

> Homicide is most prevalent, or the highest rates of homicide occur, among a relatively homogeneous subcultural group in any large urban community. . . . The value system of this group, as we are contending, constitutes a subculture of violence. From a psychological viewpoint, we might hypothesize that the greater the degree of integration of the individual into this subculture, the higher the probability that his behavior will be violent in a variety of situations.[43]

Ferracuti and Wolfgang extend their theory of subcultural violence with the following "corollary propositions":[44]

- No subculture can be totally different from or totally in conflict with the society of which it is a part.

- To establish the existence of a subculture of violence does not require that the actors sharing in these basic value elements express violence in all situations.

- The potential to resort or willingness to resort to violence in a variety of situations emphasizes the penetrating and diffusive character of this culture theme.

- The subcultural ethos of violence may be shared by all ages in a subsociety, but this ethos is most prominent in a limited age group, ranging from late adolescence to middle age.

- The counter-norm is non-violence.

- The development of favourable attitudes toward and the use of violence in a subculture usually involves learned behaviour and a process of differential learning, association, or identification.

- The use of violence in a subculture is not necessarily viewed as illicit conduct, and the users therefore do not have to deal with feelings of guilt about their aggression.

Canadian researchers have commented on geographical distinctions between violent subcultures in different parts of Canada. National homicide rates have consistently shown a distinct east-to-west/south-to-north upward trend over the last several decades. Homicide rates during this period have been lowest in New Brunswick, highest in Manitoba, and two to three times higher in Yukon and Northwest Territories than in Manitoba. The reasons for these persistent regional differences are difficult to pinpoint. While certain elements of Canada's social structure (age, ethnicity, economic well-being) are obvious contributing factors, some researchers suggest that cultural differences among regions of Canada also need to be taken into account. Do the accumulated traditions and shared experiences shaping the values and beliefs of people in different regions contribute to varying levels of violence? Many Canadian researchers believe that this cannot be overlooked.[45]

Regional variations are found in other countries as well. In the United States, for example, a body of criminological literature claims that certain forms of criminal violence are more acceptable in the South than in northern portions of the country.[46] Some writers have also referred to variability in the degree to which interpersonal violence has been accepted in the South over time, whereas others have suggested that violence in the South might be a traditional tool in the service of social order.[47]

The wider culture often recognizes, sometimes begrudgingly and sometimes matter-of-factly, a violent subculture's internal rules, so that when one member of such a subculture kills another, the wider society may take the killing less seriously than if someone outside the subculture had been killed. As a consequence of this realization, Franklin Zimring and his associates described what he called "wholesale" and "retail" costs of homicide, in which killings that are perceived to occur within a subculture of violence (when both the victim and the perpetrator are seen as members of a violent subculture) generally result in a less harsh punishment than do killings that occur outside of the subculture.[48] Punishments relate to the perceived seriousness of the offence; if members of the subculture within which a crime occurs accept the offence as part of the landscape, so too will members of the wider culture.

Much of the original research into subcultural theory dates back to the 1950s and 1960s. However, the reality of inner-city gangs and violence, especially in the United States but also in Canada, has brought with it a renewed interest in this approach in recent decades. In his review of the research literature on gangs, Canadian criminologist John Hagan suggested that subcultural theories continue to have a role to play in understanding the serious problems of largely ethnic, urban youth who see themselves as marginalized.[49]

⊙ Watch
Cloward and Ohlin

Differential Opportunity Theory

In 1960, Richard Cloward and Lloyd Ohlin published *Delinquency and Opportunity*.[50] Their book, a report on the nature and activities of juvenile gangs, blended the subcultural thesis with ideas derived from strain theory. Cloward and Ohlin identified two types of socially structured opportunities for success: legitimate and illegitimate. While legitimate opportunities are generally available to individuals born into middle-class culture, participants in lower-class subcultures are often denied access to them; therefore, illegitimate opportunities for success are often seen as quite acceptable by participants in so-called illegitimate subcultures.

Illegitimate opportunity structure A subcultural pathway to success that is disapproved of by the wider society.

Cloward and Ohlin used the term **illegitimate opportunity structure** to describe pre-existing subcultural paths to success that are not approved of by the wider culture. Where illegitimate paths to success are not already in place, alienated individuals may undertake a process of ideational evolution through which "a collective delinquent solution" or a "delinquent means of achieving success" may be decided upon by members of a gang. Because the two paths to success—legitimate and illegitimate—differ in their availability to members of society, Cloward and Ohlin's perspective has been termed *differential opportunity*.

According to Cloward and Ohlin, delinquent behaviour may result from the ready availability of illegitimate opportunities with the effective replacement of the norms of the wider culture with expedient and "legitimate" subcultural rules. The authors wrote, "A delinquent subculture is one in which certain forms of delinquent activity are essential requirements for the performance of the dominant roles supported by the subculture."[51] Its most crucial elements are the "prescriptions, norms, or rules of conduct that define the activities required of a full-fledged member."[52] They continued, "A person attributes legitimacy to a system of rules and corresponding models of behavior when he accepts them as binding on his conduct."[53] They concluded, "Delinquents have withdrawn their support from established norms and invested officially forbidden forms of conduct with a claim to legitimacy."[54]

Cloward and Ohlin noted that there are two necessary parts to a delinquent act: "It is behavior that violates basic norms of the society, and, when officially known, it evokes a judgment by agents of criminal justice that such norms have been violated."[55] For Cloward and Ohlin, however, crime and deviance are just as normal as any other form of behaviour supported by group socialization. In their words, "Deviance and conformity generally result from the same kinds of social conditions [and] deviance ordinarily represents a search for solutions to problems of adjustment." In their view, deviance is just as much an effort to conform, albeit to subcultural norms and expectations, as is conformity to the norms of the wider society. They added, however,

> It has been our experience that most persons who participate in delinquent subcultures, if not lone offenders, are fully aware of the difference between right and wrong, between conventional behavior and rule-violating behavior. They may not care about the difference, or they may enjoy flouting the rules of the game, or they may have decided that illegitimate practices get them what they want more efficiently than legitimate practices.[56]

Cloward and Ohlin described three types of delinquent subcultures: (1) criminal subcultures, in which criminal role models are readily available for adoption by those being socialized into the subculture; (2) conflict subcultures, in which participants seek status through violence; and (3) retreatist subcultures, where drug use and withdrawal from the wider society predominate. These delinquent subcultures have at least three identifiable features: "acts of delinquency that reflect subcultural support are likely to recur with great frequency, access to a successful adult criminal career sometimes results from participation in a delinquent subculture, and the delinquent subculture imparts to the conduct of its members a high degree of stability and resistance to control or change."[57]

Cloward and Ohlin divided lower-class youth into four types according to their degree of commitment to middle-class values and/or material achievement. Type I youths desire entry to the middle class through improvement in their economic position. Type II youths desire entry to the middle class but not improvement in their economic position. Type III youths desire wealth but not entry to the middle class and are seen as the most crime prone. Type IV youths are dropouts who retreat from the cultural mainstream through drug and alcohol use (see the Who's Responsible? box).

Cloward and Ohlin had a substantial impact on social policy, resulting in government programs designed to change the structures of legitimate opportunities in poor communities. Programs such as Mobilization for Youth (MFY), Job Corps, and Opportunities for Youth created employment and educational opportunities for deprived youths and were largely based on opportunity theory.

Reaction Formation   Another criminologist whose work is often associated with both strain theory and the subcultural perspective is Albert Cohen, whose work focused primarily on the gang behaviour of delinquent youth. In Cohen's words,

> When we speak of a delinquent subculture, we speak of a way of life that has somehow become traditional among certain groups in American society. These groups are the boys' gangs that flourish most conspicuously in the "delinquency neighborhoods" of our larger American cities. The members of these gangs grow up, some to become law-abiding citizens and others to graduate to more professional and adult forms of criminality, but the delinquent tradition is kept alive by the age-groups that succeed them.[58]

Cohen argued that youngsters from all backgrounds are generally held accountable to the norms of the wider society through a "middle-class measuring rod" of expectations related to such items as school performance, language proficiency, cleanliness, punctuality,

◉ Watch
Albert K. Cohen

WHO'S RESPONSIBLE—THE INDIVIDUAL OR SOCIETY?

Like Father, Like Son

Reginald Barfield, 22, was arrested for driving under the influence of alcohol and taken to jail. A judge set bail at $500, and his mother came to the jail to post bond for him. She didn't have much money, so she used the services of a bondsman, who charged her a $70 fee and arranged for Reginald's release. As she drove her son home, she began yelling at him, telling him that he had turned out just like his father, who had had a long-standing problem with alcohol.

"You're just like your father," she said. "And if you don't change, you'll end up just like him—dead."

Reginald became angry and blurted out that he drank because that was all he had known as a child.

"What do you mean?" his mother asked.

"Whenever dad had a problem, or when you two fought," Reginald said, "dad broke open a bottle and killed the pain. It worked for him. It works for me. So, you're right, I'm just like him. But it's not my fault. I learned it from him. You didn't stop him. And you didn't stop me."

Think about it:

1. Is Reginald right—did he learn his problem behaviour from his father? What other factors might have contributed to his excessive use of alcohol?

2. Might the concept of reaction formation help explain Reginald's behaviour? If so, how?

3. If you were Reginald's mother, to what degree would you hold your son responsible for his problem-drinking behaviour? To what degree would you hold him responsible if you were a judge hearing his case in court?

4. Are questions about responsibility merely exercises in blame shifting? Is blame shifting ever appropriate when assessing criminal responsibility?

Note: This example is a fictionalized one intended to encourage critical thinking.

neatness, non-violent behaviour, and allegiance to other similar standards. But he noted that not everyone is prepared, by birth and subsequent socialization, to effectively meet such expectations.

In an examination of vandalism, Cohen found that "non-utilitarian" delinquency, in which things of value are destroyed rather than stolen or otherwise used for financial gain, is the result of middle-class values being turned upside down.[59] Delinquent youths, often alienated from middle-class values and lifestyles through deprivation and limited opportunities, can achieve status among their subcultural peers through vandalism and other forms of delinquent behaviour.

Children, especially those from deprived backgrounds, turn to delinquency because they experience status-frustration when judged by others according to middle-class standards and goals that they are unable to achieve, Cohen claimed. Because it is nearly impossible for them to succeed in middle-class terms, they also may overcome anxiety through the process of **reaction formation**, in which hostility toward middle-class values develops. (Cohen adapted reaction formation from psychiatric perspectives and used it to mean "the process in which a person openly rejects that which he wants, or aspires to, but cannot obtain or achieve."[60])

Reaction formation The process by which a person openly rejects that which he or she wants or aspires to but cannot obtain or achieve.

Cohen discovered the roots of delinquent subcultures in what he termed the "collective solution to the problem of status."[61] When youths who experience the same kind of alienation from middle-class ideals band together, they achieve a collective and independent solution and create a delinquent subculture. Cohen wrote,

> The delinquent subculture, we suggest, is a way of dealing with the problems of adjustment. . . . These problems are chiefly status problems: certain children are denied status in the respectable society because they cannot meet the criteria of the respectable status system. The delinquent subculture deals with these problems by providing criteria of status that these children can meet.[62]

Cohen's approach is effectively summarized in a theoretical scenario offered by Donald J. Shoemaker, who said that lower-class youths undergo a working-class socialization that combines lower-class values and habits with middle-class success values.[63] Lower-class youths experience failure in school because they cannot live up to the middle-class norms operative in educational institutions, suffer a consequent loss of self-esteem and increased feelings of rejection, drop out of school and associate with delinquent peers, and experience hostility and resentment toward middle-class standards through reaction formation. Such alienated youths achieve status and a sense of improved self-worth through participation in a gang of like-minded peers. Delinquency and crime are the result.

CRIME IN THE NEWS
Murder Showed Gang Would Stop at Nothing

On Sept. 6, 1995, John Wartley Richardson walked out of Millhaven penitentiary in Kingston, Ontario. He'd just turned 24, a hardened and violent Ottawa street thug with a previous conviction for robbery. Now, he was free again after serving part of a 30-month prison term for pimping.

National Parole Board file No. 233185C, obtained by the *Citizen*, reveals officials had little doubt Mr. Richardson would strike again. In fact, it took just 50 days.

The crime would be murder. The victim would be Sylvain Leduc.

The file shows Mr. Richardson, now 26, has never held a legitimate job. He's been a pimp and a brute, involved in narcotics and the misery of vulnerable, strung-out young women trapped in Ottawa's street sex trade.

In prison, he was sometimes locked in segregation for "negative behaviour." He showed no remorse for anything. An area woman who helped put him away for procuring was so scared afterwards, the file notes, she had police help her relocate to a new town.

>

In the fall of 1994, Mr. Richardson was rejected for early parole.

"The board is satisfied that reasonable grounds exist to believe that, if released, you are likely to commit an offence involving violence and directs that you not be released."

But 11 months later, parole officials had little choice but to let him go because of a federal statute that grants all but the most dangerous inmates parole after serving two-thirds of their sentences.

"You remain a high risk to reoffend," officials wrote in his file. "Strict adherence to release conditions (including regularly reporting in to authorities) will be required in order to render that risk manageable."

Mr. Richardson, unmanageable as ever, ignored the conditions. He finally met with authorities Jan. 2, 1996, when heavily armed police in Winnipeg arrested him as an armed-and-dangerous fugitive wanted for the Leduc homicide.

A subsequent parole board document added a grim footnote to the file: "The risk you represent is clearly not manageable and the board orders that your statutory release be revoked."

Yesterday, a judge and jury went further. The jury revoked much of what's left of Mr. Richardson's life by finding him guilty of first-degree murder. Justice Douglas Rutherford then shipped him back to a bleak federal cellblock for life, with no chance of parole for at least 25 years. He also sentenced him to an additional 73 years, to be served concurrently, for various other crimes.

Sylvain Leduc was killed because he innocently strayed into the nasty underworld of urban street gangs, where extreme violence and revenge are rewarded with criminal status and power.

Mr. Leduc, 17, offended a dangerous collection of mostly young, Black men who called themselves Ace Crew and sold $20-hits of crack cocaine on the streets of Lowertown. His death sentence was sealed with one ugly, unfortunate word: he called them "niggers."

Mr. Leduc's timing was particularly bad. In the fall of 1995, the gang's members were feeling threatened on several fronts.

Police, they worried, might be on to them. And at least one of the teenage girls the gang used for drug-running and sex—she was Mr. Leduc's cousin—wanted out, undermining the group's authority and its all-important reputation on the street. As well, rival drug dealers, they suspected, were muscling in on their turf, on their money.

Ace Crew was, at best, disorganized crime. But in late October 1995, it appeared to be losing its grip on even that existence. And that made it potentially lethal.

Enter John Richardson, fresh out of Millhaven. He was a friend of Mark Williams, the then 19-year-old reputed leader of Ace Crew. Mr. Richardson was just the type of crime consultant who could help the outfit rebuild.

Sylvain Leduc was tortured and killed by members of the Ace Crew gang because he had been disrespectful toward them. Was Sylvain Leduc a victim of a violent subculture?

QMI Agency

If Ace was struggling, perhaps Mr. Richardson and his pal, Kurton Edwards, 28, could teach the gang a thing or two about becoming so bad, so feared, that people would be afraid to walk the streets of Ottawa.

At least that's how it appeared in the hours leading up to the Leduc murder, as Mr. Richardson regaled the group with violent tales about how notorious U.S. Black ghetto gangs ruthlessly maintain their turf. He talked about violence. He talked about retribution. He talked about torture. And he had a gun.

Ace Crew, police believe, has now largely disbanded. Six members and associates have been convicted for various roles in Mr. Leduc's slaying. Another was imprisoned for 11 years for the bold March 1997 shooting of two men inside the crowded Rideau Centre. Five other members and associates, all non-Canadians, have been deported to their native countries because of their criminal activities here.

Discussion Questions

1. What subcultural elements (beliefs, behaviour patterns, etc.) may have contributed to Sylvain Leduc's death?

2. Does the subculture of violence thesis help to explain the behaviour of gang members, such as the named Ace Crew who killed Leduc? If so, how?

3. What explanations, other than a subculture of violence thesis, might be offered to explain the death of Leduc?

Source: Ian MacLeod, "The Rise and Fall of the Ace Crew: Murder Showed Gang Would Stop at Nothing," *Ottawa Citizen*, April 15, 1998, p. B1. Reprinted with permission.

Gangs Today   Street gangs have become a major source of concern in contemporary North American society, particularly in the United States. Although the writings of investigators such as Cohen, Thrasher, and Cloward and Ohlin focused on the illicit activities of juvenile gangs in inner cities, most gang-related crimes of the period involved vandalism, petty theft, and battles over turf. Today, the ethnic distinctions that gave rise to gang culture in the 1920s through the 1950s are largely forgotten. Italian, Hungarian, Polish, and Jewish immigrants, whose children made up many of the early gangs, have been, for the most part, successfully integrated into modern North American society.

Today's gang are quite different. Members appear more violent, involved with drugs, and intransigent than those studied by early researchers. Although the United States is the nation with the most gangs (and has the best information about them), Canada is not exempt from them. One of the challenges in determining accurate amounts of gang activity in Canada stems from issues surrounding the definition of *gang* and *gang member*. Law enforcement officials and the media often refer to small groups of offenders as gangs, even though the members of these groups do not see themselves that way. In a comprehensive study of gangs in the Greater Vancouver area, this concern with definition was addressed and distinctions were made between *criminal business organizations*, *street gangs*, and *wannabe groups*.[64] In a recent report entitled *Promising Practices for Addressing Youth Involvement in Gangs*, Mark Totten defined gangs as

> visible, hardcore groups that come together for profit-driven criminal activity and severe violence. They identify themselves through the adoption of a name, common brands/colours of clothing, and tattoos to demonstrate gang membership to rival gangs. Street gangs are not part of larger criminal organizations and often have a geographic "turf" (often specific social housing projects and/or areas they claim to be their own for drug distribution) that they protect from rival gangs. Youth and adults carry out planned and profitable crimes and gratuitous violence against rival gangs. Ethnic and racial composition of gangs is an important defining feature.[65]

Bill C-24, known as the Organized Crime Bill, was enacted in February 2002 and includes the current legal definition of an organized crime group such as a gang. See Box 8.1 for this definition.

Box 8.1 DEFINITION OF CRIMINAL ORGANIZATION

As stated in the *Criminal Code*, section 467.1(1), a "criminal organization" means a group, however organized, that

- is composed of three or more persons in or outside Canada; and,

- has as one of its main purposes or main activities the facilitation or commission of one or more serious offences, that, if committed, would likely result in the direct or indirect receipt of a material benefit, including a financial benefit, by the group or by any one of the persons who constitute the group.

It does not include a group of persons that form randomly for the immediate commission of a single offence.

In determining whether an individual participates in OR actively contributes to any activity of a criminal organization, the Court may look at the following:

- If they use a name, word, symbol, or other representation that identifies, or is associated with, that criminal organization;

- If they frequently associate with any of the persons who constitute the criminal organization;

- If they receive any benefit from the criminal organization;

- If they repeatedly engage in activities at the instruction of any of the persons who constitute the criminal organization.

Source: Edmonton Police Service, http://www.edmontonpolice.ca/CommunityPolicing/OrganizedCrime/Gangs/OrganizedCrime Legislation.aspx [Accessed April 8, 2012].

In its 2010 *Annual Report on Organized Crime*, the Criminal Intelligence Service of Canada (CISC) reported that street gangs are characterized by their involvement in the street-level trafficking of illicit drugs such as crack cocaine, ecstasy and marijuana. Other activities include street-level prostitution, theft, robbery, fraud, and weapons offences. CISC contended that while some street gangs across Canada work on behalf of other organized crime groups and may engage in more sophisticated crimes such as drug importation or manufacturing, most street gangs operate with relatively low criminal capabilities and within a defined area of operation. Trends show that street gangs are increasingly using technology to not only conceal their criminal activity but also conduct it, such as credit card fraud. Social networking sites are used to advertise and connect with possible recruits. Youth gang member collaboration with established criminal organizations (such as the Hell's Angels, Big Circle Boys, and Indian Posse) involves criminal activities such as chemical trafficking, intimidation/extortion, kidnapping, and sophisticated auto theft rings.[66]

According to the most recent statistics available, over 300 street gangs have been identified in Canada, with an estimated 11 000 gang members and associates operating across the country. The gangs are primarily local in scope, with only a limited number having interprovincial and international criminal links. Street gangs are composed primarily of males and almost half are 17 years of age or younger. Gang members are predominantly African-Canadian (25 percent), Aboriginal (22 percent), and Caucasian (18 percent). Over one-third of gangs in Canada are composed of two or more ethno-racial groups (hybrid gangs). Nationally, almost half of Canadian police forces believe that the return of adult or youth gang member inmates to the community has a negative influence on street gangs on the outside, particularly those young males on the periphery and those who are in the process of being tested out for membership.[67]

While street gang-related violence is not a new phenomenon, a recent increase in gang-related violence is being reported and appears to be related to street gang expansion, recruitment, and encroachment on the territory of other criminal groups. The degree of street gang violence differs by region and gang. Violence may be planned—to promote and protect the gang's interests, such as targeting rival gang members or resources—or be spontaneous and opportunistic, resulting in intentional or unintentional harm to the general public from drive-by shootings, street gang cross-fire, and mistaken identities. Street gangs use a wide variety of weapons, including swords, knives, machetes, hammers, screwdrivers, and firearms. Illicit firearms used by street gangs are typically acquired through residential or commercial thefts, or are smuggled into the country from the United States.[68]

Information about gangs in the United States is much more detailed. The annual National Gang Center (NGC) survey (conducted by the Office of Juvenile Justice and Delinquency Prevention) compiles gang-related information from thousands of law enforcement agencies across the United States. The National Gang Crime Research Center's Project, Gangfact, provides a profile of gangs and gang members throughout the United States, though its data are older than the data available through the NGC. The most recent Gangfact report, based on data collected by 28 researchers in 17 states, presents much detailed information specific to the United States but shows characteristics similar to the Canadian reality:[69]

- The average age for joining a gang nationally is 12.8 years of age.
- Over half who joined gangs have tried to quit.
- More than two-thirds of gangs have written rules for members to follow.
- Over one-half of all gangs hold regular weekly meetings.
- Nearly 30 percent of gangs require their members to pay dues.
- Approximately 55 percent of gang members were recruited by other gang members; the remainder sought out gang membership.

- Most gang members (79 percent) say they would leave the gang if given a second chance in life.

- Four-fifths of gang members report that their gangs sell crack cocaine.

- Most gangs (70 percent) are not racially exclusive and consist of members drawn from a variety of ethnic groups.

- One-third of gang members report that they have been able to conceal their gang membership from their parents.

- Most gangs (83 percent) report having female members, but few allow female members to assume leadership roles.

- Many gang members (40 percent) report knowing male members of their gangs who had raped females.

Contemporary researchers are drawing some new distinctions between gangs and violence. Some years ago, G. David Curry and Irving A. Spergel, in a study of Chicago communities, distinguished between juvenile delinquency and gang-related homicide.[70] They found that communities characterized by high rates of delinquency do not necessarily experience exceptionally high rates of crime or of gang-related homicides, and they concluded that although gang activity may be associated with homicide, "gang homicide rates and delinquency rates are ecologically distinct community problems." Gang-related homicide seems to be well explained by classical theories of social disorganization and is especially prevalent in areas of the city characterized by in-migration and by the "settlement of new immigrant groups." In their study, high rates of juvenile delinquency seemed to correlate more with poverty, which the researchers defined as "social adaptation to chronic deprivation." According to Curry and Spergel, "Social disorganization and poverty rather than criminal organization and conspiracy may better explain the recent growth and spread of youth gangs to many parts of the country. Moreover, community organization and social opportunity in conjunction with suppression, rather than simply suppression and incapacitation, may be more effective policies in dealing with the social problem."[71] In devising strategies to counter gang activity, policymakers must remember that many gang members are delinquent before they become associated with gangs and that merely suppressing gangs should not replace other youth crime intervention and prevention strategies.[72]

Members of the Manitoba Warriors leave a courthouse in Winnipeg after being sentenced to time already served following their conviction on drug charges. Gangs have become a concern in today's society. What social structure theories might explain the proliferation of gangs and gang-related activity in Canada?

Phil Hossack/Winnipeg Free Press/ Canadian Press Images

POLICY IMPLICATIONS OF SOCIAL STRUCTURE THEORIES

THEORETICAL APPROACHES THAT LOOK TO THE SOCIAL STRUCTURE AS THE ROOT cause of crime point in the direction of social action as a panacea. In the 1930s, for example, Clifford Shaw, in an effort to put his theories into practice and to reduce delinquency in transitional neighbourhoods, established the Chicago Area Project. Shaw analyzed oral histories gathered from neighbourhood citizens to determine that delinquents were essentially normal youngsters who entered into illegal activities at early ages, often through street play, so he worked to increase opportunities for young people to embark on successful work careers.

The Chicago Area Project attempted to reduce social disorganization in slum neighbourhoods through the creation of community committees staffed with local residents rather than professional social workers. The project had three broad objectives: (1) improving the physical appearance of poor neighbourhoods, (2) providing recreational opportunities for youth, and (3) involving project members directly in the lives of troubled youth through school and courtroom mediation. The program also made use of "curbside counsellors," streetwise workers who could serve as positive role models for inner-city youth. Although no effective assessment programs were established to evaluate the Chicago Area Project during the program's tenure, in 1984 a 50-year review of the program was published that declared the program "effective in reducing rates of juvenile delinquency."[73]

Mobilization for Youth (a programmatic outgrowth of Cloward and Ohlin's theory of differential opportunity) provides a bold example of the treatment implications of social structure theories seeking not only to provide new opportunities but also to change the fundamental arrangements of society through direct social action and thereby address the root causes of crime and deviance. Leaders of Mobilization for Youth decided that "what was needed to overcome formidable barriers to opportunity was not community organization but community action" that attacked entrenched political interests, so the program promoted "boycotts against schools, protests against welfare policies, rent strikes against 'slum landlords,' lawsuits to ensure poor people's rights, and voter registration."[74] A truly unusual government-sponsored program for its time, Mobilization for Youth was eventually disbanded amid protests that its mandate was to reduce delinquency, not reform urban society or test sociological theories.[75]

A contemporary example of social intervention efforts based on sociological theories is the Youth Violence Project: A Community-Based Violence Prevention Project, introduced in a Vancouver Island school district. It is a community-based initiative designed to address the problem of youth violence and involves teachers, counsellors, parents, students, and representatives from health and social service agencies. Consisting of 13 individual anti-violence initiatives, it is intended to educate and train students and community members in a preventative approach to violence by helping individuals change their behaviour and acquire skills that enable them to use non-violent responses in circumstances where violence might previously have been used.[76]

Mobilization for Youth and the Youth Violence Project both stand as examples of the kinds of programs that theorists who focus on the social structure typically seek to implement. Social programs of this sort are intended to change the cultural conditions and societal arrangements that lead people into crime.

CRITIQUE OF SOCIAL STRUCTURE THEORIES

THE FUNDAMENTAL ASSUMPTION OF SOCIAL STRUCTURE APPROACHES IS THAT social injustice, racism, and poverty are the root causes of crime. Hence, the social structure perspective is intimately associated with the first part of this textbook's theme, the social problems approach (described in Chapter 1). If the assumptions that inform social structure theories are true, they largely negate the claims of those who advocate our theme's other part, the social responsibility perspective.

Social structure explanations for criminality that portrayed social inequality and stifled opportunity as fundamental causes of crime were popular during the 1960s. Later, a number of social commentators began to question the nature of the relationship among poverty, apparent social inequities, and crime.[77] Some argued the inverse of the root causes argument: poverty and social inequality are produced by crime, rather than the other way around. Disorder, fear, and crime, they suggested, undermine positive social and economic institutions; families, schools, churches, businesses, and other institutions cannot function properly in social settings where crime is a taken-for-granted part of the social landscape. If this proposed inverse relationship is even partially true, then addressing poverty and social inequality as the root causes of crime is an ineffective crime-prevention strategy.

This chapter has identified three types of social structure theory, and each can be critiqued. Some authors have suggested that social disorganization theories give too much credence to the notion that special location determines crime and delinquency because the nature of any given location changes over time, and evolutions in land-use patterns (such as a movement away from home ownership and toward rental or low-income housing) may seriously affect the nature of a neighbourhood and the concomitant quality of its social organization. Rates of neighbourhood crime and delinquency may be "an artifact of police decision-making practices" and bear little objective relationship to the actual degree of law violation in an area.[78] If police bias (the focus on low-income inner-city areas) exists, it may seriously mislead researchers into categorizing certain areas as high in crime when enforcement decisions made by police administrators merely make them appear that way.

Another critique of the ecological school can be found in its seeming inability to differentiate between the condition of social disorganization and the things such a condition is said to cause. What is the difference between social disorganization and high rates of delinquency? Isn't delinquency a form of the very thing said to cause it? As Stephen Pfohl observed, early ecological writers sometimes used the incidence of delinquency as "both an example of disorganization and something caused by disorganization,"[79] making it difficult to gauge the efficacy of their explanatory approach.

Those who criticize the ecological approach note that many crimes occur outside of geographic areas characterized by social disorganization. Murder, sexual assault, burglary, incidents of drug use, and assault all occur in affluent, well-established neighbourhoods. White-collar crime, cybercrime, and environmental crime may actually occur more often in well-established neighbourhoods. Hence, the ecological approach is clearly not an adequate explanation for all crime or all types of crime.

From a social responsibility perspective, those who criticize strain theory note that Merton's strain theory is probably less applicable to North American society today than it was in the 1930s because in the ensuing decades considerable effort has been made toward improving success opportunities for all, regardless of ethnicity, race, or gender. Travis Hirschi criticized contemporary strain theory for its inability "to locate people suffering from discrepancy" and noted that human beings are naturally optimistic—a fact that "overrides [the] aspiration-expectation disjunction," concluding that "expectations appear to affect delinquency, but they do so regardless of aspirations, and strain notions are neither consistent with nor required by the data." [80]

Culture conflict approaches (the last of the three types of social structure explanations for crime discussed in this chapter) have been questioned by some criminologists who see them as lacking explanatory power. Canadian criminologist Gwynn Nettler called the notion of violent subcultures tautological, or circular, arguing that saying that people fight because they are violent or that "they are murderous because they live violently" does little to explain their behaviour. Attributing fighting to "other spheres of violence" may be true, but it is fundamentally "uninformative." [81]

The subcultural approach has also been criticized for being racist because many so-called violent subcultures are said to be populated primarily by minorities. Margaret Anderson said that "the problem with this explanation is that it turns attention away from the relationship of black communities to the larger society and it recreates dominant stereotypes about blacks as violent, aggressive, and fearful. Although it may be true that rates of violence are higher in black communities, this observation does not explain the fact."[82] In sociological jargon, an observed correlation between race and violence does not necessarily provide a workable explanation for the relationship.

According to Nettler, social structure theories suffer from another shortcoming that generally affects most other sociological perspectives on crime causation:

> The conceptual bias of social scientists emphasizes environments—cultures and structures—as the powerful causes of differential conduct. This bias places an intellectual taboo on looking elsewhere for possible causes as, for example, in physiologies. This taboo is … strongly applied against the possibility that ethnic groups may have genetically transmitted differential physiologies that have relevance for social behavior.[83]

In other words, social scientists downplay the causative role of non-sociological factors. Many outside of sociology believe that such factors are important, but since sociological theorizing has captured most of the academic attention over the past few decades, the role of other causative factors in the etiology of criminal behaviour stands in danger of being shortchanged.

Finally, some see the inability of social structure theories to predict which individuals—or what proportion of a given population—will turn to crime as a crucial failure of such perspectives. Although the large majority of persons growing up in inner-city, poverty-ridden areas probably experience an inequitable opportunity structure firsthand, only a relatively small number of those people become criminal. Even if substantially more people living under such conditions become criminal compared to those living in other types of social environments, a large proportion of persons being raised in deviant subcultures and experiencing strain still embrace non-criminal lifestyles. In his book *The Moral Sense*, James Q. Wilson suggested that most people—regardless of socialization experiences and the structural aspects of their social circumstances—may still carry within themselves an inherent sense of fairness and interpersonal morality.[84] If what Wilson suggested is even partially true, then the explanatory power of social structure theories may be limited by human nature itself.

SOCIAL STRUCTURE THEORIES AT A GLANCE

STRAIN
holds that crime is a result of the disjuncture between socially and subculturally sanctioned means and goals.
The three youths who killed Nicholas Battersby lacked the socially acceptable means (education, saleable skills) to achieve the socially acceptable goals.

Crime is a result of the economic and social arrangements in society. When these arrangements are unfair and relatively unchangeable, they perpetuate the fundamental conditions that are conducive to crime, such as poverty, lack of education, absence of saleable skills, social injustice, racism, feelings of disenfranchisement, and subcultural values.

How can the actions of Rubens Henderson, Cory Cyr, and Brian Raymond be explained using the social structure perspective?

CULTURE CONFLICT
holds that crime is a result of a clash of values between variously socialized groups over what is acceptable or proper behaviour. The behaviours of the three youths who were involved in the killing of Nicholas Battersby were a result of beliefs in subcultural values of excitement, autonomy, and violence.

SOCIAL DISORGANIZATION
holds that society is a kind of organism and crime and deviance are a kind of disease that is rooted in social conditions.
The three youths who killed Nicholas Battersby were a product of their individual location in the social structure and of social and economic conditions including lack of education, lack of employment, and disenfranchisement.

SUMMARY OF LEARNING OBJECTIVES

8.1 Sociological theories explore relationships between and among groups and institutions and see crime as the result of social processes, as the consequence of aspects of social structure, or as the result of economic and class struggle.

8.2 Although different kinds of social structure theories have been advanced to explain crime, they all have one thing in common: they highlight those arrangements within society that contribute to the low socio-economic status of identifiable groups—poverty, lack of education, absence of marketable skills, and subcultural values—as significant causes of crime and view members of socially and economically disadvantaged groups as being more likely to commit crime.

8.3 Three subtypes of social structure theories can be identified: social disorganization theory, strain theory, and culture conflict theory. Social disorganization theory encompasses social pathology, seeing society as a kind of organism and crime and deviance as a kind of disease (or social pathology), and is often associated with social ecology and the Chicago school of criminology. Strain theory points to a lack of fit between socially approved success goals and availability of socially approved means to achieve those goals; individuals unable to succeed through legitimate means turn to other avenues (crime) that promise economic and social recognition. Culture conflict theory suggests that the root cause of criminality can be found in a clash of values between differently socialized groups over what is acceptable or proper behaviour.

8.4 Because theories of social structure look to the organization of society for their explanatory power, intervention strategies based on them typically seek to alleviate the social conditions thought to produce crime through social programs that increase socially acceptable opportunities for success and meaningful employment.

8.5 Social structure theories are open to criticisms. Social structure approaches assume that social inequality, racism, and poverty are the root causes of crime, but some argue the inverse. Poverty and social injustices are produced by crime rather than the other way around. If this proposed inverse relationship is even partially true, then addressing poverty and social inequality as the root causes of crime is an ineffective crime-prevention strategy.

Questions for Review

1. What is the nature of sociological theorizing? What are the assumptions upon which sociological perspectives on crime causation rest?

2. What do sociologists mean by the term *social structure*? How might the organization and structure of a society contribute to criminality?

3. What are the three types of social structure theories that this chapter describes? What are the major differences among them?

4. What are the policy implications of the theories discussed in this chapter? What kinds of changes in society and in government policy might be based on the theories discussed here? Would they be likely to bring about a reduction in crime?

5. What are the shortcomings of the social structure approaches to understanding and preventing crime? Can these shortcomings be overcome?

Multiple-Choice Questions

1. _____ emphasize the structure of society, the relationship between social institutions, and the types of behaviour that tend to characterize groups of people.

    a. Strain theories

    b. Conduct norms

    c. Sociological theories

    d. Culture conflicts

    e. Subcultural theories

2. Included among the social structure theorists are _____

    a. Cloward and Ohlin, Merton, and Sutherland

    b. Cloward and Ohlin, Ferracuti, and Lemert

    c. Shaw, Merton, and Cloward and Ohlin

    d. Merton, Quinney, and Cohen

    e. Merton, Quinney, and Chambliss

3. In the 1930s, Clifford Shaw attempted to put his theories into practice by establishing the _____, which sought to reduce social disorganization in transitional neighbourhoods through the creation of community committees. Shaw staffed these committees with local residents rather than professional social workers.

    a. Ethnographic Mapping Project

    b. Chicago Area Project

    c. Atlanta Demographic Transition Project

    d. St. Louis Area Community Project

    e. Chicago Land Relocation Project

4. Social structure approaches assume that social inequality, racism, and poverty are the root causes of crime. According to _____, it is poverty and social injustices that are produced by crime rather than the other way around.

    a. Franco Ferracuti

    b. Albert Cohen

    c. Thorsten Sellin

    d. Henry McKay

    e. Gwynn Nettler

5. Which of the following is not one of Walter Miller's focal concerns?

    a. trouble

    b. autonomy

    c. toughness

    d. control

    e. fate

Multiple Choice Answers: 1c, 2c, 3b, 4d, 5d

Chapter 9

The Meaning of Crime: Social Process Perspective

Tomas Zelezny/ctk/AP Photo

Children learn to become delinquents by becoming members of groups in which delinquent conduct is already established.

—*Albert K. Cohen*[1]

LEARNING OBJECTIVES

After reading this chapter, you should be able to

9.1 Recognize how the process of social interaction between people contributes to criminal behaviour.

9.2 Understand and distinguish between a number of social process theories.

9.3 Identify social policy initiatives that reflect the social process approach.

9.4 Assess the shortcomings of the social process perspective.

INTRODUCTION

Andrew Leyshon-Hughes continues to live in the centre of controversy. Leyshon-Hughes had been found not guilty by reason of insanity for the brutal sexual assault and stabbing murder of Nancy Eaton many decades ago, in 1985. Eaton, the great-great-granddaughter of Timothy Eaton, founder of Eaton's department store empire, had befriended Leyshon-Hughes, himself a member of an established Toronto family of lawyers. The murder shocked high society, as did the court's ruling. Leyshon-Hughes's lawyer argued that his client, who was 17 at the time, suffered from brain damage at birth and that only the primitive part of his brain was functioning when he killed Nancy Eaton. Leyshon-Hughes was sentenced to treatment in the Ontario psychiatric hospital system and remained in psychiatric custody for the next 15 years.

In 2001, the community was shocked to learn that Leyshon-Hughes had been granted a number of privileges, including the right to leave the grounds of the psychiatric hospital to attend college or to socialize. His request for longer, overnight visits to stay with family in northern Ontario and British Columbia had the community asking questions about their safety, especially since, a few years earlier, Leyshon-Hughes had been considered too dangerous to leave hospital grounds.

His psychiatrist believed that Leyshon-Hughes wanted to eventually have a normal life and raise a family. Forensic psychiatrist John Bradford argued that his patient was not a sexual deviant or psychopath, testifying that the risk was manageable: "A manageable risk means that a person is in the community and we have procedures and treatment in place that reduces that level of risk," he said. "I don't think there's ever such a thing as a zero-risk. That's not feasible."[2]

Marlys Edwardh, who had been Leyshon-Hughes's lawyer since he was 17, said that her client was misdiagnosed. Once he was locked up, no one took into consideration that he could be treated and rehabilitated.[3]

The case of Andrew Leyshon-Hughes provides an example of how society's continued reaction to what it identifies as criminal behaviour can change the course of an offender's life. As some would say, while there are plenty of ex-cons, there is no such thing as an "ex–ex-con." Or "once a con, always a con." A book entitled *A Question of Murder* by William Scoular, an episode dedicated to the case by the Canadian investigative program *W5*, and a made-for-television movie called *Deadly Friends (The Death and Life of Nancy Eaton)* have kept this controversy alive.

9.1 **LEARNING OBJECTIVE**

THE SOCIAL PROCESS PERSPECTIVE

Social process theory The theory that criminal behaviour is learned in interaction with others and that the socialization processes that occur as a result of group membership are the primary route through which this learning occurs. Also called interactionist theory.

⊙ Watch

Major Principles of Social Process

THE THEORIES DISCUSSED IN THE FIRST PART OF THIS CHAPTER ARE TYPICALLY called **social process theories**, or *interactionist perspectives*, because they emphasize the process of interaction between individuals and society. Social process theories of crime causation assume that everyone has the potential to violate the law and that criminality is not an innate human characteristic. According to social process theories, criminal behaviour is learned in interaction with others, and the socialization process that occurs as the result of group membership is seen as the primary route through which learning occurs. Among the most important groups contributing to the process of socialization are family, peers, work groups, and reference groups with which one identifies. Such groups instill values and norms in their members and communicate what are (for their members) acceptable world views and patterns of behaviour.

Social process perspectives hold that the process through which criminality is acquired, deviant self-concepts are established, and criminal behaviour results is active, open-ended, and ongoing throughout a person's life. They suggest that individuals who have weak ties to conformity are more likely to be influenced by the social processes and experiences that lead to crime and that criminal choices tend to persist because they are reinforced by the reaction of society to those whom it has identified as deviant.

TYPES OF SOCIAL PROCESS THEORIES

9.2 LEARNING OBJECTIVE

A NUMBER OF THEORIES CAN BE CLASSIFIED UNDER THE SOCIAL PROCESS UMBRELLA: social learning theory, labelling theory, reintegrative shaming, social control theory, and social development theories (see Table 9.1). Social learning theory places primary emphasis upon the role of communication and socialization in the acquisition of learned patterns of criminal behaviour and the values that support that behaviour. Labelling theory points to the special significance of society's response to the criminal and sees the process through which a person becomes defined as criminal, along with society's imposition of the label *criminal*, as a significant contributory factor in determining future criminality. Reintegrative shaming, a contemporary offshoot of labelling theory, emphasizes possible positive outcomes of the labelling process. Social control theory focuses on the strength of the bond people share with institutions and individuals around them, especially as those relationships shape their behaviour. Finally, social development theory integrates theories of human development that examine psychological, biological, familial, interpersonal, cultural, societal, and ecological aspects of that development.

Social Learning Theory

Social learning theory states that all behaviour is learned in much the same way and such learning includes the acquisition of norms, values, and patterns of behaviour conducive to crime, meaning that crime is also learned and that people learn to commit crime from others. Criminal behaviour is a product of the social environment, not an innate characteristic of particular people.

Differential Association   One of the earliest and most influential forms of social learning theories was advanced by Edwin Sutherland in 1939. Sutherland's thesis was that criminality is learned through a process of **differential association** with others who communicate criminal values and who advocate the commission of crimes.[4] He emphasized the role of social learning as an explanation for crime because he believed that many of the concepts popular in the field of criminology at the time—including social pathology, genetic inheritance, biological characteristics, and personality flaws—were inadequate to explain the process by which an otherwise normal individual turns to crime. Sutherland was the first well-known criminologist to suggest that all significant human behaviour is learned behaviour and that crime is not substantively different from any other form of behaviour.

◉ **Watch**
Burgess and Akers

Social learning theory
A perspective that places primary emphasis on the role of communication and socialization in the acquisition of learned patterns of criminal behaviour and the values that support that behaviour.

◉ **Watch**
Introduction to Edwin H. Sutherland

◉ **Watch**
Differential Association

◉ **Watch**
The Influence of Romantic Relationships and Family on Criminal Behaviour

Differential association   The sociological thesis that criminality, like any other form of behaviour, is learned through a process of association with others who communicate criminal values.

Table 9.1	Social Process Theories			
Theory	**Social Learning**	**Labelling**	**Social Control**	**Social Development**
Period	1930s–1960s	1960s–1980s, 1990s	1950s–present	1980s–present
Theorists	Edwin Sutherland and others	Edwin M. Lemert and others	Travis Hirschi and others	Sheldon and Eleanor Glueck and others
Concepts	Differential association, neutralization techniques, crime as learned	Tagging, primary and secondary deviance, reintegrative shaming	Social bond, inner and outer containment	Life course, evolutionary ecology, developmental pathways

Sutherland's nine principles of differential association were presented in complete form three years before his death in the fourth edition of his famous book, *Principles of Criminology:*[5]

1. *Criminal behaviour is learned.* Criminal behaviour is learned in the same manner as learning how to read or write. In other words, criminal behaviour is not seen as an inherent character trait.

2. *Criminal behaviour is learned in interaction with other persons in a process of communication.* The learning of criminal behaviour is very much dependent on the association between individuals. Those who are already criminal serve as "teachers" to others.

3. *The principal part of the learning of criminal behaviour occurs within intimate personal groups.* Individuals are influenced by those closest to them—family members, peers, and friends. Relationships with these individuals will control the way one sees the world. For example, studies have shown that children who grow up in households where parents abuse alcohol tend to develop the attitudes that support such behaviour.[6] The belief that many young people are pressured by peers to commit illegal acts is inherent in this third principle. It is the intimate peer group that most significantly influences youth.

4. *When criminal behaviour is learned, the learning includes (a) techniques of committing the crime, which are sometimes very complicated, sometimes very simple, and (b) the specific direction of motives, drives, rationalizations, and attitudes.* Since learning criminal behaviour is like learning any other kind of behaviour, the actual techniques of committing the crime must be taught and learned. Offenders learn from others how to pick locks, get involved in prostitution, obtain and use illicit drugs, or shoplift, for example. In addition to learning the actual techniques of criminal behaviour, offenders also learn the attitudes necessary to justify the behaviour. Some of these justifications are discussed in the Neutralization Techniques section later in this chapter.

5. *The specific direction of motives and drives is learned from definitions of the legal codes as favourable or unfavourable.* There are a variety of attitudes toward both the legal code and notions of right and wrong behaviour. The attitudes toward criminal behaviour held by the significant people in an individual's life have the greatest impact on the attitudes developed by the individual, through differential association.

6. *A person becomes delinquent because of an excess of definitions favourable to violation of law over definitions unfavourable to violation of law.* Interaction with those people or events that promote a disregard for the law will serve to strengthen and solidify those attitudes in another. For example, if a person spends more time in the company of someone who is constantly stealing CDs from music stores than with parents who extol the virtues of honesty and respect for the property of others, then disregard for the law becomes reinforced.

7. *Differential associations may vary in frequency, duration, priority, and intensity.* Whether a person learns to disobey the law depends upon the quality of the social interactions experienced. The more often one interacts with a deviant group, the greater the likelihood of learning the behaviour. The length of the interaction also influences the likelihood of learning a given behaviour. Priority has been interpreted to mean the age at which a person first encounters criminality. It is believed that contacts made at an earlier age are likely to have a more significant impact on that person's behaviour than those made later in life. For example, for many youth at a certain stage of development, peer groups take priority over parents and can significantly influence a young person's behaviour.

8. *The process of learning criminal behaviour by association with criminal and anti-criminal patterns involves all the mechanisms that are involved in any other learning.* Learning criminal behaviour occurs the same way as learning any other behaviour and does not simply involve imitation.

9. *While criminal behaviour is an expression of general needs and values, it is not explained by those general needs and values, since non-criminal behaviour is an expression of the same needs and values.* The motive for criminal behaviour is not the same as that for non-criminal behaviour. In other words, the desire for a leather jacket in and of itself does not foster criminal behaviour. Why one person will work to earn money to buy the jacket and someone else will steal it is largely determined by the different norms learned through associations with various groups. The learning of deviant norms from deviant groups produces criminal behavior.

Differential association found considerable acceptance among theorists of the mid-20th century because it combined then-prevalent psychological and sociological principles into a coherent perspective on criminality. Crime as a form of learned behaviour became the catchword, and biological and other perspectives were largely abandoned by those involved in the process of theory testing.

Neutralization Techniques   Of particular interest to proponents of differential association is the manner in which various rationalizations are employed by those involved in criminal behaviour. Those who disobey the law are, at least to some degree, participants in the larger culture that surrounds them. How is it, then, that they may choose behavioural alternatives that seemingly negate the norms and values of the larger society? While social learning theorists such as Sutherland contend that criminal behaviour is learned through the mastery of techniques, values, and attitudes needed to commit deviant acts, neutralization theory holds that most offenders learn **techniques of neutralization** to allow them to go against conventional values and attitudes. Gresham Sykes and David Matza put forth this notion in their 1957 article, "Techniques of Neutralization."[7] Sykes and Matza suggested that offenders are aware of conventional values and understand that their offending is wrong, but engage in neutralizing self-talk before offending to mitigate the anticipated shame and guilt associated with violating societal norms.[8] Offenders can overcome feelings of responsibility when involved in crime commission by using five types of justifications (see Figure 9.1).

Techniques of neutralization
Learned justifications that can provide criminal offenders with the means to disavow responsibility for their behaviour.

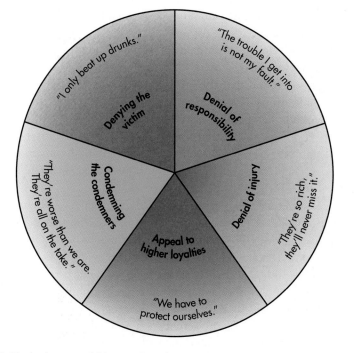

Figure 9.1 Techniques of Neutralization

1. *Denying responsibility*. They point to their backgrounds of poverty, abuse, and lack of opportunity: "The trouble I get into is not my fault," or "They made me do it."

2. *Denying injury*. They explain that everyone does it or that individuals or companies can afford it: "They're so rich, they'll never miss it."

3. *Denying the victim*. They justify the harm done by claiming that the victim deserved the victimization: "I only beat up drunks," or "She had it coming."

4. *Condemning the condemners*. They assert that authorities are corrupt or responsible for their own victimization and that society has made them what they are and must now suffer the consequences: "They're worse than we are. They're all on the take," or "If I don't do it to him, he'll do it to me."

5. *Appealing to higher loyalties*. They use the defence of their family honour, gang, girl-friend, or neighbourhood: "I have to protect myself."

In the words of Sykes and Matza, "It is our argument that much delinquency is based on what is essentially an unrecognized extension of defenses to crimes, in the form of justifications for deviance that are seen as valid by the delinquent but not by the legal system or society at large."[9]

A few years later, Matza went on to suggest that delinquents tended to drift into crime when available techniques of neutralization combined with weak or ineffective values espoused by the controlling elements in society, stating that the delinquent "drifts between criminal and conventional action," choosing whichever is the more expedient at the time. By employing techniques of neutralization, delinquents need not be fully alienated from the larger society because these techniques provide an effective way of overcoming feelings of guilt so they can commit crimes. Matza used the phrase "soft determinism" to describe drift, saying that delinquents are neither forced to make choices because of fateful experiences early in life nor entirely free to make choices unencumbered by the realities of their situation.

More recent studies have found that whereas "only a small percentage of adolescents generally approve of violence or express indifference to violence … [a] large percentage of adolescents … accept neutralizations justifying the use of violence in particular situations."[10] Studies have found that young people who disapprove of violence but associate with delinquent peers will often use neutralization techniques as justifications for violence in which they personally engage.[11]

A 2003 study of remorse and neutralization among violent male offenders was based on interviews with 27 men who had committed serious violent crimes. Sociologist Lois Presser found that the men excused or justified their violent actions through five rationalizations: (1) victims were to blame for harms they sustained that resulted from provoking the offender, (2) victims were themselves offenders or deserving of harm, (3) harm to a victim that was not premeditated or intended carried no blame, (4) the legal sanctioning of an offender negated any harm, and (5) harms to the offender and his family stemming from the crime negated any harms caused by the offender.[12]

In innovative research published in 2008, Orly Turgeman-Goldschmidt of Israel's Bar-Ilan University conducted 54 unstructured, in-depth face-to-face interviews with malicious Israeli computer vandals (hackers) in order to determine what kinds of neutralization techniques they employed and found that the hackers used neutralization techniques common to other offenders, although their language reflected the cyber-realm.[13] Some hackers were found to be like political criminals, assuming responsibility by means of internal justifications (by attacking al-Qaeda websites or bringing down computers of the Arab news network Al-Jazeera and seeing the activity as a positive contribution to their socio-political environment); these "hacktivists" defined themselves as hackers with political consciences.[14] Other hackers justified illegal hacking as simply being fun, rewarding, or self-fulfilling and argued that anyone or anything affected, such as financial institutions, could afford it and that no one was physically hurt.

Labelling Theory

Another social process perspective is based on the study of societal reactions to deviance. Society's response to known or suspected offenders is important not only because it determines the individual futures of those who are labelled as offenders, but also because it may contribute to a heightened incidence of criminality by reducing behavioural options available to labelled offenders.

Tagging   An early description of lasting societal reaction to deviance can be found in the work of Frank Tannenbaum, whose 1938 book *Crime and the Community* popularized the term **tagging** to explain what happens to offenders following arrest, conviction, and sentencing. Tannenbaum told his readers that crime was essentially the result of two opposing views—those of the delinquent and those of the community at large:

> This conflict over the situation is one that arises out of a divergence of values. As the problem develops, the situation gradually becomes redefined. The attitude of the community hardens definitely into a demand for suppression. There is a gradual shift from the definition of the specific acts as evil to a definition of the individual as evil, so that all his acts come to be looked upon with suspicion. From the community's point of view, the individual who used to do bad and mischievous things has now become a bad and unredeemable human being. . . . There is a persistent demand for consistency in character. The community cannot deal with people whom it cannot define.[15]

After the process whereby an offender comes to be seen as ultimately and irrevocably bad has been completed, Tannenbaum said, the offender "now lives in a different world. He has been tagged. The process of making the criminal, therefore, is a process of tagging."[16] Once a person has been defined as bad, he or she finds that few legitimate opportunities remain open and that only other people who have been similarly defined by society as bad are available to associate with him or her, and this continued association with negatively defined others leads to continued crime.

Primary and Secondary Deviance   Using terminology developed by Edwin M. Lemert, it became fashionable to call an offender's initial acts of deviance *primary deviance* and continued acts of deviance, especially those resulting from forced association with other offenders, *secondary deviance*. **Primary deviance** may be undertaken to solve some immediate problem or to meet the expectations of one's subcultural group. For example, the robbery of a convenience store by a college student temporarily desperate for tuition money may be the first serious criminal offence ever committed by the student, and he or she may well intend for it to be the last, but if arrest ensues and the student is tagged with the status of a criminal, then secondary deviance may occur as a means of adjustment to the negative status. In Lemert's words, "When a person begins to employ his deviant behavior or a role based upon it as a means of defense, attack, or adjustment to the overt and covert problems created by the consequent societal reaction to him, his deviation is secondary."[17]

Secondary deviance is especially important because of the forceful role it plays in causing tagged individuals to internalize the negative labels that have been applied to them and to assume the role of the deviant. According to Lemert, "Objective evidences of this change will be found in the symbolic appurtenances of the new role, in clothes, speech, posture, and mannerisms, which in some cases heighten social visibility, and which in some cases serve as symbolic cues to professionalization."[18]

Watch
Introduction to Labelling
Watch
Societal Reaction

Tagging   The process whereby an individual is negatively defined by agencies of justice.

Watch
Edwin Lemert

Primary deviance   Initial deviance often undertaken to deal with transient problems in living.

Secondary deviance   Deviant behaviour that results from official labelling and from association with others who have been so labelled.

👁 Watch
Howard Becker

Labelling An interactionist perspective that sees continued crime as a consequence of limited opportunities for acceptable behaviour that follow from the negative responses of society to those defined as offenders. Also, the process by which a negative or deviant label is imposed.

Labelling   The person most often associated with labelling theory is Howard Becker, who published *Outsiders: Studies in the Sociology of Deviance*, the work in which the perspective of **labelling** found its fullest development.[19] Labelling is the idea that society's response to the criminal and the process through which a person comes to be defined as a criminal and labelled criminal are significant contributory factors in future criminality. In *Outsiders*, Becker described the deviant subculture in which jazz musicians live and the process by which an individual becomes a marijuana user. His primary focus, however, was to explain how a person becomes labelled an outsider, as "a special kind of person, one who cannot be trusted to live by the rules agreed on by the group."[20] The central fact is that society creates both deviance and the deviant person by responding to circumscribed behaviours. In Becker's words,

> Social groups create deviance by making the rules whose infraction constitutes deviance, and by applying those rules to particular people and labeling them as outsiders. From this point of view, deviance is not a quality of the act the person commits, but rather a consequence of the application by others of rules and sanctions. The deviant is one to whom that label has been successfully applied.[21]

For Becker and other labelling theorists, no act is intrinsically deviant or criminal but must be defined as such by others; becoming deviant involves a sequence of steps that eventually leads to commitment to a deviant identity and participation in a deviant career.

In developing labelling theory, Becker attempted to explain how some rules come to carry the force of law, while others have less weight or apply only within the context of marginal subcultures. His explanation centred on the concept of **moral enterprise**, meaning all the efforts a particular interest group makes to have its sense of propriety embodied in law. "Rules are the products of someone's initiative, and we can think of the people who exhibit such enterprise as moral entrepreneurs."[22] An early example of moral enterprise can be found in the Women's Christian Temperance Union (WCTU), a group devoted to the idea of prohibition in the United States. In Canada, the *Dominion Temperance Act*, passed in 1878, left the decision about prohibition with the provinces, and it wasn't until World War I that prohibition became a national reality.[23]

Moral enterprise Efforts made by an interest group to have its sense of propriety enacted into law.

Becker was especially interested in describing deviant careers and the processes by which individuals become members of deviant subcultures and take on the attributes associated with the deviant role. Becker argued that most deviance is likely to be transitory and unlikely to occur again. For example, a youth who shoplifts a candy bar from a convenience store will probably not make a habit out of this behaviour. However, transitory deviance can be effectively stabilized in a person's behavioural repertoire through the labelling process. If that youth is caught and charged by the police, then he or she becomes known as a shoplifter or young offender. Once a person is labelled as deviant, opportunities for conforming behaviour are seriously reduced and behavioural opportunities that remain open are primarily deviant ones. The budding deviant increasingly exhibits deviant behaviour because his or her choices are restricted by society. Successful deviants must acquire the techniques and resources necessary to undertake the deviant act (drug use, bank robbery, breaking and entering) and develop the mindset characteristic of others like them. Near the end of a deviant career, the person labelled a deviant has internalized society's negative label, has assumed a deviant self-concept, and is likely a member of a deviant subgroup (see the Who's Responsible? box). "A drug addict once told me that the moment she felt she was really 'hooked' was when she realized she no longer had any friends who were not drug addicts."[24] In this way, explained Becker, deviance becomes a self-fulfilling prophecy. Labelling, then, is a cause of crime insofar as the actions of society in defining the rule breaker as deviant push the person further in the direction of continued deviance.

Living in Shame

When her son was sent to prison for pedophilia, Sheila was plunged into a world of secrecy and loneliness.

Lance, 21, was convicted last year of sexually assaulting an eight-year-old girl and a ten-year-old boy. He was sentenced to 20 months in jail.

"When I first found out he was charged, I was horrified, and immediately thought, 'What have I done wrong?'" says Sheila, who prefers to be identified only as a Lower Mainland teacher.

"I didn't know what to do. It was a nightmare. And because I didn't know what was going on, I wasn't in any kind of position to offer support to my son—who was terrified."

The experience left Sheila feeling isolated and abandoned. She still hasn't told other members of Lance's family—including her ex-husband—about his crime.

"I was feeling so alone. I mean, who could I talk to about this?

"You have a sense of isolation because you cut off all your friends.

"I was worried that everyone would find out. I was worried it would reflect on me and put my job in jeopardy. I have shared with only a few friends.

"Even some of my friends who do understand . . . their attitude has changed and they stay away. It's like we're all tarred with the same brush.

"People say he's not really a pedophile, and I have to say, 'Yes he is.'"

The system, Sheila says, is just as mystifying to the families of offenders as it is to the victims. For one thing, there are few if any support groups.

"I went to court with my son time after time. I would sit in that courtroom . . . and I was alone."

Lance, she says, was totally unprepared for the prison system.

"When he was taken into jail you would not believe the harassment from staff, and the filthy comments they made.

"This is a first-time offender, a young kid. He was so frightened.

"The day he was pronounced guilty he wrapped piano wire around his top button. He was afraid he'd end up getting raped because of the hatred towards pedophiles."

It was Lance's first conviction. Sheila believes he had never sexually molested children before.

But she admits he was a difficult child. Being expelled from kindergarten was only the start.

When she divorced Lance's father, things got worse. The next man she married was an alcoholic.

By the time he reached his teens, Lance was stealing and doing drugs.

Finally, in desperation, Sheila had him placed in a foster home.

"It was the hardest thing I've ever done, signing those papers."

The papers she signed declared that she was legally "abandoning" him. That's the official language of B.C.'s *Family Child Services Act*, but Sheila insists that was never her intention.

Within weeks, Sheila says, Lance was sexually molested by his foster mother.

Within months he was sexually molesting two other kids in the home, resulting in the two charges of sexual assault.

"She (the foster mother) has admitted it to me," say Sheila.

"We have not pressed charges because my son did not want me to go through any more trauma.

"I have a lot of anger toward her (the foster mom). But I have a lot of guilt because I feel that if I hadn't been with an alcoholic husband, I would have been more aware.

"But Lance himself said, 'Mom, I made those choices, I did those things.'"

That admission, and confrontation with his past, came after months of therapy at Stave Lake, a minimum-security institution near Maple Ridge for sex offenders.

Sheila has nothing but praise for the staff and program. Now she does volunteer work with sex offenders, helping them upgrade their education, and with victims, helping them understand offenders.

Lance was released from prison after six months and has moved away from the Lower Mainland.

He lives with a family, Sheila says, which is aware of his conviction, and he is supervised at all times.

She's anxious for him to get back into counselling, but she says his probation officer won't let him because of his living arrangements.

"They want him to move to a family apartment building where there would be no supervision."

Sheila wonders what kind of life Lance will have.

"I look down the road and I really wonder what chance my son has for having a good, wholesome, healthy life—like having a family.

"I just have to turn it over to God."

Think about it:

1. How did the label of "pedophile" affect others associated with Lance? Is there a danger in using such labels?

2. Do you feel any differently about Lance once you know a little about his background and what led him to commit the sexual assaults? Is it possible to separate the offender from the offence?

3. Do you think the names of sexual offenders should be made known to the public? Defend your position.

Source: S. Jiwa and C. Ogilvie, "Living in Shame," *The Province*, February 21, 1993, p. 58. Reprinted with permission from Pacific Newspaper Group.

Contributions of Labelling Theory Labelling theory contributed a number of unique ideas to the criminological literature:

■ Deviance is the result of social processes involving the imposition of definitions rather than the consequence of any quality inherent in human activity itself.

■ Deviant individuals achieve their status by virtue of social definition rather than because of inborn traits.

■ The reaction of society to deviant behaviour and to actors who engage in such behaviour is the major element in determining the criminality of the person and of the behaviour in question.

■ Negative self-images follow from processing by the formal criminal justice system, rather than preceding delinquency.

■ Labelling by society and handling by the justice system tend to perpetuate crime and delinquency rather than reduce them.

Becker's typology of delinquents—the pure deviant, the falsely accused deviant, and the secret deviant—helped explain the labelling approach. The pure deviant is one who commits norm-breaking behaviour, who is accurately appraised by society, and who is tried, convicted, and sentenced. The falsely accused individual is one who is not guilty but is labelled deviant nonetheless, who experiences the impact of conviction and the experiences that attend prison life, and who is left with a negative self-concept and with group associations practically indistinguishable from those of the true deviant. This person demonstrates the power of social definition—the life of the falsely accused is changed just as thoroughly as is the life of the pure deviant by the process of labelling. The secret deviant violates social norms, but his or her behaviour is not noticed, so negative societal reactions do not follow. A secret deviant again demonstrates the power of societal reaction, but in this case by the very lack of consequences.

Although labelling theory fell into disregard during the late 1970s and early 1980s due to allegations that it was vague and ambiguous, some contemporary criminologists have recast the approach as a developmental theory of structural disadvantage. The theory is now seen as one that points out the cumulative effects over time of official intervention on future life chances and opportunities for approved success. Contemporary proponents of the labelling perspective generally see labelling as only one factor contributing to cumulative disadvantages in life chances. A recent study considered the impact of negative official interventions on young men from the time they were about 13.5 years old until they reached the age of 22. In keeping with what labelling theory would predict, the study found that official intervention during adolescence led to increased criminality in early adulthood because it reduced life chances for educational achievement and successful employment and that poor people were more negatively affected by official processing, probably because they were already disadvantaged along other important social dimensions.[25]

The transition from primary to secondary deviance is outlined in Box 9.1.

Reintegrative Shaming

In a more contemporary offshoot of labelling theory, John Braithwaite and colleagues at the Australian National University reported initial results of their 1997 studies on reintegrative shaming, which describes processes by which a deviant is labelled and sanctioned but then is brought back into a community of conformity through words, gestures, or rituals.[26]

Called RISE (for Reintegrative Shaming Experiments), the project assessed the efficacy of each approach using several criteria: (1) prevalence and frequency of repeat offending, (2) victim satisfaction with the process, (3) estimated cost savings within the

Box 9.1 THE DEVIANCE PROCESS

1. A person commits a deviant/criminal act (if undetected, the act remains primary deviance).

2. Society reacts in a retributive or punitive way.

3. The individual responds by committing more infractions (secondary deviation), which in turn draws additional attention to the criminal. The deviant cycle begins to escalate (e.g., in frequency and/or intensity), a self-fulfilling process.

4. The labelled individual develops more hostility and resentment toward criminal justice agents.

5. Society and the legal system respond by further labelling and stigmatizing the offender.

6. As the individual's options become increasingly restricted, the criminal justice system sees the offender

as a problem and the offender sees him- or herself as deviant.

7. The probability for future acts of deviance increases—deviance amplification. Therefore, once labelled and stigmatized, the offender's identity and self-concept evolve around deviance.

General Model of Labelling Process

Primary deviance → information reaction → continuance of deviance → escalation of response (e.g., stereotyping, rejection, alienation of tagged actor) → more delinquency (secondary deviance) → formal intervention → individual begins to see self as delinquent → self-fulfilling process.

Source: J.A. Winterdyk, *Canadian Criminology* (Toronto: Prentice Hall, 2000), p. 241. Reprinted with permission of Pearson Education Canada.

---

justice process, (4) changes in drinking or drug use behaviour among offenders, and (5) perceptions of procedural justice, fairness, and protection of rights.[27]

At the core of the study is Braithwaite's belief that two different kinds of shame exist. **Stigmatic shaming** is thought to destroy the moral bond between the offender and the community, whereas **reintegrative shaming** is thought to strengthen the moral bond between the offender and the community. According to Braithwaite and Strang,

> Stigmatic shaming is what American judges employ when they make an offender post a sign on his property saying "a violent felon lives here'" or a bumper sticker on his car saying "I am a drunk driver." Stigmatic shaming sets the offender apart as an outcast—often for the rest of the offender's life. By labeling him or her as someone who cannot be trusted to obey the law, stigmatic shaming says the offender is expected to commit more crimes.[28]

Their alternative to stigmatic humiliation is "to condemn the crime, not the criminal."[29] Through carefully monitored diversionary conferences, Braithwaite and Strang hoped to give offenders the opportunity to rejoin the community as law-abiding citizens, but to earn the right to a fresh start, offenders had to express remorse for their past conduct, apologize to any victims, and repair the harm caused by the crime.

Preliminary results from the RISE study supported the claimed value of reintegrative shaming, but most of these results were measured through interviews with offenders following diversionary conferences and consisted primarily of anecdotal evidence based on the reported feelings of the respondents. These findings showed that offenders were far more likely to feel ashamed of their crimes if handled through conferences rather than through formal court processing and that both offenders and victims reported finding conferences fairer than official court proceedings. See the discussion on the related topic of restorative justice in Chapter 10.

Social Control Theories

Social control theories seek to identify those features of the personality (Chapter 7) and the environment (Chapter 8) that keep people from committing crimes. Social control

Stigmatic shaming A form of shaming, imposed as a sanction by the criminal justice system, that is thought to destroy the moral bond between the offender and the community.

Reintegrative shaming A form of shaming, imposed as a sanction by the criminal justice system, that is thought to strengthen the moral bond between the offender and the community.

Social control theories Perspectives predicting that when social constraints on anti-social behaviour are weakened or absent, delinquent behaviour emerges. Rather than stressing causative factors in criminal behaviour, social control theory asks why people actually obey rules instead of breaking them.

⊙ Watch

Introduction to Social Control

theories take a step beyond static aspects of the personality and physical features of the environment in order to focus on the *process* through which social integration develops. The extent of a person's integration with positive social institutions and with significant others determines that person's resistance to criminal temptations. Social control theories focus on the process through which such integration develops. Rather than stressing causal factors in criminal behaviour, social control theories tend to ask why people actually obey rules instead of breaking them.[30]

Containment Theory

In the 1950s, a student of the Chicago school of criminology, Walter C. Reckless, wrote *The Crime Problem*.[31] He tackled head-on the realization that most sociological theories, although conceptually enlightening, offered less than perfect predictability, being unable to predict which individuals (even those exposed to various "causes" of crime) would become criminal. Reckless thought that the sociological perspectives prevalent at the time offered only half of a comprehensive theoretical framework, writing that crime was the consequence of both social pressures to become involved in violations of the law and failures to resist such pressures. Reckless called his approach **containment theory** and compared it with a biological immune response, saying that only some people exposed to a disease actually come down with it. Sickness, like crime, results from the failure of control mechanisms, some internal to the person and others external.

In the case of crime, Reckless wrote that *external containment* consists of "the holding power of the group."[32] Under most circumstances, Reckless said that "the society, the state, the tribe, the village, the family, and other nuclear groups are able to hold the individual within the bounds of the accepted norms and expectations."[33] In addition to setting limits, he saw society as providing individuals with meaningful roles and activities, another important factor of external containment.

Reckless stated that *inner containment* "represents the ability of the person to follow the expected norms, to direct himself."[34] This ability was enhanced by a positive self-image, a focus on socially approved goals, personal aspirations in line with reality, a tolerance for frustration, and a general adherence to society's norms and values. A person with a positive self-concept can avoid the temptations of crime simply by thinking, "I'm not that kind of person." A focus on approved goals helps keep one on the proverbial straight and narrow path. "Aspirations in line with reality" are simply realistic desires. In other words, if one seriously desires to be the richest person in the world, disappointment will probably result. Even when aspirations are reasonable, however, disappointments will occur—hence the need for a tolerance for frustration. Adherence to the norms and values of the larger society are a basic component of inner containment.

In Figure 9.2, "pushes toward crime" represents those factors in an individual's background that might propel him or her into criminal behaviour and include a criminogenic background or upbringing involving participation in a delinquent subculture, deprivation, biological propensities toward deviant behaviour, and psychological maladjustment. "Pulls toward crime" signifies all the perceived rewards crime may offer, including financial gain, sexual satisfaction, and higher status that crime may offer. **Containment** is a stabilizing force that blocks such pushes and pulls from leading the individual into crime.

Reckless believed that inner containment was far more effective than external containment in preventing law violations. "As social relations become more impersonal, as society becomes more diverse and alienated, as people participate more and more for longer periods of time away from a home base, the self becomes more and more important as a controlling agent."[35]

◉ Watch
Travis Hirschi

◉ Watch
Self-Control Theory

Social Bond Theory

An important form of social control theory was popularized by Travis Hirschi in his 1969 book *Causes of Delinquency*.[36] Hirschi argued that, through successful socialization, a bond forms between individuals and the social group, but when that bond is weakened or broken, deviance and crime may result. Hirschi described four components

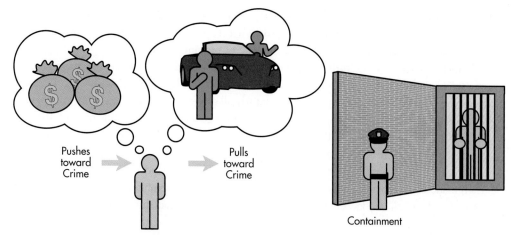

Pushes toward Crime

Pulls toward Crime

Containment

The Criminal Event

Figure 9.2 A Diagrammatic Representation of Containment Theory

of the **social bond**: (1) attachment (a person's shared interests with others), (2) commitment (the amount of energy and effort put into activities with others), (3) involvement (the amount of time spent with others in shared activities), and (4) belief (a shared system of values and morals).

Regarding *attachment*, Hirschi cited the psychopath as an example of a kind of person whose attachment to society is nearly non-existent.[37] Other relatively normal individuals may find their attachment to society loosened through "the process of becoming alienated from others, [which] often involves or is based on active interpersonal conflict. Such conflict could easily supply a reservoir of socially derived hostility sufficient to account for the aggressiveness of those whose attachments to others have been weakened."[38]

The second component of the social bond—*commitment*—reflects a person's investment of time and energies into conforming behaviour and the potential loss of rewards that he or she has already gained from that behaviour. In Hirschi's words,

> The idea, then, is that the person invests time, energy, himself, in a certain line of activity—say, getting an education, building up a business, acquiring a reputation for virtue. Whenever he considers deviant behavior, he must consider the costs of this deviant behavior, the risk he runs of losing the investment he has made in conventional behavior.[39]

For such a traditionally successful person, committing a petty theft is stupid because the potential loss far exceeds any possible gains. Recognizing that his approach applies primarily to individuals who have been successfully socialized into conventional society, Hirschi added, "The concept of commitment assumes that the organization of society is such that the interests of most persons would be endangered if they were to engage in criminal acts."[40]

Involvement, the third aspect, means "engrossment in conventional activities" and is similar to Reckless's concept of meaningful roles.[41] In explaining the importance of involvement in determining conformity, Hirschi cited the colloquial saying that "idle hands are the devil's workshop"—time and energy are limited, so if a person is busy at legitimate pursuits, he or she will have little opportunity for crime and deviance.

Belief, the last of Hirschi's four aspects of the social bond, sets his control theory apart from subcultural approaches because "control theory assumes the existence of a common value system within the society or group whose norms are being violated. We not only assume the deviant has believed the rules, [but also] assume he believes the rules even as he violates them."[42] How can a person simultaneously believe it is wrong to commit a

Social bond The link, created through socialization, between individuals and the society of which they are a part.

crime and still commit it? Hirschi's answer is that "many persons do not have an attitude of respect toward the rules of society."[43] Although they know the rules exist, they basically do not care and invest little of their sense of self in moral standards.

In 1990, Michael R. Gottfredson, in collaboration with Hirschi, proposed a general theory of crime based on the concepts advanced earlier in control theory.[44] Gottfredson and Hirschi began by asking, "What is crime?" Because nearly all crimes are mundane, simple, trivial, easy acts aimed at satisfying desires of the moment, their general theory is built on a classical or rational choice perspective— the belief that crime is a natural consequence of unrestrained human tendencies to seek pleasure and avoid pain. Crime, said Gottfredson and Hirschi, is little more than a subset of general deviant behaviour. They concluded that crime is little more than a subset of general deviant behaviour and bears little resemblance to the explanations offered in the media, by law enforcement officials, or by most academic thinkers on the subject.

According to Gottfredson and Hirschi, the offender is neither the diabolical genius of fiction nor the ambitious seeker of the "American Dream" often portrayed by other social scientists. Offenders appear to have little control over their own desires, so when personal desires conflict with long-term interests, those who lack self-control often opt for the desires of the moment, thus contravening legal restrictions and becoming involved in crime.[45] Central to Gottfredson and Hirschi's thesis is the belief that a well-developed social bond will result in the creation of effective mechanisms of self-control. "For Gottfredson and Hirschi, self-control is the key concept in the explanation of all forms of crime as well as other types of behavior. Indeed, they believe that all current differences in rates of crime between groups and categories may be explained by differences in the management of self-control."[46]

◉─Watch

Abuse of Anna: Sideshow

Social Development Theories

Over the past 25 years, an appreciation for the process of human development (the relationship between the maturing individual and his or her changing environment and to the social processes that relationship entails) has played an increasingly important role in helping us understand criminality.[47] Students of human development recognize that the process of development occurs through reciprocal dynamic interactions that take place between individuals and various aspects of their environment, and the **social development perspective** posits that development, which begins at birth (and perhaps even earlier), occurs primarily within a social context. Unlike social learning theory (discussed earlier in this chapter), social development sees socialization as only one feature of that context. If socialization were the primary determinant of criminality, then we might expect that all problem children would become criminals as adults, but since that doesn't happen, there must be other aspects to the development process that social learning theories don't fully cover.

Social development perspective An integrated view of human development that examines multiple maturation levels simultaneously, including psychological, biological, familial, interpersonal, cultural, societal, and ecological levels.

According to the social development perspective, human development simultaneously occurs on many levels—psychological, biological, familial, interpersonal, cultural, societal, and ecological—so social development theories tend to be integrated theories, or theories combining various points of view. The rest of this chapter looks briefly at the social development perspective.

Most sociological explanations for crime involve the study of groups and the identification of differences among groups of offenders, but social development theories focus more on individual rates of offending and seek to understand both increases and decreases in rates of offending over the individual's lifetime. Social development theories generally employ longitudinal (over time) measurements of delinquency and offending, and they pay special attention to the transitions that people face as they move through the life cycle.

Most theories of social development recognize that a critical transitional period occurs as a person moves from childhood to adulthood. Life course theorists have identified at least seven developmental tasks that adolescents must confront: (1) establishing identity,

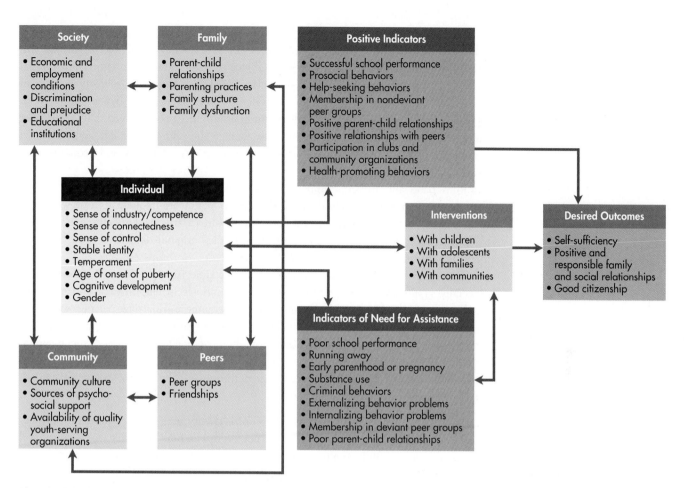

Figure 9.3 A Conceptual Model of Adolescent Development

Source: Family and Youth Services Bureau, *Understanding Youth Development: Promoting Positive Pathways of Growth* (Washington, DC: U.S. Department of Health and Human Services, 2000).

(2) cultivating symbiotic relationships, (3) defining physical attractiveness, (4) investing in a value system, (5) obtaining an education, (6) separating from family and achieving independence, and (7) obtaining and maintaining gainful employment.[48] Youths are confronted with many obstacles or risks in their attempts to resolve these issues as they work to make a successful transition to adulthood. Figure 9.3 provides a conceptual model of the developmental processes that a maturing youth experiences during adolescence.

Life Course Perspective   Traditional explanations for crime and delinquency often lack a developmental perspective because they generally ignore developmental changes throughout the life course and frequently fail to distinguish between different phases of criminal careers.[49] In contrast, development theories draw attention to the fact that criminal behaviour tends to follow a distinct pattern across the life cycle. Criminality is relatively uncommon during childhood, tends to begin as sporadic instances of delinquency during late adolescence and early adulthood, and then diminishes and sometimes completely disappears from a person's behaviour repertoire by age 30 or 40. Of course, some people never commit crimes or do so only rarely, while others become career criminals and persist in lives of crime.

The life course perspective (also called life course criminology) shifted the traditional focus away from the reasons why people begin offending to questions about what the dimensions of criminal offending are over the entire life course.[50] This perspective is supported by research dating back to the 1930s. For example, Sheldon and Eleanor Glueck studied the life cycles of delinquent boys.[51] The Gluecks followed the careers of known delinquents in an effort to identify the causes of delinquency. Data were originally collected through psychiatric interviews with subjects, parent and teacher reports, and official records obtained from police, court, and correctional files. Surviving subjects were again interviewed between 1949 and 1965. The Gluecks found that family dynamics played an especially significant role in the development of criminality and observed that "the deeper the roots of childhood maladjustment, the smaller the chance of adult adjustment."[52] Delinquent careers, said the Gluecks, tend to carry over into adulthood and frequently lead to criminal careers.

John Laub and Robert Sampson[53] reanalyzed the data originally gathered by the Gluecks and found that children who turn to delinquency are frequently those who have trouble at school and at home and who have friends already involved in delinquency. Using a sophisticated computerized analysis of the Gluecks' original data, Laub and Sampson identified "turning points" in a criminal career.

Turning points, they found, may occur at any time in such a career, although two especially significant turning points centre on the choice of employment and marriage. Employers who are willing to give "troublemakers" a chance and marriage partners who insist on conventional lifestyles can successfully redirect the course of a budding offender's life, according to these authors. Laub and Sampson also developed the concept of **social capital** in reference to the number of positive relationships with other persons and social institutions that individuals build up over the course of their lives. The greater one's social capital, the less the chance of criminal activity.[54]

Evolutionary Ecology
Because life course theory uses a developmental perspective in the study of criminal careers, life course researchers typically use longitudinal research designs involving **cohort analysis**, which usually begins at birth and traces the development of a population whose members share common characteristics until they reach a certain age. One well-known analysis of a birth **cohort**, undertaken by Marvin Wolfgang during the 1960s, found that a small nucleus of chronic juvenile offenders accounted for a disproportionately large share of all juvenile arrests.[55] Wolfgang studied male individuals born in Philadelphia in 1945, following them until they reached age 18. He concluded that a relatively small number of violent offenders were responsible for most of the crimes committed by the cohort—6 percent of cohort members accounted for 52 percent of all arrests. A follow-up study found that the seriousness of offences among the cohort increased in adulthood, but that the actual number of offences decreased as the cohort aged.[56] Wolfgang's analysis has since been criticized for its lack of a second cohort, or control group, against which the experiences of the cohort under study could be compared.[57]

The ecological perspective on crime control, pioneered by Lawrence E. Cohen and Richard Machalek, provides a more contemporary example of a life course approach.[58] **Evolutionary ecology** builds on the approach of social ecology while emphasizing developmental pathways encountered early in life. Criminologist Bryan Vila stated that "the evolutionary ecological approach draws attention to the ways people develop over the course of their lives. Experiences and environment early in life, especially those that affect child development and the transmission of biological traits and family management practices across generations, seem particularly important."[59] According to Vila, evolutionary ecology "attempts to explain how people acquire criminality—a predisposition that disproportionately favors criminal behavior—when and why they express it as crime, how individuals and groups respond to those crimes, and how all these phenomena interact as a dynamic self-reinforcing system that evolves over time."[60]

Developmental Pathways
Researchers have found that manifestations of disruptive behaviours in childhood and adolescence are often age dependent, reflecting a

Social capital The number of positive relationships with other persons and social institutions that individuals build up over the course of their lives.

Cohort analysis A social scientific technique that studies a population that shares common characteristics over time. Cohort analysis usually begins at birth and traces the development of cohort members until they reach a certain age.

Cohort A group of individuals sharing certain significant social characteristics, such as gender and time and place of birth.

Evolutionary ecology An approach to understanding crime that draws attention to the ways people develop over the course of their lives.

◉─▐Watch
Juvenile Corrections

developing capability to display different behaviours with age.[61] One of the most comprehensive studies to date that has attempted to detail life pathways leading to criminality began in 1986. The study, a cohort analysis, has compiled data on 4500 youths from three distinct but coordinated projects throughout the United States.[62] A survey sampled youngsters at high risk for serious delinquency and drug use and found that (1) "the more seriously involved in drugs a youth was, the more seriously that juvenile was involved in delinquency," (2) "greater risks exist for violent offending when a child is physically abused or neglected early in life," (3) students who are not highly committed to school have higher rates of delinquency, (4) "poor family life exacerbates delinquency and drug use," and (5) affiliation with street gangs and illegal gun ownership are both predictive of delinquency. The study also found that "peers who were delinquent or used drugs had a great impact on [other] youth." Perhaps the most significant result of the study is the finding that three separate developmental pathways to delinquency exist:[63]

1. *Authority conflict pathway.* Subjects appear to begin quite young (3 or 4 years of age) on the authority conflict pathway. "The first step," said the study authors, "was stubborn behavior, followed by defiance around age 11, and authority avoidance—truancy, staying out late at night, or running away."

2. *Covert pathway.* "Minor covert acts such as frequent lying and shoplifting usually [start] around age 10." Delinquents following the covert pathway quickly progress "to acts of property damage, such as fire starting or vandalism, around age 11 or 12, followed by moderate and serious forms of delinquency."

3. *Overt pathway.* The first step on the overt pathway is minor aggression such as "annoying others and bullying—around age 11 or 12." Bullying was found to escalate into "physical fighting and violence as the juvenile progressed along this pathway." The overt pathway eventually leads to violent crimes like rape, robbery, and assault.

Researchers have found that these three different pathways are not necessarily mutually exclusive and can at times converge. Self-report data have shown that simultaneous progression along two or more pathways leads to higher rates of delinquency.[64]

Another study that could potentially produce substantially significant results began in 1990.[65] Project directors described their ongoing research as "the major criminologic investigation of this century." The project is actually two studies combined into a single, comprehensive design. The first, an intensive study of Chicago's neighbourhoods, is evaluating the social, economic, organizational, political, and cultural components of each neighbourhood. It seeks to identify changes that took place in the neighbourhoods over the study's eight-year data-gathering period. The second project component consists of a series of coordinated longitudinal evaluations of 7000 randomly selected children, adolescents, and young adults. This aspect of the study is looking at the changing circumstances of people's lives and is attempting to identify personal characteristics that may lead toward or away from anti-social behaviour. A variety of study methodologies are utilized, including self-reports, individualized tests and examinations, direct observation, the examination of existing records, and reports by informants. Researchers hope to provide answers to the following questions: (1) "How and why do anti-social and criminal behaviours originate?" (2) "What causes some individuals to continue those behaviours?" and (3) "How and why do some individuals cease law-violating behaviours while others continue?"

Life course theories often point to the need for early intervention through nurturant strategies that build self-control through positive socialization. As Vila pointed out, "There are two main types of nurturant strategies: those that improve early life experiences to forestall the development of strategic styles based on criminality, and those that channel child and adolescent development in an effort to improve the match between individuals and their environment."[66]

POLICY IMPLICATIONS OF SOCIAL PROCESS THEORIES

As has been noted throughout this chapter, both offenders and victims are stigmatized through social processes involving the formal and informal imposition of labels. Removal of the stigma would, at least theoretically, restore both to their pre-crime state.

Labelling theory, in particular, cautions against too much intervention, since it is often through contact with various types of rehabilitative programs that individuals become even further labelled. Even well-intentioned programs such as special education programs or support groups for released offenders can serve to label participants as "stupid" or "ex-con." Current restitution and court diversion programs are examples of policy initiatives that recognize the principles of labelling theory. Adult diversion projects or alternative measures for youth are designed to divert the offender away from formal contact with the criminal justice system, thereby avoiding the imposition of a label. For example, a man who is arrested for seeking the services of a prostitute but who has no previous criminal convictions may be ordered to attend "john school." Successful attendance means the offender has no further contact with the criminal justice system and is free of a criminal record. Diversion programs are usually joint initiatives involving the Crown's office and the local police service. Likewise, restitution initiatives are attempts to prevent the stigmatization of the offender. In lieu of the trial and court process, the offender is required to compensate either the victim or the community for the loss or for harm done. Since their inception, diversion programs have been surrounded by controversy. Whether they actually prevent the imposition of a negative label and thereby prevent future criminal activity is open to debate.[67]

Social learning perspectives have also had an impact on program initiatives dealing with offenders and those at risk of becoming offenders. Social learning is based on the principle that since criminal behaviour and attitudes can be learned through association with criminal types, conventional values can be learned by interaction with those holding them. Well-known programs such as "Night Hoops" or "After-4 Drop-ins" are aimed at "at-risk" youth and provide an opportunity for them to associate with positive role models. Well-known sports figures will often participate and deliver positive messages telling kids to "Stay in school" or "Say no to drugs." The Ottawa Police Service runs a youth centre in a neighbourhood once ridden with youth crime and has reported a significant decrease in illegal activity in the area since the centre's opening.

Closely linked to the idea of learned behaviour are the notions of commitment and attachment put forth by social control theorists. Not only do recreation programs run by such organizations as Boys and Girls Clubs and the YM/YWCA promote positive learning, but they help to develop a positive bond between individual participants and the program. Individuals, in turn, will not want to risk losing the privilege of being a member of the program if they break the rules. Similarly, educational programs such as Head Start work to socialize children at the preschool stage to help make their school experiences more enjoyable and thereby decrease the chances of early withdrawal. Social control theorists believe that a strong commitment to school, family, employment, and recreation—assuming these environments are all positive ones—can help decrease an individual's likelihood of succumbing to a criminal lifestyle.

Another contemporary example of social intervention efforts tied to a developmental model is Targeted Outreach, a program operated in the United States by Boys and Girls Clubs of America.[68] Using a wide referral network made up of local schools, police departments, and various youth service agencies, club officials work to end what they call the "inappropriate detention of juveniles."[69] The program's primary goal is to provide a positive, productive alternative to gangs for the youths who are most vulnerable to their influences or are already entrenched in gang activity. Currently, the program recruits at-risk youngsters—many as young as 7 years old—and diverts them into activities that are intended to promote a sense of belonging, competence, usefulness, and self-control. A sense of belonging is fostered through clubs that provide familiar settings where each child is accepted. Competence and usefulness are developed through opportunities for meaningful activities, which young people in the club program can successfully undertake. Finally, Targeted Outreach provides its youthful participants with a chance to be heard and, consequently, with the opportunity to influence decisions affecting their future. To date, Targeted Outreach has served more than 10 000 at-risk youths. Organizers hope that the program will eventually involve more than 1.5 million youngsters between the ages of 7 and 17.[70]

Life course theories have been widely applied to develop programs aimed at youth in conflict with the law. Most of these programs centre around a number of principles, which include strengthening the role of the family in providing guidance and discipline, supporting core social institutions such as schools and community organizations, promoting prevention strategies, and intervening immediately and consistently when delinquent behaviour first occurs. Examples of programs that reflect these principles are found in Chapter 11 in the discussion of nurturant crime-control policies.

CRITIQUE OF SOCIAL PROCESS THEORIES

9.4 LEARNING OBJECTIVE

SOCIAL PROCESS THEORIES SHARE SOME OF THE LIMITATIONS OF SOCIAL STRUCTURE theories, discussed in Chapter 8. Most notable of these is the disregard for biological and/or psychological contributions to criminal behaviour; indeed, all these theories are concerned with the social reality surrounding individuals and their interaction with all or some segments of it. In addition, like social structure theories, the social process perspective fails to fully explain why some individuals who are surrounded by negative environments and poor role models manage to avoid becoming involved in criminal behaviour. How is it that some manage to resist the peer pressure to get involved in deviant activity? How are they able to desist from "learning" from what they see all around them? If socialization is so crucial to an understanding of criminal behaviour, how is it that crime rates fluctuate from region to region in Canada? Are youth in the western provinces, where crime rates are generally higher, socialized differently than those in the eastern parts of the country, where crime rates are generally lower?

A critical examination of the individual theories presented in this chapter confirms these questions. Perhaps the most potent criticism against the concept of differential association, for example, is the claim that the perspective is virtually untestable, even though much use has been made of the insights it appears to offer. Other critics also suggest that differential association alone is not a sufficient explanation for crime. If it were, then we might expect correctional officers, for example, to become criminals by virtue of their constant and continued association with prison inmates. Similarly, wrongly imprisoned persons might be expected to turn to crime upon release from confinement. Little evidence suggests that either of these scenarios actually occurs. In effect, differential association does not seem to provide for free choice in individual circumstances, nor for the fact that some individuals, even when surrounded by associates who are committed to lives of crime, are still able to hold on to other, non-criminal values.

Although the labelling approach delineates how an individual might have reasons for continuing in deviance and suffering stabilization in deviant identities, it does little to explain the origin of crime and deviance. Likewise, few, if any, studies seem to support the basic tenets of the theory. Critics of labelling have pointed to its "lack of firm empirical support for the notion of secondary deviance," and observed that "many studies have not found that delinquents or criminals have a delinquent or criminal self-image."[71] In addition, there is a lack of unequivocal empirical support for the claim that contact with the justice system is fundamentally detrimental to the personal lives of criminal perpetrators. Although labelling theory suggests that official processing makes a significant contribution to continued criminality, it is questionable whether offenders untouched by the system would forgo the rewards of future criminality. Rather, it is the *type* of contact with the criminal justice system that many feel influences the future behaviour of an offender.

SOCIAL PROCESS THEORIES APPLIED

SOCIAL LEARNING
holds that all behaviour is learned in much the same way and that crime, like other forms of behaviour, is learned.
Andrew Leyshon-Hughes came from a well-established family. Where might he have learned the deviant behaviour that he exhibited? How might he have justified his behaviour?

Crime is a result of interaction between individuals and society. Criminal behaviour is learned in interaction with others and through the socialization process that occurs as a result of group membership. Among the most important groups contributing to this process of socialization are family, peers, and work groups. These groups instill the values and norms in their members and determine what is acceptable and unacceptable. The process through which criminality is learned, deviant self-concepts are established, and criminal behaviour results is active, open-ended, and ongoing throughout a person's life. Criminal choices, once made, tend to persist because they are reinforced by the reaction of society to those whom it has identified as deviant.

How can society's reaction to Andrew Leyshon-Hughes's criminal behaviour be explained using the social process perspective?

SOCIAL DEVELOPMENT
holds that crime is a result of the relationship between the maturing individual and his or her changing environment and of the social processes that relationship entails.
Andrew Leyshon-Hughes's lawyer argued that his client suffered from brain damage at birth. Is this an example of poor social development?

LABELLING
holds that crime is a result of limited opportunities for acceptable behaviour that follow from the negative responses of society to those defined as offenders.
Andrew Leyshon-Hughes was unable to escape from the label of psychopath, despite the efforts of his psychiatrist to deem him well enough to live in the community.

SOCIAL CONTROL
holds that crime is a result of weak or absent social constraints on anti-social behaviour.
Is there evidence that Andrew Leyshon-Hughes lacked strong social bonds? Why might have these been weak or absent?

SUMMARY OF LEARNING OBJECTIVES

9.1 According to social process theories, criminal behaviour is learned in interaction with others. The socialization process occurring as the result of group membership—in families, peer groups, work groups, and reference groups—is seen as the primary route through which learning occurs. Social process theories suggest that individuals who have weak stakes in conformity are more likely to be influenced by the social processes and contingent experiences that lead to crime and that criminal choices tend to persist because they are reinforced by the reaction of society to those whom it has identified as deviant.

9.2 This examination of the social process perspective looks at several distinct approaches. Social learning theory places primary emphasis upon the role of communication and socialization in the acquisition of learned patterns of criminal behaviour and the values that support that behaviour. Labelling theory points to the special significance of society's response to the criminal and sees society's imposition of the label *criminal* as a significant contributory factor in determining future criminality. Reintegrative shaming emphasizes possible positive outcomes of the labelling process, while social control theory focuses on the strength of the bond people share with institutions and individuals around them, especially as those relationships shape their behaviour. Finally, the social development approach integrates theories of human development that examine psychological, biological, familial, interpersonal, cultural, societal, and ecological aspects of that development.

9.3 Social process theories suggest that crime-prevention programs should work to enhance self-control and to build prosocial bonds (bonds that strengthen conformity). Labelling theory, in particular, cautions against too much intervention, since it is often through contact with various types of rehabilitative programs that individuals become even further labelled. Even well-intentioned programs such as special education programs or support groups for released offenders can serve to label participants.

9.4 Criticisms of social process theories are varied. The social process perspective fails to fully explain why some individuals who are surrounded by negative environments and poor role models manage to avoid becoming involved in criminal behaviour. If socialization is so crucial to an understanding of criminal behaviour, why is it that some manage to resist the peer pressure to get involved in deviant activity and to desist from "learning" from what they see all around them?

Questions for Review

1. How does the process of social interaction contribute to criminal behaviour?
2. Compare and contrast the theories discussed in this chapter, citing differences and similarities between and among them.
3. What kinds of social policy initiatives might be suggested by social process theories? Identify some already in place in Canadian society.
4. Describe the various shortcomings of the social process perspective of criminality.

Multiple-Choice Questions

1. Which of the following perspectives sees continued crime as a consequence of limited opportunities for acceptable behaviour that follow from the negative responses of society to those defined as offenders?

    a. reintegrative shaming

    b. life course theory

    c. labelling theory

    d. containment theory

    e. social control theory

2. According to Edwin Lemert, _____ is the initial deviant act that results in being caught and labelled as a deviant.

    a. primary deviance

    b. secondary deviance

    c. tagging

    d. labelling

    e. reaction formation

3. According to differential association theory, how does learning criminal behaviour differ from learning other types of behaviour?

    a. Learning criminal behaviour is much more a peer group exercise.

    b. Learning criminal behaviour is a matter of imitation.

    c. Learning criminal behaviour is more difficult.

    d. There is no difference between learning criminal behaviour and noncriminal behaviour.

    e. Learning criminal behaviour is greater in intensity.

4. The technique of neutralization, which involves a young offender claiming that the unlawful acts were "not my fault," is known as _____.

    a. denial of injury

    b. denial of responsibility

    c. appeal to higher loyalties

    d. condemnation of the condemners

    e. denial of the victim

5. Rather than stressing causative factors in criminal behaviour, _____ asks why people actually obey rules instead of breaking them.

    a. social control

    b. subcultural

    c. strain

    d. differential association

    e. labelling

Multiple Choice Answers: 1c, 2a, 3d, 4b, 5a

Chapter 10
The Meaning of Crime: Social Conflict Perspective

Fred Lum/The Globe and Mail/Canadian Press Images

Crime is an opportunity, not a problem. It's an opportunity to find out what's wrong in the relationship that exists in our community.

—Justice Barry Stuart[1]

LEARNING OBJECTIVES

After reading this chapter, you should be able to

10.1 Recognize the ways in which power conflict between social groups contributes to crime and criminal activity.

10.2 Understand the distinctions between a number of social conflict theories.

10.3 Assess the shortcomings of the social conflict perspective.

10.4 Identify those policy initiatives that reflect the social conflict approach.

INTRODUCTION

On March 11, 1990, a small Mohawk Aboriginal band erected a barricade along the border of the Mohawk Nation reserve of Kanesatake. The nearby city of Oka, Quebec, was proceeding with plans to enlarge a golf course on 22 hectares of land known as "The Pines" that had been given to the city but was claimed by the Mohawks as a sacred ancestral burial ground. Since the courts had rejected the Mohawks' claim to the land, the band concluded that their only option was to hold a standoff. It lasted 78 days.

Initially, the barricade was guarded mostly by women and children. The standoff intensified, however, as the Mohawks of Kanesatake were joined by Mohawks from other reserves in Canada and the United States, some of whom belonged to a society of heavily armed Mohawk Warriors. The introduction of high-powered firearms and other weapons increased the tension between the Mohawks and authorities, represented largely by the Quebec provincial police force, the Sûreté du Québec (SQ). The city of Oka was successful in obtaining a court order to evict the Mohawks, and on July 10, 1990, about 100 SQ personnel attempted to enforce this injunction on behalf of the municipality. Armed Mohawks were positioned to one side in the woods while police equipped with gas masks and assault rifles advanced on the barricade. An armed conflict erupted, and hundreds of rounds of ammunition were fired from both sides, resulting in the wounding and eventual death of a 31-year-old SQ corporal. The standoff had reached crisis proportions, and each side blamed the other for the death of the police officer.

Thirty kilometres to the south of the Kanesatake reserve, Mohawks from the Kahnawake reserve were outraged by the actions of the police. In a show of support, they blocked off all roads into the reserve. These included two major highways, one of which led to the Mercier Bridge linking the city of Montreal to the residential neighbourhood of Châteauguay, which forced thousands of commuters to take a two-hour daily detour. Threatening to "bring down the bridge" if there was another police assault at Oka, the Mohawks dug in. Over 100 chiefs from across Canada met at Kahnawake in a show of solidarity.

The crisis captured national attention, and throngs of media personnel transmitted interviews and pictures across the country. As the standoff continued throughout the summer of 1990, both sides in the conflict became more entrenched. Arms and ammunition were smuggled from Native communities in the United States to bolster the Mohawk cause. Mohawk Warriors with monikers such as "Lasagna" and "Kadahfi" appeared before television cameras in army fatigues, with bandanas covering their faces. Two hundred or so RCMP officers bolstered the 1400 to 1800 SQ forces throughout the duration of the crisis. As the standoff dragged on through the summer, with no progress made toward negotiating a settlement, then prime minister Mulroney called in the Canadian Armed Forces at the request of Quebec premier Bourassa and the provincial government. Approximately 1000 military personnel took over police positions established at Kanesatake and Kahnawake. Numerous violent clashes erupted as each side stood its ground. Canadians witnessed scenes of armoured personnel carriers, barbed-wire barricades, and shouting matches between the two sides as the group of Mohawk Warriors resisted advances by the authorities. Eventually, on September 6, 1990, the Kahnawake Mohawks ended their occupation of the Mercier Bridge. On September 26, after often heated negotiations, the standoff ended when the Mohawk Warriors agreed to lift the barricade. The golf course has not since been expanded.

The Oka crisis cost the Canadian people $200 million, including the expense of extra policing and army intervention. The incident at Oka ended relatively peacefully. However, in the ensuing years there have been numerous similar standoffs: April

In a standoff at the Kanesatake reserve in Oka, Quebec, on September 1, 1990, a Canadian soldier comes face-to-face with a Mohawk warrior.

str-Shaney Komulainen/Canadian Press Images

1995—members of the Adams Lake band in British Columbia stopped equipment from reaching a planned park near Chase, British Columbia, on an ancient burial site; June 1995—Micmacs from Nova Scotia set gill nets in New Brunswick's Miramichi River and blockaded the road to the Native-run fishing camp; September 1995—members of the Stoney Point Ojibway band occupied Ipperwash Provincial Park in southwestern Ontario, saying it was a sacred burial ground, during which three Aboriginal protesters were shot by police in a gunfight and one protester, Dudley George, died; October 2005—a seven-hour standoff by the Stoney First Nations group prevented the planned construction of a $27 million casino project on land west of Calgary; April 2006—protesters from the Six Nations of the Grand River Territory occupied a new subdivision construction site in Caledonia, in southwestern Ontario, claiming that the land belonged to them; and January 2010, 20 years after the Oka crisis, the Mohawks of Kanesatake called upon the federal government to return to the negotiating table to discuss plans by housing developer Normand Ducharme to cut down a number of pine trees on "The Pines." Grand Chief Sohenrise Paul Nicholas, citing outstanding land claim negotiations, was quoted as saying, "We don't want a second Oka crisis—we want this matter resolved."[2] Ducharme subsequently withdrew his plans.

THE SOCIAL CONFLICT PERSPECTIVE

SOCIAL CONFLICT THEORIES EMPHASIZE SOCIAL, ECONOMIC, AND POLITICAL REALITIES AND place crime within this context. As with social process theories, the **social conflict perspective** focuses on the interaction between groups but views this interaction as one of conflict. Various groups within society, defined in terms of their political, economic, or social standing, are seen to compete with one another to promote their own best interests.

Crime and criminal activity are the outcome of this struggle, according to social conflict theories. The creation and application of criminal laws is crucial to determining who becomes criminalized; social conflict criminologists see these roles largely filled by that segment of society holding the economic and political power. This segment uses the law as a means of controlling the dissatisfied and less powerful groups within society while maintaining its position of power. As various groups struggle for power, conflict ensues,

10.1 LEARNING OBJECTIVE

Social conflict perspective   An analytical perspective on social organization which holds that conflict is a fundamental aspect of social life itself and can never fully be resolved.

⊙ Watch
Introduction to Conflict Perspective

⊙ Watch
Definition of Conflict Theory

⊙ Watch
Basic Principles of Conflict Theory

⊙ Watch
Religion and Polarization

which promotes crime. Social conflict theories are also concerned with the role of government and the state in producing crime, since what is considered acceptable and unacceptable behaviour is determined by state-sanctioned laws designed to set boundaries governing such behaviour (see the Who's Responsible? box).

Most social conflict theories of crime causation make the following fundamental assumptions:

- Society is divided by conflict rather than integrated by consensus.
- Society is made up of groups based on political and economic power.
- Differences in social class, and in particular those arrangements within society that maintain class differences, are the focus for criminological study.
- Powerful groups make laws that reflect and protect their interests.
- Crime is an outcome of conflict between those who have and those who have not.

10.2 | LEARNING OBJECTIVE

TYPES OF SOCIAL CONFLICT THEORIES

VARIOUS THEORIES FOUND UNDER THE RUBRIC OF THE SOCIAL CONFLICT PERSPECtive emphasize different root causes of the conflict. This chapter considers a number of these theories, including radical and critical criminology, feminist criminology, the peacemaking model, restorative justice, and the left-realist perspective. Radical criminology is based on Marxist political thought and contends that current inequities in social standing and economic power are the main contributors to the reality of crime. Critical criminology is distinguished from radical criminology by its emphasis on a critique of the relationship between social classes; it is generally viewed as more reactive than the proactive approach taken by the radical criminological outlook. Feminist criminology sees the inequities that exist within society as drawn along gender lines. Peacemaking criminology advocates the reduction of crime through the cooperative efforts of criminal justice agencies and the citizens they serve. Restorative justice and alternative dispute resolution models have their roots in this perspective. Finally, the left-realist perspective moves away from a political-ideological explanation of crime and criminality toward the contention that crime is very "real," especially for marginalized segments of society. Table 10.1 provides an overview of the social conflict theories discussed in this chapter.

◉─[Watch
Karl Marx

Radical Criminology

The conflict perspective is thoroughly entrenched in radical criminology, which is also diversely known as, or related to, schools of thought referred to as *new*, *critical*, or *Marxist*

Table 10.1 Social Conflict Theories			
Theory	**Radical Criminology**	**Left-Realist Criminology**	**Feminist Criminology**	**Peacemaking Criminology**
Period	1960s–present	1980s–present	1970s–present	1980s–present
Theorists	Karl Marx and others	Walter DeKeseredy and others	Freda Adler and others	Harold Pepinsky and others
Concepts	Social class, bourgeoisie, proletariat	Radical realism, critical realism, street crime, social justice, crime control	Power control, gender socialization, empowerment	Compassionate criminology, restorative justice

criminology. **Radical criminology**, which appeared on the criminology scene in the 1970s, has its roots in the writings of 19th-century social utopian thinkers. Primary among them is Karl Marx, whose writings on the conflicts inherent in capitalism led to the formulation of communist ideals and, many would say, to the rise of communist societies the world over.

According to Marx, two fundamental social classes exist in any capitalist society: the haves or the **bourgeoisie**, who are capitalists and wealthy owners of the means of production (factories, businesses, land, natural resources), and the have-nots or the **proletariat**, who are relatively uneducated workers without power. Although Marx was German, the terms *proletariat* and *bourgeoisie* were taken from Marx's knowledge of the French language and are in turn derived from Latin. In ancient Rome, for example, that city's lowest class was propertyless, and its members were individually referred to as *proletarius*.

According to Marx, the members of the proletariat, possessing neither capital nor the means of production, must earn their living by selling their labour. The bourgeoisie, on the other hand, are the capitalist class who, by nature of their very position within society, stand opposed to the proletariat in an ongoing class struggle. Marx saw such struggle between classes as inevitable to the evolution of any capitalistic society and believed that the natural outcome of such struggle would be the overthrow of capitalistic social order and the birth of a truly classless, or communist, society.

Radical criminology   A perspective that holds that the causes of crime are rooted in social conditions that empower the wealthy and the politically well organized but disenfranchise those less fortunate. Radical criminology is sometimes called Marxist criminology.

Bourgeoisie   In Marxist theory, the class of people that owns the means of production.

Proletariat   In Marxist theory, the working class.

WHO'S RESPONSIBLE—THE INDIVIDUAL OR SOCIETY?

"Compassionate Homicide": The Law and Robert Latimer

Robert Latimer, a farmer working a spread in Saskatchewan northwest of Saskatoon, killed his 12-year-old daughter, Tracy, on October 24, 1993. There has never been any doubt about this.

Latimer told police he did it. He said he loved his daughter and could not bear to watch her suffer from a severe form of cerebral palsy. So he placed her in the cab of his Chevy pickup, ran a hose from the exhaust to the cab, climbed into the box of the truck, sat on a tire, and watched her die.

Tracy was a 40-pound quadriplegic, a 12-year-old who functioned at the level of a three-month-old. She had been repeatedly operated on and at the time of her murder was due for more surgery, this time to remove a thigh bone. She could not walk, talk, or feed herself, though she responded to affection and occasionally smiled. Tracy was in constant, excruciating pain yet, for reasons not entirely clear, could not be treated with a painkiller stronger than Tylenol.

On November 4, 1993, Latimer was charged with first-degree murder. A year later, he was convicted of second-degree murder.

End of story?

No.

The issues arising from the Latimer case are momentous. Should courts abide by the letter or the spirit of the law? Would a decision favourable to Latimer legalize euthanasia, mercy killing? Would it put the disabled in danger? Would it mean the end of mandatory minimum sentences for convicted persons?

The killing of Tracy Latimer has been called an act of "compassionate homicide." Others warn that leniency for Latimer, by means of a constitutional exception, would have shown that the disabled are regarded as second-class citizens.

Following his first conviction, the Latimer case became horrendously complex. The Supreme Court ordered a new trial when it was learned that the RCMP, acting on orders from the Crown, had possibly tainted the case by questioning potential jurors on their views on religion, abortion, and mercy killing.

Latimer stood trial again in October 1997. A month later he was convicted, again, of second-degree murder.

The jury recommended he be eligible for parole after a year, even though the minimum sentence for second-degree murder is 25 years with no chance of parole for 10 years. (Automatic minimum sentences for first- and second-degree murder have been mandatory since 1976, as a trade-off for the abolition of capital punishment.)

New legal ground was broken in December 1997, when Justice Ted Noble—trying to distinguish between mercy killing and cold-blooded murder—granted Latimer a constitutional exemption from the minimum sentence for second-degree murder. He explained that, for Latimer, the minimum sentence would constitute "cruel and unusual punishment."

(Continued)

"Compassionate Homicide": The Law and Robert Latimer

Noble carefully detailed the reasons for his decision, anticipating the controversy it would provoke—and the likelihood it would be appealed. He said the law "recognizes that the moral culpability or the moral blameworthiness of murder can vary from one convicted offender to another." He called Tracy Latimer's murder a "rare act of homicide that was committed for caring and altruistic reasons. That is why for want of a better term this is called compassionate homicide."

Noble also described Latimer's relationship with Tracy as "that of a loving and protective parent" who wanted to end his daughter's suffering. Noble said Latimer "is not a threat to society, nor does he require any rehabilitation."

The Crown argued that Tracy was a relatively cheerful child, and her rights were violated by being killed by her father. According to the Crown brief presented at Latimer's second trial:

"Tracy enjoyed outings, one of which was to the circus, where she smiled when the horses went by. She also responded to visits by her family, smiling and looking happy to see them.

"There is no dispute that through her life, Tracy at times suffered considerable pain. As well, the quality of her life was limited by her severe disability. But the pain she suffered was not unremitting, and her life had value and quality."

Nearly a year later, in November 1998, the Saskatchewan Court of Appeal overturned Noble's ruling, imposing the mandatory minimum sentence: 25 years, with no parole before 10 years.

Then, on January 18, 2001, the Supreme Court of Canada upheld his conviction and life sentence.

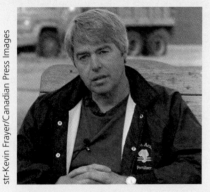

str-Kevin Frayer/Canadian Press Images

Robert Latimer

His first bid for day parole in December 2007 was denied after a hearing at a Victoria prison. However, that decision was overturned two months later, and Latimer was ultimately released for day parole on March 13, 2008.

At the time of the 2001 Supreme Court ruling, critics worried that a decision soft on Latimer would send a signal to many convicted murderers that they, too, may be victims of "cruel and unusual punishment" and are eligible for constitutional exceptions to reduce their mandatory minimum sentences.

In February 2010 the National Parole Board approved Latimer's application to continue day parole in British Columbia, where he was working and studying to become an electrician. Latimer was allowed to be at work or school during the day and return to a halfway house five evenings a week. He asked the Parole Board to reverse those conditions so he could spend five days a week at an apartment he rented and two at the halfway house. In November 2010, Latimer was granted full parole.

Unusual as the Latimer case is, there are related cases, such as battered women who have killed their batterers—often their husbands—and received leniency from the courts. Special legislation is being considered for victims who kill their oppressors, based on self-defence. It's more difficult when the victim, like Tracy Latimer, is so clearly blameless.

An old legal maxim is "Hard cases make bad law." Whether this applies to the case of Robert Latimer remains to be seen.

Think about it:

1. How is it that some people view Robert Latimer as a common criminal, while others see him as a hero? How can otherwise law-abiding citizens condone the killing of a child with severe disabilities?

2. What does the debate over euthanasia have to tell us about the role of law in society and about how laws are made and enforced?

3. What other issues can you identify that are officially law violations but that have numerous proponents?

Source: Adapted from Martin O'Malley and Owen Wood, "'Compassionate Homicide': The Law and Robert Latimer," *CBC News Online*, December 6, 2012, http://www.cbc.ca/news/canada/story/2010/12/06/f-robert-latimer-compassionate-homicide.html [Accessed January 22, 2012]. © CBC News Online.

Social class Distinctions made between individuals on the basis of important defining social characteristics.

Central to the perspective of radical criminology is the notion of **social class** (distinctions made between individuals based on characteristics such as race, religion, education, profession, income, wealth, family background, housing, artistic tastes, aspirations, cultural pursuits, child-rearing habits, speech, and accent). Some maintain that "class is nothing but an abbreviation to describe a way of living, thinking, and feeling."[3] Individuals are assigned to classes by others and by themselves on the basis of characteristics that are both ascribed and achieved. Ascribed attributes are those with which a person is born, such as race or gender, while achieved characteristics are acquired through personal effort or chance over the course of one's life and include such things as level of education, income, place of residence, and profession.

Although Marx concerned himself with only two social classes, most social scientists today talk in terms of at least three groups: upper, middle, and lower classes. Some have distinguished between five hierarchically arranged classes (the real upper, semi-upper, limited-success, working, and real lower) while further subdividing classes "horizontally" according to ascribed characteristics such as race and religion.[4]

Within the discipline of criminology, George Vold helped to create the field of radical criminology. In his 1958 work entitled *Theoretical Criminology*, Vold described crime as the product of political conflict between groups, seeing it as a natural expression of the ongoing struggle for power, control, and material well-being.[5] Conflict is "a universal form of interaction," and groups are naturally in conflict as their interests and purposes "overlap, encroach on one another and (tend to) be competitive."[6] Vold's most succinct observation of the role conflict plays in contributing to crime was expressed in these words: "The whole political process of law making, law breaking, and law enforcement becomes a direct reflection of deep-seated and fundamental conflicts between interest groups. . . . Those who produce legislative majorities win control over the power, and dominate the policies that decide who is likely to be involved in violation of the law."[7]

From Vold's point of view, powerful groups make laws, and those laws express and protect their interests. Hence, the body of laws that characterizes any society is a political statement, and crime is a political definition imposed largely upon those whose interests lie outside of that which the powerful, through the law, define as acceptable. In his writings about conflict, Vold went so far as to compare the criminal to a soldier, fighting, through crime commission, for the very survival of the group whose values he or she represents. Vold's analogy, probably influenced by the fact that he wrote in the wake of World War II, was meant to express the idea that crime is a manifestation of denied needs and values— that is, the cultural heritage of disenfranchised groups who are powerless to enact their interests in legitimate fashion. So, theft becomes necessary for many poor people, especially those left unemployed or unemployable by the socially acceptable forms of wealth distribution defined by law.

Conflict theorists of the early and mid-1900s saw in the concept of social class the rudimentary ingredients of other important concepts like authority, power, and conflict. Ralf Dahrendorf wrote that "classes are social conflict groups the determinant of which can be found in the participation in or exclusion from the exercise of authority."[8] For Dahrendorf, conflict was ubiquitous, fundamental, and coextensive: "Not the presence but the absence of conflict is surprising and abnormal, and we have good reason to be suspicious if we find a society or social organization that displays no evidence of conflict."[9]

From Dahrendorf's perspective, power and authority are most at issue between groups and the cause of class conflicts. It is out of conflict that change—either destructive or constructive—arises. Destructive change brings a lessening of social order, whereas constructive change increases cohesiveness within society.

Another mid-20th-century conflict theorist, Austin Turk, said that in the search for an explanation of criminality, "one is led to investigate the tendency of laws to penalize persons whose behavior is more characteristic of the less powerful than of the more powerful and the extent to which some persons and groups can and do use legal processes and agencies to maintain and enhance their power position vis-à-vis other persons and groups."[10] In his 1969 seminal work, *Criminality and Legal Order*, Turk wrote that in any attempt to explain criminality, "it is more useful to view the social order as mainly a pattern of conflict" rather than to offer explanations for crime based on behavioural or psychological approaches.[11] Turk, like most other conflict criminologists, saw the law as a powerful tool in the service of prominent social groups seeking continued control over others and crime as a natural consequence of such intergroup struggle, resulting from the definitions imposed by the laws of the powerful upon the disapproved strivings of the unempowered.

Radical Criminology Today

⊙┤Watch
Jeffery Reiman
⊙┤Watch
Richard Quinney

Radical criminologists are considerably more sophisticated than their Marxist forebears. Contemporary radical criminology holds that the causes of crime are rooted in social conditions that empower the wealthy and the politically well organized, but disenfranchise those less fortunate. William J. Chambliss, a well-known spokesperson for radical thinkers, summarized the modern perspective in these words: "What makes the behavior of some criminal is the coercive power of the state to enforce the will of the ruling class."[12]

In 1971, Chambliss, along with Robert T. Seidman, published a critically acclaimed volume entitled *Law, Order, and Power*. Their work represented something of a bridge between earlier conflict theorists and the more radical approach of Marxists. Through its emphasis on social class, class interests, and class conflict, *Law, Order, and Power* presented a Marxist perspective stripped of any overt references to capitalism as the root cause of crime. "The more economically stratified a society becomes," Chambliss and Seidman wrote, "the more it becomes necessary for the dominant groups in the society to enforce through coercion the norms of conduct which guarantee their supremacy."[13] Chambliss and Seidman outlined their position in four propositions:[14]

1. The conditions of one's life affect one's values and norms.
2. Complex societies are composed of groups with widely different life conditions and highly disparate and conflicting sets of norms.
3. The probability of a given group's having its particular normative system embodied in law is not distributed equally but is closely related to the political and economic position of that group.
4. The higher a group's political or economic position, the greater the probability that its views will be reflected in laws.

Chambliss also believed that middle- and upper-class criminals are more apt to escape apprehension and punishment by the criminal justice system, not because they are any smarter or more capable of hiding their crimes than are lower-class offenders, but because of a "very rational choice on the part of the legal system to pursue those violators that the community will reward them for pursuing and to ignore those violators who have the capability for causing trouble for the agencies."[15]

By the 1970s, Chambliss's writings assumed a much more Marxist flavour. In a 1975 article, Chambliss once again recognized the huge power gap separating the "haves" from the "have-nots," saying that crime is created by actions of the ruling class, who define as criminal any undertakings and activities contravening their interests yet sometimes violate the criminal law with impunity because it is their own creation.[16]

Soon the Marxist flavour of Chambliss's writing had become undeniable. "As capitalist societies industrialize and the gap between the bourgeoisie and the proletariat widens, penal law will expand in an effort to coerce the proletariat into submission."[17] For Chambliss, the economic consequences of crime within a capitalistic society are partially what perpetuate it. Socialist societies, he wrote, should reflect much lower crime rates than capitalist societies because a "less intense class struggle should reduce the forces leading to and the functions of crime."[18]

Although Chambliss provided much of the intellectual bedrock of contemporary radical criminology, that school of thought found its most eloquent expression in the writings of Richard Quinney, who attempted to challenge and change American social life for the better by setting forth in 1974 his six Marxist propositions for an understanding of crime:[19]

1. American society is based on an advanced capitalist economy.

2. The state is organized to serve the interests of the dominant economic class, the capitalist ruling class.

3. Criminal law is an instrument of the state and ruling class to maintain and perpetuate the existing social and economic order.

4. Crime control in capitalist society is accomplished through a variety of institutions and agencies established and administered by a governmental elite, representing ruling class interests, for the purpose of establishing domestic order.

5. The contradictions of advanced capitalism—the disjunction between existence and essence—require that the subordinate classes remain oppressed by whatever means necessary, especially through the coercion and violence of the legal system.

6. Only with the collapse of capitalist society and the creation of a new society, based on socialist principles, will there be a solution to the crime problem.

A few years later, Quinney published *Class, State, and Crime*, in which he argued that almost all crimes committed by members of the lower classes are necessary for the survival of individual members of those classes and are actually an attempt by the socially disenfranchised "to exist in a society where *survival* is not assured by other, collective means."[20] He concluded, "Crime is inevitable under capitalist conditions" because crime is "a response to the material conditions of life. Permanent unemployment—and the acceptance of that condition—can result in a form of life where criminality is an appropriate and consistent response."[21] The solution offered by Quinney to the problem of crime was the development of a socialist society. "The *ultimate meaning* of crime in the development of capitalism is the need for a socialist society."[22]

Contemporary radical criminology attributes much of the existing propensity toward criminality to differences in social class, and in particular to those arrangements within society that maintain class differences. Quinney explained, "Classes are an expression of the underlying forces of the capitalist mode of production."[23]

Today's radical criminologies can be divided into two schools: structuralist and instrumentalist. **Structural Marxism** sees capitalism as a self-maintaining system in which the law and the justice system work together to perpetuate the existing system of power relationships. Even the rich are subject to certain laws designed to prevent them from engaging in forms of behaviour that might undermine the system of which they are a part. Laws regulating trade practices and monopolies, for example, regulate the behaviour of the powerful and serve to ensure the survival of the capitalist system. **Instrumental Marxism** sees the criminal law and the justice system as tools that the powerful use to control the poor and to keep them disenfranchised. The legal system serves not only to perpetuate the power relationships that exist within society, but also to keep control in the hands of those who are already powerful. A popular book by Jeffrey H. Reiman, entitled *The Rich Get Richer and the Poor Get Prison* is built upon this premise, contending that the criminal justice system is biased against the poor from start to finish and that well-to-do members of society control the criminal justice system from the definition of crime through the process of arrest, trial, and sentencing.[24]

Reiman also claimed that many of the actions taken by well-off people, such as refusal to make workplaces safe, refusal to curtail deadly industrial pollution, promotion of unnecessary surgery, and prescription of unnecessary drugs, should be defined as criminal but

Structural Marxism A perspective that holds that the structural institutions of society influence the behaviour of individuals and groups by virtue of the type of relationships created. The criminal law, for example, reflects class relationships and serves to reinforce those relationships.

Instrumental Marxism A perspective that holds that those in power intentionally create laws and social institutions that serve their own interests and that keep others from becoming powerful.

are not. This kind of self-serving behaviour creates occupational and environmental hazards for the poor and for those who are less well off and produces as much death, destruction, and financial loss as the so-called crimes of the poor.

Critical Criminology

Some writers distinguish between critical criminology and radical criminology, claiming that the former is simply a way of critiquing social relationships leading to crime, whereas the latter constitutes a proactive call for a radical change in the social conditions that lead to crime.

Gresham Sykes explained **critical criminology** this way: "It forces an inquiry into precisely how the normative content of the criminal law is internalized in different segments of society, and how norm-holding is actually related to behavior."[25] As David A. Jones stated in his *History of Criminology*, "Sometimes, it may be difficult to distinguish 'critical' from a truly Marxist criminology. One basis, advanced by Marvin Wolfgang, is that 'critical' criminology is 'more reactive than proactive,' meaning that 'critical' criminology does not aim to overthrow the 'ruling class' so much as it may criticize the way it believes such a group dominates society."[26]

A cogent example of the critical perspective in contemporary criminology can be had in the work of Elliott Currie. Currie, who claimed that "'market societies'—those in which the pursuit of private gain becomes the dominant organizing principle of social and economic life—are especially likely to breed high levels of violent crime."[27] Market societies are characterized by more than free enterprise and a free market economy; they are societies in which the striving after personal economic gain runs rampant and becomes the hallmark of social life. The conditions endemic to market societies lead to high crime rates because they undercut and overwhelm more traditional principles that "have historically sustained individuals, families, and communities." North American society, and the United States in particular, is the world's premier market society and its culture provides "a particularly fertile breeding ground for serious violent crime." According to Currie, seven "profoundly criminogenic and closely intertwined mechanisms" operate in a market society to produce crime:

1. "The progressive destruction of livelihood," which results from the long-term absence of opportunities for stable and rewarding work and is a consequence of the fact that market societies view labour "simply as a cost to be reduced" rather than as an asset with intrinsic value.

2. "The growth of extremes of economic inequality and material deprivation," which causes many children to spend their developmental years in poverty.

3. "The withdrawal of public services and supports, especially for families and children," resulting from the fact that "it is a basic operating principle of market society to keep the public sector small."

4. "The erosion of informal and communal networks of mutual support, supervision, and care," which is brought about by the high mobility of the workforce characteristic of market societies.

5. "The spread of a materialistic, neglectful, and 'hard' culture," which exalts brutal forms of individualized competition.

6. "The unregulated marketing of the technology of violence," which includes ready availability of guns, an emphasis on advancing technologies of destruction (such as the military), and mass-marketed violence on television and in other media.

7. "The weakening of social and political alternatives," which leaves people unable to cope effectively with the forces of the market society, undermines their communities, and destroys valuable interpersonal relationships.

Currie suggested that as more nations emulate the "market society" culture of the United States, crime rates throughout the world will rise, and that an increasing emphasis

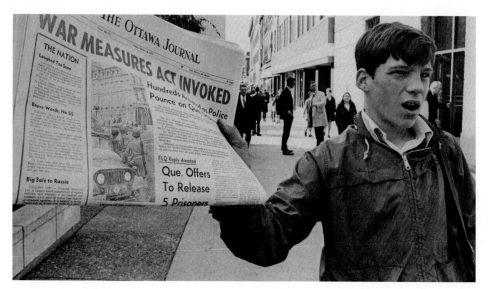

In October 1970, the Front de libération du Québec (FLQ) kidnapped British diplomat James Cross and murdered Quebec cabinet minister Pierre Laporte to bring attention to its struggle for independence for French-speaking Quebec. The Canadian government responded by invoking the *War Measures Act*. How would the radical criminology perspective interpret the actions of the FLQ? The Canadian government?

Peter Bregg/Canadian Press Images

on punishment and the growth of huge prison systems will consequently characterize most of the world's nations in the 21st century.

Critique of Radical Criminology

10.3 LEARNING OBJECTIVE

Radical criminology has been criticized for its nearly exclusive emphasis on methods of social change at the expense of well-developed theory. As William Pelfrey stated, "It is in the Radical School of Criminology that theory is almost totally disregarded, except as something to criticize, and radical methods are seen as optimum."[28]

Radical criminology can also be criticized for failing to recognize what appears to be at least a fair degree of public consensus about the nature of crime—that is, that crime is undesirable and that criminal activity is to be controlled. If criminal activity was a true expression of the sentiments of the politically and economically disenfranchised, as some radical criminologists claim, then public opinion might be expected to offer support for at least certain forms of crime, but even the sale of illicit drugs (a type of crime that may provide an alternative path to riches for the otherwise disenfranchised) is frequently condemned by residents of working-class communities.[29]

An effective criticism of Marxist criminology, in particular, centres on the fact that Marxist thinkers appear to confuse issues of personal politics with what could otherwise be social reality, allowing personal values and political leanings to enter the criminological arena and sacrificing their objectivity. Jackson Toby claimed that Marxist and radical thinkers are simply building upon an "old tradition of sentimentality toward those who break social rules."[30] Such sentimentality can be easily discounted when we realize that "color television sets and automobiles are stolen more often than food and blankets."[31]

Marxist criminology has also been refuted by contemporary thinkers who find that it falls short in appreciating the multiplicity of problems that contribute to the problem of crime. Some years ago, for example, Hermann Mannheim critiqued Marxist assumptions by showing how "subsequent developments" have revealed that "Marx was wrong in thinking" in several areas: (1) that "there could be only two classes in a capitalist society," (2) that "class struggle was entirely concerned with the question of private property in the means of production," (3) that "the only way in which fundamental social changes could be effected was by violent social revolution," and (4) that "all conflicts were class conflicts and all social change could be explained in terms of class conflicts."[32] Mannheim also pointed out that the development of a semi-skilled workforce along with the advent of highly skilled and well-educated workers has led to the creation of a multiplicity of classes within contemporary capitalistic societies. The growth of such classes, said Mannheim, effectively spreads the available wealth in those societies where such workers are employed and reduces the likelihood of revolution.

Marxist criminology has suffered a considerable loss of prestige among many would-be followers in the wake of the collapse of the former Soviet Union and its client states in Eastern Europe and other parts of the world and seems to have lost some of its impetus. Many would argue that, in fact, the work of writers such as Quinney and Chambliss presaged the decline of Soviet influence and had already moved Marxist and radical criminology into new areas. The work of Currie and others has since led in a post-Marxist direction while retaining a critical emphasis on the principles out of which radical criminology was fashioned. Today's radical criminologists have largely rescinded calls for revolutionary change and escalated their demands for the eradication of gender, racial, and other inequalities within the criminal justice system; the elimination of prisons; the abolition of capital punishment; and an end to police misconduct.

Emerging Conflict Theories

The radical ideas associated with mid-20th-century Marxist criminology contributed to the formation of a number of new and innovative approaches to crime and criminology, such as left-realist criminology, feminist criminology, and peacemaking criminology (including restorative justice). It is to these perspectives that we now turn our attention.

Left-realist criminology A conflict perspective that insists on a pragmatic assessment of crime and its associated problems.

Left-Realist Criminology **Left-realist criminology** is a natural outgrowth of practical concerns with street crime, the fear of crime, and everyday victimization. Left-realist criminology faults radical-critical criminologists for romanticizing street crime and the criminals who commit it. It does not reject the conflict perspective inherent in radical-critical criminology, but rather shifts the centre of focus onto a pragmatic assessment of crime and the needs of crime victims, seeking to portray crime in terms understandable to those most often affected by it—victims and their families, offenders, and criminal justice personnel. The test insisted upon by realist criminology is not whether a particular perspective on crime control or an explanation of crime causation complies with rigorous academic criteria, but whether the perspective speaks meaningfully to those faced with crime on a daily basis. "For realists crime is no less harmful to its victims because of its socially constructed origins."[33]

Left-realist criminology is generally considered synonymous with left realism (also called *radical realism* or *critical realism*) but tends to distance itself from some of the more visionary claims of early radical and Marxist theory.[34]

Daniel J. Curran and Claire M. Renzetti portrayed left realism as a natural consequence of increasingly conservative attitudes toward crime and criminals in both Europe and North America: "Though not successful in converting many radicals to the right, this new conservatism did lead a number of radical criminologists to temper their views a bit and to take what some might call a less romanticized look at street crime."[35]

Some authors have credited Walter DeKeseredy[36] with popularizing left-realist notions in North America, and Jock Young[37] has been identified as a major source of left-realist writings in England. Prior to the writings of DeKeseredy and Young, radical criminology, with its emphasis upon the crime-inducing consequences of existing power structures, tended to portray the ruling class as the "real criminals" and saw street criminals as social rebels who were acting out of felt deprivation. In contrast, DeKeseredy and Young were successful in refocusing leftist theories onto the serious consequences of street crime and upon the crimes of the lower classes. Left realists argued that victims of crime are often the poor and disenfranchised who fall prey to criminals with similar backgrounds and saw the criminal justice system and its agents not as pawns of the powerful, but rather as institutions that could offer useful services if modifications were made to reduce their use of force and increase their sensitivity toward the public.

A central tenet of left realism is the claim that radical ideas must be translated into realistic social policies if contemporary criminology is to have any practical relevance. Concrete suggestions with respect to community policing models are indicative of the direction left realists are headed. Instead of seeing the police as oppressors working on behalf of the state, left realists recommend that police work with, and answer to, the communities they serve.[38] The major goal of left realism is to achieve "a fair and orderly society" through a practical emphasis on social justice.[39]

Critique of Left-Realist Criminology Left-realist criminology has been convincingly criticized for representing more of an ideological emphasis than a theory. As Don C. Gibbons explained, "Left realism can best be described as a general perspective centered on injunctions to 'take crime seriously' and to 'take crime control seriously' rather than as a well-developed criminological perspective."[40] Realist criminologists appear to build upon pre-existing theoretical frameworks, but rarely offer new propositions or hypotheses that are testable. They do, however, frequently suggest crime-control approaches that are in keeping with the needs of the victimized. Policies promulgated by left realists understandably include an emphasis on community policing, neighbourhood justice centres, and dispute-resolution mechanisms. Piers Beirne and James W. Messerschmidt summarized the situation this way: "What left realists have essentially accomplished is an attempt to theorize about conventional crime realistically while simultaneously developing a 'radical law and order' program for curbing such behavior."[41]

10.3 | LEARNING OBJECTIVE

Feminist Criminology As some writers have observed, "Women have been virtually invisible in criminological analysis until recently and much theorizing has proceeded as though criminality is restricted to men."[42] Others have put it this way: "Criminological theory assumes a woman is like a man."[43] But beginning in the 1970s, advances in feminist theory were applied to criminology, resulting in what has been called a **feminist criminology** (a model redirecting criminologists' thinking to include gender awareness).

Feminism is a way of seeing the world, not a sexual orientation. To be a feminist is to "combine a female mental perspective with a sensitivity for those social issues that influence primarily women."[44] Central to understanding feminist thought is the realization that feminism views gender in terms of power relationships. According to feminist approaches, men have traditionally held much more power in the patriarchal structure of Western society than women and have excluded women from much decision making in socially significant areas, and sexist attitudes—deeply ingrained notions of male superiority—have perpetuated inequality between the sexes. The consequences of sexism and the unequal gender-based distribution of power have been far-reaching, affecting fundamental aspects of social roles and personal expectations at all levels.

Five strands of feminist thought inform feminist criminology today: liberal feminism, radical feminism, Marxist feminism, socialist feminism, and postmodern feminism. Each of these perspectives argues that conflict in society is based on inequalities focused around issues of gender.

Liberal feminism sees gender-role socialization as the primary source of women's oppression.[45] Liberal feminists describe a power-based and traditional domination of women's bodies and minds by men throughout history and blame present inequalities on the development within culture and society of "separate and distinct spheres of influence and traditional attitudes about the appropriate role of men and women."[46] Liberal feminists call for elimination of traditional divisions of power and labour between the sexes as a way of eliminating inequality and promoting social harmony.

⊙ Watch
What is "Social" about Sexuality?

⊙ Watch
Social Norms and Conformity

Feminist criminology A self-conscious corrective model intended to redirect the thinking of mainstream criminologists to include gender awareness.

Liberal feminism A perspective that holds that gender-role socialization is the primary source of women's oppression.

Radical feminism sees **patriarchy**, or male dominance, as the cause of women's oppression, depicting men as being fundamentally brutish, aggressive, and violent and controlling women through sexuality by taking advantage of both women's biological dependence during childbearing years and their lack of physical strength relative to men. The exploitation of women by men triggers women's deviant behaviour, because young women who are sexually or physically exploited may run away or abuse substances and become criminalized, so the elimination of male domination should reduce crime rates for women and "even precipitate a decrease in male violence against women."[47]

The oppression of women caused by their subordinate working-class status in capitalist societies is the main tenet of **Marxist feminism**. Within capitalist society, women may be drawn into crime commission in an effort to support themselves and their children; men commit violent street crimes more often, whereas women commit property and vice crimes.[48]

Socialist feminism, a fourth perspective, sees gender oppression as a consequence of the interaction between the economic structure of society and gender-based roles. Egalitarian societies would be built around socialist or Marxist principles with the aim of creating a society that is free of gender and class divisions.

The social construction of concepts typically used in any discussion of criminology—including concepts like justice and crime—are questioned by **postmodern feminism**. According to criminologist Amanda Burgess-Proctor, postmodern feminism departs from the other feminist perspectives by questioning the existence of any one "truth," including "women's oppression," and "postmodern feminists reject fixed categories and universal concepts in favor of multiple truths and as such examine the effects of discourse and symbolic representation on claims about knowledge."[49]

Feminist criminology points out the inequities inherent in patriarchal forms of thought. Patriarchy can be defined as a "set of social relations of power in which the male gender appropriates the labour power of women and controls their sexuality."[50] Early works in the field of feminist criminology include Freda Adler's *Sisters in Crime*[51] and Rita J. Simon's *Women and Crime*,[52] both published in 1975. In these books, the authors attempted to explain existing divergences in crime rates between men and women as being due primarily to socialization rather than biology. Women were taught to believe in personal limitations, faced reduced socio-economic opportunities, and, as a result, suffered from lower aspirations. As gender equality increased, these authors said, it could be expected that male and female criminality would take on similar characteristics, but such has not been the case and the approach of Adler and Simon has not been validated by observations surrounding increased gender equality over the past few decades. Another early work, *Women, Crime and Criminology*, published in 1977 by British sociologist Carol Smart, sensitized criminologists to sexist traditions within the field.[53] Smart pointed out that men and women perceive and experience the world in different ways. She showed how important it is for women to have a voice in interpreting the behaviour of other women, as opposed to having the behaviour of other women interpreted from a male standpoint.

Early feminist theorizing may not have borne the fruit that some researchers anticipated, but it has led to a heightened awareness of gender issues within criminology. Two of the most insightful proponents of the usefulness of applying feminist thinking to criminological analysis, Kathleen Daly and Meda Chesney-Lind, pointed out that "gender differences in crime suggest that crime may not be so normal after all."[54] Traditional understandings about what is "typical" about crime are derived from a study of men only, or, more precisely, from that relatively small group of men who commit crimes. In general terms, Daly and Chesney-Lind identified the following five elements of feminist thought that set it apart from other types of social and political thought:[55]

1. Gender is not a natural fact but a complex social, historical, and cultural product that is related to, not simply derived from, biological sex differences and differing reproductive capacities.

2. Gender and gender relations order social life and social institutions in fundamental ways.

3. Gender relations and constructs of masculinity and femininity are not symmetrical but are based on an organizing principle of men's superiority and their socio- and political-economic dominance over women.

4. Systems of knowledge reflect men's views of the natural and social world; the production of knowledge is gendered.

5. Women should be at the centre, not the periphery, of intellectual inquiry; they should not be invisible or treated as appendages to men.

In a more recent analysis of feminist criminology, Susan Caulfield and Nancy Wonders described "five major contributions that have been made to criminological thinking by feminist scholarship and practice":[56] (1) a focus on gender as a central organizing principle of contemporary life; (2) an awareness of the importance of power in shaping social relationships; (3) a heightened sensitivity to the way in which social context helps shape human relationships; (4) the recognition that social reality must be understood as a process, and that the development of research methods must take this into account; and (5) a commitment to social change as a crucial part of feminist scholarship and practice.[57] John Hagan built upon defining features of power relationships in his book *Structural Criminology*, in which he explained that power relationships existing in the wider society are effectively "brought home" to domestic settings and are reflected in everyday relationships between men, women, and children within the context of family life.[58] Hagan's approach, termed *power-control theory*, suggested that "family class structure shapes the social reproduction of gender relations, and in turn the social distribution of delinquency."[59] In most middle- and upper-middle-class families, said Hagan, a paternalistic model, in which the father works and the mother supervises the children, is the norm. Under the paternalistic model, girls are controlled by both parents—through male domination and by female role modelling. Boys, however, are less closely controlled and are relatively free to deviate from social norms, resulting in higher levels of delinquency among males. In lower-middle- and lower-class families, however, the paternalistic model is frequently absent.

In a work supportive of Hagan's thesis, Evelyn K. Sommers recently conducted a series of four hour-long interviews with 14 female inmates in a Canadian medium-security prison.[60] Focusing on what led to violations of the criminal law, Sommers identified four common themes to explain the criminality of the women she interviewed: (1) economic and financial need, (2) drug involvement, (3) personal anger rooted in sexual and physical abuse or a sense of loss, and (4) fear. Because "need" was identified as the cause of law-breaking behaviour by the majority of the women interviewed, Sommers concluded that women's criminality is based on two underlying issues: the effort to maintain connection within relationships (such as between mother and child) and a personal quest for empowerment (as single mothers are expected to be independent and capable of providing for themselves and their children).

In a cogent analysis encompassing much of contemporary feminist theory, Daly and Chesney-Lind suggested that feminist thought is more important for the way it informs and challenges existing criminology than for the new theories it offers. Much current feminist thought within criminology emphasizes the need for gender awareness. Theories of crime causation and prevention, it is suggested, must include women, and more research on gender-related issues in the field is badly needed. Daly and Chesney-Lind explained that "criminologists should begin to appreciate that their discipline and its questions are

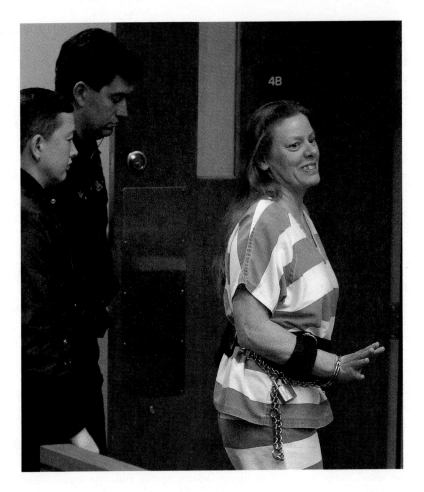

Aileen Wuornos, convicted female serial killer. Although some women are moving into areas of traditional male criminality, the number of women committing most forms of crime is still far lower than that of men. How does the criminality of women appear to differ from that of men?

Doug Engle/AP Photo

a product of white, economically privileged men's experiences"[61] and that rates of female criminality, which are lower than those of males, may highlight the fact that criminal behaviour is not as "normal" as once thought. Because modern-day criminological perspectives were mostly developed by Caucasian, middle-class men, the propositions and theories they advanced failed to take into consideration women's "ways of knowing."[62] Hence, the fundamental challenge posed by feminist criminology is this: Do existing theories of crime causation apply as well to women as they do to men? Or, as Daly and Chesney-Lind asked, given the current situation in theory development, "Do theories of men's crime apply to women?"[63]

Other feminists have analyzed the process by which laws are created and legislation passed and concluded that modern-day statutes frequently represent characteristically masculine modes of thought. Such analysts have concluded that existing criminal laws are overly rational and hierarchically structured, reflecting traditionally male ways of organizing the social world.[64] Until recently, many jurisdictions viewed assault victims differently based on the gendered relationships involved in the offence. *Assault* is defined as an attack by one person upon another, but until the last few decades of the 20th century, domestic violence statutes tended to downplay the seriousness of the attacks involved, giving the impression that because they occurred within the home and the victims were typically women, they weren't as important to the justice system as other forms of assault. Similarly, some have argued that legal definitions of such behaviours as prostitution, pornography, and sexual assault are defined primarily by men's understanding of the behaviour in question and not by the experiences of women. Hence, in traditional criminology, women receive protection because they are considered vulnerable to crime, but the experiences of women do not define the nature of the law or of the justice system's response. Consequently, some analysts have suggested, existing laws need to be replaced by, or complemented with, "a system of justice based upon ... the specifically feminine principles of care, connection, and community."[65]

In the area of social policy, feminist thinkers have pointed to the need for increased controls over men's violence toward women, the creation of alternatives (to supplement the home and traditional family structures) for women facing abuse, and the protection of children. They have also questioned the role of government, culture, and the mass media in promulgating pornography, prostitution, and sexual assault and have generally portrayed ongoing crimes against women as characteristic of continuing traditions in which women are undervalued and controlled. Many radical feminists have suggested the replacement of men with women in positions of power, especially within the justice system and government organizations, while others have noted that such a replacement still would not address needed changes in the structure of the system itself, which is gender-biased due to years of male domination. Centrists, on the other hand, have offered a more balanced approach, believing that individuals of both genders have much to contribute to a workable justice system.[66]

Critique of Feminist Criminology Some would argue that in the area of theoretical development, feminist criminology has yet to live up to its promise because few comprehensive feminist theories of crime were proposed; feminist criminology focused instead on descriptive studies of female involvement in crime.[67] Male violence against women was seen as adding support to the central tenet of feminist criminology (that the relationship between the sexes is primarily characterized by the exercise of power), but that did not make for broad theory building. As one writer explained regarding the current state of feminist criminology, "Feminist theory is a theory in formation."[68] A fair assessment of the current situation would probably conclude that the greatest contributions of feminist thought to criminological theory building are yet to come.

10.3 | **LEARNING OBJECTIVE**

Feminist criminology has faced criticism from many other directions. Predicted increases in female crime rates have failed to materialize as social opportunities available to both genders have become more balanced. The gender gap in crime—with males accounting for much more law violation than females—continues to exist. Other critics have pointed to fundamental flaws in feminist thought, asking questions such as, "If men have more power than women, then why are so many more men arrested?"[69] Where studies do exist, gender disparities in arrest are rarely found, nor do sentencing practices seem to favour women.[70] The chivalry hypothesis of many years ago, under which it was proposed that women are apt to be treated more leniently by the justice system because of their gender, does not appear to operate today.[71]

Some critics have even argued that a feminist criminology is impossible. Daly and Chesney-Lind, for example, agreed that although feminist thought may inform criminology, "a feminist criminology cannot exist because neither feminism nor criminology is a unified set of principles and practices."[72] A criminology built solely on feminist principles is unlikely because neither feminist thought nor criminology meets the strict requirements of formal theory building.

Peacemaking Criminology

Throughout much of history, formal agencies of social control—the police, officials of the courts, and corrections personnel—have been seen as pitted against criminal perpetrators and would-be wrongdoers. Crime control has been traditionally depicted in terms of a kind of epic struggle in which diametrically opposed antagonists continuously engage one another, but in which only one side can emerge as victorious. Another point of view has come to the fore: **peacemaking criminology**, a form of criminology that has its roots in Christian and Eastern philosophies and advances the notion that crime-control agencies and the citizens they serve should work together to alleviate social problems and human suffering and thus reduce crime.[73]

Peacemaking criminology A perspective that holds that crime-control agencies and the citizens they serve should work together to alleviate social problems and human suffering and thus reduce crime.

Peacemaking criminology, which includes the notion of service, has also been called *compassionate criminology* and suggests that "compassion, wisdom, and love are essential for understanding the suffering of which we are all a part and for practising a criminology of nonviolence."[74]

Peacemaking criminology was popularized by the works of Harold E. Pepinsky[75] and Richard Quinney[76] beginning in 1986. Both Pepinsky and Quinney restated the problem of crime control from one of how to stop crime to one of how to make peace within society and between citizens and criminal justice agencies. Peacemaking criminology draws attention to many issues: (1) perpetuation of violence through the continuation of social policies based on dominant forms of criminological theory; (2) role of education in peacemaking; (3) common-sense theories of crime; (4) crime control as human rights enforcement; and (5) conflict resolution within community settings.[77]

Common-sense theories of crime are derived from everyday experience and beliefs and are characteristic of the "person in the street." Unfortunately, in the view of peacemaking criminologists, fanciful common-sense theories all too often provide the basis for criminological investigations, which in turn offer support for the naïve theories themselves. One common-sense theory criticized by peacemaking criminologists is the "black-male-as-savage theory,"[78] which holds that men of African descent are far more crime-prone than their Caucasian counterparts. Such a perspective, frequently given added credence by official interpretations of criminal-incidence data, only increases the crime-control challenge by further distancing these males from government-sponsored crime-prevention policies. A genuine concern for the problems facing all citizens, according to peacemaking criminologists, would more effectively serve the ends of crime control.

Richard Quinney and John Wildeman summarized well the underpinnings of peacemaking criminology by stating that "a criminology of peacemaking—a nonviolent criminology of compassion and service—seeks to end suffering and thereby eliminate crime."[79]

Other contributors to the peacemaking movement include Bo Lozoff, Michael Braswell, and Clemmons Bartollas. In *Inner Corrections*, Lozoff and Braswell claimed that "we are fully aware by now that the criminal justice system in this country is founded on violence. It is a system that assumes that violence can be overcome by

The principles of restorative justice are reflected in community sentencing conferences such as the one shown here at the Aboriginal Ganootamaage Justice Service Centre in Winnipeg, Manitoba. Do you think this approach is more effective at controlling crime than the adversarial approach? Why or why not?

Joe Bryksa/Canadian Press Images

violence, evil by evil. Criminal justice at home and warfare abroad are of the same principle of violence. This principle sadly dominates much of our criminology."[80] *Inner Corrections*, which is primarily a compilation of previous works on compassion and prison experience, provides meditative techniques and prayers for those seeking to become more compassionate and includes a number of letters from inmates who demonstrate the book's philosophy.

In a work entitled "Correctional Treatment, Peacemaking, and the New Age Movement," Bartollas and Braswell applied New Age principles to correctional treatment:[81] "Most offenders suffered abusive and deprived childhoods. Treatment that focuses on the inner child and such qualities as forgiveness and self-esteem could benefit offenders."[82] In a fundamental sense, peacemaking criminologists exhort their colleagues to transcend personal dichotomies to end the political and ideological divisiveness that separates people.

Restorative Justice Peacemaking criminology suggests that effective crime prevention can best be achieved by the adoption of a **peace model** based on cooperation rather than on retribution and focused on effective ways of developing a shared consensus on critical issues that have the potential to seriously affect the quality of life. Major issues include crimes like murder and sexual assault but extend to property rights, rights to the use of new technologies, and the ownership of information; minor issues, including sexual preference, non-violent sexual deviance, gambling, drug use, noise, child-custody claims, and publicly offensive behaviour, can be dealt with in ways that require few resources beyond those immediately available in the community.

Peace model An approach to crime control that focuses on effective ways for developing a shared consensus on critical issues that have the potential to seriously affect the quality of life.

The concept of **restorative justice** stems from these notions of cooperation and reconciliation rather than from retribution and punishment. The Canadian criminologist Ezzat Fattah has been a proponent of alternative forms of justice for several decades. In an article entitled "Restorative and Retributive Justice Models: A Comparison," Fattah critically examined the ineffectiveness of the punishment model.[83] He argued that the punishment model is a costly one, with incarceration being the most expensive sentencing option. Moreover, punishment serves only to treat human beings as a means to an end since it has little positive effect on those being punished. Even though the public and the victim may feel somewhat vindicated by a harsh punitive sentence, punishment, Fattah contended, does nothing to assist either in the healing process. It is toward the goal of healing that the restorative-justice approach reaches.

Restorative justice A perspective that stresses remedies and restoration rather than prison, punishment, and neglect of victims.

Restorative justice is defined as an approach to justice that focuses on dealing with the harmful effects of crime by engaging victims, offenders, and the community in a process of reparation and healing. The pain and suffering of victims is central to defining the harm that has resulted from the crime and the manner in which it is to be resolved. The community is active in offering support to victims and in holding offenders accountable for their crimes while giving the offenders the opportunity to make amends.[84]

Whereas the traditional adversarial system of justice defines crime as a violation of rules and a harm to the state, the restorative-justice approach views crime as a harm done to the victim and the community. The adversarial system blames and punishes the offender and assumes a win–loss outcome; the restorative-justice approach looks to a win–win outcome by focusing on the process of problem solving, including the reintegration of the offender into the community and the preservation of his or her dignity.

Restorative-justice models are not new. In Canada, Australia, and the United States, Aboriginal groups have traditionally practised what is commonly referred to as **circle sentencing conferences**, which are based on traditional Aboriginal principles of peacemaking, mediation, and consensus building. Sentencing circles involve participation by the judge, victim, offender, family or supporters, elders, and other justice and community

Circle sentencing conferences Groups of community members who actively assist justice authorities by participating in discussions about available sentencing options and plans to reintegrate the offender back into the community.

representatives. Each has input, and the needs of each are considered equally important and worthy of representation. The conference results in sentencing recommendations, which are passed on to the judge with a view to ensuring the protection of the community, healing the victim, and rehabilitating the offender. The judge may accept or reject the recommendations, and community members are responsible for ensuring that the eventual sentence is carried out.

Circle sentencing conferences have been revived in many parts of Canada. Introduced in Yukon, they have become more widely used in other parts of the country, primarily in rural communities. Programs such as the Peigan Nation Youth Traditional Justice Circle on the Peigan Reserve near Lethbridge, Alberta, enable adult and youth criminals to access the circle through pre- or post-charge diversion or even after a guilty plea is entered. The recommendations of the circle are forwarded to the Crown prosecutor, who then endeavours to have the presiding judge incorporate them into the court's final decision. In this way, the circle works in conjunction with the existing criminal justice system. Crown prosecutors screen cases coming through the courts and select those that appear suitable for referral to the circle. It is ultimately the circle's decision whether it wishes to accept any case. Interestingly, in cases where the Crown feels that a sentence of incarceration is warranted, the circle is advised of this at the time of referral. If the circle decides to accept the referral, it will often make a recommendation to the court that will not contradict the Crown's position, thereby ensuring that the court will not have to make a decision contrary to the wishes of the circle.[85]

The principles of restorative justice can be seen in a number of other Canadian criminal justice initiatives. The first **Victim–Offender Reconciliation Program (VORP)** was established by the Mennonite community in Kitchener, Ontario, in 1974, and the model spread rapidly, in various forms, throughout Canada, the United States, and Europe. There are now dozens of programs across Canada, hundreds in the United States, and more than 500 throughout Europe.[86] Based on mediation and alternative dispute resolution principles, the VORP involves face-to-face meetings between victim and offender, facilitated by a trained mediator, to discuss the events of the crime and its effects and reach an agreed-upon outcome. The program is usually used with young offenders, in the post-charge phase of the criminal justice process or as an alternative measure. The proliferation of community and neighbourhood justice centres has enabled expansion of VORPs and other similar mediation and dispute resolution programs that deal with both criminal and civil cases.

Since the inception of VORPs, restorative-justice principles have been manifest in a number of other criminal justice initiatives. **Family group conferencing** provides a forum for dealing with unanswered questions, emotions, and the victim's right to restitution and reparation resulting from a crime. These conferences involve participation of the victim, the offender, and their family members and supporters. **Community sentencing panels** are composed of volunteers from the community and focus on restorative measures such as restitution, reparation, mediation, and victim involvement. These panels also consider crime prevention by addressing social factors that may contribute to crime. The principles of **community policing**, which emphasize a proactive approach to law enforcement through the establishment of partnerships with the community, can be seen to be compatible with much of the philosophy of restorative justice. The community policing approach has been formally adopted by the Royal Canadian Mounted Police and the Ontario Provincial Police and is practised by most police services across Canada.

The restorative-justice philosophy has been embraced and endorsed by all levels of government in Canada as well as by voluntary and community organizations. The federal department Public Safety Canada and the Department of Justice Canada, along

Victim–Offender Reconciliation Program (VORP) A program that gives the offender the opportunity to meet face-to-face with the victim in the presence of a trained mediator in an attempt to reduce the victim's fears while establishing accountability and reparation for the crime.

Family group conferencing A forum for dealing with unanswered questions, emotions, and the victim's right to restitution and reparation resulting from a crime.

Community sentencing panels Groups composed of volunteers from the community who focus on restorative measures such as restitution, reparation, mediation, and victim involvement.

Community policing A philosophy of policing involving proactive collaboration between the police and the community to prevent and respond to crime and other community problems.

with the National Parole Board and Correctional Service of Canada, are exploring the scope of restorative approaches and developing strategies for implementing them. Restorative Resolutions is a community-based sentencing program that has been operating in Winnipeg, Manitoba since 1993. It is a unique partnership between the John Howard Society of Manitoba and the province of Manitoba's Department of Justice. The high success rate of the program, as demonstrated by its consistently low recidivism rate, can be attributed to a blend of restorative justice principles along with the "what works model" of intervention providing a viable and more effective alternative to incarceration.

Clients must be facing a minimum sentence of six months to be considered. The key to acceptance into the program is a client's willingness to take responsibility for his or her actions by pleading guilty and making a commitment to try to repair the harm done to the victim and the community as a whole. Restorative practices usually take the form of letters of apology to victims, direct restitution paid to victims and community service work. In terms of intervention, clients often take part in groups which are cognitive behavioural and provide them with tools to connect how they think impacts how they feel which impacts how they behave and victim empathy. Experience demonstrates that clients do make pro-social lifestyle changes more readily after the education and support from a group setting. However, the one-to-one work between client and Restorative Resolutions staff also addresses issues related to education and employment, relationships, attitudes, companions, leisure and recreation, addictions, and social patterns. Restorative Resolutions clients are involved in treatment programs, educational upgrading, and/or employment searches. It is always up to the victims to decide how much or even if they want to be involved in the process. Victims who do participate give the program high satisfaction marks and report feeling well served by the program.

One client of the program, reflecting on her experience in the program, stated,

> Going to jail would have been easier for me because I would not have had to be accountable for what I'd done. Restorative Resolutions challenged me to be honest with myself and others for the first time in my life. They forced me to figure out the real reasons why I did what I did, whom I had hurt, what I needed to do to fix it, and most important, how not to fall back into that destructive pattern. My victims now receive money from me on a monthly basis.[87*]

Alternative dispute resolution is another example of the restorative-justice approach and peacemaking perspective. Mediation programs such as dispute-resolution centres are characterized by cooperative efforts to reach dispute resolution rather than by the adversarial proceedings characteristic of most Canadian courts. Dispute-resolution programs are based on the principle of **participatory justice**, in which all parties to a dispute accept a kind of binding arbitration by neutral parties.

The Ontario Mandatory Mediation Program, operating in a number of centres across Ontario, is designed to help parties involved in civil litigation and estate matters attempt to settle their cases before they get to trial. Under this program, cases are referred to a mediation session early in the litigation process to give parties an opportunity to discuss the issues in dispute. With the assistance of a trained mediator, the parties explore settlement options and may be able to avoid the pre-trial and trial process. The benefits of the program include resolutions that are tailored to the needs of the parties and a greater sense of satisfaction because participants play an active role in resolving their dispute rather than having a solution determined by a judge.

The restorative-justice approach has often been criticized for its vagueness of definition and direction. The term *community*, for example, is an abstract one and has been used indiscriminately. Not all communities are clearly defined, nor are they all capable of engaging in partnerships that will sustain a restorative-justice approach;

Participatory justice A relatively informal type of justice case processing which makes use of local community resources rather than requiring traditional forms of official intervention.

---

*Excerpted with permission from The John Howard Society of Manitoba, Inc., www.johnhoward.mb.ca/pages/home.php [Accessed January 24, 2012].

for some, involving the community in restorative justice is seen as a "quick fix" for a crime issue that may require a more traditional approach. Some critics claim that the lack of due process and unclear legal procedures all serve to render the restorative-justice approach ineffective. Concern around disparity of sentencing has been raised, especially if not all accused persons are afforded access to restorative-justice programs. Whether or not power imbalances between those in positions of authority and the accused can be rectified to allow for the true implementation of restorative-justice initiatives has been questioned as well. Finally, some critics charge that existing structural and legislative realities restrict or prevent widespread acceptance of the restorative-justice approach. Table 10.2 compares retributive- and restorative-justice approaches.

10.3 LEARNING OBJECTIVE

Critique of Peacemaking Criminology Peacemaking criminology has been criticized as being naïve and utopian and for failing to recognize the realities of crime control and law enforcement, because few victims would expect to gain much during the victimization process from attempting to make peace with their victimizers (although such strategies do occasionally work). Such criticisms may be improperly directed at a level of analysis that peacemaking criminologists have not assumed. While it involves work with individual offenders, peacemaking criminology envisions positive change on the societal and institutional levels and does not suggest to victims that they attempt to effect personal changes in offenders.

Table 10.2 Differences between Retributive and Restorative Justice

Retributive Justice	Restorative Justice
Crime is an act against the state, a violation of a law, an abstract idea.	Crime is an act against another person or the community.
The criminal justice system controls crime.	Crime control lies primarily with the community.
Offender accountability is defined as taking punishment.	Offender accountability is defined as assuming responsibility and taking action to repair harm.
Crime is an individual act with individual responsibility.	Crime has both individual and social dimensions of responsibility.
Victims are peripheral to the process of resolving a crime.	Victims are central to the process of resolving a crime.
The offender is defined by deficits.	The offender is defined by the capacity to make reparation.
The emphasis is on adversarial relationships.	The emphasis is on dialogue and negotiation.
Pain is imposed to punish, deter, and prevent.	Restitution is a means of restoring both parties; the goal is reconciliation.
The community is on the sidelines, represented abstractly by the state.	The community is the facilitator in the restorative process.
The response is focused on the offender's past behaviour.	The response is focused on harmful consequences of the offender's behaviour; the emphasis is on the future and on reparation.
There is dependence on criminal justice professionals.	There is direct involvement by both the offender and the victim.

Source: Adapted from Gordon Bazemore and Mark S. Umbreit, *Balanced and Restorative Justice: Program Summary* (Washington, DC: Office of Juvenile Justice and Delinquency Prevention, 1994), p. 7.

POLICY IMPLICATIONS OF SOCIAL CONFLICT THEORIES

THE POLICY IMPLICATIONS OF THE SOCIAL CONFLICT THEORY ARE FAIRLY CLEAR: bring about social change and redistribute the wealth in society, and crime rates will fall. At one extreme, radical-Marxist criminologists argue that the only effective way of reducing conflict is through a total dismantling of the existing capitalist state and its replacement by a socialist economic structure. Most radical-critical criminologists of today have come to recognize that this is highly unlikely. As a consequence, such theorists have begun to focus on promoting a gradual transition to socialism and to socialized forms of government activity. These middle-range policy alternatives include "equal justice in the bail system, the abolition of mandatory sentences, prosecution of corporate crimes, increased employment opportunities, and promoting community alternatives to imprisonment."[88] Likewise, programs to reduce prison overcrowding, efforts to highlight injustices within the current system, the elimination of racism and other forms of inequality in the handling of both victims and offenders, growing equality in criminal justice system employment, and the like are all frequently mentioned as mid-range strategies for bringing about a justice system that is more fair and closer to the radical ideal.

At the other extreme are the calls of peacemaking criminologists for a practical application of the principles of conflict resolution. Between these two extremes lie left-realist and feminist criminology; the solutions they offer vary from the reduction of paternalism to a practical recognition of the consequences of crime to victims.

SOCIAL CONFLICT THEORIES APPLIED

RADICAL CRIMINOLOGY

holds that the causes of crime are rooted in social conditions that empower the wealthy and the politically well organized, but disenfranchise those less fortunate. In the Oka crisis, the city of Oka, supported by the army and the police, is considered to be the "haves," while the members of the Mohawk Nation are the "have-nots."

Crime is a result of constant conflict and struggle between groups attempting to promote their own disparate interests. These groups have different amounts of power, and as the groups struggle for power, conflict ensues, which promotes crime.

How can the Oka crisis be explained using the social conflict perspective?

FEMINIST CRIMINOLOGY

holds that the conflict and inequality in society are based on gender. Women are more likely to be victims of crime, and females who commit crime do so for different reasons and are treated differently by the criminal justice system. The crisis in Oka would equate the lack of rights afforded to First Nations peoples as similar to the realities for women.

PEACEMAKING CRIMINOLOGY

holds that crime and violence are perpetuated through social policy based on the dominant perspective of crime control, which tends to be based on naïve theories and to disregard human rights. The Oka crisis is an example of disharmony around human rights that serves to perpetuate the naïve theory that First Nations peoples are more crime-prone.

LEFT-REALIST CRIMINOLOGY

holds that crime is a real social problem experienced by the lower classes and that the criminal justice system can be an effective crime-reduction tool through reduced use of force and increased awareness of the plight of the have-nots. Throughout the Oka crisis, the use of force and confrontation by the agents of the justice system represented them as the oppressors working on behalf of the state.

SUMMARY OF LEARNING OBJECTIVES

10.1 The social conflict perspective holds that the root causes of crime are found in social conditions empowering the wealthy and the politically well organized but disenfranchising the less successful. Various groups within society, defined in terms of their political, economic, or social standing, are seen to complete with one another to promote their own best interests. Crime and criminal activity are the outcome of this struggle, according to social conflict theories.

10.2 Three perspectives offer explanations of crime and criminality: left-realist criminology, feminist criminology, and peacemaking criminology. Left-realist criminology is concerned with street crime, fear of crime, and everyday victimization and embraces radical and Marxist criminology. Feminist criminology believes that sexism and an unequal gender-based distribution of power in our patriarchal society affect both crime and its understanding in the field of criminology. Peacemaking criminology restates the problem of crime control from how to stop crime to how to make peace within society and between citizens and criminal justice agencies.

10.3 The social conflict perspective has been criticized for its nearly exclusive emphasis on methods of social change at the expense of well-developed theory. This perspective can also be criticized for failing to recognize what appears to be at least a fair degree of public consensus about the nature of crime—that is, that crime is undesirable and that criminal activity is to be controlled. Today's radical criminologists have largely rescinded calls for revolutionary change and escalated their demands for the eradication of gender, racial, and other inequalities within the criminal justice system; the elimination of prisons; the abolition of capital punishment; and an end to police misconduct.

10.4 Conflict theories hold that social conflict and its manifestations are the root causes of crime; the crime-control implications involve redressing injustices to end the marginalization of the politically and economically disadvantaged.

Questions for Review

1. Does the social conflict perspective hold any significance for contemporary Canadian society? Why or why not?

2. How do the social conflict perspectives discussed in this chapter purport to explain crime and criminality? Use examples of specific theories.

3. Does the radical nature of the social conflict theories fall short in explaining crime in contemporary Canadian society? Why or why not?

4. What are the social policy implications of social conflict theories? Give an example.

Multiple-Choice Questions

1. According to _____, classes are an expression of the underlying forces of the capitalist mode of production.

   a. Karl Marx

   b. William Chambliss

   c. Roscoe Pound

   d. Austin Turk

   e. Richard Quinney

2. Central to the perspective of radical criminology is the notion of _____.

   a. terrorism

   b. state organized crime

   c. consensus

   d. social class

   e. pluralism

3. Which of the following is not a strategy proposed by radical-critical criminologists to bring about a justice system closer to the radical ideal?

   a. increasing equality in criminal justice system employment

   b. programs designed to reduce prison overcrowding

   c. promotion of mandatory sentencing

   d. prosecution of corporate crime

   e. equal justice in the bail system

4. _____ criminology believes that in order to reduce crime, crime-control agencies and citizens must work together to alleviate social problems.

   a. Peacemaking

   b. Feminist

   c. Realist

   d. Marxist

   e. Radical

5. _____ involve(s) participation by the judge, victim, offender, family or supporters, elders, and other justice and community representatives.

   a. Instrumental Marxist panels

   b. Sentencing circles

   c. Community policing

   d. Power-control circles

   e. Left-realism participation circles

Multiple Choice Answers: 1e, 2d, 3c, 4a, 5b

Chapter 11
Criminology and Social Policy

Jonathan Hayward/Canadian Press Images

While the justice system is necessary to hold offenders accountable for their actions, it is only part of the solution to crime. A better solution is to prevent crime in the first place.

— *National Crime Prevention Council*[1]

LEARNING OBJECTIVES

After reading this chapter, you should be able to

11.1 Understand how crime-prevention and public policy is developed.

11.2 Recognize and understand the various types of crime-prevention philosophies and strategies.

11.3 Relate various crime-prevention strategies to recent Canadian crime-prevention policy initiatives and discuss the strengths and weaknesses of each.

11.4 Consider how the political reality of Canada has an impact on the effectiveness of crime-prevention policies.

INTRODUCTION

On June 12, 2012, criminologist Professor Jan van Dijk of the University of Tilburg in the Netherlands stepped up to a podium in the Chinese Theatre in central Stockholm, Sweden, to be recognized at the awards ceremony of the International Stockholm Criminology Symposium as the recipient of the 2012 Stockholm Prize in Criminology.

Van Dijk was recognized for his sustained leadership of the International Crime Victimization Survey (ICVS) since 1987, when he initiated the the first survey. He subsequently supervised five rounds of implementation, covering over 80 countries worldwide. The most recent survey was completed in 2008. As officer in charge of the United Nations International Centre for Crime Prevention, Van Dijk played a significant role in developing the protocols for the United Nations Convention on Transnational Organized Crime, adopted in 2000. In 2005 he co-authored a United Nations report on trends in crime in justice.

First awarded in 2006, the Stockholm Prize in Criminology recognizes outstanding achievements in criminological research or in the practical implementation of research findings in order to combat crime and promote human rights. It carries a cash award of one million Swedish kronor (about $150 000). Financed by the Jerry Lee Centre of Criminology in the United States, the Japanese Correctional Association and Hitachi Mirai Foundation in Japan, and the Söderberg Foundations of Sweden, the prize intends to promote

- improved knowledge of causes of crime on an individual and structural level
- more effective and humane public policies for dealing with criminal offenders
- greater knowledge of alternative crime-prevention strategies inside and outside the judicial system
- policies for helping victims of crime
- better ways to reduce the global problem of illegal or abusive practices that may occur in the administration of justice

Past recipients include John Braithwaite of Australia National University and Friedrich Lösel of Cambridge University (2006) for their work on reintegrative shaming (see Chapter 9) and their systematic reviews of empirical evidence on the effectiveness of correctional treatment. The 2007 prize was awarded to Alfred Blumstein of Carnegie-Mellon University in Pittsburgh and Terrie E. Moffit of the University of London and Duke University, North Carolina, for their discoveries about the development of criminal behaviour over the life course of individuals (see Chapter 9). In 2008, Professors David Olds from the University of Colorado and Jonathan Shepherd of Cardiff University were recognized for their field experiments in policies for crime and injury prevention, while the 2009 recipients—Eugenio Raúl Zaffaroni of the Supreme Court of Argentina and John Hagan of Northwestern University in Illinois—received the prize for their pioneering research regarding the causes and prevention of genocide. In 2010, David L. Weisburg of Hebrew University, Israel, was recognized for a series of experiments showing that intensified police patrol has a positive effect on crime control, and in 2011, John Laub of the U.S. National Institute of Justice and Robert Sampson of Harvard University received the award for their research into explanations of why and how criminals stop offending (see Chapter 9).[2]

In Chapter 1, we made reference to the importance of the link between objective findings of well-conducted criminological research and the development of effective social policy. The Stockholm Prize in Criminology is one very recent recognition that this link is indeed being made. This chapter will examine a number of Canadian public policies related to crime prevention. We will begin with an outline of current crime-prevention directions.

CRIME PREVENTION AND PUBLIC POLICY

SOME UNDERSTANDING OF HOW PUBLIC POLICY—ESPECIALLY CRIME-PREVENTION policy—is created is essential to the study of criminology. Before we consider a number of current public policies in the criminal justice area, a definition of the term *public policy* is in order. **Public policy**, also called *social policy*, can be defined as "those standing directives, formulated by public organizations, on behalf of the public good"[3] or "a course of action that government takes in an effort to solve a problem or to achieve an end."[4] Other definitions contend that public policy is an expression of meaning: "A policy statement in the criminal justice system constitutes a declaration of social value, and it is upon the basis of the declared value that subsequent decisions are shaped."[5] Social values, in turn, are defined as ideals, customs, or institutions that society regards either positively (such as freedom) or negatively (such as cruelty). There are various types of public policy. Descriptors such as "social," "fiscal," "housing," "health," and "economic" can all be attached to the word *policy*. Generally, policy dealing with issues of crime and its prevention and control fall under the rubric of social policy, which can be defined as policy "concerned with the betterment of social life, the amelioration of social ills, and the allocation of public money to accomplish that end."[6]

Public policy Government-formulated directives made on behalf of the public good to solve a problem or achieve an end.

Analysts of public policy have observed that policies undergo five stages in their development:[7]

1. identification of the problem
2. agenda setting or the prioritization of problems
3. policy formation
4. program implementation
5. program evaluation and reassessment

Compare these stages to those described in Box 11.1.

The issue of criminal justice policymaking in Canada is a concentrated interest for the field of criminology, yet there is debate within Canadian criminology circles as to the impact of criminological research on the development of public crime policy. As John Ekstedt and Curt Griffiths have noted,

> Public policy making in areas of critical social awareness has taken on the atmosphere of political "campaigns" with all the attention to the marketing of ideas, the testing of public reaction, and the selling of policy positions normally associated with an election process. Governments seek to promote policies that can contribute to the common good without resulting in political disruption.[8]

The outline in Box 11.1 illustrates this process by examining legislation introduced to address the public's concern with impaired driving. Others have made the comment, "As all criminologists know, criminality is decided as much by legal and political authorities, and by their strategies of criminalization, enforcement, and control, as by criminals themselves."[9] Yet others have argued that Canadian political scientists pay more attention to criminal justice issues than is commonly believed. Troy Riddell argued, for example, that political scientists are well positioned to study how the policy process influences the formation of criminal justice policy.[10]

Box 11.1 STAGES OF CRIMINAL JUSTICE POLICY IN CANADA

Identification of a problem

Increase in reported incidence of violent crime by youth.

Agenda setting/Prioritization of the problem

Interested groups respond and a critical mass of attention is established. Responses come from:

government bureaucracy (collects and reports data on youth crime, shifts or increases resources from another social problem, provides/enforces sanctions to fight youth crime)

media (reports on incidences of youth violent crime, focuses public attention/sensationalizes the reality of violent youth crime, provides editorial insight on the reasons for and how to combat youth crime)

political (manages perceived threat to political stability as public demands political response, maintains balance in designation of resources to government services, uses media to respond to issue by pledging to address the matter of youth crime)

Policy formation

Government announces and implements a major initiative to combat youth violent crime. Resources (money and personnel) are committed, a program is described, legal changes to powers of arrest/criminal sanctions are initiated.

Program implementation

As pressure from the public and the media continue and/or mount and threaten political stability, the bureaucracy responsible implements the program to tackle youth violent crime. Procedures for implementation of the program include:

laws/regulations changes are made to the criminal law (increased sanctions) and regulations (*Youth Criminal Justice Act*)

enforcement additional police and correctional/aftercare resources/personnel are committed

Program evaluation and reassessment

Research, data gathering and analysis continues. Effectiveness of the program from efficiency, ability to meet objectives and cost perspectives is determined.

Sources: Nancy E. Marion, *A History of Federal Crime Control Initiatives, 1960–1993* (Westport: Praeger, 1994), p. 3. For a more detailed analysis of the process by which crime control policies are created, see Paul Rock, "The Opening Stages of Criminal Justice Policy Making," *British Journal of Criminology,* vol. 35, no. 1 (Winter 1995) and *Canadian Criminology: Perspectives on Crime and Criminality,* Second Edition by Jackson/Griffiths, 1995. Reprinted with permission of Nelson, a division of Thomson Learning: www.thomsonrights.com. Fax 800-730-2215.

11.2 LEARNING OBJECTIVE

CRIME-PREVENTION PHILOSOPHIES TODAY

TODAY'S POLICY RESPONSE TO CRIME HAS TWO PRONGS. ONE PRONG DEFINES CRIME as an issue of individual responsibility. The other sees crime and criminal behaviour as resulting from poor social conditions and dysfunctional social structures. In Chapter 1, the first prong was termed the *social responsibility perspective*, and the second approach was called the *social problems perspective*.

Each of these perspectives sees the root causes of crime very differently and dictates a different approach to its resolution. Our American neighbours, for example, appear to have embraced the social responsibility perspective, which is clearly reflected in their current criminal justice policies. Since 1980, the United States has been "waging a war" on crime, criminals, and, most recently, terror, resulting in such legislation as the *Comprehensive Crime Control Act* (1984), the *Omnibus Anti-Drug Abuse Act* (1988), the *Violent Crime Control and Law Enforcement Act* (1994), and the *USA PATRIOT Act* (2001). (The full name of this act is "Uniting and Strengthening America by Providing Appropriate Tools Required to Intercept and Obstruct Terrorism.") All of these pieces of legislation have introduced harsher penalties and increased law enforcement powers. Currently, policies at both the state and federal levels are becoming more and more focused on strict enforcement of existing laws and on strict punishments.[11] Americans continue to push their political representatives for the creation of conservative policy tools to deal with crime and the fear it engenders. At recent count, there were some 2.29 million people incarcerated in the United States, or roughly 760 per 100 000 population (see Figure 11.1). In fact, the United States now imprisons more people per capita than any other country in the Western world.

Detractors of such "get-tough" policies claim that they may not provide the solution sought by those advocating them. They argue that those crime-prevention strategies that attempt to resolve the root causes of crime are more effective in the long run. "We know full well that the most serious and intractable types of crime have their roots in the very child welfare problems that are neglected as we trash through one ineffective war on crime after another," said one American commentator. "Political support for nurturant programs might be obtainable," he argued, "if we could reverse the vicious cycle of media sensationalism, short-sighted policy, and public impatience that encourages ineffective 'quick fixes' for crime."[12]*

By way of contrast, the history of criminal justice policymaking in Canada is largely based on the social problems perspective. Traditionally, the federal government and others have decried the "get-tough" approach to crime prevention as being purely reactive and failing to address the underlying causes of crime and criminality. Decades of crime-prevention policymaking have reflected the sentiments of a former federal minister of justice:

We do not think for a moment that violent crime is going to be resolved in this society by tinkering with statutes or changing Acts. The fact of the matter is that the criminal

Figure 11.1 Canada's Incarceration Rate Compared to Other Western European Countries, 2008/2009

Canada's incarceration rate is higher than the rates in most Western European countries but much lower than the United States, which had an incarceration rate of 760 per 100 000 general population in 2009. While the incarceration rate in Canada has been decreasing from 131 per 100 000 in 1996 to 108 per 100 000 in 2007–08, it increased by 1 percent between 2008 and 2009, owing largely to the numbers of adults held in remand.

Note: The incarceration rate in this figure is a measure of the number of people (i.e., adults and youth) in custody per 100 000 people in the general population.

Source: Adult and Youth Correctional Services: Key Indicators, Statistics Canada, 2008/2009. Reproduced and distributed on an "as is" basis with the permission of Statistics Canada.

---

*Bryan Vila, "Could We Break the Crime Control Paradox?" Paper presented at the annual meeting of the American Society of Criminology, Miami, Florida, November 1994. Reprinted with permission from Professor Bryan Vila, Washington State University.

justice system itself is not going to end violent crime. It only deals with the consequences of the underlying social problems. It is crime prevention that must have at least the equal focus of the House of Commons.[13]

By addressing social problems and the need for improvements in the social infrastructure, the social problems perspective takes a *proactive* rather than *reactive* approach to the reality of crime. Within this context, Canadian crime policy initiatives overall have stressed strategies designed to prevent crime. The National Strategy on Community Safety and Crime Prevention (discussed in more detail later in this chapter) is anchored in the belief that crime prevention is best promoted through social development and that "in order to prevent crime, action must take place at the community level. It is the people who live, work and play in a community who best understand their area's resources, problems, needs and capacities."[14]

Recently, a shift away from this social problems-based approach to crime prevention has been apparent. The Conservative government of Stephen Harper has proposed legislation that would appear closer to the "get-tough" approach to crime and criminality. In 2006, the federal government announced plans to scrap previously proposed legislation to decriminalize the possession of small amounts of marijuana as well as to bring in tougher sentences for those convicted of a criminal offence. The same year, the federal government introduced legislation designed to get tough with high-risk and sex offenders. The proposed reforms targeted *Criminal Code* provisions governing dangerous offenders, to make it easier for Crown prosecutors to obtain dangerous offender designations. A cornerstone of the reforms was that an offender found guilty of a third conviction of a designated violent or sexual offence must prove that he or she does not qualify as a dangerous offender. At the time, the Minister of Public Safety declared, "It is time to implement effective preventative measures to safeguard communities and children from individuals identified as dangerous or high-risk offenders, and at the same time, to strengthen the ability of law enforcement agencies to deal with these individuals. This government is serious about getting tough on crime."[15] The *Tackling Violent Crime Act* of 2008 increased mandatory minimum sentences for gun crimes and impaired driving and requires those convicted of three serious sexual or violent offences to prove why they should not be jailed indefinitely.

The trend toward a tough-on-crime approach is continuing, and in 2012, the passage of the *Safe Streets and Communities Act* (Bill C-10) increased penalties for sexual offences against children and for drug-related crimes, increased the use of adult sentences for youth, limited the use of judicial discretion in issuing conditional sentences, and extended the ineligibility period for criminal pardons. "By moving expeditiously to reintroduce the *Safe Streets and Communities Act*, our Government is fulfilling its commitment to protect families and hold criminals accountable. By imposing sentences that are in proportion to the crimes committed, this Bill recognizes that victims have suffered and gives them confidence in Canada's justice system," said the Minister of Justice and Attorney General of Canada when the bill received Royal Assent.[16] Bill C-10 will be discussed in more detail later in this chapter.

Types of Crime-Prevention Strategies

The range of effective crime-prevention alternatives available to today's policymakers can be classified into three types of strategies. These three strategies differ in terms of strategic focus.[17] That is, they are distinguishable from one another "by whether they attempt to block opportunities for crime, alter the outcome of conscious or unconscious decision making that precedes a criminal act, or alter the broad strategic style with which people approach many aspects of their lives."[18] The three strategies are

1. nurturant strategies
2. protection/avoidance strategies
3. deterrence strategies

Nurturant strategies "attempt to forestall development of criminality by improving early life experiences and channelling child and adolescent development" into desirable directions. They "focus on prevention of criminality rather than its remediation or control."[19] Nurturant strategies include increased infant and maternal health care, child care for low-income families, training in parenting skills, enhanced public education, and stay-in-school programs.

Protection/avoidance strategies "attempt to reduce criminal opportunities by changing people's routine activities, increasing guardianship, or incapacitating convicted offenders."[20] Incapacitating convicted offenders through incarceration or the use of electronic monitoring would be considered examples of protection/avoidance strategies. Target hardening or opportunity reduction through the use of architectural design, crime-prevention programs such as neighbourhood watch, and increased policing also fit into this category.

Deterrence strategies "attempt to diminish motivation for crime by increasing the perceived certainty, severity, or celerity of penalties."[21] New and tougher laws, quicker trial-court processing, harsher punishments, and faster imposition of sentences are all deterrence strategies.

A comprehensive crime-prevention strategy, according to some criminologists, would be "a balanced mix of protection/avoidance, deterrence, and nurturant strategies."[22] Achieving the most effective balance in a politically sensitive world, however, is a difficult undertaking. In Canada, many crime-prevention initiatives continue to emphasize the nurturant approach. Influential political constituencies, however, have increased the pressure for crime-prevention measures that have protection/avoidance and deterrence strategies as their focus.

Nurturant strategy A crime-prevention strategy that attempts to forestall development of criminality by improving early life experiences and channelling child and adolescent development into desirable directions.

Protection/avoidance strategy A crime-prevention strategy that attempts to reduce criminal opportunities by changing people's routine activities, increasing guardianship, or incapacitating convicted offenders.

Deterrence strategy A crime-prevention strategy that attempts to diminish motivation for crime by increasing the perceived certainty, severity, or celerity of penalties.

Aboriginal sweat lodges within Canadian correctional facilities allow Aboriginal inmates to continue to practise traditional customs. What type of crime-prevention strategy does this represent?

Judy Waytiuk/Alamy

CURRENT CRIME-PREVENTION POLICY INITIATIVES

The National Crime Prevention Strategy

Over the past two decades, the Canadian federal and provincial governments have been paying greater attention to crime and community safety, targeting resources to understanding and addressing risk factors associated with crime and victimization. In the 1990s, parliamentary committee reports called for a more concerted, national approach to crime prevention. In 1993, the Standing Committee on Justice and the Solicitor General tabled a report in Parliament that sent a clear message to the federal government about crime prevention. It advised that traditional "police, courts, and corrections" approaches to crime and community safety are limited in their scope and stated that "it is time to translate the rhetoric of crime prevention into policies, legislation, and programs if we are to make real progress in our attempt to protect Canadians. . . ."[23]

National Strategy on Community Safety and Crime Prevention A federal crime-prevention initiative designed to create safer communities by supporting community-based crime-prevention efforts, enhancing communities' knowledge and experience with respect to crime prevention, and fostering partnerships and collaboration.

The federal government responded in 1994 by introducing the **National Strategy on Community Safety and Crime Prevention**.[24] The broad vision of the strategy was to encourage federal and provincial cooperation and the inclusion of citizens at the local level in a national crime-prevention initiative. The specific objectives of the National Strategy are as follows:

- to promote the integrated action of key governmental and non-governmental partners to reduce crime and victimization

- to assist communities in developing and implementing community-based solutions to problems that contribute to crime and victimization, particularly as they affect children, youth, women, and Aboriginal people

- to increase public awareness of and support for effective approaches to crime prevention

Referred to as "crime prevention through social development," this initiative is emblematic of a nurturant strategy.

Phase I of the National Crime Prevention Strategy (NCPS) set the groundwork for its national implementation. The creation of the National Crime Prevention Council, with the mission to "develop strategies to empower individuals and their communities to improve their safety, security and well-being," resulted in the identification of children and youth as the immediate focus for a national crime-prevention policy. The council concluded that

Nurturant crime-prevention strategies are largely aimed at improving the social conditions and experiences of youth such as these living in Toronto's Regent Park housing development prior to its redevelopment. Do you think the focus on preventing crime through social development is an effective crime-prevention approach?

Dick Hemingway

the failure of Canadians to invest in the social development of children and youth has had serious implications in the areas of criminal activity and victimization. It stated that what is needed in Canada is "a comprehensive approach to systemic crime prevention through social development" to best address "the combination of social, systemic, personal, and situational factors which place children and youth at risk and contribute to crime."

Phase II of the National Strategy was launched in 1998 with a mandate to "provide national leadership on effective and cost-efficient ways to both prevent and reduce crime by addressing known risk factors in high-risk populations and places." To achieve its mission, the National Crime Prevention Council (NCPC) develops policies, gathers and disseminates knowledge to Canadian communities, and cooperates with the provinces and territories to manage funding programs that support community crime-prevention projects through time-limited grants and contributions.

The council identified various risk factors for engaging in crime, including (1) individual-related factors (impulsiveness, alienation, early aggressiveness, early use of substances), (2) family-related factors (parent or family member involved in crime, addictions or substance abuse, family violence), (3) peer-related factors (deviant or criminalized friends, friends who are gang members, little social commitment), (4) school-related factors (poor school performance, low attachment to school, dropping out of school, exclusion or suspension from school) and (5) community-related factors (availability of firearms or drugs, weak or poor social networks).

The initiative focuses on groups identified as being most at risk of offending, categorized as (1) children aged 6–11 (to prevent their initiation to criminal activity), (2) young people aged 12–17 (to reduce pressures brought about by known risk factors), (3) young adults aged 18–24 (particularly those who have a history of offending), and (4) offenders who have completed sentences and have been released to the community (to prevent or reduce recidivism). In all four of these groups, a particular emphasis has been placed on Aboriginal populations.

Currently, the NCPS consists of four funding programs:

- The Communities at Risk: Security Infrastructure Program provides time-limited funding to enhance the security infrastructure of communities that are targeted by hate-motivated crime.

- The Crime Prevention Action Fund provides time-limited grant and contribution funding that supports evidence-based crime-prevention initiatives in communities.

- The Northern and Aboriginal Crime Prevention Fund supports the adaptation, development, and implementation of innovative and promising culturally sensitive crime-prevention practices that address known risk and protective factors to reduce offending among at-risk children and youth and high-risk offenders in communities; the dissemination of knowledge and the development of tools and resources for Aboriginal and northern populations; and capacity building as a means to explore ways to develop or implement culturally sensitive crime-prevention practices among Aboriginal and northern populations.

- The Youth Gang Prevention Fund provides time-limited grant and contribution funding for initiatives in communities where youth gangs are an existing or emerging threat and supports initiatives that clearly target youth in gangs or at greatest risk of joining gangs.

Since 2008, the government of Canada has invested $63 million annually to this initiative. In 2011 alone, the government funded 138 community-based crime-prevention programs through the National Crime Prevention Strategy, in which nearly 16 000 at-risk youth participated.

Box 11.2 highlights three recent crime-prevention projects from across Canada that have received funding.

Box 11.2 CANADIAN CRIME-PREVENTION PROJECTS

Aboriginal Peoples—the Aboriginal EMPATHIC Program

A school-based curriculum designed for students in grades one to five, the Aboriginal Emotional Maturity Problem-Solving and Awareness Targeting Higher Impulse Control (EMPATHIC) program was implemented between 2003 and 2006 in the Eskasoni Elementary and Middle School in Nova Scotia. The goal of the EMPATHIC program is to develop emotional awareness and impulse control among Aboriginal children as a means of reducing the likelihood of future violent and criminal behaviour. Students at each of the five levels of the program are required to attend 40 lessons. Important modules are repeated from year to year for positive reinforcement. The lesson activities include role playing, journal writing, picture-based scenarios, and story telling. In addition to the curriculum, a program representative conducts selected home visits each week to create a positive focus on the child.

Families, Children, and Youth at Risk—Family Adolescent Straight Talk (FAST) Day Suspension Project

Family Adolescent Straight Talk (FAST) is an outpatient treatment centre in Halton Region, Ontario, that helps adolescents and families in crisis. FAST's services include crisis intervention, adolescent assessment, psychological and addictions counselling, parent counselling, anger and stress management programs, and relapse prevention programs. Funded by the NCPC from 2007 to 2009, the program targets high-risk

youth aged 12 to 18 who have been suspended from elementary or high school as a result of drug use or other anti-social behaviours, including bullying, physical violence, and truancy. The primary objective of the program is to ensure that youth remain drug free during their school suspension. The program features a 12-week therapy cycle: youth participate in weekly one-on-one counselling sessions (at a minimum), undergo regular drug testing, and have follow-up contact and support.

General Crime Prevention—Drug Treatment Court of Vancouver

Implemented between 2001 and 2005, the goal of Drug Treatment Court of Vancouver (DTCV) is to reduce heroin and cocaine use in adults charged with offences motivated by drug addiction. Persons charged under the *Controlled Drugs and Substances Act* are eligible for the drug treatment court program. In exchange for less severe sentences, offenders plead guilty and participate in a supervised drug treatment program, which includes individual and group counselling and social activities. In addition to the program activities, participants regularly report to the DTCV judge to review their progress. The judge provides participants with positive reinforcements for success and increasingly firm legal sanctions for lack of progress.

Source: Adapted from Public Safety Canada, "National Crime Prevention Centre Publications—Building the Evidence," March 7, 2013, http://www.publicsafety.gc.ca/prg/cp/ncpc-pubs-eng.aspx [Accessed April 7, 2013].

Crime Prevention Through Environmental Design

Crime Prevention Through Environmental Design (CPTED) A crime-prevention strategy based on the premise that the proper design and effective use of the built environment can lead to a reduction in the incidence and fear of crime.

Indicative of the protection/avoidance approach to crime prevention is the notion of **Crime Prevention Through Environmental Design (CPTED)**. In 1971, C. Ray Jeffery's work entitled *Crime Prevention Through Environmental Design* introduced the concept to North America.[25] CPTED is based on the concept of *defensible space*, which holds that crime can be prevented through proper residential and commercial architectural design and the layout of the physical environment. The concept was introduced to Canada in the early 1980s by the Peel Regional Police Service and has since been endorsed by a great number of police services throughout the country (including the RCMP), many of whom have trained CPTED officers.

The concept of CPTED has not been formally incorporated into any federal or provincial crime-prevention policies but has been widely incorporated into crime-prevention plans at the national and municipal levels. The RCMP provides a general overview of CPTED for professionals who work in urban development and related areas.[26] Local governmental crime-prevention plans in an increasing number of cities, including Toronto, Edmonton, Vancouver, Kingston, and Mississauga, include CPTED concepts in building codes and zoning bylaws, as do the mandates of numerous police services, such as the Peel Regional Police Service in Ontario. Box 11.3 illustrates examples of CPTED principles in practice.

Box 11.3 CPTED PRINCIPLES IN PRACTICE

Natural Surveillance

This basement computer lab has no natural observation.

Improved natural observation of the same lab is achieved by the addition of windows.

Natural Access Control

This photo illustrates natural observation from a business reception area to an elevator lobby area and natural access control. Visitors can clearly identify where they may go.

The use of landscape prevents easy access to a rooftop, providing a deterrent to graffiti.

Territorial Reinforcement

These apartments lack clear definition. The ground level provides a source of easy authorized access and criminal activity.

A fence clearly demarcates public from private space.

Source: CPTED Ontario, "What Is CPTED?" 2002, http://www.cptedontario.ca/index.php [Accessed April 7, 2012].

Traditional "target hardening" crime-prevention approaches have employed physical or artificial barriers such as locks, alarms, fences, and gates to deny access to a crime target. The CPTED model recognizes that these traditional methods often tend to place constraints on use, access, and enjoyment of the "hardened" environment. As an alternative, CPTED focuses on *natural surveillance* (keeping potential intruders under observation), *natural access control* (decreasing the opportunity for crime), and *territorial reinforcement* (creating or extending the sphere of influence through physical design to develop a sense of ownership). Further, the CPTED model insists upon an assessment of the physical environment to be protected. The designated purpose of the space; the social, cultural, legal, or physical definitions that suggest desired and acceptable behaviours for it; and the appropriateness of the design in the productive use of the space are included in this assessment.[27] The Crime Prevention Association of New Brunswick identified the following CPTED tactics that can be employed in a variety of settings:[28]

Neighbourhoods

- Minimize the number of entry and exit points on a block.
- Design roadways to discourage through-traffic.
- Maximize residents' ability to view public spaces.
- Encourage residents' use of public spaces.
- Provide appropriate lighting for streets, paths, alleys, and parks.
- Encourage residents to watch over each other.

Houses

- Clearly delineate private property (e.g., yard, driveway) from public space (e.g., street, sidewalk) using shrubbery, alternative paving stone colour, and changes in grade.
- Use solid-core exterior doors.
- Use solid door frames with proper strike plates.

Apartment Buildings

- Provide common spaces to ensure tenant interaction.
- Minimize the number of units sharing a common entrance.
- Equip shared entrances with an intercom.
- Ensure hallways are well lit.
- Provide a children's area that can be easily observed.
- Provide windows in laundry rooms that allow for surveillance.

Parking Lots and Garages

- Avoid enclosed, underground, multi-storey garages.
- Install bright lights over driving lanes and parking spaces.
- Use paint to increase light levels.
- Control access and egress with automatic doors and gates.
- Avoid pillars and recesses that may hide offenders.

Public Spaces

- Encourage use by legitimate users.
- Avoid locating dark and/or hidden areas near activity nodes.
- Install appropriate lighting.
- Avoid locating covered outdoor areas where loitering may be a problem.

Advocates of CPTED stress that it should be considered only part of a comprehensive approach to crime prevention. Modifications to the physical environment will be effective only if they complement community-policing efforts and social programs that address some of the root causes of crime. One of CPTED's most ardent supporters, Greg Saville, claimed, "On the one hand, a CPTED that pretends to solve problems with physical designs alone, while ignoring the psychological response of those living there, is doomed to failure. . . . On the other hand, also doomed is a socio-psychological CPTED that ignores all the advances we have learned in architecture and urban design since the 1970s."[29] Saville insisted that there must be a balance struck between the physical aspects of CPTED, such as access control and natural surveillance, with psycho-social crime-prevention strategies, such as community building, neighbourhood accords, school programs, and community policing. For Saville, initial analysis and diagnosis of the problem is crucial to striking that balance.[30]

Safe Streets and Communities Act

Since 2007, the federal government of Canada has promoted a series of "tackling community crime bills" to address the issue of public safety. Included in this series is an intended National Anti-Drug Strategy, a comprehensive review of the *Youth Criminal Justice Act*, the introduction of the *Tackling Violent Crime Act*, and most recently, the *Safe Streets and Communities Act*.

The **Safe Streets and Communities Act**, which came into force in March 2012, is an example of a deterrence strategy, or an attempt to diminish crime by making penalties more severe. Passed as Bill C-10, the *Safe Streets and Communities Act*, the act legislates increased penalties and a number of get-tough approaches to sentencing. "I am proud today to announce that our Government has fulfilled its commitment to Canadians to bring forward legislation to make our streets, families and communities safer," said Rob Nicholson, minister of justice and attorney general of Canada. "We campaigned on a promise to get tough on child sexual offenders, crack down on illegal drug trafficking, and improve the overall efficiency of our judicial system. Canadians gave us a strong mandate to bring forward these reforms."[31]

Highlights of the *Safe Streets and Communities Act* include the following:

1. **Increased penalties and mandatory sentences of incarceration**

   New mandatory minimum penalties have been created for seven existing offences related to child exploitation, including prohibiting anyone from providing sexually explicit material to a child or from using any means of telecommunications, including the internet, to agree or make arrangements with another person for the purpose of committing a sexual offence against a child.

   New mandatory minimum penalties have been introduced for serious drug offences, when such offences are carried out for organized crime purposes or if they involve targeting youth. Mandatory minimum penalties have also been increased for nine existing offences related to child exploitation.

   The maximum penalty for the production of drugs has been increased. Sentencing provisions for violent and repeat offenders have been strengthened and barriers to custody reduced for these same offenders. All young offenders under 18 given a conditional sentence are to serve it in a youth facility.

2. **Changes to court discretion**

   The discretion of judges, the Crown, and police officers has been limited by some of the provisions of the *Safe Streets and Communities Act*. Pretrial detention rules have been amended to help ensure that, when necessary, violent and repeat young offenders are kept off the streets while awaiting trial. In addition, the act requires the Crown to consider seeking adult sentences for youth convicted of the most serious violent crimes (murder, attempted murder, manslaughter, and aggravated sexual assault), while provinces and territories maintain the discretion to set the age at which this requirement would apply.

   Courts are now required to consider lifting the publication ban on the names of young offenders who are convicted of "violent offences" when youth sentences are given, and police are required to keep records when informal measures are used in order to make it easier to identify patterns of reoffending. Finally, the list of offences for which a conditional sentence is not a sentencing option is expanded.

Safe Streets and Communities Act Canadian legislation that introduces changes to the *Criminal Code of Canada* including increased penalties for sexual offences against children and for drug crimes, denial of release for violent and repeat young offenders, adult sentences for and the publication of the names of youths convicted of the most serious crimes, and the reduction of judicial discretion in sentencing for crimes involving serious personal injury, which carry a maximum prison term of 14 years or more.

3. **Changes to offender accountability**

The *Safe Streets and Communities Act* requires the Parole Board to consider the seriousness of the offender's offence in its decision making and authorizes police to arrest an offender who appears to be breaking his or her release conditions without the need for a warrant. It extends the ineligibility periods for an application for a pardon to five years from three years for a summary conviction offence and to ten years from five years for an indictable offence, and makes those convicted of a sexual offence in relation to a minor or those convicted of more than three offences unable to apply for a pardon. Finally, a number of additional factors must now be considered before an offender can be granted a transfer back to Canada, including whether he or she will endanger public safety, continue to engage in criminal activity, or endanger the safety of any child.

Detractors of the *Safe Streets and Communities Act* have been many. Groups like the Canadian Bar Association, the Canadian Centre for Policy Alternatives, and the Canadian Civil Liberties Association argue that the act ignores decades of research and experience that show that what actually reduces crime is the focus on child poverty, provision of services for the mentally ill, diversion of young offenders from the adult justice system, and rehabilitation of prisoners to assist with their reintegration into society. Others argue that the increased punishments outlined in the act eclipse the crimes. The elimination of the use of conditional sentences for more than the most serious crimes will result in more offenders being given sentences of incarceration. Is roughly $100 000 per year to incarcerate someone a good use of taxpayers' money, they ask? With mandatory minimum prison sentences replacing conditional sentences, people in remote, rural, and northern communities will be moved far from their families to serve time. Aboriginals currently represent up to 80 percent of inmates in institutions in the Prairie provinces, and the direction of the *Safe Streets and Communities Act* will not reverse this trend.

The changes to the treatment of young offenders mean that more youth will spend months in custodial centres before trial. Experience has shown that at-risk youth learn or reinforce criminal behaviour in custodial centres; only when diverted to community options are they more likely to be reformed.

Finally, longer and harsher sentences will increase the strains on a justice system already at the breaking point. Courts and Crown prosecutors' offices are currently overwhelmed, legal aid plans are at the breaking point, and police services don't have the resources to do their jobs properly. Critics argue that the *Safe Streets and Communities Act* addresses none of these problems and will serve to make these realities much worse.

Another Deterrent Approach to Crime Control

Another initiative in the Canadian government's move to get tough on crime includes a recent review of the operation of the Correctional Service of Canada. A public panel appointed by the Minister of Public Safety produced a report entitled *A Roadmap to Strengthening Public Safety*. The report recommended a number of changes within the correctional system, including the elimination of statutory release and the movement toward earned parole for inmates. Detractors of this get-tough approach decry the current direction being pursued in Canada. "We've had this get-tough movement for three decades now," said Marc Mauer, executive director of the Sentencing Project in the United States. "If that's the best way to produce safety, we should be the safest country in the world, and clearly that's not the case."[32] Other detractors of the federal government's apparent move toward a get-tough approach to crime have presented it as a human rights issue. For a summary of two points of view, see Box 11.4.

The following is a summary of two points of view.

The first is expressed by the federal government of Canada in its review of the correctional system and is presented in *A Roadmap to Strengthening Public Safety*.

The second is held by Michael Jackson, lawyer and prison rights advocate, and Graham Stewart, past director of the Canadian John Howard Society, and is expressed in *A Flawed Compass: A Human Rights Analysis of the Roadmap to Strengthening Public Safety*.

Which point of view do you agree with, and why?

A Roadmap to Strengthening Public Safety

1. Offender Accountability

It is the responsibility of Correctional Service of Canada (CSC) to provide the offender with ample opportunity to learn the skills required to correct behaviour. However, to change his or her behaviour, the offender must seize opportunities offered to change—to pick up the tools of rehabilitation and use them. The principles of the *Corrections and Conditional Release Act* (CCRA) have to be strengthened to further emphasize offender responsibility and accountability. (*A Roadmap to Strengthening Public Safety*, p. 11)

2. Eliminating Drugs from Prison

The presence of drugs means that the institutions are not safe and secure environments where offenders can focus on rehabilitation. The panel recommends that CSC strengthen its interdiction initiatives on all fronts, including enhanced perimeter control, increased use of technology, more drug detector dogs, and better search of vehicles and individuals entering the penitentiary. (*A Roadmap to Strengthening Public Safety*, p. 11)

3. Employability/Employment

There is a need to enhance both the quantity and quality of work opportunities available in penitentiaries leading to opportunities in the community.

The panel recommends that CSC implement a more structured workday to allow for the proper balance among work, education, and correctional programs. (*A Roadmap to Strengthening Public Safety*, p. 12)

4. Physical Infrastructure

The panel recommends that CSC explore building regional "complexes." The development, design, and implementation of such regional complexes across the country serves to reinforce an overall correctional management model and moves away from a facility development approach that relies on stand-alone facilities. (*A Roadmap to Strengthening Public Safety*, p. 12)

5. Eliminating Statutory Release; Moving to Earned Parole

The panel recommends that rehabilitation must be a shared accountability and the offender must work to address his or her risks and needs. Mirroring Canadian society—earning your own way—should be a core concept of life inside penitentiaries. Any arbitrary release that is not made based on rehabilitation is counterproductive and, when aggravated by shorter sentences, reduces public safety. (*A Roadmap to Strengthening Public Safety*, p. 12)

A Flawed Compass: A Human Rights Analysis of the Roadmap to Strengthening Public Safety

1. Offender Accountability

"There are many recommendations of the Roadmap which reflect ideological and populist views that being 'tough on crime' is a sufficient and defensible basis for public policy. . . . Not only will implementation of many of the key recommendations undermine respect for human rights but they will also do nothing to enhance public safety." (*A Flawed Compass*, p. iv)

2. Eliminating Drugs from Prison

"We have seen no evidence to support the case that 'a more rigorous approach to drug interdiction' [including the allocation of new money to introduce more Ionscan equipment, more drug dogs, and more security intelligence officers] would have any more success within prisons than the array of increased enforcement and tougher sentencing has had on stemming the flow of drugs coming into Canadian cities and communities." (*A Flawed Compass*, pp. 92–93)

3. Employability/Employment

"We do not deny the need for work and trades related programming. However, in the interests of both public safety and fiscal accountability we feel obliged to raise the question of why the Roadmap gives such overwhelming attention to work and minimal attention to education when, dollar-for-dollar, and demonstrated effects on recidivism, good education programs appear to offer much greater cost-effectiveness and logistically are much easier to implement." (*A Flawed Compass*, p. 146)

4. Physical Infrastructure

"The Panel's assessment is blind to the likely impact of the government's current criminal justice policies, as well as to their own recommendations, on the size of future prison populations. . . . Any plan, especially one as massive and permanent as regional complexes, must

(Continued)

be seriously challenged in the planning stages if we are to avoid having many future generations saddled with expensive, obsolete structures." (*A Flawed Compass*, p. 171)

5. Eliminating Statutory Release; Moving to Earned Parole

The conditional release of an inmate is no longer based on clemency. It is not something that is given on the basis of desert, but rather on the basis of risk. Statutory release was introduced, not because prisoners deserve it but because the community needs it to maximize the potential for successful reintegration without subsequent new offences. The principle of "least restrictive measures," when considered in combination with the first principle of public safety, requires that the focus be entirely on risk—not desert. (*A Flawed Compass*, p. 117)

Sources: Adapted from Minister of Public Works and Government Services Canada, *Report of the Correctional Service of Canada Review Panel: A Roadmap to Strengthening Public Safety*, 2007, http://www.publicsafety.gc.ca/csc-scc/cscrprprt-eng.pdf [Accessed May 6, 2012]; and Michael Jackson and Graham Stewart, *A Flawed Compass: A Human Rights Analysis of the Roadmap to Strengthening Public Safety*, September 2009, http://www.justicebehindthewalls.net/resources/news/flawed_Compass.pdf [Accessed May 6, 2012].

CAN WE SOLVE THE PROBLEM OF CRIME?

Kriminalpolitik The political handling of crime, or a criminology-based social policy.

IN 1956, EUROPEAN WRITER H. BIANCHI EMPHASIZED WHAT HE SAW AS THE DIFference between criminology and what he termed **Kriminalpolitik**, meaning the political handling of crime or a criminology-based social policy.[33] Criminology, according to Bianchi, should be considered a "metascience" or "a science of wider scope (than that of criminal law, jurisprudence, criminal justice, or corrections) whose terminology can be used to clarify the conceptions of its subdisciplines. Far from being a mere auxiliary to the criminal law, it is therefore superior to it."[34] Bianchi believed that if criminology were to remain pure, it could not afford to sully its hands, so to speak, with political concerns.

Today, the image esteemed by criminologists and the expectations they hold for their discipline are quite different than in Bianchi's time. Many criminologists expect to work hand-in-hand with politicians and policymakers forging crime-prevention agendas based on scientific knowledge and criminological theorizing and would say that this change in attitude represents a maturation of the discipline of criminology.

Whether effective crime-prevention policies can ever be implemented, however, is another question. Central to any discussion of public-policy development in Canada is the political reality of the country. Without going into a lot of detail on the impact of our decentralized, federalist political system, suffice it to say that the division of powers between the two levels of government in Canada—federal and provincial/territorial—has a profound impact on the creation and implementation of crime-prevention policy. Briefly, in criminal justice matters the federal government, through the Parliament of Canada, has exclusive jurisdiction to make criminal laws and set sanctions for their violation. The provinces and territories, on the other hand, are responsible for the implementation of the criminal laws, otherwise known as the "administration of justice." A number of provincial/territorial statutes, such as those regulating liquor licensing and highway traffic, are the sole responsibility of each individual provincial/territorial government. Needless to say, there is an overlap between the two governmental jurisdictions in the area of crime prevention, and, in many cases, joint decision-making mechanisms must be implemented before any policy can be developed—especially federal government initiatives with a national scope. Often referred to as federal/provincial/territorial conferences or task forces, these forums allow federal and provincial/territorial leaders to discuss issues of concern within the area of crime prevention and control. For example, a recent federal government initiative to explore strategies for managing offenders resulted in the creation of the Federal/Provincial/

Territorial Task Force on High-Risk and Violent Offenders. The task force's work resulted in changes to legislation dealing with long-term dangerous offenders, including a new long-term offender designation that targets sex offenders and adds a period of long-term supervision of up to ten years following release from prison, as well as changes to the dangerous offender provisions of the *Criminal Code* to require that anyone classified as a dangerous offender must be given an indefinite sentence.

Matters of criminal justice are also dealt with at the municipal level of government. Essentially, municipalities are responsible for the enforcement of all laws and the creation of local bylaws.[35] In this way, a crime-prevention approach taken by a particular municipality through its police service may not necessarily dovetail neatly into crime-prevention approaches being taken at the provincial or federal levels.[36] In short, crime prevention and control is not as simple as implementing a federally developed policy across the country. Each level of government may interpret, implement, or challenge a policy, with the result that its uniform application across the country often takes many years. The following Who's Responsible? box presents the case of a fictitious, yet typical, offender and emphasizes the importance of investing in young people at the early stages of a delinquent lifestyle. The crime-prevention philosophy—be it a nurturant, protection/avoidance, or deterrence approach—will determine the tone and type of intervention policies adopted.

The Costs to Society of a Young Person in Trouble

Problems start early for many future offenders, especially those who will become chronic and persistent offenders. Patterns of troublesome behaviour are often apparent by the age of 3. The costs to society start early as well, and increase as the years go by.

Identifying all the costs of a delinquent career would be an impossible task. But it is possible to identify some elements and make estimates or educated guesses of what they might cost in the life of a repeat young offender before he or she reaches the age of 18. Take the fictional, but typical, case of Jack. He is a troubled child who needs special help and preventive services early in his life—but the appropriate services are not available to him and his family.

Jack's First Three Years:

The child welfare authorities become aware of serious problems in Jack's home during his first year. His parents often have arguments, many of which end with the exchange of blows, especially after they have been drinking. Their parenting is affectionate, but erratic. Child welfare staff regularly visit Jack and his parents during his first three years of life. Social workers make a number of suggestions about his care and the special help he may need, but because of a lack of community resources, they are not able to refer Jack to appropriate support services.

Costs: Three years child welfare services at $2300 a year. Total = $6900

Jack Aged 3 to 5:

Jack is showing a number of developmental problems, both physical and psychological. By the age of 3 he is difficult to manage. His parents do not know how to cope with his impulsive behaviour, and he shows no awareness of the consequences of his actions. The child welfare services, in conjunction with the family doctor and child psychiatric services, conclude that Jack would benefit from being placed in a subsidized child-care centre. Jack's mother qualifies for the subsidized service, but the staff at the centre are not trained to provide the remedial care he really needs. Jack tends to bully the other children, disrupt their play, and be insensitive to the needs of others.

Costs: Three years child welfare services at $2300 a year, child care at $12 000 a year, and health and psychiatric services at $2000 a year. Total = $48 900

Jack Aged 6 to 10:

Although Jack has benefited from the child-care services, and is better behaved in group settings, his home situation has gone from bad to worse. His parents have separated, and his mother is now living with a young man who appears

(Continued)

The Costs to Society of a Young Person in Trouble

jealous of the affection she shows toward Jack and is abusive toward him. The child welfare services decide, reluctantly, that they have to take him into care; this requires an appearance in family court. Jack is placed in the first of a series of foster homes. Separation from his mother upsets him and reawakens his behaviour problems. He has difficulty relating to his foster parents and their children. In five years he lives in five foster homes. These moves disrupt his education and he has difficulty getting along with other children. Consequently, he is involved with school guidance counsellors and child psychiatric services.

Costs: Five years child welfare services at $2300 a year, foster care at $7300 a year, guidance counsellors and special education services at $2000 a year, health and child psychiatric services at $2000 a year, and court services for one appearance at $1000. Total = $69 000

Jack Aged 11 to 14:

By the age of 11, Jack is big for his age and precocious in his behaviour toward his peers, particularly girls. The child welfare services recognize that he has never settled down in the various foster homes he has lived in. In conjunction with the education and child health services, they conclude that a group home placement may be the only way to contain Jack's "acting-out."

The "acting-out" continues in the group home setting, however. He comes to the notice of the police several times before he turns 12, partly through misbehaviour at school and partly through various delinquent acts in the community.

Finally, at the age of 12 he is charged in relation to a number of incidents of shoplifting, vandalism, and rowdy behaviour in a local shopping mall. He goes to Youth Court for the first time and is ordered to provide restitution services to make up for the damage he has done. He remains in the care of the child welfare services. Jack's contact with his mother is spasmodic after years of living away from her. When he does see her, it usually results in a period of disturbed behaviour in the group home and at school. At the age of 13, he gets involved with drugs at school, starts selling them to schoolmates, and becomes physically abusive in collecting his debts.

On one occasion, he hurts a boy seriously enough for the boy to receive in-patient care at a local hospital. Charges are laid, and Jack goes to Youth Court for a second time, where he is found guilty. The court is in a quandary over what sentence to give him. One possibility is to send him to a youth custodial facility, but this is seen as extreme for a boy of his age. Instead, he is placed on probation for a year, while

continuing in the care of the child welfare services.

Jack is able to complete the year's probation without any further major incidents, with the help of the child welfare services, including the group home staff, the probation officer, and the school authorities. The probation ends when he has passed his 14th birthday. He is by now a physically mature young man, but he still has difficulty restraining his temper.

One weekend Jack leaves the group home without permission and meets some friends at a local mall. They obtain alcohol and drugs, and steal a car. Jack is the ringleader. They are caught after running the car off the road. On his third appearance in the Youth Court, Jack is remanded to the local detention facility for assessment reports. When he next returns to court, for his fourth appearance, the Youth Court sentences him to an open custodial placement followed by probation supervision of a year. He is sent to a youth centre for three months and meets other youths with similar backgrounds. Jack receives some educational services, but is found to be backward for his age. The court had recommended psychological and psychiatric services, but no professional treatment other than assessments is provided in the open facility.

Costs: Four years of group home care at $36 500, special education services at $2000 a year, child welfare supervision at $2300 a year; probation supervision for one year at $1200; police contacts before age 12, $1000; three police investigations at $1500 each; four court sessions at $1000 each; four police attendances at court at $250 each; two psychological and psychiatric assessments at $2000 each; three months open custody $19 250. Total = $198 150.

Jack Aged 15 to 17:

When he leaves the open custody facility, Jack is 15 years old. He returns to the same group home, continues to have contact with the child welfare social worker, and attends school when he feels like it. He is again under probation supervision, but is very unsettled. He meets some of his former friends from the youth centre, and they decide to break into a local pharmacy to steal drugs. They trip the alarm and are apprehended. After a further remand in a detention facility, the Youth Court (where he has now made his fifth and sixth appearances) sends Jack to another open custody facility for six months, with supervision to follow. Halfway through his sentence, Jack escapes with some of his fellow inmates. They steal a car, but their erratic driving alerts a patrolling police car. In the subsequent chase with Jack at the wheel, they crash into another vehicle, killing the driver. It is now his

(Continued)

The Costs to Society of a Young Person in Trouble

seventh appearance. The Youth Court, without asking for further reports, sends him to a secure custody facility for two years with supervision to follow.

By the time Jack is released, he is approaching the age of 18. He has a girlfriend, and their relationship is unstable and often violent. She soon becomes pregnant, and it is all too likely that the cycle of Jack's early life is about to repeat itself.

Costs: Special education services, about $2000; two psychological and psychiatric assessments at $2000 each; three years for child welfare supervision at $2300 a year; one year for group home care at $36 500; three appearances in Youth Court at $1000; two police investigations at $1500 each and three police court attendances at $250 each; two years of probation supervision etc. at $1200; six months open custody at $38 500; one year closed custody at $91 500. Total = $188 550.

Grand Total for Jack's Career to Age 17 = $511 500.

The Moral of the Story

Jack's career as a repeat young offender illustrates some of the common features of how children and young people pass through the child welfare and young offender systems. Not only are these services expensive to provide, but also the offences themselves result in a cost to society in terms of the physical costs, personal injuries, and psychological harm experienced by victims.

Jack has a painful early life, and his offences cause pain to others. The cost of such pain is enormous and not easily calculated in dollar terms, which would require placing a figure on a lost life, or lost employment and lost enjoyment of life by victims and families. In addition, the costs of crime have to be calculated over time, because pain and suffering are not necessarily short-term in their effects.

Jack's story is not intended to suggest that the various services do not succeed in helping many young people. What it shows, in fact, is how important it is to invest early in helping young people and their families. Without this help, too many young people end up just like Jack, poised at the age of 18 to enter on a life of adult offending and to bring further costs to society and all who come in contact with them.

Think about it:

1. Identify and explain examples of each of the crime-prevention initiatives in the story of Jack's life. Is one approach more apparent?

2. How would a deterrent approach to crime prevention manifest itself in the ways in which society would deal with a person like Jack?

3. Does Canadian society have an obligation to support youth like Jack and incur the costs of doing so? Why or why not?

Source: Prevention, (Volume 1, Issue 1, p. 7), http://www.ps-sp.gc.ca/res/cp/nwslet/_f1/issue_1-en.pdf, National Crime Prevention Centre, 1999; Prevention, (Volume 1, Issue 2, p. 7), http://www. ps-sp.gc.ca/res/cp/nwslet/_fl/issue_2-en.pdf. National Crime Prevention Centre, 2000. Reproduced with the permission of the Minister of Public Works and Government Services, 2010.

MySearchLab® with eText offers you access to an online interactive version of the text, extensive help with your writing and research projects, and provides round-the-clock access to credible and reliable source material.

SUMMARY OF LEARNING OBJECTIVES

11.1 Policies dealing with issues of crime and its prevention and control fall under social policy. Policies undergo five stages in their development: identification of the problem; agenda setting, or the prioritization of problems; policy formation; program implementation; and program evaluation and reassessment.

11.2 Most crime-prevention strategies can be described as nurturant, protection/avoidant, or deterrent in nature. Nurturant approaches focus on improving early life experiences and child and adolescent development as the way to effectively prevent crime. Protection/avoidant strategies seek to attempt to reduce criminal opportunities by changing routine patterns, increasing guardianship, or incapacitating offenders. Deterrent strategies attempt to reduce motivation for crime by increasing certainty and severity of penalties.

11.3 Examples of all three crime-prevention strategies exist in Canada. The nurturant approach is exemplified in the National Crime Prevention Strategy; examples of the protection/avoidant approach are found in the Crime Prevention Through Environmental Design initiatives across the country; and the recent *Safe Streets and Communities Act* embodies the notions of increased certainty and severity of penalties as a means of controlling crime.

11.4 Crime prevention is a matter of public policy. Efforts to reduce crime are fraught with political uncertainties that rest largely upon fundamental disagreements within Canadian society itself as to the sources of crime and the most appropriate means of preventing and combatting it.

Questions for Review

1. What are the typical stages in the development of public policy? Does criminal justice policy-making in Canada follow these stages? Why or why not?

2. What are the three types of crime-prevention strategies described in this chapter? Which comes closest to your own philosophy? Why?

3. Provide one recent Canadian example for each of the three crime-prevention strategies outlined in this chapter. Outline one strength and one weakness for each of the three crime-prevention strategies.

4. How does Canada's political system affect the successful implementation of crime-prevention policies?

Multiple-Choice Questions

1. The National Strategy on Community Safety and Crime Prevention is an example of a _____ strategy.
   a. nurturant
   b. retributive
   c. defensive

d. protection/avoidance

e. social epidemiology

2. _____ crime-control strategies include infant and maternal health care, child care for the working poor, and training in parental skills.

    a. Social epidemiology

    b. Restorative

    c. Protection/avoidance

    d. Deterrent

    e. Nurturant

3. _____ attempt(s) to reduce criminal opportunities by changing people's routine activities or by incapacitating convicted offenders.

    a. Social epidemiology

    b. Nurturant strategies

    c. Public health

    d. Deterrent strategies

    e. Protection/avoidance strategies

4. Which of the following is an example of a protection/avoidance strategy?

    a. decreasing the age for which one is considered a young offender

    b. developing an anger management program for youth

    c. reducing the number of entry and exit points on a neighbourhood block

    d. increasing penalties for offences committed using a firearm

    e. introducing a parenting skills group for men

5. The last stage of public policy development is _____.

    a. policy formation

    b. program evaluation and reassessment

    c. identification of the problem

    d. agenda setting or the prioritization of problems

    e. program implementation

Chapter 12
Future Directions and Emerging Trends

Victor Habbick Visions/Science Photo Library/Corbis

As surely as the future will bring new forms of technology, it will bring new forms of crime.

—*Cynthia Manson and Charles Ardai*[1]

LEARNING OBJECTIVES

After reading this chapter, you should be able to

12.1 Explain globalization and understand its impact on contemporary transnational criminal activity.

12.2 Recognize the global and transnational nature of emerging crime trends.

12.3 Realize the role of technology in emerging crime trends.

12.4 Describe some of the crime trends predicted to emerge and grow in the future.

INTRODUCTION

Canadian criminologist Gwynn Nettler once told a story of two people passing on a street in New York City.[2] One carried a pint of whiskey; the other carried $100 in gold coins. In March 1933, near the end of the Prohibition era, the person with the alcohol would have been committing a crime, but the person carrying the gold would have been regarded as law-abiding. A year later, however, the same two people passing on the street would have occupied exactly the opposite legal positions. The repeal of Prohibition legalized carrying whiskey in most places, but gold hoarding became a federal crime in 1934, and remained so until 1974.

It is easy to look back in time and assess the legal standing of people like those in Nettler's story, but predicting what crimes the future will bring is far more difficult. The future is an abstract concept through which human beings bring symbolic order to the present and meaning to past endeavours.[3] From our present point of view, multiple futures exist, each of which is more or less probable and may or may not come to pass. In other words, the future contains an almost limitless number of possibilities, any of which might unfold but only a few of which actually will. Those who study the future are called **futurists**, and their task is to effectively distinguish among these impending possibilities, assessing the likelihood of each and making more or less realistic forecasts based on such assessments. **Future criminology** is the study of likely futures as they relate to crime and its control, and futurists working in the area of criminology try to imagine how crime will appear in both the near and the distant future.

Some assumptions about the future, such as estimates of future world populations, can be based on existing and highly credible public or private statistics and mathematical analyses of trends. Others are more intuitive and result from the integration of a wide range of diverse materials derived from many different sources. As one futurist explained,

> Before we can plan the future, we must make some assumptions about what that future will be like. Assumptions about the future are not like assumptions in a geometry exercise. They are not abstract statements from which consequences can be derived with mathematical precision. But we need to make some assumptions about the future in order to plan it, prepare for it, and prevent undesired events from happening.[4]

International organizations such as the World Future Society bring ideas, people, and knowledge together to prepare for the future. Within criminology, the Society of Police Futurists International (PFI) represents the cutting edge of research into future crime-prevention and control policy.[5]

Another group actively attempting to discern the future is the United Kingdom's government-led Foresight program, which "brings people, knowledge, and ideas together to look ahead and prepare for the future."[6] Foresight's Crime Prevention Panel released a report in 2001 entitled *Just around the Corner*, which focused on the year 2020 and provided a summation of the views of 60 experts given three tasks: to describe crimes of the near future, to identify methods to reduce and detect those crimes, and to decide what role science and technology will play in future criminality and crime prevention.[7] According to Foresight's Crime Prevention Panel, there are a number of social characteristics affecting future crimes in Great Britain and throughout the world. One of these is what the panel calls "individuality and independence." The panel believed that greater individuality and personal independence will arise as traditional family forms continue to decline over the next decade or two. Once traditional families no longer provide the "foundation" of society and more people find themselves living in single-person households, "there will be more self-centered, self-indulgent, and hedonistic psychologies." Traditional limits on anti-social behaviour

Futurists Those who study the future; in the case of criminology, criminologists who try to imagine how crime will appear in both the near and distant future.

Future criminology The study of likely futures as they relate to crime and its control.

will erode, the panel predicted, as individuals gravitate toward membership in like-minded groups, many of which "may reinforce rather than challenge anti-social views."

A second social characteristic that will affect crime in the future, according to the panel, is what it termed "Information Communication Technology (ICT) usage." The panel predicted that crimes like electronic theft and fraud will occur with increasing rapidity, reducing the likelihood that offenders will be caught. Websites will become highly targeted properties, with sites in English being the hardest hit. Such attacks will require that digital evidence in courts be increasingly accepted and that jurors, judges, and attorneys be educated in relevant technologies.

Technology is also leading to the growth of an impersonal society in which people meet and interact in virtual space rather than in physical society. As a consequence, physical space may become an increasingly hostile and dangerous place, or what the panel termed "a dehumanized environment" in which "people may become less 'real' to one another leading to more extreme reactions, interactions, and the reluctance to intervene in conflicts."

A third social characteristic, according to the panel, that is relevant to understanding and predicting future forms of criminality and that is having an impact on much of society—including technology, commerce, communication, and crime—is globalization, the increasingly international character of social life. "Already, crimes on the Internet, drug dealing, and smuggling show the power of global crime and the difficulties it poses for local level law enforcement." Local crimes and small-time perpetrators will be replaced or supplemented by crimes and criminal groups with global scope. The panel noted that criminal organizations, like organizations everywhere, "are adapting to the opportunities offered by the flexibility of the Internet." Modern technology offers individuals new opportunities to commit crimes that may be virtually unsolvable: "The clear danger is being at the mercy of a small technologically knowledgeable elite." At the same time, the panel warned, large numbers of people either won't have the opportunity to acquire advanced technological skills or will be unable to learn them; the consequence will be a technologically disenfranchised underclass whose existence will "further fuel crime and reduce the opportunities for access to mainstream society."

12.1 | LEARNING OBJECTIVE

GLOBALIZATION

IN 2007, OFFICIALS OF U.S.-BASED CHIQUITA BRANDS INTERNATIONAL ADMITTED in federal court that executives with the company had paid protection money to Colombian terrorists to help secure their most profitable banana-growing operations.[8] Under a plea arrangement, the company pleaded guilty to one count of doing business with a terrorist organization and was ordered to pay a $25 million fine. The deal, however, allowed the identities of several senior executives involved in the illegal protection payments to remain anonymous. Attorneys for Chiquita said that the company was forced to make the payments and was acting only to ensure the safety of its workers.

The payment of protection monies to a South American terrorist organization by an American-based banana importer illustrates the complexity of contemporary international business operations, which often occur in the midst of intricate political situations and which can be affected by the interests of a wide variety of groups. On a global scale, society is experiencing a period of unprecedented change in both substance and pace. Sequences of events are no longer occurring in relative isolation and are happening ever more quickly; there is greater simultaneity of occurrences, swifter interpenetration of various groups, and increased feedback of one set of changes upon another.[9]

The increasing integration of previously isolated events in all spheres of endeavours affects people far and wide. The economist Thomas L. Friedman said that globalization will likely be the most pervasive influence on the entire world in the first part of the 21st century.[10] **Globalization** can be defined as a process of social homogenization by which the experiences of everyday life, marked by the diffusion of commodities and ideas, can foster a standardization of cultural expressions around the world.[11] Globalization, occurring in communications, economics, science, education, and business, involves the progressive erosion of the influence of nation-states and the rise in influence of global decision makers at both public and private levels.

Globalization is making it impossible for policymakers to ignore criminal activity in other parts of the world, especially crimes perpetrated by transnational criminal and terrorist organizations. **Transnational organized crime** (also called *transnational crime*) refers to unlawful activity undertaken and supported by organized criminal groups operating across national boundaries. The growing globalization of crime has necessitated the enhanced coordination of law enforcement efforts in different parts of the world and the expansion of North American law enforcement activities beyond national borders.

TRANSNATIONAL CRIMES

According to the National Institute of Justice (NIJ) in the United States, transnational crime groups have profited more from globalization than legitimate businesses, which are subject to domestic and host country laws and regulations, pointing out that transnational criminal syndicates and networks, abetted by official corruption, blackmail, and intimidation, can use open markets and open societies to their full advantage.[12] The list of transnational crimes is long and ranges from relatively simple fraudulent email and phishing schemes that are globally perpetrated, to the much more dangerous and threatening illegal trafficking in human beings, human organs, and illicit drugs. Included are the activities of multinational drug cartels, the support of terrorist groups by criminal organizations seeking armed protection, and well-funded and politically sophisticated efforts by organized criminal groups seeking to supplant the ruling regime in countries or regions with others sympathetic to their operations. At the 2005 summit meeting in England, G-8 leaders identified transnational criminal activity as one of the three major challenges facing the world in the 21st century.[13] In 2003, the United Nations (UN) made the issue of organized crime one of its priorities for the 21st century and ratified [14]

As a signatory to the UN Convention and its protocols, Canada is a world partner in the effort to seek ways to prevent and control transnational organized crime. The Criminal Intelligence Service Canada (CISC) is an organization that provides the facilities to unite the criminal intelligence units of Canadian law enforcement agencies in the fight against organized crime and other serious crime in Canada. CISC provides an overview of selected global trends and highlights some of the threats and opportunities that have the potential to develop within specific criminal markets. CISC contends that transnational criminal activity is a growing problem in Canada and that technological advances over the past 20 years have made national borders irrelevant to telecommunications and financial transactions and have enabled the globalization of criminal activity.

Although statistics vary, CISC reports that there appear to be anywhere from 5 to 18 active transnational criminal organizations represented in Canada. This includes Asian triads, Colombian cartels, Italian Mafia groups (the most influential being the Sicilian Mafia), Russian/Eastern European *mafiyas*, Nigerian crime groups, and major outlaw motorcycle gangs. Whereas crime syndicates of the past were involved in illegal street-level activities such as drug trafficking, prostitution, illegal gambling, loan sharking, and extortion, CISC reports that today's organized crime syndicates have become quasi-corporate in their activities and are now involved in arms dealing, large-scale insurance and financial fraud, environmental crime, the trafficking and smuggling of humans, money laundering, bank fraud, and gasoline tax fraud.[15]

Globalization A process of social homogenization by which the experiences of everyday life, marked by the diffusion of commodities and ideas, can foster a standardization of cultural expressions around the world.

Transnational organized crime Any unlawful activity undertaken and supported by organized groups operating across national boundaries.

12.2 LEARNING OBJECTIVE

Trafficking and Smuggling of Humans

According to the UN, smuggling of persons and human trafficking, two distinct crimes, are two of the fastest-growing areas of international criminal activity today.[16] The *United Nations Convention against Transnational Organized Crime* defines **human smuggling** as the "procurement for financial or other material benefit of illegal entry of a person into a State of which the person is not a national or resident."[17]

Human smuggling may be conducted to obtain financial or other benefits for the smuggler, although sometimes people engage in smuggling for other motives, such as to reunite their families. It generally occurs with the consent of the persons being smuggled, who often pay a smuggler for his or her services; once in the country they've paid to enter, they usually are no longer in contact with the smuggler. The vast majority of people who are assisted in illegally entering a country annually are smuggled rather than trafficked.

In contrast to smuggling, **trafficking in persons (TIP)**—the exploitation of unwilling or unwitting people through force, coercion, threat, or deception—can be compared to modern-day slavery. Trafficking can involve human rights abuses such as debt bondage, deprivation of liberty, or lack of control over freedom and labour.

Trafficking involves the delivery of persons to individuals or organizations who have paid for their delivery and the repayment of those debts to the traffickers by the trafficked persons, usually through prostitution or forced labour.[18] Reports estimate that there are millions of TIP victims in the world each year. At least 136 different nationalities were trafficked and detected in 118 different countries. Women account for 55 to 60 percent of all trafficking victims detected globally; women and girls together account for about 75 percent. Children make up 27 percent of all victims detected globally. Of every three child victims, two are girls and one is a boy.[19] Although human trafficking is often an international crime that involves the crossing of borders, it is important to note that human trafficking victims can be trafficked within their own countries and communities. Traffickers can move victims between locations within the same country and often sell them to other trafficking organizations. The International Labor Organization (ILO), the UN agency charged with addressing labour standards, employment, and social protection issues, estimates that there are 20.9 million people in forced labour, bonded labour, forced child labour, and sexual servitude throughout the world today.[20]

It is sometimes difficult to distinguish between smuggling and trafficking because trafficking may include an element of smuggling (that is, the illegal crossing of a national border), and some trafficking victims may believe they are being smuggled when they are really being trafficked but are unaware of their eventual fate. For example, women trafficked for sexual exploitation thought they were agreeing to work in legitimate industries for decent wages, part of which they may have agreed to pay to the trafficker who smuggled them, not knowing the trafficker would keep them in bondage, subject them to physical force or sexual violence, force them to work in the sex trade, and take most or all of their income. (Table 12.1 provides a guide to distinguish human trafficking from human smuggling.)

According to the United Nations, human smuggling and trafficking have become a worldwide industry affecting millions of people and involving billions of dollars. Many of the routes used by smugglers—from Mexico and Central America to the United States, from West Asia through Greece and Turkey to Western Europe, and within East and Southeast Asia—have become well established and are widely known. The UN has attributed the flourishing smuggling routes to weak legislation, lax border controls, corrupt officials, and organized crime's power and influence. While there are significant differences between human smuggling and TIP, the underlying conditions that give rise to both are similar: extreme poverty, lack of economic opportunity, civil unrest, and political uncertainty.

A comprehensive report released in 2012 by the United Nations Office on Drugs and Crime (UNODC) entitled *Global Report on Trafficking in Persons* identified countries

Human smuggling A type of illegal immigration in which an agent is paid to help a person cross a border clandestinely.

Trafficking in persons (TIP) The exploitation of unwilling or unwitting people by means of coercion, threat, or deception.

Table 12.1 Differences between Human Trafficking and Smuggling

Trafficking	Smuggling
Trafficking contains an element of force, fraud, or coercion (actual, perceived, or implied). (Force, fraud, or coercion is not required if the person is under age 18 and is involved in commercial sex acts.)	The person being smuggled is generally cooperating.
Trafficking involves forced labour and/or exploitation.	Smuggling involves no forced labour or other exploitation.
Persons trafficked are victims.	Persons smuggled are not victims; they are violating the law.
Trafficked persons are enslaved, are subjected to limited movement or isolation, and have their documents confiscated.	Smuggled persons are free to leave, change jobs, etc.
Trafficking need not involve the actual movement of the victim.	Smuggling facilitates the illegal transportation of the person from one country into another.
Trafficking does not need to cross an international border.	Smuggling always crosses an international border.
Trafficked persons must be involved in labour/services or commercial sex acts (that is, must be "working").	Smuggled persons must be attempting entry or already be in a country illegally.

Note: This table is meant to be conceptual and is not intended to provide precise legal distinctions between trafficking and smuggling.

Source: Adapted from U.S. Department of State, Bureau for International Narcotics and Law Enforcement Affairs, Human Smuggling and Trafficking Center, *Fact Sheet: Distinctions Between Human Smuggling and Trafficking*, April 2006, http://www.state.gov/documents/organization/90541.pdf (Accessed April 10, 2013).

of origin, transit, and destination as they pertain to the trafficking of human beings. The report noted that Canada ranks high in terms of a destination country; however, the scope of these criminal activities in Canada remains a small percentage of the international (or even the North American) criminal market. Canada is largely a destination and a transit country for women who are trafficked for the purposes of sexual exploitation. Most arrive from Asia, Latin America, Russia, and Eastern Europe.[21] According to the latest strategic intelligence assessment on human trafficking produced by the RCMP,

> Human trafficking may as likely be orchestrated by transnational organized criminal networks as it may be coordinated by a few family-based opportunists with little formal structure. It is also a borderless crime that victimizes vulnerable persons regardless of their nationality. Human trafficking is a crime that thrives in stigmatized facets of the work force, like the sex trade and illegal labour, and hides in the privacy of homes and businesses.[22]

Based on various reports, the RCMP estimates that anywhere between 1500 and 2200 persons are trafficked from Canada into the United States each year.[23]

Trafficking in human beings is a global issue, and illegal migrants and trafficking victims have become another commodity in a larger arena of criminal commerce involving other commodities, such as narcotic drugs, firearms or other weapons, and money laundering, all of which generate illicit revenues or seek to reduce risks for traffickers. To date, the lack of systematic research in this area means that reliable data on the trafficking of human

A poster designed by the RCMP to raise public awareness about the growing issue of human trafficking. How does this type of criminal activity represent the globalization of crime?

© 2013 HER MAJESTY THE QUEEN IN RIGHT OF CANADA as represented by the Royal Canadian Mounted Police

beings that would allow comparative analyses and the design of preventative measures are limited. The relatively low risks associated with trafficking and the potential for substantial profits have, in some cases, induced criminals to become involved as an alternative to other, riskier criminal pursuits. Furthermore, victims are intimidated by traffickers, both in destination countries, where they fear deportation or prosecution for offences such as prostitution or illegal immigration, and in their countries of origin, where they are often vulnerable to retaliation or re-victimization. As a result, many are reluctant to cooperate with criminal justice authorities, making detection and prosecution difficult. Supporting and protecting victims are critical elements in the fight against trafficking to increase their willingness to cooperate with authorities and as a necessary means of rehabilitation.

The adoption of the UNODC's *Protocol to Prevent, Suppress, and Punish Trafficking in Persons, Especially Women and Children* in 2000 has initiated the cooperation of all signing countries to work together to produce and share greater information on the trafficking of humans, to enact domestic laws making human trafficking an offence, to ensure that such legislation applies to victims of all ages and both sexes, and to implement measures to provide for the physical, psychological, and social recovery of victims. More recently, the UNODC has launched a human trafficking case law database that aims at assisting judges and prosecutors by making available details of real cases with examples of how the respective national laws can be used to prosecute trafficking in persons. Since very little is currently known internationally about the cases where prosecutions have been carried out, the case law database serves to provide immediate public access to officially documented instances of this crime and contains details on victims' and perpetrators' nationalities, trafficking routes, verdicts, and other information related to prosecuted cases from across the world.[24] In Canada, trafficking in humans wasn't recognized as an offence until November 2001, when Bill C-11 amended the former *Immigration Act* to include fines of up to $1 million and life imprisonment for the trafficking of people. The new *Immigration and Refugee Protection Act (IRPA)* was proclaimed in June 2002. In 2005, the *Criminal Code of Canada* was amended, creating three additional offences to cover all forms of trafficking. Section 279 includes the prohibition of trafficking in persons, defined as the recruitment, transport, transfer, receipt, concealment, or harbouring of a person, or the exercise of control, direction, or influence over the movements of a person, for the purpose of exploitation. It also prohibits a person from benefiting economically from trafficking, as well as prohibiting the withholding or destroying of identity, immigration, or travel documents to facilitate trafficking in persons.

Even with the appropriate legislation in place, it is difficult to lay charges for human trafficking as these are not regular criminal cases. The low number of human trafficking charges in Canada speaks in large part to the very covert nature of these crimes, the reluctance of victims to come forward, and the complexity of human trafficking investigations that often span multiple international jurisdictions. In 2004, the RCMP established a new human trafficking unit to provide guidance and analytical support for domestic investigations across Canada and to mount joint investigations with foreign law enforcement agencies. The unit shares information with the Canadian Security and Intelligence Service (CSIS) and works to coordinate domestic efforts of individual police services across the country and to link these efforts to the protocols, investigative standards, and training in the international arena. Within its Immigration and Passport Branch, the RCMP has created the Human Trafficking National Coordination Centre (HTNCC), which oversees six regional immigration and passport sections, employing about 160 officers who are mandated to investigate immigration and human trafficking offences.[25]

TECHNOLOGY AND CRIME

IN 2010 A NEW TERM, *CYBERBANGING*—REFERRING TO THE USE OF THE INTERNET and social networking websites by street gangs to tout their exploits, recruit new members, post threats, and socialize—entered the law enforcement lexicon. Videos and lyrics glorifying gang activities can be found on Facebook, MySpace, and Twitter, and some gangs have their own home pages and even run their own servers.[26] Law enforcement experts have said that gangs sometimes use social networking sites to circumvent court injunctions forbidding members from meeting face-to-face. Not to be outdone, police agencies and criminal prosecutors have begun scouring social networking sites looking for evidence they can use to disrupt gang activities or to prosecute gang members for crimes they've committed.

Technology and crime have always been closely linked. The con artist who uses a telephone in a financial scam, the robber who uses a firearm and drives a getaway car, even the murderer who wields a knife—all employ at least rudimentary forms of technology in the crimes they commit. Early forms of technology, including the telegraph, the telephone, and the automobile, were embraced by agents of law enforcement as soon as they became available. Evidence derived from fingerprint and ballistics analysis is routinely employed by prosecutors, and emerging technologies promise to keep criminologists and law enforcement agents in step with high-tech offenders.

As technology advances, it facilitates new forms of behaviour, so we can be certain that tomorrow's crimes will differ from those of today. Personal crimes of violence and traditional property crimes will continue to occur, but advancing technology will create new and as yet unimaginable opportunities for criminals positioned to take advantage of it and of the power it will afford. The very nature of this criminal activity makes it a global concern and transnational in scope—indeed, technology is one of the easiest ways to organize and undertake unlawful activity that transcends national borders.

Cybercrime refers to any crime that involves the use of computers or the manipulation of digital data and is generally defined as "a criminal offence involving a computer as the object of the crime, or the tool used to commit a material component of the offence."[27] Many argue that only those crimes that employ computer technology as central to their commission and that could not be committed without it may properly be called "cybercrimes." The Canadian Police College recognizes two broad categories of cybercrime—one in which the computer is the *tool* of the crime and one in which the computer is the *object* of the crime.

Types of criminal behaviour in which the computer is the *tool* of the crime include traditional crimes that are now being perpetrated more widely through the use of the internet.

Cybercrime Any crime that involves a computer as the object of the crime or as the tool used to commit a material component of the offence.

They include child pornography, child luring, criminal harassment, cyberbullying, fraud, theft of intellectual property and information, and the sale of humans, illegal goods, and substances. (For a more in-depth look at cyberbullying, see the Crime in the News box.)

The second category of cybercrime, in which the computer is the *object* of the crime, speaks to relatively new crimes that are related more specifically to computer technology. This category includes such activities as hacking or unauthorized use of computer systems, defacing of websites, and the creation and malicious dissemination of computer viruses.[28] The FBI in the United States recognizes five types of computer crime: (1) internal computer crimes, such as viruses, (2) internet and telecommunications crimes such as illegal hacking, (3) support of criminal enterprises such as databases supporting drug distribution, (4) computer manipulation crimes including embezzlement, and (5) hardware, software, and information theft.[29] (See Table 12.2 for a more detailed breakdown of the categories of computer crimes as defined by the FBI.)

Computers as a Tool of Crime

The 21st century has been described by some as the epitome of the post-industrial information age. Information is vital to the success of any endeavour, and certain forms of information hold nearly incalculable value. Patents on new products, the chemical composition of innovative and effective drugs, corporate marketing strategies, and the financial resources of competing corporations are all forms of information whose illegitimate access might bestow unfair advantages upon unscrupulous competitors. Imagine the financial wealth and

Table 12.2 Categories of Cybercrime	
Internal Cybercrimes	***Support of Criminal Enterprises***
Trojan horses	Databases to support drug distribution
Logic bombs	Databases to support loan-sharking
Trapdoors	Databases to support illegal gambling
Viruses	Databases to keep records of illegal client transactions
	Electronic money laundering
	Communications in furtherance of criminal conspiracies
Internet and Telecommunications Crimes	
Phone phreaking	***Computer-Manipulation Crimes***
Hacking	Embezzlement
Denial of service attacks	Electronic fund transfer fraud
Illegal websites	Other fraud/phishing
Dissemination of illegal material (such as child pornography)	Extortion threats/electronic terrorism
Misuse of telephone systems	***Hardware, Software, and Information Theft***
Theft of telecommunications services	Software piracy (Warez)
Illegal eavesdropping	Theft of computers
Illegal internet-based gambling	Theft of microprocessor chips
	Theft of trade secrets and proprietary information
	Identify theft

Cyberbullying-Linked Suicides Rising

Cases of suicides linked to cyberbullying have grown over the past decade, but being tormented over the internet is rarely the main factor involved, a new Canadian study shows.

There have been 41 suicides since 2003 involving cyberbullying in the United States, Canada, Australia, and the United Kingdom, but most of the victims were also bullied in school and many suffered from mental illness, including depression, said John C. LeBlanc, a professor at Dalhousie University in Halifax who conducted the research.

"Although cyberbullying is a new and fairly awful modern manifestation of bullying . . . it is not a cause of suicide. It's only one factor among many. . . . People who are cyberbullied have, for the most part, been bullied in more traditional manners as well."

The case of British Columbia teen Amanda Todd, who took her own life in December 2012 after posting a video on YouTube describing how she had been tormented by bullying online and struggling with depression, has shone a spotlight on the problem of cyberbullying and the tragic consequences that can result. Her death sparked a firestorm of international attention, prompted RCMP to investigate the contributing factors, including cyberbullying, and pushed MPs to call for a national anti-bullying strategy. There have been other high-profile cases in Canada, such as Jenna Bowers-Bryanton, a 15-year-old Nova Scotia girl who took her own life in January 2011.

Seventy-Eight Percent of Victims Bullied Online and in Person

LeBlanc and his team of researchers analyzed English-language media reports of suicides in which cyberbullying was mentioned. They identified 41 cases, stemming as far back as 2003. Their research showed that the incidence increased over time, with 23 cases (56 percent) taking place between 2003 and 2010. But in 2011 and the first four months of 2012, there were 18 cases of suicides with a cyberbullying link.

There is no clear reason why the cases appear to be growing, but exposure and use of social media has increased, LeBlanc said. "While it is catastrophic, it is rare. These 41 cases, over four countries in eight years illustrate that ... but it's rare and therefore very difficult to study," he said.

The vast majority of cases, 23, were in the U.S., followed by six in Australia, five in the U.K., and four in Canada. Of the victims, 78 percent of them who committed suicide were bullied both at school and online—with only 17 percent targeted on the internet only, the study showed. A mood disorder was present in 32 percent of the teens, and another 15 percent also had depression symptoms. Another notable finding was that all of the victims were between the ages of 13 to 18, likely stemming from the pressures of adolescence, LeBlanc said.

"Teenagers are very vulnerable that way," he said. "Adults use social media, particularly young adults. So, it's not exposure to social media, but about being a young adolescent that is trying to form his or her identity, and cares very much about what people think."

Social Networking Sites Used in Nearly Half of Cases

The victims were more often female, with 24 female cases compared with 17 males, researchers found. The researchers also catalogued the type of electronic media or social media used. Social networking sites were used in 48 percent of all the suicide cases, while messaging (text, pictures, or video) were used in 25 percent of the cases. Facebook was used in cyberbullying most often, cited in 27 percent of cases, while Facebook combined with messaging of pictures, videos, and texts were used in 13 percent. Also, it appeared that most of the suicides took place in September and January, coinciding with the beginning of a new school semester, though there were not enough cases to be statistically significant, LeBlanc said.

The takeaway message from the study, he said, is like with traditional bullying, people must intervene when they suspect someone is being bullied.

Amanda Todd's suicide is a "striking example," he said, of a troubled person putting out a cry for help, but no one coming to her aid.

Because bullying usually takes places out of the view of most adults, other young people need to step in, whether online or in person, LeBlanc said.

"Youth themselves have to develop a code of ethics or civility ... where, when things like this happen, they actually jump in to protect the other person, and they actually post things online that says this is inappropriate," he said.

Source: Adapted with permission from The Canadian Broadcasting Corporation from *CBCNews*, "Cyberbullying-linked suicides rising, study says", October 20, 2012. http://www.cbc.ca/news/technology/story/2012/10/19/cyberbullying-suicide-study.html.

market share that would accrue to the first pharmaceutical company to patent an effective AIDS cure and the potential profitability inherent in the information describing the chemical composition of that drug (especially to a competitor who might beat the legitimate originator of the substance to the patent desk or who might use stolen information in a later bid to challenge patents already issued).

High-tech criminals seeking illegitimate access to computerized information and to the databases that contain it have taken a number of routes. One is the path of direct access, by which office workers or corporate spies, planted as seemingly innocuous employees, violate positions of trust and use otherwise legitimate work-related entry to a company's computer resources to acquire wanted information, stealing data during business hours under the guise of normal work routines.

Another path of illegal access, called "computer trespass," involves remote access to targeted machines. Anyone equipped with a home computer and some knowledge about computer modems, telecommunications, and log-on procedures has easy access to numerous computer systems across the country because many of these systems have few (if any) security procedures in place (see the following Who's Responsible? box). In one case, for example, a Silicon Valley software company learned that a software developer who had been fired had been using her telephone to enter the company's computers. By the time she was caught, she had copied several million dollars' worth of the company's programs.[30] It was later learned that the stolen software had been slated for illicit transmission to collaborators in Taiwan, and if the scheme had succeeded, thousands of pirated copies of the software would have been distributed at great financial loss to the legitimate copyright owners.

Some cybercriminals intend simply to destroy or alter data without otherwise accessing or copying the information. Disgruntled employees, mischievous computer **hackers**, business competitors, and others may all have varied degrees of interest in destroying a company's records or computer capabilities.

In 1988, the first criminal prosecution of a person accused of creating a computer virus took place. According to Richard Baker, author of the respected *Computer Security Handbook*, "The greatest threat to your computers and data comes from inside your company, not outside. The person most likely to invade your computer is not a gawky youngster in some other part of the country but an employee who is currently on your payroll."[31]

Software piracy, the unauthorized and illegal copying of software programs, is rampant, and global estimates of lost revenues owing to pirated software (known as "Warez" in the computer underground) dwarfed those cybercrime amounts. The Software and Information Industry Association (SIIA) distinguishes among various forms of software piracy.[32] According to the Business Software Alliance, global losses from software piracy totaled nearly $51.4 billion in 2009.[33] The Alliance notes that 43 percent of software in use worldwide is illegally copied. Some countries have especially high rates of illegal use. Of all the computer software in use in China, for example, it is estimated that 82 percent has been illegally copied.

According to some experts, losses like these may be just the beginning. One technological visionary observed, "Our society is about to feel the impact of the first generation of children who have grown up using computers. The increasing sophistication of hackers suggests that computer crime will soon soar, as members of this new generation are tempted to commit more serious offenses."[34]

While the theft or damage of information represents one area of illegitimate criminal activity, using different technologies in direct furtherance of criminal enterprise constitutes another and is as varied as the technologies themselves. Nuclear blackmail may represent the extreme technologically based criminal threat, whereas telephone fraud and phone phreaking are examples of low-end crimes that depend on modern technology for their commission.

One of the earliest forms of cybercrime was committed by **phone phreaks**, who use special dial-up access codes and other restricted technical information to avoid long-distance charges. Some are able to place calls from pay phones, while others fool telephone equipment into billing other callers. "Many organizations discover they have been victims of telephone fraud only after their telephone bill arrives in a carton instead of an envelope."[35]

Criminal Activity or Performing a Good Deed?

His second academic year had barely begun in September 2008 when Mansour Moufid withdrew from his math program at Carleton University in Ottawa amid controversy surrounding his involvement in an attempt to expose the weaknesses of the university's security system.

In a 16-page report sent to university administrators and students under the pseudonym "Kasper Holmberg," Moufid showed that he had accessed the campus card accounts of 32 students. His letter indicated that, while he could have accessed student emails, course registrations, library records, and personal financial information, as well as any money students put on their cards, he did not, stating that he was only interested in encouraging the university to improve its security.

Cited for violation of the school's Student Rights and Responsibilities Policy, the university administration imposed six sanctions on Moufid, including paying $608 for the cost of 32 new student cards; paying $2160 for the cost of extra security staff for the residence buildings due to the unknown risk caused by the breach of the campus card system; seven hours of community service per week at a local food bank; and the completion of an ethics course. It was made very clear that if Moufid violated the university's student policy again, he would face expulsion.

The controversy about the situation and what ultimately resulted in Moufid's withdrawal from Carleton University was the university's requirement that he write a letter of apology to all 32 students, the university, and the university community, admitting that he had lied about alerting the university before distributing his report. Moufid refused, insisting that he had mailed a copy of his report to Carleton's Information Privacy Officer and its Information Coordinator two weeks

before he sent it to the affected students and campus media. In his statement of defence, Mr. Moufid indicated that he never had any intention of harming his fellow students or Carleton University in any way, and that his ultimate goal was to see security improved.

"To be clear: I did not create any security problem, but simply revealed it; I did not alter or destroy any data although I could have; I did not take any advantage of any student, either financially or otherwise, although I could have; I was acting in good faith, with the interests of the student body—of which I am a part of—in mind," read a portion of his statement.

In addition to being submitted to the university's discipline, Mr. Moufid was also charged under the *Criminal Code* with mischief to data and unauthorized use of a computer. Both charges carry a maximum prison sentence of 10 years. Mr. Moufid said he was surprised by the severity of the charges. "Ten years in prison? That's like the Mafia or something."

Think about it:

1. Was Mansour Moufid, as he claimed, doing a service by showing weaknesses in the university's security infrastructure?

2. Might there have been better ways for Moufid to make his point? Would these ways have been as effective as the computer mischief in which he engaged? Why or why not?

Source: Adapted from "Hacker Quits School to Avoid Punishment," *Ottawa Citizen*, September 28, 2008, http://www.canada.com/ottawacitizen/news/story.html?id=ce863a37-9fb9-46d6-b90b-40be380084e6 [Accessed January 1, 2013]; and Karen Pinchin, "All Charges Against Carleton Hacker Dropped," *Maclean's On Campus*, July 27, 2009, http://oncampus.macleans.ca/education/2009/07/27/all-charges-against-carleton- hacker-dropped/ [Accessed January 1, 2013].

Another form of phone phreaking has emerged that involves the electronic theft of cellular telephone numbers and access codes. Thieves armed with simple mail-order scanners and low-end computers can "literally grab a caller's phone number and identification number out of the air."[36] According to some experts, "Those numbers are [then] used to program computer chips, which are placed inside other cellular phones—or 'clones'—so the long-distance calls appear on the victim's bill."[37]

Developments in Voice-over Internet Protocol (VoIP) technology have made the theft of telecommunications services less lucrative but have also opened the door to new kinds of crime. The rapid growth of VoIP communications services makes surveillance and wiretapping difficult and is thought to facilitate "drug trafficking, organized crime, and terrorism."[38] Legislators in some countries are considering changes to VoIP regulations to require telecommunications providers to build "back doors" into VoIP networks that would allow for court-ordered wiretaps to be successfully enforced.

Another form of high-technology fraud is termed **phishing**, a scam that uses official-looking email messages to steal valuable information such as credit card numbers, social insurance numbers, user IDs, and passwords from victims. The email messages appear to come from a user's bank, credit card company, retail store, or internet service provider (ISP) and generally inform the recipients that some vital information in their account urgently needs to be updated. Those who respond are provided with an official-looking Web form on which they can enter their private financial information; once the information is submitted, it enters the phisher's database.

The Anti-Phishing Working Group—a coalition of banks and ISPs—estimated that a typical phishing scheme reaches up to one million email inboxes and identified more than 55 600 different scams as of June 2007.[39] Some observers have noted that in addition to losses suffered by individuals and institutions, phishing has the potential to threaten the viability of e-commerce and to call into question the safety of all Web-based financial transactions.[40] A 2012 report indicated that Canada ranked second worldwide after the United States for hosted phishing sites (ahead of well-known offenders like Egypt and Russia) and hosted 170 percent more phishing sites than in 2011.[41] See Box 12.1 for some suggestions on protecting yourself from identity theft.

Computers as an Object of Crime

Not all cybercrime is committed for financial gain. Some types of cybercrime—including the creation and transmission of destructive computer viruses, "worms," and other malicious forms of programming code (often called *malware*)—might better be classified as "criminal mischief." These types of activities are typically associated with young, technologically sophisticated males seeking a kind of clandestine recognition from their computer-savvy peers. Cybercrimes committed by youthful idealistic offenders may represent a new form of juvenile delinquency—one aimed at expressing dissatisfaction with the status quo.

Computer viruses have shown signs of becoming effective terrorist-like tools in the hands of young, disaffected "technonerds" intent on attacking or destroying existing social institutions. A **computer virus** is simply a computer program that is designed to secretly invade computer systems and either to modify the way in which they operate or to alter the information they store.[42] Other types of destructive programs are logic bombs, worms, and Trojan horse routines. Distinctions among these programs are based on the way in which they infect targeted machines or the way they behave once they have managed to find their way into a computer.

Viruses may spread from one machine to another via modem or high-speed cable and digital subscriber line (DSL) connections (when files are downloaded) and through networks or direct links, DVDs, flash drives, CD-ROMs, or magnetic or optical backup media. Most viruses hide inside executable computer software in the so-called boot sectors of storage media. Rogue codes known as *macro viruses* have been secreted into text documents; the most famous of these, the Concept virus, affects users of Microsoft's Word software. Hypertext markup language (HTML) files, which form the backbone of the World Wide Web, may be infected with viruses lurking inside Java script or Macromedia Shockwave-generated code. Some users also worry that "cookies" (small programs sent to users' machines by servers on the Web) may spread viruses. Viruses infect not only desktop computers and laptops but also popular handheld devices, including personal digital assistants (PDAs) and mobile phones.

Perhaps the most insidious forms of destructive programming making the rounds of the computer world today are polymorphic viruses, which use advanced encryption techniques to assemble varied (yet entirely operational) clones of themselves and have the ability to

Box 12.1 IDENTITY THEFT: WHAT IT IS AND WHAT YOU CAN DO ABOUT IT

Identity theft is the unauthorized collection and use of personal information, usually for criminal purposes. Name, date of birth, address, credit card, social insurance number (SIN), and other personal identification numbers can be used to open credit card and bank accounts; redirect mail; establish cellular phone service; rent vehicles, equipment, or accommodation; and even secure employment. Victims can be left with the bills, charges, bad cheques, and taxes. In 2010, Bill S-4 became law in Canada, making it illegal to possess another person's identity information for criminal purposes. Section 402 of the *Criminal Code of Canada* addresses identity theft.

Every year, thousands of Canadians are victims of identity theft. While recent developments in telecommunications and computer processing make it easier for companies and consumers to reach each other, they can also scatter your personal information more widely, making life easier for criminals. In 2011, 17 002 victims of identity fraud reported a combined loss of over $13 million (see Figure 12.1).

Prevention is the best way to deal with identity theft:

- Identity theft can occur over the internet or telephone, or via fax or regular mail. Therefore, be particularly wary of unsolicited emails, telephone calls, or mail attempting to extract personal or financial information from you.

- Ask yourself if you really need all the identity documents you carry in your wallet or purse. Remove any you don't need and keep them in a secure place instead.

- Periodically check your credit reports and bank and credit card statements and report any irregularities promptly to the relevant financial institution and to the credit bureaus.

- During transactions, it's safer to swipe your cards yourself than it is to allow a cashier to do it for you. If you must hand over your card, never lose sight of it.

- Always shield your personal identification number when using an ATM or a PIN pad.

- Memorize all personal identification numbers for payment cards and telephone calling cards. Never write them on the cards.

- Familiarize yourself with billing cycles for your credit and debit cards.

- Trash bins are a goldmine for identity thieves. Make sure you shred personal and financial documents before putting them in the garbage.

- When you change your address, make sure you notify the post office and all relevant financial institutions (your bank and credit card companies).

Sources: Canadian Anti-Fraud Centre Criminal Intelligence Analytical Unit, *Annual Statistical Report 2011*, http://www.anti-fraudcentre-centreantifraude.ca/english/documents/Annual%20 2011%20CAFC.pdf [Accessed January 4, 2013]; and "Identity Theft and Identity Fraud," Royal Canadian Mounted Police website, April 27, 2012, http://www.rcmp-grc.gc.ca/scams-fraudes/id-theft-vol-eng.htm [Accessed January 4, 2013].

Figure 12.1 Total Reported Dollar Loss by Canadian Identity Fraud Victims, 2011

Source: Canadian Anti-Fraud Centre Criminal Intelligence Analytical Unit, *Annual Statistical Report 2011*, p. 18, http://www. antifraudcentre-centreantifraude.ca/english/documents/Annual%202011%20CAFC.pdf [Accessed April 7, 2011].

alter themselves once they have infected a computer. This strategy is effective in circumventing most security devices that depend on scanning techniques to recognize viral signatures—when viruses change, they can no longer be recognized. In typical leapfrog fashion, as when crime-fighting techniques are overtaken and surpassed by new technologies favouring lawbreakers and then later regain ascendancy, polymorphic viruses have largely rendered signature-based antivirus-scanning technologies obsolete.

Although many hardware devices and software products now on the market offer some degree of virus protection to individual and commercial users, new viruses are constantly being created that may soon have the ability to circumvent all security procedures now in place. The only fully effective technique for avoiding viral contamination is the complete and total isolation of computer equipment—a strategy as unlikely to be maintained as it is to be implemented. Once certain forms of malicious software code have successfully invaded a computer, they can take over the machine and use it to send out additional copies of themselves or send spam and other information (including the legitimate user's personal information) to various places on the internet.

Technology in the Fight against Crime

Technology is a double-edged sword: it arms evildoers with potent new weapons of crime commission, yet it provides police agencies and criminal justice personnel with powerful tools useful in the battle against crime. Criminally useful or evasive technologies and law enforcement capabilities commonly leapfrog one another. Consider traffic radar, which has gone from early always-on units through trigger-operated radar devices to today's sophisticated laser-based speed-measuring apparatus—each change being an attempt by enforcement agencies to keep a step ahead of increasingly sophisticated radar-detection devices marketed to drivers. Although cutting-edge laser units are invisible to most radar detectors, laser radar detectors *do* exist; their usefulness is open to debate because they generally alert the speeding driver too late. Radar-jamming devices and laser jammers are also now used by people apparently intent on breaking speed-limit laws.

Other potent technologies in law enforcement today are computer databases of known offenders (including public access to sex-offender databases), machine-based expert systems, cellular communications, video surveillance (often combined with face-recognition technology), electronic eavesdropping, deoxyribonucleic acid (DNA) analysis, and less-lethal weapons (such as electroshock weapons, also known as Tasers). Transponder-based automated vehicle location (AVL) systems now use patrol car–based transmitters in tandem with orbiting global positioning satellites (GPS) to pinpoint locations of police vehicles so that dispatchers can better allocate available resources on a given shift and substantially reduce police response times in crisis situations. (Chip-based transponders are also installed in private vehicles to deter thieves and to help trace stolen automobiles.)

As new technologies are developed, their potential usefulness in law enforcement activities is evaluated by the RCMP, the FBI, and other agencies. The U.S. National Institute of Justice Technology Assessment Program (TAP), for example, focuses on four areas of advancing technology: protective equipment, such as bullet-proof vests and other body armour; forensic sciences, including advances in DNA technology; transportation and weapons, such as electronic stun guns and other less-lethal weapons; and communications and electronics, including computer security and electronic eavesdropping.[43]

The widespread use of computers and computer applications in a diversity of professions has been one of the most far-reaching social phenomena of recent years. As crime-fighting tools, computers assist in the design of new technologies and aid in the assignment of resources to problem areas: police departments, prisons, and courts now employ computer software to schedule facilities and personnel; to keep track of defendants, witnesses, and cases; and to keep account of budgetary matters.

Computers also connect people. The internet contains a large number of law enforcement–oriented blogs and discussion groups and provides access to United Nations and worldwide crime data through its link to the United Nations Criminal Justice Information Network (uncjin.org). Other computer services offer access to security information and to software useful in law enforcement administration. Specialized websites, such as the Society of Police Futurists International's home page (policefuturists.org), the International Association of Chiefs of Police site (theiacp.org), and the SEARCH Group (search.org), link law enforcement professionals and criminologists throughout the world.

Other innovative computer technologies—the automated fingerprint identification system (AFIS) with international links, a computerized crime-scene simulation and reenactment, expert systems, and online clearinghouses with data on criminal activity and offenders—facilitate the work of law enforcement agents. AFIS allows investigators to match a suspect's fingerprints against stored records in a matter of minutes (instead of weeks or months) because its computers are able to compare and eliminate many thousands of fingerprints per second, sometimes leading to the identification of a suspect in a short time. "Live-scan" technology permits easy inkless digitizing of fingerprints from suspects, and the U.S. Bureau of Alcohol, Tobacco, and Firearms has new software that takes a 360-degree picture of a bullet's ballistic characteristics and then compares them with others stored in a database to isolate a small universe of potential matches.

The automated measurement of human traits and identifiers such as face, finger, and iris recognition is now a wide-spread practice among law enforcement agencies. These biometric technologies are used for two main purposes: to identify individuals in a database and to support identity assurance, meaning that a user of a system is who he or she claims to be. See Box 12.2 for a more detailed look at the use of biometric technologies in Canada.

Box 12.2 BIOMETRIC TECHNOLOGIES IN CANADA

Biometric technologies are a deeply personal subject—they relate to the automated measurement of human physiological traits (such as face, finger, and iris) or behavioural traits (such as walking gait or typing style). By definition, we are all attached to our biometric attributes. But to get to the heart of a technology that has been around for a couple of decades (predated by many non-automated systems), one has to poke around a bit under the surface.

What are biometric technologies used for?

Biometric technologies are used for two main purposes: to identify individuals in a database and to support identity assurance, meaning that a user of a system is who he or she claims to be.

Along this line, the use of biometric technologies has migrated from its historical role in isolated applications such as forensic investigation to a broader role supporting applications such as crossing a border or authorizing a financial transaction.

The acceptable degree of identity assurance for any transaction depends on the particular risk assessed in that environment. For example, a higher degree of identity assurance would be required for crossing a border than for buying a bag of groceries. Biometric technologies can enable

such a high degree of identity assurance that they can largely mitigate any malfeasance by imposters. In other words, the stronger that an individual can assert a claim of identity assurance, the less chance there is for someone else to be able to access that person's data or services.

How Canada Uses Biometric Technologies

So what does this all mean for Canada? Canada's keen sense of privacy and personal data control is embodied by its legislation. As biometric technologies are deployed in Canada, both in the private and public sectors, their effect on the existing infrastructure is typically evaluated through both a security evaluation and a privacy impact assessment. This is particularly true of large-scale government deployments such as the use of electronic passports.

Maintaining both security and privacy is integral to Canada's well-being, and the use of biometric technologies is assessed with this in mind. In Canada, biometric technologies are currently being used in many commercial environments such as protection of physical and computer assets, and time and attendance applications. Often, a single biometric technology such as facial recognition will be used (for example, with the e-passports for some countries); in other cases, a combination of several technologies will be used to increase the degree of identity assurance (for example,

(Continued)

As of 2012, Canadian passports include an electronic chip for increased security. The chip stores the passport holder's photo and personal information.

B Calkins/Shutterstock

fingerprint and facial recognition are typically combined for border and immigration applications).

Canada has been operating expedited traveller systems for the last decade, first with the CANPASS border clearance system, which expedites border clearance for low-risk, pre-approved travellers into Canada, and more recently with the NEXUS system for travellers into both Canada and the United States. Canada was one of the first nations in the world to strengthen its airport security using biometric technologies to access secure areas with the Restricted Area Identification Card deployed by the Canadian Air Transport Security Authority.

In 2012, Canada joined the 100 or so countries around the world that use e-passports, which allow automated facial recognition to positively authenticate that the holder is who he or she claims to be. The standards for e-passports were developed by the International Civil Aviation Organization, headquartered in Montreal.

Canada will also soon include biometric technologies in its visa application process—as the United Kingdom and the United States currently do. The use of biometric technologies for visa application prevents known criminals from entering Canada and maintains integrity throughout the visit by ensuring that no one has stolen the correct holder's visa entitlement.

What's the Future of Biometrics in Canada?

Four main trends are driving biometric technologies to more commonplace applications: (1) people are becoming increasingly aware of the well-being of their personal data and the need to protect it using strong authentication techniques such as biometric technologies, (2) the use of remote cloud applications to store important corporate or personal data means that identity assurance needs to be increasingly strong, (3) the use of mobile devices such as smart phones to remotely access data and services can be strengthened using on-board biometric capabilities, and (4) the continued security and performance characterization of biometric technologies will allow them to be further used alongside other authentication technologies.

Canada's strong technology and privacy base will ensure that technologies are designed with the appropriate safeguards and principles in place, and that biometric technologies can continue to be used as a tool to maintain our personal information, assets, and access to entitlements.

Source: Biometric technologies in Canada: Finding a balance between security and privacy, National Research Council Canada, 2012 Reproduced with the permission of the Minister of Public Works and Government Services Canada, 2013.

Once crime-related information or profiles of criminal offenders have been generated, they are typically stored in a database and made accessible to law enforcement agencies at other sites. The RCMP's Violent Crime Linkage Analysis System (ViCLAS) is used internationally (and is described in more detail in Chapter 7). Other specialized database programs now track inner-city gang activity and gang membership, contain information on known sexual predators, and describe missing children.

PC radios, combinations of laptop computers and police radios, provide another high-tech approach to the fight against crime. Officers use PC radios to obtain motor vehicle information, get detailed information when answering a call, and report incidents either by saving data on disk or by transmitting them to other locations such as police headquarters. PC radios have also helped mislead offenders who routinely use police scanners to keep abreast of enforcement activities, because the digitized transmissions consist of machine code that cannot be easily read by those trying to outsmart the police.

Expert systems deploy machine-based artificial intelligence to duplicate decision-making processes used by skilled investigators in analyzing evidence and recognizing patterns that such evidence might represent to draw conclusions and make recommendations to police investigators and others interested in solving problems related to crime and its commission. One system being used by the FBI's National Center for the Analysis of Violent Crime (NCAVC) attempts to profile serial killers by matching clues left at a crime scene with individual personality characteristics. While the NCAVC system is becoming increasingly sophisticated, it has not yet replaced human investigators. A number of other specialized computer programs, such as ImAger (by Face Software, Inc.) and Compusketch (by Visatex Corporation), assist police artists in rendering composite images of suspects and missing victims.

Cybercrime and the Law

The internet is now available around the world and its borderless nature allows for crimes to be committed through a number of different countries. Challenges to the prevention and control of cybercrime are that a criminal can commit a crime from any country in the world, target victims all over the world, hide his or her identity by using computer systems located in many different countries, and store evidence in remote locations. Given this transnational reality of cybercrime, initiatives for combating and preventing computer-based crime largely rely on international cooperation. The Council of Europe *Convention on Cybercrime*, signed by Canada and 29 other nations, is the first international treaty on crimes that are committed via the internet and that involve the use of computer networks. Critics of the convention contend that the treaty fails to provide meaningful privacy and civil liberties protections and that its scope is too broad and covers much more than computer-related crimes. Moreover, they argue, the treaty lacks a "dual criminality" provision, under which an activity must be considered a crime in both countries before one nation can demand cooperation from another.[44] In 2005, Canada signed the *Additional Protocol to the Convention on Cybercrime*, which addresses material and acts of a racist or xenophobic nature committed through computer networks. At home, the Canadian government launched Canada's Cyber Security Strategy in 2010, designed to enhance the protection from cyberthreats for Canadian governments, industries, and families. Committing $8 million of funding over five years, the strategy is built on three pillars: (1) securing government systems—putting in place the necessary structures, tools, and personnel to meet the government's obligations for cybersecurity; (2) partnering to secure vital cybersystems outside the federal government—supporting initiatives and strengthening Canada's cyber resiliency, including that of its critical infrastructure sectors, in cooperation with provincial/territorial governments and the private sector; and (3) helping Canadians to be secure online—assisting Canadians in getting the information they need to protect themselves and their families online. The Canadian Auditor General's 2012 report criticized the country's commitment on battling cybercrime and showed how far behind Canada is on cybersecurity. The Auditor General found that federal departments have lost track of how millions of dollars have been spent on cybersecurity over the past decade and that there are no benchmarks to determine whether the spending is having its intended effect. Also missing is a detailed plan that lays out who is responsible for what in terms of keeping federal systems safe and helping secure the vast private networks that control the country's telephone, banking, and transportation systems.[45]

One of the challenges within Canada in the battle against cybercrime is the difficulty of applying existing legislation to criminal activities that involve new technologies. Nevertheless, Canada is well ahead of many nations in enacting laws to address cybercrime. Amendments to the *Criminal Code of Canada* have addressed theft of telecommunications services, possession of a device to obtain computer services, computer fraud, and mischief in relation to data, among criminal acts. In many instances, revisions to legislation ensure that existing offences are defined in such a way as to address the new technological aspects of the crime. For example, revisions to legislation making the possession of child pornography illegal have now made it also illegal to download and view child pornography online.[46]

12.4 LEARNING OBJECTIVE

EMERGING CRIMES

MURDER, THEFT, SEXUAL ASSAULT, AND THE OTHER TYPES OF "EVERYDAY" CRIME that have become mainstays of contemporary criminological analysis will continue to occur in the future, but other new and emergent forms of criminality will grow in frequency and number. One prediction contended that by the year 2025, "socially significant crime—that is, the crimes that have the widest negative effects—in the advanced nations will be increasingly economic and computer based. Examples include disruption of business, theft, introduction of maliciously false information, and tampering with medical records, air traffic control, or national-security systems."[47] Another futurist predicted that "the top guns of 21st-century criminal organizations will be educated, highly sophisticated, computer-literate individuals who can wield state-of-the-art information technology to the best advantage—for themselves and for their organizations."[48]

In a wide-ranging overview of future crimes, Richter H. Moore, Jr., painted a picture of future criminality that includes many dimensions: "Computer hackers are changing bank records, credit accounts and reports, criminal-history files, and educational, medical, and even military records."[49] Identity manipulation will be a nexus of future criminality. "By the 21st century," Moore wrote, "genetic-based records will include a birth-to-death dossier of a person and will be the method of criminal identification." The U.S. military is presently using genetic testing to assign unique identification codes to each of its soldiers; in the event of war, such codes will allow for the identification of human remains from as little as a single cell. DNA coding may form the basis for nearly foolproof identification technologies, taking the science of personal identification far beyond fingerprinting, blood-type matching, or photography. The science of bioengineering, now undergoing clinical trials in the treatment of various diseases, could also be clandestinely employed for the illegal modification of human DNA, with the goal of effectively altering a person's identity, and the theft of computer-based genetic identification records could make it possible for one person to effectively imitate another in our future society.

Moore described many other crimes of the future. Within a few decades, "criminal organizations will be able to afford their own satellites." Drug trafficking and money laundering operations could be coordinated via satellite communications, couriers and shipments could be tracked, and satellite surveillance could provide alerts of enforcement activity. Moore went on to say that "prostitution rings will use modern technology to coordinate global activities," and that children and fetuses may "become subject to unlawful trafficking." The illegal disposal of toxic materials, an activity already perpetrated by organized crime, may become even more profitable for criminal entrepreneurs as many more hazardous substances are produced in the face of ever-tighter controls. The supply of nuclear materials and military-quality armaments to "private armies, terrorists, hate groups, questionable regimes, independent crime groups, and individual criminals" will be a fact of life in the 21st century, as will the infiltration of governments and financial institutions by sophisticated criminals whose activities are supported by large, illegally acquired fortunes.

SUMMARY OF LEARNING OBJECTIVES

12.1 Globalization refers to the increasing integration of previously isolated events in all areas of life and to its effects on people throughout the world. Globalization makes it impossible for Canadian policymakers to ignore criminal activity in other parts of the world.

12.2 Transnational crime refers to unlawful activity undertaken and supported by organized criminal groups operating across national boundaries whose activities include fraudulent email and phishing schemes, drug running, sex tourism, illegal trafficking in human beings and human organs, and international trade in weapons of mass destruction.

12.3 Technology and criminology have always been closely linked—as technology advances, it facilitates new forms of criminal behaviour. High-technology offences can dramatically change our understanding of crime. Some forms of high-tech crime, committed without regard for national borders or even the need for physical travel, hold dangers never before imagined. High technology provides new criminal opportunities by making available to perpetrators new tools and advanced techniques useful in the commission of crime, and by contributing to the development of items of value, such as computer codes, that did not previously exist. Technology in law enforcement today involves computer databases of known offenders, expert systems, cellular communications, video surveillance and face-recognition technology, electronic eavesdropping, DNA analysis, and less-lethal weapons.

12.4 Crimes of the future are predicted to be "socially significant," having wide-ranging negative effects. Future crimes will be increasingly economic and computer based.

Questions for Review

1. What is globalization? How does it affect criminal activity in today's world?

2. Do you believe that transnational crimes will eventually surpass the abilities of enforcement agencies to prevent or solve them? Why?

3. What are the differences between cybercrime and traditional forms of criminal activity? How does high technology provide new criminal opportunities?

4. What are some likely future crimes, and how will future criminal activity differ from criminal activity today?

Multiple-Choice Questions

1. The task of the futurist is to distinguish effectively between the impending possibilities of multiple futures, assess the likelihood of each, and _____.

   a. make unrealistic assumptions about technology

   b. make realistic forecasts based on each assessment

   c. make realistic arrest forecasts about transnational criminal activities

   d. make realistic assumptions about biometric interventions

   e. make unrealistic economic forecasts about law enforcement costs

2. All of the following statements indicate different challenges to the prevention and control of cybercrime except _____.

   a. a criminal can target victims all over the world

   b. a criminal can store evidence in remote locations

   c. a criminal can commit a crime from any country in the world

   d. a criminal can hide his or her identity by using computer systems located in many different countries

   e. a criminal can commit crimes at any time of the day or night

3. _____ refers to the displacement of an individual by means of coercion, deceit, or violence for the purpose of exploitation.

   a. Human abduction

   b. Human smuggling

   c. Migrant smuggling

   d. Human trafficking

   e. Migrant trafficking

4. Foresight's Crime Prevention Panel outlines three social characteristics that are relevant to understanding and predicting future forms of criminality. They are individuality and independence, Information Communication Technology usage, and _____.

   a. technology

   b. criminality

   c. defensible space

   d. globalization

   e. territorial reinforcement

5. _____ has been identified as one of the three major challenges facing the world in the 21st century.

   a. Transnational criminal activity

   b. The globalization of criminal behaviour

   c. Information technology

   d. Human trafficking

   e. Cybercrime

Multiple Choice Answers: 1b, 2e, 3d, 4d, 5a

Notes

Chapter 1

1. Thomas Gabor, *Everybody Does It! Crime by the Public* (Toronto: University of Toronto Press, 1994), p. 307.

2. Robert Seidman, "'NCIS' Voted America's All-Time Favorite Show," *TV by the Numbers*, May 5, 2011, http://tvbythenumbers.zap2it.com/2011/05/05/ncis-voted-americas-all-time-favorite-tv-show-two-and-a-half-men-bones-house-several-current-shows-rank/91686/ [Accessed November 11, 2012].

3. Sarah Bibel, "'CSI: Crime Scene Investigation' Is the Most-Watched Show in the World," *TV by the Numbers*, June 14, 2012, http://tvbythenumbers.zap2it.com/2012/06/14/csi-crime-scene-investigation-is-the-most-watched-show-in-the-world-2/138212/ [Accessed November 11, 2012].

4. From the standpoint of the law, the proper word is *conduct* rather than *behaviour*, because the term *conduct* implies intentional and wilful activity, whereas *behaviour* refers to any human activity—even that which occurs while a person is unconscious, as well as that which is unintended.

5. Paul W. Tappan, "Who Is the Criminal?" in Gilbert Geis and Robert F. Meier, eds., *White Collar Crime* (New York: Free Press, 1947), p. 277.

6. Edwin Sutherland, *Principles of Criminology*, 4th ed. (New York: J.B. Lippincott, 1947).

7. "The Fight for the Right to Die," *CBC News*, June 15, 2012, http://www.cbc.ca/news/canada/story/2012/06/15/f-assisted-suicide.html [Accessed November 11, 2012].

8. Marlisa Tiedemann and Dominique Valiquet, *Euthanasia and Assisted Suicide in Canada*, (Ottawa: Library of Parliament, Law and Government Division, July 2008).

9. "The Fight for the Right to Die."

10. C.D. Shearing, "Criminologists Must Broaden Their Field of Study beyond Crime and Criminals," in R. Boostrom, ed., *Enduring Issues in Criminology* (San Diego, CA: Greenhaven, 1995).

11. Ezzat Fattah, *Introduction to Criminology* (Burnaby, BC: School of Criminology, Simon Fraser University, 1989).

12. Hermann Mannheim, *Comparative Criminology* (Boston: Houghton Mifflin, 1965).

13. Ron Claassen, *Restorative Justice: Fundamental Principles*, http://peace.fresno.edu/docs/rjprinc.html [Accessed November 11, 2012].

14. H. Schwendinger and J. Schwendinger, "Defenders of Order or Guardians of Human Rights?" *Issues in Criminology*, vol. 5, no. 2 (Summer 1970), pp. 123–157.

15. Jeffrey H. Reiman, *The Rich Get Richer and the Poor Get Prison*, 4th ed. (Boston: Allyn & Bacon, 1997), p. 49.

16. Fattah, *Introduction to Criminology*.

17. Matthew B. Robinson, "Defining 'Crime,'" http://www.appstate.edu/~robinsnmb/smokeharms.htm [Accessed November 4, 2006].

18. Piers Beirne and James W. Messerschmidt, *Criminology* (San Diego, CA: Harcourt Brace Jovanovich, 1991), p. 20.

19. See this site maintained by the Canadian Automobile Association (CAA) for an overview of each province's legislation: http://distracteddriving.caa.ca/education/distracted-driving-laws-in-canada.php [Accessed November 11, 2012].

20. Raymond J. Michalowski, "Perspectives and Paradigm: Structuring Criminological Thought," in Robert F. Meier, ed., *Theory in Criminology* (Beverly Hills, CA: Sage, 1977), pp. 17–39.

21. Ibid.

22. Ibid.

23. *The American Heritage Dictionary*, CD-ROM (Boston: Houghton Mifflin, 1992).

24. *The American Heritage Dictionary of the English Language*, 3rd ed. (Boston: Houghton Mifflin, 1996).

25. This list is not meant to be exclusive. There are many other journals in the field, too many to list here.

26. A paper entitled *Public Policing and Private Security: Canadian Jurisprudence in International Perspective* by Tom Quigley, Faculty of Law, University of Saskatchewan, contends that the ratio of private security personnel outnumbers police officers in Canada by two to one. The 2006 statistics from Statistics Canada report that there are three private security personnel (102 000) for every two police officers (68 000). See G. Li, "Private Security and Public Policing in Canada, 2006," *Juristat*, vol. 28, no. 10 (Ottawa: Minister of Industry, 2009).

27. Piers Beirne, *Inventing Criminology* (Albany: State University of New York Press, 1993).

28. See also Paul Topinard, *Anthropology* (London: Chapman and Hall, 1984).

29. Edwin H. Sutherland, *Criminology* (Philadelphia: Lippincott, 1924), p. 11.

30. Edwin H. Sutherland, *Principles of Criminology* (Chicago: University of Chicago Press, 1934).

31. Edwin H. Sutherland and Donald R. Cressey, *Criminology*, 9th ed. (Philadelphia: Lippincott, 1974), p. 3.

32. Gennaro F. Vito and Ronald M. Holmes, *Criminology: Theory, Research, and Policy* (Belmont, CA: Wadsworth, 1994), p. 3.

33. Clemens Bartollas and Simon Dinitz, *Introduction to Criminology: Order and Disorder* (New York: Harper & Row, 1989), p. 548.

34. Marvin E. Wolfgang and Franco Ferracuti, *The Subculture of Violence: Towards an Integrated Theory in Criminology* (London: Tavistock, 1967).

35. European Society of Criminology, Constitution, Section 1(d), http://www.esc-eurocrim.org/constitution.shtml [Accessed November 14, 2012].

36. Jack P. Gibbs, "The State of Criminological Theory," *Criminology*, vol. 25, no. 4 (November 1987), pp. 822–823.

37. *Theoretical Criminology*, vol. 1, no. 1 (February 1997), pp. 5–141. Available through Sage Publications, Thousand Oaks, CA.

38. There are, however, those who deny that criminology deserves the name "discipline." See, for example, Don C. Gibbons, *Talking about Crime and Criminals: Problems and Issues in Theory Development in Criminology* (Englewood Cliffs, NJ: Prentice Hall, 1994), p. 3.

39. Gibbons, *Talking about Crime and Criminals*, p. 4.

40. Sutherland, *Principles of Criminology*.

41. Don M. Gottfredson, "Criminological Theories: The Truth as Told by Mark Twain," in William S. Laufer and Freda Adler, eds., *Advances in Criminological Theory*, vol. 1 (New Brunswick, NJ: Transaction, 1989), p. 1.

42. Gregg Barak, *Integrating Criminologies* (Boston: Allyn & Bacon, 1998), p. 5.

43. Don G. Gibbons, "Talking About Crime: Observations on the Prospects for Causal Theory in Criminology," *Criminal Justice Research Bulletin*, vol. 7, no. 6 (Huntsville, TX: Sam Houston State University, 1992).

44. Ibid.

45. Hermann Mannheim, *Comparative Criminology* (Boston: Houghton Mifflin, 1967), p. 20.

46. Details for this story come from Paul Stokes, "Extra Police Put on the Beat for Full Moon," *The Telegraph*, June 7, 2006, http://www.telegraph.co.uk/news/uknews/1553751/Extra-police-put-on-the-beat-for-full-moon.html [Accessed November 23, 2012].

47. Gottfredson, "Criminology Theories," p. 3.

48. Kenneth R. Hoover, *The Elements of Social Scientific Thinking*, 5th ed. (New York: St. Martin's Press, 1992), p. 34.

49. Bernard P. Cohen, *Developing Sociological Knowledge: Theory and Method*, 2nd ed. (Chicago: Nelson-Hall, 1989), p. 71.

50. Susette M. Talarico, *Criminal Justice Research: Approaches, Problems and Policy* (Cincinnati, OH: Anderson, 1980), p. 3.

51. For a good review of secondary research, see J.H. Laub, R.J. Sampson, and K. Kiger, "Assessing the Potential of Secondary Data Analysis: A New Look at the Gluecks' Unraveling Juvenile Delinquency Data," in Kimberly L. Kempf, ed., *Measurement Issues in Criminology* (New York: Springer-Verlag, 1990), pp. 241–257; and Robert J. Sampson and John H. Laub, *Crime in the Making* (Cambridge, MA: Harvard University Press, 1993).

52. Sampson and Laub, *Crime in the Making*, p. 3.

53. According to Denise C. Gottfredson, "Midnight basketball programs are not likely to reduce crime." Gottfredson cites research (J.G. Ross et al., "The Effectiveness of an After-School Program for Primary Grade Latchkey Students on Precursors of Substance Abuse," *Journal of Community Psychology*, OSAP Special Issue [1992], pp. 22–38) showing that such programs may actually increase the risk for delinquency by increasing risk taking and impulsiveness. See Denise C. Gottfredson, "School-Based Crime Prevention," in Lawrence W. Sherman et al., *Preventing Crime: What Works, What Doesn't, What's Promising* (Washington, DC: National Institute of Justice, 1998).

54. Frank E. Hagan, *Research Methods in Criminal Justice and Criminology* (New York: Macmillan, 1993), p. 103.

55. Canadian Centre for Justice Statistics, *The Juristat Reader: A Statistical Overview of the Criminal Justice System* (Toronto: Thompson Educational Publishing, 1999), p. v.

56. As with almost anything else, qualitative data can be assigned to categories and the categories numbered. Hence qualitative data can be quantified, although the worth of such effort is subject to debate.

57. Patrick J. Desroches, *Behind the Bars—Experiences in Crime* (Toronto: Canadian Scholars' Press, 1996), pp. 27–28.

58. Hagan, *Research Methods in Criminal Justice and Criminology*, p. 43.

59. Ibid.

60. Faye S. Taxman, "Research and Relevance: Lessons from the Past, Thoughts for the Future," *Criminology and Public Policy*, vol. 3, no. 2 (March 2004), p. 170.

61. Julian Leigh, "Mandatory Arrest Laws Can Reduce Domestic Violence," in Tamara L. Roleff, ed., *Domestic Violence: Opposing Viewpoints* (San Diego, CA: Greenhaven Press, 2000).

62. Kevin D. Haggerty, "Displaced Expertise: Three Constraints on the Policy Relevance of Criminological Thought," *Theoretical Criminology*, vol. 8, no. 2 (2004), pp. 211–231.

63. The Campaign for an Effective Crime Policy, *The Impact of Three Strikes and You're Out Laws: What Have We Learned?* (Washington, DC: CECP, 1997).

64. Fox Butterfield, no headline, *New York Times News Service Online*, April 16, 1997.

65. Sherman et al., *Preventing Crime: What Works, What Doesn't, What's Promising* (Washington, DC: National Institute of Justice, 1998).

66. Mennonite Central Committee, "Harsher Penalities Not Answer to Canada's Crime Problem," *Mennonite Central Committee News Service*, October 26, 1994, http://www.acbr.com/fas/crime1.htm [Accessed November 24, 2012].

67. Carol La Prairie, "The Impact of Aboriginal Justice Research on Policy: A Marginal Past and an Even More Uncertain Future," *Canadian Journal of Criminology*, vol. 41, no. 2 (April 1999), p. 249.

68. Ibid., p. 250.

69. Alfred Blumstein, "Making Rationality Relevant: The American Society of Criminology 1992 Presidential Address," *Criminology*, vol. 31, no. 1 (February 1993), p. 1.

70. Julian V. Roberts, *Fear of Crime and Attitudes to Criminal Justice: A Review of Recent Trends, 2001–02*. Report for the Ministry of the Solicitor General (Ottawa: Public Works and Government Services Canada, 2001), pp. 24–26.

71. Angus Reid Strategies, *Canadians Endorse Federal Government's Anti-Crime Proposals*, June 26, 2009, http://www.angus-reid.com/polls/40374/canadians-endorse-federal-governments-anti-crime-proposals/ [Accessed November 24, 2012].

72. Karin Stein, *Public Perception of Crime and Justice in Canada: A Review of Opinion Polls* (Ottawa: Department of Justice Canada, 2001), p. x.

73. For an especially good discussion of this issue, see Theodore Sasson, *Crime Talk: How Citizens Construct a Social Problem* (Hawthorne, NY: Aldine de Gruyter, 1995).

74. Dan Gardner, *Risk: The Science and Politics of Fear* (Toronto: McClelland & Stewart, 2008).

75. Public Safety Canada, *Supporting the Successful Implementation of the National Crime Prevention Strategy*, http://www.public-safety.gc.ca/res/cp/res/ssincps-amosnpc-eng.aspx [Accessed November 24, 2012].

76. Frank Schmalleger, *Criminology Today: An Integrative Introduction* (Upper Saddle River, NJ: Prentice Hall, 2012), p. 16.

77. For a good overview of this issue, see Wesley G. Skogan, ed., *Reactions to Crime and Violence: The Annals of the American Academy of Political and Social Science* (Thousand Oaks, CA: Sage, 1995).

78. For an excellent discussion of crime as a social event, see Leslie W. Kennedy and Vincent F. Sacco, *Crime Counts: A Criminal Event Analysis* (Toronto: Nelson Canada, 1996).

79. For a good discussion of the social construction of crime, see Leslie T. Wilkins, "On Crime and Its Social Construction: Observations on the Social Construction of Crime," *Social Pathology*, vol. 1, no. 1 (January 1995), pp. 1–11.

80. For a parallel approach, see Terance D. Miethe and Robert F. Meier, *Crime and Its Social Context: Toward an Integrated Theory of Offenders, Victims, and Situations* (Albany: State University of New York Press, 1995).

81. Joan McCord, "Family Relationships, Juvenile Delinquency, and Adult Criminality," *Criminology*, vol. 29, no. 3 (August 1991), pp. 397–417.

82. Elizabeth Candle and Sarnoff A. Mednick, "Perinatal Complications Predict Violent Offending," *Criminology*, vol. 29, no. 3 (August 1991), pp. 519–529.

83. Carol W. Kohfeld and John Sprague, "Demography, Police Behavior, and Deterrence," *Criminology*, vol. 28, no. 1 (February 1990), pp. 111–136.

84. Leslie W. Kennedy and David R. Forde, "Routine Activities and Crime: An Analysis of Victimization in Canada," *Criminology*, vol. 28, no. 1 (February 1990), pp. 137–152.

85. William G. Doerner, "The Impact of Medical Resources on Criminally Induced Lethality: A Further Examination," *Criminology*, vol. 26, no. 1 (February 1988), pp. 171–177.

86. Ibid., p. 177.

87. James F. Gilsinan, "They Is Clowning Tough: 911 and the Social Construction of Reality," *Criminology*, vol. 27, no. 2 (May 1989), pp. 329–344.

88. See, for example, Miethe and Meier, *Crime and Its Social Context*.

89. For a good discussion of the historical development of criminology, see Don C. Gibbons, *Talking about Crime and Criminals:*

Problems and Issues in Theory Development in Criminology (Englewood Cliffs, NJ: Prentice Hall, 1994); Don C. Gibbons, *The Criminological Enterprise* (Englewood Cliffs, NJ: Prentice Hall, 1979); and Leon Radzinowicz, *In Search of Criminology* (Cambridge, MA: Harvard University Press, 1962).

90. Diana Fishbein, as quoted in W. Wayt Gibbs, "Trends in Behavioral Science: Seeking the Criminal Element," *Scientific American*, vol. 272, no. 3 (1995), pp. 100–107.

Chapter 2

1. F. Schmalleger, D. MacAlister, P.F. McKenna, and J. Winterdyk, *Canadian Criminal Justice Today: An Introductory Text for the Twenty-First Century* (Toronto: Prentice Hall Allyn & Bacon Canada, 2000), p. 29.

2. This section adapted from CBC News, "'Black Widow' Charged with Attempted Murder," *CBC News*, October 2, 2012, http://www.cbc.ca/news/canada/nova-scotia/story/2012/10/02/ns-black-widow-charged.html [Accessed December 10, 2012]; The Canadian Press, "Man Who Wed Black Widow Says Marriage Unregistered," *CBC News*, October 18, 2012, http://www.cbc.ca/news/canada/nova-scotia/story/2012/10/18/ns-black-widow-marriage-weeks.html [Accessed December 10, 2012]; and "Trial for 'Internet Black Widow' Set for June," *CBC News*, December 3, 2012, http://www.cbc.ca/news/canada/nova-scotia/story/2012/12/03/ns-black-widow-trial-june.html [Accessed December 10, 2012].

3. A number of contemporary criminologists continue to study the effect of weather on crime. See, for example, Ellen G. Cohn, "The Effect of Weather and Temporal Variations on Calls for Police Service," *American Journal of Police*, vol. 15, no. 1 (1996), pp. 23–43; Ellen G. Cohn, "The Prediction of Police Calls for Service: The Influence of Weather and Temporal Variables on Rape and Domestic Violence," *Environmental Psychology*, vol. 13 (1993), pp. 71–83; Ellen G. Cohn, "Weather and Crime," *British Journal of Criminology*, vol. 30, no. 1 (1990), pp. 51–64; and Derral Cheatwood, "Is There a Season for Homicide?" *Criminology*, vol. 26, no. 2 (May 1988), pp. 287–306.

4. B.J. Ennis and T.R. Litwack, "Psychiatry and the Presumption of Expertise: Flipping Coins in the Classroom," *California Law Review*, vol. 62 (1974), pp. 693–725.

5. Canadian Centre for Justice Statistics, *The Juristat Reader. A Statistical Overview of the Canadian Justice System* (Toronto: Thompson Educational Publishing, 1999), p. v.

6. R.A. Silverman, J.T. Teevan, and V.F. Sacco, eds., *Crime in Canadian Society* (Toronto: Harcourt Brace, 1996), pp. 62–63.

7. Shannon Brennan, "Police-Reported Crime Statistics in Canada, 2011," *Juristat*, Cat. no. 85-002-X (Ottawa: Ministry of Industry, July 2012).

8. Ibid.

9. Ibid.

10. K. AuCoin, "Children and Youth as Victims of Violent Crime," *Juristat*, vol. 25, no. 1 (Ottawa: Minister of Industry, 2005).

11. Solicitor General of Canada, "Victims of Crime," *Canadian Urban Victimization Survey* (Ottawa: Solicitor General of Canada, 1983).

12. J. Short and F. Nye, "Extent of Unrecorded Juvenile Delinquency: Tentative Conclusions," *Journal of Criminal Law, Criminology and Police Science*, vol. 49 (1958), pp. 296–302.

13. M. LeBlanc and M. Fréchette, *Male Criminal Activity from Childhood through Youth: Multilevel and Developmental Perspectives* (New York: Springer-Verlag, 1989).

14. For an overview of the reliability of self-report studies, see M.J. Hindelang, T. Hirschi, and J.G. Weis, *Measuring Delinquency* (Beverly Hills, CA: Sage, 1981).

15. For an excellent overview of the social dimensions of crime, see John Hagan and Ruth D. Peterson, *Crime and Inequality* (Stanford, CA: Stanford University Press, 1995); and James W.

Messerschmidt, *Crime as Structured Action: Gender, Race, Class and Crime in the Making* (Thousand Oaks, CA: Sage, 1997).

16. V.P. Bunge, H. Johnson, and T. Baldé, "Exploring Crime Patterns in Canada," *Crime and Research Justice Research Paper Series*, Cat. no. 85-561-MIE (Ottawa: Minister of Industry, 2005).

17. Alfred Blumstein, "Violence by Young People: Why the Deadly Nexus?" *National Institute of Justice Journal*, no. 229 (August 1995).

18. John J. Dilulio, Jr., "The Question of Black Crime," *The Public Interest* (Fall 1994), pp. 3–12.

19. James Alan Fox, *Trends in Juvenile Violence: A Report to the United States Attorney General on Current and Future Rates of Juvenile Offending* (Washington, DC: Bureau of Justice Statistics, 1996); and Gary Fields, "Youth Violent Crime Falls 9.2%," *USA Today*, October 3–5, 1997, p. 1A (quoting James Fox).

20. James Q. Wilson and Joan Petersilia, *Crime* (San Francisco: Institute of Contemporary Studies, 1995).

21. Bunge, Johnston, and Baldé, "Exploring Crime Patterns in Canada."

22. Marc Ouimet, "Explaining the American and Canadian Crime 'Drop' in the 1990s," *Canadian Journal of Criminology*, vol. 45, no. 2 (2002), pp. 33–50.

23. Samuel Perreault and Shannon Brennan, "Criminal Victimization in Canada, 2009," *Juristat*, vol. 30, no. 2 (Ottawa: Minister of Industry, 2010).

24. K. AuCoin, "Children and Youth as Victims of Violent Crime," *Juristat*, vol. 25, no. 1 (Ottawa: Minister of Industry, 2005).

25. Stephen E. Brown, Finn-Aage Esbensen, and Gilbert Geis, *Criminology: Explaining Crime and Its Context*, 2nd ed. (Cincinnati, OH: Anderson, 1996), p. 198.

26. Tina Hotton Mahony, "Women and the Criminal Justice System," *Women in Canada: A Gender-Based Statistical Report*, Cat. no. 89-503-X (Ottawa: Minister of Industry, April 2011).

27. Elizabeth Cormack, "Women and Crime," in R. Linden, ed., *Criminology: A Canadian Perspective* (Toronto: Harcourt Brace Canada, 1996), pp. 139–175.

28. Leanne Fiftal Alarid, James W. Marquart, Velmer S. Burton, Jr., Francis T. Cullen, and Steven J. Cuvelier, "Women's Roles in Serious Offenses: A Study of Adult Felons," *Justice Quarterly*, vol. 13, no. 3 (September 1996), pp. 432–454.

29. Nicole Bermbach, "Putting Increase in Female Crime Rates in Context," *Pathways: The Elizabeth Fry Society of Calgary*, vol. 1, no. 5 (September/October 2012), http://www.elizabethfrycalgary.ca/files/pdf/Newsletter_Vol-1_Iss-5_2012-SeptemberOctober.pdf [Accessed December 29, 2012].

30. Ibid.

31. Perreault and Brennan, "Criminal Victimization in Canada, 2009."

32. Statistics Canada, *Violence Against Women Survey: Survey Highlights* (Ottawa: Minister of Industry, 1993).

33. Public Safety Canada, *Corrections and Conditional Release Statistical Overview 2011* (Ottawa: Public Works and Government Services Canada, 2011).

34. P. Havemann, K. Couse, L. Foster, and R. Matonovich, *Law and Order for Canada's Indigenous People* (Regina: Prairie Justice Research, School of Human Justice, University of Regina, 1985); John Hagan, "Criminal Justice in Rural and Urban Communities," *Social Forces*, vol. 55, no. 3 (1977), pp. 597–612; and D.F. Wayne and T.F. Hartnagel, "Race and Plea Negotiation," *Canadian Journal of Sociology*, vol. 1, no. 2 (1975), pp. 147–155.

35. J.H. Hylton, "The Native Offender in Saskatchewan," *Canadian Journal of Criminology*, vol. 24, no. 2 (1982), pp. 121–131; and Carol La Prairie, "Aboriginal Crime and Justice," *Canadian Journal of Criminology*, vol. 34 (1992), pp. 281–297.

36. Carol La Prairie, "Aboriginal Over-representation in the Criminal Justice System: A Tale of Nine Cities," *Canadian Journal of Criminology*, vol. 44, no. 2 (2002), pp. 181–208.

37. Havemann et al., *Law and Order for Canada's Indigenous People*.

38. John Hagan, "Criminal Justice and Native People," *Canadian Review of Sociology and Anthropology*, Special Issue (August 1974), pp. 220–236.

39. Samuel Perreault, "Violent Victimization of Aboriginal Peoples in the Canadian Provinces, 2009," *Juristat*, Cat. no. 85-002-X (Ottawa: Minister of Industry, March 11, 2011).

40. For a good review of the issues involved, see John Hagan, *Structural Criminology* (New Brunswick, NJ: Rutgers University Press, 1989).

41. Charles R. Tittle, Wayne Villemez, and Douglas Smith, "The Myth of Social Class and Criminality: An Empirical Assessment of the Empirical Evidence," *American Sociological Review*, vol. 43, no. 5 (1978), pp. 643–656; see also Charles R. Tittle, "Social Class and Criminality," *Social Forces*, vol. 56, no. 2 (1977), pp. 474–502.

42. John Braithwaite, "The Myth of Social Class and Criminality Reconsidered," *American Sociological Review*, vol. 46, no. 1 (1981), pp. 36–57.

43. Margaret Farnworth, Terence P. Thornberry, and Marvin D. Krohn, "Measurement in the Study of Class and Delinquency: Integrating Theory and Research," *Journal of Research in Crime and Delinquency*, vol. 31, no. 1 (1994), pp. 32–61.

44. J. Hagan and B. McCarthy, "Street Life and Delinquency," *British Journal of Sociology*, vol. 43, no. 4 (1992), pp. 533–561.

45. J. Savoie, "Youth Self-Reported Delinquency, Toronto, 2006," *Juristat*, vol. 27, no. 5 (Ottawa: Minister of Industry, 2007).

46. Bunge, Johnston, and Baldé, "Exploring Crime Patterns in Canada."

47. Perreault and Brennan, "Criminal Victimization in Canada, 2009."

Chapter 3

1. Anthony Doob, quoted in "Crime Rate Continues to Drop Across Canada," *National Post*, August 25, 2011, http://news.nationalpost.com/2011/07/21/crime-rate-down-across-canada/ [Accessed December 1, 2012].

2. Jeremy Mercer, "'Locker Room Bandit' Benched," *Ottawa Citizen*, March 6, 1999, pp. A1–A2.

3. Shannon Brennan, "Police-Reported Crime Statistics in Canada, 2011," *Juristat*, Cat. no. 85-002-X (Ottawa: Ministry of Industry, July 2012).

4. "Teenager Gets Nine Years in Dagenais Murders," *CBC News*, http://www.cbc.ca/canada/ottawa/story/2003/12/09/ot_dagenais20031209.html [Accessed November 27, 2012].

5. Bureau of Justice Statistics, *Report to the Nation on Crime and Justice* (Washington, DC: U.S. Government Printing Office, 1988), p. 4.

6. Frank Schmalleger, *Criminology Today: An Integrated Introduction* (Upper Saddle River, NJ: Prentice Hall, 1999), p. 63.

7. Bureau of Justice Statistics, *Report to the Nation on Crime and Justice*, p. 4.

8. Detailed information about homicide in Canada is from Tina Hotton Mahony, "Homicide in Canada, 2010," *Juristat*, Cat. no. 85-002-X (Ottawa: Minister of Industry, October 26, 2011).

9. Federal Bureau of Investigation, *Crime in the United States, 2011* (Washington, DC: U.S. Department of Justice, 2011), http://www.fbi.gov/about-us/cjis/ucr/crime-in-the-u.s/2011/crime-in-the-u.s.-2011 [Accessed December 1, 2012].

10. See Elizabeth Cormack, "Women and Crime," in Rick Linden, ed., *Criminology: A Canadian Perspective* (Toronto: Harcourt Brace Canada, 1996), pp. 139–175.

11. Maire Gannon, "Canadian Crime Statistics, 2005," *Juristat*, vol. 26, no. 4 (Ottawa: Minister of Industry, 2006).

12. Samuel Perreault and Shannon Brennan, "Criminal Victimization in Canada, 2009," *Juristat*, vol. 30, no. 2 (Ottawa: Minister of Industry, 2010).

13. Perreault and Brennan, "Criminal Victimization in Canada, 2009"; and Brennan, "Police-Reported Crime Statistics in Canada, 2011."

14. Martha R. Burt, "Cultural Myths and Supports for Rape," *Journal of Personality and Social Psychology*, vol. 38 (1980), pp. 217–230.

15. For example, see Mary P. Koss et al., "Nonstranger Sexual Aggression: A Discriminant Analysis of the Psychological Characteristics of Undetected Offenders," *Sex Roles*, vol. 12 (1985), pp. 981–992.

16. Martha R. Burt, "Rape Myths," in Andrea Parrot and Laurie Bechhofer, eds., *Acquaintance Rape: The Hidden Crime* (New York: John Wiley & Sons, 1991).

17. Brennan, "Police-Reported Crime Statistics in Canada, 2011."

18. Shelly Milligan, "Criminal Harassment in Canada, 2009," *Juristat*, Cat no. 85-005-X (Ottawa: Minister of Industry, March 2011).

19. Brennan, "Police-Reported Crime Statistics in Canada, 2011."

20. The most recent data are from 1999. See Karen Hackett, "Criminal Harassment," *Juristat*, vol. 20, no. 11 (Ottawa: Minister of Industry, 2000).

21. Milligan, "Criminal Harassment in Canada, 2009."

22. Mia Dauvergne, "Police-Reported Robbery in Canada, 2009," *Juristat*, vol. 30, no. 1 (Ottawa: Minister of Industry, March, 2010).

23. Phil Walsh and Mia Dauvergne, "Police-Reported Hate Crime in Canada, 2008," *Juristat*, vol. 30, no. 2 (Ottawa: Ministry of Industry, March 2010).

24. All statistics taken from Walsh and Dauvergne, "Police-Reported Hate Crime in Canada, 2007."

25. Peter Hum, "Compassion for a Child Killer," *Ottawa Citizen*, December 28, 1999, p. B1.

26. Cathy S. Widom, "The Intergenerational Transmission of Violence," in Neil Warner and Marvin Wolfgang, eds., *Pathways to Criminal Violence* (Newbury Park, CA: Sage, 1989).

27. Orest Fedorowycz, "Breaking and Entering in Canada—2002," *Juristat*, vol. 24, no. 5 (Ottawa: Minister of Industry, July 2004).

28. R. Barnhorst and S. Barnhorst, *Criminal Law and the Canadian Criminal Code* (Toronto: McGraw-Hill Ryerson, 2009), p. 303.

29. Mia Dauvergne, "Motor Vehicle Theft in Canada, 2007," *Juristat*, vol. 28, no. 10 (Ottawa: Minister of Industry, 2008).

30. Ibid.

31. Taylor Shire, "Car Thefts Down: RCMP," *The Star Phoenix*, January 14, 2011, http://www2.canada.com/saskatoonstarphoenix/news/local/story.html?id=81f15494-4384-4af0-8c5a-e2738cb9095f [Accessed December 2, 2012].

32. Criminal Intelligence Service Canada (CISC), *2010 Report on Organized Crime*, 2010, http://www.cisc.gc.ca/annual_reports/annual_report_2010/document/report_oc_2010_e.pdf [Accessed December 2, 2012].

33. *Bank of Canada Review Supplement*, June 2011, http://www.bankofcanada.ca/wp-content/uploads/2011/06/spencer.pdf [Accessed December 2, 2012].

34. L.J. Siegel and C. McCormick, *Criminology in Canada* (Scarborough: ITP Nelson, 1999), p. 427; and Nicholas D. Kristof and Sheryl WuDunn, *Half the Sky: Turning Oppression into Opportunity for Women Worldwide* (New York: Alfred A. Knopf, 2009).

35. Mia Dauvergne, "Trends in Police-Reported Drug Offences in Canada," *Juristat*, vol. 29, no. 2 (Ottawa: Minister of Industry, 2009).

36. "Drug Situation in Canada—2009," Royal Canadian Mounted Police (RCMP) website, 2009, http://www.rcmp-grc.gc.ca/drugs-drogues/index-eng.htm [Accessed December 2, 2012].

37. CISC, *2010 Report on Organized Crime*.

Chapter 4

1. Alan Young, *The Role of the Victim in the Criminal Process: A Literature Review—1989 to 1999*, Victims of Crime Research Series (Ottawa: Department of Justice, 2001).

2. G. Dimmock and J. Rupert, "Student Dies Trying to Stop Bar Fight," *Ottawa Citizen*, December 24, 1998, http://andymoffitt.org/newspapers/ottawacitizen/sep152003/story.asp_modified.html [Accessed March 8, 2007].

3. Dimmock and Rupert, "Student Dies Trying to Stop Bar Fight."

4. D. Campbell, "Mother Haunted by Son's Dying Screams," *Ottawa Citizen*, March 18, 2003, http://andymoffitt.org/newspapers/ottawacitizen/mar182003/story/story.asp_modified.html [Accessed October 5, 2012].

5. Hans von Hentig, *The Criminal and His Victim: Studies in the Sociobiology of Crime* (Hamden, CT: Archon Books, 1967). Reprinted from the 1948 Yale University Press edition.

6. As noted by Stephen Schafer, *The Victim and His Criminal: A Study in Functional Responsibility* (New York: Random House, 1968).

7. Benjamin Mendelsohn, "Method to Be Used by Counsel for the Defence in the Researches Made into the Personality of the Criminal," *Revue de Droit Pénal et de Criminologie* (Brussels, Belgium: Fall 1937), p. 877.

8. See Henry Ellenberger, "Relations Psychologiques entre le Criminel et sa Victime," *Revue Internationale de Criminologie et de Police Technique*, no. 2 (Geneva, Switzerland: 1954).

9. Thorsten Sellin and Marvin E. Wolfgang, *The Measurement of Delinquency* (New York: John Wiley & Sons, 1964).

10. Michael Hindelang, Michael R. Gottfredson, and James Garofalo, *Victims of Personal Crime: An Empirical Foundation for a Theory of Personal Victimization* (Cambridge, MA: Ballinger, 1978).

11. Lawrence E. Cohen and Marcus Felson, "Social Change and Crime Rate Trends: A Routine Activity Approach," *American Sociological Review*, vol. 44, no. 4 (August 1979), pp. 588–608.

12. Lawrence E. Cohen, J.R. Kluegel, and Kenneth Land, "Social Inequality and Predatory Criminal Victimization: An Exposition and Test of a Formal Theory," *American Sociological Review*, vol. 46, no. 5 (October 1981), pp. 505–524.

13. Ezzat Fattah, "Victimology Today: Recent and Applied Developments." Paper presented at the 112 International Training Course, Tokyo, 2000, http://www.unafei.or.jp/english/pdf/RS_No56/No56_09VE_Fattah2.pdf [Accessed October 5, 2012].

14. Samuel Perreault and Shannon Brennan, "Criminal Victimization in Canada, 2009," *Juristat*, vol. 30, no. 2 (Ottawa: Minister of Industry, 2010).

15. Rosa Casarez-Levison, "An Empirical Investigation of the Coping Strategies Used by Victims of Crime: Victimization Redefined," in Emilio Viano, ed., *Critical Issues in Victimology: International Perspectives* (New York: Springer, 1992).

16. Morton Bard and Dawn Sangrey, *The Crime Victim's Book*, 2nd ed. (New York: Brunner/Mazel, 1986).

17. Elisabeth Kübler-Ross, *On Death and Dying* (New York: Macmillan, 1969).

18. For an excellent review of many of these studies, see Alan Young, *The Role of the Victim in the Criminal Process: A Literature Review—1989 to 1999*, Victims of Crime Research Series (Ottawa: Department of Justice, 2001), pp. 57–59.

19. D. Kilpatrick and R. Otto, "Constitutionally Guaranteed Participation in Criminal Proceedings for Victims: Potential Effects on Psychological Functioning," *Wayne Law Review*, vol. 37, no. 7 (1987), p. 27.

20. Solicitor General of Canada, *The Psychological Impact of Crime: A Review* (Ottawa: Solicitor General of Canada, 1990–1991); and Solicitor General of Canada, *The Psychological Impact of Nonsexual Criminal Offences on Victims* (Ottawa: Solicitor General of Canada, 1992).

21. W. McDonald, "Towards a Bicentennial Revolution in Criminal Justice: The Return of the Victim," *American Criminal Law Review*, vol. 13 (1976); and S. Schafer, *Victimology: The Victim and His Criminal* (Reston: Reston Publishing, 1977).

22. Schafer, *Victimology*.

23. Nils Christie, "Conflicts as Property," *British Journal of Criminology*, vol. 1, no. 1 (1977), pp. 3–4.

24. See D. Hall, "Victims' Voices in Criminal Court: The Need for Restraint," *American Criminal Law Review*, vol. 28 (1991); J. Acker, "Social Sciences and the Criminal Law: Victims of Crime—Plight vs. Rights," *Criminal Law Bulletin*, vol. 28 (1992); and R. Black, "Forgotten Penological Purposes: A Critique of Victim Participation in Sentencing," *American Journal of Jurisprudence*, vol. 39 (1994).

25. Herbert Packer, *The Limits of the Criminal Process* (Stanford, CA: Stanford University Press, 1968).

26. Kent Roach, *Due Process and Victims' Rights: The New Law and Politics of Criminal Justice* (Toronto: University of Toronto Press, 1999).

27. Ibid., pp. 30–31.

28. Ibid., pp. 33–34.

29. V.F. Sacco and H. Johnson, *Patterns of Criminal Victimization in Canada* (Ottawa: Statistics Canada, 1990); and M. Baril, S. LaFlamme-Cusson, and S. Beauchemin, *Working Paper No. 12. Crime Victims Compensation: An Assessment of the Quebec IVAC Program* (Ottawa: Policy Planning and Development Branch, Department of Justice, 1984).

30. André Marin, *Investigation into the Treatment of Victims by the Criminal Injuries Compensation Board. "Adding Insult to Injury."* Ombudsman of Ontario, 2007.

31. "Ontario Commits $20M to Clear Criminal Injuries Backlog," *CBC News*, http://www.cbc.ca/canada/toronto/story/2007/03/02/criminal-injuries-ont.html [Accessed October 5, 2012].

32. Fattah, "Victimology Today," p. 61.

33. For more information about the role of the National Office for Victims, visit http://www.publicsafety.gc.ca/prg/cor/nov/nov-bnv-eng.aspx [Accessed October 5, 2012].

34. For a detailed look at the Office of the Federal Ombudsman for Victims of Crime, see http://www.victimsfirst.gc.ca/index.html [Accessed October 5, 2012].

35. Visit the website for the Policy Centre for Victim Issues at http://www.justice.gc.ca/eng/pi/pcvi-cpcv/ [Accessed October 5, 2012].

36. I. Waller, "Victims, Safer Communities and Sentencing," *Canadian Journal of Criminology*, vol. 32, no. 2 (1990), pp. 461–469.

37. J. Sauvé, "Victim Services in Canada, 2007/2008," *Juristat*, vol. 29, no. 4 (Ottawa: Minister of Industry, 2009).

38. Ibid.

39. Joseph Moylan, *Victim Services and Canadian Police Agencies—A Source Book* (Ottawa: Canadian Association of Chiefs of Police and Solicitor General of Canada, 1990). See also the overview of victim services on the Office of the Federal Ombudsman for Victims of Crime website at http://www.victimsfirst.gc.ca/serv/vsc-svc.html [Accessed October 5, 2012].

40. W. Jamieson and R.R. Ross, "An Evaluation of the Victim/Witness Assistance Programme, Ministry of the Attorney

General of Ontario," *Canadian Journal of Program Evaluation*, vol. 6, no. 1 (1991), pp. 83–96. See also the Victim Witness Assistance website at http://www.attorneygeneral.jus.gov.on.ca/english/service_standards/service_standards_victim_services.asp [Accessed October 5, 2012].

41. A. Hatch Cunningham and C.T. Griffiths, *Canadian Criminal Justice: A Primer* (Toronto: Harcourt Brace Canada, 1997), p. 79.

42. Jeff Latimer and Norman Desjardins, *The 2007 National Justice Survey: Tackling Crime and Public Confidence* (Ottawa: Department of Justice, 2007), p. 33.

43. Ezzat Fatah, "Victims and Victimology: The Facts and the Rhetoric," *International Review of Victimology*, vol. 1 (1989), p. 43.

44. R. Elias, *Victims Still: The Political Manipulation of Crime Victims* (Thousand Oaks, CA: Sage, 1993), p. 26.

45. Young, *The Role of the Victim in the Criminal Process*, p. 29.

46. Irvin Waller, *Less Law, More Order* (Westport, CT: Praeger, 2006). Waller also maintains a very informative website at http://irvinwaller.org/ [Accessed October 5, 2012].

47. Ibid.

Chapter 5

1. Cesare Beccaria, *Essay on Crimes and Punishments*, translated by Henry Paolucci (New York: Bobbs-Merrill, 1963); first printed 1764.

2. William Graham Sumner, *Folkways* (New York: Dover, 1906).

3. Marvin Wolfgang, "The Key Reporter," *Phi Beta Kappa*, vol. 52, no. 1.

4. Roman influence in England had ended by 442 AD, according to Crane Brinton, John B. Christopher, and Robert L. Wolff, *A History of Civilization*, 3rd ed., vol. 1 (Englewood Cliffs, NJ: Prentice Hall, 1967), p. 180.

5. Howard Abadinsky, *Law and Justice* (Chicago: Nelson-Hall, 1988), p. 6.

6. Edward McNall Burns, *Western Civilization*, 7th ed. (New York: W.W. Norton, 1969), p. 339.

7. Ibid.

8. Brinton, Christopher, and Wolff, *A History of Civilization*, p. 274.

9. Referred to in official transcripts as Rudolf Franz Ferdinand Hoess.

10. International Military Tribunal, "One Hundred and Eighth Day, Monday, 4/15/1946, Part 03," in *Trial of the Major War Criminals before the International Military Tribunal*, Volume XI. Proceedings: 4/8/1946–4/17/1946 (Nuremberg: IMT, 1943), pp. 398–400.

11. The quotations attributed to Beccaria in this section are from Cesare Beccaria, *Essay on Crimes and Punishments* (Livorno, Italy: Tipografia Coltellini, 1764).

12. The quotations attributed to Bentham in this section are from Jeremy Bentham, *An Introduction to the Principles of Morals and Legislation* (Oxford: Clarendon Press, 1907); reprint of the 1823 edition, first printed 1780.

13. R. Martinson, "What Works? Questions and Answers about Prison Reform," *Public Interest*, vol. 35 (1974).

14. James Q. Wilson, *Thinking about Crime* (New York: Vintage, 1975).

15. Felton M. Earls and Albert J. Reiss, *Breaking the Cycle: Predicting and Preventing Crime* (Washington, DC: National Institute of Justice, 1994), p. 49.

16. Lawrence E. Cohen and Marcus Felson, "Social Change and Crime Rate Trends: A Routine Activity Approach," *American Sociological Review*, vol. 44, no. 4 (August 1979), pp. 588–608. Also, see Marcus Felson and L.E. Cohen, "Human Ecology and Crime: A Routine Activity Approach," *Human Ecology*, vol. 8, no. 4 (1980), pp. 389–406; Marcus Felson, "Linking Criminal

Choices, Routine Activities, Informal Control, and Criminal Outcomes," in Derek B. Cornish and Ronald V. Clarke, eds., *The Reasoning Criminal: Rational Choice Perspectives on Offending* (New York: Springer-Verlag, 1986), pp. 119–128; and Ronald V. Clarke and Marcus Felson, eds., *Advances in Criminological Theory: Routine Activity and Rational Choice* (New Brunswick, NJ: Transaction, 1993).

17. Cohen and Felson, "Social Change and Crime Rate Trends," p. 595.

18. For a test of routine activities theory as an explanation for victimization in the workplace, see John D. Wooldredge, Francis T. Cullen, and Edward J. Latessa, "Victimization in the Workplace: A Test of Routine Activities Theory," *Justice Quarterly*, vol. 9, no. 2 (June 1992), pp. 325–335.

19. Marcus Felson, *Crime and Everyday Life: Insight and Implications for Society* (Thousand Oaks, CA: Pine Forge Press, 1994).

20. Gary LaFree and Christopher Birkbeck, "The Neglected Situation: A Cross-National Study of the Situational Characteristics of Crime," *Criminology*, vol. 29, no. 1 (February 1991), p. 75.

21. Ronald V. Clarke and Derek B. Cornish, eds., *Crime Control in Britain: A Review of Police and Research* (Albany: State University of New York Press, 1983), p. 8.

22. See Derek B. Cornish and Ronald V. Clarke, "Understanding Crime Displacement: An Application of Rational Choice Theory," *Criminology*, vol. 25, no. 4 (November 1987), p. 933.

23. See Tomislav V. Kovandzic, Lynne M. Vieraitis, and Denise Paquette Boots, "Does the Death Penalty Save Lives? New Evidence from State Panel Data, 1977 to 2006," *Criminology and Public Policy*, vol. 8, no. 4 (2009), pp. 803–843.

24. Werner Einstadter and Stuart Henry, *Criminological Theory: An Analysis of Its Underlying Assumptions* (Fort Worth, TX: Harcourt Brace, 1995), p. 70.

25. Daniel J. Curran and Claire M. Renzetti, *Theories of Crime* (Boston: Allyn & Bacon, 1994), p. 18.

26. The quotations attributed to Weisburd in this section are from David Weisburd, "Reorienting Crime Prevention Research and Policy: From the Causes of Criminality to the Context of Crime," *NIJ Research Report* (Washington, DC: NIJ, June 1997).

27. See P.J. Brantingham and P.L. Brantingham, "Situational Crime Prevention in Practice," *Canadian Journal of Criminology* (January 1990), pp. 17–40; and R.V. Clarke, "Situational Crime Prevention: Achievements and Challenges," in M. Tonry and D. Farrington, eds., *Building a Safer Society: Strategic Approaches to Crime Prevention, Crime and Justice: A Review of Research*, vol. 19 (Chicago: University of Chicago Press, 1995).

28. Quotations in this paragraph and the next are taken from Weisburd, "Reorienting Crime Prevention Research and Policy."

29. See, for example, J.E. Eck and D. Weisburd, eds., *Crime and Place: Crime Prevention Studies*, vol. 4 (Monsey, NY: Willow Tree Press, 1995).

30. Marcus Felson and Ronald V. Clarke, *Opportunity Makes the Thief: Practical Theory for Crime Prevention* (London: British Home Office, 1998), p. 33.

31. Laura J. Moriarty and James E. Williams, "Examining the Relationship between Routine Activities Theory and Social Disorganization: An Analysis of Property Crime Victimization," *American Journal of Criminal Justice*, vol. 21, no. 1 (1996), pp. 43–59.

32. Ibid., p. 43.

33. Ibid., p. 46.

34. Kenneth D. Tunnell, "Choosing Crime: Close Your Eyes and Take Your Chances," *Justice Quarterly*, vol. 7 (1990), pp. 673–690.

35. See R. Barr and K. Pease, "Crime Placement, Displacement and Deflection," in M. Tonry and N. Morris, eds., *Crime and*

Justice: A Review of Research, vol. 12 (Chicago: University of Chicago Press, 1990).

36. For a good summation of target hardening, see Ronald V. Clarke, *Situational Crime Prevention* (New York: Harrow and Heston, 1992).

37. For a good summation of studies on displacement, see R. Hesseling, "Displacement: A Review of the Empirical Literature," in R.V. Clarke, ed., *Crime Prevention Studies*, vol. 3 (Monsey, NY: Willow Tree Press, 1994).

38. For a good overview of the challenges in defining recidivism and determining rates of recidivism, see T. Nouwens, L. Motiuk, and R. Boe, "So You Want to Know the Recidivism Rate," *Forum on Correctional Research*, vol. 5, no. 3 (1993), pp. 22–26.

39. J. Bonta, T. Rugge, and M. Dauvergne, *The Reconviction Rate of Federal Offenders 2003–2004* (Ottawa: Solicitor General of Canada, 2003).

40. See, for example, W.C. Bailey, "Deterrence and the Death Penalty for Murders in Utah: A Time Series Analysis," *Journal of Contemporary Law*, vol. 5, no. 1 (1978), pp. 1–20; and "An Analysis of the Deterrent Effect of the Death Penalty for Murders in California," *Southern California Law Review*, vol. 52, no. 3 (1979), pp. 743–764.

41. See, for example, B.E. Forst, "The Deterrent Effect of Capital Punishment: A Cross-State Analysis of the 1960s," *Minnesota Law Review*, vol. 61 (1977), pp. 743–764.

42. Scott H. Decker and Carol W. Kohfeld, "Capital Punishment and Executions in the Lone Star State: A Deterrence Study," *Criminal Justice Research Bulletin* (Criminal Justice Center, Sam Houston State University), vol. 3, no. 12 (1988).

43. Lawrence W. Sherman, "Reason for Emotion: Reinventing Justice with Theories, Innovations and Research: 2002 ASC Presidential Address," *Criminology*, vol. 41, no. 1 (2003), pp. 1–38.

44. Ibid.

45. Mia Dauvergne, "Adult Correctional Services in Canada, 2010/2011," *Juristat*, Cat. no. 85-0002-X (Ottawa: Minister of Industry, October 11, 2012).

46. Heather C. West, *Prisoners at Yearend 2009—Advance Counts* (Washington, DC: Bureau of Justice Statistics, 2010).

47. Marvin Wolfgang, Thorsten Sellin, and Robert Figlio, *Delinquency in a Birth Cohort* (Chicago: University of Chicago Press, 1972).

48. Sherman, "Reason for Emotion," p. 7.

49. Randy Martin, Robert J. Mutchnick, and W. Timothy Austin, *Criminological Thought: Pioneers Past and Present* (New York: Macmillan, 1990), p. 17.

50. Ibid., p. 18.

Chapter 6

1. Julian V. Roberts and Thomas Gabor, "Lombrosian Wine in a New Bottle: Research on Crime and Race," *Canadian Journal of Criminology*, vol. 32, no. 2 (April 1990), p. 309.

2. "Brain Tumour Causes Uncontrollable Paedophilia," *New Scientist*, October 21, 2002.

3. C. Ray Jeffery, "Biological Perspectives," *Journal of Criminal Justice Education*, vol. 4, no. 2 (Fall 1993), pp. 292–293.

4. Anthony Walsh, "Biological Theories of Criminal Behavior," in Richard A. Wright and J. Mitchell Miller, eds., *Encyclopedia of Criminology*, Vol. 1 (New York: Routledge, 2005), p. 106.

5. Ibid.

6. Ibid.

7. Jeffery, "Biological Perspectives," p. 298.

8. Konrad Lorenz, *On Aggression* (New York: Harcourt, Brace & World, 1966).

9. Ibid., p. 23.

10. Ibid., p. 38.

11. Ibid., p. 249.

12. Ibid., p. 225.

13. Cesare Lombroso, introduction to Gina Lombroso-Ferrero, *Criminal Man According to the Classification of Cesare Lombroso* (New York and London: G.P. Putnam's Sons, 1911). Reprinted in 1972, by Patterson Smith, Montclair, NJ, p. xiv.

14. Charles Darwin, *Descent of Man: And Selection in Relation to Sex*, rev. ed. (London: John Murray, 1874), p. 137.

15. Auguste Comte, *A System of Positive Polity*, translated by John Henry Bridges (New York: Franklin, 1875). Originally published in four volumes, 1851–1854.

16. See K.L. Henwood and N.F. Pidgeon, "Qualitative Research and Psychological Theorising," *British Journal of Psychology*, vol. 83 (1992), pp. 97–111.

17. Lombroso, "Introduction," p. xv.

18. Della Fossetta Cerebellare Mediana in un Criminale, Institute Lombardo di Scienze e Lettere, 1872, pp. 1058–1065, as cited and translated by Thorsten Sellin, "A New Phase of Criminal Anthropology in Italy," *The Annals of the American Academy of Political and Social Science, Modern Crime*, 525 (May 1926), p. 234.

19. The English language version appeared in 1895 as Cesare Lombroso, *The Female Offender* (New York: D. Appleton & Co., 1895).

20. Marvin Wolfgang, "Cesare Lombroso," in Hermann Mannheim, *Pioneers in Criminology*, 2nd ed. (Montclair, NJ: Patterson Smith, 1972), p. 254.

21. Charles Goring, *The English Convict: A Statistical Study* (London: His Majesty's Stationary Office, 1913). Reprinted in 1972 by Patterson Smith, Montclair, NJ, p. 15.

22. Ibid., p. 15.

23. Earnest A. Hooton, *Crime and the Man* (Cambridge, MA: Harvard University Press, 1939). Reprinted in 1972 by Greenwood Press, Westport, CT.

24. Ibid., p. 75.

25. Ibid., p. 388.

26. Ernest A. Hooton, *The American Criminal: An Anthropological Study* (Cambridge, MA: Harvard University Press, 1939).

27. Stephen Schafer, *Theories in Criminology: Past and Present Philosophies of the Crime Problem* (New York: Random House, 1969), p. 187.

28. L. Arseneault et al., "Minor Physical Anomalies and Family Adversity as Risk Factors for Violent Delinquency in Adolescence," *American Journal of Psychiatry*, vol. 157, no. 6 (June 2000), pp. 917–923.

29. William H. Sheldon, *Varieties of Delinquent Youth* (New York: Harper & Brothers, 1949).

30. Ibid.

31. Sheldon Glueck and Eleanor Glueck, *Unraveling Juvenile Delinquency* (Cambridge, MA: Harvard University Press, 1950).

32. D. Hill and W. Sargent, "A Case of Matricide," *Lancet*, vol. 244 (1943), pp. 526–527.

33. William Dufty, *Sugar Blues* (Pandor, PA: Chilton, 1975).

34. Nanci Hellmich, "Sweets May Not Be Culprit in Hyper Kids," *USA Today*, February 3, 1994, p. 1A (reporting on a study reported in the *New England Journal of Medicine*).

35. Ibid., p. 1A.

36. See, for example, A.R. Mawson and K.J. Jacobs, "Corn Consumption, Tryptophan, and Cross National Homicide Rates," *Journal of Orthomolecular Psychiatry*, vol. 7 (1978), pp. 227–230; and A. Hoffer, "The Relation of Crime to Nutrition," *Humanist in Canada*, vol. 8 (1975), p. 8.

37. See, for example, C. Hawley and R.E. Buckley, "Food Dyes and Hyperkinetic Children," *Academy Therapy*, vol. 10 (1974), pp. 27–32; and Alexander Schauss, *Diet, Crime and Delinquency* (Berkeley, CA: Parker House, 1980).

38. "Special Report: Measuring Your Life with Coffee Spoons," *Tufts University Diet and Nutrition Letter*, vol. 2, no. 2 (April 1984), pp. 3–6.

39. See, for example, "Special Report: Does What You Eat Affect Your Mood and Actions?" *Tufts University Diet and Nutrition Letter*, vol. 2, no. 12 (February 1985), pp. 4–6.

40. See *Tufts University Diet and Nutrition Newsletter*, vol. 2, no. 11 (January 1985), p. 2; and "Special Report: Why Sugar Continues to Concern Nutritionists," *Tufts University Diet and Nutrition Letter*, vol. 3, no. 3 (May 1985), pp. 3–6.

41. A. Hoffer, "Children with Learning and Behavioral Disorders," *Journal of Orthomolecular Psychiatry*, vol. 5 (1976), p. 229.

42. I.B. Helland, L. Smith, K. Saarem, O.D. Saugstad, and C.A. Drevon, "Maternal Supplements with Very-Long-Chain Omega-3 Fatty Acids during Pregnancy and Lactation Augments Children's IQ at 4 Years of Age," *Pediatrics*, vol. 111, no. 1 (January 2003), pp. 39–44.

43. C. Iribarren, J.H. Markovitz, D.R. Jacobs, Jr., P.J. Schreiner, M. Daviglus, and J.R. Hibbeln, "Dietary Intake of Omega-3, Omega-6 Fatty Acids and Fish: Relationship with Hostility in Young Adults—The CARDIA Study," *European Journal of Clinical Nutrition*, vol. 50, no. 1 (January 2004), pp. 24–31.

44. David Benton, "The Impact of Diet on Anti-social, Violent and Criminal Behaviour," *Neuroscience and Biobehavioral Reviews*, vol. 31 (2007), pp. 752–774.

45. C. Bernard Gesch, Sean M. Hammond, Sarah E. Hampson, Anita Eves, and Martin J. Crowder, "Influence of Supplementary Vitamins, Minerals and Essential Fatty Acids on the Antisocial Behaviour of Young Adult Prisoners: Randomized, Placebo-Controlled Trial," *British Journal of Psychiatry*, vol. 181 (July 2002), pp. 22–28.

46. S. Schoenthaler and I.D. Bier, "Addiction and Criminal Behaviour," in J. Brostoff and S. Challacombe, eds., *Food Allergy and Intolerance*, 2nd ed. (London: W.B. Saunders, 2002), pp. 985–1000.

47. Roger D. Masters, Brian Hone, and Anil Doshi, "Environmental Pollution, Neurotoxicity, and Criminal Violence," in J. Rose, ed., *Environmental Toxicology* (London and New York: Gordon and Breach, 1997), pp. 13–48.

48. Peter Montague, "Toxics and Violent Crime," *Rachel's Environment and Health Weekly*, no. 551 (June 19, 1997).

49. See, for example, Jeffrey Halperin et al., "Serotonergic Function in Aggressive and Nonaggressive Boys with ADHD," *American Journal of Psychiatry*, vol. 151, no. 2 (February 1994), pp. 243–248.

50. Masters, Hone, and Doshi, "Environmental Pollution, Neurotoxicity, and Criminal Violence."

51. See, for example, Rick Nevin, "How Lead Exposure Relates to Temporal Changes in IQ, Violent Crime, and Unwed Pregnancy," *Environmental Research*, vol. 83, no. 1 (May 2000), pp. 1–22.

52. Alison Motluck, "Pollution May Lead to a Life of Crime," *New Scientist*, vol. 154, no. 2084 (May 31, 1997), p. 4.

53. See Alexander G. Schauss, "Tranquilizing Effect of Color Reduces Aggressive Behavior and Potential Violence," *Journal of Orthomolecular Psychiatry*, vol. 8, no. 4 (1979), pp. 218–221; and David Johnston, "Is It Merely a Fad, Or Do Pastel Walls Stop Jail House Brawls?" *Corrections Magazine*, vol. 7, no. 3 (1981), pp. 28–32.

54. Questions were raised, however, about the long-term effects of confinement in pink cells, and some researchers suggested that extended exposure to the colour pink could generate suicidal impulses. See Alexander G. Schauss, "Tranquilizing Effect of Color Reduces Aggressive Behavior and Potential Violence," *Journal of Orthomolecular Psychiatry*, vol. 8, no. 4 (1979), pp. 218–221; and David Johnston, "Is It Merely a Fad, or Do Pastel Walls Stop Jail House Brawls?" *Corrections Magazine*, vol. 7,

no. 3 (1981), pp. 28–32.

55. L. Goldschmidt, N.L. Day, and G.A. Richardson, "Effects of Prenatal Marijuana Exposure on Child Behavior Problems at Age 10," *Neurotoxicology and Teratology*, vol. 22, no. 3 (May/June 2000), pp. 325–336.

56. David Fergusson, Lianne Woodward, and L. John Horwood, "Maternal Smoking during Pregnancy and Psychiatric Adjustment in Late Adolescence," *Archives of General Psychiatry*, vol. 55 (August 1998), pp. 721–727.

57. Jacob F. Orlebeke, Dirk L. Knol, and Frank C. Verhulst, "Increase in Child Behavior Problems Resulting from Maternal Smoking during Pregnancy," *Archives of Environmental Health*, vol. 52, no. 4 (July/August 1997), pp. 317–321.

58. Travis C. Pratt, Jean Marie McGloin, and Noelle E. Fearn, "Maternal Cigarette Smoking during Pregnancy and Criminal/Deviant Behavior: A Meta-Analysis," *International Journal of Offender Therapy and Comparative Criminology*, vol. 50, no. 6 (2006), pp. 672–690.

59. Ann Pytkowicz Streissguth et al., "Fetal Alcohol Syndrome in Adolescents and Adults," *Journal of the American Medical Association*, vol. 265, no. 15 (April 17, 1991).

60. Tresa M. Roebuck, Sarah N. Mattson, and Edward P. Riley, "Behavioral and Psychosocial Profiles of Alcohol-Exposed Children," *Alcoholism: Clinical and Experimental Research*, vol. 23, no. 6 (June 1999), pp. 1070–1076.

61. See, for example, R.T. Rada, D.R. Laws, and R. Kellner, "Plasma Testosterone Levels in the Rapist," *Psychomatic Medicine*, vol. 38 (1976), pp. 257–268.

62. "The Insanity of Steroid Abuse," *Newsweek*, May 23, 1988, p. 75.

63. Dan Olweus, Mattsson Ake, Daisy Schalling, and Hans Low, "Testosterone, Aggression, Physical and Personality Dimensions in Normal Adolescent Males," *Psychosomatic Medicine*, vol. 42 (1980), pp. 253–269.

64. Richard Udry, "Biosocial Models of Adolescent Problem Behaviors," *Social Biology*, vol. 37 (1990), pp. 1–10.

65. Dan Olweus, "Testosterone and Adrenaline: Aggressive Antisocial Behavior in Normal Adolescent Males," in Sarnoff A. Mednick, Terrie E. Moffitt, and Susan A. Stack, eds., *The Causes of Crime: New Biological Approaches* (Cambridge, England: Cambridge University Press, 1987), pp. 263–282.

66. Alan Booth and D. Wayne Osgood, "The Influence of Testosterone on Deviance in Adulthood: Assessing and Explaining the Relationship," *Criminology*, vol. 31, no. 1 (1993), p. 93.

67. Paul C. Bernhardt, "Influences of Serotonin and Testosterone in Aggressions and Dominance: Convergence with Social Psychology," *Current Directions in Psychological Science*, vol. 6. no. 2 (1997), pp. 44–48.

68. Richard Udry, Luther Talbert, and Naomi Morris, "Biosocial Foundations for Adolescent Female Sexuality," *Demography*, vol. 23 (1986), pp. 217–227.

69. James M. Dabbs, Jr., and Marian F. Hargrove, "Age, Testosterone, and Behavior among Female Prison Inmates," *Psychosomatic Medicine*, vol. 59 (1997), pp. 447–480.

70. See D. Asso, *The Real Menstrual Cycle* (Toronto: Wiley, 1984).

71. Anastasia Toufexis, "Seeking the Roots of Violence," *Time*, April 19, 1993, pp. 52–54.

72. Terrie E. Moffitt et al., "Whole Blood Serotonin Relates to Violence in an Epidemiological Study," *Biological Psychiatry*, vol. 43, no. 6 (1998), pp. 446–457.

73. H. Soderstrom, K. Blennow, A.K. Sjodin, and A. Forsman, "New Evidence for an Association between the CSF HVA:5–HIAA Ratio and Psychopathic Traits," *Journal of Neurology, Neurosurgery and Psychiatry*, vol. 74 (2003), pp. 918–921.

74. See E.G. Stalenheim, L. von Knorring, and L. Wide, "Serum Levels of Thyroid Hormones as Biological Markers

in a Swedish Forensic Psychiatric Population," *Biological Psychiatry*, vol. 43, no. 10 (1998), pp. 755–761; and P.O. Alm et al., "Criminality and Psychopathy as Related to Thyroid Activity in Former Juvenile Delinquents," *Acta Psychiatrica Scandinavica*, vol. 94, no. 2 (1996), pp. 112–117.

75. Stalenheim, von Knorring, and Wide, "Serum Levels of Thyroid Hormones as Biological Markers in a Swedish Forensic Psychiatric Population."

76. Michael Kosfeld, Markus Heinrichs, Paul J. Zak, Urs Fischbacher, and Ernst Fehr, "Oxytocin Increases Trust in Humans," *Nature*, vol. 435 (2005), pp. 673–676.

77. "'Trust' Hormone Identified," *Red Herring*, June 2, 2005.

78. Richard Louis Dugdale, *The Jukes: A Study in Crime, Pauperism, Disease, and Heredity*, 3rd ed. (New York: G.P. Putnam's Sons, 1895).

79. Arthur H. Estabrook, *The Jukes in 1915* (Washington, DC: Carnegie Institute of Washington, 1916).

80. Henry Herbert Goddard, *The Kallikak Family: A Study in the Heredity of Feeblemindedness* (New York: Macmillan, 1912).

81. Samuel Hopkins Adams, "The Juke Myth," *Saturday Review*, vol. 38, no. 13 (1960), pp. 48–49.

82. See Nicole Hahn Rafter, *Creating Born Criminals* (Urbana: University of Illinois Press, 1997).

83. T.L. Chapman, "The Early Eugenics Movement in Western Canada," *Alberta History*, vol. 25 (1977), pp. 9–17. See also A. McLaren, "The Creation of a Haven for Human Thoroughbreds," *Canadian Historical Review*, vol. 67 (1986), pp. 264–268.

84. P.A. Jacobs, M. Brunton, and M. Melville, "Aggressive Behavior, Mental Subnormality, and the XXY Male," *Nature*, vol. 208 (1965), p. 1351.

85. Biologists often define *karyotype* as "a photomicrograph of metaphase chromosomes in a standard array." The process of karyotyping typically involves drawing a small sample of blood.

86. See David A. Jones, *History of Criminology: A Philosophical Perspective* (Westport, CT: Greenwood Press, 1986), p. 124.

87. Many of which have been summarized in J. Katz and W. Chambliss, "Biology and Crime," in J.F. Sheley, ed., *Criminology* (Belmont, CA: Wadsworth, 1991), pp. 245–272.

88. As reported by S.A. Mednick and J. Volavka, "Biology and Crime," in N. Morris and M. Tonry, *Crime and Justice: An Annual Review of Research*, vol. 2 (Chicago: University of Chicago Press, 1980), pp. 85–158; and D.A. Andrews and James Bonta, *The Psychology of Criminal Conduct* (Cincinnati, OH: Anderson, 1994), pp. 126–127.

89. T. Sarbin and J. Miller, "Demonism Revisited: The XYY Chromosomal Anomaly," *Issues in Criminology*, vol. 5 (1970), p. 199.

90. Geoffrey Cowley and Carol Hallin, "The Genetics of Bad Behavior: A Study Links Violence to Heredity," *Newsweek*, November 1, 1993, p. 57.

91. Johannes Lange, *Verbrechen als Schicksal* (Leipzig, Germany: Georg Thieme, 1929).

92. Karl O. Christiansen, "A Preliminary Study of Criminality among Twins," in Sarnoff Mednick and Karl Christiansen, eds., *Biosocial Bases of Criminal Behavior* (New York: Gardner Press, 1977).

93. Peter McGuffin and Anita Thapar, "Genetic Basis of Bad Behaviour in Adolescents," *Lancet*, vol. 350 (August 9, 1997), pp. 411–412.

94. Wendy Slutske et al., "Modeling Genetic and Environmental Influences in the Etiology of Conduct Disorder: A Study of 2,682 Adult Twin Pairs," *Journal of Abnormal Psychology*, vol. 106, no. 2 (1997), pp. 266–279.

95. C. Ray Jeffery, "Biological Perspectives," *Journal of Criminal Justice Education*, vol. 4, no. 2 (Fall 1993), p. 300.

96. Diana Kendall, Jane L. Murray, and Rick Linden, *Sociology in Our Times: The Essentials* (Toronto: ITP Nelson, 2008).

97. Frank Schmalleger, *Criminology Today: An Integrative Introduction* (Upper Saddle River, NJ: Prentice Hall, 2012, p. 110.

98. D. Thomas, *Criminality among the Foreign Born: Analysis of Federal Prison Population* (Ottawa: Immigration and Employment Canada, 1992).

99. Robert Silverman and Leslie Kennedy, *Deadly Deeds: Murder in Canada* (Scarborough, ON: Nelson Canada, 1993).

100. Mary Hyde and Carol La Prairie, *American Police Crime Prevention* (Working Paper) (Ottawa: Solicitor General of Canada, 1987).

101. S. Perreault and R. Kong, "The Incarceration of Aboriginal People in Adult Correctional Services," *Juristat*, vol. 29, no. 3 (Ottawa: Ministry of Industry, 2009).

102. Schmalleger, *Criminology Today*, p. 110.

103. See, for example, D.H. Fishbein, "The Psychobiology of Female Aggression," *Criminal Justice and Behavior*, vol. 19 (1992), pp. 99–126.

104. Robbin S. Ogle, Daniel Maier-Katin, and Thomas J. Bernard, "A Theory of Homicidal Behavior among Women," *Criminology*, vol. 33, no. 2 (1995), pp. 173–193.

105. Ibid., p. 177.

106. Ibid., p. 179.

107. Arthur Fisher, "A New Synthesis Comes of Age," *Mosaic*, vol. 22, no. 1 (Spring 1991), pp. 2–9.

108. The quotations attributed to Wilson in this section are from Edward O. Wilson, *Sociobiology: The New Synthesis* (Cambridge, MA: The Belknap Press of Harvard University Press, 1975).

109. Ibid., p. 327.

110. Research by Martin Daly and Margo Wilson of McMaster University in Hamilton, Ontario, as reported in Arthur Fisher, "A New Synthesis II: How Different Are Humans?" *Mosaic*, vol. 22, no. 1 (Spring 1991), p. 14.

111. Arthur Fisher, "A New Synthesis II: How Different Are Humans?" *Mosaic*, vol. 22, no. 1 (Spring 1991), p. 11.

112. John H. Beckstrom, *Evolutionary Jurisprudence: Prospects and Limitations on the Youth of Modern Darwinism throughout the Legal Process* (Urbana: University of Illinois Press, 1989).

113. John Madison Memory, "Sociobiology and the Metamorphoses of Criminology: 1978–2000," unpublished manuscript.

114. Ibid, p. 33.

115. Gail S. Anderson, *Biological Influences on Criminal Behavior* (Boca Raton, FL: CRC Press, 2006).

116. See also Arnold L. Lieber, *The Lunar Effect: Biological Tides and Human Emotions* (Garden City, NY: Anchor Press, 1978).

117. James Q. Wilson and Richard J. Herrnstein, *Crime and Human Nature* (New York: Simon & Schuster, 1985).

118. Quoted in Karen J. Winkler, "Criminals Are Born as Well as Made, Authors of Controversial Book Assert," *Chronicle of Higher Education*, January 16, 1986, p. 5.

119. Wilson and Herrnstein, *Crime and Human Nature*.

120. Winkler, "Criminals Are Born as Well as Made," p. 8.

121. Quotes in the list are taken from Jeffery, "Biological Perspectives," p. 303.

122. Ibid.

123. Julian V. Roberts and Thomas Gabor, "Lombrosian Wine in a New Bottle: Research on Crime and Race," *Canadian Journal of Criminology*, vol. 32, no. 2 (April 1990), p. 309.

124. Toufexis, "Seeking the Roots of Violence," p. 53.

125. Lee Ellis and Anthony Walsh, "Gene-Based Evolutionary Theories in Criminology," *Criminology*, vol. 35, no. 2 (1997), pp. 229–230.

126. Nicole Hahn Rafter, *Creating Born Criminals* (Urbana: University of Illinois Press, 1997).

127. Glenn D. Walters and Thomas W. White, "Heredity and Crime: Bad Genes or Bad Research?" *Criminology*, vol. 27,

no. 3 (1989), pp. 455–485. See also P.A. Brennan and S.A. Mednick, "Reply to Walters and White: Heredity and Crime," *Criminology*, vol. 28, no. 4 (November 1990), pp. 657–661.

128. Walters and White, "Heredity and Crime," p. 476.

129. Ibid., p. 478.

Chapter 7

1. Robert D. Hare, *Without Conscience: The Disturbing World of the Psychopaths Among Us* (New York: Pocket Books, 1993), p. xi.

2. "Manslaughter Verdict for Cannibal," *BBC News*, January 30, 2004, http://news.bbc.co.uk/2/hi/europe/3443293.stm [Accessed October 21, 2102].

3. K. Connolly, "Cannibal Filmed Himself Killing and Eating His 'Willing' Victim," *The Telegraph*, December 4, 2003, http://www.telegraph.co.uk/news/worldnews/europe/germany/1448497/Cannibal-filmed-himself-killing-and-eating-his-willing-victim.html [Accessed October 21, 2012].

4. "German Cannibal Guilty of Murder," *BBC News*, May 6, 2006, http://news.bbc.co.uk/2/hi/europe/4752797.stm [Accessed October 21, 2012].

5. Barry Came, "Montreal Massacre," *Maclean's Magazine*, December 18, 1989, p. 14.

6. Bruce Wallace, "The Making of a Mass Killer," *Maclean's Magazine*, December 18, 1989, p. 22.

7. D.A. Andrews and James Bonta, *The Psychology of Criminal Conduct* (Cincinnati, OH: Anderson, 1998), p. 93.

8. See Adrian Raine, *The Psychopathology of Crime: Criminal Behavior as a Clinical Disorder* (Orlando, FL: Academic Press, 1993).

9. American Board of Forensic Psychology, brochure, 2012, http://www.abfp.com/brochure.asp [Accessed October 21, 2012].

10. Canadian Academy of Psychiatry and the Law home page, 2011, http://www.capl-acpd.org/ [Accessed October 21, 2012].

11. Cathy Spatz Widom and Hans Toch, "The Contribution of Psychology to Criminal Justice Education," *Journal of Criminal Justice Education*, vol. 4, no. 2 (Fall 1993), p. 253.

12. Curt R. Bartol, *Criminal Behavior: A Psychosocial Approach*, 3rd ed. (Englewood Cliffs, NJ: Prentice Hall, 1991), p. 16.

13. For additional information, see S. Giora Shoham and Mark C. Seis, *A Primer in the Psychology of Crime* (New York: Harrow and Heston, 1993); and Frederic L. Faust, "A Review of A Primer in the Psychology of Crime," in *Social Pathology*, vol. 1, no. 1 (January 1995), pp. 48–61.

14. "Human Ecology," *Encyclopaedia Britannica* online, 2012, http://britannica.com [Accessed October 21, 2012].

15. Nicole Hahn Rafter, "Psychopathy and the Evolution of Criminological Knowledge," *Theoretical Criminology*, vol. 1, no. 2 (May 1997), pp. 235–259.

16. Nolan D.C. Lewis, foreword to David Abrahamsen, *Crime and the Human Mind* (Montclair, NJ: Patterson Smith, 1969), p. vii. Originally published in 1944.

17. Abrahamsen, *Crime and the Human Mind*.

18. P.Q. Roche, *The Criminal Mind: A Study of Communications between Criminal Law and Psychiatry* (New York: Grove Press, 1958), p. 52.

19. "Nationline: Book Thief," *USA Today*, August 1, 1991, p. 3A.

20. Mark Solms, "Freud Returns," *Scientific American*, vol. 290, no. 5 (2004), pp. 82–90.

21. Eric R. Kandel, "Biology and the Future of Psychoanalysis: A New Intellectual Framework for Psychiatry Revisited," *American Journal of Psychiatry*, vol. 156 (1999), pp. 505–524.

22. Hans J. Eysenck, *Crime and Personality* (Boston: Houghton Mifflin, 1964).

23. Hans J. Eysenck, "Personality and Criminality: A Dispositional Analysis," in William S. Laufer and Freda Adler, eds., *Advances in Criminology Theory*, vol. 1 (New Brunswick, NJ: Transaction, 1989), p. 90.

24. Eysenck, *Crime and Personality*, pp. 35–36.

25. J. Dollard, L. Doob, N. Miller, O. Mowrer, and R. Sears, *Frustration and Aggression* (New Haven, CT: Yale University Press, 1939).

26. Maria Bohuslawsky, "Troubled Killer Was Once Fired," *Ottawa Citizen*, April 7, 1999, p. C1.

27. Andrew F. Henry and James F. Short, Jr., *Suicide and Homicide: Economic, Sociological, and Psychological Aspects of Aggression* (Glencoe, IL: Free Press, 1954).

28. Stewart Palmer, *A Study of Murder* (New York: Crowell, 1960).

29. "40-Year-Old Suspect Held in Gruesome Manitoba Bus Killing," *CBC News*, July 31, 2008, http://www.cbc.ca/canada/story/2008/07/31/greyhound-transcanada.html [Accessed October 22, 2012]; "Vince Li Not Criminally Responsible for Beheading," *CTV News*, March 5, 2009, http://www.ctv.ca/servlet/ArticleNews/story/CTVNews/20090304/bus_verdict_090305/20090305/ [Accessed October 22, 2012].

30. Gwynn Nettler, *Killing One Another* (Cincinnati, OH: Anderson, 1982), p. 159.

31. Ibid., p. 155.

32. Abrahamsen, *Crime and the Human Mind*, p. 99.

33. Ibid., p. 100.

34. As noted by Nicole Hahn Rafter in "Psychopathy and the Evolution of Criminological Knowledge." See Richard von Krafft-Ebing, *Psychopathia Sexualis* (New York: Stein and Day, 1965), reprint of the original 1886 edition; and *Text-Book of Insanity* (Philadelphia: F.A. Davis Company, 1904), first German edition, 1879.

35. Bernard H. Glueck, *Studies in Forensic Psychiatry* (Boston: Little, Brown, 1916).

36. William Healy, *The Individual Delinquent* (Boston: Little, Brown, 1915).

37. Early writings about the psychopath personality focused almost exclusively on men, and most psychiatrists appeared to believe that very few women (if any) possessed such traits.

38. Hervey M. Cleckley, *The Mask of Sanity*, 4th ed. (St. Louis, MO: C.V. Mosby, 1964).

39. Quoted in Joseph P. Newman and Chad A. Brinkley, "Psychopathy: Rediscovering Cleckley's Construct," *Psychopathology Research*, vol. 9, no. 1 (1998).

40. Nettler, *Killing One Another*, p. 179.

41. Ralph Serin, "Can Criminal Psychopaths Be Identified?" *Correctional Service of Canada*, October 22, 1999.

42. Robert D. Hare, "Checklist for the Assessment of Psychopathy in Criminal Populations," in M.H. Ben-Aron, S.J. Hucker, and C.D. Webster, eds., *Clinical Criminology* (Toronto: University of Toronto, Clarke Institute of Psychiatry, 1985), pp. 157–167.

43. Adapted from Laurence Steinberg, "The Juvenile Psychopath: Fads, Fictions, and Facts," *National Institute of Justice Perspectives on Crime and Justice: 2001 Lecture Series*, vol. 5 (Washington, DC: NIJ, 2002), pp. 35–64.

44. Kent A. Kiehl, Andra M. Smith, Adrianna Mendrek, Bruce B. Forster, Robert D. Hare, and Peter F. Liddle, "Temporal Lobe Abnormalities in Semantic Processing by Criminal Psychopaths as Revealed by Functional Magnetic Resonance Imaging," *Psychiatry Research: Neuroimaging*, vol. 130 (2004), pp. 27–42.

45. Ibid.

46. Ivan Semeniuk, "How We Tell Right from Wrong: An Interview with Marc Hauser," *New Scientist*, March 3, 2007, p. 44.

47. American Psychiatric Association, *Diagnostic and Statistical Manual of Mental Disorders*, 2nd ed. (Washington, DC: American Psychiatric Association, 1968).

48. Ibid., p. 43.

49. A.L. Rabin, "The Antisocial Personality—Psychopathy and Sociopathy," in Hans Toch, *Psychology of Crime and Criminal Justice* (Prospect Heights, IL: Waveland, 1979), p. 330.

50. For recent research in this area, see A. Tengstrom et al., "Psychopathy as a Predictor of Violent Recidivism among Criminal Offenders with Schizophrenia in Sweden," *Law and Behavior*, vol. 23, no. 1 (2000), pp. 45–58. For additional information, see V.L. Quinsey et al., *Violent Offenders: Appraising and Managing Risk* (Washington, DC: American Psychological Association, 1998); and V.L. Quinsey, M.E. Rice, and G.T. Harris, "Actuarial Prediction of Sexual Recidivism," *Journal of Interpersonal Violence*, vol. 10, no. 1 (1995), pp. 85–105.

51. R.D. Hare, *Psychopathy: Theory and Research* (New York: John Wiley & Sons, 1970).

52. L.N. Robins, *Deviant Children Grow Up* (Baltimore, MD: Williams and Wilkins, 1966).

53. S.B. Guze, *Criminality and Psychiatric Disorders* (New York: Oxford University Press, 1976).

54. S. Hodgins and G. Cote, "The Prevalence of Mental Disorders Among Penitentiary Inmates in Quebec," *Canada's Mental Health*, vol. 38 (1990), pp. 1–4.

55. H. Prins, *Offenders, Deviants or Patients? An Introduction to the Study of Socio-Forensic Problems* (London: Tavistock, 1980).

56. American Psychiatric Association website, http://www.psych.org/ [Accessed October 22, 2012].

57. Abrahamsen, *Crime and the Human Mind*, p. 26.

58. Nancy Gibbs, "The Devil's Disciple," *Time*, January 11, 1993, p. 40.

59. Seymour L. Halleck, *Psychiatry and the Dilemmas of Crime: A Study of Causes, Punishment and Treatment* (Berkeley: University of California Press, 1971).

60. Ibid., p. 77.

61. Ibid., p. 80.

62. Ibid.

63. Ibid.

64. Arnold S. Linsky, Ronet Bachman, and Murray A. Straus, *Stress, Culture, and Aggression* (New Haven, CT: Yale University Press, 1995).

65. Ibid., p. 7.

66. Gabriel Tarde, *The Laws of Imitation*, trans. E.C. Parsons (Gloucester, MA: Peter Smith, 1962). Originally published in 1890.

67. Albert Bandura, "The Social Learning Perspective: Mechanisms of Aggression," in Toch, *Psychology of Crime and Criminal Justice*, p. 198.

68. Ibid.

69. Ibid., p. 199.

70. M.M. Lefkowitz, L.D. Eron, L.O. Walder, and L.R. Huesmann, "Television Violence and Child Aggression: A Follow-up Study," in G.A. Comstock and E.A. Rubinstein, eds., *Television and Social Behavior*, vol. 3 (Washington, DC: U.S. Government Printing Office, 1972), pp. 35–135.

71. C.A. Anderson et al., "Violent Video Game Effects on Aggression, Empathy, and Prosocial Behavior in Eastern and Western Countries," *Psychological Bulletin*, vol. 136 (2010), pp. 151–173.

72. Widom and Toch, "The Contribution of Psychology to Criminal Justice Education."

73. Ibid., p. 253.

74. C.R. Hollin, *Psychology and Crime: An Introduction to Criminological Psychology* (London: Routledge, 1989), p. 42.

75. Ibid., p. 254.

76. *R. v. Parks* (1992), 75 C.C.C. (3d) 287 (S.C.C.).

77. R. Barnhorst and S. Barnhorst, *Criminal Law and the Canadian Criminal Code* (Toronto: McGraw-Hill Ryerson, 2009), p. 59.

78. Halleck, *Psychiatry and the Dilemmas of Crime*, p. 213.

79. *R. v. Swain* (1991), 63 C.C.C. (3d) 481 (S.C.C.).

80. Minister of Justice and Attorney General of Canada, *Justice Communiqué*, January 30, 1992, p. 2.

81. F. Schmalleger, *Criminology Today: An Integrated Introduction* (Upper Saddle River, NJ: Prentice-Hall, 2012), pp. 141–142.

82. *Martin's Annual Criminal Code* (Aurora, ON: Canada Law Book, 2007), s. 672.5(2).

83. M.A. Jackson and C.T. Griffiths, *Canadian Criminology: Perspectives on Crime and Criminality* (Toronto: Harcourt Brace and Co., 1995), p. 73.

84. Shirley Steller, *Canadian Centre for Justice Statistics, Special Study on Mentally Disordered Accused in the Criminal Justice System* (Ottawa: Minister of Industry, 2003).

85. Pauline Tam, *Ottawa Citizen*, October 29, 1996, p. C3.

86. See, for example, D.P. Farrington, "Childhood Aggression and Adult Violence: Early Precursors and Later Life Outcomes," in D.J. Pepler and K.H. Rubin, eds., *The Development and Treatment of Childhood Aggression* (Hillsdale, NJ: Erlbaum, 1990), pp. 2–29; and R.E. Tremblay, B. Masse, D. Perron, M. LeBlanc, A.E. Schwartzman, and J.E. Ledingham, "Early Disruptive Behavior: Poor School Achievement, Delinquent Behavior and Delinquent Personality: Longitudinal Analyses," *Journal of Consulting and Clinical Psychology*, vol. 60, no. 1 (1992), pp. 64–72.

87. R. Loeber, "Questions and Advances in the Study of Developmental Pathways," in D. Cicchetti and S. Toth, eds., *Models and Integration: Rochester Symposium on Developmental Psychopathology* (Rochester, NY: University of Rochester Press, 1991), pp. 97–115.

88. Joanne Laucius, "Pedophile's Trail of Destruction," *Ottawa Citizen*, April 28, 1999, p. B1.

89. Jennifer L. White, Terrie E. Moffitt, Felton Earls, Lee Robins, and Phil A. Silva, "How Early Can We Tell? Predictors of Childhood Conduct Disorder and Adolescent Delinquency," *Criminology*, vol. 28, no. 4 (1990), pp. 507–528.

90. Daniel S. Nagin and David P. Farrington, "The Stability of Criminal Potential from Childhood to Adulthood," *Criminology*, vol. 30, no. 2 (1992), pp. 235–260.

91. Paul Gendreau, Tracy Little, and Claire Goggin, "A Meta-Analysis of the Predictors of Adult Offender Recidivism: What Works!" *Criminology*, vol. 34, no. 4 (November 1996), pp. 575–607.

92. For one of the first and still definitive works in the area of selective incapacitation, see Peter Greenwood and Allan Abrahamsen, *Selective Incapacitation* (Santa Monica, CA: Rand Corporation, 1982).

93. M.A. Peterson, H.B. Braiker, and S.M. Polich, *Who Commits Crimes?* (Cambridge: Oelgeschlager, Gunn and Hain, 1981).

94. J. Monahan, *Predicting Violent Behavior: An Assessment of Clinical Techniques* (Beverly Hills, CA: Sage, 1981).

95. Public Safety Canada Portfolio Corrections Statistics Committee, *Corrections and Conditional Release Statistical Overview: Annual Report, 2011* (Ottawa: Public Works and Government Services Canada, 2011).

96. Jill Peay, "Dangerousness—Ascription or Description," in M.P. Feldman, ed., *Developments in the Study of Criminal Behavior, vol. 2, Violence* (New York: John Wiley & Sons, 1982), p. 211, citing N. Walker, "Dangerous People," *International Journal of Law and Psychiatry*, vol. 1 (1978), pp. 37–50.

97. See, for example, Michael Gottfredson and Travis Hirschi, *A General Theory of Crime* (Stanford, CA: Stanford University Press, 1990); and Travis Hirschi and Michael Gottfredson, "Age and the Explanation of Crime," *American Journal of Sociology*, vol. 89 (1983), pp. 552–584.

98. David F. Greenberg, "Modeling Criminal Careers," *Criminology*, vol. 29, no. 1 (1991), p. 39.

99. D.A. Andrews and James Bonta, *The Psychology of Criminal Conduct* (Cincinnati, OH: Anderson, 1998).

100. Ibid., p. 1.
101. Ibid.
102. Ibid., pp. 20–21.
103. Ibid., p. 227.
104. Ibid
105. Ibid., p. 236.
106. Robert R. Hazelwood and John E. Douglas, "The Lust Murderer," *FBI Law Enforcement Bulletin* (Washington, DC: U.S. Department of Justice, April 1980).
107. Ibid.
108. Ibid.
109. Anastasia Toufexis, "Mind Games with Monsters," *Time*, May 6, 1991, pp. 68–69.
110. "Violent Crime Linkage System (ViCLAS)," RCMP website, n.d., http://www.rcmp-grc.gc.ca/tops-opst/bs-sc/viclas-salvac-eng.htm, [Accessed October 24, 2012].
111. Ibid.

Chapter 8

1. Frank Tannenbaum, *Crime and the Community* (Boston: Ginn and Company, 1938), p. 25.
2. P. Tam, "Driver in Battersby Killing Sent to Adult Jail," *Ottawa Citizen*, November 8, 1996, p. D1; and M. Blanchfield, "Crossed Paths," *Ottawa Citizen*, February 17, 1996, p. B2.
3. See Anthony Walsh, *Biosocial Criminology: Introduction and Integration* (Cincinnati, OH: Anderson, 2002).
4. Emile Durkheim, *The Division of Labor in Society*, trans. George Simpson (New York: Free Press, 1947). Originally published in 1893.
5. Durkheim, *The Division of Labor in Society*, p. 80.
6. W.I. Thomas and Florian Znaniecki, *The Polish Peasant in Europe and America* (Boston: Gorham, 1920).
7. Robert Park and Ernest Burgess, *The City* (Chicago: University of Chicago Press, 1925).
8. Clifford R. Shaw et al., *Delinquency Areas* (Chicago: University of Chicago Press, 1929).
9. David Matza, *Becoming Deviant* (Englewood Cliffs, NJ: Prentice Hall, 1969).
10. C.P. La Prairie, "Community Types, Crime and Police Services on Canadian Indian Reserves," *Journal of Research in Crime and Delinquency*, vol. 25 (1987), pp. 375–391.
11. C.P. La Prairie, "Seen But Not Heard: Native People in the Inner City," in *City-By-City Differences: Inner Cities and the Criminal Justice System, Report 2, Aboriginal Justice Directorate* (Ottawa: Department of Justice, 1994).
12. Lawrence W. Sherman, Patrick R. Gartin, and Michael E. Buerger, "Hot Spots of Predatory Crime: Routine Activities and the Criminology of Place," *Criminology*, vol. 27, no. 1 (1989), pp. 27–55.
13. Rodney Stark, "Deviant Places: A Theory of the Ecology of Crime," *Criminology*, vol. 25, no. 4 (1987), p. 893.
14. Ibid., pp. 895–899.
15. James Q. Wilson and George L. Kelling, "Broken Windows: The Police and Neighborhood Safety," *Atlantic Monthly*, March 1982, http://www.theatlantic.com/politics/crime/windows.htm [Accessed February 15, 2010].
16. Ibid.
17. David Thacher, "Order Maintenance Reconsidered: Moving beyond Strong Causal Reasoning," *Journal of Criminal Law and Criminology*, vol. 94, no. 2 (2004), pp. 381–414.
18. Oscar Newman, *Architectural Design for Crime Prevention* (Washington, DC: U.S. Department of Justice, 1973). See also Oscar Newman, *Defensible Space* (New York: Macmillan, 1972); and Oscar Newman, *Creating Defensible Space* (Washington, DC: Office of Housing and Urban Development, 1996).
19. Oscar Newman, *Defensible Space: Crime Prevention Through Urban Design* (New York: Macmillan, 1972), p. 3. See also

Ralph B. Taylor and Adele V. Harrell, *Physical Environment and Crime* (Washington, DC: National Institute of Justice, May 1996).
20. "Crime Prevention Through Environmental Design," Peel Regional Police website, 2012, http://www.peelpolice.on.ca/en/crimeprevention/crimepreventionthroughenvironmentaldesign.asp [Accessed May 6, 2012].
21. Bernard E. Harcourt, *Illusion of Order: The False Promise of Broken Windows Policing* (Cambridge, MA: Harvard University Press, 2001).
22. Robert J. Sampson and Stephen W. Radenbush, "Systematic Social Observation of Public Spaces: A New Look at Disorder in Urban Neighborhoods," *American Journal of Sociology*, vol. 105 (1999), p. 603.
23. Thomas M. Arvanites and Robert H. Defina, "Business Cycles and Street Crime," *Criminology*, vol. 44, no. 1 (2006), pp. 141.
24. Émile Durkheim, *Suicide: A Study in Sociology* (New York: Free Press, 1897). Reprinted and translated in 1951.
25. Robert K. Merton, "Social Structure and Anomie," *American Sociological Review*, vol. 3 (October 1938), pp. 672–682; and Robert K. Merton, *Social Theory and Social Structure*, rev. ed. (New York: Free Press, 1957).
26. Robert K. Merton, *Social Theory and Social Structure* (New York: Glencoe, 1957), p. 190.
27. Merton, "Social Structure and Anomie," p. 681.
28. M. Beare, *Criminal Conspiracies: Organized Crime in Canada* (Toronto: McClelland & Stewart, 1996); and Criminal Intelligence Service of Canada, *2008 Report on Organized Crime*, 2008, http://www.cisc.gc.ca/annual_reports/annual_report_2008/frontpage_2008_e.html [Accessed May 7, 2012].
29. Robert Agnew, "Foundation for a General Strain Theory of Crime and Delinquency," *Criminology*, vol. 30, no. 1 (1992), pp. 47–87.
30. Ibid.
31. Ibid.
32. Ibid.
33. Raymond Paternoster and Paul Mazerolle, "General Strain Theory and Delinquency: A Replication and Extension," *Journal of Research in Crime and Delinquency*, vol. 31, no. 3 (1994), pp. 235–263.
34. Robert Agnew and Helene Raskin White, "An Empirical Test of General Strain Theory," *Criminology*, vol. 30, no. 4 (1992), pp. 475–499.
35. Thorsten Sellin, *Culture Conflict and Crime* (New York: Social Science Research Council, 1938).
36. Ibid., p. 68.
37. Frederick M. Thrasher, *The Gang* (Chicago: University of Chicago Press, 1927).
38. William F. Whyte, *Street Corner Society: The Social Structure of an Italian Slum* (Chicago: University of Chicago Press, 1943).
39. The quotations attributed to Miller in this section are from Walter Miller, "Lower Class Culture as a Generating Milieu of Gang Delinquency," *Journal of Social Issues*, vol. 14, no. 3 (1958), pp. 5–19.
40. Elijah Anderson, *The Code of the Street: Decency, Violence, and the Moral Life of the Inner City* (New York: W.W. Norton, 1990).
41. Franco Ferracuti and Marvin Wolfgang, *The Subculture of Violence: Toward an Integrated Theory of Criminology* (London: Tavistock, 1967).
42. Ibid.
43. Ibid., p. 151.
44. Ibid., p. 151.
45. Jeffrey I. Ross, *Violence in Canada: Sociopolitical Perspectives* (Toronto: Oxford University Press, 1995), pp. 195–196.
46. For an excellent review of the literature, see F. Frederick Hawley, "The Southern Violence Construct: A Skeleton in the

Criminological Closet." Paper presented at the annual meeting of the American Society of Criminology, 1988.

47. Bertram Wyatt-Brown, *Southern Honor: Ethics and Behavior in the Old South* (Oxford: Oxford University Press, 1983).

48. Franklin Zimring et al., "Punishing Homicide in Philadelphia: Perspectives on the Death Penalty," *University of Chicago Law Review*, vol. 43 (1976), pp. 227–252.

49. John Hagan, "Structural and Cultural Disinvestment and the New Ethnographies of Poverty and Culture," *Contemporary Sociology*, vol. 22, no. 3 (1993), pp. 327–331.

50. Richard A. Cloward and Lloyd E. Ohlin, *Delinquency and Opportunity: A Theory of Delinquent Gangs* (Glencoe, IL: Free Press, 1960).

51. Ibid., p. 7.

52. Ibid., p. 13.

53. Ibid., p. 16.

54. Ibid., p. 19.

55. Ibid., p. 3.

56. Ibid., p. 37.

57. Ibid., pp. 12–13.

58. Albert H. Cohen, *Delinquent Boys: The Culture of the Gang* (Glencoe, IL: Free Press, 1955).

59. Ibid., p. 13.

60. Donald J. Shoemaker, *Theories of Delinquency: An Examination of Explanations of Delinquent Behavior* (New York: Oxford University Press, 1984), p. 102, citing Cohen.

61. Cohen, *Delinquent Boys*, p. 76.

62. Ibid., p. 121.

63. Shoemaker, *Theories of Delinquency*, p. 105.

64. Robert M. Gordon, "Criminal Business Organizations, Street Gangs and 'Wanna Be' Groups: A Vancouver Perspective," *Canadian Journal of Criminology*, vol. 42, no. 1 (January 2000), pp. 39–60.

65. Mark Totten, *Promising Practices for Addressing Youth Involvement in Gangs*, April 2008, http://www.pssg.gov.bc.ca/crimeprevention/publications/docs/totten-report.pdf [Accessed May 10, 2012].

66. Criminal Intelligence Service of Canada, *2010 Annual Report on Organized Crime*, May 2010, http://www.cisc.gc.ca/annual_reports/annual_report_2010/document/report_oc_2010_e.pdf [Accessed May 10, 2012].

67. Totten, *Promising Practices for Addressing Youth Involvement in Gangs*.

68. Criminal Intelligence Service Canada, *2009 Annual Report on Organized Crime*, May 2009, http://www.cisc.gc.ca/annual_reports/annual_report_2009/document/report_oc_2009_e.pdf [Accessed May 10, 2012].

69. National Gang Crime Research Center, *Achieving Justice and Reversing the Problem of Gang Crime and Gang Violence in America Today: Preliminary Results of the Project Gangfact Study* (Chicago: National Gang Crime Research Center, 1996).

70. G. David Curry and Irving A. Spergel, "Gang Homicide, Delinquency, and Community," *Criminology*, vol. 26, no. 3 (1988), pp. 381–405.

71. Ibid., p. 401.

72. Cited in Mary H. Glazier, a review of J. Mitchell Miller and Jeffrey P. Rush, eds., *Gangs: A Criminal Justice Approach* (Cincinnati, OH: Anderson, 1996), in *The Criminologist* (July/April 1996), p. 29.

73. Steven Schlossman et al., *Delinquency Prevention in South Chicago: A Fifty-Year Assessment of the Chicago Area Project* (Santa Monica, CA: Rand Corporation, 1984).

74. J. Robert Lilly, Francis T. Cullen, and Richard A. Ball, *Criminological Theory: Context and Consequences* (Newbury Park, CA: Sage, 1989), p. 80.

75. Lamar T. Empey, *American Delinquency: Its Meaning and Construction* (Homewood, IL: Dorsey, 1982), p. 243.

76. Sibylle Artz, *Sex, Power and the Violent School Girl* (Toronto: Trifolium Books, 1998), p. 24.

77. See, for example, George L. Kelling, "Crime Control, the Police, and Culture Wars: Broken Windows and Cultural Pluralism," in *National Institute of Justice, Perspectives on Crime and Justice: 1997–1998 Lecture Series* (Washington, DC: National Institute of Justice, 1998).

78. Robert J. Bursik, "Social Disorganization and Theories of Crime and Delinquency: Problems and Prospects," *Criminology*, vol. 26, no. 4 (1988), p. 519.

79. Stephen J. Pfohl, *Images of Deviance and Social Control* (New York: McGraw-Hill, 1985), p. 167.

80. Travis Hirschi, review of Delbert S. Elliott, David Huizinga, and Suzanne S. Ageton, *Explaining Delinquency and Drug Use*, in *Criminology*, vol. 25, no. 1 (February 1987), p. 195.

81. Gwynn Nettler, *Killing One Another* (Cincinnati, OH: Anderson, 1982), p. 67.

82. Margaret Anderson, "Review Essay: Rape Theories, Myths, and Social Change," *Contemporary Crises*, vol. 5 (1983), p. 237.

83. Nettler, *Killing One Another*, p. 54.

84. James Q. Wilson, *The Moral Sense* (New York: The Free Press, 1993).

Chapter 9

1. Albert K. Cohen, *Delinquent Boys: The Culture of the Gang* (Glencoe, IL: Free Press, 1995), p. 11.

2. "Killer Seeks Family Visits," *CBC News*, February 14, 2001, http://www.cbc.ca/news/story/2001/02/14/hearing010214.html [Accessed February 19, 2010].

3. "Freedom Weighed for Killer of Heiress," *CBC News*, February 13, 2001, http://www.cbc.ca/news/story/2001/02/13/ott_eatonkiller010213.html [Accessed February 19, 2010].

4. Edwin Sutherland, *Principles of Criminology* (New York: Lippincott, 1939).

5. Edwin H. Sutherland and Donald R. Cressey, *Criminology* (New York: Lippincott, 1978).

6. S. Brown, V. Creamer, and B. Stetson, "Adolescent Alcohol Expectancies in Relation to Personal and Parental Drinking Patterns," *Journal of Abnormal Psychology*, vol. 96 (1987), pp. 117–121.

7. Gresham Sykes and David Matza, "Techniques of Neutralization: A Theory of Delinquency," *American Sociological Review*, vol. 22 (December 1957), pp. 664–670.

8. See Volkan Topalli, "When Being Good Is Bad: An Expansion of Neutralization Theory," *Criminology*, vol. 43 (2005), p. 797.

9. Ibid., pp. 664–670.

10. Robert Agnew, "The Techniques of Neutralization and Violence," *Criminology*, vol. 32, no. 4 (1994), pp. 555–580.

11. Ibid., pp. 555–580.

12. Lois Presser, "Remorse and Neutralization among Violent Male Offenders," *Justice Quarterly*, vol. 20, no. 4 (2003), pp. 801–825.

13. Orly Turgeman-Goldschmidt, "The Rhetoric of Hackers' Neutralizations," in Frank Schmalleger and Michale Pittaro, eds., *Crimes of the Internet* (Upper Saddle River, NJ: Prentice Hall, 2008).

14. See, for example, Dorothy E. Denning, "Activism, Hacktivism, and Cyberterrorism: The Internet as a Tool for Influencing Foreign Policy," *Computer Security Journal*, vol. 16 (2000), pp. 15–35; and Tim Jordan and Paul Taylor, *Hacktivism and Cyberwars: Rebels with a Cause?* (New York: Routledge, 2004).

15. Frank Tannenbaum, *Crime and the Community* (New York: Atheneum Press, 1938), pp. 17–18.

16. Ibid., p. 19.

17. Edwin M. Lemert, *Social Pathology: A Systematic Approach to the Theory of Sociopathic Behavior* (New York: McGraw-Hill, 1951), p. 76.

18. Ibid.
19. Howard Becker, *Outsiders: Studies in the Sociology of Deviance* (New York: Free Press, 1963).
20. Ibid., p. 1.
21. Ibid., p. 9.
22. Ibid., p. 147.
23. M.A. Jackson and C.T. Griffiths, *Canadian Criminology: Perspectives on Crime and Criminality* (Toronto: Harcourt Brace Canada, 1995), pp. 261–263.
24. Becker, *Outsiders*, pp. 37–38.
25. Jon Gunnar Bernburg and Marvin D. Krohn, "Labeling, Life Chances, and Adult Crime: The Direct and Indirect Effects of Official Intervention in Adolescence on Crime in Early Adulthood," *Criminology*, vol. 41, no. 4 (2003), pp. 1287–1318.
26. A number of papers have been released in the Reintegrative Shaming Experiments (RISE) series to date: Lawrence W. Sherman and Heather Strang, *The Right Kind of Shame for Crime Prevention* (Canberra: Australian National University, 1997); Heather Strang and Lawrence W. Sherman, *The Victim's Perspective* (Canberra: Australian National University, 1997); Lawrence W. Sherman and Geoffrey C. Barnes, *Restorative Justice and Offenders' Respect for the Law* (Canberra: Australian National University, 1997); Lawrence W. Sherman and Heather Strang, *Restorative Justice and Deterring Crime* (Canberra: Australian National University, 1997); and Nathan Harris and Jamie B. Burton, *The Reliability of Observed Reintegrative Shaming, Shame, Defiance and Other Key Concepts in Diversionary Conferences* (Canberra: Australian National University, 1997).
27. *RISE Working Papers: Introduction* (Canberra: Australian National University, 1997).
28. Cited in Lawrence W. Sherman and Heather Strang, *The Right Kind of Shame for Crime Prevention* (Canberra: Australian National University, 1997).
29. Ibid.
30. For a good overview of social control approaches, see George S. Bridges and Martha Myers, eds., *Inequality, Crime, and Social Control* (Boulder, CO: Westview Press, 1994).
31. Walter C. Reckless, *The Crime Problem*, 4th ed. (New York: Appleton-Century-Crofts, 1967).
32. Ibid., p. 470.
33. Ibid.
34. Ibid., p. 475.
35. Ibid.
36. Travis Hirschi, *Causes of Delinquency* (Berkeley: University of California Press, 1969).
37. Ibid.
38. Ibid.
39. Ibid.
40. Ibid.
41. Ibid.
42. Ibid.
43. Ibid.
44. Michael Gottfredson and Travis Hirschi, *A General Theory of Crime* (Stanford, CA: Stanford University Press, 1990).
45. See also Michael R. Gottfredson and Travis Hirschi, "Criminality and Low Self-Control," in John E. Conklin, ed., *New Perspectives in Criminology* (Boston: Allyn & Bacon, 1996).
46. Werner Einstadter and Stuart Henry, *Criminological Theory: An Analysis of Its Underlying Assumptions* (Fort Worth, TX: Harcourt Brace, 1995), p. 189.
47. For some influential writings of the period, see K.F. Riegel, "Toward a Dialectical Theory of Development," *Human Development*, vol. 18 (1975), pp. 50–64; and U. Bronfenbrenner, *The Ecology of Human Development* (Cambridge: Harvard University Press, 1979).
48. R.M. Lerner, "Early Adolescence: Towards an Agenda for the Integration of Research, Policy and Intervention," in R.M. Lerner, ed., *Early Adolescence: Perspectives on Research, Policy, and Intervention* (Hillsdale, NJ: Erlbaum, 1993), pp. 1–13.
49. See T.P. Thornberry, *Developmental Theories of Crime and Delinquency* (Piscataway, NJ: Transaction, 1997).
50. A. Blumstein et al., eds., *Criminal Careers and Career Criminals* (Washington, DC: National Academy Press, 1986).
51. See, for example, the collected papers of Sheldon Glueck, 1916–1972, which are part of the David L. Bazelon collection at Harvard University Law School (Cambridge, MA). Results of the Gluecks' work were reported in S. Glueck and E. Glueck, *Unraveling Juvenile Delinquency* (New York: The Commonwealth Fund, 1950).
52. Sheldon Glueck and Eleanor Glueck, *Delinquents and Nondelinquents in Perspective* (Cambridge, MA: Harvard University Press, 1968).
53. John H. Laub and Robert J. Sampson, "Turning Points in the Life Course: Why Change Matters to the Study of Crime," *Criminology*, vol. 31, no. 3 (1993), pp. 301–325. See also Robert J. Sampson and John H. Laub, "Crime and Deviance in the Life Course," *Annual Review of Sociology*, vol. 18 (1992), pp. 63–84.
54. Robert J. Sampson and John H. Laub, *Crime in the Making* (Cambridge, MA: Harvard University Press, 1993).
55. Marvin Wolfgang, Robert Figlio, and Thorsten Sellin, *Delinquency in a Birth Cohort* (Chicago: University of Chicago Press, 1972).
56. Marvin Wolfgang, Terence Thornberry, and Robert Figlio, *From Boy to Man, From Delinquency to Crime* (Chicago: University of Chicago Press, 1987).
57. Steven P. Lab, "Analyzing Change in Crime and Delinquency Rates: The Case for Cohort Analysis," *Criminal Justice Research Bulletin*, vol. 3, no. 10 (Huntsville, TX: Sam Houston State University, 1988), p. 2.
58. Lawrence E. Cohen and Richard Machalek, "A General Theory of Expropriative Crime: An Evolutionary Ecological Approach," *American Journal of Sociology*, vol. 94, no. 3 (1988), pp. 465–501; and Lawrence E. Cohen and Richard Machalek, "The Normalcy of Crime: From Durkheim to Evolutionary Ecology," *Rationality and Society*, vol. 6 (1994), pp. 286–308.
59. Bryan Vila, "Human Nature and Crime Control: Improving the Feasibility of Nurturant Strategies," *Politics and the Life Sciences* (March 1997), pp. 3–21.
60. Ibid.
61. Barbara Tatem Kelley et al., *Developmental Pathways in Boys' Disruptive and Delinquent Behavior* (Washington, DC: Office of Juvenile Justice and Delinquency Prevention, December 1997).
62. See Stuart Greenbaum, "Drugs, Delinquency, and Other Data," in *Juvenile Justice*, vol. 2, no. 1 (Spring/Summer 1994), pp. 2–8.
63. For another interesting analysis, see Robert J. Sampson and John H. Laub, *Crime in the Making* (Cambridge, MA: Harvard University Press, 1993).
64. Kelley et al., *Developmental Pathways in Boys' Disruptive and Delinquent Behavior*, p. 14.
65. See Felton J. Earls and Albert J. Reiss, *Breaking the Cycle: Predicting and Preventing Crime* (Washington, DC: National Institute of Justice, 1994).
66. Vila, "Human Nature and Crime Control," p. 10.
67. C.T. Griffiths and S. Verdun-Jones, *Canadian Criminal Justice* (Toronto: Harcourt Brace Canada, 1994), p. 559.
68. Robert W. Sweet, Jr., "Preserving Families to Prevent Delinquency," *Office of Juvenile Justice and Delinquency Prevention Model Programs, 1990* (Washington, DC: U.S. Department of Justice, April 1992).

69. Ibid.
70. Frank Schmalleger, *Criminology Today: An Integrative Introduction* (Upper Saddle River, NJ: Pearson Education, 2009), p. 336.
71. Randy Martin, Robert J. Mutchnick, and W. Timothy Austin, *Criminological Thought: Pioneers Past and Present* (New York: Macmillan, 1990), p. 368.

Chapter 10

1. *Communities and the Challenge of Conflict: Perspectives on Restorative Justice* [Monograph]. Law Commission of Canada, 2000.
2. Katherine Wilton, "'We Don't Want a Second Oka Crisis': Kanesetake Mohawks," *The Gazette*, January 25, 2010, http://www.montrealgazette.com/technology/want+second+crisis+Kanesatake+Mohawks/2483648/story.html [Accessed February 28, 2010].
3. Richard Quinney, *Class, State, and Class: On the Theory and Practice of Criminal Justice* (New York: David McKay, 1977), p. 145.
4. Vance Packard, *The Status Seekers* (London: Harmondsworth, 1961).
5. George B. Vold, *Theoretical Criminology* (New York: Oxford University Press, 1958).
6. Ibid., p. 205.
7. Ibid., pp. 208–209.
8. Ralf Dahrendorf, *Class and Class Conflict in Industrial Society* (Stanford, CA: Stanford University Press, 1959).
9. Ralf Dahrendorf, "Out of Utopia: Toward a Reorientation of Sociological Analysis," *American Journal of Sociology*, vol. 64 (1958), pp. 115–127.
10. Austin Turk, *Criminality and Legal Order* (Chicago: Rand McNally, 1969), p. vii.
11. Ibid.
12. William J. Chambliss, "Toward a Political Economy of Crime," in C. Reasons and R. Rich, eds., *The Sociology of Law* (Toronto: Butterworth, 1978), p. 193.
13. William Chambliss and Robert T. Seidman, *Law, Order, and Power* (Reading, MA: Addison-Wesley, 1971), p. 33.
14. Adapted from Chambliss and Seidman, *Law, Order, and Power*, pp. 473–474.
15. William J. Chambliss, *Crime and the Legal Process* (New York: McGraw-Hill, 1969), p. 88.
16. William J. Chambliss, "Toward a Political Economy of Crime," *Theory and Society*, vol. 2 (1975), pp. 152–153.
17. Ibid.
18. Ibid., p. 152.
19. Richard Quinney, *Critique of the Legal Order: Crime Control in Capitalist Society* (Boston: Little, Brown, 1974), p. 16.
20. Quinney, *Class, State, and Class*, p. 58.
21. Ibid.
22. Ibid., p. 61.
23. Ibid., p. 65.
24. Jeffrey H. Reiman, *The Rich Get Richer and the Poor Get Prison: Ideology, Class and Criminal Justice* (Boston: Allyn & Bacon, 2000).
25. Gresham M. Sykes, "Critical Criminology," *Journal of Criminal Law and Criminology*, vol. 65 (1974), pp. 206–213.
26. David A. Jones, *History of Criminology: A Philosophical Perspective* (Westport, CT: Greenwood, 1986), p. 200.
27. Elliott Currie, "Market, Crime, and Community," *Theoretical Criminology*, vol. 1, no. 2 (May 1997), pp. 147–172.
28. William V. Pelfrey, *The Evolution of Criminology* (Cincinnati, OH: Anderson, 1980), p. 86.
29. For a good overview of critiques of radical criminology, see J.F. Galliher, "Life and Death of Liberal Criminology," *Contemporary Crisis*, vol. 2, no. 3 (July 1978), pp. 245–263.
30. Jackson Toby, "The New Criminology Is the Old Sentimentality," *Criminology*, vol. 16 (1979), pp. 516–526.
31. Ibid.
32. Hermann Mannheim, *Comparative Criminology* (Boston: Houghton Mifflin, 1965), p. 445.
33. Werner Einstadter and Stuart Henry, *Criminological Theory: An Analysis of Its Underlying Assumptions* (Fort Worth, TX: Harcourt Brace, 1995), p. 233.
34. For an excellent review of critical realism in a Canadian context, see John Lowman and Brian D. MacLean, eds., *Realist Criminology: Crime Control and Policing in the 1990s* (Toronto: University of Toronto Press, 1994).
35. Daniel J. Curran and Claire M. Renzetti, *Theories of Crime* (Boston: Allyn & Bacon, 1994), p. 283.
36. See M.D. Schwartz and W.S. DeKeseredy, "Left Realist Criminology: Strengths, Weaknesses, and the Feminist Critique," *Crime, Law, and Social Change*, vol. 15, no. 1 (January 1991), pp. 51–72; W.S. DeKeseredy and B.D. MacLean, "Exploring the Gender, Race, and Class Dimensions of Victimization: A Left Realist Critique of the Canadian Urban Victimization Survey," *International Journal of Offender Therapy and Comparative Criminology*, vol. 35, no. 2 (Summer 1991), pp. 143–161; and W.S. DeKeseredy and M.D. Schwartz, "British and U.S. Left Realism: A Critical Comparison," *International Journal of Offender Therapy and Comparative Criminology*, vol. 35, no. 3 (Fall 1991), pp. 248–262.
37. See Jock Young, "The Failure of Criminology: The Need for a Radical Realism," in R. Matthews and J. Young, eds., *Confronting Crime* (Beverly Hills, CA: Sage, 1986), pp. 4–30; Jock Young, "The Tasks of a Realist Criminology," *Contemporary Crisis*, vol. 11, no. 4 (1987) pp. 337–356; and "Radical Criminology in Britain: The Emergence of a Competing Paradigm," *British Journal of Criminology*, vol. 28 (1988), pp. 159–183.
38. D. Brown and R. Hogg, "Essentialism, Radical Criminology, and Left Realism," *Australian and New Zealand Journal of Criminology*, vol. 25 (1992), pp. 195–230.
39. Roger Matthews and Jock Young, "Reflections on Realism," in Jock Young and Roger Matthews, eds., *Rethinking Criminology: The Realist Debate* (Newbury Park, CA: Sage, 1992).
40. Don C. Gibbons, *Talking About Crime and Criminals: Problems and Issues in Theory Development in Criminology* (Englewood Cliffs, NJ: Prentice Hall, 1994), p. 170.
41. Piers Beirne and James W. Messerschmidt, *Criminology* (New York: Harcourt Brace Jovanovich, 1991), p. 501.
42. Gibbons, *Talking About Crime and Criminals*, p. 165, citing Loraine Gelsthorpe and Alison Morris, "Feminism and Criminology in Britain," *British Journal of Criminology* (Spring 1988), pp. 93–110.
43. Sally S. Simpson, "Feminist Theory, Crime and Justice," *Criminology*, vol. 27, no. 4 (1989), p. 605.
44. Roslyn Muraskin and Ted Alleman, eds., *It's a Crime: Women and Justice* (Upper Saddle River, NJ: Prentice Hall, 1993), p. 1.
45. As stated in Amanda Burgess-Proctor, "Intersections of Race, Class, Gender, and Crime: Future Directions for Feminist Criminology," *Feminist Criminology*, vol. 1, no. 27 (2006), p. 29.
46. Carol Pateman, "Feminist Critiques of the Public/Private Dichotomy," in Anne Phillips, ed., *Feminism and Equality* (Oxford, England: Blackwell, 1987).
47. F.P. Williams III and M.D. McShane, *Criminological Theory* (Upper Saddle River, NJ: Prentice Hall, 1994), p. 238.
48. Ibid.
49. Burgess-Proctor, "Intersections of Race, Class, Gender, and Crime," p. 29.
50. James W. Messerschmidt, *Capitalism, Patriarchy, and Crime: Toward a Socialist Feminist Criminology* (Totowa, NJ: Rowman and Littlefield, 1986).

51. Freda Adler, *Sisters in Crime: The Rise of the New Female Criminal* (New York: McGraw-Hill, 1975).

52. Rita J. Simon, *Women and Crime* (Lexington, MA: Lexington Books, 1975).

53. Carol Smart, *Women, Crime and Criminology: A Feminist Critique* (London: Routledge, 1977).

54. Kathleen Daly and Meda Chesney-Lind, "Feminism and Criminology," *Justice Quarterly*, vol. 5, no. 5 (December 1988), pp. 497–535.

55. The following list is adapted from Daly and Chesney-Lind, "Feminism and Criminology," pp. 497–535.

56. Susan Caulfield and Nancy Wonders, "Gender and Justice: Feminist Contributions to Criminology," in Gregg Barak, ed., *Varieties of Criminology: Readings from a Dynamic Discipline* (Westport, CT: Praeger, 1994), pp. 213–229.

57. Caufield and Wonders, "Gender and Justice," pp. 213–229.

58. John Hagan, *Structural Criminology* (New Brunswick, NJ: Rutgers University Press, 1989), p. 130.

59. Ibid.

60. Evelyn K. Sommers, *Voices from Within: Women Who Have Broken the Law* (Toronto: University of Toronto Press, 1995).

61. Daly and Chesney-Lind, "Feminism and Criminology," p. 506.

62. Ibid.

63. Ibid.

64. For an intriguing analysis of how existing laws tend to criminalize women and their reproductive activities, see Susan O. Reed, "The Criminalization of Pregnancy: Drugs, Alcohol, and AIDS," in Muraskin and Alleman, eds., *It's a Crime*, pp. 92–117; and Drew Humphries, "Mothers and Children, Drugs and Crack: Reactions to Maternal Drug Dependency," in Muraskin and Alleman, eds., *It's a Crime*, pp. 131–145.

65. Dawn H. Currie, "Feminist Encounters with Postmodernism: Exploring the Impasse of the Debates on Patriarchy and Law," *Canadian Journal of Women and the Law*, vol. 5, no. 1 (1992), p. 10.

66. For an excellent overview of feminist theory in criminology, and for a comprehensive review of research regarding female offenders, see Joanne Belknap, *The Invisible Woman: Gender Crime and Justice* (Belmont, CA: Wadsworth, 1996).

67. Such studies are still ongoing and continue to add to the descriptive literature of feminist criminology. See, for example, Deborah R. Baskin and Ira Sommers, "Female Initiation into Violent Street Crime," *Justice Quarterly*, vol. 10, no. 4 (December 1993), pp. 559–583; Scott Decker, Richard Wright, Allison Redfern, and Dietrich Smith, "A Woman's Place Is in the Home: Females and Residential Burglary," *Justice Quarterly*, vol. 10, no. 1 (March 1993), pp. 143–162; and Jill L. Rosenbaum, "The Female Delinquent: Another Look at the Role of the Family," in Muraskin and Alleman, eds., *It's a Crime*, pp. 399–420.

68. Ronald L. Akers, *Criminological Theories: Introduction and Evaluation* (Los Angeles: Roxbury, 1994), p. 39.

69. Daly and Chesney-Lind, "Feminism and Criminology," p. 512.

70. See, for example, Darrell J. Steffensmeier and Emile Andersen Allan, "Sex Disparities in Arrests by Residence, Race, and Age: An Assessment of the Gender Convergence/Crime Hypothesis," *Justice Quarterly*, vol. 5, no. 1 (March 1988), pp. 53–80; and Darrell Steffensmeier, John Kramer, and Cathy Streifel, "Gender and Imprisonment Decisions," *Criminology*, vol. 31, no. 3 (August 1993), pp. 411–446. Gender-based differences, however, have been discovered in some instances of probation- and parole-related decision making. See Edna Erez, "Gender, Rehabilitation, and Probation Decisions," *Criminology*, vol. 27, no. 2 (1989), pp. 307–327; and Edna Erez, "Dangerous Men, Evil Women: Gender and Parole Decision-Making," *Justice Quarterly*, vol. 9, no. 1 (March 1992), pp. 106–126.

71. See, for example, Kathleen Daly, "Neither Conflict nor Labeling nor Paternalism Will Suffice: Intersections of Race, Ethnicity, Gender, and Family in Criminal Court Decisions," *Crime and Delinquency*, vol. 35, no. 1 (January 1989), pp. 136–168.

72. Cited in Allison Morris, *Women, Crime and Criminal Justice* (New York: Blackwell, 1987).

73. For examples of how this might be accomplished, see F.H. Knopp, "Community Solutions to Sexual Violence: Feminist/Abolitionist Perspectives," in Harold E. Pepinsky and Richard Quinney, eds., *Criminology as Peacemaking* (Bloomington: Indiana University Press, 1991), pp. 181–193; and S. Caringella-MacDonald and D. Humphries, "Sexual Assault, Women, and the Community: Organizing to Prevent Sexual Violence," in Pepinsky and Quinney, eds., *Criminology as Peacemaking*, pp. 98–113.

74. Richard Quinney, "Life of Crime: Criminology and Public Policy as Peacemaking," *Journal of Crime and Justice*, vol. 16, no. 2 (1993), pp. 3–9.

75. See, for example, Harold E. Pepinsky, "This Can't Be Peace: A Pessimist Looks at Punishment," in W.B. Groves and G. Newman, eds., *Punishment and Privilege* (Albany, NY: Harrow and Heston, 1986); Harold E. Pepinsky, "Violence as Unresponsiveness: Toward a New Conception of Crime," *Justice Quarterly*, vol. 5 (1988), pp. 539–563; and Pepinsky and Quinney, eds., *Criminology as Peacemaking*.

76. See, for example, Richard Quinney, "Crime, Suffering, Service: Toward a Criminology of Peacemaking," *Quest*, vol. 1 (1988), pp. 66–75; Richard Quinney, "The Theory and Practice of Peacemaking in the Development of Radical Criminology," *Critical Criminologist*, vol. 1, no. 5 (1989), p. 5; and Richard Quinney and John Wildeman, *The Problem of Crime: A Peace and Social Justice Perspective*, 3rd ed. (Mayfield, CA: Mountain View Press, 1991), originally published as *The Problem of Crime: A Critical Introduction to Criminology* (New York: Bantam, 1977).

77. All these themes are addressed, for example, in Pepinsky and Quinney, eds., *Criminology as Peacemaking*.

78. For a good discussion of this "theory," see John F. Galliher, "Willie Horton: Fact, Faith, and Commonsense Theory of Crime," in Pepinsky and Quinney, eds., *Criminology as Peacemaking*, pp. 245–250.

79. Quinney and Wildeman, *The Problem of Crime*, pp. vii–viii.

80. Bo Lozoff and Michael Braswell, *Inner Corrections: Finding Peace and Peace Making* (Cincinnati, OH: Anderson, 1989).

81. Clemmons Bartollas and Michael Braswell, "Correctional Treatment, Peacemaking, and the New Age Movement," *Journal of Crime and Justice*, vol. 16, no. 2 (1993), pp. 43–58.

82. Ibid.

83. E.A. Fattah, "Restorative and Retributive Justice Models: A Comparison," in H.H. Kuhne, ed., *Festschrift fur Koichi Miyazawa* (Baden-Baden, Germany: Nomos Verlagsgesllschaft, 1995).

84. J. Bonta, S. Wallace-Capretta, and J. Rooney, *Restorative Justice: An Evaluation of the Restorative Justice Project*, User Report 1998–05 (Ottawa: Solicitor General Canada, 1998). See also *Restorative Justice in Canada: A Consultation Paper*, Department of Justice Canada, May 2000.

85. Robin Dann, *Restorative Justice Initiatives in South Eastern Alberta* (unpublished paper, 2000). See also Heino Lilles, Territorial Judge, Whitehorse, Yukon, *Circle Sentencing: Part of the Restorative Justice Continuum*, Plenary Speaker, August 9, 2002, Third International Conference on Conferencing, August 8–10, 2002, Minneapolis, Minnesota.

86. Bonta et al., *Restorative Justice*.
87. "Restorative Resolutions," The John Howard Society of Manitoba website, 2006, http://www.johnhoward.mb.ca/pages/home.php [Accessed January 24, 2012].
88. Michael J. Lynch and W. Byron Groves, *A Primer in Radical Criminology*, 2nd ed. (Albany, NY: Harrow and Heston, 1989), p. 128.

Chapter 11

1. National Crime Prevention Council (NCPC), "Working Together for Safer Communities," National Crime Prevention Strategy (Ottawa: NCPC, 1997).
2. "The Stockholm Prize in Criminology," Stockholm University website, n.d., http://www.criminologyprize.com/extra/pod/?module_instance=3 [Accessed April 10, 2012].
3. John Ekstedt, "Canadian Justice Policy," in Margaret A. Jackson and Curt T. Griffiths, eds., *Canadian Criminology: Perspectives on Crime and Criminality* (Toronto: Harcourt Brace Canada, 1995), p. 311.
4. James E. Anderson, *Public Policymaking: An Introduction* (Boston: Houghton Mifflin, 1990).
5. Ekstedt, "Canadian Justice Policy," p. 308.
6. Ibid., p. 312.
7. Nancy E. Marion, *A History of Federal Crime Control Initiatives, 1960–1993* (Westport, CT: Praeger, 1994), p. 3. For a more detailed analysis of the process by which crime-control policies are created, see Paul Rock, "The Opening Stages of Criminal Justice Policy Making," *British Journal of Criminology*, vol. 35, no. 1 (Winter 1995).
8. Ekstedt, "Canadian Justice Policy," p. 308.
9. Jeff Ferrell, "Criminological Verstehen: Inside the Immediacy of Crime," *Justice Quarterly*, vol. 14, no. 1 (1997), p. 16.
10. Troy Q. Riddell, "What Can Political Science Contribute to the Study of Criminal Justice in Canada?" *Canadian Journal of Criminology and Criminal Justice*, vol. 52, no. 3 (June 2010), p. 321.
11. For an excellent discussion of the policies associated with law, punishment, and social control, see Thomas G. Blomberg and Stanley Cohen, eds., *Punishment and Social Control: Essays in Honor of Sheldon L. Messinger* (Hawthorne, NY: Aldine de Gruyter, 1995).
12. Bryan Vila, "Could We Break the Crime Control Paradox?" Paper presented at the annual meeting of the American Society of Criminology, Miami, Florida, November 1994 [abstract].
13. From an address to the Standing Committee on Justice and the Solicitor General, 1993.
14. Department of Justice Canada, *The National Strategy on Community Safety and Crime Prevention: Building Safer Communities*, n.d., http://www.acsa-caah.ca/Portals/0/Member/PDF/en/documents/nationalstrat.pdf [Accessed April 7, 2012].
15. Department of Justice Canada, "Minister of Justice Proposes Stringent New Rules to Protect Canadians from Dangerous and High-Risk Offenders," October 17, 2006, http://www.justice.gc.ca/eng/news-nouv/nr-cp/2006/doc_31908.html [Accessed April 7, 2012].
16. Department of Justice Canada, "Statement by the Government of Canada on the Royal Assent of Bill C-10," March 13, 2012, http://www.justice.gc.ca/eng/news-nouv/nr-cp/2012/doc_32714.html [Accessed April 7, 2012].
17. Bryan Vila, "A General Paradigm for Understanding Criminal Behavior: Extending Evolutionary Ecological Theory," *Criminology*, vol. 32, no. 3 (August 1994), pp. 311–359.
18. Vila, "Could We Break the Crime Control Paradox?"
19. Bryan Vila, "Human Nature and Crime Control: Improving the Feasibility of Nurturant Strategies," *Politics and the Life Sciences*, March 1997, p. 10.
20. Ibid., pp. 3–21.
21. Vila, "A General Paradigm."
22. Vila, "Human Nature and Crime Control," p. 11.
23. Canada, House of Commons, Standing Committee on Justice and the Solicitor General, "Crime Prevention in Canada: Toward a National Strategy," Twelfth Report of the Standing Committee on Justice and the Solicitor General, 1993.
24. Information for this section has been obtained from Public Safety Canada website, http://www.publicsafety.gc.ca/prg/cp/index-eng.aspx [Accessed April 8, 2012].
25. C. Ray Jeffery, *Crime Control Through Environmental Design* (Beverley Hills, CA: Sage, 1971).
26. Royal Canadian Mounted Police, *Crime Control through Environmental Design*, March 16, 2011, http://www.rcmp-grc.gc.ca/pubs/ccaps-spcca/safecomm-seccollect-eng.htm [Accessed April 7, 2012].
27. Peel Regional Police, *Fact Sheet: Crime Prevention Through Environmental Design*, May 2008, http://www.peelpolice.on.ca/en/crimeprevention/resources/cpted.pdf [Accessed April 7, 2012].
28. Crime Prevention Association of New Brunswick website, http://jaba.net/cpanb/ [Accessed April 7, 2012].
29. Greg Saville, "Balancing the CPTED Response," n.d., http://www.cpted.net [Accessed May 25, 2007].
30. Ibid.
31. Department of Justice Canada, "Government of Canada Introduces the *Safe Streets and Communities Act*," September 20, 2011, http://www.justice.gc.ca/eng/news-nouv/nr-cp/2011/doc_32631.html [Accessed April 29, 2012].
32. "Tough-On-Crime Policies Ineffective, U.S. Sentencing Expert Contends," *Ottawa Citizen*, May 24, 2008, http://www.canada.com/topics/news/politics/story.html?id=4c4d7eec-daff-4a7e-b53a-057dd7102746&k=85304 [Accessed November 12, 2009].
33. H. Bianchi, *Position and Subject-Matter of Criminology* (Amsterdam: North Holland Pub., 1956).
34. Hermann Mannheim, *Comparative Criminology* (New York: Houghton Mifflin, 1965), p. 18.
35. For an interesting look at jurisdictional complexities, see the discussion about the attempts to regulate lap dancing in Ontario in Alison Hatch Cunningham and Curt T. Griffiths, *Canadian Criminal Justice: A Primer* (Toronto: Harcourt Brace Canada, 1997), pp. 13–14.
36. Ekstedt, "Canadian Justice Policy," pp. 307–329.

Chapter 12

1. Cynthia Manson and Charles Ardai, eds., *Future Crime: An Anthology of the Shape of Crime to Come* (New York: Donald I. Fine, 1992), p. ix.
2. This story is adapted from Gary LaFree et al., "The Changing Nature of Crime in America," in Gary LaFree, ed., *Criminal Justice 2000: Volume III—the Nature of Crime—Continuity and Change* (Washington, DC: National Institute of Justice, 2000).
3. Darlene E. Weingand, "Futures Research Methodologies: Linking Today's Decisions with Tomorrow's Possibilities." Paper presented at the Sixty-First International Federation of Library Associations and Institutions annual conference, August 20–25, 1995, http://www.ifla.org/IV/ifla61/61-weid.htm [Accessed March 26, 2010].
4. Joseph F. Coates, "The Highly Probable Future: 83 Assumptions about the Year 2025," *The Futurist*, vol. 28, no. 4 (July/August 1994), p. 51.
5. Although this chapter cannot cover all aspects of the criminal justice system, readers are referred to C.J. Swank, "Police in the Twenty-first Century: Hypotheses for the Future," *International Journal of Comparative and Applied Criminal Justice*, vol. 17, nos. 1 and 2 (Spring/Fall 1993), pp. 107–120, for an excellent analysis of policing in the future.
6. Foresight home page, http://www.foresight.gov.uk [Accessed December 31, 2012].

7. The quotations attributed to the panel in this section are from Foresight Crime Prevention Panel, *Just around the Corner: A Consultation Document*, n.d., http://www.bis.gov.uk/assets/foresight/docs/crime-prevention/just-around-the-corner-march-2000.pdf [Accessed December 31, 2013].

8. "Chiquita Pleads Guilty to Paying Terrorists to Protect Workers," *USA Today*, March 20, 2007, http://usatoday30.usatoday.com/money/industries/food/2007-03-19-chiquita-terrorism_N.htm [Accessed December 31, 2013].

9. Adapted from John McHale, "Futures Critical: A Review," in *Human Futures: Needs, Societies, Technologies* (Guildford, Surrey, UK: IPC Business Press Limited, 1974), p. 13.

10. Thomas L. Friedman, *The Lexus and the Olive Tree* (New York: Anchor Books, 2000).

11. Frank Schmalleger, *Criminology Today: An Integrative Introduction* (Upper Saddle River, NJ: Pearson Education, 2009), p. 618.

12. National Institute of Justice, *Asian Transnational Organized Crime and Its Impact on the United States* (Washington, DC: NIJ, 2007).

13. Department of Justice, Canada, G8 *Recommendations on Transnational Crime*, December 12, 2008, http://www.canadainternational.gc.ca/g8/ministerials-ministerielles/2002/transnational_crime-criminalite_transnationale.aspx?lang=eng&view=d [Accessed December 31, 2012].

14. United Nations Office on Drugs and Crime, *United Nations Convention against Transnational Organized Crime and the Protocols Thereto*, 2004, http://www.unodc.org/documents/treaties/UNTOC/Publications/TOC%20Convention/TOCebook-e.pdf [Accessed December 31, 2012].

15. Criminal Intelligence Service Canada, *2008 Report on Organized Crime*, http://www.cisc.gc.ca/annual_reports/annual_report_2008/frontpage_2008_e.html [Accessed December 31, 2012].

16. Bureau for International Narcotics and Law Enforcement Affairs, Human Smuggling and Trafficking Center, *Distinctions between Human Smuggling and Human Trafficking* (Washington, DC: The Bureau, January 2005).

17. United Nations Office on Drugs and Crime (UNODC), "Migrant Smuggling," 2004, http://www.unodc.org/unodc/en/human-trafficking/smuggling-of-migrants.html [Accessed December 31, 2012].

18. Kristiina Kangaspunta, "Mapping the Inhuman Trade: Preliminary Findings of the Database on Trafficking in Human Beings," *Forum on Crime and Society*, vol. 3, nos. 1 and 2 (2003), p. 83.

19. United Nations Office on Drugs and Crime (UNODC), *Global Report on Trafficking in Persons, 2012*, p. 3, http://www.unodc.org/documents/data-and-analysis/glotip/Trafficking_in_Persons_2012_web.pdf [Accessed January 1, 2013].

20. Ibid.

21. Ibid.

22. RCMP Criminal Intelligence, *Human Trafficking in Canada*, March 2012, p. 44, http://publications.gc.ca/collections/collection_2011/grc-rcmp/PS64-78-2010-eng.pdf [Accessed April 14, 2013].

23. RCMP, *Gazette*, vol. 66, no. 3 (2004).

24. UNODC, *Global Report on Trafficking in Persons, 2012*, p. 91.

25. RCMP, *Gazette*, vol. 66, no. 2 (2004).

26. Tony Castro, "Valley Gangs Leave Trail on Web," *Los Angeles Daily News*, December 5, 2009, http://www.dailynews.com/news/ci_13931149 [Accessed January 1, 2013].

27. Melanie Kowalski, Canadian Centre for Justice Statistics, *Cyber-Crime: Issues, Data Sources, and Feasibility of Collecting Police-Reported Statistics* (Ottawa: Minister of Industry, 2002), p. 6.

28. Ibid.

29. Catherine H. Conley and J. Thomas McEwen, "Computer Crime," *NIJ Reports* (January/February 1990).

30. Kenneth Rosenblatt, "Deterring Computer Crime," *Technology Review*, vol. 93, no. 2 (February/March 1990), pp. 34–41.

31. Richard H. Baker, *The Computer Security Handbook* (Blue Ridge Summit, PA: TAB Books, 1985).

32. Software and Information Industry Association, *Report on Global Software Piracy 2000*, p. 7, http://www.siia.net/estore/GPR-00.pdf [Accessed January 1, 2013].

33. Business Software Alliance, *Seventh Annual BSA/IDC Global Software Piracy Study*, May 2010, http://portal.bsa.org/globalpiracy2009/index.html [Accessed January 1, 2013].

34. Gary H. Anthes, "Software Pirates' Booty Topped $13B, Study Finds," *Computerworld*, January 6, 1997, p. 24.

35. Stephen R. Purdy, "Protecting Your Telephone Systems against Dial-Tone Thieves," *Infosecurity News*, July/August, 1993, p. 43.

36. Paul Keegan, "High Tech Pirates Collecting Phone Calls," *USA Today*, September 23, 1994, p. 4A.

37. Ibid.

38. Fraser Lovatt, "U.S. Department of Justice: VoIP Fosters Crime, Drugs and Terrorism," *Digital-Lifestyles.info*, June 18, 2004, http://digital-lifestyles.info/2004/06/18/us-department-of-justice-voip-fosters-crime-drugs-and-terrorism/ [Accessed January 1, 2013].

39. The Anti-Phishing Working Group, *Phishing Activity Trends*, April 2007, http://www.antiphishing.org/reports/apwg_report_april_2007.pdf [Accessed January 1, 2013].

40. Gregg Keizer, "Gartner: Phishing Attacks Threaten E-Commerce," *Network Computing*, May 6, 2004, http://www.networkcomputing.com/data-protection/gartner-phishing-attacks-threaten-ecomm/229621154 [Accessed January 4, 2013].

41. "Cybercrime in Canada Said to Be Skyrocketing," *CBC News*, May 9, 2012, http://www.cbc.ca/news/technology/story/2012/05/08/cyber-security-phishing-bots-malicious.html [Accessed January 4, 2013].

42. Donn B. Parker, *Computer Crime: Criminal Justice Resource Manual* (Washington, DC: National Institute of Justice, 1989).

43. For a complete look at the research, analysis, and evaluation performed by the National Institute of Justice, see their website at http://www.nij.gov/welcome.html [Accessed January 4, 2013].

44. "The Council of Europe's Convention on Cyber-Crime," Electronic Privacy Information Center, 2005, http://www.epic.org/privacy/intl/ccc.html [Accessed January 4, 2013].

45. Jordan Press, "Canada's Cyber Security Lacking, Says Report," *The Province*, October 24, 2012, http://www.theprovince.com/technology/Canada+cyber+security+lacking+says+report/7437712/story.html [Accessed January 4, 2013].

46. Kowalski, *Cyber-Crime*.

47. Joseph F. Coates et al., *2025: Scenarios of U.S. and Global Society Reshaped by Science and Technology* (Winchester, VA: Oakhill Press, 1997).

48. Richter H. Moore, Jr., "Wiseguys: Smarter Criminals and Smarter Crime in the Twenty-First Century," *Futurist*, vol. 28, no. 5 (September/October 1994), p. 33.

49. The quotations attributed to Moore in this section are from "Wiseguys," pp. 33–37.

Glossary

Alloplastic adaptation a form of adjustment resulting from changes in the environment surrounding an individual.

Anomie a social condition in which norms are uncertain or lacking.

Anti-social personality disorder (ASPD) a psychological condition exhibited by individuals who are basically unsocialized and whose behaviour pattern brings them repeatedly into conflict with society.

Anti-social personality or **asocial personality** an individual who is unsocialized and whose behaviour pattern brings him or her into repeated conflict with society.

Applied research Research based on scientific inquiry that is designed and carried out with practical application in mind.

Assault the intentional or threatened application of force on another person without consent. The categories of assault include level 1—assault or common assault; level 2—assault that involves the use of a weapon or that causes bodily harm; and level 3—assault that results in wounding or endangering the life of the victim.

Atavism a concept used by Cesare Lombroso to suggest that criminals are physiological throwbacks to earlier stages of human evolution.

Autoplastic adaptation a form of adjustment resulting from changes within an individual.

Behaviour theory a psychological perspective positing that individual behaviour that is rewarded will increase in frequency and behaviour that is punished will decrease.

Biological theory a theory that maintains that the basic determinants of human behaviour, including criminality, are constitutionally or physiologically based and often inherited.

Biosocial criminology a theoretical perspective that sees the interaction between biology and the environment as key to understanding human behaviour, including criminality.

Born criminal an individual who is born with a genetic predilection toward criminality.

Bourgeoisie in Marxist theory, the class of people that owns the means of production.

Breaking and entering the unlawful entry of a place to commit an indictable offence.

Broken windows thesis a perspective on crime that holds that physical deterioration in an area leads to increased concerns for personal safety among area residents and to higher crime rates in that area.

Canadian Statement of Basic Principles of Justice for Victims of Crime a document promoting access to justice, fair treatment, and provision of assistance for victims of crime.

Capital punishment the legal imposition of a sentence of death upon a convicted offender. Another term for the death penalty.

Case study an investigation into an individual case.

Chicago school of criminology an ecological approach to explaining crime that examines how social disorganization contributes to social pathology.

Circle sentencing conferences groups of community members who actively assist justice authorities by participating in discussions about available sentencing options and plans to reintegrate the offender back into the community.

Classical school a criminological perspective of the late 18th and early 19th centuries that had its roots in the Enlightenment. It held that men and women are rational beings, that crime is the result of the exercise of free will, and that punishment can be effective in reducing the incidence of crime to the degree that it negates the pleasure to be derived from crime commission.

Code of Hammurabi an early set of laws established by the Babylonian King Hammurabi, who ruled the ancient city from 1792 to 1750 BC.

Cohort a group of individuals sharing certain significant social characteristics, such as gender and time and place of birth.

Cohort analysis a social scientific technique that studies a population that shares common characteristics over time. Cohort analysis usually begins at birth and traces the development of cohort members until they reach a certain age.

Common law law originating from usage and custom rather than from written statutes. The term refers to non-statutory customs, traditions, and precedents that help guide judicial decision making.

Community policing a philosophy of policing involving proactive collaboration between the police and the community to prevent and respond to crime and other community problems.

Community sentencing panels groups composed of volunteers from the community who focus on restorative measures such as restitution, reparation, mediation, and victim involvement.

Computer virus a computer program designed to secretly invade computer systems in order either to modify the way in which they operate or to alter the information they store.

Conditioning a psychological principle holding that the frequency of any behaviour can be increased or decreased through reward, punishment, or association with other stimuli.

Conduct norms shared expectations of a social group relative to personal conduct.

Conflict perspective an analytical approach to social organization that holds that conflict is a fundamental aspect of social life and can never be fully resolved.

Confounding effect a rival explanation, or competing hypothesis, that is a threat to the internal or external validity of research design.

Consensus perspective an analytical perspective on social organization that holds that most members of society agree about what is right and wrong and that various elements of society work together toward a common vision of the greater good.

Constitutional theory a theory that explains criminality by reference to offenders' body types, inheritance, genetics, or external observable physical characteristics.

Containment aspects of the social bond that act as a stabilizing force to prevent individuals from committing crimes and that keep them from engaging in deviance.

Containment theory a form of control theory that suggests a series of both internal and external factors contributes to law-abiding behaviour.

Controlled experiment an experiment that attempts to hold conditions (other than the intentionally introduced experimental intervention) constant.

Correctional psychology the branch of forensic psychology concerned with the diagnosis and classification of offenders, the treatment of correctional populations, and the rehabilitation of inmates and other law violators.

Correlates of crime those variables observed to be related to criminal activity such as age, sex and gender, ethnicity, and social class.

Correlation a causal, complementary, or reciprocal relationship between two measurable variables.

Counterfeiting any unauthorized reproduction of a thing with the intention that it be accepted as genuine. It can thus refer to anything that is capable of reproduction, including things that are subjects of rights of private property. It also includes the reproduction of documents for identification, such as passports, or any paper that represents value (e.g., stamps, travellers' cheques, or negotiable instruments).

Crime human conduct in violation of the criminal laws of a state, the federal government, or a provincial or local jurisdiction that has the power to make such laws and for which there is some form of authorized sanction.

Crime Prevention Through Environmental Design (CPTED) a crime-prevention strategy based on the premise that the design and effective use of the built environment can lead to a reduction in the incidence and fear of crime.

Crime rate crime per capita based on the number of recorded crimes calculated per 100 000 population.

Criminal anthropology the scientific study of the relationship between human physical characteristics and criminality.

Criminal behaviour a way of acquiring valued resources from others by exploring and deceiving them.

Criminal harassment also known as stalking, the repeated following, watching, or communicating with a person or someone known to that person in a way that causes the person to fear for his/her safety or for the safety of someone known to him/her.

Criminal justice the scientific study of crime, the criminal law, and components of the criminal justice system, including the police, courts, and corrections.

Criminal justice system the various agencies of justice, especially police, courts, and corrections, whose goal it is to apprehend, convict, sanction, and rehabilitate law violators.

Criminality a behavioural predisposition that disproportionately favours criminal activity.

Criminalist a specialist in the collection and examination of the physical evidence of crime.

Criminalize to make illegal.

Criminaloids a term used by Cesare Lombroso to describe occasional criminals who were pulled into criminality primarily by environmental influences.

Criminologist one who is trained in the field of criminology; also, one who studies crime, criminals, and criminal behaviour.

Criminology an interdisciplinary profession built around the scientific study of crime and criminal behaviour, including their form, causes, legal aspects, prevention, and control.

Criminology of place or environmental criminology an emerging perspective that emphasizes the importance of geographic location and architectural features as they are associated with the prevalence of criminal victimization.

Critical criminology a perspective focused on challenging traditional understandings and on uncovering false beliefs about crime and criminal justice.

Culture conflict theory a sociological perspective on crime that suggests that the root cause of criminality can be found in a clash of values between variously socialized groups over what is acceptable or proper behaviour.

Cybercrime any crime that involves a computer as the object of the crime or as the tool used to commit a material component of the offence.

Cycloid a term developed by Ernst Kretschmer to describe a particular relationship between body build and personality type. The cycloid personality, which was associated with a heavyset, soft type of body, was said to vacillate between normality and abnormality.

Dark figure of crime refers to that the portion of criminal activity that goes unreported and/or undetected by official sources.

Data confidentiality The ethical requirement of social scientific research to protect the confidentiality of individual research participants while preserving justified research access to the information participants provide.

Defensible space the range of mechanisms that combine to bring an environment under the control of its residents.

Demographics the characteristics of population groups, usually expressed in statistical form.

Determinate sentencing a criminal punishment strategy that mandates a specified and fixed amount of time to be served for every offence category.

Deterrence the prevention of crime.

Deterrence strategy a crime-prevention strategy that attempts to diminish motivation for crime by increasing the perceived certainty, severity, or celerity of penalties.

Deviant behaviour human activity that violates social norms.

Differential association the sociological thesis that criminality, like any other form of behaviour, is learned through a process of association with others who communicate criminal values.

Displacement a shift of criminal activity from one spatial location to another.

Displastics a mixed group of offenders described by theorist Ernst Kretschmer as highly emotional and often unable to control themselves.

Dizygotic twins twins who develop from a separate ovum and carry the genetic material shared by siblings.

Ecological theory a type of sociological approach that emphasizes demographics (the characteristics of population groups) and geographics (the mapped location of such groups relative to one another) and sees the social disorganization that characterizes delinquency areas as a major cause of criminality and victimization.

Ectomorph a body type described as thin and fragile, with long, slender, poorly muscled extremities, and delicate bones.

Ego the reality-testing part of the personality; also called the *reality principle*. More formally, it is the personality component that is conscious, most immediately controls behaviour, and is most in touch with external reality.

Electroencephalogram (EEG) electrical measurements of brain-wave activity.

Endomorph a body type described as soft and round, or overweight.

The Enlightenment a social movement that arose during the late 17th and 18th centuries and built upon ideas such as empiricism, rationality, free will, humanism, and natural law.

Eugenics the study of hereditary improvement by genetic control.

Evolutionary ecology an approach to understanding crime that draws attention to the ways people develop over the course of their lives.

Family group conferencing a forum for dealing with unanswered questions, emotions, and the victim's right to restitution and reparation resulting from a crime.

Feminist criminology a self-conscious corrective model intended to redirect the thinking of mainstream criminologists to include gender awareness.

First-degree murder culpable homicide that is planned and deliberate.

Focal concerns the key values of any culture, and especially the key values of a delinquent subculture.

Folkways time-honoured customs. Although folkways carry the force of tradition, their violation is unlikely to threaten the survival of the group.

Forensic psychiatry a branch of psychiatry having to do with the study of crime and criminality.

Forensic psychology the application of the science and profession of psychology to questions and issues relating to law and the legal system. Also known as criminal psychology.

Future criminology the study of likely futures as they relate to crime and its control.

Futurists those who study the future; in the case of criminology, criminologists who try to imagine how crime will appear in both the near and distant future.

General deterrence a goal of criminal sentencing that seeks to prevent others from committing crimes similar to the one for which a particular offender is being sentenced.

General theory a theory that attempts to explain all (or at least most) forms of criminal conduct through a single, overarching approach.

Globalization a process of social homogenization by which the experiences of everyday life, marked by the diffusion of commodities and ideas, can foster a standardization of cultural expressions around the world.

Hacker a person who uses computers for exploration and exploitation.

Hard determinism the belief that crime results from forces beyond the control of the individual.

Hate crime a criminal act directed toward a person or group because of race, national or ethnic origin, religion, language, colour, sex, age, sexual orientation, or mental or physical disability. Also referred to as hate-motivated crime, or bias crime.

Hedonistic calculus or utilitarianism the belief, first proposed by Jeremy Bentham, that behaviour holds value to any individual undertaking according to the amount of pleasure or pain that it can be expected to produce for that person.

Homicide when a person, directly or indirectly, by any means, causes the death of a human being. Homicide can be culpable or non-culpable.

Human smuggling a type of illegal immigration in which an agent is paid to help a person cross a border clandestinely.

Hypoglycemia a condition characterized by low blood sugar.

Hypothesis 1. an explanation that accounts for a set of facts and that can be tested by further investigation. 2. something that is taken to be true for the purpose of argument or investigation.

Id the aspect of the personality from which drives, wishes, urges, and desires emanate. More formally, it is the division of the psyche associated with instinctual impulses and demands for immediate satisfaction of primitive needs.

Illegitimate opportunity structure a subcultural pathway to success that is disapproved of by the wider society.

Incapacitation the use of imprisonment or other means to reduce the likelihood that an offender will be capable of committing future offences.

Infanticide when a female considered disturbed from the effects of giving birth causes the death of her newborn child (under age 1).

Informed consent the ethical requirement of social scientific research that research subjects be informed as to the nature of the research about to be conducted, their anticipated role in it, and the uses to which the data they provide will be put.

Instrumental Marxism a perspective that holds that those in power intentionally create laws and social institutions that serve their own interests and that keep others from becoming powerful.

Integrated theory an explanatory perspective that merges (or attempts to merge) concepts drawn from different sources.

Juke family a well-known "criminal family" studied by Richard L. Dugdale.

Just deserts model the notion that criminal offenders deserve the punishment they receive at the hands of the law and that punishments should be appropriate to the type and severity of the crime committed.

Kallikak family a well-known "criminal family" studied by Henry H. Goddard.

Kriminalpolitik the political handling of crime, or a criminology-based social policy.

Labelling an interactionist perspective that sees continued crime as a consequence of limited opportunities for acceptable behaviour that follow from the negative responses of society to those defined as offenders. Also, the process by which a negative or deviant label is imposed.

Left-realist criminology a conflict perspective that insists on a pragmatic assessment of crime and its associated problems.

Liberal feminism a perspective that holds that gender-role socialization is the primary source of women's oppression.

Life course theories explanations for criminality that recognize criminogenic influences as having their greatest impact during the early stages of life and that see formative childhood experiences as catalysts in shaping children for the rest of their lives.

Lifestyle model the theory that the likelihood that an individual will suffer a personal victimization depends heavily on the concept of lifestyle.

Mala in se an act thought to be wrong in and of itself.

Mala prohibita an act that is wrong only because it is prohibited.

Manslaughter all non-intentional homicide.

Marxist feminism a perspective in feminist criminology that sees the oppression of women as caused by their subordinate class status within capitalist societies.

Mass murder the illegal killing of four or more victims at one location, within one event.

McNaughten rule a standard for judging legal insanity that requires that offenders did not know what they were doing, or if they did, that they did not know it was wrong.

Mental disorder (law) a legally established inability to understand right from wrong, or to conform one's behaviour to the requirements of the law. Also, a defence allowable in criminal courts.

Mental disorder (psychological) disease of the mind including schizophrenia, paranoia, senile dementia, melancholia, various types of epilepsy, and delirium tremens caused by alcohol abuse.

Mesomorph a body type described as athletic and muscular.

Modelling theory a form of social learning theory that asserts that people learn how to behave by observing others.

Monozygotic twins twins who develop from the same egg and carry virtually the same genetic material.

Moral enterprise efforts made by an interest group to have its sense of propriety enacted into law.

Mores behavioural proscriptions covering potentially serious violations of a group's values. Examples might include strictures against murder, sexual assault, and robbery.

Motor vehicle theft the taking of a vehicle without the owner's authorization. A motor vehicle is defined as a car, truck, van, bus, recreational vehicle, semi-trailer truck, motorcycle, construction machinery, agricultural machinery, or other land-based motor vehicle (such as a go-kart, snowmobile, all-terrain vehicle, or dune buggy).

Murder when a person intentionally causes the death of another human being or intends to cause bodily harm likely to result in death.

National Strategy on Community Safety and Crime Prevention a federal crime-prevention initiative designed to create safer communities by supporting community-based crime-prevention efforts, enhancing communities' knowledge and experience with respect to crime prevention, and fostering partnerships and collaboration.

Natural law the philosophical perspective that certain immutable laws are fundamental to human nature and can be readily ascertained through reason. Human-made laws, in contrast, are said to derive from human experience and history—both of which are subject to continual change.

Natural rights rights that, according to natural law theorists, individuals retain in the face of government action and interests.

Neo-classical criminology a contemporary version of classical criminology that emphasizes deterrence and retribution, with reduced emphasis on rehabilitation.

Neurosis a functional disorder of the mind or of the emotions involving anxiety, phobia, or other abnormal behaviour.

Not criminally responsible on account of mental disorder (NCRMD) a finding that offenders are responsible for committing the offence that they have committed and because of their prevailing mental condition, should be sent to a psychiatric hospital for treatment rather than to prison. The maximum length of stay is predetermined.

Nurturant strategy a crime-prevention strategy that attempts to forestall development of criminality by improving early life experiences and channelling child and adolescent development into desirable directions.

Operant behaviour behaviour that affects the environment so as to produce responses or further behavioural cues.

Opportunity model the contention that the risk of criminal victimization depends largely on people's lifestyle and daily activities that bring them and their property into direct contact with potential offenders in the absence of capable guardians.

Panopticon a prison designed by Jeremy Bentham that was to be a circular building with cells along the circumference, each clearly visible from a central location staffed by guards.

Paradigm an example, model, or theory.

Paranoid schizophrenic a schizophrenic individual who suffers from delusions and hallucinations.

Participant observation a strategy in data gathering in which the researcher observes a group by participating, to varying degrees, in the activities of the group.

Participatory justice a relatively informal type of justice case processing which makes use of local community resources rather than requiring traditional forms of official intervention.

Patriarchy the tradition of male dominance.

Peace model an approach to crime control that focuses on effective ways for developing a shared consensus on critical issues that have the potential to seriously affect the quality of life.

Peacemaking criminology a perspective that holds that crime-control agencies and the citizens they serve should work together to alleviate social problems and human suffering and thus reduce crime.

Penal couple a term that describes the relationship between victim and criminal.

Phishing an internet-based scam to steal valuable information such as credit card numbers, social insurance numbers, user IDs, and passwords.

Phone phreak a person who uses switched, dialed-access telephone services for exploration and exploitation.

Phrenology the study of the shape of the head to determine anatomical correlates of human behaviour.

Pluralistic perspective an analytical approach to social organization that holds that a multiplicity of values and beliefs exists in any complex society but that most social actors agree on the usefulness of law as a formal means of dispute resolution.

Positivism the application of scientific techniques to the study of crime and criminals.

Post-crime victimization or secondary victimization problems in living that tend to follow from initial victimization, some of which may be related to the victim's interaction with the criminal justice system.

Postmodern feminism a perspective in modern criminology that questions the social construction of concepts typically used in discussions of crime and justice.

Primary deviance initial deviance often undertaken to deal with transient problems in living.

Primary research research characterized by original and direct investigation.

Proletariat in Marxist theory, the working class.

Prostitution most commonly used to refer to the illegal activities of publicly communicating with another person for the purposes of buying or selling sexual services, running a bawdy house, or living on the avails of the prostitution of another person.

Protection/avoidance strategy a crime-prevention strategy that attempts to reduce criminal opportunities by changing people's routine activities, increasing guardianship, or incapacitating convicted offenders.

Psychiatric criminology theories derived from the medical sciences, including neurology, which, like other psychological theories, focus on the individual as the unit of analysis. Psychiatric theories form the basis of psychiatric criminology.

Psychoanalysis the theory of human psychology founded by Freud and based on the concepts of the unconscious, resistance, repression, sexuality, and the Oedipus complex.

Psychological profiling the attempt to categorize, understand, and predict the behaviour of certain types of offenders based on behavioural clues they provide; also called *criminal profiling* and *behavioural profiling*.

Psychological theory a theory derived from the behavioural sciences that focuses on the individual as the unit of analysis. Psychological theories place the locus of crime causation within the personality of the individual offender.

Psychopath or **sociopath** a person with a personality disorder, especially one manifested in aggressively anti-social behaviour, and who is lacking in empathy.

Psychopathology the study of pathological mental conditions.

Psychosis a form of mental illness in which sufferers are said to be out of touch with reality.

Psychotherapy a form of psychiatric treatment based on psychoanalytical principles and techniques.

Public policy government-formulated directives made on behalf of the public good to solve a problem or achieve an end.

Punishments undesirable behavioural consequences likely to decrease the frequency of occurrence of that behaviour.

Pure research research undertaken simply for the sake of advancing scientific knowledge.

Qualitative method a research technique that produces subjective results or results that are difficult to quantify.

Quantitative methods a research technique that produces measurable results.

Quasi-experimental design an approach to research that, although less powerful than an experimental design, is deemed worthy of use when better designs are not feasible.

Radical criminology a perspective that holds that the causes of crime are rooted in social conditions that empower the wealthy and the politically well organized but disenfranchise those less fortunate. Radical criminology is sometimes called Marxist criminology.

Radical feminism the perspective that patriarchy is the cause of women's oppression.

Rape myth a false assumption about sexual assault, such as "When a woman says no, she really means yes."

Rational choice theory a perspective holding that criminality is the result of conscious choice and predicting that individuals choose to commit crime when the benefits outweigh the costs of disobeying the law.

Reaction formation the process in which a person openly rejects that which he or she wants, or aspires to, but cannot obtain or achieve.

Recidivism the repetition of criminal behaviour.

Recidivism rate the percentage of convicted offenders who have been released from prison and who are later rearrested for a new crime.

Reintegrative shaming a form of shaming, imposed as a sanction by the criminal justice system, that is thought to strengthen the moral bond between the offender and the community.

Research the use of standardized, systematic procedures in the search for knowledge.

Research design the logic and structure inherent in an approach to data gathering.

Restitution a criminal sanction, in particular the payment of compensation by the offender to the victim.

Restorative justice a perspective that stresses remedies and restoration rather than prison, punishment, and neglect of victims.

Retribution the act of taking revenge upon a criminal perpetrator.

Rewards desirable behavioural consequences likely to increase the frequency of occurrence of that behaviour.

Robbery the unlawful taking or attempted taking of property that is in the immediate possession of another by threatened or actual use of force or violence.

Routine activities theory or **lifestyle theory** a brand of rational choice theory posited by Lawrence Cohen and Marcus Felson that suggests that lifestyles contribute significantly to both the volume and the type of crime found in any society.

Routine activity approach the theory that occurrences of personal victimization are dependent upon the "routine" or "daily activities" of people and are the outcome of three elements: the motivated offender, a suitable target, and the absence of a capable guardian.

Safe Streets and Communities Act Canadian legislation that introduces changes to the *Criminal Code of Canada* including increased penalties for sexual offences against children and for drug crimes, denial of release for violent and repeat young offenders, adult sentences for and the publication of the names of youths convicted of the most serious crimes, and the reduction of judicial discretion in sentencing for crimes involving serious personal injury, which carry a maximum prison term of 14 years or more.

Schizoid a person characterized by a schizoid personality disorder. Such disordered personalities appear to be aloof, withdrawn, unresponsive, humourless, dull, and solitary to an abnormal degree.

Schizophrenic a mentally ill individual who is out of touch with reality and suffers from disjointed thinking.

Secondary analysis the reanalysis of existing data.

Secondary deviance deviant behaviour that results from official labelling and from association with others who have been so labelled.

Secondary research new evaluations of existing information collected by other researchers.

Second-degree murder all murder that is not first-degree murder.

Selective incapacitation a social policy that seeks to protect society by incarcerating those individuals deemed to be the most dangerous.

Self-report study a data collection method requiring subjects to reveal their own participation in criminal behaviour.

Self-reports a research investigation of subjects in order to record and report their behaviours.

Serial murder culpable homicide that involves the killing of several victims in three or more separate events.

Sexual assault an assault committed in circumstances of a sexual nature such that the sexual integrity of the victim is violated. The degree of violence used determines whether the sexual assault is level 1, level 2, or level 3.

Situational choice theory a brand of rational choice theory that views criminal behaviour "as a function of choices and decisions made within a context of situational constraints and opportunities."

Situational crime prevention   a social policy approach that looks to develop greater understanding of crime and more effective crime-prevention strategies through concern with the physical, organizational, and social environments that make crime possible.

Social bond   the link, created through socialization, between individuals and the society of which they are a part.

Social capital   the number of positive relationships with other persons and social institutions that individuals build up over the course of their lives.

Social class   distinctions made between individuals on the basis of important defining social characteristics.

Social conflict perspective   an analytical perspective on social organization which holds that conflict is a fundamental aspect of social life itself and can never be fully resolved.

Social contract   the Enlightenment-era concept that human beings abandon their natural state of individual freedom to join together and form society. Although in the process of forming a social contract individuals surrender some freedoms to society as a whole, government, once formed, is obligated to assume responsibilities toward its citizens and to provide for their protection and welfare.

Social control theories   perspectives predicting that when social constraints on anti-social behaviour are weakened or absent, delinquent behaviour emerges. Rather than stressing causative factors in criminal behaviour, social control theory asks why people actually obey rules instead of breaking them.

Social development perspective   an integrated view of human development that examines multiple levels of maturation simultaneously, including psychological, biological, familial, interpersonal, cultural, societal, and ecological levels.

Social disorganization theory   a perspective on crime and deviance that sees society as a kind of organism and crime and deviance as a kind of disease, or social pathology.

Social ecology   an approach to criminological theorizing that attempts to link the structure and organization of a human community to interactions with its localized environment.

Social epidemiology   the study of social epidemics and diseases of the social order.

Social learning theory   a perspective that places primary emphasis on the role of communication and socialization in the acquisition of learned patterns of criminal behaviour and the values that support that behaviour.

Social life   the ongoing structured interaction—including socialization and social behavior in general—that occurs between persons in a society.

Social policy   a government initiative, program, or plan intended to address problems in society.

Social problems perspective   the belief that crime is a manifestation of underlying social problems such as poverty, discrimination, pervasive family violence, inadequate socialization practices, and the breakdown of traditional social institutions.

Social process   the interaction between and among social institutions, groups, and individuals.

Social process theory   the theory that criminal behaviour is learned in interaction with others and that the socialization processes that occur as a result of group membership are the primary route through which learning occurs. Also called interactionist theory.

Social relativity   the notion that social events are differently interpreted according to the cultural experiences and personal interests of the initiator, the observer, or the recipient of that behaviour.

Social responsibility perspective   the belief that individuals are fundamentally responsible for their own behaviour and that they choose crime over other, more law-abiding courses of action.

Social structure   the pattern of social organization and the interrelationships among institutions characteristic of a society.

Social structure theory   a theory that explains crime by reference to the economic and social arrangements in society. This type of theory emphasizes relationships among social institutions and describes the types of behaviour that tend to characterize groups of people rather than individuals.

Socialist feminism   a perspective that examines social roles and the gender-based division of labour within the family, seeing both as a significant source of women's insubordination within society.

Socialization   the lifelong process of social experience whereby individuals acquire the cultural patterns of their society.

Sociobiology   the systematic study of the biological basis of all social behaviour.

Sociological theory   a perspective that focuses on the nature of the power relationships that exist between social groups and on the influences that various social phenomena bring to bear on the types of behaviours that tend to characterize groups of people.

Soft determinism   the belief that human behaviour is the result of choices and decisions made within a context of situational constraints and opportunities.

Software piracy   the unauthorized and illegal copying of software programs.

Somatotyping   the classification of human beings into types according to body build and other physical characteristics.

Specific deterrence   a goal of criminal sentencing that seeks to prevent a particular offender from engaging in repeat criminality.

Statistical school   a criminological perspective with roots in the early 19th century that seeks to uncover correlations between crime rates and other types of demographic data.

Statute   a formal written enactment of a legislative body.

Statutory law   law in the form of statutes or formal written stricture made by a legislature or governing body with the power to make law.

Stigmatic shaming   a form of shaming, imposed as a sanction by the criminal justice system, that is thought to destroy the moral bond between the offender and the community.

Strain theory   a sociological approach that posits a disjuncture between socially and subculturally sanctioned means and goals as the cause of criminal behaviour.

Structural Marxism   a perspective that holds that the structural institutions of society influence the behaviour of individuals and groups by virtue of the type of relationships created. The criminal law, for example, reflects class relationships and serves to reinforce those relationships.

Subcultural theory   a sociological perspective that emphasizes the contribution made by variously socialized cultural groups to the phenomenon of crime.

Subculture   a collection of values and preferences that is communicated to subcultural participants through a process of socialization.

Sublimation   the psychological process whereby one aspect of consciousness comes to be symbolically substituted for another.

Superego   the moral aspect of the personality; much like the conscience. More formally, it is the division of the psyche that develops by the incorporation of the perceived moral standards of the community, is mainly unconscious, and includes the conscience.

Supermale   a male individual displaying the XYY chromosomal structure.

Survey research   research using a social science data-gathering technique that involves the use of questionnaires.

Tagging   the process whereby an individual is negatively defined by agencies of justice.

Target hardening   the reduction in criminal opportunity for a particular location, generally through the use of physical barriers, architectural design, and enhanced security measures.

Techniques of neutralization   learned justifications that can provide criminal offenders with the means to disavow responsibility for their behaviour.

Testosterone   the primary male sex hormone. It is produced in the testes, and its function is to control secondary sex characteristics and sexual drive.

Thanatos   a death wish.

Theft   the act of dishonestly taking property belonging to another person with the intention of depriving its owner of it either permanently or temporarily.

Theory   a series of interrelated propositions that attempt to describe, explain, predict, and ultimately control some class of events. A theory gains explanatory power from inherent logical consistency and is "tested" by how well it describes and predicts reality.

Trafficking in persons (TIP)   the exploitation of unwilling or unwitting people by means of coercion, threat, or deception.

Transnational organized crime   any unlawful activity undertaken and supported by organized groups operating across national boundaries.

Twelve Tables   early Roman laws written circa 450 BC that regulated family, religious, and economic life.

Typologies of crime   classifications of crime useful in identifying patterns of criminal activity and motivations for criminal behaviour.

Unicausal   having one cause. Unicausal theories posit only one source for all that they attempt to explain.

Uniform Crime Report Survey (UCR)   a summation of crime statistics tallied annually by the Canadian Centre for Justice Statistics (CCJS) and consisting primarily of data on crimes reported to the police.

Victim impact statement   a written document that describes the losses, suffering, and trauma experienced by the crime victim or by the victim's survivors. Judges are expected to consider these effects in arriving at an appropriate sentence for the offender.

Victim surcharge   a mandatory, judicial imposition of a monetary fine administered in addition to a criminal sentence and used to finance victim services.

Victimization Survey   first conducted as the Canadian Urban Victimization Survey in 1981 by Statistics Canada and then every five years since 1988 as part of the General Social Survey. It provides data on surveyed households reporting that they had been affected by crime.

Victim–Offender Reconciliation Program (VORP)   a program that gives the offender the opportunity to meet face-to-face with the victim in the presence of a trained mediator in an attempt to reduce the victim's fears while establishing accountability and reparation for the crime.

Victimogenesis   the contribution to victimization made by the background of a victim.

Victim-proneness   the degree of an individual's likelihood of victimization.

Victim/Witness Assistance Program   a program in Ontario that counsels victims, orients them to the justice process, and provides a variety of other services such as transportation to court, child care during court appearances, and referrals to social service agencies.

Victimology   the study of victims and their contributory role, if any, in the criminal event.

Violent Crime Linkage Analysis System (ViCLAS)   a centralized computer bank containing details of violent crimes that assists police in recognizing patterns among violent offences and offenders.

Youth Criminal Justice Act   Canadian legislation that determines the way in which youth are prosecuted under the criminal justice system. It replaced the *Young Offenders Act* in 2003.

Name Index

Subject Index

A

abnormal behaviours, 171, 174
Aboriginal communities, 203
Aboriginal Emotional Maturity
    Problem-Solving and Awareness
    Targeting Higher Impulse Control
    (EMPATHIC) program, 282
Aboriginal Ganootamaage Justice Service
    Centre, 264
Aboriginal peoples
    Aboriginal EMPATHIC Program,
      282
    alcohol consumption, 60
    circle sentencing conferences,
      265–266
    crime rates, 203
    discrimination of, 60
    ecological approach, 203
    gangs, 217
    Good Intentions, Disappointing
      Results, 61
    Oka crisis, 248–249
    over-representation in criminal
      justice system, 59–61, 159
    self-government movement, 27
    socio-economic realities, 60–61
    substance abuse, 60
    victimization, 61
abortion, 120
academic criminologists, 11
Ace Crew, 210, 215
adaptive behaviour, 181–182
Adding Insult to Injury (Ombudsman of
    Ontario), 100
Additional Protocol to the Convention on
    Cybercrime, 311
administration of justice, 288
administrative law, 4
adolescent development, 238–239, 239f
After-4 Drop-ins, 242
age
    See also youth
    and crime, 56–57
    property and violent crimes
      by, 56f
    and victimization, 57, 95
Age of Reason, 118–120
Aggregate Uniform Crime Reporting
    Survey, 45
aggression
    biological roots of, 142–155
    crowding, 142
    and frustration, 79–80
    frustration-aggression theory, 176
    reward from, 183

self-regulatory mechanisms,
    183–184
and serotonin, 150, 151, 153–154,
    157
and testosterone, 152–153
alcohol consumption, 151
    Aboriginal peoples, 60
    driving under the influence of
      alcohol, 213
    young offenders, 62
allergic reactions, 149
Alliance for the Rights of Children,
    114
alloplastic adaptation, 181
alternative dispute resolution, 267
altruism, 160
American Neurological Association,
    140
American Psychiatric Association
    (APA), 179
American Psychological Association, 161
American Society of Criminology, 11
amphetamines, 88
anabolic steroids, 88
An Act Respecting Victims of Crime—Victims'
    Bill of Rights (Ontario), 102–103
Annual Report on Organized Crime (CISC), 217
anomie, 205
Anti-Counterfeiting Network, 86
Anti-Phishing Working Group, 306
anti-social personality, 179
anti-social personality disorder (ASPD),
    180–181
APD. *See* anti-social personality disorder
    (ASPD)
applied research, 19
A Question of Murder (Scoular), 226
A Roadmap to Strengthening Public Safety,
    286–288
artificial intelligence, 311
asocial personality, 179
assault, 77, 262
assisted suicide, 4–5
A System of Positive Policy (Comte), 144
atavism, 144, 145–147
attachment, 237, 242
attempted murder, 70, 72
Australian and New Zealand Journal of
    Criminology, 11
authority, 253
authority conflict pathway, 241
automated fingerprint identification
    system (AFIS), 309
autonomy, 209
autoplastic adaptation, 181

B

balanced type, 148
Bank of Canada, 85–86
barbiturates, 88
Barbra Schlifer Commemorative
    Clinic, 75
behavioural profiling, 192–193
behaviour theory, 185–186
belief, 237–238
Bentham, Jeremy, 121–123
Beyond Borders, 114
Bill C-10, 26, 278, 285
Bill C-11, 300
Bill C-24, 216
Bill C-393, 93
Bill C-562, 5
Bill S-4, 307
biological theories
    aggression, biological roots of,
      142–155
    applied, 165
    atavism, 144, 145–147
    body types, 147–148, 148f
    chemical and environmental
      precursors of crime, 149–152
    chromosomes, 157
    constitutional theories, 147
    criminal families, 155–156
    critique of, 163–164
    defined, 141–142
    early biological theories, 143–147
    genetics, 155–160
    hormones, 152–155
    major principles of, 141–142
    male-female differences in
      criminality, 158–160
    policy implications of,
      162–163
    positivist school, 144–145
    sociobiology, 160–161
    supermale, 156–157
    twin studies, 157–158
biometric technologies, 309–310
biosocial criminology, 161–162, 165
Black Death, 116
black-male-as-savage theory, 264
blogs, 309
body chemistry, 165
body types, 147–148, 148f
born criminal, 145
bourgeoisie, 251
Boys and Girls Clubs, 242
brain tumour, 140
breaking and entering, 81–82, 82f
British Journal of Criminology, 11

federal government, 288–289

Federal-Provincial Conference of Ministers Responsible for Criminal Justice, 100

Federal-Provincial Task Force on Justice for the Victims of Crime, 101

feedback loop, 34

The Female Offender (Lombroso), 145

feminism, 259

feminist criminology
  critique of, 263
  defined, 259
  liberal feminism, 259
  major contributions, 261
  Marxist feminism, 260
  patriarchy, 260
  postmodern feminism, 260
  power-control theory, 261
  public order crimes, 89
  radical feminism, 260
  sexist traditions in criminology, 261
  socialist feminism, 260
  and social policy, 263
  violent crime, 81

feminization of poverty, 58

fingerprinting, 309

first-degree murder, 71

First Nations. *See* Aboriginal peoples

fitness to stand trial, 188–190

A Flawed Compass: A Human Rights Analysis of the Roadmap to Strengthening Public Safety (Jackson), 287

focal concerns, 208–209

folkways, 116

food additives, 149

forensic psychiatrists, 171

forensic psychiatry, 172

forensic psychology, 170–171, 190–192
  See also psychological theories

Foresight program, 295

fraternal twins, 157

Front de libération du Québec (FLQ), 257

frustration, and aggression, 79–80

frustration-aggression theory, 176

functional magnetic resonance imaging (fMRI), 178

Fundamentalist Church of Jesus Christ of Latter Day Saints (FLDS), 9

future criminology, 295

future directions
  emerging crimes, 312
  globalization, 296–297
  human smuggling, 298–301
  social characteristics affecting crime, 295–296
  technology and crime, 301–312
  trafficking in persons (TIP), 298–301
  in victimology, 109–110

futurists, 295

G

The Gang (Thrasher), 208

Gangfact, 217

gangs
  Ace Crew, 215
  in Canada, 216–218
  cyberbanging, 301
  defined, 216
  delinquent neighbourhoods, 213
  gang-related violence, 217–218
  and subcultural theories, 208
  today's gangs, 216–218
  in United States, 216–217

gender. *See* sex

general deterrence, 129

general public. *See* the public

General Social Survey (GSS), 49, 53t, 55, 59, 63, 77, 96

general strain theory (GST), 206–207

general theory, 15

genetic determinism, 141

genetics
  chromosomes, 157
  criminal families, 155–156
  male-female differences in criminality, 158–160
  supermale, 156–157
  twin studies, 157–158

geographic profiling, 20, 125

Gesch study, 150

get tough on crime policies, 123, 277, 278

globalization, 296–297

Global Report on Trafficking in Persons, 298–299

goals and means, 205–206

Golden Age of the Victim, 97

Good Intentions, Disappointing Results: A Progress Report on Federal Aboriginal Corrections (Office of the Correctional Investigator), 61

guilty but mentally ill (GBMI), 188

H

habitual offenders, 190

hacker, 304

hacking, 230–231, 302

hard determinism, 123

hardened environment, 283

hate crime, 77–78, 78f

haves and have-nots, 254

heavy equipment theft, 83–84

hedonism, 123

hedonistic calculus, 122

helping behaviour, 160

heroine, 88

History of Criminology (Jones), 256

Hitachi Mirai Foundation, 274

Holocaust, 116

homicide
  compassionate homicide, 251–252
  culpable homicide, 71
  defined, 71
  first-degree murder, 71
  gang-related, 218
  infanticide, 71
  intimate partners, 73
  justifiable homicide, 71
  male-female differences in criminality, 158t
  manslaughter, 71
  mass murder, 72
  murder, 71
  non-culpable homicide, 71
  occupations of victims, 73
  rates, 72–73, 210
  regional variations in homicide rates, 211
  retail costs of, 211
  second-degree murder, 71
  serial murder, 71
  weapons, use of, 73
  wholesale costs of, 211
  and women, 158–160

hormones, 152–155

House of Commons Standing Committee on Justice and Human Rights, 102

human development, 238

human ecology movement, 201

human rights, 123

human smuggling, 298–301

human trafficking. *See* trafficking in persons (TIP)

Human Trafficking National Coordination Centre (HTNCC), 301

hybrid offences, 4

hypoglycemia, 149

hypothesis, 20

I

id, 79, 173

identical twins, 157

identity theft, 307, 312

illegitimate opportunity structure, 212

illicit drugs, 88–89

ImAger, 311

Immigration Act, 300

Immigration and Refugee Protection Act (IRPA), 88, 300

incapacitation, 133–134

Incident-Based UCR, 45

income inequality, 62

indefinite hospitalization, 189

independence, 295

indictable offences, 4

individuality, 295

individual responsibility perspective, 30, 89

infanticide, 71

X

XYY supermale, 156–157

Y

YM/YWCA, 242
young offenders
    age, and crime, 56–57, 56f
    alcohol consumption, 62
    concentric zone model (Chicago),
      202f
    lower class crime, 62
    self-report questions from the
      Montreal Youth Study, 54t
    self-report studies, 52–53
    substance abuse, 62
youth
    See also children
    costs of young person in trouble,
      289–291
    delinquent subcultures, 212–213
    developmental pathways, 240–241
    lower-class, 213
    programs, 213, 242–243
Youth Criminal Justice Act, 285
Youth Gang Prevention Fund, 281
Youth Violence Project: A Community-
    Based Violence Prevention Project, 219
YouTube, 303